Refugees from Revolution

Refugees from Revolution

U.S. Policy and Third-World Migration

Peter H. Koehn

Westview Press

BOULDER • SAN FRANCISCO • OXFORD

This Westview softcover edition is printed on acid-free paper and bound in library-quality, coated covers that carry the highest rating of the National Association of State Textbook Administrators, in consultation with the Association of American Publishers and the Book Manufacturers' Institute.

Copyright © 1991 by Westview Press, Inc.

Published in 1991 in the United States of America by Westview Press, Inc., 5500 Central Avenue, Boulder, Colorado 80301-2847 in the United Kingdom by Westview Press, 36 Lonsdale Road, Summertown, Oxford OX2 7EW

Library of Congress Cataloging-in-Publication Data
Koehn, Peter H.
  Refugees from revolution : U.S. policy and Third-World Migration /
by Peter H. Koehn.
    p. cm.
  Includes bibliographical references and index.
  ISBN 0-8133-7719-6
  1. Refugees—Government policy—United States. 2. Refugees.
I. Title.
JV6601.R4K642 1991
325′.21′0973—dc20   91-31275
                                                                                          CIP

Printed and bound in the United States of America

        The paper used in this publication meets the requirements
   ∞   of the American National Standard for Permanence of Paper
        for Printed Library Materials Z39.48-1984.

10   9   8   7   6   5   4   3   2   1

Contents

Tables and Figures

Figures

Acknowledgments

It is a pleasure to acknowledge here that many people generously assisted with various aspects of *Refugees from Revolution*. Although only a few can be singled out for individual recognition, all are remembered. I am most grateful to:

-Girma Negash and Elsabet Tesfaye for the insights which inspired the decision to become professionally involved with exile communities;

-The Rockefeller Foundation's Population Sciences Program, especially Mary Kritz, and to the University of Montana for financial assistance and support;

-Girma Negash, Mohammad Amjad, Tsehaye Teferra, Fisseha Tekie, Abdul Mohamed, each of the project interviewers, Jon Gundersen, Aminata Diop, Konjit Bekele, Bereket Habte Sellassie, and Carolyn Waller for encouragement and special assistance during the field-work stage;

-Dick Lane, Janet McMaster, Dell McCann, Annajeannette Presnell, Sue Koehn, and Faith Lane for work on various stages of data processing and manuscript preparation;

-Paul G. Lauren, Shahin Monshipour, Mehrdad Kia, Richard Drake, Abraham Demoz, Carolyn Waller, Tewolde Habte Michael, Elsabet Tesfaye, and Girma Negash, for time spent reading and commenting on various portions of the manuscript;

-Robert E. Mazur for valuable suggestions at the conceptualization stage as well as a thorough review of the entire manuscript;

-Miriam Gilbert, Barbara Ellington, and, especially, Rebecca Ritke at Westview Press for their interest, patience, and useful contributions.

Above all, I am indebted to the many refugees from revolution who have taken time over the past eight years of involvement on this project to share their personal and often traumatic experiences and who have generously and patiently explained their migration decisions. It is to their future, and to the well being of others similarly situated or in the position of a potential refugee, that this book is dedicated.

Peter H. Koehn
Missoula, Montana

Introduction to Contemporary Cross-National Population Movements: Challenges for International Relations and U.S. Policy

Ours is the age of the refugee, the displaced person, mass immigration.
—Edward Said

The movement of vast human populations across porous borders provides a striking indication of the declining relevance of the nation state at the dawn of the 21st century. East German authorities could not keep young people in; the United States Border Patrol cannot keep undocumented migrant workers from Central America out. Chinese students engaged in overseas study, distressed by their government's response to events in Tiananmen Square, delay their return home. In the wake of the Iraqi invasion of Kuwait, a mass multinational exodus of third-country citizens occurs. Wealthy German and Scandinavian tourists maintain "second homes" on East African beaches. Not far away, on both sides of two borders in the Horn of Africa, hundreds of thousands of people subsist in squalor following involuntary population exchanges between Ethiopia and Sudan, and Ethiopia and Somalia. Another generation of Fulani herders in West Africa, undeterred by political boundaries arbitrarily established by self-interested and long-departed imperialist powers, continues to follow the rains. In Western Europe, meanwhile, government leaders in the former colonialist states plan the erosion of their countries' own archaic boundaries by 1993.

Population Movements and International Relations

In today's interdependent world, more people traverse national borders than ever before. Massive population movements across permeable boundaries present fundamental challenges to prevailing approaches in the study of national politics and international relations.[1]

International migrants also generate complex problems for national and transnational policy makers. The most recent and challenging pressures more often stem from the "temporary" movement of nationals out of their place of origin than from the familiar authorized permanent migration of new immigrants. The temporary departure phenomenon, which frequently extends far beyond the anticipated duration, involves migrant laborers, expatriate executives employed by transnational corporations and international agencies, students, entertainers, tourists, the victims of famine and environmental disasters, and political refugees.[2] Together, those forced to leave their country of origin and persons living and working temporarily outside of their homeland probably outnumber "traditional" emigrants by four to one.[3] The complexity and strength of the forces behind these developments, as well as the number of people affected and threatened, affirm the central place of refugee movements and economic migrations in the study of contemporary international relations.

South-North Population Flows

The world's principal population exchanges no longer occur among industrialized countries. In both volume and impact, the predominant axes of the new transnational migration are South-South and, increasingly, South-North.[4] The South-North nexus is of principal concern in this book. Although it is important to understand all of the streams which comprise the new migration, this study focuses on the cross-continental movement of refugees following Third World revolutions.

The "temporary" migration of masses of Third World residents into industrialized nations constitutes a late 20th-century phenomenon with far-reaching implications for international relations that are not yet fully appreciated by scholars and public-policy makers. In the prevailing world system, wealthy Western nations export manufactured goods, technical services, food, and weapons to poor countries in the Third World. The South continues to send raw materials to the North. Some of its impoverished regions now return more capital, in the form of debt repayment, than they receive.[5] Finally, the Third World is exporting people to industrialized nations—particularly to the United States.[6]

Although their admission has provoked controversy, official refugees actually have constituted a minor part of overall migration to the United States; legal immigrants and undocumented migrants far outnumber resettled refugees and asylum grantees. Typically, about 600,000 new immigrants—including 70,000 to 100,000 official refugees—have been granted legal admission to the U.S. each year.[7] The estimated number of residents who *emigrate* annually from the United States is higher than the statutory refugee-admission ceiling.[8]

Among the South's three net exports, people are likely to offer the most promising prospect for redressing the present imbalances in global power and wealth through a process which Ali Mazrui refers to as "demographic counter-penetration."[9] Radical redistribution of the world's consumable resources might be brought about through unarmed invasion of the North by poor and desperate Third World squatters. A creeping invasion may have begun.[10] However, as a percentage of the total U.S. population and of population growth, net in-migration exerted a greater impact in the first decade of this century than it has recently.[11] Nevertheless, important demographic changes are in motion[12] and fear of a "people invasion" from the South shapes the thinking of those already "in" the North who favor strict controls on further immigration.[13]

Although barely visible on the current U.S. political horizon, the threat of continuous mass South-North migrations, coupled with the exercise of internal political influence by an expanding population that possesses family and other ties to the Third World, eventually might provide sufficient incentive for industrialized countries to make major concessions in international economic policy and fundamental revisions in foreign policy.[14] Certainly, the issue of South-North migration will intrude ever more forcefully on the public-policy agenda of the wealthy nations. The dilemmas are complex, the trade-offs costly, the options far-reaching, and the resolution long-term. At issue are humanitarian impulses and norms, basic human rights, and perceived national interests.[15]

In short, migration and immigration decision making are located at the crossroads of compelling internal and international pressures.[16] Refugee issues provide a particularly revealing illustration of the interconnected nature of foreign and domestic policy and the growing power of the Third World to direct attention to previously neglected concerns.[17] The refugee phenomenon arises from and generates major human conflicts and opportunities for social change, commands scarce resources, and raises fundamental political and ethical challenges. A systematic comparative analysis of contemporary transnational population movements promises to yield important insights regarding relations among distant and neighboring nations.[18]

4

Foreign-policy analysts and actors frequently ignore vital domestic immigration concerns.[19] In sharp contrast to this tendency, the interrelationship of foreign, refugee, and immigration policy constitutes the recurring theme of this book. The first step toward improved policy making on all three fronts is increased understanding—of the issues and connections involved, the underlying factors, and the actors themselves.

There are four distinct components in the current South-North population flow: economic migrants, official refugees, the displaced, and persons seeking reunification with a family member in one of the first three categories. Some people migrate primarily for economic reasons. They are typically labeled economic migrants. Others move principally due to considerations that are related to exposure to violence and the denial of human rights and government protection in their homeland. Although all persons in the second situation can be considered legitimate refugees, for political reasons only part of the total number is officially counted and treated as such by nation states and the international community.[20] Finally, spouses, parents, siblings, and children seeking family reunification on humanitarian grounds constitute a major part of the current legal immigration to the north from the Third World.[21]

In an increasing number of instances, a reinforcing and inseparably linked combination of economic policies and political forces propels transnational population movement. As a result, some Third World migrants possess mixed and tangled economic and political motives.[22] At the analytical level, convincing arguments have been advanced for treating a substantial part of this group as *de facto* or "sociological" refugees.[23] In practice, however, migrants who flee life-threatening circumstances that do not involve persecution have not been widely accepted as refugees.

In the absence of prior consensus regarding the nature of certain population movements, the acknowledged experience of "displacement" serves as a convenient definitional focal point. Thus, it is useful to consider *uprooting* as the common and overarching element in involuntary South-North migration. From this analytical perspective, officially recognized refugees constitute "one category of forcibly displaced people."[24]

The next sections present an overview of the contributing factors and consequences associated with population dislocation in the Third World. Following a brief discussion of the forces that propel mass economic migration, we will consider the politically displaced. From this encompassing perspective, the focus of attention is progressively narrowed to official refugees and, finally, to refugees from revolution.

Economic Migrants. The compelling considerations at the individual level in large-scale South-North economic migration are poverty, unemployment, and "binational kinship-employer networks."[25] The connection with prevailing global economic relations is revealed by dependency theorists. It is useful to review their conclusions before turning our attention to political dislocation.

Undocumented and legal economic migrants are "pushed" abroad by forces operating in the international economy as well as by the impoverished state of economic conditions in the country of origin, and "pulled" north by the attraction of perceived employment opportunities and consumption prospects. In the dependency framework, the key structural features dominating the global economy are multinational corporations and lending institutions, controlled commodity prices on the world market, state enterprises and economic agencies in the Third World, and transnational ruling-class networks. The prevailing exploitative nature of international economic relations is held to induce migration among both the highly skilled and the unskilled. Firms deeply involved in the global economy endeavor to promote the fluid or mobile state of all factors of production—including labor—so that they might be shifted rapidly across national boundaries in the interest of accelerated capital accumulation.[26]

The economic policies foisted upon receptive Third World states tend to facilitate South-North population movements. For instance, the highly mechanized, export-oriented, agricultural-production strategies advocated by the Western aid establishment have exacerbated income inequities, triggered rural unemployment and outmigration, and invited political repression.[27] Large-scale, direct foreign investment by U.S. firms in export manufacturing and agricultural-commodity production is a characteristic feature of the economies principally associated with recent labor migration to the United States.[28] Although U.S.-based corporations favor overseas investments in manufacturing operations that employ a large number of laborers, Saskia Sassen-Koob finds that two intervening factors still act to stimulate South-North migration. First, traditional work patterns are severely disrupted. Specifically, corporate concentration upon hiring low-paid women workers in the new industrial sector directly and indirectly encourages emigration among unemployed and underemployed males.[29] Second, the spread of foreign capital and cultural influences fosters awareness of, along with structural and ideological links to, migration networks in the principal urban areas of the North. As a result of frequent contact, for instance, persons "employed in services and office work necessary for the export sector" are especially prone "to become part of the pool of migrants." It is no accident, therefore, that most leading sources of immigrants from the Third World to the United States are countries that host large numbers of U.S. personnel and accept a high volume of capital investment and/or military-security assistance.[30]

In addition, advanced industrial economies have become structurally dependent upon foreign-born labor. In order to keep labor costs down on manufacturing operations, multinational corporations endeavor to utilize low-wage workers either in countries where labor is strictly controlled or in free-trade zones. Most industrialized nations also increasingly rely upon large populations of immigrant workers.[31] Sustained capital accumulation at the center of the global economy requires the availability of "a large, mobile, relatively unskilled labor force that can be drawn upon to perform low-status, repetitious, physically demanding tasks that cannot be mechanized."[32] From the exploitation-oriented employer's point of view, illegal but infrequently apprehended workers constitute the preferred labor force because they will be docile and work hard for little pay.[33] Economic migrants are treated as "a modern reserve industrial army that cushions capitalism through its booms and busts with foreign labor recruitment and then expulsion."[34]

Cities such as New York, Washington, D.C., and Los Angeles have become global centers for international management-control and/or producer-service functions. These large urban centers simultaneously are experiencing shrinkage in medium-income jobs and growth in (1) highly remunerated professional and technical positions at the hub of powerful global institutions and (2) in poorly paid non-exportable service employment that is characterized by unattractive working conditions and extremely limited opportunities for advancement. Sassen-Koob explains that "the demand for low-wage workers to service the high-income lifestyles of the rapidly expanding top level work force is one key factor in the expansion of an informal sector in cities like New York and Los Angeles." The labor-intensive, informal-sector employment opportunities created by "high-income gentrification" include waiters and waitresses, porters, nannies, "residential building attendants, workers producing services or goods for speciality shops and gourmet food shops, dog walkers, errand runners, cleaners of all sorts. . . ."[35]

It is inaccurate, therefore, to view contemporary economic migration from poor countries to the industrialized world exclusively in terms of push factors related to domestic poverty. South-North labor migration also is stimulated by the increasing demand emanating from influential growth sectors and middle-sized enterprises in the Western capitalist countries for low-wage, non-unionized and powerless workers.[36] By 1990, millions of migrant workers had invaded the industrialized world. A diverse set of legal and illegal avenues, including surreptitious border crossings, are available for those intent on taking this step.[37]

The Politically Displaced. In the contemporary Third World, millions of people have been uprooted from their homes by armed hostilities, foreign interventions, and government policies such as forced resettlement.[38] This category includes persons internally as well as externally displaced. Major refugee-generating countries also tend to produce sizeable populations of internally dislocated nationals. Many of these individuals would qualify for refugee status on the basis of persecution and continued harassment if they succeeded in crossing an international border.[39] Estimates of *internally displaced* populations are especially imprecise, but two regions of special interest in this book—the Horn of Africa and Iran/Iraq—presently rank with southern Africa among the areas of the world that possess the highest total number of "internal refugees."[40]

The *externally displaced* include individuals and families who seek but have not yet been granted political asylum, Palestinians outside of UNRWA's area of operations, the victims of urban warfare in religiously divided Beirut and of nationality struggles in rural Africa, Kurds escaping attacks by the Iraqi army, and impoverished Latin Americans who have fled armed conflict and economic or environmental disasters induced by government policies. A conservative estimate of 4 million people could be counted in this category at the end of the 1980s.[41] In response to the needs of the internationally dislocated, members of the Organization of African Unity consciously updated and expanded the organization's definition of a refugee to encompass persons compelled to flee "'external aggression, occupation, foreign domination or events seriously disturbing public order'" and, in some cases, the United Nations High Commission for Refugees (UNHCR) has extended its protection to externally displaced populations. In Latin America, for instance, UNHCR aids Salvadoreans and Guatemalans who have fled violence and terror in their homeland and are living in refugee-like situations.[42]

Leon Gordenker provides a helpful introduction to the different types of actions that lead to displacement and generate refugees. His classification scheme includes international wars, revolutions, *coups d'état*, insurrections, and brutal governments as "causal elements in contemporary refugee incidents."[43] "Cross-fire refugees," usually members of peasant families, are the victims of violent actions unleashed by government, quasi-governmental, or guerrilla forces and death squads that frequently are supported and supplied by external powers.[44]   Displacement also is associated with kidnapping and assassination attempts, unsolved disappearances, forced relocation in strategic settlements, bombing and strafing, and scorched-earth military tactics.[45]   The random, unrestrained, and apparently uncontrollable nature of these vicious methods of so-called "low-intensity conflict" frequently are not accidental. In many cases, such actions either are part of a deliberate strategy of state terrorism or counterterrorism designed "to silence through fear anyone who might possibly consider opposition in the future"[46] or to deprive guerrilla forces of a civilian support base.[47]

Various dislocating forces often are simultaneously at work in countries experiencing mass displacement. Although low-intensity conflicts fall short of "full-scale combat between modern armies," their total dislocating effect can be extensive.   Low-intensity conflict encompasses terrorism, anti-terrorism and anti-drug operations, counter-insurgency, and inter-ethnic violence.[48]   In southern Sudan, the forcible interdiction of food relief has been employed as a weapon of war—especially by the government side—in the conflict between the Sudan People's Liberation Army and the state's armed forces.[49]   Forced resettlement schemes usually are intended, at least in part, to enhance the ability of the state to exert military control over rural populations and/or to extract surplus from sedentary cultivators.[50]

In short, the techniques of armed conflict and citizen control that have become commonplace in many Third World countries turn innocent bystanders into victims of violence. Whether calculated or random, the effect is to instill fear into rural and urban populations in the affected areas. A former Deputy High Commissioner for Refugees explains that "they may have seen their houses, shops or land burned, seized, pillaged or invaded, their countrymen—often friends or relatives—taken away without explanation." Their experiences in the conflict zone leave them in a state of "fear for their lives, for their families, for their future."[51]

Refugees. The year 1989 opened with roughly 14.5 million recognized refugees living outside their homelands. Afghanistan stood out far above the other refugee-producing states; nearly 6 million persons had fled that war-torn country.   Considered together, African refugees comprised 28 percent of the world total at the end of 1988.   The Horn of Africa remained the source of the third largest refugee population—after the 2.3 million Palestinians. In the Horn, an estimated 355,000 Sudanese, 350,000 Somalis, and 1,100,000 refugees from Ethiopia lived in need of external protection and/or assistance. Mozambique and Angola in southern Africa came next, with 1,100,000 and 400,000 refugees, respectively.   Iraq and Iran followed, with a combined total of nearly one million.[52] By mid 1991, fighting in Kuwait and Iraq and regime overthrows in Somalia and Ethiopia had triggered massive new waves of refugees to neighboring countries.

Persons who have been accepted for permanent resettlement are no longer counted among those needing protection and/or assistance. Between 1975 and 1987, the United States accommodated 1.2 million official refugees, or 58 percent of the permanently resettled total.[53] In relation to national population size, however, total U.S. refugee admissions only rank seventh in the world. Among the other Western industrialized nations, Canada (224,000), France (169,000), and Australia (over 150,000) have been the most active in third-country resettlement.[54]

Refugees from Indochina have been the most successful in securing third-country resettlement. According to the U.S. State Department, "since 1975, over 1.5 million Vietnamese, Cambodians, and Laotians have been resettled in third countries."[55] Most other Third World refugees spend lengthy periods in camps or other facilities designed for temporary settlement. For those still living in such circumstances, prospects are dim that they or their children will be able to return to their homeland or qualify for resettlement. Palestinian refugees present the most striking illustration of the contemporary phenomenon of perpetual refugee-camp populations. Many refugees from Ethiopia in Sudan and Somalia have lived in exile for approximately 15 years, and vast numbers from Afghanistan have resided in Iran and Pakistan for about a decade.[56]

Refugees from Revolution. Revolutions typically resemble other refugee-producing incidents in terms of the experience of armed conflict, the effort to displace the governing elite, the occurrence of violent internal struggles to consolidate power, and the intolerance of opposition. Revolutions are uniquely powerful refugee-generating events, however, because they also involve a deliberate and simultaneous attempt to transform social and economic relations and to construct a radically different political system.[57]

China became the first Third World country to experience revolution in the post-war period. Within the next 30 years, Cuba, Vietnam, Cambodia, Laos, Ethiopia, Afghanistan, Iran, Angola, Mozambique, and Nicaragua experienced massive population outflows in the wake of revolutionary transformation of their political and social landscapes and the "internationalization" of armed conflict.[58]

National revolutions are likely to provoke international conflicts because they typically are perceived to promote or threaten superpower interests. Thus, all post-war U.S. administrations have actively opposed revolutionary change in the Third World in an effort to ´preserve the global status quo. The forms of intervention are diverse; they range from direct and overt military action (Vietnam and Cambodia) to the abrupt termination of security assistance and indications of support for hostile neighbors (Ethiopia and Iran). Other destabilization techniques include organizational, material, and logistical support for exile invasion forces (Cuba, Nicaragua) and the provision of extensive covert and overt paramilitary assistance for (frequently ethnically based) guerrilla armies engaged in insurgency campaigns against revolutionary Marxist regimes (Vietnam, Laos, Angola, Cambodia, and Afghanistan).[59] Each type of intervention has produced similar outcomes. The externally supported opposition proves insufficient, especially in the face of revolutionary nationalism, to overcome the new regime. However, the revolutionary political system faces prolonged armed conflict with debilitating consequences in terms of economic crisis, reduced state legitimacy, and population out-migration.

As a result of the radical changes introduced and their tendency to attract external intervention, Third World revolutions have produced a major proportion of the combined global total of refugees who have been permanently resettled and who still require protection. Table I.1 provides a rough indication of the number of refugees who have escaped from each of the eleven revolution-experiencing countries in the Third World. The estimates include persons who have been permanently resettled outside of their homeland, the few who have returned, and those who live in camps or in self-settled situations. In terms of the total numbers of citizens affected, Afghanistan, China, Iran, and Ethiopia are at the top of the list. When we consider the proportion that refugees constitute of each country's population, Afghanistan and China stand at extreme opposite ends of the spectrum. In the other post-revolution societies, with the exception of Cambodia, between three and ten percent of all citizens opted for exile. The magnitude of such population losses is indicative of the extraordinary devastation that has occurred in Third World countries that experience revolution.

Distribution Patterns. Roughly eight million officially recognized refugees from Afghanistan, Ethiopia, Cambodia, Iran, Laos, Vietnam, and Nicaragua had not been permanently resettled by the end of the 1980s— although new departures from these countries had at least temporarily declined from their previous levels.[60] Less than one percent of the world's refugee population manages to go North.

These aggregate statistics mask three distinct patterns. In the first and least-common situation, *most* of those who flee revolutionary conditions in a Third World country eventually resettle in the industrialized West. The United States has served as the country of first asylum for nearly all post-

TABLE I.1 Estimates of Total Refugee Population from Third-World Countries Experiencing Revolution

Sending Country	Estimated Total # Refugees ('000s)	Estimated Current Pop. ('000s)	Refugees as % Total Population
Afghanistan	6,000	18,600	32.3%
China	3,500	1,200	0.3
Iran	2,000	40,000	5.0
Ethiopia	1,500	44,000	3.4
Mozambique	1,100	15,000	7.3
Vietnam	1,100	63,000	1.7
Cuba	1,000	10,000	10.0
Cambodia	800	6,000	13.3
Angola	400	9,000	4.4
Laos	300	3,300	9.1
Nicaragua	300	3,700	8.1

Source: *World Refugee Survey—1988 in Review*, pp. 32–33, 73; Jones, *Iranian Refugees*, p. 7; *National Resistance Movement Newspaper* (Paris), 15 July 1986; Suhrke and Klink, "Vietnamese and Afghan," p. 88; Bach, "Cubans," p. 77; Ebihara, "Khmer," pp. 133–134; Van Esterik, "Lao," pp. 151, 154; Zolberg *et al.*, *Refugee Crisis*, pp. 126–127, 150, 156–168, 184, 206–212; Jo Sullivan, *Global Studies*: *Africa*, 3rd edition (Guilford: Dushkin Publishing Group, 1989), pp. 94, 128, 137; *Europa World Yearbook 1989* (London: Europa Publications, 1989), Vol. I, p. 281; Vol. II, p. 2932.

revolution exiles who arrived in several waves from Cuba, and as the primary place of resettlement for those from Indochina.[61] Although countries near to Vietnam have served as the principal areas of first asylum, they have made no effort to integrate sizeable numbers of Vietnamese refugees and, on occasion, have not allowed them to enter at all.[62]

In the second type of situation, the majority of refugees from revolution tend to remain in their region of origin—though *large numbers* are accepted for "third-country" resettlement in the North. Thus, most people who have fled from Ethiopia still are found today in Sudan and Somalia, although those living outside of the Horn are located primarily in the United States—where they constitute the largest group of resettled refugees from Africa.[63] One also encounters substantial populations of Iranian exiles in

12

the U.S.A. and France, although the majority remain in the South.[64] About 250,000 refugees from Iran live in Turkey, with other large communities located in Iraq and Pakistan. Refugees from the Chinese revolution have established themselves on Taiwan, Hong Kong, and elsewhere in Southeast Asia. Over half a million Chinese immigrants have entered the United States since 1965. Although few Chinese have been officially admitted as refugees, most of those accepted as regular immigrants initially fled from the mainland.[65] Nicaraguans mainly have fled to Costa Rica, Honduras, Guatemala, Mexico, and the United States.[66]

In the final pattern, regional resettlement prevails and there is *extremely limited* South-North migration. Out of nearly 6 million Afghan refugees, only 22,000 had been admitted to the United States by mid-1988.[67] Even fewer refugees from Mozambique and Angola have been resettled in this country.[68] In 1990, Pakistan and Iran continued to host most of those who fled from Afghanistan. The vast majority of refugees from Mozambique resided in Malawi, and Angolans remained in Zaire and Zambia.[69]

Post-Revolution Exile Communities in the United States

As the principal final destination to date for refugees from revolution who seek asylum or are resettled in the North, U.S. communities provide valuable research settings. *Refugees from Revolution* focuses on four sending countries—Cuba, Vietnam, Iran, and Ethiopia—that cover the main regions of the Third World and include a balanced mix of predominantly first-asylum and third-country resettled situations. Figure I.1 graphically displays the share of the total refugee population from each country of origin that resides in the United States.

The migrant communities that provide the principal basis for the studies drawn upon in writing this book consist mainly of self-imposed exiles, but encompass some economic migrants as well.[70] Exiles include official (or resettled) refugees, political-asylum grantees, and others with legitimate claims to refugee status that remain unrecognized by the state. In the latter category are individuals who maintain temporary non-immigrant status, those who entered without INS inspection (EWI), visa abusers, and unrecognized refugees who have been granted amnesty or regular-immigrant status.

Cubans and Indochinese

The Cuban and Indochinese post-revolution exile populations are of particular interest because of their size and because they constitute the first

Figure I.1 Estimated Proportion of Total Refugee Population from Cuba, Vietnam, Iran, and Ethiopia Currently Living in the United States

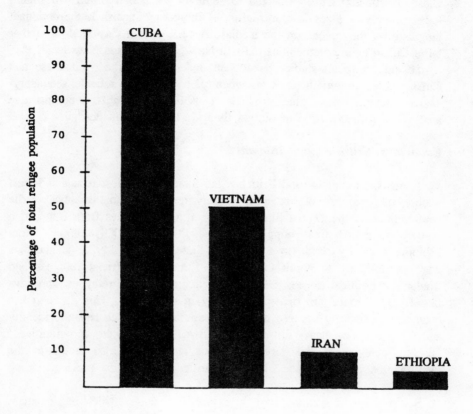

groups to resettle predominantly in the United States rather than to remain in the South. Roughly 900,000 Indochinese refugees entered this country between 1975 and 1989. The majority of these resettled refugees are Vietnamese.[71] Extensive migration from Vietnam to the United States, including about 30,000 regular refugee admissions per year, continues to occur. Within the past decade, moreover, 75,000 Vietnamese have resettled here under the Orderly Departure Program (ODP); another 100,000 are likely to arrive eventually under an agreement reached between the U.S. and the Socialist Republic of Vietnam in July 1989.[72]

Nearly one million Cuban exiles also have resettled in the United States. Close to 700,000 Cubans elected to settle in southern Florida. In Miami today, largely as a result of the influx of refugees, "Spanish is the dominant language on the streets, on the media airwaves, and in City Hall."[73] Other large Cuban exile communities exist in New York City and New Jersey.[74]

Several thorough studies have been undertaken of the Vietnamese and Cuban exile communities. Consequently, a wealth of reliable secondary-source material exists that provides a useful basis for the comparative analysis of refugees from revolution living in the United States.[75]

Ethiopians, Eritreans, and Iranians

Iranians, Ethiopians, and Eritreans are three of the most recent and least understood groups of refugees from revolution to establish exile communities in the United States. Perhaps 200,000 exiles from Iran and a crudely estimated total population of 40,000 to 75,000 migrants from Ethiopia currently reside in the United States.[76] Until 1985, gatekeepers were more likely to admit exiles from Ethiopia as official refugees and Iranians as political asylees. Eritreans, a major group of refugees who have fled from Ethiopia, are treated separately in this book. This decision has been made primarily because many Eritreans insist on their separate identity and, in practice, have formed their own unique exile communities.[77] Discrete analysis of this large group of respondents also facilitates the identification of differences and similarities in decision making among political migrants with diverse backgrounds.

South-North migration from Iran and Ethiopia provides an excellent basis for controlled comparison because the two countries share certain features in common and remain quite dissimilar in other ways. The most important common element is the nature of U.S. foreign relations with the pre-revolution imperial regimes and with their post-revolution successor governments. Combined analysis of the two experiences with external intervention and with ruling monarchical political systems is likely to promote understanding of the refugee-generating impact of the U.S. government's response to revolutionary change. On the other hand, the two countries remain quite different in terms of the cultural background of the people, the type of post-revolution regime, and the nature of their economies. For instance, Ethiopia's economy is characterized by considerably less industrialization and multinational corporate penetration.

Finally, the protracted and consuming nature of the Eritrean struggle for independence sets Ethiopia apart from Iran.

Unlike the Indochinese and Cuban cases, little has been published on Iranians, Ethiopians, and Eritreans. These three exile communities also differ from the former because they include substantial proportions of non returnees as well as émigrés. One of the central objectives of this volume, therefore, is to review previous conclusions in light of new findings based upon the analysis of recent migration from Iran and Ethiopia. The primary-source data contribution rests in large part upon field work conducted among the Ethiopian and Eritrean communities in the District of Columbia metropolitan area and with Iranians in D.C. and in the Los Angeles metropolitan area. The L.A. area is the central locale for Iranian migrants to the United States, while the highest concentration of exiles from Ethiopia have settled in the District of Columbia and its environs.

In addition to official interviews, documents, and contemporary accounts, *Refugees from Revolution* draws upon five distinct data sets gathered by the author: (1) basic demographic information regarding 10,000 refugees admitted to the United States from Ethiopia, supplied in 1984 by the Refugee Data Center (RDC); (2) more detailed information coded from a systematic 10 percent sample of the refugee bio-data forms kept on file at the RDC (a total of 796 household heads or independent entrants from Ethiopia and Iran); (3) analysis of officially reported reasons for emigration and information on migration avenues collected from 197 refugee files (approximately 20 percent of the total) made available by Church World Service, a major resettlement agency; (4) data coded from 59 political-asylum applications filed mainly in the New York City and Washington, D.C., metropolitan areas through 1990; and (5) 317 extensive interviews conducted with randomly selected members of the Ethiopian, Eritrean, and Iranian communities carried out during 1984–85 in the Washington, D.C., and Los Angeles metropolitan areas.[78] The research design and sampling results for the D.C./L.A. study are described more fully in the Appendix to this volume. Chapter 6 provides a profile of the three post-revolution exile communities in the U.S. that is based principally upon the above sources.

The Refugee-Policy Community

The complexity of refugee policy-making in the United States is an outgrowth of the country's devotion to a system of shared powers among different governmental and non-governmental institutions. The U.S. government's refugee policy operates at two levels: international and domestic. The international level is concerned with external issues of protection, resettlement, and repatriation. Policies in this area are largely shaped by the foreign-policy establishment; i.e., the Department of State and congressional foreign affairs and immigration committees and subcommittees.[79] Although policy proposing and implementation fall within the State Department's domain under the 1980 Refugee Act, Congress must approve admission ceilings and budgets.[80] The Bureau for Refugee Programs at the Department of State oversees the distribution of U.S. assistance to refugees living abroad.

The Refugee Act created the Office of Refugee Coordinator within the State Department and established an annual consultation process between the executive and legislative branches. The Coordinator is responsible for initiating refugee policy, conducting international negotiations on refugee issues, preparing official reports, and coordinating both domestic and overseas programs.[81] In practice, little cooperative decision-making has resulted and Congress rarely challenges the determinations, priority-setting decisions, allocations, and re-allocations made by the Department of State.[82] However, "the office of the refugee coordinator never attained the stature or the presence that the Refugee Act envisioned" and the occupant "has been able to exercise only limited authority over the large array of federal agencies involved with refugee issues."[83]

The domestic dimensions of refugee policy primarily involve issues of admission, settlement, and adjustment. Admission decisions are matters of national legislative and executive policy making—even though their principal immediate effect is on state and local political jurisdictions and on particular urban communities. There are two potential tracks available for refugee admission in the United States: resettlement and political asylum. The Bureau for Refugee Programs advises Immigration and Naturalization (INS) field officers and is responsible for major administrative decisions regarding refugee processing as well as for preparing the information used in consultation documents. The Immigration and Naturalization Service of the Justice Department, assisted by voluntary-agency (volag) personnel, plays the key overseas role in selecting "official" refugees for resettlement in the United States. Under authority delegated by the Attorney General, INS district directors and immigration judges have held primary responsibility for asylum determinations—although the State Department's "advisory" opinions usually have been decisive. Asylum decisions frequently involve the legal community and independent expert testimony. On occasion, a highly contested case will be appealed to the courts.

Refugees admitted through the first track are assisted in the adjustment process by a voluntary resettlement agency. Moreover, the Department of Health and Human Services' Office of Refugee Resettlement (ORR), together with state and local welfare offices, implement the welfare provisions of the Refugee Act and other congressional enactments. ORR exercises primary responsibility for coordinating domestic resettlement-assistance programs.[84]

The unrecognized refugees who succeed in entering the United States operate outside of these formal systems. They include migrants entering without inspection (EWI), individuals admitted on a legal temporary basis who overstay their visa and become undocumented aliens, and immigrants arriving with permanent status but not as legally recognized refugees. Among the undocumented group, refugees who do not secure political asylum can still take advantage of immigration procedures which allow them to become permanent residents. These include regularization of status through marriage or other relation to a U.S. citizen or permanent resident, labor certification, and amnesty.[85]

In the international arena, U.S. policy makers attempt to influence multinational organizations with responsibility for refugee assistance—including the U.N. High Commission for Refugees (UNHCR) and the private voluntary agencies at work in the field. The High Commissioner, who is nominated by the Secretary-General, is appointed by, and dependent for instructions upon, the General Assembly.[86] Nevertheless, decisions reached by the international refugee establishment "primarily reflect the interests and priorities of the major donor countries" in the North.[87]

In recent years, UNHCR has been under pressure to improve the coordination of refugee-assistance activities with other international organizations—including the United Nations Development Programme (UNDP), the International Labor Organization (ILO), the World Food Programme, and the World Bank. Non-governmental organizations (NGOs) also play an important role in the reception and settlement of refugees.[88]

Conceptual Framework

A consensus is developing among scholars concerned with migration theory that it is essential to treat population movements within a framework that links social-structural and individual levels of analysis.[89] An important objective of this book is to relate social constraints and opportunities to micro-level exile decision making. The structural analysis should encompass global, national, and local conditions, incorporate insights drawn from historical perspective, and locate transnational refugee movements within the political and economic contexts of sending and receiving societies.[90]   The impact of the U.S. government's foreign and immigration policies is a recurring theme in this discussion.   The individual level is captured through case-history analysis, survey research, and process study.[91]

In analyzing post-revolution migration from South to North, therefore, it is necessary to link "international relations, migration studies, public policy analysis, and that part of comparative politics that deals with causes of violent societal conflict."[92]   The conceptual framework set forth in Chapter 1 develops the key linkages and avoids a narrow view of refugee migrations as isolated and unique events.[93]   Subsequent chapters apply the framework through cross-national comparisons that are designed to identify common motivating factors, assist in the analysis of prevailing outcomes, and present a comprehensive understanding of the refugee condition.   In the application of integrated structural-individual analysis to each stage of the refugee experience, *Refugees from Revolution* utilizes the method of intensive controlled comparison rather than the cross-national manipulation of aggregate statistical data of questionable reliability.[94]

The nature of refugee formation constitutes the focus of Part 1.   Why do some citizens of Third World countries seek exile in the first place?   In attempting to answer this question, the first three chapters devote special attention to external intervention, class relations, ideological commitments, and national political developments.   Understanding the political and historical context of exile formation is important for service providers who are responsible for assisting refugees from revolution as well as for students of international relations and for those interested in addressing the underlying forces that provoke transnational population movement.

Part 2 is concerned with avenues of post-revolution migration. Resettlement in the industrialized world usually occurs only at the end of a lengthy step-migration process.   How do cross-national, micro-level networks facilitate the migration of refugees and their households?   Which refugees from revolution wind up in the United States?   Why?   What are the principal barriers to entry and how are they overcome?   This section includes a critical assessment of the application of U.S. immigration policy.

Part 3 deals with the reception of refugees from revolution after they arrive in the United States.   It profiles five exile communities and explores economic adjustment and social adaptation within the context of existing obstacles and opportunities.   Interesting differences between and within exile communities in terms of economic and social adaptation are identified and their implications are analyzed in these chapters.

Part 4 treats the important but frequently neglected issue of repatriation. Repatriation constitutes a potential final stage in the refugee-migration process. Many social-service workers, policy makers, and scholars hold that secure resettlement in the country of origin offers the preferred resolution of the refugee crisis. Do refugees from revolution who reach the North continue to hope for return to the country of origin? Under what conditions are they likely to make that move? Chapter 8 presents new research findings that address these questions and Chapter 9 links the results of this analysis with prevailing national and transnational obstacles to repatriation.

The interconnectedness of domestic and foreign issues is a unifying theme in *Refugees from Revolution*. Part 5 explores how an unplanned component of contemporary international relations—refugee migration—is shaped by foreign-policy actions and, in turn, how it affects foreign and domestic policy making. Chapter 10 reviews the principal conclusions drawn from the analysis of the experiences of exiles living in the United States, considers the public-policy implications, and offers recommendations for change in U.S. foreign policy toward the Third World and in immigration policy toward political migrants. The final chapter reconsiders the challenges raised by South-North population movements in light of the U.S. experience with refugees from revolution. Specifically, it explores the future implications of current migration trends for sending and receiving countries, and for the conduct of international relations in the 21st century.

Notes

1. Elizabeth Ferris confirms that "political scientists have traditionally paid little attention to refugee movements, largely interpreting such migrations as marginal to the central processes of international politics." Elizabeth G. Ferris, "Overview: Refugees and World Politics," in *Refugees and World Politics*, edited by Elizabeth G. Ferris (New York: Praeger, 1985), p. 1; also see Gil Loescher, "Introduction: Refugee Issues in International Relations," in *Refugees and International Relations*, edited by Gil Loescher and Laila Monahan (Oxford: Oxford University Press, 1989), p. 7. According to Myron Weiner, "the literature on international relations says relatively little about population movements, except insofar as the refugee phenomenon is described as an outcome of conflicts." Myron Weiner, "On International Migration and International Relations," *Population and Development Review* 11, No. 3 (September 1985):441. Frederic Wakeman's trenchant criticism

that "our research strategies in international and area studies are ordered in such a way as to permit important problem-oriented issues to slip through our analytical nets" certainly is applicable with respect to transnational migration. Frederic E. Wakeman, Jr., "Transnational and Comparative Research," *Social Science Research Council Items* 42, No. 4 (December 1988):85–88. For an insightful critique of the prevailing international-relations paradigm, see Dennis Pirages, *Global Technopolitics: The International Politics of Technology & Resources* (Pacific Grove, California: Brooks/Cole Publishing Company, 1989), pp. 19–20.

2. See Mary M. Kritz, "The Global Picture of Contemporary Immigration Patterns," in *Pacific Bridges: The New Immigration from Asia and the Pacific Islands*, edited by James T. Fawcett and Benjamin V. Cariño (Staten Island: Center for Migration Studies, 1987), pp. 29, 45–48; Robin Cohen, "Citizens, Denizens and Helots: The Politics of International Migration Flows in the Post-War World" (paper presented at an international symposium, Hitotsubashi University, Tokyo, September 1988), p. 13; Michael J. Piore, *Birds of Passage: Migrant Labor and Industrial Societies* (Cambridge: Cambridge University Press, 1979), pp. 50, 52; Demetrios G. Papademetriou, "International Migration in a Changing World," *International Social Science Journal* 36, No. 3 (1984):417–418; and Elsa M. Chaney, "Migrant Workers and National Boundaries: The Basis for Rights and Protections," in *Boundaries: National Autonomy and Its Limits*, edited by Peter G. Brown and Henry Shue (Totowa: Rowman and Littlefield, 1981), p. 57.

3. Michael S. Teitelbaum, "International Relations and Asian Migrations," in *Pacific Bridges: The New Immigration from Asia and the Pacific Islands*, p. 73.

4. See Leon Gordenker, *Refugees in International Politics* (New York: Columbia University Press, 1987), pp. 52–53; Ferris, "Overview," p. 10; W. R. Smyser, "Refugees: A Never-Ending Story," *Foreign Affairs* 64, No. 1 (Fall 1985):160, 162; Saskia Sassen-Koob, "Towards a Conceptualization of Immigrant Labor," *Social Problems* 29, No. 1 (October 1981):68, 75. The end of the decade of the 1980s witnessed a dramatic surge in East-West population movement and predictions that millions of Eastern Europeans will invade Western Europe, but intra-South exchanges continued to involve more people even if they receive less attention in the North. See Gervase Coles, "Approaching the Refugee Problem Today," in *Refugees and International Relations*, p. 373; Jonas Widgren, "Demography and Democracy," *Refugees* (March 1990):11; *New York Times*, 14 December 1990, p. A6. The terms "South" and "Third World" are used interchangeably in this book to refer generally to countries other than the United States, Canada, Australia, New Zealand, Japan, the Soviet Union, and all of Europe. Also see J. P. Dickenson *et al.*, *A Geography of the Third World* (London: Methuen, 1983), pp. 1–14.

Third World peoples have predominated among legal U.S. immigrants since 1965. In 1988, thirteen of the fifteen leading sources of immigrants to the United

States, including Vietnam, Cuba, Iran, and Laos, were located in the Third World. Over 70 percent of all immigrants now originate in Asia or Latin America. U.S., Immigration and Naturalization Service, *Statistical Yearbook of the Immigration and Naturalization Service, 1987* (Washington, D.C.: U.S. Government Printing Office, 1988), p. xix; Vincent N. Parrillo, *Strangers to these Shores: Race and Ethnic Relations in the United States*, 3rd edition (New York: Macmillan Publishing Company, 1990), pp. 534–535; Leon F. Bouvier, "U.S. Immigration: Effects on Population Growth and Structure," in *U.S. Immigration and Refugee Policy: Global and Domestic Issues*, edited by Mary M. Kritz (Lexington: D.C. Heath and Company, 1983), p. 195. Annual Asian immigration ranged between 268,000 and 281,000 in the late 1980s. About one-third of the new entrants, who came primarily from the Philippines, China, Taiwan, Hong Kong, South Korea, and India, settled in California. *New York Times*, 2 March 1990, p. A12. Recent Canadian immigration also is overwhelmingly from the South—including 80,000 wealthy Chinese from Hong Kong who have mainly settled in Vancouver and Toronto since 1984. *New York Times*, 17 March 1990, p. A4.

On the history of U.S. immigration policy, including the racial-exclusion laws which inhibited South-North migration, see David M. Reimers, *Still the Golden Door: The Third World Comes to America* (New York: Columbia University Press, 1985), pp. xii–xiii, 2, 9, 156, 176, 243; Paul G. Lauren, *Power and Prejudice: The Politics and Diplomacy of Racial Discrimination* (Boulder: Westview, 1988), p. 38.

5. Chandra S. Hardy, "Africa's Debt: Structural Adjustment with Stability," in *Strategies for African Development*, edited by Robert G. Berg and Jennifer S. Whitaker (Berkeley: University of California Press, 1986), pp. 472, 467; Peter H. Koehn, *Public Policy and Administration in Africa: Lessons from Nigeria* (Boulder: Westview Press, 1990), p. 134.

6. Currently, the U.S. receives roughly half of the world's international migrants. Constance Holden, "Debate Warming Up on Legal Migration Policy," *Science* 241 (15 July 1988):287. Papademetriou and DiMarzio refer to the South-North migration process as "a subsidy of the rich by the poor." Demetrios G. Papademetriou and Nicholas DiMarzio, "An Exploration into the Social and Labor Market Incorporation of Undocumented Aliens: The Case of the New York Metropolitan Area" (report to the Center for Migration Studies and the Tinker Foundation, 1985), p. 184.

The movement of people to industrialized nations includes gradually increasing legal and illegal migration to Japan from China, Vietnam, the Philippines, and other Asian countries. See *Washington Post*, 22 October 1989, p. A40; *New York Times*, 12 October 1989, p. A6; 12 December 1989, p. A18; and 3 January 1990, p. A8. From a continent of out-migration to other parts of the world, Western Europe has become a land of immigrants. On European Community efforts to prevent Third

World migrants from entering the newly integrated region and from transferring legal residence and work authorization from one country to another after 1992, see *New York Times*, 20 December 1989, p. 9; 16 April 1990, p. A5.

South Korea, among other Third World countries, has officially exported workers as part of an overall economic-development strategy. On the receiving side, "immigration policies in western Europe and the Arab oil-exporting countries increasingly treat immigrants as a commodity." Sassen-Koob, "Immigrant Labor," 79; Illsoo Kim, "Korea and East Asia: Premigration Factors and U.S. Immigration Policy," in *Pacific Bridges: The New Immigration from Asia and the Pacific Islands*, pp. 336–337. On the transformation of labor into a transnational component of the world capitalist economic system, see Papademetriou, "International Migration," 412–415.

7. Holden, "Debate," 241. Petitioners filed a total of 26,107 asylum applications with INS district directors in FY 1987; 5,093 individuals received asylum in the United States in that fiscal year. U.S., INS, *1987 Yearbook*, p. 57. In contrast, refugees and asylum seekers have accounted for a large proportion of Western European in-migration since 1979. Applicants for asylum, mostly from the Third World, outnumbered legally admitted workers for the first time in 1985. Cohen, "Citizens, Denizens and Helots," pp. 6, 8; Widgren, "Europe," 52; Guy S. Goodwin-Gill, "Refugees: The Functions and Limits of the Existing Protection System," in *Human Rights and the Protection of Refugees under International Law*, edited by Alan E. Nash (Halifax: Institute for Research on Public Policy, 1988), p. 152; Smyser, "Refugees," 162.

8. Norman L. Zucker and Naomi F. Zucker, *The Guarded Gate: The Reality of American Refugee Policy* (San Diego: Harcourt Brace Jovanovich, 1987), p. 95. U.S. Bureau of the Census estimates place annual emigration at 160,000. Cited in U.S., INS, *1987 Yearbook*, p. xxiii.

9. Ali A. Mazrui, "The New Interdependence: From Hierarchy to Symmetry," in *The U.S. and World Development: Agenda for Action 1975*, comp. by James W. Howe (New York: Praeger, 1975), p. 126; also see Bouvier, "Growth," 194. According to Papademetriou ("International Migration," 415), advanced industrial societies are "more vulnerable to population movements originating in less-developed countries than they are to any other resource except perhaps energy."

10. See, for instance, *New York Times*, 26 March 1990, p. A9.

11. Zucker and Zucker, *Guarded Gate*, p. 146; Parrillo, *Strangers*, p. 534.

12. See, for instance, Parrillo, *Strangers*, pp. 534–535; Leon F. Bouvier and Anthony J. Agresta, "The Future Asian Population of the United States," in *Pacific Bridges: The New Immigration from Asia and the Pacific Islands*, pp. 297–298. Recent entrants tend to be young in age and from diverse social and cultural backgrounds. In terms of residential distribution, they are concentrated in seven

metropolitan areas—including Los Angeles, New York, and Washington, D.C. Thomas Muller and Thomas J. Espenshade, *The Fourth Wave: California's Newest Immigrants* (Washington, D.C.: Urban Institute, 1985), pp. 14–15. On southern California immigrants, also see *New York Times*, 16 June 1990, pp. 1, 7.

13. Among others, Richard Lamm, former governor of the state of Colorado, and former President Ronald Reagan have endeavored to fan invasion fears among the U.S. public. See Peter W. van Arsdale and Laurel J. Bagan, "The Development of Refugee Policy and Mental Health Programming in Colorado," in *Refugee Law and Policy: International and U.S. Responses*, edited by Ved P. Nanda (Westport: Greenwood Press, 1989), p. 156; Silvia Pedraza-Bailey, *Political and Economic Migrants in America: Cubans and Mexicans* (Austin: University of Texas Press, 1985), p. 166; Zucker and Zucker, *Guarded Gate*, p. 146; Michael S. Teitelbaum, "Immigration, Refugees, and Foreign Policy," *International Organization* 38, No. 3 (Summer 1984):434–435. For a brief discussion of the opposing positions on controlling immigration and refugee numbers advocated by various interest groups in the United States, see Reimer, *Golden Door*, p. xi.

14. See Weiner, "International Relations," pp. 451, 453. Mazrui ("New Interdependence," p. 126) predicts that "the 'brain drain' from the developing into the developed world could one day become a source of Southern influence within the North—comparable in principle to the role played by Jewish intellectuals and businessmen in Europe and North America in defense of Israeli interests." For a discussion of the actual impact and potential influence within the North of autonomous non-national political actors, including permanent residents and students, see Mark J. Miller and Demetrios G. Papademetriou, "Immigration and U.S. Foreign Policy," in *The Unavoidable Issue: U.S. Immigration Policy in the 1980s*, ed. by Papademetriou and Miller (Philadelphia: Institute for the Study of Human Issues, 1983), pp. 169, 178. By 1990, U.S. Supreme Court rulings had protected efforts to establish single-member electoral districts that promised to advance the political influence of naturalized immigrants—particularly Hispanic Americans. See Rafael Valdivieso and Cary Davis, *U.S. Hispanics: Challenging Issues for the 1990s* (Washington, D.C.: Population Reference Bureau, 1988), pp. 14–15.

15. See Loescher, "Issues," p. 8.

16. Pedraza-Bailey, *Migrants*, pp. 138–139.

17. Also see Pirages, *Global Technopolitics*, pp. 21, 34.

18. Most of the concepts traditionally examined by students of international relations are sharply illustrated in this policy arena. See Loescher, "Issues," pp. 7–8. Moreover, as Ferris ("Overview," p. 1) points out, "the study of refugee movements presents fascinating opportunities for understanding the interplay between political, social, economic, cultural, and psychological phenomena."

19. Miller and Papademetriou, "Foreign," 155–157; Loescher, "Issues," p. 4.

24

20. Suhrke and Klink note that "some sociological refugees are legally recognized while others are not; and some who would not meet a sociological criterion of refugee nevertheless may be given legal status as such." Astri Suhrke and Frank Klink, "Contrasting Patterns of Asian Refugee Movements: The Vietnamese and Afghan Syndromes," in *Pacific Bridges: The New Immigration from Asia and the Pacific Islands*, p. 87.

21. Jonas Widgren, "Europe and International Migration in the Future: The Necessity for Merging Migration, Refugee, and Development Policies," in *Refugees and International Relations*, p. 52; Bill Frelick, "No Place to Go: Controlling Who Gets In," in *Forced Out: The Agony of the Refugee in Our Time*, compiled by Carole Kismaric (Washington, D.C.: Human Rights Watch and the J. M. Kaplan Fund, 1989), p. 164. Most legal immigrants to the U.S. in the 1980s arrived under family-reunification priorities. See *New York Times*, 2 March 1990, p. A12.

22. For instance, dissatisfaction with political and economic conditions and career opportunities in the homeland constituted the major factors associated with migration from the Philippines to the United States during Ferdinand Marcos' rule. Josefina J. Card, "Push and Pull Factors at Origin and Destination as Determinants of Migration," in Select Commission on Immigration and Refugee Policy, *U.S. Immigration Policy and the National Interest*, Appendix B to the Staff Report (Washington, D.C.: Commission, 1981), p. 290. With regard to the Cuban revolution, Bach notes that "as the government consolidated its control of all sectors of the society and economy, the differences between economic and political motivations became virtually impossible to disentangle, if ever they could be." Robert L. Bach, "Cubans," in *Refugees in the United States: A Reference Handbook*, edited by David W. Haines (Westport: Greenwood Press, 1985), p. 82; also see Stephen B. Young, "Who is a Refugee? A Theory of Persecution," in *In Defense of the Alien*, Vol. V, edited by Lydio F. Tomasi (New York: Center for Migration Studies, 1983), p. 44; *Chronicle of Higher Education*, 12 September 1990, p. A6. In a 1980 district court case, Judge James L. King found much of Haiti's poverty to be a function of the Duvalier political system. Therefore, Judge King reasoned, Haitian migrants for economic reasons still qualified as refugees under the 1980 Refugee Act. See Teitelbaum, "Foreign Policy," 440–441; Gil Loescher and John A. Scanlan, *Calculated Kindness: Refugees and America's Half-Open Door, 1945 to Present* (New York: Free Press, 1986), p. 177. For a historical perspective on these issues, see Aristide R. Zolberg, Astri Suhrke, and Sergio Aguayo, *Escape from Violence: Conflict and the Refugee Crisis in the Developing World* (New York: Oxford University Press, 1989), pp. 31–32.

23. See, for instance, Zolberg, Suhrke, and Aguayo, *Refugee Crisis*, pp. 28–32; Johan Cels, "Responses of European States to *de facto* Refugees," in *Refugees and International Relations*, p. 188. In behavioral terms, economic migrants differ from

refugees most basically in that the latter are "not drawn but driven." Zucker and Zucker, *Guarded Gate*, p. xiv; United States, Agency for International Development, International Development Corporation Agency, "The Relationship of U.S. Aid, Trade, and Investment to Migration Pressures in Major Countries of Origin," in Select Commission on Immigration and Refugee Policy, *U.S. Immigration Policy and the National Interest*, Appendix B to the Staff Report (Washington, D.C.: Commission, 1981), p. 13. Zolberg *et al.* (*Refugee Crisis*, pp. 31, 33) consider individuals to be refugees when their movement "is forced—that is, when it occurs as a response to life-threatening violence, exercised by an agent or occurring as a by-product of circumstances. . . ." This includes "people cast abroad by famine" when the famine is attributed to violent acts and government policies. On the rights of civilian "war refugees" under international humanitarian law, see Karen Parker, "The Rights of Refugees under International Humanitarian Law," in *Refugee Law and Policy: International and U.S. Responses*, pp. 36–39.

24. Michael J. Schultheis, "Refugees in Africa: The Dynamics of a Global Justice Issue" (paper presented at the Annual Meeting of the African Studies Association held in Denver, November 1987), pp. 2, 11–12.

25. On the latter, see Wayne A. Cornelius, "Mexican Migration to the United States," *Proceedings of the Academy of Political Science* 34, No. 1 (1981):69–71; Alejandro Portes, "Migration and Underdevelopment," *Politics and Society*, 8, No. 1 (1978):43.

26. Robin Cohen argues that today's migrants are often recruited, selected, channeled, and controlled by agencies, firms, and state administrative organs. Robin Cohen, *The New Helots: Migrants in the International Division of Labour* (Brookfield: Gower Publishing Company, 1987), p. 39.

27. See Peter Koehn, "Agricultural Policy and Environmental Destruction in Ethiopia and Nigeria," *Rural Africana* 25–26 (Spring-Fall 1986):28, 41; Saskia Sassen-Koob, "Direct Foreign Investment: A Migration Push-Factor?" *Environment and Planning: Government and Policy* 2, No. 4 (1984):412n; Josh DeWind and David H. Kinley III, *Aiding Migration: The Impact of International Development Assistance on Haiti* (Boulder: Westview Press, 1988), pp. 138–144. Similarly, the capital-intensive technologies and contract-farming system introduced in Mexico by U.S.-based multinational corporations have resulted in labor displacement and migration. Wayne A. Cornelius, "Mexican Immigration: Causes and Consequences for Mexico," in *Sourcebook on the New Immigration: Implications for the United States and the International Community*, edited by Roy S. Bryce-Laporte (New Brunswick: Transaction Books, 1980), pp. 71–72, 76. Portes ("Underdevelopment," 11, 18) points out that the imbalances which result in labor displacement "are first induced from the outside but in time become internal to the structure of the weaker societies."

26

28. Sassen-Koob, "Direct Foreign Investment," 399–401, 404; Alejandro Portes, "International Labor Migration and National Development," in *U.S. Immigration and Refugee Policy: Global and Domestic Issues*, pp. 80, 88.

29. This discussion of intervening factors is based upon Sassen-Koob, "Direct Foreign Investment," 401–402, 408–413. Robin Cohen (*New Helots*, pp. 224, 244) also points out that exploitative firms operating factories in Third World countries prefer to hire young women, who encounter particular difficulties organizing themselves in male-dominated societies and possess "limited commitment to life-time wage labour." This strategy is most noticeable in the newly industrialized countries (NICs) of Southeast Asia.

30. Roy S. Bryce-Laporte, "The New Immigration: A Challenge to Our Sociological Imagination," in *Sourcebook on the New Immigration: Implications for the United States and the International Community*, pp. 459, 467; Fred Arnold, Urmil Minocha, and James T. Fawcett, "The Changing Face of Asian Immigration to the United States," in *Pacific Bridges: The New Immigration from Asia and the Pacific Islands*, pp. 120–121; Teitelbaum, "Asian Migrations," pp. 75, 77; Kim, "Korea," pp. 333–335, 339–340; Zolberg *et al.*, *Refugee Crisis*, p. 165.

31. Sassen-Koob, "Immigrant Labor," 74, 77, 81; Sassen-Koob, "Direct Foreign Investment," 402, 405n; Cohen, *New Helots*, pp. 224–225; Demetrios G. Papademetriou and Mark J. Miller, "U.S. Immigration Policy: International Context, Theoretical Parameters, and Research Priorities," in *The Unavoidable Issue: U.S. Immigration Policy in the 1980s*, p. 21.

32. Cornelius, "Mexican Migration," 72–73; also see Piore, *Migrant Labor*, pp. 81, 120–121. The rapid growth of high-tech industries in southern California, for instance, produced a "massive expansion in low-wage assembly line jobs, mostly not unionized and held by immigrant or native minority women." Major U.S. urban centers have witnessed an increase in readily exploited sweatshops for garment work and electronics homework. Saskia Sassen-Koob, "The New Labor Demand in Global Cities," in *Cities in Transformation: Class, Capital, and the State*, edited by Michael P. Smith (Beverly Hills: Sage Publications, 1984), pp. 148–149, 162–163; *New York Times*, 30 May 1990, p. A15. On the lure of Japan and the imported-labor needs of its economy, see *Japan Times*, 8 June 1989, p. 3; *Washington Post*, 22 October 1989, p. A40.

33. Piore, *Migrant Labor*, p. 175.

34. Miller and Papademetriou, "Foreign Policy," 164.

35. Sassen-Koob, "New Labor," pp. 141–163; Sassen-Koob, "Immigrant Labor," 81; Cohen, *New Helots*, pp. 250–251; Miller and Papademetriou, "Foreign," 164.

36. Sassen-Koob, "New Labor Demand," pp. 158, 165; Piore, *Migrant Labor*, pp. 183, 189; Cohen, *New Helots*, p. 251. On the advantages for advanced industrialized economies of dependent and powerless immigrant labor, see Sassen-

Koob, "Immigrant Labor," 70–73, 77; Alejandro Portes, "One Field, Many Views: Competing Theories of International Migration," in *Pacific Bridges: The New Immigration from Asia and the Pacific Islands*, pp. 59, 61; Portes, "Underdevelopment," 39–40. Due to their illegal immigration status, undocumented workers are particularly easily exploited by unscrupulous employers. See Piore, *Migrant Labor*, p. 183; Cohen, *New Helots*, p. 70.

37. Although most Third World residents who seek to work in the U.S. are denied legal permanent entry under prevailing immigration laws, many economic migrants find ways to shift from temporary visitor or worker status into long-term residency. See Kim, "Korea," pp. 329, 339. Mexican nationals constitute approximately 90 percent of all apprehended undocumented entrants and perhaps 50 percent of the total pool of unauthorized immigrants in the United States. Kritz, "Contemporary Immigration," p. 45; Piore, *Migrant Labor*, pp. 167, 172, 180–181. By 1986, an estimated 4–5 million migrant workers had entered this country without inspection; about 3.1 million received amnesty and legal temporary residency under the Immigration Control and Reform Act of 1986. *New York Times*, 5 March 1990, p. A12; Parrillo, *Strangers*, p. 535. Few of those who arrived in the U.S. after the 1982 cutoff date contained in the legislation returned to their homeland as a result of the 1986 Act. Most of these illegal migrants, including many spouses of persons granted amnesty, continue to function under undocumented conditions. Undocumented migrants have not become unemployable due to the employer sanctions provisions of the Act, but their range of job options has been reduced. Some work with fraudulent identity papers. The rest are drawn deeper into the underground economy where the potential for exploitation—particularly by sweatshop owners and other employers who pay workers off the books—remains high and INS enforcement of employer sanctions has been limited. See *New York Times*, 9 October 1989, pp. 1, 7; 2 January 1990, p. 9; and 5 March 1990, p. 12.

Furthermore, with expanding world-travel opportunities, more visitors are arriving in the United States and electing to stay. The U.S. higher-education system is particularly attractive. By 1986, more than 200,000 students and nearly three million temporary visitors from Asia entered this country annually. Arnold *et al.*, "Asian Immigration," p. 119; also see Reimer, *Golden Door*, pp. 203, 216; Kim, "Korea," pp. 329, 340; Parrillo, *Strangers*, p. 306.

38. Lance Clark contends that "it is no accident that projects that displace local populations. . . are often implemented by governments made up primarily of members of certain powerful ethnic groups and displace those in areas populated mostly by other, less powerful groups." Lance Clark, "Internal Refugees—The Hidden Half," *World Refugee Survey—1988 in Review* (Washington, D.C.: U.S. Committee for Refugees, 1989), p. 21. Also see Thayer Scudder and Elizabeth Colson, "From Welfare to Development: A Conceptual Framework for the Analysis

of Dislocated People," in *Involuntary Migration and Resettlement: The Problems and Responses of Dislocated People*, edited by Art Hansen and Anthony Oliver-Smith (Boulder: Westview Press, 1982), pp. 268, 271.

39. Clark, "Internal Refugees," pp. 18–19, 23. On the connection between the creation of internal refugees in Vietnam and third-country resettlement, see Suhrke and Klink, "Vietnamese and Afghan," p. 89.

40. *World Refugee Survey—1988 in Review*, pp. 34, 41, 73; Dawit Wolde Giorgis, *Red Tears: War, Famine and Revolution in Ethiopia* (Trenton: Red Sea Press, 1989), p. 370. Ruiz and Frelick estimate that there are 2 million internal refugees in Mozambique, and 1.5 million displaced southern Sudanese living in the Khartoum area alone. Hiram A. Ruiz and Bill Frelick, "Africa's Uprooted People: Shaping a Humanitarian Response," *Issue* 18, No. 1 (Winter 1989):32–33. On the impact of fighting in Southern Sudan on the local population, see Zolberg *et al.*, *Refugee Crisis*, p. 55. Brennan notes that between 1975 and 1987 an estimated 3.5 million "civilians—roughly 40 percent of the entire population—fled the war-torn countryside of Angola for the comparative safety of its towns and cities." T. O. Brennan, *Uprooted Angolans: From Crisis to Catastrophe* (Washington, D.C.: U.S. Committee for Refugees, 1987), pp. 22–23. Angela Delli Sante reports that there are roughly one million internal refugees in both El Salvador and Guatemala. Angela Delli Sante, "Central American Refugees: A Consequence of War and Social Upheaval," in *Refugee Law and Policy: International and U.S. Responses*, pp. 103–104.

41. *World Refugee Survey—1988 in Review*, p. 34; *New York Times*, 9 April 1990, pp. A1, 4. The 1990 exodus from Kuwait and Iraq also involved over half a million Asians who had been employed there in skilled and unskilled capacities. See *New York Times*, 4 September 1990, p. A1; 7 September 1990, p. 1; 19 September 1990, p. 1; Lawrence S. Eagleburger, "Proposed FY 1991 Refugee Admissions Levels," *Current Policy* 1307 (October 1990):3. The displaced include groups, such as the Dinka of southern Sudan, that are threatened by genocide. See Bill Frelick, "Refugees: A Barometer of Genocide," in *World Refugee Survey—1988 in Review*, p. 14.

42. Cited in Andrew E. Shacknove, "Who is a Refugee?" *Ethics* 95 (January 1985):275–276. Also see Cels, "Responses," 190; Zolberg *et al.*, *Refugee Crisis*, pp. 29, 245, 269; Astri Suhrke, "Global Refugee Movements and Strategies of Response," in *U.S. Immigration and Refugee Policy: Global and Domestic Issues*, p. 160; John R. Rogge, ed., *Refugees: A Third World Dilemma* (Totowa: Rowman & Littlefield, 1987), pp. 3–4; Margarita B. Melville, "Salvadoreans and Guatemalans," in *Refugees in the United States: A Reference Handbook*, pp. 170–173. In addition, the Cartagena Declaration of 1984 "has given impetus to *de facto* application of its broader refugee definition by several Latin American countries—"efforts which have

been "supported by United Nations General Assembly resolutions. . . ." Fiorella
Capelli, "UNHCR and the Plight of Refugees: International Protection and Solutions
in a Changing World Context," in *Human Rights and the Protection of Refugees
under International Law*, pp. 30–31.

43. Gordenker, *Refugees*, pp. 64–76.

44. Elizabeth G. Ferris, "Regional Responses to Central American Refugees:
Policy Making in Nicaragua, Honduras, and Mexico," in *Refugees and World
Politics*, ed. by Elizabeth Ferris (New York: Praeger, 1985), p. 193; Aryeh Neier,
"Drain the Sea, Scorch the Earth: An Outline of the Counterinsurgency Strategy," in
Forced Out: The Agony of the Refugee in Our Time, pp. 66–68; Schultheis,
"Refugees in Africa," p. 11. On indiscriminate bombing by the armed forces in El
Salvador, death-squad operations, and human-rights violations on the part of the
rebels, see *New York Times*, 25 November 1989, p. 5.

45. Melville, "Salvadoreans and Guatemalans," pp. 169, 171; Neier,
"Counterinsurgency," p. 66; Mekuria Bulcha, *Flight and Integration: Causes of Mass
Exodus from Ethiopia and Problems of Integration in the Sudan* (Uppsala:
Scandinavian Institute of African Studies, 1988), p. 83; Robert Gersony, "Why
Somalis Flee: Conflict in Northern Somalia," *Cultural Survival Quarterly* 13, No. 4
(1989):46–50, 56; Jane Perlez, "Sudan Again Bombs Civilians in Rebel Areas," *New
York Times*, 26 November 1990, p. A3. In an effort to punish anti-government
population centers, Myanmar authorities engaged in the forcible relocation of
roughly 500,000 Burmese in late 1989 and early 1990. Approximately 50,000
Burmese subsequently took refuge in Thailand. *New York Times*, 21 March 1990,
p. 1; 18 April 1990, p. A3.

46. Raymond D. Duvall and Michael Stohl, "Governance by Terror," in *The
Politics of Terrorism*, 2nd edition, edited by Michael Stohl (New York: Marcel
Dekker, 1983), pp. 193–194.

47. Neier, "Counterinsurgency," pp. 67–68.

48. Michael T. Klare, "The Development of Low-Intensity Conflict Doctrine," in
Intervention in the 1980s: U.S. Foreign Policy in the Third World, edited by Peter
J. Schraeder (Boulder: Lynne Rienner Publishers, 1989), pp. 31, 39.

49. Ruiz and Frelick, "Uprooted People," 30–32; *New York Times*, 15 February
1990, p. A12.

50. On resettlement in Somalia, see Peter J. Schraeder, "Involuntary Migration
in Somalia: The Politics of Resettlement," *Journal of Modern African Studies* 24,
No. 4 (1986):642, 648.

51. Smyser, "Refugees," 157; also see Gary E. Rubin, *The Asylum Challenge to
Western Nations* (Washington, D.C.: U. S. Committee for Refugees, 1984), p. 7.

52. *World Refugee Survey—1988 in Review*, pp. 32, 35; Zolberg, Suhrke, and
Aguayo, *Refugee Crisis*, pp. 23–24, 240–241; *New York Times*, 22 April 1991, p. 5.

On estimating refugee numbers, see Rogge, *Refugees*, p. 3. Not included in the refugee estimates for 1988 are the approximately 40,000 black residents expelled from Mauritania in 1989 and the 500,000 Liberians who fled their home country in 1990. See *New York Times*, 22 July 1989, p. 1; Eagleburger, "FY 1991," 3. When the slave trades are considered along with recent developments, there can be no doubt that "relative to its population, Africa has produced more exiles than any other continent." Roger G. Thomas, "Exile, Dictatorship and the Creative Writer in Africa: A Selective Annotated Bibliography," *Third World Quarterly* 9, No. 1 (January 1987):271.

53. By comparison, this country received well over 2 million refugees at the conclusion of World War II. Reimer, *Golden Door*, p. 241.

54. Zucker and Zucker, *Guarded Gate*, p. 95; *World Refugee Survey—1988 in Review*, p. 36. Canada and Australia are among the leading countries both in terms of the number of refugees admitted in comparison with total population size and in per capita contributions to international refugee-assistance agencies. Freda Hawkins, *Critical Years in Immigration: Canada and Australia Compared* (Kingston and Montreal: McGill-Queen's University Press, 1989), p. 182.

55. Lawrence S. Eagleburger, "Indochina Refugee Situation: Toward a Comprehensive Plan of Action," *Current Policy*, No. 1184 (June 1989):1.

56. See Smyser, "Refugees," 157–158.

57. See Bach, "Cubans," p. 80; Theda Skocpol, *States and Social Revolutions* (Cambridge: Cambridge University Press, 1979). With few exceptions, such as Iran in the late 1970s, Third World revolutions "have been directed toward the construction of socialist alternatives." Richard R. Fagen, Carmen D. Deere, and José L. Coraggio, "Introduction," in *Transition and Development: Problems of Third World Socialism*, edited by Richard R. Fagen, Carmen D. Deere, and José L. Coraggio (New York: Monthly Review Press, 1986), p. 9.

58. The social transformation of Kampuchea, which included the forced evacuation of Phnom Penh and other urban centers, proved particularly brutal. Perhaps one million people perished out of the total 1975 population of seven million. May Ebihara, "Khmer," in *Refugees in the United States: A Reference Handbook*, pp. 130–131. Post-revolution measures imposed by the Lao People's Democratic Republic included restrictions on population movement, price controls, nationalization of factories, and mandatory attendance at political seminars. John L. Van Esterik, "Lao," in *Refugees in the United States: A Reference Handbook*, pp. 153–154. Roughly 5 percent of the population of the southern part of Vietnam exited after 1975 in the wake of political change, imposition of a new economic order, and hostile relations with China. The collectivization of agriculture during the Great Leap Forward, the radical social upheaval of the Cultural Revolution, and the government's brutal repression of dissent in June 1989 all resulted in renewed

population exodus from post-revolution China. In general, however, the refugee exodus from China has been remarkably modest when considered in light of the country's population size, the magnitude of the revolution, and the scope of the overseas Chinese network. See Zolberg *et al., Refugee Crisis*, pp. 127, 157–160, 164.

On the revolutionary measures adopted by the FRELIMO leadership in Mozambique, see James H. Mittelman, *Out from Underdevelopment: Prospects for the Third World* (New York: St. Martin's Press, 1988), pp. 132–147; Zolberg *et al., Refugee Crisis*, p. 94. On the forced removal of several thousand unemployed urbanites from Maputo to state farms in the interior of Mozambique, see Jeffery Crisp, ed., *Refugees: The Dynamics of Displacement* (London: Zed Books, 1986), p. 103. For Ethiopia, see John M. Cohen and Peter H. Koehn, "Rural and Urban Land Reform in Ethiopia," *African Law Studies* 14 (1977):3–62; Christopher Clapham, *Transformation and Continuity in Revolutionary Ethiopia* (Cambridge: Cambridge University Press, 1988), p. 5. Although the overthrow of the monarchy in 1973 and the seizure of power in 1978 by Marxists intent on instituting radical social change created some Afghan exiles, the massive population outflow began following the Soviet invasion in December 1979, the application of indiscriminate firepower against the nationalist resistance, and the extension of massive U.S. military assistance to the guerrilla forces via Pakistan. Suhrke and Klink, "Vietnamese and Afghan," pp. 85, 93–94; Zolberg *et al., Refugee Crisis*, pp. 150–153, 254, 267. In Nicaragua, the Sandinistas introduced moderate economic, political, and agrarian reforms upon attaining power. Zolberg *et al., Refugee Crisis*, pp. 206, 211–213.

59. Historically, the President, in consultation with his advisors, has taken the lead in such ventures. With the most notable exception of the (later repealed) Clark Amendment of 1976 which prohibited further aid to FNLA guerrilla forces in Angola, the U.S. Congress generally has followed presidential leadership in this foreign-policy area. Peter J. Schraeder, "Paramilitary Intervention," in *Intervention in the 1980s: U.S. Foreign Policy in the Third World*, pp. 115—122; Klare, "Low-Intensity Conflict," p. 41. The pro-insurgency dimension of the Reagan Doctrine was pursued most aggressively in Nicaragua (through the *contras*) and in Afghanistan (*mujahedin*). For a penetrating historical analysis of the Nicaraguan effort, which degenerated into "vicious attacks on small villages, state-owned agricultural cooperatives, rural health clinics, bridges, electrical generators, and, finally, civilian noncombatants," consult Peter Kornbluh, "Nicaragua," in *Intervention in the 1980s: U.S. Foreign Policy in the Third World*, pp. 240–245; also see Mary B. Vanderlaan, *Revolution and Foreign Policy in Nicaragua* (Boulder: Westview Press, 1986), pp. 189, 205, 208.

60. *World Refugee Survey—1988 in Review*, pp. 32—33, 35, 41, 73; Roger P. Winter, "The Year in Review," *World Refugee Survey—1988 in Review*, p. 3; Hiram

A. Ruiz, *Beyond the Headlines: Refugees in the Horn of Africa* (Washington, D.C.: U.S. Committee for Refugees, 1988), pp. 37–38; Ruiz and Frelick, "Uprooted People," 30; Dennis McNamara, "The Origins and Effects of 'Humane Deterrence' Policies in South-east Asia," in *Refugees and International Relations*, p. 128.

Both Iran and Ethiopia also have become major refugee-receiving countries. Nearly 2.5 million refugees from Afghanistan and another million from Iraq resided in Iran by 1991. Armed conflicts in northern Somalia and southern Sudan pushed nearly 700,000 unprotected persons into Ethiopia at the end of the 1980s. Most of the Somali refugees who crossed into Ethiopia after May 1988 are city dwellers from Hargeisa. Ground combat and government bombing had nearly destroyed Hargeisa, Somalia's second largest city, by 1989. *New York Times*, 7 August 1989; *World Refugee Survey—1988 in Review*, pp. 41, 44.

61. Reimer, *Golden Door*, pp. 157, 169–170, 175; Timothy Dunnigan and Douglas P. Olney, "Hmong," in *Refugees in the United States: A Reference Handbook*, p. 117; Ebihara, "Khmer," pp. 134–135; Van Esterik, "Lao," p. 155.

62. Suhrke and Klink, "Vietnamese and Afghan," p. 88; Zolberg *et al.*, *Refugee Crisis*, pp. 165–166; McNamara, "'Humane Deterrence,'" 125. Non-resettled Cambodians languish in border camps in Thailand, while refugees from Vietnam are spread among Hong Kong, Thailand, Malaysia, Indonesia, and the Philippines. Under the Comprehensive Plan of Action (CPA) adopted in Geneva on 14 June 1989, the United States promised to resettle 50 percent of the Vietnamese reaching neighboring countries who "are determined by the screening procedures to be bona fide refugees." Robert L. Funseth, "U.S.-Vietnam Relations and Emigration," *Current Policy* 1238 (November 1989):3.

In December 1989, British authorities forcibly repatriated 51 Vietnamese from Hong Kong and threatened to return up to 44,000 post-1988 arrivals out of the 57,000 boat people living in detention camps in the crown colony. *New York Times*, 12 December 1989, p. 1; 13 December 1989, p. A13; 20 December 1989, p. 6; and 16 January 1990, p. A3. The status of Vietnamese residing in Hong Kong is further complicated by official indications that the People's Republic of China wants the Vietnamese 'burden' resolved before the transfer of sovereignty in 1997. Michael G. Aldridge, "Economics or Racism: The Vietnamese Refugees and Hong Kong," *Asian Perspective* (April 1989):2–3; *New York Times*, 31 December 1989. In 1990, the government of Malaysia turned Vietnamese refugees back to sea with increasing frequency and ASEAN nations pressured the United States to withdraw its opposition to the forced return of people they believe are economic migrants from Vietnam. See *New York Times*, 17 April 1990, p. A4; 12 August 1990, p. 16; 12 July 1990, p. A3. Historically, refugees with a compelling reason to flee from their homeland have not been deterred by the threat of inhumane treatment in receiving countries. McNamara, "'Humane Deterrence,'" 123.

63. The largest concentration of refugees from Ethiopia is in Sudan (approximately 660,000); roughly 400,000 others reside in Somalia. *World Refugee Survey–1988 in Review*, pp. 32–33; Zolberg *et al., Refugee Crisis*, p. 119. Although the exact numbers are unknown, sizeable communities of Ethiopian exiles exist in several European and Middle Eastern countries. Mekuria Bulcha, *Flight*, pp. 15, 164. About 30,000 Beta Israel have resettled in Israel since 1979. Zolberg *et al., Refugee Crisis*, p. 120.

64. See Allen K. Jones, *Iranian Refugees: The Many Faces of Persecution* (Washington, D.C.: U.S. Committee for Refugees, 1984), pp. 14–16.

65. Reimers, *Golden Door*, p. 103; William S. Bernard, *Chinese Newcomers in the United States: A Sample Study of Recent Immigrants and Refugees* (New York: American Immigration and Citizenship Conference, 1974), pp. 7–8, 10–11; Zolberg *et al., Refugee Crisis*, p. 178.

66. Zolberg *et al., Refugee Crisis*, pp. 211–212. As many as 100,000 Nicaraguans currently live in the Miami area.

67. Zolberg *et al., Refugee Crisis*, p. 154. The lack of a pervasive pre-revolution U.S. presence in Afghanistan has resulted in little demand by Afghan refugees for resettlement in the United States. Suhrke and Klink, "Vietnamese and Afghan," pp. 95, 98.

68. In FY 1986, the United States only admitted 47 African refugees (roughly 150 in FY 1987) who had not fled from Ethiopia. George Shultz, "Proposed Refugee Admissions for FY 1988," *Current Policy* 1004 (September 1987):4.

69. Zolberg *et al., Refugee Crisis*, p. 153; Suhrke and Klink, "Vietnamese and Afghan," pp. 85, 95; *World Refugee Survey—1988 in Review*, pp. 32–33.

70. One also finds people who are not migrants living among the members of these communities. Non migrants include students and short-term visitors who are intent on returning to the homeland after a fixed period of time. In the D.C./L.A. study, only 12 respondents (2 percent of the sample from Ethiopia and 5 percent from Iran) had not decided to live in exile at the time of interview. The small number of non exiles severely limits opportunities for control-group analysis.

71. The total refugee-admission figure includes over half a million Vietnamese, at least 200,000 Laotians, and close to 200,000 Cambodians. Eagleburger, "Indochina," pp. 1–2; Suhrke and Klink, "Vietnamese and Afghan," p. 88; Nguyen Manh Hung, "Vietnamese," in *Refugees in the United States: A Reference Handbook*, pp. 195, 201; Parrillo, *Strangers*, p. 304.

72. Shultz, "FY 1988," 3–4; Robert L. Funseth, "Orderly Departure of Refugees from Vietnam," *Current Policy* 1199 (June 1989):1–2; *New York Times*, 1 August 1989, p. 4 and 6 January 1990, p. 6. Vietnam issued a much larger number of exit permits in 1989, and roughly 26,000 persons departed for the United States under the ODP. Funseth, "Relations," 3.

73. Al Santoli, *New Americans: An Oral History* (New York: Viking, 1988), p. 368.

74. Santoli, *New Americans*, p. 368; Parrillo, *Strangers*, p. 419; Margaret S. Boone, "The Social Structure of a Low-Density Cultural Group: Cubans in Washington, D.C.," *Anthropological Quarterly* 54, No. 2 (1981):103.

75. A profile of the Cuban and Indochinese exile communities is presented in Chapter 6.

76. Santoli, *New Americans*, p. 87. The Iranian estimate is particularly imprecise because of the continued presence of large numbers of students who may or may not return to the homeland upon concluding their studies.

77. On the roots of Eritrean identity and its pervasiveness among exiles in the North, see John Sorenson, "Opposition, Exile and Identity: The Eritrean Case," *Journal of Refugee Studies* (forthcoming).

Distinguishing Eritreans for the purpose of analysis does not infer recognition of the claim to a separate political identity. That issue only can be resolved through negotiation among the parties to the conflict.

78. A grant from the Rockefeller Foundation supported most of these research activities. The author also acknowledges the matching assistance received from the University of Montana.

79. See Patricia W. Fagen, *Resource Paper on Political Asylum and Refugee Status in the United States* (Washington, D.C.: Refugee Policy Group, 1985), p. 17. Prevailing congressional structural arrangements provide one indication that U.S. refugee policy is overshadowed by concern with enforcing immigration controls. Specifically, the "committees that have the lead responsibility for refugees and refugee issues of a broader nature are those committees that are preoccupied with immigration issues." Roger P. Winter, "The International Refugee Protection System," in *Human Rights and the Protection of Refugees under International Law*, p. 40.

80. Prior to passage of the 1980 Refugee Act, the executive branch unilaterally allowed the influx of large numbers of recognized refugees through the exercise of the "parole power." Reimers, *Golden Door*, p. 163. Also see Chapter 5. The 1980 Act itself reflects congressional initiative in changing refugee-admission policy "from an artifact of the cold war into something with broader humanitarian roots." Loescher and Scanlan, *Kindness*, pp. 68—69.

81. Jeff Crisp, "Interview: Jewel S. Lafontant," *Refugees* (October 1989):39; Fagen, *Political Asylum*, pp. 15–16. President Jimmy Carter appointed former U.S. Senator Dick Clark as the first Coordinator. Loescher and Scanlan, *Kindness*, pp. 154, 68–69.

82. On the other hand, the formulation of U.S. *immigration* policy has been dominated by Congress and domestic interest groups. See Miller and

Papademetriou, "Foreign Policy," 180. In 1990, the "pro-immigration" coalition of interest groups included religious organizations, Hispanic and Asian associations, civil-rights lawyers, large corporations and industrial associations, and conservative think tanks. See *New York Times*, 15 August 1990, p. A12.

83. Zucker and Zucker, *Guarded Gate*, pp. 69–76, 127–129; Richard H. Feen, "Domestic and Foreign Policy Dilemmas in Contemporary U.S. Refugee Policy," in *Refugees and World Politics*, p. 109. In March 1989, Jewel S. Lafontant, former deputy solicitor general in the Nixon administration, replaced Jonathan Moore as U.S. Coordinator for Refugee Affairs. *Washington Post*, 1 March 1989; Crisp, "Lafontant," 38–40.

84. See Fagen, *Political Asylum*, pp. 15–16; Susan S. Forbes, *Adaptation and Integration of Recent Refugees to the United States* (Washington, D.C.: Refugee Policy Center, 1985), pp. 2–3; Zucker and Zucker, *Guarded Gate*, p. 129. Many local-government authorities have claimed that their implementation role results in serious non-reimbursed financial consequences. Robert L. Bach, "Third Country Resettlement," in *Refugees and International Relations*, p. 325.

85. These issues are discussed in Chapters 4 and 5.

86. Gordenker, *Refugees*, p. 32. When Thorvald Stoltenberg of Norway resigned as High Commissioner for Refugees in November 1990, the U.N. Secretary General announced the selection of Professor Sadako Ogata of Sophia University in Tokyo as his replacement. The U.S. contributes 25 to 30 percent of UNHCR's annual budget of roughly $500 million. Japan is the second-largest contributor. Feen, "Refugee Policy," p. 117; *New York Times*, 14 December 1990, p. A9; 20 December 1990, p. A8; 27 December 1990, p. A3.

87. Loescher, "Issues," 10. UNHCR's dependence upon voluntary contributions allows major donor states, particularly the United States, the opportunity "to influence the setting of the organization's priorities." Shelly Pitterman, "Determinants of International Refugee Policy: A Comparative Study of UNHCR Material Assistance to Refugees in Africa, 1963–1981," in *Refugees: A Third World Dilemma*, pp. 18, 32, 35.

88. Goodwin-Gill, "Protection System," pp. 154, 155. The Intergovernmental Committee for Migration provides transportation, orientation, and language-training services and frequently assists displaced persons who do not fit under UNHCR's definition of a refugee. Hawkins, *Canada and Australia*, p. 160.

89. See Peter Koehn, "The Migration of Post-Revolution Exiles to the United States: Determinant Factors and Policy Implications in the Ethiopian Case" (paper presented at the 26th Annual Meeting of the African Studies Association, 10 December 1983), pp. 1–2, 13–14; Papademetriou, "International Migration," 414. According to Sylvia Pedraza-Bailey (*Migrants*, p. 16), "the theoretical and empirical

36

challenge now facing immigration research lies in its capacity to capture both individuals and structure."

90. On the latter point, see Papademetriou and Miller, "Parameters," 5. Also see Mekuria Bulcha, *Flight*, p. 221.

91. Research at this level is valuable, in part, because it allows authors to convey "the sheer bloody-mindedness of unshackled rulers." Thomas ("Exile," 274) claims that political scientists tend not to deal effectively with personal experiences of persecution as a result of their preoccupation with structural features.

92. Suhrke, "Movements," pp. 170, 183; also see Mary M. Kritz, "Introduction and Overview," in *U.S. Immigration and Refugee Policy: Global and Domestic Issues*, p. 3.

93. Also see Egon F. Kunz, "The Refugee in Flight: Kinetic Models and Forms of Displacement," *International Migration Review* 7, No. 2 (Summer 1973):127, 129; Ferris, "Overview," p. 7; Kritz, "Contemporary Immigration," p. 46; Marta Tienda, "Socioeconomic and Labor Force Characteristics of U.S. Immigrants: Issues and Approaches," in *U.S. Immigration and Refugee Policy: Global and Domestic Issues*, p. 222.

94. See Alexander L. George, "Case Studies and Theory Development: The Method of Structured, Focused Comparison," in *Diplomacy: New Approaches in History, Theory, and Policy*, edited by Paul G. Lauren (New York: Free Press, 1979), p. 50.

PART ONE

Third-World Refugee Formation

1

Framework for Analysis:
National Politics, External Intervention, and Individual Motivation

Self-imposed exile is one of the most interesting and important political phenomena of the post-war world.
—Richard R. Fagen and Richard A. Brody

Part 1 of *Refugees from Revolution* is concerned with the initial step in the migration process. Why and how are refugees created? The answers are related to global and national political conditions and to individual motivations. With the aid of historical analysis, Chapter 2 focuses on key dimensions of the political economy of Third World revolutions. Chapter 3 deals with individual exile decision making.

One goal of this chapter is to show why it is important to consider both institutional forces and individuals in the analysis of refugee formation. A second objective is to present the conceptual framework that will be applied in the discussion of post-revolution migration. The value of this overall scheme as a guide in understanding international-migration outcomes must be assessed in terms of the explanatory power of the insights it provides with respect to past and future population movements.

In the study of refugee formation, two levels of analysis are crucial: the social-structural and the individual. By shaping the political-economy context, institutional conditions, both transnational and national, indirectly charge population movement.[1] Most immediately, however, exiles are the product of individual or collective decision making.[2] While scholars have recognized the importance of both structural and individual levels of analysis, there have been few explicit attempts to link them.[3]

By incorporating global, national, and individual inquiry, the framework presented here is designed to generate a comprehensive analysis of determinant factors in exile formation. Events, policies, and incidents constitute the concrete manifestations of the structural context that function as catalysts in exile decision making. The focus of application is on refugees from Third World revolutions.

The Interaction of External and Domestic Forces

Third World exile formation is rooted in the interaction of external and domestic forces. The processes responsible for the creation of post-revolution refugees are explained most thoroughly by a framework that draws upon dependency theory along with class and political-regime analysis.[4]

The creation of post-revolution exiles is a concrete manifestation of dependency that has been neglected by most conventional approaches to the study of international relations. National political dynamics and transnational economic penetration tend to be overlooked by scholars who concentrate on power, security, and diplomatic relations among states.[5] The dependency perspective's strength lies in explicating the connection between features of the global economy (particularly unequal terms of international trade and finance, and external penetration by multinational corporations) and processes of underdevelopment (uneven economic growth, fragmentation, marginalization and exploitation) in Third World societies.[6] The dependency approach has demonstrated particular utility in identifying the forces that generate the transnational migration of populations for economic reasons.[7] However, labor-flow theories fail to explain refugee movements.[8]

In exploring the genesis of political exiles, the analysis of class conflict, regime structure, revolutionary change, and external involvement needs to be incorporated with insights suggested by the dependency approach in a fashion that does not preclude the possibility of autonomous political action by Third World states and individual decision makers.[9] A complete understanding of the South-North movement of refugees must treat social-structural factors at the sending and receiving ends of the migration process.[10]

In the framework presented here, the interaction of national and transnational political and economic institutions shapes and conditions internal developments and policy actions which, in turn, influence exile decision making.[11] The energizing relationship of superpower foreign policy to global economic conditions, regime characteristics, class and nationality relations, and post-revolution politics constitutes a critical process feature in this conceptualization.[12]

Class Analysis

Class analysis is useful in revealing the social-structural context of political migration from the Third World to industrialized countries. In the formulation incorporated here, class is primarily "determined by relations of power. . . ."[13] The focus is on class *relationships*. The dynamics of dominant-class exploitation of subordinate classes for purposes of capital accumulation are particularly pertinent in the analysis of revolutionary situations.

The dominant class consists of those who utilize control over the means of compulsion and consumption to exploit poor and powerless members of society. In the Third World, this class generally is based upon superior educational attainments, high income, managerial or technical occupation, and/or control over large-scale economic activity. It is tightly linked politically to external foreign-policy actors, donors, and military personnel. Partners, directors, and technical experts affiliated with multinational industrial, commercial, and agricultural firms, along with top-level economic planners and parastatal officials, share common interests and work closely with the international corporate bourgeoisie.[14] These relationships raise the prospect that the dominant domestic class and Western capitalists will coalesce in a transnational ruling class. Consequently, class formation and conflict constitute vitally important dimensions of international relations.[15]

Conflict between the dominant and subordinate classes is a crucial political dynamic in Third World societies. Of particular interest in the analysis of refugee formation is the nature and extent of class conflict and the response of the state to pressures from subordinate classes.[16] The outcome of the public policy-formation process with respect to key distributive issues such as land reform and allocation, development strategies, the management of foreign debt and external investment, ethnic and gender privilege, and internal credit distribution reveals the nature of regime response to class struggle.

In addition, the South is prone to intra-class divisions and conflicts over nationality sentiments, ideological orientations, tactical paths of action, and/or capital-accumulation strategies. As a result, control of the state can pass among competing "elements" in the dominant class. Divisions within the transnational ruling class and conflicts among external actors also allow for autonomous political action by indigenous elites and revolutionary forces operating at the national and local level.[17]

Pre-Revolution Regime Characteristics and Western Foreign Policy

The intersection of transnational class interests and external political intervention provides a fruitful focal point for inquiry into pre-revolution regime characteristics in the Third World. The penetration of multinational capital, with support from Western foreign-policy actions, reinforces the position of the domestic ruling class and entrenched leaders who oppose balanced development and significant sharing of power and material resources with excluded and exploited members of society.[18] The presence of extensive foreign-capital investments and loans generates external pressures on compliant regimes to suppress radical political opinion, to resist fundamental land reform and peasant empowerment, to force subsistence farmers off land coveted for export agriculture, to undermine labor unions, and to impose unpopular and inappropriate structural-adjustment and economic-policy measures. At the same time, the introduction of Western social and consumptive influences and shallow political mobilization lead to increasing class conflict and political instability, and to even greater reliance upon foreign support and intervention.[19]

This volatile situation arises in large measure because the inclination of authoritarian rulers to resist demands for wider political participation and to be preoccupied with personal aggrandizement typically is reinforced by superpower involvement. U.S. military and economic aid encourages regimes confronting a narrow base of domestic support and legitimacy to resist demands for fundamental change in prevailing socio-economic relations and to defer the creation of institutional mechanisms for effective mass participation.[20] The exclusion of leftist groups from politics, in particular, effectively precludes political and social change through non-revolutionary channels.[21]

With avenues for non-violent change blocked by a repressive regime, the opposition acts covertly and in more strident fashion.[22] The ruling class increasingly resorts to the externally supported state coercive apparatus in dealing with opposition movements that threaten its dominant social position.[23] Reliance on violence in an attempt to crush popular dissent accelerates revolutionary insurgency and necessitates further dependence upon foreign involvement on the part of the threatened regime.[24]

Foreign-policy leaders in the United States have been eager to take actions aimed at preserving or installing authoritarian Third World regimes that are receptive to external penetration.[25] Foreign involvement occurs directly and indirectly through:

1. application of military force in order to prop up "regimes considered friendly to perceived economic and security interests" or "to thwart radical insurgencies;"[26]
2. bolstering internal-security apparatuses, supplying arms and extensive military assistance, and backing counter-insurgency efforts in an attempt to block revolutionary processes and/or to eliminate guerrilla movements;[27]
3. covert intervention in domestic leadership struggles;
4. advancing key economic and political advisors;
5. political pressure and material support for measures such as privatization and structural-adjustment packages that promote corporate investment and marketing interests in the periphery;[28] and
6. providing extensive bilateral cultural and professional opportunities in the North for educators, media representatives, military officers, businesspeople, labor leaders, etc.

These practices further the transnational incorporation of the domestic ruling class, alienation of the exploited rural and urban masses, and expansion of the gulf between state and society. In the case of U.S. interventions against leaders possessing nationalist legitimacy, moreover, one common outcome is to empower successors who are vulnerable to revolutionary movements.[29]

Revolutionary Change in the Third World

By insulating brutal authoritarian regimes from domestic pressures for social and political change, U.S. intervention increases the likelihood of an explosive upheaval.[30] The experience of persistent state coercion in response to urgent political demands convinces some of those who are exploited by the ruling class that a violent revolutionary strategy offers the only viable course to fundamental social and economic transformation. Political transformation occurs in the Third World when class conflict and exploitation, exacerbated by the alliance of agents of transnational capitalism and comprador bureaucratic structures, are effectively manipulated by

42

revolutionary forces.[31]   At this stage, the historical context of extensive
foreign interference facilitates mass mobilization behind revolutionary
objectives.   However, as a result of limited political insight, the vanguard's
perceived preoccupation with gaining control over means of coercion, and lack
of unity within the opposition movement, effective collective action on behalf
of the subordinate class by revolutionary forces remains an exceptional
development. Consequently, revolutions are uncommon political events.[32]

In the framework presented here, the feedback loop between external
military, economic, and cultural intervention on one side and dependency on
the other can be severed as well as reinforced by political action in the
periphery.[33]   When class conflict reaches revolutionary proportions, one
outcome is the emigration of discredited elements in the former ruling
class—particularly individuals who had been closely allied with Western
interests. Overthrow of the old regime sweeps members of the ruling class
out of positions of authority and severs their transnational links with class
allies in the global-capitalist economy.   The survivors are especially
vulnerable to "revolutionary justice" because they constitute conspicuous
symbols of pre-revolution exploitation, they represent a potential counter-
revolutionary threat to the new regime, and they have been cut off from
previously controlled means of compulsion and self-protection.[34]   Since
emigration offers one of the few viable avenues for ensuring self-preservation
open to formerly leading elements in the ruling class, they are inclined to
exit in the wake of the revolution.   The rupture of economic relations,
cultural ties, and foreign-policy association with the United States following
a revolution generates and sustains additional exile formation.

Post-Revolution Consolidation of Power

In the post-revolution interval, an escalating pattern of violence ensues
when the new leading element within the ruling class moves to consolidate
power, to introduce radical social change, and to institutionalize the new
regime. During this period, those who gain control often turn upon their
former allies.[35]   The surviving members of factions and movements that
unsuccessfully challenged the post-revolution consolidation of power by the
emergent ruler(s) become the principal targets of state repression.[36]

Persons who actively oppose, or are suspected of opposing, the new
regime on ideological and/or nationality grounds are especially vulnerable to
persecution. In an effort to complete the transformation of society and to
secure greater popularity, radical Third World regimes are prone to move

with military force against nationality movements and to suppress religious practices and political values that are viewed as threatening.

Internationalization of Conflict

Revolutionary change overthrows vested ruling-class interests and promises to provide an alternative route to improving the social and economic position of the masses. The superpowers are prone to become involved on opposite sides again—although their orientations toward the regime in power are reversed in the post-revolution period. For reasons of perceived self-interest, U.S. administrations typically have opposed revolutions and radical regimes while Soviet governments have been favorably oriented toward them.[37]

Since the revolutionary alternative in the Third World typically advocates a self-reliant path to development that involves a fundamental break with global-capitalist institutions and reduced opportunities for external manipulation and exploitation, it has attracted the overt or covert opposition of powerful forces in the West.[38] In an attempt to divert attention and scarce resources from social change, retard the success of the revolution, and sustain the prevailing weak and dependent position of peripheral countries, U.S. policy makers seek to exacerbate existing divisions or to instigate competing (non-class-based) conflicts. Concomitantly, the initial post-revolution phase provides an inviting opportunity for invasion or destabilization by regional powers.[39]

The prevailing globalist perspective on U.S. foreign and military policy has viewed revolutionary change and the subsequent adoption of socialist policies as automatically resulting in expansion of Soviet influence in the South and as directly threatening vital national interests. This simplistic perspective, which ignores the independent and nationalist characteristics of contemporary Third World revolutions, provides a potent rationale for containment and roll-back actions.[40] Thus, globalists in the U.S. foreign-policy establishment are prone to advocate measures designed to drain the energy and resources of revolutionary regimes as a strategy deemed necessary for countering Soviet ambitions in the South. In the absence of an acceptable alternative group, they are inclined to support the remobilization of forces associated with the former regime.[41]

In the face of radical societal transformation, post-revolution regime consolidation, and heightened emigration among the politically disaffected, intervention-minded external actors are likely to be frustrated by declining prospects of locating an ideologically suitable, popular, and pro-Western opposition group that is capable of effectively challenging the new rulers. Therefore, they indirectly and often covertly support actions aimed at exacerbating nationality and inter-state conflicts at this juncture.[42]   U.S. policy makers, working in conjunction with powerful transnational capitalist institutions, also are prone to apply economic and diplomatic sanctions aimed at weakening and demoralizing post-revolution societies.[43] Concomitantly, the Soviet Union typically provides weapons that encourage post-revolution regimes to pursue military rather than political solutions to internal social conflicts and externally supported threats.   Blinded by the global-rivalry perspective, both superpowers have underestimated and underplayed the indigenous roots of conflict.[44]

While nationality movements generally secure external support, the level of assistance they receive proves sufficient for sustaining the struggle but not for victory over the government's forces and achieving the goal of establishing a new political community.   On the other hand, the heavily armed post-revolution regime finds itself incapable of suppressing popular liberation movements that operate on familiar terrain and receive support from a local population increasingly alienated by indiscriminate government attacks.   The end result is widespread, costly, and protracted armed confrontations.[45] Resort to the counter-insurgency strategy of attacking the source population ensures recurring refugee outflows among groups inhabiting border areas. Furthermore, militarization diverts attention away from implementing popular reforms and constructing the basis for mass legitimacy.[46]

In the political-transition phase, "the class nature of the measures taken by the revolutionary government necessarily intensifies the antagonisms of those in whose favor the revolution is *not* being made."   Many post-revolution governments become increasingly repressive in the face of extended conflict.[47]   In other cases, the impetus for social transformation and for the reconstruction of political legitimacy is diminished by the need to divert scarce national resources into military activity in a desperate attempt to defend against externally supported armed forces.[48]   Although revolutionary regimes typically survive foreign-inspired and supported destabilization efforts, the economic toll is debilitating[49] and the dislocation of populations living in and near conflict zones escalates and is prolonged.

Summary

The social-structural dimension of the analytical framework presented here articulates the powerful link between global capitalist economic relations and superpower interventions on the one hand and revolutionary political conflict and national-liberation movements on the other. In light of the small margin of survival available to most citizens in dependent economies, the interaction of class conflict and other indigenous pressures with U.S.-Soviet competition produces particularly volatile conditions that are amenable to manipulation in revolutionary directions. External intervention is inextricably linked to the forces and events that motivate exile formation: repressive rule, revolution, insurgency, and liberationist struggles. The life-threatening experiences that ensue compel many to seek protection elsewhere.

Individual Decision Making

Surprisingly little scholarly attention has been devoted to the actual process of becoming a refugee.[50] Just as economic migration is not a universal reaction to poverty,[51] refugee flight does not occur as an automatic and direct response to unfavorable political conditions.[52] Becoming an exile depends upon the outcome of two related, but distinct, mental processes: (1) contemplating emigration and (2) deciding to leave, or not to return to, the homeland. Considerable time might elapse between the first stage and the final decision, or the two processes can occur virtually simultaneously. The act of flight might take place immediately following the decision to exit, or be postponed in anticipation of more conducive circumstances.

Most fundamentally, involuntary migration is a response to perceived stress in satisfying basic survival needs.[53] Four types of intolerable stress perceptions can result in the act of emigration or not returning to one's homeland: (1) physical dislocation and rootlessness, (2) economic destitution, (3) personal or family danger, and (4) ideological alienation. Violence, or the fear of violence induced by prevailing political conditions and/or personal experience, can be associated with each type of stress perception. Thus, physical dislocation can result from war or forced removal. Economic destitution can be a consequence of the violent destruction or expropriation of one's means of production, the interdiction of relief and rehabilitation items, and the coerced loss or elimination of employment. Danger can be attributed to acts of random violence, war-zone conditions, and the threat of imprisonment, torture, and execution. Ideological alienation can result from fear of execution and torture by the state apparatus and/or the suppression of alternative political discourse by force.

In repressive political systems, it is not uncommon to encounter all four forms of life-threatening violence and for diverse types of social conflict to persist.[54]   The extent to which each is present and active as a motivating factor is an empirical question of considerable scholarly and practical interest.   Although many refugees actually experience and survive one or more forms of violence, prospects alone can be perceived as sufficiently stressful and threatening to one's survival to warrant emigration.   The fact that some people react by opting for exile and others do not is a complex phenomenon related to personal background and orientations, exposure to harrowing incidents, reactions to political events and policy directions, and the opportunity and capacity to escape.

Personal Background and Orientations

In immediate post-revolution circumstances, stress levels are likely to be highest among the former leading elements in the ruling class—particularly those closely associated with agents of Western foreign policy and multinational firms.   In addition to their connection with the repressive pre-revolution regime, the class status of such persons generally provides cause for alarm in the face of revolutionary rhetoric directed against enemies of previously exploited members of society.   The fears of the discredited leading element in the pre-revolution ruling class include loss of livelihood, lengthy prison terms, the immediate application of "revolutionary justice," and execution following summary trial.

During the regime-consolidation interval, people actively involved in an unsuccessful opposition movement or factional dispute typically perceive the gravest threats to their survival requirements.   Individuals who oppose the new regime in less overt and active fashion, as well as the neutral victims of prolonged armed conflict, also fear for their own physical safety.   While sympathetic to the need for radical political transformation of the old regime, many intellectuals find that they are unable to commit themselves fully to the objectives and methods pursued by those who have assumed power.   Moreover, they are not trusted by leaders of the new regime.   In light of their central position in the formation of public opinion, intellectuals and educators are subjected to particularly heavy pressure to accept the principal ideological tenets that the faction in power aims to inculcate in the population.   Then, led by the urge to create their own intelligentsia, those in control of the new revolutionary state move to discredit and to eliminate individuals with "deviant" ideological perspectives.   This action completes the alienation of pre-revolution intellectuals.[55]

Later on, the bases for persecution expand to encompass all forms of organized and individual opposition or perceived opposition (especially movements linked to ethnic and religious identity), and the application of force becomes increasingly indiscriminate. As a result, the fear of violence cuts across all class lines within several years following the overthrow of the old regime.

Intervening Events, Incidents, and Policies

The social-structural context defines the choices available in exile decision making.[56] In light of the strength of attachments to the homeland and the prevailing reluctance to uproot oneself, however, refugee formation requires a mix of individual motivations, milieu factors, their concrete impact on people, and negative perceptions of change that result in the conviction that conditions have become or are about to become intolerable.[57]

The historical occurrences that shape migration decision making constitute one manifestation of the interaction of national and global relations. It is useful to distinguish such migration-inducing events according to their primary nature and impact (political, economic, social, or natural disaster) and location (inside or outside of the homeland). The revolution itself is likely to be the overriding event. Revolutions also spawn strong "aftershocks" that influence exile decision making.

In addition to responding to major triggering events, people become refugees in reaction to feared policies or rumored programs that are rooted in the pre- and post-revolution structural milieu.[58] Personal incidents and/or confrontations affecting a family member constitute other salient stress experiences in exile decision making. The connection between such micro-level incidents and political developments, including revolution itself, can be clear-cut or difficult to discern.

The Capacity and Opportunity to Escape

In order to emigrate successfully, the potential refugee from revolution must be aware of existing opportunities to exit, and possess the capacity and courage to take advantage of an opening. This requires, first of all, the development of a "flight perspective." The requisite orientation emerges through social interaction, some knowledge of possible destination(s), and growing awareness that leaving the homeland behind is "an appropriate, feasible, and logical course of action."[59] The migration process also requires that a second decision be made concerning the selection of an initial foreign destination.

Particularly useful means for safe exit are money, contacts, access to reliable sources of information, links to networks abroad,[60] and proximity to an unguarded border. With the possible exception of border proximity, members of the former ruling class usually possess superior access to most of the requisite means for successful exit.[61] At this point, micro-level ties developed during the pre-revolution period as a result of the extensive presence in the sending country of Western institutions and nationals, as well as migratory networks built up through prior transnational population movements, become active facilitating conditions.[62]

Emigration Vintages

In all refugee situations, distinct "vintages," or groups, of emigrants can be identified according to the temporal dimension of the decision to break with one's homeland.[63] In light of the conditions and events that lead people to be inclined to exit under revolutionary circumstances, the perceptions that precipitate an individual's decision to flee, and the means that can be employed for successful flight, the defining characteristic of Third World political exiles in the initial post-revolution vintage is expected to be class. Specifically, former leading elements in the old regime, particularly persons with close ties to the Western foreign-policy establishment and to institutions of global capitalism, are the most likely to emigrate in the immediate post-revolution period.[64]

Individuals linked to an opposition faction, either to the right or left of the new regime, and/or associated with a nationality movement are expected to take flight during and after the power-consolidation interval. The second exodus of refugees will consist of surviving members of revolutionary factions that have been excluded from positions of power and driven into opposition,[65] people adversely affected by radical social change,[66] and remnants of the former political order.[67] Victims of the violent transformation of society join this flight group.[68] This less "pure" vintage, which also includes persons who opt for exile while physically located outside of their homeland, will assume larger proportions, encompass more members of subordinate classes, and be prolonged when opposition sentiments are inflamed by nationality or religious issues, assisted by exile organizations, and/or supported by external powers.[69]

In the next two chapters, the framework presented here will be applied, first, to the social-structural and historical context of refugee creation in the focal countries and, then, to exile decision making. The structural/historical application includes an analysis of critical events and policies at the pre-revolution, revolution, and post-revolution stages. Cuba and Indochina are treated briefly; Iran and Ethiopia in greater depth.

Notes

1. The structural factors that *constrain* migration opportunities are most relevant in the analysis of step-migration. See Robin Cohen, *The New Helots: Migrants in the International Division of Labour* (Brookfield: Gower Publishing Company, 1987), pp. 35–36.

2. Sylvia Pedraza-Bailey warns that the danger of exclusive reliance upon structural analysis is "the tendency to obliterate people, to lose sight of the individual migrants who do make decisions." Sylvia Pedraza-Bailey, *Political and Economic Migrants in America: Cubans and Mexicans* (Austin: University of Texas Press, 1985), p. 16.

3. For instance, Elizabeth Ferris maintains that "the level of analysis used by a researcher determines in large measure the causes to which refugee phenomena are attributed, the evaluation of the seriousness of the problem, assessment of the consequences of such flows as well as prescriptions for dealing with refugees" and contends that the global, national, and individual levels "interact continuously." Yet, she implies that scholars must choose "which level of analysis to use in conducting refugee research" rather than pursue all three levels of inquiry. Elizabeth G. Ferris, "Overview: Refugees and World Politics," in *Refugees and World Politics*, edited by Elizabeth G. Ferris (New York: Praeger, 1985), pp. 11, 14, 18. A good example of the type of overgeneralized and unsupported analysis of refugee formation that results from exclusive reliance upon the structural level is W. R. Smyser, *Refugees: Extended Exile* (New York: Praeger, 1987), especially pp. 64–65.

4. Edwin Winkler, "Authoritarianism and Dependency in East Asia," *Social Science Research Council Items* 35, Nos. 1/2 (1981):14–16; Frederick Cooper, "Africa and the World Economy," *African Studies Review* 24, Nos. 2/3 (1981):21; Demetrios G. Papademetriou, "Rethinking International Migration: A Review and Critique," *Comparative Political Studies* 15, No. 4 (1983):478; Theda Skocpol, *States and Social Revolutions* (Cambridge: Cambridge University Press, 1979), p. 24; Richard R. Fagen, "A Funny Thing Happened on the Way to the Market: Thoughts on Extending Dependency Ideas," *International Organization* 32 (Winter 1978):289.

5. See James A. Caporaso, "Dependence, Dependency, and Power in the Global System: A Structural and Behavioral Analysis," *International Organization* 32 (Winter 1978):24.

6. Steven Langdon and Lynn Mytelka, "Africa in the Changing World Economy," in *Africa in the 1980s: A Continent in Crisis* (New York: McGraw-Hill, 1979), pp. 123–125, 168–169; Theotonio Dos Santos, "The Structure of Dependence," *American Economic Review* 60, No. 2 (1970):231–236; Fernando Cardoso and Enzo Faletto, *Dependent Development in Latin America* (Berkeley: University of California Press, 1979), pp. 180–188; Peter Evans, *Dependent Development: The Alliance of Multinationals, State, and Local Capital in Brazil* (Princeton: Princeton University Press, 1979), pp. 14–54; Johan Galtung, "A Structural Theory of Imperialism," *Journal of Peace Research* 8, No. 2 (1971):81–117; Raymond Duvall et al., "A Formal Model of 'Dependencia Theory': Structure and Measurement," in *From National Development to Global Community*, edited by Richard L. Merritt and Bruce M. Russett (London: George Allen and Unwin, 1981), pp. 316–317, 323, 331–332.

7. See the Introduction to this book; Saskia Sassen-Koob, "Direct Foreign Investment: A Migration Push-Factor?" *Environment and Planning C: Government and Policy* 2, No. 4 (1984):399–414; Alejandro Portes, "Illegal Immigration and the International System: Lessons from Recent Legal Mexican Immigrants to the United States," *Social Problems* 26, No. 4 (1979):434, 436; Demetrios G. Papademetriou, "International Migration in a Changing World," *International Social Science Journal* 36, No. 3 (1984):412; Papademetriou, "Rethinking," 471–475, 478, 490; Elizabeth M. Petras, "Towards a Theory of International Migration: The New Division of Labor," in *Sourcebook on the New Immigration: Implications for the United States and the International Community*, edited by Roy S. Bryce-Laporte (New Brunswick: Transaction Books, 1980), pp. 439–440.

The principal weakness of dependency theory, which is most pronounced among world-system theorists, is foreclosure of (1) the capacity for autonomous action by states located in the periphery and (2) the possibility of change in prevailing relations of international exploitation. On the latter point, see Alejandro Portes, "Migration and Underdevelopment," *Politics & Society* 8, No. 1 (1978):9. Moreover, "the content of Marxist theory must be modified to allow for the contributions of human action and motivation as integrated parts of the totality of history." Otwin Marenin, "Essence and Empiricism in African Politics," *Journal of Modern African Studies* 19, No. 1 (1981):24–25, 29–30.

8. See Alejandro Portes, "One Field, Many Views: Competing Theories of International Migration," in *Pacific Bridges: The New Immigration from Asia and the Pacific Islands*, edited by James T. Fawcett and Benjamin V. Cariño (Staten Island: Center for Migration Studies, 1987), pp. 53–54.

9. Cooper, "Africa," 10, 20, 48; Skocpol, *Revolutions*, pp. 14, 22–23, 30–31; Bruce Andrews, "Political Economy of World Capitalism: Theory and Practice," *International Organization* 36 (Winter 1982):149–153; Richard L. Sklar, "A Class

Analysis of Multinational Corporate Expansion," in *Transnational Enterprises: Their Impact on Third World Societies and Cultures*, edited by Krishna Kumar (Boulder: Westview Press, 1980), p. 92; Richard L. Sklar, "The Nature of Class Domination in Africa," *Journal of Modern African Studies* 17 (December 1979):550; Papademetriou, "Rethinking," 477–478.

10. Cohen, *New Helots*, p. 41.

11. Although Zolberg, Suhrke, and Aguayo recognize that "internal factors themselves often are part of patterns of social change determined by a combination of closely intertwined external and internal processes," they have treated dependent incorporation into the global capitalist network as a factor that exacerbates "inherent" domestic tensions and conflicts. In their analysis of the "root causes" of refugee flows, these scholars fail to address the possibility that economic inequities imposed by the prevailing system of global capitalism generate revolutionary forces. See Aristide R. Zolberg, Astri Suhrke, and Sergio Aguayo, *Escape from Violence: Conflict and the Refugee Crisis in the Developing World* (Oxford: Oxford University Press, 1989), pp. vi, 230, 261–262; and their "International Factors in the Formation of Refugee Movements," *International Migration Review* 22, No. 2 (Summer 1986):154–158.

12. On the utility of incorporating foreign-policy considerations in the analysis of refugee formation, see Astri Suhrke and Frank Klink, "Contrasting Patterns of Asian Refugee Movements: The Vietnamese and Afghan Syndromes," in *Pacific Bridges: The New Immigration from Asia and the Pacific Islands*, edited by James T. Fawcett and Benjamin V. Cariño (Staten Island: Center for Migration Studies, 1987), p. 99.

13. The following discussion draws upon Sklar, "Class Domination;" and James A. Bill, "Class Analysis and the Dialectics of Modernization in the Middle East," *International Journal of Middle East Studies* 3 (October 1972):417–434.

14. See Sklar, "Class Analysis," 94–96; Issa G. Shivji, *Class Struggles in Tanzania* (New York: Monthly Review Press, 1976), pp. 88–89.

15. See James F. Petras and Morris H. Morley, "Development and Revolution: Contradictions in the Advanced Third World Countries—Brazil, South Africa, and Iran," *Studies in Comparative International Development* 10 (Spring 1981):39–40. In Nigeria, for instance, Beckman finds that "the relations of domination originating from outside have been built into the fabric of domestic class relations." Bjorn Beckman, "Whose State? State and Capitalist Development in Nigeria," *Review of African Political Economy* 23 (January-April 1982):50, 45.

16. While the framework developed here focuses on the interaction of class and political regime, Zolberg *et al.* (*Refugee Crisis*, p. vi) emphasize other types of "social conflict."

52

17. See the discussion in Peter H. Koehn, *Public Policy and Administration in Africa: Lessons from Nigeria* (Boulder: Westview Press, 1990), pp. 282–283.

18. Langdon and Mytelka, "Africa," pp. 126–127, 176; Fagen, "Dependency," 292–294; Sklar, "Class Domination," 532–533, 544; "Class Analysis," pp. 90–91, 94–95; Ali A. Mazrui, "The Impact of Transnational Corporations on Educational Processes and Cultural Change: An African Perspective," in *Transnational Enterprises: Their Impact on Third World Societies and Cultures*, edited by Krishna Kumar (Boulder: Westview Press, 1980), pp. 207–229; Evans, *Dependent Development*, pp. 48–49.

19. Winckler, "Authoritarianism," 14; Cooper, "Africa," 4–6, 17–20; Christopher Chase-Dunn, "The Effects of International Economic Dependence on Development and Inequality," in *National Development and the World System: Educational, Economic and Political Change*, edited by John Meyer and Michael Hannan (Chicago: University of Chicago Press, 1979), p. 148; Duvall *et al.*, "Model," pp. 338, 341; Timothy M. Shaw and Malcolm J. Grieve, "Dependency as an Approach to Understanding Continuing Inequalities in Africa," *Journal of Developing Areas* 13 (April 1979):232, 239–240; Andrews, "World Capitalism," 149; L. S. Stavrianos, *Global Rift: The Third World Comes of Age* (New York: William Morrow and Company, 1981), p. 477.

20. Stavrianos, *Global Rift*, pp. 468, 473; Peter J. Schraeder, "U.S. Intervention in Perspective," in *Intervention in the 1980s: U.S. Foreign Policy in the Third World*, ed. by Peter J. Schraeder (Boulder: Lynne Rienner Publishers, 1989), p. 292; Doug Bandow, "Economic and Military Aid," in *Intervention in the 1980s: U.S. Foreign Policy in the Third World*, edited by Peter J. Schraeder (Boulder: Lynne Rienner Publishers, 1989), p. 78.

Restrictions on political participation are particularly widespread under traditional monarchies that allow Western penetration—due to the inherent contradiction between the traditional norms underlying political authority and secular democratic values. Samuel Huntington, *Political Order in Changing Societies* (New Haven: Yale University Press, 1968), pp. 151–187. Consequently, an exceptionally high proportion of successful revolutions have occurred in countries governed by a traditional monarchy or by a politically inept regime with a narrow base of legitimacy that briefly replaces the monarchy. Christopher Clapham, *Transformation and Continuity in Revolutionary Ethiopia* (Cambridge: Cambridge University Press, 1988), p. 4.

21. Schraeder, "U.S. Intervention," p. 288. The principal objectives shared by groups on the radical left are "(1) production and distribution oriented toward meeting the basic needs of the majority of the population; (2) an ending of class, gender, racial, ethnic, and other forms of privilege in access to 'valued goods' such as income, culture, justice, and recreation; and (3) the reconstitution of state-society

3

relations such that the 'popular classes' have a high degree of participation in determining public policy at all levels." Richard R. Fagen, Carmen D. Deere, and José L. Coraggio, "Introduction," in *Transition and Development: Problems of Third World Socialism*, edited by Richard R. Fagen, Carmen D. Deere, and José L. Coraggio (New York: Monthly Review Press, 1986), pp. 10–11.

22. For instance, in Nicaragua, where the historical record of U.S. intervention has been particularly overt, "Somoza's escalating repression. . . only served to radicalize the situation, empowering the opposition to organize and unify and contributing to the growing popularity of the Sandinista guerrilla movement." Peter Kornbluh, "Nicaragua," in *Intervention in the 1980s: U.S. Foreign Policy in the Third World*, edited by Peter J. Schraeder (Boulder: Lynne Rienner Publishers, 1989), p. 239; Zolberg *et al.*, *Refugee Crisis*, p. 205. Also see Peter Koehn and Louis D. Hayes, "Student Politics in Traditional Monarchies," *Journal of Asian and African Studies* 13, Nos. 1-2 (January-April 1978):37–42.

23. Duvall *et al.*, "Model," pp. 317, 338–339; Chase-Dunn, "Inequality," pp. 136–137; John W. Sloan, "Political Terrorism in Latin America," in *The Politics of Terrorism*, 2nd ed., ed. by Michael Stohl (New York: Marcel Dekker, 1983), p. 386.

24. Michael T. Klare, "The Development of Low-Intensity Conflict Doctrine," in *Intervention in the 1980s: U.S. Foreign Policy in the Third World*, edited by Peter J. Schraeder (Boulder: Lynne Rienner Publishers, 1989), p. 41.

25. Mary B. Vanderlaan, *Revolution and Foreign Policy in Nicaragua* (Boulder: Westview Press, 1986), p. 133; Klare, "Low-Intensity Conflict," pp. 43–44.

26. Ted G. Carpenter, "Direct Military Intervention," in *Intervention in the 1980s: U.S. Foreign Policy in the Third World*, ed. by Peter J. Schraeder (Boulder: Lynne Rienner Publishers, 1989), p. 131; Peter J. Schraeder, "Concepts, Relevance, Themes, and Overview," in *Intervention in the 1980s*, p. 2.

In the wake of its experience in Vietnam, the U.S. government favored indirect involvement over direct military intervention in Third World conflicts. Klare, "Low-Intensity Conflict," pp. 31, 37–38. In Grenada and Panama, however, U.S. Presidents did not refrain from direct military intervention in situations where local resistance was not expected to be protracted. These actions, along with the often-cited justification of "self-defense" against the spread of Soviet ideological influence, clearly are in violation of international law. Christopher Joyner points out that "to argue otherwise is to suggest the right of the United States to supersede the limits of self-defense and thereby mutate these doctrines into potential instruments for legitimizing the use of U.S. force throughout the Third World." Christopher Joyner, "International Law," in *Intervention in the 1980s: U.S. Foreign Policy in the Third World*, edited by Peter J. Schraeder (Boulder: Lynne Rienner Publishers, 1989), pp. 191, 201.

54

27. Klare, "Low-Intensity Conflict," p. 41; Raymond D. Duvall, "Governance By Terror," in *The Politics of Terrorism*, 2nd ed., edited by Michael Stohl (New York: Marcel Dekker, 1983), p. 195; Vanderlaan, *Revolution*, pp. 134, 175. The basis for this type of intervention by U.S. administrations has been the assumption or allegation that leftist groups and leaders are "pro-Soviet." See S. Neil Macfarlane, "Superpower Rivalry in the 1990s," *Third World Quarterly* 12, No. 1 (January 1990):8. With the left in ideological retreat at the end of the 1980s, the United States government promoted a new strategy that invited electoral participation by diverse and competing interests—partly in an effort to build legitimacy for regimes that could be counted on to resist fundamental social change.

28. See Koehn, *Public Policy*, pp. 109–142; Robert L. Curry, "The African Private Sector and U.S. Policy," *Journal of Modern African Studies* 20, No. 3 (1982):510–511.

29. Richard W. Cottam, *Iran and the United States: A Cold War Case Study* (Pittsburgh: University of Pittsburgh Press, 1988), p. 262; Fred Halliday, "The Arc of Revolutions: Iran, Afghanistan, South Yemen, Ethiopia," *Race and Class* 20, No. 4 (Spring 1979):377.

30. Bandow, "Aid," pp. 79, 83.

31. Skocpol, *Revolutions*, pp. 29–30, 287, 350; Fred Halliday and Maxine Molyneux, *The Ethiopian Revolution* (London: Verso Editions, 1981), p. 12; Koehn and Hayes, "Student Politics," 35–42; Duvall *et al.*, "Model," p. 342; Fagen, "Dependency," 293.

32. While decayed monarchies can be brought down by urban-based revolutionaries, rural guerrilla struggle also is required in nationalist revolutions. See Clapham, *Revolutionary Ethiopia*, p. 5. For an insightful analysis of strategies of nationalist revolution in the Third World, see Frantz Fanon, *Wretched of the Earth* (New York: Grove Press, 1963), pp. 107–147.

33. Duvall *et al.*, "Model," pp. 317, 344; Galtung, "Imperialism," 184; Skocpol, *Revolutions*, pp. 289–292; Rudolfo Stavenhagen, "The Future of Latin America: Between Underdevelopment and Revolution," in *From Dependency to Development: Strategies to Overcome Underdevelopment and Inequality*, edited by Heraldo Munoz (Boulder: Westview Press, 1981), p. 217.

34. John Markakis and Nega Ayele, *Class and Revolution in Ethiopia* (Nottingham: Spokesman, 1978), p. 73.

35. Following Marxist revolutions, the theoretical justification for the suppression of dissent is likely to be reliance upon the vanguard elite, which possesses the "correct" interpretation of history and, therefore, can identify counter-revolutionary actions. Marenin, "Empiricism," 25.

36. Clapham, *Revolutionary Ethiopia*, p. 6.

55

37. Zolberg *et al., Refugee Crisis*, p. 249; Roy Allison and Phil Williams, "Superpower Competition and Crisis Prevention in the Third World," in *Superpower Competition and Crisis Prevention in the Third World*, edited by Roy Allison and Phil Williams (Cambridge: Cambridge University Press, 1990), p. 4.

38. Zolberg *et al.* ("International Factors," 157, 159) maintain that "internal regime changes among Third World countries tend to be perceived as having implications for the wider system, and are therefore likely to provoke some sort of response by outsiders." Also see their *Refugee Crisis*, pp. 231–232.

39. Invasion examples are Kampuchea by the Vietnamese army, Ethiopia by armed forces from Somalia, and Iran by Iraqi troops. Clapham, *Revolutionary Ethiopia*, p. 11. South African support for UNITA in Angola and RENAMO in Mozambique constitutes the prime destabilization case. See Fantu Cheru, "The Politics of Desperation: Mozambique and *Nkomati*," *TransAfrica Forum* 3, No. 3 (Spring 1986):29-46; Robert E. Mazur, "The Political Economy of Refugee Creation in Southern Africa: Micro and Macro Issues in Sociological Perspective," *Journal of Refugee Studies* 2, No. 4 (1989):441–464; *New York Times*, 25 February 1989.

40. Klare, "Low-Intensity Conflict," pp. 38–40; Schraeder, "Concepts," p. 7; Zolberg *et al., Refugee Crisis*, pp. 208–209; Vanderlaan, *Nicaragua*, pp. 132, 134–135, 209. For a thorough critical review of the globalist approach to U.S. foreign policy, see Charles F. Doran, "The Globalist-Regionalist Debate," in *Intervention in the 1980s: U.S. Foreign Policy in the Third World*, ed. by Peter J. Schraeder (Boulder: Lynne Rienner Publishers, 1989), pp. 45, 48–49.

41. Richard R. Fagen, "The Politics of Transition," in *Transition and Development: Problems of Third World Socialism*, edited by Richard R. Fagen, Carmen D. Deere, and José L. Coraggio (New York: Monthly Review Press, 1986), p. 252.

42. See Peter Koehn, "The Ethiopian Revolution: Events, Interpretations, and Implications," *Africa Today* 27, No. 1 (1980):44; Stavrianos, *Global Rift*, p. 467. In the U.S.A., the Reagan administration proved most committed to preaching and practicing the strategy of "proinsurgency." Klare, "Low-Intensity Conflict," p. 41. Its tactics included the mobilization of refugees for military purposes—that is, the organization and support of *contra* refugee-warriors. On this phenomenon and U.S. support for UNITA forces in Angola following repeal of the Clark amendment, see Zolberg *et al., Refugee Crisis*, pp. 93, 218; T. O. Brennan, *Uprooted Angolans: From Crisis to Catastrophe* (Washington, D.C.: U.S. Committee for Refugees, 1987), p. 24.

43. For a comprehensive case study of U.S. government-inspired economic sanctions against the Sandinista regime, see Vanderlaan, *Nicaragua*, pp. 172–174.

44. Macfarlane, "Superpower Rivalry," 7.

56

45. Zolberg *et al., Refugee Crisis*, pp. 243–245; Fagen, "Transition," pp. 259–260.

46. Also see Zolberg *et al., Refugee Crisis*, p. 251.

47. Fagen, "Transition," pp. 258–259. Leon Gordenker points out that members of foreign-supported opposition groups are particularly likely to face persecution at the hands of the threatened regime. Leon Gordenker, *Refugees in International Politics* (New York: Columbia University Press, 1987), p. 85.

48. Fagen, "Transition," p. 252; Zolberg *et al.*, "Refugee Movements," 160–161; Clapham, *Revolutionary Ethiopia*, p. 11; Vanderlaan, *Nicaragua*, pp. 175, 188, 206, 209.

49. See, for instance, Vanderlaan, *Nicaragua*, pp. 202–209.

50. Rebecca Allen and Harry H. Hiller, "The Social Organization of Migration: An Analysis of the Uprooting and Flight of Vietnamese Refugees," *International Migration* 23, No. 4 (1985):440.

51. Sassen-Koob, "Direct Foreign Investment," 413–414.

52. Thus, some people living in the same social-structural context fail to become refugees because they are not affected by events, policies, or incidents, because they deliberately choose not to become exiles, or because they are unable to link up with the social organization for flight that facilitates exit. See Allen and Hiller, "Refugees," 448.

53. Julian Wolpert, "Migration as an Adjustment to Environmental Stress," *Journal of Social Issues* 22 (October 1966):92–102.

54. Zolberg *et al., Refugee Crisis*, p. vi.

55. Mehrdad Kia contributed greatly to the discussion of ideological alienation among the intelligentsia in the post-revolution state.

56. Papademetriou, "International Migration," 414.

57. Allen and Hiller, "Refugees," 440–444. Milieu forces include the extent of state incorporation into the global political economy, regime characteristics and actions, and population pressures. See the transnational-migration model developed by Demetrios G. Papademetriou and Mark J. Miller, "U.S. Immigration Policy: International Context, Theoretical Parameters, and Research Priorities," in *The Unavoidable Issue: U.S. Immigration Policy in the 1980s*, edited by Demetrios G. Papademetriou and Mark J. Miller (Philadelphia: Institute for the Study of Human Issues, 1983), p. 4.

58. See Jeffery Crisp, editor, *Refugees: The Dynamics of Displacement* (London: Zed Books, 1986), p. 132.

59. Allen and Hiller, "Refugees," 442; also see Mekuria Bulcha, *Flight and Integration: Causes of Mass Exodus from Ethiopia and Problems of Integration in the Sudan* (Uppsala: Scandinavian Institute of African Studies, 1988), p. 82; Richard

R. Fagen, Richard A. Brody, and Thomas J. O'Leary, *Cubans in Exile: Disaffection and the Revolution* (Stanford: Stanford University Press, 1968), p. 101. Feasibility calculations include the financial cost involved in reaching one's destination.

60. See Mary M. Kritz, "The Global Picture of Contemporary Immigration Patterns," in *Pacific Bridges: The New Immigration from Asia and the Pacific Islands*, edited by James T. Fawcett and Benjamin V. Cariño (Staten Island: Center for Migration Studies, 1987), p. 46.

61. Fagen *et al., Cubans in Exile*, pp. 106–107.

62. See Sassen-Koob, "Direct Foreign Investment," 402. The presence of highly developed migratory networks is more powerful than the disposition of neighboring countries is in promoting exit and prolonging the exodus of refugees.

63. Egon F. Kunz, "The Refugee in Flight: Kinetic Models and Forms of Displacement," *International Migration Review* 7, No. 2 (1973):139–140.

64. Also see Zolberg *et al., Refugee Crisis*, p. 250.

65. Skocpol, *Revolutions*, pp. 29, 285–287.

66. Zolberg *et al.*, "Refugee Movements," 160.

67. Kunz, "Flight," 137–141.

68. Zolberg *et al., Refugee Crisis*, p. 250.

69. Halliday and Molyneux, *Ethiopian Revolution*, pp. 156–159; Aristide Zolberg, "Contemporary Transnational Migrations in Historical Perspective: Patterns and Dilemmas," in *U.S. Immigration and Refugee Policy: Global and Domestic Issues*, edited by Mary M. Kritz (Lexington: D.C. Heath and Company, 1983), p. 19; Zolberg *et al., Refugee Crisis*, p. 251.

2

Revolutions and Refugees: The Global and National Context in Historical Perspective

Persons expressing opposition to the regime or who are believed not to support it are routinely arrested by security police and subjected to torture in varying degrees; some executions have been reported as well. The individual citizen enjoys no legal protection and may be detained at any time without explanation and be held indefinitely without any prospect of trial.
— U.S. Department of State, *Country Report for Ethiopia,* 1985

Revolutionary conflicts attract the attention of the superpowers because ideological solidarity is an instrument of international hegemony.
— Aristide R. Zolberg, Astri Suhrke, and Sergio Aguayo

Chapter 2 is devoted to analyzing the historical background and social-structural context of the four recent Third World revolutions of particular interest in this book.[1] The principal purpose is to identify the underlying conditions associated with the phenomenon of mass post-revolution refugee movements from South to North by comparing situations in Latin America, Asia, Africa, and the Middle East. Moreover, the specific details surrounding each revolution are important for policy makers and service providers who seek to approach Third World refugees in an understanding and sensitive manner. Following this discussion, we will be positioned to treat individual motivations and links between social-structural and individual decision-making levels in refugee formation.

The Cuban Revolution

The origins of the Cuban exodus lie in its pre-revolutionary history. During this period, U.S. economic interests dominated the Cuban economy. Foreign capitalists controlled the industrial, agricultural, and tourist sectors.[2] U.S. domination encouraged exploitation of the laboring classes and largely shaped the social composition of the post-revolution exodus.[3]

Cuba's dependent social and political structure constituted the target of a revolutionary movement that sought to improve the status of the subordinated classes.[4] The revolution introduced a massive redistribution of political power and wealth "away from those entrenched groups that benefitted from the prerevolutionary order and toward those who had been disadvantaged," and eventually brought about the most equitable intra-national distribution of income in Latin America.[5]

Although Fidel Castro's takeover occurred in 1959, it is between 1961 and 1962 that Cuba experienced transition "from the relatively ambiguous early revolutionary period to the clearly defined Marxist-Leninist period."[6] The leaders of the Cuban revolution treated persons who refused to adapt to the new order in ruthless fashion, but they generally did not invoke state brutality and extermination. Thus, the size of the population exodus from Cuba must be understood in terms of the pervasiveness of the revolution. Castro's cataclysmic transformation of pre-revolution social structure, economic activity, and political institutions left no sector unaffected. Consequently, persons negatively affected by the process of revolutionary change, including those dependent upon nationalized U.S. holdings, provided a large pool of potential refugees.[7]

After 1965, the revolutionary leadership strictly limited the supply of consumer goods. As a result, the Cuban middle class suffered even more than previously from the regime's redistributive policies. In the late 1960s, Castro ordered a new round of nationalizations that primarily affected small businesses. When the government allowed exile families to return in 1978 and 1979, more than 100,000 Cuban-Americans visited the island. Their presence offered Cubans who had remained in the homeland a close-up demonstration of "consumer possibilities in the United States."[8]

In general, "Castro's policies created the potential for a mass exodus, [and] U.S. policies made the exodus possible."[9] Although they remained hostile to one another, the sending and receiving governments at times perceived that their separate interests would be served by coordinating Cuban migration to the United States.[10] The availability of occasional windows during which both sides agreed to remove restrictions on emigration and immigration fueled population movement to the U.S.A.

U.S. foreign-policy actions also contributed to the post-revolution exodus from Cuba. As early as 1960, strategic planners in the U.S. government considered schemes designed to assassinate Fidel Castro and to overthrow his regime. The Kennedy administration activated several of these abortive plans, including the Bay of Pigs invasion in 1961 by U.S.-trained exiles and covert CIA attempts to kill the Cuban leader.[11] Successive U.S. administrations refused to accept the legitimacy of the revolution, endeavored to isolate Castro's regime diplomatically, and applied economic sanctions that disrupted the Cuban economy. Rather than destabilizing the post-revolution regime, however, "these actions served as focal points whereby Castro strengthened his position on the island by whipping up 'anti-yankee' nationalism and painting those elements still opposed to his rule as mere lackeys of U.S. imperialism."[12] In addition, as Silvia Pedraza-Bailey points out:

> the exodus also performed an important political function: it lessened the capacity of those politically disaffected from the revolution to undermine it. In externalizing dissent, the Cuban government in effect controlled it. As a result, the revolution grew stronger.[13]

Revolution in Indochina

Nationalist revolutions are energized by the perceived need to overthrow foreign domination as a fundamental prerequisite for introducing radical political and social change. The nationalist dimension of the struggle for social and political transformation assumed particular importance in Indochina because of the presence of foreign military advisors, intelligence gatherers, and combatants in large numbers. In addition, more than half of the over 300,000 Asian military personnel participating in the U.S. Defense Department's International Military Education and Training Program between 1950 and mid-1980 came from Vietnam, Cambodia, and Laos.[14]

Vietnam

Economic exploitation of the subordinate class provided the principal impetus for Vietnamese nationalism in the early twentieth century.[15] About 900,000 political migrants moved from North to South Vietnam following partition according to the Geneva Accords of 1954. This mass movement consisted of people closely associated with the French colonialists, including "soldiers, functionaries, and a large number of Catholics," who became anti-communist pillars of the southern regime.[16]

At the peak of its involvement in Vietnam, the U.S. government committed nearly half a million combat troops. They engaged in saturation bombing, chemical warfare, and the forced relocation of peasants into "strategic hamlets." During this period, the CIA-directed "Phoenix Program" encouraged the systematic assassination of villagers suspected of ties to the Vietcong opposition forces.[17]

Nevertheless, the U.S.-backed pre-revolution regime could not withstand the onslaught of revolutionary nationalism. The introduction of foreign troops and weapons on a massive scale eventually resulted in the internal dislocation of perhaps half of the 20 million people living in South Vietnam. In sum, U.S. intervention in Vietnam prolonged the nationalist struggle and dramatically expanded "the fire zone which indiscriminately engulfed civilians."[18]

While Western countries and global-capitalist institutions applied an embargo on trade and economic assistance, the post-revolution regime endeavored to bring about a socialist transformation of the capitalist economy entrenched in the south.[19] The government immediately sent thousands of people who had fled to the cities during the war back to villages and transferred 800,000 urban dwellers to 'new economic zones' established to place unused rural land under cultivation.[20]

In 1978, the post-revolution government threatened to force citizenship and military service on the Chinese population, moved to control the urban economy of the entire country, and forced people of Chinese descent out of cities and strategic areas. In the face of these developments, about 150,000 Chinese crossed the northern border into China. Many others left by boat after making payments to Vietnamese officials, who then allowed their "illegal" emigration.[21]

Persons associated with the pre-revolution regime or with the U.S. war effort, some of whom have spent time in government reeducation centers, continue to suffer in Vietnam.[22] Thus, although the exodus from Vietnam has abated, it has not ceased. Nearly 40,000 new refugees from Vietnam arrived in first-asylum areas during 1987.[23]

62

Cambodia

Lon Nol introduced few changes in government structure after overthrowing Norodom Sihanouk in a 1970 rightist coup. Between 1970 and 1975, however, the Cambodian countryside suffered considerable destruction in the face of fighting between Lon Nol's troops and the rapidly expanding Khmer Rouge, as well as due to U.S. saturation bombing.[24] When the U.S.-backed regime in Saigon fell, so did the one in Phnom Penh.[25]

The Khmer Rouge overran Phnom Penh and established Democratic Kampuchea in April 1975. Once in power, they immediately cleared urban dwellers and internal refugees out of the cities and forced them to live in the countryside. Many urban Chinese managed to flee the country.[26]

In the regime-consolidation phase, factional disputes within the Kampuchean Communist Party resulted in a new round of executions. As the Pol Pot group gained power, moreover, it purged many high public officials. The Pol Pot regime, through the widespread application of terror and coercion, collectivized the economy, separated family members, and suppressed Buddhism.[27] The Khmer Rouge's program involved "forced internal migrations, massive purges and liquidation of party cadres, elimination of whole social segments, and. . . 'final solution' campaigns against ethnic minorities." Its victims cut across class lines and included Marxists, peasants, and others who had never been associated with Western intervention in Cambodian affairs. In total, the Pol Pot government bears responsibility for the killing of an estimated one million people—especially Khmer Muslims, Vietnamese, and Chinese.[28]

An invasion force led by 150,000 Khmer exiles who had been organized, trained, and armed by the government of Vietnam, captured Phnom Penh in January 1979. Following the defeat of the Pol Pot regime, hundreds of thousands of refugees fled to the Thai border. This population movement included former urban dwellers who had been traumatized by Pol Pot's policies and the remnants of the Khmer Rouge army and its civilian followers.[29] Nearly 150,000 Cambodians entered Thailand at this time.[30] In the mid 1980s, the Lawyers' Committee for International Human Rights reported that the areas of Cambodia still controlled by the Khmer Rouge were characterized by police-state repression and that the population under the Hun Sen regime experienced little respect for civil rights and the brutal treatment of political prisoners.[31]

Until 1990, the U.S. government consistently "supported a noncommunist resistance to Hanoi's imposition of a surrogate regime in Phnom Penh."[32] This effort—as well as similar actions in Afghanistan,

Nicaragua, and Angola—has its roots in the Reagan policy of promoting counter-revolutionary insurgency campaigns.[33] By the end of the 1980s, the various anti-Vietnamese resistance movements, each supplied and armed by external forces, had established *de facto* zones of governance along the border with Thailand. Their periodic clashes with Vietnamese-backed government troops resulted in renewed displacement and refugee outflows.[34] The prevailing alignment in Cambodia pit the Hun Sen government, assisted by Vietnam and the Soviet Union, against Sihanouk loyalists backed by the United States and Pol Pot forces supported by China and North Korea.[35] Superpower rivalry clearly had prolonged the fighting in Cambodia.[36]

Laos

In Laos, a coalition government of princes, generals, and neutralists formed in 1974 and disintegrated in 1975. U.S. withdrawal left the right wing without support.[37] After assessing developments in Vietnam, the king abdicated, other old-regime officials fled, and the Communist Party proclaimed establishment of the Lao People's Democratic Republic in December 1975.

A sizeable population outflow, which included members of the defeated army and former government officials, commenced immediately following creation of the new political system. Severe persecution, including detention under harsh conditions at "reeducation" camps, affected thousands of Laotians who remained in the country.[38] Many of the Hmong who had been trained by the CIA and had served as the mainstay of the royalist forces during the war either exited or resisted the Pathet Lao's integration efforts.[39] Continued fighting eventually pushed survivors from the Hmong resistance movement into refugee camps in Thailand.[40]

Between 1975 and 1980, about 300,000 people left Laos.[41] When the out-migration subsided in 1981, nearly one-tenth of the total population of the country had fled.[42] Serious abuses of basic human rights, including arbitrary arrests, continued through the 1980s.[43]

Iran: Islamic Revolution

The analysis of the Iranian revolution presented here consists of four parts. First, we explore the pre-revolution context. This is followed by consideration of the revolution itself, discussion of post-revolution developments, and an assessment of the role of superpower intervention.

Pre-Revolution Context

In 1953, at the urging of British intelligence, the CIA guided the overthrow of Iran's democratically elected and popular Prime Minister and his replacement by Shah Mohammad Reza Pahlavi. Prime Minister Mohammad Mosaddeq had nationalized the Anglo-Iranian Oil Company in 1951. London and Washington viewed the Shah as amenable to Western influence and supportive of foreign corporate interests.[44] The CIA's actions helped to eliminate a government that "symbolized Iran's search for national integrity and dignity" and ensured that Iranians would view the Shah as a traitor who could never achieve nationalist legitimacy.[45]

The Shah immediately invited increased U.S. economic involvement in Iran. Within a year, he had awarded a newly formed consortium of major U.S. and European petroleum companies control over the production, pricing, and export of Iranian oil.[46] Large and small multinational corporations rushed to invest in Iran during the oil-boom period of the 1970s. Japanese involvement emphasized familiar manufacturing operations and petro-chemicals. U.S.-based firms played a substantial role— particularly in petroleum-related industrial activity, supplying military equipment, and in the manufacturing, entertainment, and banking sectors.[47] During the 1970s, the United States purchased roughly 16 percent of the oil produced in Iran and exported billions of dollars worth of manufactured products to Tehran. In 1976, "the two countries signed an agreement that projected an annual nonoil, nonmilitary trade of $15 billion by 1981, almost all of it in the form of U.S. exports to Iran."[48] By the end of 1978, the Iranian state, together with domestic private enterprises, had entered into commitments to purchase about $20 billion worth of imports from U.S. firms.[49] In addition, "total capital exposure by U.S. banks in Iran" reached $2.2 billion, and "direct investment by about 500 U.S. companies amounted to a total of $8.82 billion."[50]

After being installed in power, the Shah "met regularly with the CIA station chief in Tehran" and made 11 official visits to the United States. The U.S. government spent $485 million on aid projects in Iran between 1953 and 1966 and assigned 500 A.I.D. personnel to the country.[51] By 1975, Iran had received roughly $1.5 billion in economic assistance from the United States and more than $1 billion in credit from international financial institutions.[52]

The U.S. government also assisted in the formation of the Iranian secret police force known as SAVAK in 1957. The Shah used the U.S.-trained SAVAK to silence critics of his person or his regime.[53] In June 1963, massive urban protest demonstrations broke out following "the arrest of Ayatollah Ruhollah Khomeini, a senior clergyman who in 1962 had begun preaching sermons increasingly critical of the shah's foreign policy, especially his dependence upon the United States." Iran's U.S.-equipped security forces violently put down the demonstrations. The Shah deported Khomeini, intensified the suppression of opposition organizations, and set in motion a dramatic escalation of Iran's military budget.[54] The regime also forced political activists from the left and from the National Front to go underground or to flee from Iran.[55] This reaction would have a major impact on the future course of the Iranian revolution. As a result of "the sustained and systematic repression of the Left opposition by the Pahlavi regime during the 1960s and 1970s, none of the Left groups was in a position either to play a leadership role in the mass movement or to define or influence the discourse and strategy of the anti-Shah struggle."[56] Meanwhile, from his place of exile in Iraq and later on in Paris, Khomeini inspired and directed the Islamic revolution.[57] In the absence of legal political organizations, the network of mosques and other Islamic religious institutions controlled by the mullahs proved to be the most effective vehicle for the mobilization of opposition to the pre-revolutionary regime.[58]

As the Shah became increasingly dictatorial, he grew even more dependent upon the United States. In 1963, Iran ranked among the largest recipients of U.S. military and economic assistance. When the country's increased oil revenues rendered external aid unnecessary, the Shah became the most important purchaser of U.S.-manufactured armaments. He ordered over $20 billion worth of weapons from U.S. firms between 1970 and 1978.[59] Between 1972 and 1979, the U.S. government delivered over $9 billion in military purchases that generated additional billions of Iranian government expenditures to accommodate the buildup.[60] In 1978, on the eve of the revolution, "Iran purchased $2.6 billion of the U.S. total world arms sales of $13.6 billion. . . ."[61]

Furthermore, "thousands of Iranian personnel including virtually all senior officers attended training courses in the United States and thousands of U.S. military personnel and dependents added to the growing American population in Iran. . . ."[62] The population of U.S. citizens in Iran numbered 54,000 in 1978 and U.S. institutions were heavily and visibly involved in economic, military, intelligence, and private investment projects.[63]

Revolution

The Iranian revolution drew its strength from three sources. First, it constituted "a nationalist revolt against the imposition of western advisers and culture. . . ." In the second place, it involved "a political revolt against twenty-five years of monarchical leadership" and, finally, it derived considerable energy from popular reaction "against the increasing inequalities and material problems associated with the pattern of capitalist development in Iran."[64]

The successful overthrow of the Shah is due primarily to the collaboration of militant clerics, bazaaris (merchants, artisans, and others), the intelligentsia (students and teachers), and leftist organizations in a carefully planned and orchestrated popular uprising.[65] The multitude of small groups on the Iranian left lacked strong ties to the urban poor and to the peasantry, and their leaders did not make a serious attempt to forge a united front.[66] With the help of financial contributions to the mosque from bazaar merchants, the ulama won the support of poor urban inhabitants.[67] The Fedaii-e, the Mujahedin, and the Tudeh (Communist) Party cooperated fully with the mosque-based organizations prior to the Shah's overthrow.[68] Public servants, professionals, industrial workers, the urban poor, and rural migrants participated in later stages of the revolution.[69] It is the mosque-centered network, however, that provided the decisive organizational base for revolutionary activity.[70] The mosque-bazaar alliance organized nearly two-thirds of the 2,500 demonstrations that occurred during the revolution. Although university and secondary-school students and teachers only *initiated* 23 per cent of the demonstrations, they "participated more actively than any other social group in every form of protest and revolutionary activity from peaceful marches, to strikes, to guerrilla warfare and armed insurrection. Relative to their size in the population, more members of this group were arrested, wounded, or killed than any other group."[71]

The Shah responded to opposition with sporadic brutality.[72] His vacillation between ineffective repression and appeasement "in turn led to a temporary retreat by the opposition, a widening of its support base, and the effort to develop new modes of mobilization and organization preparatory to a new and escalated assault on the state."[73] Thus, the process of escalating confrontation facilitated effective revolutionary action.

The events which precipitated the overthrow of the monarchical regime occurred in 1978. Workers and public servants engaged in a protracted strike, eventually joined by students and teachers, against continued rule by the Shah.[74] By this time, only the armed forces supported the monarch. In the face of widespread opposition, Shah Mohammed Reza Pahlavi appointed Shapur Bakhtiar as Prime Minister in January 1979 and left Iran on an "extended vacation." The last vestiges of the monarchical regime crumbled quickly. In February, the military leadership, weakened by internal rivalries, desertions, and mutinies, surrendered following a brief confrontation with urban guerrillas.[75]

Post-Revolution Developments

The first vintage of refugees escaped at the end of the Shah's reign and shortly after his overthrow. Richard Cottam reports that, in 1978, far-sighted individuals among those closest to the Shah's regime "began to slip quietly out of the country, taking with them as much of their wealth as could easily be transferred."[76] This vintage of émigrés belonged to the former ruling class. It included members of the royal family, top government officials, multinational corporate managers, and other successful businesspersons.[77]

After the overthrow of the monarchy, revolutionary courts conducted cursory public trials of individuals who had served the Shah, expropriated "excessive" wealth and property, and ordered numerous summary executions. Those executed included a former prime minister, two previous heads of SAVAK, and "almost all of the leading military officers who remained in Iran."[78] Associates of the Shah, high-level civil servants, professionals, and university professors became prime targets of the post-revolution regime. In the face of the widesread internments and executions that followed in the wake of Khomeini's return to Iran, many opted for exile.[79]

On the other hand, Iranians living in the West who supported the revolution returned to the homeland to further its objectives after Khomeini's reentry in February 1979. Allen Jones notes that "in the early, heady days of the revolution, most Iranians were filled with hope for greater freedom and justice than they had known under the Shah. As the revolution progressed, however, that hope faded as it became clear that only certain Iranians—those close to the Ayatollah or believers in his vision for Iran—were to benefit from the revolution."[80] Consequently, a large proportion of the returnees would become disillusioned with the Islamic revolution and seek to flee Iran again.[81]

Regime Consolidation. Leftist groups mobilized mass demonstrations of support following the Shah's abdication. The People's Mujahedin demonstrated wide appeal among activist teachers, professionals, and educated young people. The Mujahedin adhered to a radical version of

Islamic ideology that incorporated neo-Marxist thinking.[82] Its leader, Masud Rajavi, possessed "the greatest popularity not derived from association with Khomeini."[83] Nevertheless, the People's Mujahedin proved unable to compete with Ayatollah Khomeini in terms of appeal to low-income urban dwellers.[84] The strategic failure of the Mujahedin resulted from lack of a solid class base and an appealing alternative ideology.[85] Its followers among the intelligentsia were not positioned to paralyze the economy. Moreover, in advocating an Islamic regime, the People's Mujahedin could not compete with the mullahs. The Islamic clergy had closer ties with the masses and far greater legitimacy with the population in terms of interpretating the Koran. Although the Mujahedin desired to link the two, its radicalized version of Islam appealed neither to conservative bazaaris nor to the secular left.

Instead of uniting in defense of their position, the Iranian left divided over the nature of the new regime and whether or not to support it.[86] The Tudeh party quickly sided with the mullahs. Other groups, including Peykar, attacked the principle of ayatollahs holding political power.[87] In June of 1980, the People's Fedaii-e, the largest armed group on the left, split into "Minority" and "Majority" factions.[88] In addition to problems with internal disunity and state repression, the Iranian left as a whole failed to appreciate the central political, strategic, and ethical importance of protecting basic human rights and supporting democratic freedoms, and neglected the issue of establishing an equitable and sustainable economic system.[89]

The original post-revolution coalition, composed of "liberal nationalists" who had long opposed the Shah and fundamentalist clergy, did not last long. The ouster of liberals from key government positions culminated in the June 1981 removal of President Abolhassan Bani-Sadr and consolidation of Islamic Republic Party (IRP) control over all major institutions of government.[90] The post-revolution regime also swiftly turned against most leftist organizations, with the exception of the Tudeh Party, in its effort to consolidate the Islamic Republic.[91]

The Mujahedin-e-Khalq openly challenged the new regime in 1981. They opposed the dictatorial concentration of power in Khomeini's hands and demanded a reduction in the political role of the clergy. Viewed as the only viable alternative to the Khomeini regime, the Mujahedin turned out huge crowds that registered disapproval of government policy. The People's Mujahedin became one of the Ayatollah's principal targets after August 1981; the new regime arrested and executed thousands of its supporters. The Mujahedin responded with violent attacks on Revolutionary Guards and assassinated several leading government figures.[92]

In the wake of mass arrests, summary executions, and the regime's intensified search for opposition leaders, the newly formed Council of National Resistance (which included followers of Bani-Sadr, the People's Mujahedin, the National Democratic Front, the Democratic Party of Kurdistan, and several small leftist groups) moved its base of operations to France and many of those associated with anti-Khomeini groups attempted to flee.[93] By 1983, the Khomeini regime had banned all leftist groups, including the Tudeh, and "executed, imprisoned, forced underground or otherwise eliminated from the scene" many of their active members.[94]

Ruhollah Khomeini probably viewed the Moslem Peoples' Republican Party and its spiritual leader, Ayatollah Shariatmadari, as one of the most serious threats to his regime.[95] He forced the leaders of this organization to flee Iran in late 1979 and 1980.[96] Other Iranian opposition groups include the monarchists, who favor restoration of the Pahlavi dynasty, and the National Front, a secular party with a liberal-democratic program. The principal actors on the right are Shahpur Bakhtiar, Ali Amini, and Reza Pahlavi (the Shah's son).[97] Amini's group, which is based in Paris and receives support from U.S. sources, advocates policies that "appeal to the members of the privileged classes, namely big landowners, wealthy industrialists, and well-to-do professionals who fled Iran either before or immediately after the 1979 revolution and who reside presently in Western European countries and the United States."[98] In 1989, Mehdi Bazaragan, the first prime minister after the flight of the Shah and the leader of the Liberation Movement of Iran, was the only National Front political leader who remained in Iran.[99] Many of the unorganized, Westernized professionals initially welcomed the revolution, but "quickly became disillusioned with the intolerance and vengefulness of the new leadership manifested by summary trials and executions and by a narrow prescription for proper Islamic behavior in all areas of life."[100]

In addition to cancelling contracts for U.S. weapons and nuclear reactors and substantially reducing imports of U.S. products,[101] the Khomeini regime nationalized banks, insurance companies, and most large-scale mining and manufacturing firms and dismissed "non-Iranian executives as well as culturally Western Iranian personnel."[102] The former owners of industrial firms connected to foreign capital went into hiding or fled from Iran and workers seized control through locally organized councils.[103] Some workers' councils later found it necessary to invite the return of professional managers in order to deal with technical and administrative problems.[104] Many professionals with specialized expertise and management skills had opted for self-exile, however.[105] This situation facilitated the appointment of politically loyal and religiously and ideologically committed managers who aimed to restore the productivity of nationalized firms at the same time that they expanded Islamic consciousness among the workers.[106] With the return of managers, "the executive power of the councils tended to change gradually from determination of the organization of work and production to consultation and cooperation with the management." After July 1981, the regime completely suppressed independent workers' councils; pro-IRP associations dominated the workplace. Assef Bayat concludes that the workers' movement initially contributed "democratic institutions and a nascent democratic tradition at the workplace. . . , [but] failed to act as an effective force to maintain the *political democracy* that had been generated in the aftermath of the Revolution."[107]

The new regime also immediately replaced at least five per cent of all high-level government personnel because of "political-SAVAK association, Shah-worshipping, leftist ideology, and personal reasons."[108] The 1979–1980 ideological-purification purge of the armed forces affected more than 10,000 ground personnel and an additional 2,000 from the navy and air force—including about 4,000 field-grade officers.[109] Between 1979 and 1982, purge committees drastically reduced the overall size of the civilian public service. From 1983 to the present time, however, the regime has emphasized the recruitment and training of technical experts and professionals, and state activity has been rebureaucratized.[110]

Members of religious minorities, particularly the Baha'i, Jewish, and Armenian Christian communities, also encountered violence and state-sponsored persecution. Nationality movements seeking increased autonomy from Tehran, especially among Kurds living in western Iran, continued to come in conflict with the new regime.[111] Perhaps 25,000 anti-Khomeini Kurds moved into Iraq prior to the outbreak of the Iran-Iraq war.[112] Furthermore, non-Farsi speakers continue to be excluded from inner decision-making circles within the ruling class.[113]

Ruhollah Khomeini used Iraq's invasion of western Iran in 1980 to bolster the state's repressive apparatus and to divert attention from internal conflict, social and economic problems, and political opposition.[114] The post-revolution regime encouraged the mobilization of boys as young as nine years of age into children's brigades.[115] Devoted teenaged members of the Revolutionary Guards' *Basij-i Mustaz'afin* (Mobilization of the Oppressed) militia often found themselves in the forefront of Iran's human-wave attacks against professional Iraqi armed forces in hotly contested border areas.[116]

When the shooting ceased in the Iran-Iraq war, "it produced the ironic result of new waves of repression against the internal enemies of both Saddam Hussein and Ayatollah Khomeini." Arrests and executions escalated in Iran.[117] The United Nations Commission on Human Rights reported in late 1986 on the continuation of lengthy arrests without trial, torture, denial of legal counsel, and summary executions. The victims included persons affiliated with the Tudeh Party, the People's Fedaii-e, the People's Mujahedin, and the Baha'i International Community.[118] In 1987 and 1988, regime authorities engaged in another wave of political executions on a large scale.[119]

Under the post-Khomeini leadership of President Hojatolislam Rafsanjani and Ayatollah Ali Khamenei, internal discontent spread over rising prices and declining living standards.[120] Leaders of the Islamic Republic have alienated the Iranian working class by suppressing trade unions and workers' councils.[121] Serious divisions have emerged between senior clerics and secular leaders over rural land ownership and other issues involving property rights and social justice.[122] In addition, the post-revolution regime has been plagued by conflicting economic objectives and approaches, competing ideological orientations regarding the role of the state, the IRP, and cooperatives, external destabilization campaigns, the high cost of post-war reconstruction, and persistent overcentralization.[123]

In the face of widespread economic hardship and diminished political support, leaders of the Islamic Republic must continue to resort to mass repression in order to maintain power.[124] The lack of secure human rights and democratic freedoms in Iran reflects both the legacy of the the Shah's U.S.-supported rule and the extreme actions taken by the post-revolution regime against all voices of opposition. The institutional vehicles of political repression created following the departure of the Shah from the Iranian political scene include the Islamic Revolutionary Guards Corps, the elite Strike Group (military police and revolutionary guards), Islamic workplace associations, neighborhood *komitehs*, and a wide variety of strictly enforced rules of personal conduct.[125] The decentralized and unpredictable nature of the current reign of terror invoked by these groups "is one of its most frightening features for its targets."[126]

Impact of Post-Revolution Emigration. Iranian émigrés "consisted initially of highly politicized cadres of the previous regime or contenders in the succession struggle. Subsequently, much broader population segments tried to leave as the revolutionary regime became radicalized and increasingly repressive, partly in response to external pressures and a devastating war with its neighbor."[127] The massive post-revolution exodus dramatically reduced opposition to the Islamic Republic within Iran and the potential base of support for alternative politics.[128]

The remnants of internal opposition have not posed a serious threat to the post-consolidation regime and exile groups have been ineffective.[129] For instance, Rajavi moved the headquarters of the Organization of the People's Mujahedin of Iran to Baghdad and Mujahedin forces participated on the Iraqi side of the Iran-Iraq war.[130] As a result of this decision and other actions taken by its leaders, "the Mojahedin have lost considerable popular sympathy among the Iranian population at large."[131] The Tudeh Party has "disappeared as a visible actor on the domestic political scene."[132] Moreover, the Khomeini regime decimated the leadership of the Fedaii-e Minority.[133] In 1990, the Iranian left remained in disarray, "polarized and riven by deep ideological cleavages."[134] The monarchists, most of whom opted for exile early in the revolutionary period, are equally divided and ineffective. Moreover, the leaders of these groups enjoy little popularity within Iran.[135] Annabelle Sreberny-Mohammadi and Ali Mohammadi explain that:

> "the exile groupings are, after all, in part the products of the Pahlavi era and suffer its same deformities of political culture: severe mistrust amongst participants, an intense egoistic jostling for leadership, and an individualism which constantly prevents any coalition of forces from lasting very long. Many groups also manifest an ideological rigidity which allows the 1 per cent of disagreement to triumph over the 99 per cent of shared views, thus preventing compromise or a more pragmatic, and therefore more effective, politics."[136]

The Role of Superpower Intervention

The preceding historical analysis reveals that superpower intervention played an important, but indirect, role in revolutionary change. In Iran, revolution occurred without substantial external support.[137] In fact, the revolutionaries succeeded largely because of extensive U.S. involvement on behalf of the pre-revolution regime.[138] The Iranian revolution provides further evidence that, in the long-run, foreign superpowers and their local agents are unable to suppress a popular nationalist revolutionary movement in the Third World that succeeds in generating a massive and dedicated support base.[139]

The globalist objective of keeping Iran free from Soviet influence dominated U.S.-Iranian relations from the end of the Second World War through the overthrow of the Shah.[140]   Cold War blinders consistently prevented U.S. foreign-policy makers from understanding the depth of nationalist sentiment among the population and the significance of local political developments.[141]   As a result, they did not respond in an effective and sensitive manner to popular aspirations.   Under the Shah, moreover, Iran served as a willing surrogate for U.S. military intervention in the immediate post-Vietnam era.   The Shah showed no reservations over serving as "Washington's policeman in the Persian Gulf" by curbing radical regimes and movements.[142]

In sum, U.S. intervention in Iran and support for the autocratic Shah undermined his legitimacy and "contributed to the creation of the revolutionary state."[143]   The externally stimulated emphasis on regional police functions simultaneously promoted overdevelopment of the internal repressive apparatus and reinforced the dictatorial tendencies of a discredited and unpopular ruler.[144]   Moreover, widespread public perception of the Shah's subservience to U.S. exploitation of Iran's resources and strategic position constituted an important stimulus in the nationalist revolutionary turmoil of 1978/1979 that paved the way for a regime "determined to end the prospects for U.S. intervention in Iran's internal affairs."[145]   In spite of its official human-rights position, the evidence is overwhelming that "the Carter administration did not waiver in its support for the regime until its disintegration was almost complete."[146]

In addition to sharing responsibility for the revolutionary events that triggered the mass exodus of exiles discussed earlier, U.S. foreign-policy actions contributed to refugee formation in the post-revolution period.   The Reagan administration initially emphasized covert assistance for anti-regime groups[147] and lent support to the Iraqi war effort.   This approach failed to undermine the Khomeini regime.   The dominant forces within the Reagan government then switched to clandestine attempts to influence the Khomeini regime through weapons sales, periodic economic sanctions and diplomatic pressures, and, finally, to increasingly hostile and confrontational military-containment actions—including armed attacks on Iranian vessels and air strikes at targets within Iran.[148]   Throughout its term, the Reagan administration showed no interest in and little understanding of internal Iranian developments even though the globalist view of international relations clearly bore no relationship to the local situation.[149]   The Bush administration retained economic sanctions against Iran, including a "near-total ban" on U.S. imports and "extensive controls" on exports with military applications.[150]   The destabilization and isolation campaigns adopted by three successive U.S. administrations did not succeed in reducing the strength of forces within Iran that are committed to eliminating opposition and curtailing democratic tendencies.[151]

Ethiopia: Revolution from Above

Analysis of the Ethiopian revolution reveals strong parallels with Iran in terms of the external and internal conditions that preceded revolutionary political transformation and the urban setting. However, the armed forces played the decisive role in the overthrow of the imperial regime in the Ethiopian case.

Pre-Revolution Context

At the same time that Emperor Haile Selassie I facilitated the spread of Western education and capital investment, he banned political parties and prohibited all other organizations from engaging in political activity, severely limited the ability of labor unions to act collectively, detained student protestors, regime opponents, and other individuals arrested arbitrarily without trial, and relied on narrow ethnic, religious, regional, and class considerations in making governmental and military appointments.[152] In retrospect, the U.S. State Department admits that, under Haile Selassie, "there were few or no guarantees of the integrity of the person. Civil and political freedoms were severely limited."[153]

From the end of World War II up to the time of the Emperor's overthrow, nevertheless, U.S. administrations issued extensive economic and military assistance to the monarchical regime. In rural Ethiopia, bilateral and multilateral donors supported mechanized agricultural schemes that benefitted a small group of wealthy entrepreneurs and progressive farmers. Multinational firms operated large-scale commercial farms principally devoted to cultivating export crops.[154] Foreign companies and expatriate managers dominated the small, but expanding, urban manufacturing sector.[155] Although the total amount of direct investment by foreign corporations in Ethiopia remained relatively meager,[156] the imperial regime's forceful intervention "on behalf of foreign capital provided clear demonstration of the collusion between the two, and created a receptive mood for radical change among the Ethiopian workers, who were among the first to be swept into the revolutionary current in 1974."[157]

The level of U.S. military aid extended to pre-revolutionary Ethiopia reached nearly $300 million, or two-thirds of total assistance to Sub Saharan

Africa.[158] Most of the officer and pilot corps—about 3,550 individuals—received training in the United States.[159] U.S. and Israeli advisors worked closely with Ethiopia's internal-security apparatus. Haile Selassie allowed the permanent presence of a U.S. military-advisory group and construction of a secret tele-communications center in Asmara. Behind the scenes, economic- and foreign-policy advisors worked to gain the confidence of the Emperor and Embassy strategists attempted to influence the outcome of domestic leadership struggles. The U.S. presence in Ethiopia also involved numerous Peace Corps volunteers and AID projects. The exceptionally deep involvement extended to government programs that supported educational, cultural, and professional visits by educators, government officials, businesspersons, labor leaders, and students.[160] In terms of levels of military assistance, presence of in-country military advisors, and numbers of officers trained in the donor country, the Ethiopian program ranked as the largest mounted by the United States on the African continent.[161]

Haile Selassie endeavored to suppress all potential challenges to the prevailing social order that perpetuated vast disparities in living conditions between the rural and urban poor and the small ruling class. In forcibly resisting popular pressures for change, the monarch relied heavily upon the tools of persecution and repression provided by Western donors. The level of U.S. foreign assistance to Ethiopia did not diminish in the face of escalating violence and the government's intransigence on the issue of land reform.[162] U.S. policy makers continued to maintain that the traditional monarchy would not be overthrown.

Revolutionary Dynamics

Urban opposition to the Emperor's autocratic rule expanded and grew more sophisticated in the 1970s. Secondary-school and university students carried out the most visible and effective demonstrations of opposition to the imperial regime.[163] The imperial regime reacted with vacillating political repression to the protests and challenges to its authority spearheaded by the student movement.[164]

Conflict over the rapidly expanding gap between rich and poor enhanced the ability of the intelligentsia to raise consciousness among the mass of unemployed and underemployed urban residents, as well as among their own relatives, regarding the government's complicity in perpetuating economic exploitation.[165] In early 1974, students seized the opportunity provided by armed-forces mutinies in two outlying areas and the aggravation of inflation in the wake of extraordinary fuel-price increases to initiate violent protests in Addis Ababa.[166] They demanded wage increases, land to the tiller, and free public education.

After being called upon to restore order, the military demanded and secured the dismissal of the Prime Minister and his Cabinet. Through a series of increasingly sweeping strokes, the Armed Forces Coordinating Committee (or Derg in Amharic) managed to substitute military rule for ruling monarchy. A general strike in the capital city, public servant work stoppages in vital sectors of the urban economy, and mass demonstrations led by students and Muslims dissatisfied with the slow pace of reform took place concurrently with military pressure during this period and hastened regime change. As Christopher Clapham concludes, the Ethiopian revolution was "an urban event, owing nothing at all to rural opposition."[167] On 12 September, 1974, the Derg placed the 82-year old Emperor under house arrest and officially terminated the ruling monarchy.

By delaying the monarch's withdrawal or overthrow, the props provided by the United States produced sharper divisions between the dominant and subordinate classes and intensified post-revolution political conflict. The new rulers eliminated the landed aristocrats who had dominated the old regime, nationalized most large businesses, and swept former political leaders and ranking members of the civilian and military ruling class out of positions of power.

Initial Post-Revolution Developments

The Provisional Military Government swiftly nationalized more than 70 large manufacturing industries, banks, insurance and mortgage companies. Within one year, the new rulers introduced revolutionary changes in rural land tenure that favored peasant cultivators and nationalized all urban land and most of the elite's housing units.[168] Concomitantly, the Derg introduced Ethiopia's first mass-based institutions of political participation: peasant associations in the countryside and urban cooperatives (kebele) in the cities.[169]

Between 1974 and 1978, bitter factional disputes and escalating political repression claimed center stage on the political scene.[170] Divisions over the right to demonstrate, labor conditions, participation in the new government, and the need for popular rule surfaced immediately after the military seized power. At its annual convention held only a few days following the arrest of the Emperor, the Confederation of Ethiopian Labor Unions (CELU) passed a resolution that demanded the removal of the military and urged its replacement by a popular government composed of representatives of workers, peasants, teachers, students, government employees, traders, soldiers, and women. The Derg responded by arresting the leaders of CELU and members of the radical intelligentsia. Student protest demonstrations, worker strikes, and unrest over political issues resumed on a wider scale in August and September of 1975. The regime reacted by declaring a state of emergency in Addis Ababa, suspending all civil rights, and granting the army and police unbridled power to maintain order in the capital city. In the countryside, the government confiscated large estates in the Humera area and instituted forced labor on newly established state farms.[171]

Post-Revolution Regime Consolidation

In the face of mounting repression and political persecution, a number of opponents of military rule went underground in early 1976 to build a clandestine organization—the Ethiopian People's Revolutionary Party (EPRP). The EPRP consistently opposed the Derg on ideological grounds. While the military government and its front organizations insisted that Ethiopia's socialist revolution be implemented from the top down and that the organization and education of the masses must precede the introduction of a political party, the radical civilian opposition viewed the creation of a people's government as an essential prelude to the attainment of a genuine revolutionary society.[172] In the fall of 1976, the EPRP instigated a wave of labor actions and strikes against government and *kebele* officials in Addis Ababa and other cities.

Following a series of violent factional conflicts that decimated the leadership of the Derg, Major Mengistu Haile Mariam consolidated his power as the sole ruler of Ethiopia in February of 1977.[173] Mengistu then decided to arm the *kebele* and employ "Red Terror" to eliminate urban opposition to his rule.[174] Torture, summary execution, indefinite detention without charge, and indiscriminate acts of violence were rampant throughout the Red Terror interval.[175]

During the period of post-revolution regime consolidation, members of radical political factions organized by the intelligentsia—first, the EPRP and, then, Me'ison—comprised the principal targets of state repression.[176] Working together with *kebele* officals and its Flame Brigade, the Derg's security unit conducted house-to-house searches and engaged in the summary execution of suspected EPRP members. John Markakis and Nega Ayele write that "unable to strike directly at the EPRP itself, the government forces turned savagely against the group they knew to be sympathetic to the opposition movement, that is, the students."[177]

The Ethiopian revolution and the struggle to consolidate and centralize the post-revolution regime also provided the impetus for mass refugee flows by rural people exposed to and unprotected from the violence that accompanies armed conflict.[178] In the countryside, the peasant associations created by the Derg "became an extension of the coercive arm of the state." Mengistu Haile Mariam used them "for detaining and punishing those suspected of opposition to the regime, for the extraction of economic surplus, forced labour and for recruitment to the people's militia."[179]

From the beginning, Siad Barre, the autocratic ruler of Somalia, saw the Ethiopian revolution "as providing an unanticipated opportunity for escalating irredentist action without fear of retaliation."[180] The Somali government's invasion of the Ogaden, encouraged in part by the unrefuted impression that the United States might support such a venture, provided an urgently needed political boost for Mengistu. By coopting the patriotic fervor that the war unleashed, the post-revolution regime "put all its domestic opponents at great disadvantage."[181] With the aid of a massive infusion of Soviet arms and advisors, Mengistu succeeded in reversing the course of the Ogaden war and in crushing all potential urban-based rivals by the end of 1978.[182] Thousands of activists who had opposed Mengistu's regime and/or military rule, joined by those who felt threatened by the new government's sweeping political, economic, and cultural disassociation with the United States, fled from political persecution or opted not to return to Ethiopia. At the same time, "the war as well as fear of Ethiopian retaliation drove hundreds of thousands of people from the three embattled provinces to Somalia to languish in sprawling refugee camps."[183]

Post-Consolidation Developments

The exodus of refugees from Ethiopia continued for more than a decade following the consolidation of Mengistu's rule. This section explores the internal and external factors that are responsible for this situation.

Internal Conditions. In 1981, the Derg revised the penal code to provide that any person who leaves or attempts to leave Ethiopia without government permission has committed an act of "treason against the country and the people" that is punishable by 5 to 25 years of rigorous imprisonment and, in exceptional cases, by life internment or execution. Nevertheless, the exodus from Ethiopia continues. According to the U.S. Department of State, "there is. . . considerable illegal emigration, undertaken either under the subterfuge of travel abroad for business or to visit relatives, or by arduous treks overland and surreptitious crossing of the border."[184]

Continued outmigration was in large measure a consequence of the coercion required to maintain the Mengistu regime. Mengistu Haile Mariam retained power largely through well-organized secret police networks and a devoted personal bodyguard, and waged war with the help of forced conscription of teen-aged boys.[185] In 1989, according to the U.S. Department of State:

> The overall human rights situation in Ethiopia remained generally deplorable. Major concerns included: widespread abuses such as summary executions by all parties to Ethiopia's civil strife; the use of torture as an accepted practice in interrogation; arbitrary, incommunicado detentions; the lack of fair public trials; serious restrictions on freedom of speech and press, assembly and association, and the right of citizens to change their government; and limitations on women's and worker rights.

With particular reference to political persecution, the State Department's 1990 report states that "Ethiopians suspected of antigovernment actions or sentiments continue to be subject to arrest or detention by the police without charge or judicial review."[186] Common grounds for detention include suspicion of support or sympathy for organizations opposed to the regime, association with a 'subversive' religious group, a family member's affiliation with a nationality movement, and failure to attend mandatory political or *kebele* meetings.

In addition to the war with Somalia and the revolutionary turmoil of the mid 1970s, successive Ethiopian governments have faced protracted nationality struggles. The most serious and costly of these armed conflicts has been the fight over the liberation of Eritrea.[187] Reliance on military tactics, including efforts to wipe out potential civilian supporters in the countryside, rather than on political negotiation as a means of resolving this conflict, and the oppression of other ethnic groups, originated under the imperial regime. It is important to recognize both that "sustained opposition and conflict began in Eritrea in 1960 when Emperor Haile Selassie manipulated the abolition of its autonomous status"[188] and that the U.S. government supported Ethiopian operations against the liberation movement throughout the latter years of the Emperor's reign.[189] As early as 1978, "around 13 per cent of the Eritrean population, or over 400,000 people, had fled to refugee camps in the Sudan."[190] The war in Eritrea ranks as one of the most protracted military struggles in modern history.

Nationality struggles remain a potent factor in post-revolution Ethiopian politics.[191]   By the 1980s, however, the conflict had widened to involve opposing revolutions: "a centralising and nationalist revolution originating in the towns, which has spread out to organise the countryside, and a decentralising and regionalist revolution organised in the countryside, seeking to surround and capture the towns."[192]   At the root of these devastating conflicts, the "common denominator is powerlessness accompanied by material deprivation and social discrimination."[193]   The Derg's 1976 promise of greater regional autonomy was never fulfilled. Instead, with costly military assistance from the Soviet Union, the Mengistu regime continued efforts to subjugate the Eritrean struggle for independence, as well as the Oromo, Tigray, and other nationality movements, through the use of force and persecution.[194]   Rigid pursuit of a military solution resulted in the disruption of pastoral and agricultural activity along with widespread population displacement.[195]   Prolonged repression induced neither support nor compliance; instead, "the polarization between the state and the oppressed nationalities was accelerated."[196]

Finally, the Mengistu regime's diversion of peasant associations into militaristic activities, its policy of forced north-to-south resettlement, and its "villagization" program were responsible for new flows of refugees to Sudan and Somalia since 1985.[197]   These uprooting schemes were pursued in part as a deliberate military strategy aimed at enhancing government control over the peasantry and denying liberation forces—particularly the Oromo Liberation Front—support in the countryside.[198]

External Involvement. For most of the post-revolution period, Ethiopia served as a stage for superpower rivalry.   The Derg's nationalization measures undermined U.S. support for the post-revolution regime.[199]   At the same time, the Ethiopian revolution and Mengistu Haile Mariam's assumption of power attracted the interest of the Soviet Union.[200]   When Washington refused to supply Ethiopia with urgently requested military equipment at the time of the Somali invasion, Mengistu turned to the Soviet Union for help.[201]

The U.S.S.R. rapidly shifted alliances, airlifted armaments valued at close to one billion dollars, and, in late 1977, guided the Mengistu government to victory over the Somali invasion forces in the Ogaden.[202] Subsequently, Soviet aid to Ethiopia primarily consisted of military assistance.   By 1981, Addis Ababa's annual interest payments on its nearly $2 billion arms debt to the Soviet Union amounted to $328 million.[203]   At the same time, the new relationship with the U.S.S.R. "failed to reduce the dependency of Ethiopia's economy on the West." [204]

In 1984, the Reagan administration demonstrated interest in destabilizing Mengistu's Marxist regime. The Central Intelligence Agency launched an abortive covert propaganda campaign against the post-revolution government that resulted in the capture of an agency operative. Frustrated by the lack of any serious non-Marxist opposition within Ethiopia, the CIA resorted to financing the London-based Ethiopian People's Democratic Alliance (EPDA)—an organization that official U.S. sources concede "has few guerrillas in the field and scant popular support inside Ethiopia."[205] In addition to the EPRP and Me'ison, all of the major nationality movements have embraced socialist principles. As in Iran and Cuba, the decimation and flight of elements on the political right dramatically reduced the ability of the U.S. strategists to shape internal developments during the post-revolution period.

Neither the United States nor the Soviet Union has placed priority on the needs and aspirations of the people living in the Horn. Instead, the foreign-policy actions of the superpowers in the post-consolidation period have exacerbated nationality and inter-state conflicts and contributed to the perpetuation of population outmigration. After 1988, however, Soviet enthusiasm for the Mengistu regime waned considerably. As a result, it withdrew military advisors and withheld permission to utilize its aircraft, threatened not to renew the military-assistance program, and pressured the Ethiopian government to reach a political settlement to the Eritrean conflict.[206] During this period, former President Jimmy Carter attempted to broker peace negotiations between the EPLF and the government of Ethiopia.[207] As the Soviet Union and Eastern European nations withdrew their support, Israel began to supply weapons and other forms of military assistance to the Mengistu regime.[208]

The current refugee situation in the Horn of Africa is a legacy of three decades of superpower arms supply. Militarization has ensured the long-term underdevelopment of Ethiopia.[209] Here, the process progressed to such an extreme extent that the world's poorest country devoted over half of its annual budget to military spending.[210] In spite of the continued emphasis on militarization and the size of its armed forces (500,000), the Mengistu regime suffered severe battlefield losses to the TPLF and the EPLF. By April 1991, the TPLF controlled Tigre, Gojjam, Begemdir, most of Wollo, and northern Shoa.[211] In rapid succession, Asmara, Assab, and Addis Ababa fell to the liberation forces in May. Mengistu Haile Mariam became an exile himself—in Zimbabwe. With both superpowers essentially sidelined, the regionalist revolution of the countryside succeeded in overthrowing the post-revolution regime. A new wave of refugees, including many military officers and collaborators in Mengistu's government, took flight to neighboring countries in the Horn.

Focused Comparisons

The four case studies analyzed in detail in this chapter have been selected to allow for focused comparisons of the phenomenon of revolutionary political transformation in the Third World and the attendant mass population exodus. The method of controlled comparison is particularly useful when the analyst is interested in many variables, but has only a few cases to work with.[212]

The results of this analysis reveal that post-revolution refugee formation is consistently associated with two pre-transformation structural conditions: (1) the maintenance of a wide gap between the ruling and subordinate classes in the sending country; and (2) denial of mass political participation and leftist opposition activity by regimes that welcome multinational capitalist advances and are propped up by extensive foreign (primarily U.S.) intervention. In the cases examined, the combination of extreme structural inequality and class conflict together with external support for the exclusion of leftist groups from participation in the political system constituted a particularly volatile revolutionary mix. The type of pre-revolution authoritarian regime that existed in the four states of special interest varied from military to monarchy, but all shared the experience of widespread U.S. presence. Massive military assistance constituted the most common prop, but the full range of supports spanned direct armed intervention through extensive economic involvement. Finally, in the Cuban, Iranian, and Ethiopian cases, the popular nature of the mass revolutionary uprisings and the uncertain outcome of political change weakened the resolve of the U.S. government to support a compliant dictator at a critical juncture in each country's political history.[213]

Once underway, refugee flows are sustained by several post-revolution conditions. Domestically, there is a tendency for revolutionary commitment to be supplanted by bureaucratic self-interest.[214] The ideological orientation and intensity of the faction that consolidates power over the post-revolution state exerts a major impact on the scope of political persecution and the extent of refugee formation at this stage. Conflicts along nationality or religious lines are exacerbated by external forces acting without respect for local aspirations. The measures instigated by U.S. foreign-policy actors devoted to destabilizing revolutionary regimes directly and indirectly create conditions, including heightened political repression by the post-revolution regime, that provoke the continued exodus of political migrants.

Notes

1. Due to space limitations, only a relatively brief discussion of each case can be presented here. An effort is made, however, to refer readers to available studies that treat the issues under consideration in a detailed and comprehensive fashion.

2. In addition, "cultural penetration was so extensive that large segments of the Cuban population had become psychologically dependent on the United States. . . ." Robert L. Bach, "Cubans," in *Refugees in the United States: A Reference Handbook*, edited by David W. Haines (Westport: Greenwood Press, 1985), pp. 78–80.

3. Bach, "Cubans," p. 80.

4. Bach, "Cubans," pp. 77–78.

5. Aristide R. Zolberg, Astri Suhrke, and Sergio Aguayo, *Escape from Violence: Conflict and the Refugee Crisis in the Developing World* (Oxford: Oxford University Press, 1989), pp. 186–187; Bach, "Cubans," p. 80; also see Charles F. Andrian, *Political Change in the Third World* (Boston: Unwin Hyman, 1988), pp. 138–142; Richard R. Fagen, "The Politics of Transition," in *Transition and Development: Problems of Third World Socialism*, ed. by Richard R. Fagen, Carmen D. Deere, and José L. Coraggio (New York: Monthly Review Press, 1986), p. 250.

6. Richard R. Fagen, Richard A. Brody, and Thomas J. O'Leary, *Cubans in Exile: Disaffection and the Revolution* (Stanford: Stanford University Press, 1968), pp. 113–115. Fidel Castro did order the nationalization of major industries in 1960.

7. Fagen *et al.*, *Cubans in Exile*, pp. 100–101; Zolberg *et al.*, *Refugee Crisis*, p. 187; Bach, "Cubans," p. 81.

8. Bach, "Cubans," p. 81; Silvia Pedraza-Bailey, "Cuba's Exiles: Portrait of a Refugee Migration," *International Migration Review* 19, No. 1 (1985):19, 26. Economic opportunities in the U.S.A. are likely to look even brighter in light of the Soviet Union's decision to restructure bilateral-trade relations with Cuba to reflect the real market value of goods exchanged. *New York Times*, 26 July 1990, p. A6.

9. Fagen *et al.*, *Cubans in Exile*, pp. 101–102.

10. Silvia Pedraza-Bailey, *Political and Economic Migrants in America: Cubans and Mexicans* (Austin: University of Texas Press, 1985), p. 16.

11. Harry H. Ransom, "Covert Intervention," in *Intervention in the 1980s: U.S. Foreign Policy in the Third World*, ed. by Peter J. Schraeder (Boulder: Lynne Rienner Publishers, 1989), p. 106; Gil Loescher and John A. Scanlan, *Calculated Kindness: Refugees and America's Half-Open Door, 1945 to the Present* (New York: Free Press, 1986), p. 61.

12. Peter J. Schraeder, "Concepts, Relevance, Themes, and Overview" in *Intervention in the 1980s: U.S. Foreign Policy in the Third World*, ed. by Peter J. Schraeder (Boulder: Lynne Rienner Publishers, 1989), p. 11; Peter J. Schraeder, "U.S. Intervention in Perspective," in *Intervention in the 1980s*, p. 290.

13. Pedraza-Bailey, "Cuba's Exiles," 7, 14. Also see Loescher and Scanlan, *Kindness*, p. 76.

14. James T. Fawcett and Benjamin V. Cariño, "International Migration and Pacific Basin Development," in *Pacific Bridges: The New Immigration from Asia and the Pacific Islands*, edited by James T. Fawcett and Benjamin V. Cariño (Staten Island: Center for Migration Studies, 1987), p. 11.

15. Zolberg *et al., Refugee Crisis*, p. 161.

16. Zolberg *et al., Refugee Crisis*, pp. 162–163; Gail P. Kelly, *From Vietnam to America: A Chronicle of the Vietnamese Immigration to the United States* (Boulder: Westview Press, 1977), pp. 13–14.

17. Fawcett and Cariño, "International Migration," p. 11; Aryeh Neier, "Drain the Sea, Scorch the Earth: An Outline of the Counterinsurgency Strategy," in *Forced Out; The Agony of the Refugee in Our Time*, compiled by Carole Kismaric (Washington, D.C.: Human Rights Watch and the J. M. Kaplan Fund, 1989), p. 67.

18. Zolberg, *Refugee Crisis*, p. 163; Kelly, *Vietnamese Immigration*, p. 15.

19. Zolberg *et al., Refugee Crisis*, pp. 164–165; William Shawcross, "A Tourist in the Refugee World," in *Forced Out: The Agony of the Refugee in Our Time*, compiled by Carole Kismaric (Washington, D.C.: Human Rights Watch and the J. M. Kaplan Fund, 1989), p. 30; Loescher and Scanlan, *Kindness*, p. 138. Most Western governments, with the exception of the United States, had relaxed economic sanctions against Vietnam by 1990. See *Washington Post*, 28 October 1990.

20. Jeffery Crisp, ed., *Refugees: The Dynamics of Displacement* (London: Zed Books, 1986), p. 102.

21. John K. Whitmore, "Chinese from Southeast Asia," in *Refugees in the United States: A Reference Handbook*, edited by David W. Haines (Westport: Greenwood Press, 1985), pp. 66–67.

22. Nguyen Manh Hung, "Vietnamese," in *Refugees in the United States: A Reference Handbook*, edited by David W. Haines (Westport: Greenwood Press, 1985), p. 199.

23. Zolberg *et al., Refugee Crisis*, p. 168; Court Robinson, "Sins of Omission: The New Vietnamese Refugee Crisis," in *World Refugee Survey—1988 in Review* (Washington, D.C.: U.S. Committee for Refugees, 1989), p. 8.

24. May Ebihara, "Khmer," in *Refugees in the United States: A Handbook*, edited by David W. Haines (Westport: Greenwood Press, 1985), pp. 128–130.

25. Zolberg *et al., Refugee Crisis*, p. 170.

26. Ebihara, "Khmer," p. 130; Whitmore, "Chinese," p. 66.

27. Ebihara, "Khmer," pp. 130–131; Crisp, *Refugees*, p. 101.

28. Zolberg *et al., Refugee Crisis*, p. 170.

29. Zolberg *et al., Refugee Crisis*, p. 171; Loescher and Scanlan, *Kindness*, p. 156. The extreme difficulty that internal refugees encountered finding a safe means of escape during the early post-revolution period accounts for the delay in international migration. Crisp, *Refugees*, p. 132.

30. Dennis McNamara, "The Origins and Effects of 'Humane Deterrence' Policies in South-east Asia," in *Refugees and International Relations*, edited by Gil Loescher and Laila Monahan (Oxford: Oxford Press, 1989), p. 125.

31. Cited in Loescher and Scanlan, *Kindness*, p. 207.

32. Richard H. Solomon, "Cambodia and Vietnam: Trapped in an Eddy of History?" *Current Policy* 1206 (September 1989):2.

33. Michael T. Klare, "The Development of Low-Intensity Conflict Doctrine," in *Intervention in the 1980s: U.S. Foreign Policy in the Third World*, ed. by Peter J. Schraeder (Boulder: Lynne Rienner Publishers, 1989), p. 41.

34. Ebihara, "Khmer," pp. 133–134.

35. John Badgley, "Cambodia and Vietnam Today" (lecture presented at the University of Montana, 8 January 1990); Ebihara, "Khmer," p. 132; *New York Times*, 1 January 1990, p. 10.

36. Zolberg *et al., Refugee Crisis*, p. 172.

37. John L. Van Esterik, "Lao," in *Refugees in the United States: A Reference Handbook*, edited by David W. Haines (Westport: Greenwood Press, 1985), p. 153.

38. Joseph Cerquone, *Refugees from Laos: In Harm's Way* (Washington, D.C.: U.S. Committee for Refugees, 1986), p. 5.

39. The identification of the Hmong people with CIA-financed armed forces contributed to their need to seek refuge outside of Laos. David M. Reimers, *Still the Golden Door: The Third World Comes to America* (New York: Columbia University Press, 1985), p. 180; Vincent N. Parrillo, *Strangers to these Shores: Race and Ethnic Relations in the United States* (New York: Macmillan, 1990), p. 304.

40. Cerquone, *Laos*, p. 5.

41. Van Esterik, "Lao," p. 154.

42. Zolberg *et al., Refugee Crisis*, p. 168; Timothy Dunnigan and Douglas P. Olney, "Hmong," in *Refugees in the United States: A Reference Handbook*, edited by David W. Haines (Westport: Greenwood Press, 1985), p. 115.

43. Cerquone, *Laos*, pp. 8, 11.

44. Ransom, "Covert Intervention," pp. 106–107; Eric Hooglund, "Iran," in *Intervention in the 1980s: U.S. Foreign Policy in the Third World*, ed. by Peter J. Schraeder (Boulder: Lynne Rienner Publishers, 1989), p. 207; Richard Falk, "Iran and American Geopolitics in the Gulf," *Horn of Africa* 2, No. 2 (April/June 1979):60.

86

45. Richard W. Cottam, *Iran and the United States: A Cold War Case Study* (Pittsburgh: University of Pittsburgh Press, 1988), p. 263; Hooglund, "Iran," p. 210.

46. Hoogland, "Iran," p. 210; Mehrdad Valibeigi, "U.S.-Iranian Trade Relations After the Revolution," in *Post-Revolutionary Iran*, edited by Hooshang Amirahmadi and Manoucher Parvin (Boulder: Westview Press, 1988), pp. 210–211.

47. G. R. Bassiry and R. Hrair Dekmejian, "MNCs and the Iranian Revolution: An Empirical Study," *Management International Review* 25, No. 2 (1985):68–73.

48. Valibeigi, "Trade," p. 211.

49. James F. Petras and Morris H. Morley, "Development and Revolution: Contradictions in the Advanced Third World Countries—Brazil, South Africa, and Iran," *Studies in Comparative International Development* 10 (Spring 1981):8–9.

50. Valibeigi, "Trade," p. 211.

51. John M. Kirk, "An Analysis of the Ethiopian, Iranian and Nicaraguan Revolutions from the Perspective of United States Involvement" (Ph.D. dissertation, University of Texas, 1985), pp. 61–62; also see Valibeigi, "Trade," p. 211.

52. Petras and Morley, "Contradictions," 9.

53. Hooglund, "Iran," pp. 210–211; Fred Halliday, "The Arc of Revolutions: Iran, Afghanistan, South Yemen, Ethiopia," *Race & Class* 20, No. 4 (Spring 1979):382.

54. Hooglund, "Iran," p. 211; Nader Entessar, "The Military and Politics in the Islamic Republic of Iran," in *Post-Revolutionary Iran*, edited by Hooshang Amirahmadi and Manoucher Parvin (Boulder: Westview Press, 1988), p. 59.

55. Nozar Alaolmolki, "The New Iranian Left," *Middle East Journal* 41, No. 2 (Spring 1987):219.

56. The People's Fedayii-e and the People's Mujahedin were particularly disadvantaged since the Shah had nearly succeeded in decimating both organizations by 1977. Val Moghadam, "The Left and Revolution in Iran: A Critical Analysis," in *Post-Revolutionary Iran*, edited by Hooshang Amirahmadi and Manoucher Parvin (Boulder: Westview Press, 1988), pp. 28–29.

57. Michael S. Teitelbaum, "Immigration, Refugees, and Foreign Policy," *International Organization* 38, No. 3 (Summer 1984):442.

58. Ahmad Ashraf and Ali Banuazizi, "The State, Classes and Modes of Mobilization in the Iranian Revolution," *State, Culture and Society* 1, No. 3 (Spring 1985):7–8, 27.

59. Hooglund, "Iran," pp. 211–213, 219; Valibeigi, "Trade," p. 211. From the standpoint of the U.S. economy, these purchases helped to recycle "petro-dollars," to reduce the balance of payments deficit, and to reward major defense contractors. Entessar, "Military," p. 59.

60. Kirk, "Revolutions," pp. 96–97.

61. Falk, "Iran," 62, 64.

62. About 15,000 Iranian military personnel received training in the U.S.A. Kirk, "Revolutions," pp. 61–61, 101. About 10,000 U.S. nationals worked on military-related projects in Iran. Entessar, "Military," p. 59.

63. Kirk, "Revolutions," pp. 63–64, 96, 263; Falk, "Iran," 62.

64. Halliday, "Arc," 378; Sohrab Behdad, "The Political Economy of Islamic Planning in Iran," in *Post-Revolutionary Iran*, edited by Hooshang Amirahmadi and Manoucher Parvin (Boulder: Westview Press, 1988), pp. 110–111; Hooshang Amirahmadi, "Middle-Class Revolutions in the Third World," in *Post-Revolutionary Iran*, edited by Hooshang Amirahmadi and Manoucher Parvin (Boulder: Westview Press, 1988), p. 225. On the state of urban inequality by 1977 and massive capital flight from Iran, see John Dunn, "Country Risk: Social and Cultural Aspects," in *Managing International Risk*, edited by Richard J. Herring (Cambridge: Cambridge University Press, 1983), p. 161; Petras and Morley, "Contradictions," 33, 37; Richard Falk, *Human Rights and State Sovereignty* (New York: Holmes & Meier Publishers, 1981), pp. 204–205.

The three principal sources of revolutionary struggle listed here also are cited by Val Moghadam, "The Left," p. 27. Moghadam argues (pp. 27–28) that the Iranian left mistakenly placed priority on national liberation from imperialism and the global economy rather than on the need for social revolution. As a result, "the Left's discourse blurred the distinction between the religious project and the Left alternative, thereby ultimately undermining the Left's position and bolstering the Islamic forces."

65. Ashraf and Banuazizi, "Mobilization," 25–26. On tactics, see Desmond Harney, "Some Explanations for the Iranian Revolution," *Asian Affairs* 67 (January 1980):135–137.

66. Bahram Alavi, "As Khomeini Government Disintegrates, Iranian Opposition Groups Revive," *Washington Report on Middle East Affairs* 8 (April 1989):4; Moghadam, "The Left," pp. 28–29. For an analysis of the competing strands of revolutionary Islamic ideology, see Ashraf and Banuazizi, "Mobilization," 30–32, 37.

67. Ashraf and Banuazizi, "Mobilization," 28–30.

68. Cottam, *Iran*, p. 203.

69. Ashraf and Banuazizi ("Mobilization," 25–26) add that the peasantry, which comprised roughly half of Iran's population, "played no significant role in any phase of the revolution."

70. On the mullahs' organizational base and effective political opposition to the Shah's regime, see Dunn, "Country Risk," pp. 159–160.

71. Ashraf and Banuazizi, "Mobilization," 25–26.

72. At least nine demonstrators died, for instance, in a January 1978 clash between police and pro-Khomeini theology students in the city of Qom. Ashraf and Banuazizi, "Mobilization," 9, 26. In addition, the Shah resorted to "strong-armed

88

bands acting ostensibly as vigilantes outside any formal government organization and committing acts of violence against seemingly arbitrarily chosen targets." Cottam, *Iran*, pp. 160–161.

73. Ashraf and Banuazizi, "Mobilization," 10–13, 20–21.

74. Ashraf and Banuazizi, "Mobilization," 12, 34; Ferrel Heady, *Public Administration: A Comparative Perspective*, 3rd revised edition (New York: Marcel Dekker, 1984), p. 301.

75. Ashraf and Banuazizi, "Mobilization," 17–18; Entessar, "Military," p. 60. The Fedaii-e Khalq played a major role in the takeover of various urban military barracks and police stations.

76. Cottam, *Iran*, pp. 176–177.

77. Mohammad Amjad, "Post-revolutionary Migration of Iranians Abroad" (paper presented at the 7th Annual Third World Studies Conference, Omaha, October 1984), pp. 10–11.

78. Cottam, *Iran*, p. 192; Behdad, "Planning," p. 111; also see Entessar, "Military," p. 63. On early post-revolution retribution in Iran, see Falk, *Human Rights*, pp. 205–208.

79. Allen K. Jones, *Iranian Refugees: The Many Faces of Persecution* (Washington, D.C.: U.S. Committee for Refugees, 1984), pp. 11–12.

80. Jones, *Iranian Refugees*, p. 4; Amjad, "Iranians Abroad," p. 4.

81. Jones, *Iranian Refugees*, pp. 4, 16.

82. Moghadam, "The Left," p. 33; Hamid Dabashi, "'Islamic Ideology': The Perils and Promises of a Neologism," in *Post-Revolutionary Iran*, ed. by Hooshang Amirahmadi and Manoucher Parvin (Boulder: Westview, 1988), p. 19.

83. Cottam, *Iran*, p. 204.

84. Moghadam, "The Left," pp. 29, 33; Cottam, *Iran*, p. 204.

85. I am indebted to Mehrdad Kia for contributing useful insights on this issue.

86. Alavi, "Opposition," 4; Moghadam, "The Left," pp. 29–30.

87. Moghadam, "The Left," pp. 29–30.

88. The original Fedaii-e drew its support base from students, teachers, workers at large manufacturing enterprises and in the oil industry, and supporters of nationality movements. Alaolmolki, "Iranian Left," 223–224; Ashraf and Banuazizi, "Mobilization," 33. The terms used following the split are misleading in that the majority of Fedaii-e supporters followed the 'minority' position. Cottam, *Iran*, pp. 204–205. The radical Fedaii-e Minority supported demands for democratic rights, the Kurdish nationality struggle, and severing imperialist economic ties. This faction viewed the new regime as reactionary and capitalist. The Majority faction emphasized the anti-imperialist struggle above all. It joined the Tudeh party in supporting the post-revolution regime. Moghadam, "The Left," pp. 35, 31; Annabelle Sreberny-Mohammadi and Ali Mohammadi, "Post-Revolutionary Iranian

Exiles: A Study in Impotence," *Third World Quarterly* 9, No. 1 (January 1987):117. The split within the People's Fedayii-e eventually led to the division and disintegration of independent workers' and students' councils and seriously weakened both the revolutionary left and the Kurdish struggle. Moghadam, "The Left," p. 35.

89. Moghadam, "The Left," pp. 32–35.

90. Cottam, *Iran*, p. 230.

91. Alaolmolki, "Iranian Left," 218–222.

92. Jones, *Iranian Refugees*, p. 4; Cottam, *Iran*, p. 231; Sreberny-Mohammadi and Mohammadi, "Impotence," 110–113.

93. Sreberny-Mohammadi and Mohammadi, "Impotence," 110, 112; Amjad, "Iranians Abroad," p. 16.

94. Alaolmolki, "Iranian Left," 218–222, 228; Cottam, *Iran*, p. 204. The Khomeini regime's 1983 "arrest of 1,500 [Tudeh] party members and the execution of the party leadership eliminated the party as a potential threat." Jones, *Iranian Refugees*, p. 9; Cottam, *Iran*, p. 232.

95. Ayatollah Shariatmadari possessed considerable popularity in the northwest province of Azerbaijan, particularly in the city of Tabriz where he received support from elements in the bazaar. Mehrdad Kia, personal communication.

96. Cottam, *Iran*, pp. 205–206.

97. Sreberny-Mohammadi and Mohammadi, "Impotence," 118–121; also see pp. 122–124 for a discussion of other opposition groups, including the National Front.

98. Alavi, "Opposition," 4.

99. Alavi, "Opposition," 4.

100. Jones, *Iranian Refugees*, pp. 9–10.

101. Valibeigi, "Trade," pp. 212–213.

102. Bassiry and Dekmejian, "MNCs," p. 75; Behdad, "Planning," pp. 107, 111.

103. Assef Bayat, "Labor and Democracy in Post-Revolutionary Iran," in *Post-Revolutionary Iran*, edited by Hooshang Amirahmadi and Manoucher Parvin (Boulder: Westview Press, 1988), p. 45; Behdad, "Planning," 111.

104. Bayat, "Labor," pp. 52–53.

105. R. K. Ramazani, "Challenges for US Policy," in *Iran's Revolution: The Search for Consensus*, edited by R. K. Ramazani (Bloomington: Indiana University Press, 1990), p. 137; Manoucher Parvin and Majid Taghavi, "A Comparison of Land Tenure in Iran Under Monarchy and Under the Islamic Republic," in *Post-Revolutionary Iran*, edited by Hooshang Amirahmadi and Manoucher Parvin (Boulder: Westview Press, 1988), p. 179; Hooshang Amirahmadi, "Economic Reconstruction of Iran: Costing the War Damage," *Third World Quarterly* 12, No. 1 (January 1990):41.

106. Bassiry and Dekmejian, "MNCs," p. 75.

107. Bayat, "Labor," pp. 52–53.

108. Ali Farazmand, "The Impacts of the Revolution of 1978–1979 on the Iranian Bureaucracy and Civil Service," *International Journal of Public Administration* 10, No. 4 (Fall 1987):340–347.

109. The abortive U.S. hostage rescue effort contributed to the size of this purge. Entessar, "Military," pp. 62–64.

110. Farazmand, "Bureaucracy," 340–347, 354–356; Cottam, *Iran*, p. 233; Heady, *Public Administration*, pp. 301–302.

111. Jones, *Iranian Refugees*, pp. 4–9; Alavi, "Opposition," 5. On the costly manipulation of Kurdish guerrillas by the Nixon administration on behalf of the client regime's (i.e., the Shah's) strategic position in the Persian Gulf, see Peter J. Schraeder, "Paramilitary Intervention," in *Intervention in the 1980s: U.S. Foreign Policy in the Third World*, ed. by Peter J. Schraeder (Boulder: Lynne Rienner Publishers, 1989), p. 119; Bill Frelick, "Refugees: A Barometer of Genocide," in *World Refugee Survey—1988 in Review* (Washington, D.C.: U.S. Committee for Refugees, 1989), pp. 13–14; and Hooglund, "Iran," p. 213. After the fall of the Shah, the Kurdish Democratic Party (KDP) agreed to a cease fire and entered into negotiations with President Bani-Sadr. However, the Khomeini regime rejected the KDP's demands for constitutional guarantees of autonomy and linguistic parity, responsibility for their own internal security, and self-administration of their region. Instead, revolutionary guards arrested and executed 21 Kurdish leaders. Mohsen Shabdar, personal communication. Nevertheless, the KDP continued to exercise control over extensive liberated zones in Kurdistan until 1983. Srebemy-Mohammadi and Mohammadi, "Impotence," 114.

112. *World Refugee Survey—1988 in Review* (Washington, D.C.: U.S. Committee for Refugees, 1989), p. 75.

113. Alavi, "Opposition," 5.

114. Alavi, "Opposition," 4; Amirahmadi, "Revolutions," pp. 228–229.

According to Cottam (*Iran*, pp. 223–224), "no major Iranian official, regardless of faction, doubted that the Iraqi attack was inspired by and orchestrated by the United States." He finds no basis for this view, and no indication that the Carter administration "was aware of the Iranian interpretation of events and of the intensity with which it was held."

115. Jones, *Iranian Refugees*, pp. 4, 10.

116. Entessar, "Military," p. 67.

117. Roger P. Winter, "The Year in Review," in *World Refugee Survey—1988 in Review* (Washington, D.C.: U.S. Committee for Refugees, 1989), p. 4.

118. *New York Times*, 13 February 1987, p. 4.

119. Amnesty International report cited in *New York Times*, 13 December 1988, p. 10; Alavi, "Opposition," 3; Richard H. Curtiss, "State Department Human Rights

Report: Only a Glimpse of Khomeini's Bloody Failure," *Washington Report on Middle East Affairs* 8 (April 1989):5–6.

120. Ramazani, "Challenges," p. 137; *New York Times*, 10 October 1989, pp. 1, 6.

121. Alavi, "Opposition," 5.

122. Shaul Bakhash, "The Politics of Land, Law, and Social Justice in Iran," in *Iran's Revolution: The Search for Consensus*, edited by R. K. Ramazani (Bloomington: Indiana University Press, 1990), pp. 27–45.

123. See, for instance, Behdad, "Planning," p. 107; Parvin and Taghavi, "Land Tenure," pp. 175–180; Amirahmadi, "Reconstruction," 34–35; Amirahmadi, "Revolutions," pp. 229, 235; Bahram Alavi, "Rafsanjani Faces Crucial Struggle," *Washington Report on Middle East Affairs* 8, No. 2 (June 1989):15; Richard Cottam, "Inside Revolutionary Iran," in *Iran's Revolution: The Search for Consensus*, edited by R. K. Ramazani (Bloomington: Indiana University Press, 1990), p. 22. Land nationalizations and the "halt in growth of foreign-owned or controlled agribusiness" constitute important changes in the political economy of post-revolution Iran. Parvin and Taghavi, "Land Tenure," pp. 179–180; Bakhash, "Land," p. 31.

124. Alavi, "Opposition," 5.

125. Entessar, "Military," pp. 65–69; Amirahmadi, "Revolutions," p. 235; *New York Times*, 16 July 1990, pp. A1, A4.

126. Cottam, "Revolutionary Iran," pp. 16, 22–23.

127. Zolberg *et al.*, *Refugee Crisis*, p. 129.

128. Sreberny-Mohammadi and Mohammadi, "Impotence," 126.

129. Shahrough Akhavi, "Institutionalizing the New Order in Iran," *Current History* 82 (February 1987):53.

130. See *Washington Post*, 1 June 1988, p. A24.

131. Sreberny-Mohammadi and Mohammadi, "Impotence," 115–116. Nevertheless, the Mujahedin retains considerable popularity among exiles and remains "the largest and perhaps the strongest opposition force." Alavi "Opposition," 4.

132. Sreberny-Mohammadi and Mohammadi, "Impotence," 117.

133. The Majority faction is barely distinguishable from the Tudeh Party today. Sreberny-Mohammadi and Mohammadi, "Impotence," 117.

134. For a thorough analysis of this situation and the emergence of Komeleh as a major and independent opposition organization, see Alaolmolki, "Iranian Left," 223–233. Also see Sreberny-Mohammadi and Mohammadi, "Impotence," 113–118; and Alavi, "Opposition," 2, 5.

135. Alavi, "Opposition," 4.

136. Sreberny-Mohammadi and Mohammadi, "Impotence," 126; also see Alavi, "Opposition," 3.

137. Cottam, *Iran*, pp. 182–183.

138. For instance, the people of Iran came to view the Imperial Armed Forces as primarily devoted to "the twin tasks of maintaining the Shah in power and serving U.S. interests in the region." Entessar, "Military," p. 59.

139. Cottam, *Iran*, pp. 252–253; Falk, *Human Rights*, p. 204.

140. The global-strategy perspective outweighed concern over human-rights abuses during the Carter administration. Hooglund, "Iran," pp. 207, 213–214; Falk, "Iran," 65–66, 69; Schraeder, "U.S. Intervention," p. 294.

141. Hooglund, "Iran," pp. 219–220.

142. Hooglund, "Iran," pp. 212–213; Klare, "Low-Intensity Conflict," p. 37; Falk, "Iran," 64; Valibeigi, "Trade," p. 211; Entessar, "Military," p. 59.

143. Bandow, "Aid," p. 78; Amirahmadi, "Revolutions," p. 225.

144. Petras and Morley, "Contradictions," p. 38.

145. Hooglund, "Iran," pp. 207–208, 219. Richard Falk ("Iran," 65) concurs that the U.S. "military build-up and foreign economic penetration of Iran only hastened the end of the Shah. . . . This augmented American presence only increased the credibility of opposition claims that the Shah had relinquished Iranian sovereignty to a foreign imperial power."

146. However, "it is also undeniable that the shah was never sure of that support." Cottam, *Iran*, pp. 186–188.

147. The CIA "provided covert financial and material support as early as 1980 to various monarchist groups in exile that were advocating the overthrow of the regime in Tehran and the re-establishment of a pro-U.S. government." Hooglund, "Iran," p. 216; Amirahmadi, "Revolutions," p. 228.

148. Ramazani, "Challenges," pp. 131–132; Hooglund, "Iran," pp. 215–218; Cottam, *Iran*, p. 251; Amirahmadi, "Revolutions," p. 228.

149. Cottam, *Iran*, pp. 237–252.

150. John H. Kelly, "The U.S. Approach to Iran: Outlook for the Future," *Current Policy*, No. 1231 (1989):3.

151. Amirahmadi, "Revolutions," pp. 228–229.

152. See Peter Koehn and Louis D. Hayes, "Student Politics in Traditional Monarchies: A Comparative Analysis of Ethiopia and Nepal," *Journal of Asian and African Studies* 13, Nos. 1–2 (January-April 1978):34–40; John Markakis, *Ethiopia: Anatomy of a Traditional Polity* (Oxford: Oxford University Press, 1974), pp. 229–252, 331–372.

153. U.S., Department of State, *Country Reports on Human Rights Practices for 1982* (Washington, D.C.: U.S. GPO, 1983), p. 98.

154. Peter Koehn, "African Approaches to Environmental Stress: A Focus on Ethiopia and Nigeria," in *International Dimensions of the Environmental Crisis*, edited by Richard N. Barrett (Boulder: Westview Press, 1982), p. 256.

155. Duri Mohammed, "Private Foreign Investment in Ethiopia," *Journal of Ethiopian Studies* 7 (July 1969):55–58; Paul H. Brietzke, *Law, Development, and the Ethiopian Revolution* (Lewisburg: Bucknell University Press, 1982), p. 264.

156. Fred Halliday and Maxine Molyneux, *The Ethiopian Revolution* (London: Verso Editions, 1981), p. 69; Marina and David Ottaway, *Ethiopia: Empire in Revolution* (New York: Africana Publishing Company, 1978), p. 193n.

157. John Markakis, *National and Class Conflict in the Horn of Africa* (Cambridge: Cambridge University Press, 1987), p. 99.

158. Richard Sherman, *Eritrea: The Unfinished Revolution* (New York: Praeger, 1980), pp. 144, 176–177.

159. Markakis, *Horn*, p. 92; Kirk, "Revolutions," p. 101.

160. Markakis, *Ethiopia*, pp. 257–258, 372–373; John M. Cohen, "Foreign Involvement in Land Reform: The Case of Ethiopia" (paper presented at the Conference on the International Dimensions of Land Reform, Mexico City, January 1983), pp. 8–37, 57n, 59n; Koehn, "Approaches," pp. 255–257; Kirk, "Revolutions," p. 51; Sherman, *Eritrea*, pp. 144–145; Marina Ottaway, *Soviet and American Influence in the Horn of Africa* (New York: Praeger, 1982), pp. 27–28, 48–53; Halliday and Molyneux, *Ethiopian Revolution*, pp. 79, 82; Aristide Zolberg and Astri Suhrke, "Social Conflict and Refugees in the Third World: The Cases of Ethiopia and Afghanistan" (paper presented at the Center for Migration and Population Studies, Harvard University, March 1984), p. 42; Robert G. Patman, *The Soviet Union in the Horn of Africa: The Diplomacy of Intervention and Disengagement* (Cambridge: Cambridge University Press, 1990), p. 35.

161. Fred Halliday, "U.S. Policy in the Horn of Africa: Aboulia or Proxy Intervention?" *Review of African Political Economy* 10 (September/December 1977):10–11; Patman, *Horn*, p. 37.

162. Michael Stahl, *Ethiopia: Political Contradictions in Agricultural Development* (Stockholm: Ruben and Sjogren, 1974), pp. 166–167; Cohen, "Foreign Involvement," pp. 6–7, 46n; Peter Koehn, "Ethiopia: Famine, Food Production, and Changes in the Legal Order," *African Studies Review* 22, No. 1 (1979):54–55.

163. Koehn and Hayes, "Student Politics," 38–42; Randi R. Balsvik, *Haile Sellassie's Students: The Intellectual and Social Background to Revolution, 1952–1977* (East Lansing: Michigan State University, 1985), p. 297.

164. Peter Koehn, "Forecast for Political Change in Ethiopia: An Urban Perspective," in *Analyzing Political Change in Africa: Applications of a New Multidimensional Framework*, edited by James R. Scarritt (Boulder: Westview Press, 1980), p. 81; Koehn and Hayes, "Student Politics," 42.

165. See Koehn, "Forecast," pp. 80–82; Balsvik, *Students*, pp. 308–309.

166. For details about events leading up to the revolution, see Peter Koehn, "Ethiopian Politics: Military Intervention and Prospects for Further Change," *Africa*

Today 22, No. 2 (1975):7–14. On the influence of the Chinese, Vietnamese, and Cuban revolutions on the Ethiopian student movement, see Gebru Mersha, "The Emergence of the Ethiopian 'Left' in the Period 1960–1970 as an Aspect of the Formation of the 'Organic Intellectuals,'" in *Proceedings of the 2nd International Conference on the Horn of Africa* (New York: New School for Social Research, 1987), p. 82.

167. Christopher Clapham, *Transformation and Continuity in Revolutionary Ethiopia* (Cambridge: Cambridge University Press, 1988), pp. 35, 40.

168. John M. Cohen and Peter Koehn, "Rural and Urban Land Reform in Ethiopia," *African Law Studies* 14, No. 1 (1977):3–55.

169. See Koehn, "Famine," 58–60; Koehn, "Forecast," pp. 88–94.

170. For details on this period, see Koehn, "Forecast," pp. 86–87; Babile Tola, *To Kill a Generation: The Red Terror in Ethiopia* (Washington, D.C.: Free Ethiopia Press, 1989), pp. 34–36, 47; Dessalegn Rahmato, "The Political Economy of Development in Ethiopia," in *Afro-Marxist Regimes: Ideology and Public Policy*, edited by Edmond J. Keller and Donald Rothchild (Boulder: Lynne Rienner Publishers, 1987), pp. 160–161.

171. Jason W. Clay and Bonnie K. Holcomb, *Politics and the Ethiopian Famine 1984–1985* (Cambridge: Cultural Survival, 1985), pp. 42, 193; Mekuria Bulcha, *Flight and Integration: Causes of Mass Exodus from Ethiopia and Problems of Integration in the Sudan* (Uppsala: Scandinavian Institute of African Studies, 1988), pp. 113–114. On the Ethiopian Democratic Union (EDU) and its defeat by government forces at Humera in 1977, see Brietzke, *Revolution*, p. 37.

172. Andreas Esheté is critical of the EPRP, as well as other leftist groups active during this period, on the grounds that they did not genuinely pursue democracy but were consumed with single-minded devotion to "the exigencies of the seizure of power." Andreas Esheté, "Beyond Scientific Socialism: A Plea for Self-governing Socialism," in *Proceedings of the 2nd International Conference on the Horn of Africa* (New York: New School for Social Research, 1987), p. 124.

173. Ottaways, *Ethiopia*, pp. 129–130, 142–144; Halliday and Molyneux, *Ethiopian Revolution*, pp. 113–118.

174. John Markakis, "The Military State and Ethiopia's Path to 'Socialism,'" *Review of African Political Economy* 21 (May/September 1981):22–24; John Markakis and Nega Ayele, *Class and Revolution in Ethiopia* (Nottingham: Spokesman, 1978), pp. 166–168; Brietzke, *Revolution*, pp. 156, 196–198; Amnesty International, "The Military Government's 'Red Terror' Campaign" (report AFR 25/04/78, March 1978, London), pp. 1–6; Ottaways, *Ethiopia*, pp. 145–148; U.S., Department of State, *Country Reports for 1982*, pp. 98–103, 106. Babile Tola argues that the Red Terror "was unleashed not to retaliate against armed actions by the EPRP but to wipe out the EPRP and all dissent" and that "killings by the EPRP

were miniscule compared to the mass murder undertaken by the Derg." Babile Tola, *Red Terror*, pp. 70–71.

175. Mekuria Bulcha, *Flight*, p. 105.

176. On relations between the Derg and these groups, as well as other smaller organizations such as Seded (Revolutionary Flame), Malered (Marxist-Leninist Revolutionary Organization), Was League (Proletarian League), and ECHAAT (Revolutionary Organization of Oppressed Ethiopians), see Bereket Habte Selassie, "The Dergue's Dilemma: The Legacies of a Feudal Empire," *Monthly Review* 32, No. 3 (July/August 1980):14–21; Babile Tola, *Red Terror*, pp. 99–100, 117–118; Edmond J. Keller, "State, Party and Revolution in Ethiopia" (mimeo, February 1984), pp. 15–19; Brietzke, *Revolution*, p. 169.

177. Markakis and Nega Ayele, *Ethiopia*, pp. 163–168. Mekuria Bulcha (*Flight*, pp. 101–105) adds that "as the persecution was generally carried out by an undisciplined militia, it affected also the innocent urban population." For details on the Red Terror, see Babile Tola, *Red Terror*, pp. 70, 137–159.

178. Also see Robin Luckham and Dawit Bekele, "Foreign Powers and Militarism in the Horn of Africa: Part I," *Review of African Political Economy* 30 (September 1984):11–12.

179. Mekuria Bulcha, *Flight*, p. 105.

180. Zolberg and Suhrke, "Social Conflict," p. 45.

181. Markakis, *Horn*, pp. 229, 231.

182. Also see Babile Tola, *Red Terror*, pp. 114, 117; Zolberg *et al., Refugee Crisis*, p. 254.

183. Markakis, *Horn*, p. 231. On the migration of Oromo refugees to Somalia during this period, see Ulrich Braukämper, "Ethnic Identity and Social Change Among Oromo Refugees in the Horn of Africa," *Northeast African Studies* 4, No. 3 (1982/1983):4–5; Mekuria Bulcha, *Flight*, pp. 107–108; *World Refugee Survey—1988 in Review*, p. 44. According to Zolberg *et al.* (*Refugee Crisis*, p. 114), "Ethiopia, which lacked the means of establishing a regular military occupation, resorted to a scorched-earth policy designed not only to cut off local support for the guerrillas but also to drive out the pastoralist population so as to make room for the settlement of non-Somali agriculturalists along the relatively fertile river valleys along the border."

184. U.S., Department of State, *Country Reports on Human Rights Practices for 1984* (Washington, D.C.: U.S. GPO, 1985), pp. 114–115.

185. See U.S., Department of State, *Country Reports 1990*, pp. 110–111, 114; Amnesty International, *Report: 1989* (London: Amnesty International Publications, 1989), p. 50; *New York Times*, 21 July 1990, p. 5; 19 February 1990, p. A4; *Washington Post*, 21 April, 1989; 10 October 1989; Dawit Wolde Giorgis, *Red Tears: War, Famine and Revolution in Ethiopia* (Trenton: Red Sea Press, 1989), p. 57.

186. U.S., Department of State, *Country Reports 1990*, pp. 110, 112. See also *Washington Post*, 26 May 1989; U.S. Department of State, *Country Reports for 1985*, pp. 107–110; Mesfin Bekele, "Prison Conditions in Ethiopia," *Horn of Africa* 2 (April/June 1979):4–11; Amnesty International, *Report: 1989*, p. 51.

187. See Asmarom Legesse, "Eritrea and Ethiopia: The Prospects for a New Political Framework" (paper presented at the United States Institute for Peace Seminar, Washington, D.C., August 1989), pp. 3–4; Kassahun Checole, "The Eritrean Struggle and the Democratic Opposition to the Ethiopian Junta" (paper presented at the Conference of the New York African Studies Association held in Ithaca, May 1976), pp. 10–13. One factor in the exodus from Ethiopia has been the desire of young men to avoid conscription by the post-revolution regime into military forces thrown with little training into northern battles. See Mekuria Bulcha, *Flight*, pp. 106–110; Luckham and Dawit Bekele, "Part I," 18. Moreover, Asmarom Legesse ("Eritrea," 6) reports that "there is a steady drift of the Eritrean population into exile, into the liberated area and into the liberation army."

188. U.S., Department of State, *Country Reports for 1982*, p. 98.

189. Halliday, "Horn," 11; Sherman, *Eritrea*, pp. 144–145.

190. Halliday and Molyneux, *Ethiopian Revolution*, p. 171.

191. Halliday and Molyneux, *Ethiopian Revolution*, pp. 40–45; Zolberg and Suhrke, "Social Conflict," pp. 4, 28.

192. Clapham, *Revolutionary Ethiopia*, p. 5.

193. Markakis, *Horn*, p. xvi.

194. Sherman, *Eritrea*, pp. 84–93; Halliday and Molyneux, *Ethiopian Revolution*, pp. 162–164, 193–209; U.S., Department of State, *Country Reports for 1982*, pp. 98–104; *Country Reports for 1984*, p. 115; Markakis, *Horn*, pp. 247–248.

195. Mary Dines, "Eritrean Refugees," *Refuge*, 6, No. 4 (May 1987):6; *New York Times*, 30 August 1988, pp. 1, 6; Asmarom Legesse, "Eritrea," 7.

196. Mekuria Bulcha, *Flight*, p. 224.

197. Jerry Tinker and John Wise, "Ethiopia and Sudan One Year Later: Refugee and Famine Recovery Needs" (staff report prepared for the Subcommittee on Immigration and Refugee Policy, Committee on the Judiciary, U.S. Senate, 99th Congress, 2nd session, April 1986), pp. 24–25; Clay and Holcolm, *Famine*, pp. 29, 86, 106, 144, 194; Taha Abdi, "The Plight of the Oromo Refugees in the Horn of Africa," *Refuge* 6, No. 4 (May 1987):7; Hiram Ruiz, *Beyond the Headlines: Refugees in the Horn of Africa* (Washington, D.C.: U.S. Committee for Refugees, 1988), pp. 16, 22, 25; Luckham and Dawit Bekele, "Part I," 18; Jeffery Crisp, editor, *Refugees: The Dynamics of Displacement* (London: Zed Books, 1986), p. 109; U.S., Department of State, *Country Reports on Human Rights Practices for 1989* (Washington, D.C.: U.S. GPO, 1990), p. 117; Amnesty International, *Report: 1989*, p. 50; Dawit Wolde Giorgis, *Red Tears*, pp. 304–307. Furthermore, the

resettlement scheme resulted in family disintegration, deforestation, soil erosion, and provoked the emigration of local peasant populations. Mekuria Bulcha, *Flight*, pp. 116–117, 121–125.

198. Robert D. Kaplan, *Surrender or Starve: The Wars Behind the Famine* (Boulder: Westview Press, 1988), pp. 120–121; Clay and Holcomb, *Famine*, p. 22; Mekuria Bulcha, *Flight*, pp. 118–119; Crisp, *Refugees*, pp. 107, 110; Dawit Wolde Giorgis, *Red Tears*, p. 307. On 21 July 1990, the *New York Times* reported that peasants had broken up villagization schemes and returned to their old farm lands in Sidamo, Bale, and Hararge provinces.

199. See Markakis and Nega Ayele, *Ethiopia*, pp. 169–171.

200. Patman, *Horn*, pp. 150–151, 163–165, 240.

201. Peter Koehn, "The Ethiopian Revolution: Events, Interpretations, and Implications," *Africa Today* 7, No. 1 (1980):44; Fred Halliday, "The U.S.S.R. and the Red Sea: Moscow's 'Panama Canal,'" in *The Red Sea: Prospects for Stability*, edited by Abdel Majid Farid (New York: St. Martin's Press, 1984), p. 127; Kirk, "Revolutions," p. 264; Patman, *Horn*, pp. 176, 204, 206.

202. David Ottaway and Marina Ottaway, *Afrocommunism* (New York: Africana Publishing Company, 1981), pp. 174–175; L. Adele Jinadu, "Soviet Influence on Afro-Marxist Regimes: Ethiopia and Mozambique," in *Afro-Marxist Regimes: Ideology and Public Policy*, edited by Edmond J. Keller and Donald Rothchild (Boulder: Lynne Rienner Publisher, 1987), pp. 232–233; Joachim Krause, "Soviet Arms Transfer to Sub-Saharan Africa," in *The Soviet Impact in Africa*, edited by R. Craig Nation and Mark V. Kauppi (Lexington: D.C. Heath and Company, 1984), pp. 130, 132; Patman, *Horn*, p. 205.

203. Jinadu, "Soviet Influence," pp. 233–236; Luckham and Dawit Bekele, "Part I," 17; Fantu Cheru, "Misplaced Optimism? Gorbachev, Perestroika and Policy Reform in Revolutionary Ethiopia," in *Proceedings of the Fourth Ethiopian Studies Conference* (New York: City University of New York, 1989), pp. 41–42, 45. On Soviet economic and technical assistance to Ethiopia between 1978 and 1987, see Patman, *Horn*, pp. 265–267, 275–277. One estimate of Ethiopia's total outstanding debt to the U.S.S.R. in 1989 came to $4 billion. Thomas D. Sisk, "Ethiopian Foes Agree to Settlement Talks," *Washington Report on Africa* 7, No. 18 (October 1989):71; Patman, *Horn*, p. 276.

204. Dessalegn Rahmato, "Development," p. 176; Jinadu, "Soviet Influence," pp. 236, 238; Fantu Cheru, "Perestroika in Revolutionary Ethiopia," pp. 45–46; Johann Wallner, "Cooperation Between the EEC and Ethiopia," *Courrier* 99 (September-October 1986):36–38; Patman, *Horn*, pp. 275–277.

205. *Washington Post*, 25 April 1986; *New York Times*, 15 March 1987.

The frustration of the U.S. right over the inability to mount a viable and "acceptable" opposition force is evident in Hense's lament that "the West has found

98

no freedom fighters in the Horn worthy of support. . . ." Paul B. Hense, "Is there Hope for the Horn of Africa? Reflections on the Political and Economic Impasses" (Rand Corporation note, June 1988), p. 25. On the crushed 1989 coup attempt by disaffected military generals, see *Washington Post*, 19, 21 May, 1989.

206. *New York Times*, 19 August 1989, p. 7; 21 July, 1990, p. A5; 17 April 1990, p. A4; *Washington Post*, 21 April 1990. As of 1990, however, the Soviet Union still provided numerous military advisors and an estimated $750 million annually in military aid. *New York Times*, 24 October 1990.

207. *New York Times*, 16 September, 1989; Sisk, "Talks," 72.

208. *New York Times*, 21 July 1990, p. 5. With the collapse of the Erich Honecker regime, East Germany terminated its contract to train Ethiopia's security forces and refused to supply further weapons. *New York Times*, 27 December 1989, p. A4.

209. See Graham Hancock, *Ethiopia: The Challenge of Hunger* (London: Victor Gollancz, Ltd., 1985), pp. 57, 121, 124; Krause, "Soviet Arms," p. 143. On Western-promoted militarization elsewhere in the Horn of Africa following the war with Somalia and on the nature of Soviet involvement in the region, see Robin Luckham and Dawit Bekele, "Foreign Powers and Militarism in the Horn of Africa: Part II," *Review of African Political Economy* 31 (December 1984):8–12, 16–23; Patman, *Horn*, p. 287.

210. U.S., Department of State, *Country Reports 1990*, p. 110; *New York Times*, 28 November 1988, p. 6; 19 August 1989, p. 3; Amare Tekle, "The Determinants of the Foreign Policy of Revolutionary Ethiopia," *Journal of Modern African Studies* 27, No. 3 (September 1989):491.

211. *New York Times*, 23 March 1991, p. A1; 21 July 1990, p. A1. In desperation, Mengistu formally embraced a mixed economy and a multi-party political system in 1990. *New York Times*, 6 March 1990, p. A4; *Africa Today* 37, No. 2 (1090):93.

212. Alexander L. George, "Case Studies and Theory Development: The Method of Structured, Focused Comparison," in *Diplomacy: New Approaches in History, Theory, and Policy*, edited by Paul G. Lauren (New York: Free Press, 1979), pp. 50–61.

213. The case-history comparisons also show that post-revolution refugee formation is not consistently associated with poverty or abrupt economic decline, religious and ethnic divisions, natural disaster, colonial history, or a particular geographical region of the Third World.

214. See Peter Koehn, "Revolution and Public Service in the Third World," in *Handbook of Comparative and Development Administration*, edited by Ali Farazmand (New York: Marcel Dekker, Inc., 1991), pp. 745–754.

3

Individual Exile Decision Making

I found the overthrow of the monarchy imminent. I knew that after the overthrow of the regime usually the armed forces are the ones that are in danger. Because of my total support of the regime and my line of work, I felt insecure and left five days before the overthrow.

—Iranian exile in L.A.

My younger brother and two of my nephews were executed during the Red Terror. I was detained, interrogated, and tortured for being suspected as a counter-revolutionary element.

—Ethiopian exile in D.C.

I left because of Ethiopian colonialism and the mass killings of the Eritrean people.

—Eritrean exile in D.C.

For six months I was in prison; I cannot talk about it because it was so terrible. Of course they tortured me—they torture everyone they suspect is part of the Tigray People's Liberation Front. . . . At last, I decided it was too dangerous for me to stay, and so, to my great sadness, I left my old life and fled to Sudan.

—Tigrean refugee in Sudan

External intervention and national conflict provide the threatening structural background for Third World societies engulfed by revolution. In the turmoil that accompanies and follows revolutionary political change, some survivors opt for self-imposed exile. What provokes human actors to make such a life-changing decision? How is the individual decision-making process related to the prevailing social-structural context?

Their public testimonies indicate that individuals decide to become refugees for multiple and diverse reasons. Self-imposed exiles perceive life in the sending country to be intolerable as the result of a complex set of experiences and reflections.[1] Some exiles speak of their fears—of death, torture, incarceration, or loss of basic human rights. The politically conscious and active often cite ideological reasons—opposition to the post-revolution regime and its policies, lack of freedom and protection of human rights, or pessimism about prospects for political change. Some individuals also choose to emigrate during a revolutionary situation due to economic deprivation at home, perceived opportunities abroad, or for purposes of family reunification.

Following an incisive analysis, Paul Tabori carefully defines an exile as a person "compelled" to leave the homeland by forces that "may be political, economic, or purely psychological."[2] One reason for this book is to identify and analyze the factors that prevail among exiles from Third World countries that experience revolution. Until recently, few systematic research findings have been available for insight into the specific individual motivations possessed by refugees, the crucial intervening factors, and the process of decision making.[3]

The absence of reliable data principally is due to flaws in research design and to interviewing obstacles.[4] The most comprehensive approach to the study of refugee formation would involve interviews with expatriates resident in industrialized countries who become exiles by refusing to return to the homeland, with persons who flee to neighboring countries of first asylum, and with displaced and non-dislocated nationals who remain in the home country. In first-asylum countries, however, host governments often restrict observation and/or prohibit scholarly investigation into the most critical issues.[5] Robert Mazur points out that "most 'research' on refugees in Africa has been in the form of consultancies rather than independent, sustained sociological efforts."[6] Moreover, refugees only represent the part of the original population that succeeds in exiting; many others are killed, internally displaced, imprisoned, or elect to remain in the homeland to fight or to engage in other forms of resistance.[7] Conducting reliable sending-country control studies that would permit valuable comparisons between the decision-making structure of exiles and those who did not succeed in emigrating or never attempted to exit is inconceivable under post-revolution circumstances in light of the inability of independent researchers to guarantee the security of interviewers and subjects.[8] Finally, in places of prospective resettlement, it is likely that information presented by petitioners to immigration authorities will be tainted by the applicant's contextual concentration on acceptance. In addition, exiles often are reluctant to participate in basic scientific research out of suspicion of investigator motives and fear of retribution.

The next section reviews the available data on decision making by Cuban and Vietnamese community members. Then, we will consider new findings based upon research among Iranian, Ethiopian, and Eritrean exiles living in two metropolitan areas in the United States.

Cuban and Vietnamese Refugees

In their 1968 study of post-revolution migration from Cuba, Richard Fagen, Richard Brody, and Thomas O'Leary secured self-administered questionnaires from 209 members of the Miami exile community. They discovered that the uncertain post-revolution situation "reinforced the scope of change to create conditions perceived as unbearable or potentially unbearable by hundreds of thousands of citizens."[9] In terms of individual decision making, personal and family experiences had an important effect on both initial thoughts and final actions among those who elected to flee from Cuba. This early group of refugees proved most likely to consider exiting due to self-initiated acts of conviction and protest, but to make the final decision to leave based upon an act directed against them—imprisonment, harassment, or threatened persecution of one sort or another.[10]

After the post-revolution regime turned its attention to transforming the Cuban economy, the new wave of migrants to the United States articulated a different mix of reasons for emigrating. Alejandro Portes, Juan Clark, and Robert Bach interviewed 590 male household heads arriving in Miami from Spain between late 1973 and early 1974. In this sample of refugees, most of whom left Cuba in 1970 and 1971, nearly all of the respondents indicated that both political considerations involving lack of freedoms *and* assessments of the future economic and social outlook in the homeland for themselves and their children played an important part in the decision to become an exile.[11] By the late 1970s, economic crises and austerity in Cuba, the desire for family reunification, and the demonstration of superior consumption opportunities in the United States created additional sources of political disaffection and emigration pressure.[12] According to Silvia Pedraza-Bailey, "the meaning of the Cuban exodus lies in the role of dissent in society. A society where the only choice possible is to 'love it or leave it' provides too few choices."[13]

Refugees from Vietnam and Cambodia also left their homeland under different circumstances and for varying reasons. The first group fled following the 1975 overthrow of U.S.-supported regimes in Saigon and Phnom Penh. Many in this vintage feared imprisonment or execution, communism, loss of social status and political freedoms. According to Gail Kelly, a sizeable proportion of these refugees "believed that the PRG would kill them if they remained in Vietnam because of their roles in South Vietnam over the previous twenty years."[14] Following conflict with China, the government forced large numbers of Chinese living in Vietnam to leave; others departed to avoid discrimination.[15] Later "boat people" and those who benefitted from the Orderly Departure Program are more likely than first-wave refugees from Vietnam are to cite economic hardship due to social discrimination and political victimization as the key factor in their decision to emigrate. Thus, the continuing exodus from Vietnam and Cambodia can be traced to "political repression, as well as worsening economic and social conditions and tales of a good life abroad. . . ."[16]

Refugee flows from the Cuban and Vietnamese revolutions, then, generally progressed in a common direction. A variety of strictly political conditions and considerations influenced the first vintage of exiles. Many who emigrated later, however, also were "'pulled out' by economic concerns and the hope for self-advancement and a better life."[17]

Refugees from Iran and Ethiopia

Iran and Ethiopia present two of the most recent cases of post-revolution population movement from the Third World to industrialized nations. This chapter is concerned with documenting the individual motives that led Iranians, Ethiopians, and Eritreans to desert their homeland. The new findings, coupled with earlier discoveries based upon work with persons of other nationalities, are intended to promote deeper understanding of decision making among refugees from revolution.

The large exile communities found on the western and eastern coasts of the United States offer valuable settings for research on contemporary refugee flows. The following discussion is based primarily on interviews conducted in 1984–1985 with a systematically identified and randomly selected sample of migrants from Ethiopia and Iran residing in the Washington, D.C., metropolitan area, and Iranians living in the Los Angeles environs.[18] We are particularly interested in (1) the role of personal experiences, national events and policies, and background factors in the exile decision-making process; (2) the specific motivations viewed as important and given greatest weight in respondent explanations regarding why they became an exile; and (3) variations in response among exiles of different nationality, gender, homeland socio-economic status, educational attainment, exposure to revolutionary conditions, political orientation, and departure interval.

Personal Experiences and Historical Events

Refugees generally do not view emigration as an opportunity to improve their socio-economic position.   Indeed, many are relatively privileged in material terms and deeply attached to their country of origin.[19] Consequently, dramatic local, national, or international events (e.g., mass executions, foreign invasion) and traumatic personal or family experiences (e.g., death of a relative, arrest) are likely to be associated with the act of breaking with the homeland.[20] We investigated this prospect by asking respondents about the time they first considered leaving or not returning and about their final decision.   This line of inquiry is aimed at uncovering links between structural and contextual factors and personal decision making.

It is interesting, in the first place, that two-thirds of both non-returnee and émigré respondents made their final decision to become an exile less than a year following the date when they initially began to think about it. Another 20 percent decided between a year and two years later.   This leaves a substantial minority of interviewees (about 15 percent) who deliberated for two years or longer before reaching their final decision to live in exile.   Non returnees, particularly those from Ethiopia who first thought about becoming an exile in the still promising years before Mengistu Haile Mariam consolidated power, took the longest time to decide.

In the D.C./L.A. study, 59 percent of the émigrés and 58 percent of the non returnees reported that a particular incident or event either caused them to consider becoming an exile and/or played an important part in their final determination that homeland conditions were no longer tolerable.[21] The finding that roughly 40 percent of the respondents in this study had not decided to become a refugee due to a particular incident or event is not consistent with the contention by Richard Fagen et al. that "people go into self-imposed exile only when they have experienced the effects of changes in economic arrangements, social structure, or political order in extremely personal and negative ways."[22]

104

Although Ethiopia has been afflicted with famine and poverty, only three of the interviewed émigrés from that country cited economic incidents or events. Natural disasters did not influence the final decision of a single Ethiopian or Eritrean respondent.[23] Over 95 percent of the 180 affected respondents included reference(s) to political events or to incidents provoked by political actors.

We observe from Table 3.1, moreover, that over 60 percent of the

TABLE 3.1 Type of Incident/Event Rated Important in Final Decision to Emigrate from or Not Return to Homeland, by Nationality

| | All Respondents | | Nationality | | |
Type of Incident/Event	N	%Tot	%Iranian (N=83)	%Ethiopian (N=62)	%Eritrean (N=35)
Personal, family only	34	18.9%	25.3%	11.3%	17.1%
Regional, national only	51	28.3	38.6	17.7	22.9
Both	95	52.8	36.1	71.0	60.0
TOTAL	180	100.0	100.0	100.0	100.0

Source: D.C./L.A. sample.

Ethiopians and Eritreans influenced by incidents and events refer to personal or family situations *and* to national or regional developments. No more than 25 percent of the interviewed migrants in each of the three groups rated personal incidents alone as important in reaching the exile decision; respondents of all three nationalities proved more likely to cite national/regional events than personal/family experiences.[24]

Émigrés. There are striking differences in the type of political incident that émigrés and non returnees cite as influential. Among those who fled from the homeland, the recurring theme involves imprisonment—of self, spouse, parent, sibling, other relative, co-worker, or friend—and/or killings (see Box 3.1).

Box 3.1

Émigré Explanations of Events and Incidents
That Shaped the Decision to Flee

Iranians

A friend of mine who was in prison was able to inform me that another prisoner whom we worked together with was forced under torture to tell about my activities. So I left home and lived underground until I could get out of the country.

My uncle and several of my friends were arrested in one week. Since I used to attend their meetings, I thought the revolutionary guards would arrest me sooner or later or they would send me to the front line of [the Iran-Iraq] war as a soldier.

The June 1981 massacre in which the government started mass execution. As a supporter of the Fedaii-e (Minority) organization, my life was in danger.

Ethiopians

I was imprisoned and my brother was killed by the Derg.

I escaped from prison and joined the Ethiopian Democratic Union (EDU). My father was killed in battle and I decided to leave my country.

There was one particular incident whereby a kebelle guard pulled a pistol on me. My father was in prison and other relatives were being harassed.

During the Red Terror campaign, almost all of my family were in prison at one time or another – father, brother, and myself [7 months].

Eritreans

[Following] imprisonment in 1979, . . . the [Eritrean] freedom fighters broke the prison and I came to Sudan. . . .

Imprisonment of people without reason and killing people on the streets. It was unsafe for a young adult at that time, and I was afraid. People had to take sides. I was badly treated by the Derg because I was secretary of the Eritrean Teacher's Association.

One day as I was going to school in my homeland, I was imprisoned and tortured.

Two brothers were killed by the government because they were Eritrean. I was the last surviving child, and my parents depended on me.

Mass killing in Eritrea.

The descriptions of critical incidents and events received from Iranian, Ethiopian, and Eritrean exiles are consistent with other findings that most refugees are not active participants in actual fighting. Nevertheless, roughly 90 percent of the interviewed émigrés opposed the post-revolution regime, and three out of every five opponents actively participated in some anti-regime activity. Most activists confined their actions to non-violent support for an opposition political or nationality organization, involvement in a strike or protest demonstration, refusal to comply with an official rule or regulation, and/or vocal opposition to the regime or to government policy.[25]

Since many non returnees have never lived in or visited their homeland since the outbreak of the revolution, the impact on decision making of exposure to war or to post-revolution violence is only likely to appear among émigré respondents. The findings from the D.C./L.A. study reveal that personal encounters with armed conflict constituted an important factor in the determination to become an exile among over half of the Eritreans (54 percent), 35 percent of the Ethiopian émigrés, and 17 percent of the Iranians.[26] These results undoubtedly reflect Eritrea's unique historical experience of protracted and hard-fought liberation struggle in the countryside in addition to revolutionary conflict in the cities.[27]

Non Returnees. Respondents who decided to become an exile *after* departing from Ethiopia or Iran are prone to have been influenced primarily by national political developments. Iranians mentioned the "Islamic revolution" itself; the fall of the Bani Sadr government; the June 1981 massacre and the onset of "intensified terror" and mass executions; the repression of political organizations, including the People's Mujahedin and the Tudeh party; the "betrayal of the revolution by the *mullahs*;" persecution of the Baha'i; the war with Iraq and attacks on Kurdistan; suppression of political and academic freedom; and the post-revolution regime's treatment of women. Ethiopian non returnees cited Mengistu Haile Mariam's violent seizure of power within the Derg; the "Red Terror;" the arrest of religious leaders; and the "state-sponsored organized terror campaign against Oromia and its people." Eritreans referred to the bombardment of Keren by Ethiopian government forces; "the execution of government officials and the massacre of many Eritreans assembled in a church at Wekidiba and other villages;" the "killing [even strangling] of innocent people in Eritrea;" and the failure to forge a unified Eritrean liberation movement.

Although non returnees are more likely than émigrés are to be influenced only by national or regional events (26 percent versus 6 percent overall), 12 percent of the former still exclusively mention personal or family incidents—including the arrest of close relatives, the execution of

returning friends, and reports that the post-revolution regime suspected them
or had singled them out for persecution. Another 21 percent of all non
returnees (43 percent of the Ethiopians) cite *both* personal and national
situations as influential.[28]

Summary. What can we conclude from respondent reports on the role
played by incidents and events in their decision to live in exile? First, we
discovered that a majority of these refugees from revolution are conscious
of specific national political developments and/or personal and family
experiences that shaped their action in important ways. The Red Terror in
Ethiopia and the June 1981 massacre in Iran head the list of political
events, although the complete set of responses offered is quite diverse.
Imprisonment and/or torture of self or family members and the execution or
random killing of a close associate or relative are common personal
considerations. It is clear, moreover, that natural disasters and economic
incidents played no role in the decisional process engaged in by the vast
majority of these U.S.-based exiles.

We also observed that the critical events that make an impact on
émigrés and non returnees are overt and tangible. From the perspective of
the individual exile, external forces and foreign crises do not play an
immediate role in triggering the decision to flee or remain abroad. This
finding is consistent with the absence of *direct* Western military intervention
in Ethiopia and Iran and with the historical analysis presented in Chapter 2
which calls attention, in particular, to the *indirect* effect of overt and covert
U.S. support for the Emperor and the Shah. Moreover, refugees of diverse
political persuasion perceive the underlying role of U.S. intervention to be a
key factor explaining the Iranian and Ethiopian revolutions.

Social Background Context

Post-revolution regimes often are accused of persecuting persons
labelled counter-revolutionary on the basis of particular social-background
characteristics. Families linked to the overthrown and discredited regime,
possessing suspect class backgrounds, and/or tied to "Western imperialist"
institutions are expected to be especially vulnerable to political persecution
in Third World countries experiencing revolutionary change.[29] However, the
reports offered by the exiles from Ethiopia and Iran interviewed in this
study indicate that these factors are not particularly prominent in individual
decision making. While persons possessing "counter-revolutionary"
backgrounds are well represented in the sampled communities, most

respondents attributed little significance to their social status and ties in the homeland when explaining why they decided to become an exile.

For instance, the fathers of over half of the sampled exiles from Ethiopia and Iran once held high-level policy-making, professional, or managerial positions in the homeland. Another 15 percent primarily engaged in large-scale farming or other commercial activity. Among the 143 respondents who had worked in their country of origin, roughly 80 percent occupied these kinds of employment niches themselves. The data on family-income levels in the homeland provide further evidence of the privileged backgrounds of these migrants. Approximately 90 percent of the Iranians, 80 percent of the Ethiopians, and 60 percent of the Eritreans rated their personal or family income as "high" or "medium" at the time they left their country of origin.[30] When asked about the role of their own or their family's position in the pre-revolution regime, however, 92 percent of the Iranians and Eritreans and 83 percent of the Ethiopians indicate that it did not constitute an important exile decision-making consideration. Furthermore, only 5 percent of the Iranians and 9 percent of the Ethiopian and Eritrean migrants report that their family's economic status or class position in the homeland had influenced the decisional process.

Similar results are encountered with regard to homeland ties to Western and international employers and agencies. About one out of every six of the exiles in this sample acknowledged personal or parental association with a multinational corporation, Western government agency, or international organization while living in Ethiopia or Iran.[31] U.S. refugee-admission policy presumes that individuals linked to such institutions are especially vulnerable to experiencing and/or fearing persecution in post-revolution circumstances. On the surface, the Marxist ideology proclaimed by the Derg and the anti-Western platform advanced by Ayatollah Khomeini lend credence to this position. However, only 9 percent of the respondents possessing ties to Western and multinational institutions indicate that these links played a role in exile decision making. In addition, association with a transnational capitalist institution or a Western government body constituted a decisional consideration for less than 10 percent of all the exiles who indicate that (fear of) political persecution played an important part in their determination to leave or not return to the homeland.

In sum, most refugees from the Ethiopian and Iranian revolutions did not place great weight on social-background factors when they decided to become an exile. Are particularly influential political or economic considerations at work? The next section explores this prospect.

Political and Economic Considerations

The D.C./L.A. study results allow us to identify the political and economic considerations that influenced and did not influence émigrés and non returnees from Ethiopia and Iran when they decided to live in exile. Five political considerations are viewed as influential by more than 60 percent of the respondents. They are general conditions of insecurity, suppression of political expression and association, ideological position or opposition to the regime in power, threat to self and/or family, and (likely) personal political persecution. More interviewees (81 percent) cited general conditions of insecurity as an important decisional consideration than any other factor. About 70 percent of the exiles referred to personal ideological commitments and to regime suppression of basic political rights. Slightly more than 60 percent indicated that the threat of physical harm and imprisonment for themselves and/or their family members and personal political persecution influenced their decision to become an exile.

The respondents who feared political persecution often did so for multiple reasons. Once again, however, social-background factors do not figure prominently in their explanations. The most frequently cited bases for fearing persecution are (suspected) association with an opposition political organization or nationality movement and the respondent's ideological commitment. The explanations mentioned least often involve background variables: family position in the pre-revolution regime; association with a Western government agency or multinational firm; religious affiliation; and, with the striking exception of the Eritrean community, nationality.[32]

At least half of the respondents in the D.C./L.A. sample confirmed that two other homeland factors played a major motivating role. These are acts of discrimination and lack of freedom of movement—domestic and/or international. Regime responses to nationality issues and the failure to realize the objectives of a nationality movement ranked as important considerations for over 70 percent of the Eritrean and Oromo exiles, but not among most other respondents. An exceptionally high percentage of the Iranians indicated that the ability of Ayatollah Khomeini to retain power affected their decision not to return to the homeland.[33] Among non returnees, 63 percent of the Iranians and 47 percent of the others stated that the experience of living overseas without fear of political persecution played an important part in the act of becoming an exile.

Roughly 40 percent of the exiles from Ethiopia interviewed in this study indicated that *superpower interference* constituted an important factor in their decision to leave or not to return to the homeland. In contrast, only 6 percent of the Iranian respondents assessed direct superpower intervention as important.[34] These differences in perspective are likely to be related to the extensive *post-revolution* involvement of the Soviet Union in Ethiopia and to the relatively independent course of action pursued by Ayatollah Khomeini.

The remaining items on the presented list affected a minority of the respondents. Roughly 35 percent referred to the socio-economic policies implemented by the regime in power, 25 percent cited the absence of academic and/or artistic freedom, and 10 percent selected the threat of military conscription and lack of religious freedom.[35] Economic factors did not constitute an important matter among most exile decision makers. Less than 20 percent of the interviewees mentioned the general state of the homeland economy and (likely) economic deprivation for self or family, and 10 percent or less cited economic prospects or benefits abroad and income-earning restrictions in the homeland. Between 22 percent and 35 percent of these exiles (mainly non returnees) were influenced by overseas educational opportunities, inability to use their education and practice their profession in the homeland, and by the presence of family members abroad.[36] In sum, this study of post-revolution exiles does not support Elizabeth Ferris' assertion that "most refugees probably leave their homelands for both political and economic reasons."[37]

Nationality. The findings presented in Table 3.2 allow us to distinguish among exiles from the three nationality groups studied in terms of the influence of the five most commonly cited factors. The issue of personal or family economic deprivation in the homeland is included for comparative purposes. Its inclusion starkly reveals the extent to which various groups of respondents place importance upon political versus economic considerations.

The Table 3.2 data show little difference by nationality on the first three items other than the tendency for Ethiopians to be somewhat less likely to view the suppression of political expression and association as important. This difference is likely to be related to the absence of such rights in Ethiopia's pre-revolution political history. The variations on the next two political factors are wider and more interesting. In this case, Eritreans are considerably more likely than Iranians are to have been influenced both by threats of physical danger and imprisonment and by political persecution. The Ethiopian respondents fall roughly in the middle on these two considerations. These findings provide evidence that the cumulative impact of revolution plus war of national liberation to which many Eritreans have been exposed manifests itself in terms of a heightened

TABLE 3.2 Important Considerations in Decision to Leave Homeland or Not
Return Permanently, by Nationality

Important Considerations	'Yes' All Respondents		% 'Yes' Iranians (Total N=148)	% 'Yes' Ethiopians (Total N=97)	% 'Yes' Eritreans (Total N=60)
	N	%Tot			
Genl condit insecurity	246	80.7%	79.7%	79.4%	85.0%
Suppression political expression,associatn	211	69.2	71.6	61.9	75.0
Ideological position, opposit regime	211	69.2	71.6	67.0	66.7
Threat to self, family	192	63.0	48.6	72.2	83.3
Polit persecution self	188	61.6	50.7	64.9	83.3
Economic deprivation	39	13.3	15.2	11.8	10.9

Source: D.C./L.A. sample.

sense of personal danger on the part of the individual exile. Finally, we note from the table that Iranians are the group most often driven by economic deprivation in the homeland. Nevertheless, the proportion influenced by this consideration pales in significance compared to the five listed political factors.

As an aid to understanding the process of exile formation, it is important to study the relationship of key respondent characteristics other than nationality to the factors that individuals identify as influential in decision making. Therefore, the following sections assess the impact of the decision maker's gender, homeland economic status, exposure to revolutionary conditions, and political orientation.

Gender. The fact that all of the respondents selected in this study were household heads or independent actors at the time they decided to become an exile provides a unique opportunity to identify commonalities and differences among male and female decision makers. Table 3.3 sets forth interviewee reactions to the six selected decisional factors, cross-tabulated by gender. The lack of variation in the results is particularly striking. With the exception of the slight difference encountered in terms of fear of physical harm, male and female exiles responded in virtually identical

TABLE 3.3   Important Considerations in Decision to Leave Homeland or Not
Return Permanently, by Gender

Important Considerations	'Yes' All Respondents		% 'Yes' Males (Total N=216)	% 'Yes' Females (Total N=89)
	N	%Tot		
Genl condit of insecurity	246	80.7%	80.1%	82.0%
Suppression polit expression,assn	211	69.2	69.0	69.7
Ideological position, opposit reg	211	69.2	68.5	70.8
Threat to self, family	192	63.0	65.7	56.2
Polit persecution self	188	61.6	63.0	58.4
Economic deprivation	39	13.3	15.2	8.4

Source: D.C./L.A. sample.

fashion when asked about the role these five political considerations played
in the decision to leave or not return to the homeland.   Economic
deprivation influenced a smaller proportion of the interviewed female
household heads.

While the overall findings from this study of three migrant communities
suggest that gender did not independently affect the principal motivations
for becoming an exile, there are some interesting differences by nationality.
Ethiopian and Eritrean males are considerably more likely than females are
to be influenced by political persecution and a considerably higher
proportion of Iranian females than males judge general conditions of
insecurity in the homeland to have been an important decisional
consideration.   On the suppression of political expression/association item,
male and female Iranians exhibit no differences, but much higher
percentages of Ethiopian women and Eritrean men indicate that this was an
important consideration.   Iranian women and Eritrean men differ from their
Ethiopian counterparts in that they are more likely to cite ideological
opposition to the regime in power as an influential factor in the exile
decision-making process.

Homeland Economic Status. Under revolutionary circumstances, one
would expect ruling-class members of society to be singled out for political
persecution.   On the other hand, citizens who are not part of the elite
segment of society would be affected more frequently by random violence

and general conditions of insecurity. The evidence compiled in this study of U.S.-based exiles offers no support for these assumptions. As Table 3.4 shows, a *smaller* percentage of the total sample of exiles who identified their homeland income level as "high" report that personal political persecution and a specific threat to themselves or a family member

TABLE 3.4   Important Considerations in Decision to Leave Homeland or Not Return Permanently, by Respondent/Family Income Level at Time

Important Considerations	'Yes' All Respondents N	%Tot	Income Level at Time Left % 'Yes' High (Total N=58)	% 'Yes' Medium (Total N=179)	% 'Yes' Low (Total N=54)
Genl condit of insecurity	246	80.7%	77.6%	81.0%	83.0%
Suppress polit exprss,assn	211	69.2	69.0	69.3	66.7
Ideolog posit, oppos regme	211	69.2	75.9	69.3	63.0
Threat to self, family	192	63.0	62.1	59.8	75.9
Polit persecution self	188	61.6	55.2	60.3	74.1
Economic deprivation	39	13.3	9.1	12.1	19.2

Source: D.C./L.A. sample.

constituted an important decisional consideration in comparison to the low-income household heads.[38]   Moreover, low-income respondents are not significantly more likely than middle- and high-income individuals are to act out of concern over general conditions of insecurity.[39]

Émigrés and non returnees from high-income homeland backgrounds do tend to be influenced more often than the others are by ideological commitments. In comparison with all exiles from Ethiopia and with their higher-income compatriots, a much greater proportion of the Iranian respondents from low-income situations report being affected by the prospect of economic deprivation in the homeland. In spite of the anti-Western platform adopted by both post-revolution regimes, moreover, there are no meaningful differences on any of these items among interviewees who possessed and did not possess a personal or parental homeland association with a multinational corporation, Western government agency, or transnational organization.

Exposure to Revolution. How deeply are exile motives affected by experiencing revolution? This study of three U.S. exile communities provides an excellent opportunity to assess the impact of such an experience. Nearly half of the total sample had lived in their country of origin during and after the revolution. The other half found themselves located outside of Ethiopia or Iran at the time of the overthrow of the Emperor or the Shah and did not return to live there afterward. Table 3.5 reveals that there is no substantial difference between the two groups in terms of influence on the decision-making process of general conditions of insecurity, suppression of political rights, and ideological convictions.[40] Respondents who had not experienced revolution are only slightly more likely than their counterparts are to be affected by (anticipated) economic deprivation in the homeland.[41]

TABLE 3.5   Important Considerations in Decision to Leave Homeland or Not Return Permanently, by Period Exile Left Homeland

Important Considerations	'Yes' All Respondents		% 'Yes' Prior Regime Overthrow	% 'Yes' After Regime Overthrow
	N	%Tot	(Total N=161)	(Total N=144)
Genl condit of insecur	246	80.7%	77.6%	84.0%
Supprss pol exprss,assn	211	69.2	72.0	66.0
Ideol pos, oppos regime	211	69.2	68.9	69.4
Threat to self, family	192	63.0	48.4	79.2
Polit persecution self	188	61.6	52.2	72.2
Economic deprivation	39	13.3	15.4	10.9

Source: D.C./L.A. sample.

The major differences revealed by Table 3.5 are that exiles who left the sending country after the revolution occurred (1) are much more likely to cite the threat of imprisonment or personal/family danger as an important influence and (2) are considerably more apt to mention fear of political persecution in comparison with the respondents who have not experienced radical political transformation in their home country.[42] These results are not surprising given that persons with first-hand knowledge of arrest, torture, and other forms of political persecution are more likely to be influenced by these fears than are those who only hear or read about revolutionary and post-revolution conditions. This does not necessarily mean, however, that nationals who departed prior to the revolution would be any less subject in practice to such consequences if they should return to their country of origin.[43]

Political Orientation. The historical discussion presented in Chapter 2 revealed the extent to which suppression of leftist political forces constituted an important dynamic of pre- and post-revolution politics in Iran. The D.C./L.A. interview data allow us to investigate the relationship between association with a leftist Iranian political organization[44] and the factors deemed important by respondents in reaching the decision to live in exile.

Table 3.6 shows that Iranian exiles associated with leftist opposition groups are more likely than their counterparts who neither supported nor

TABLE 3.6   Important Considerations in Decision to Leave Homeland or Not Return Permanently, by Association with Iranian Leftist Political Organization

Important Considerations	% 'Yes' Leftist Org (Total N=56)	% 'Yes' No Leftist Org (Total N=92)
Genl condit of insecurity	80.4%	79.3%
Suppression polit expressn, assn	87.5	62.0
Ideological position, opposit reg	83.9	64.1
Threat to self, family	83.9	27.2
Polit persecution self	83.9	30.4
Economic deprivation	8.9	19.1

Source: D.C./L.A. sample.

agreed with such organizations are to have been influenced by four of the five listed political considerations. The differences on the "physical threat" and "political persecution" dimensions are particularly striking. Of the two groups, Iranians with leftist political sympathies are far more inclined to view personal/family danger and persecution as important factors affecting exile decision making. Finally, economic deprivation in Iran influenced twice the proportion of interviewees who neither supported nor identified with a leftist organization.

Principal Motivating Factors

We observed above that migrants opted to leave or not to return to Ethiopia and Iran for multiple reasons. The factors deemed important by this sample of recent refugees from revolution are overwhelmingly political. Among the many influences shaping the decision to become an exile, a few are likely to prove decisive. In this section, we are interested in refining the analysis of expressed political considerations and identifying the *primary* motivating factors for different categories of exiles.

The principal political motives for becoming an exile reported by the respondents in this study can be arranged along a "fear of life-threatening violence" continuum bounded on one end by the desire to avoid imprisonment and/or threatened physical danger to oneself and on the other end by political convictions. Fear of political persecution and the intention to escape general conditions of insecurity fall within the two outer points of the continuum. Ideological beliefs and deeply held political convictions involve the risk of provoking violence and personal danger when individuals who feel compelled to act in accordance with their values confront repressive regimes.

The open-ended descriptions offered by émigrés and non returnees richly illustrate the full range of political motives. Box 3.2 presents selected respondent explanations when asked to describe in their own words why they decided to live in exile rather than return to Iran or Ethiopia. The unstructured explanations for exiting given by émigré respondents are remarkably similar to those presented by non returnees. Box 3.3 contains illustrative statements from Iranian, Ethiopian, and Eritrean émigrés.[45]

Most Compelling Consideration. The statements presented in Box 3.2 and Box 3.3 confirm that many refugees possess multiple reasons for leaving or not returning to the homeland. In assessing the relative importance of a particular motivation, we first consider the explanation that each respondent identified as most compelling. Table 3.7 lists the main considerations that Iranians, Ethiopians, and Eritreans chose when asked to identify the one factor that constituted the overriding or most important motivation in the decision to become an exile. It is immediately apparent

Box 3.2
Selected Respondent Explanations for Not Returning to Homeland

Iranians
The total repression [of the Khomeini regime] destroyed many political organizations. As a supporter of PAYKAR, I knew that I would at least be imprisoned. So, I decided to stay here.

Since 1983, Tudeh party members and supporters have been subject to arrest. As a Tudeh sympathizer, it is not safe for me to go back.

Due to my active support of People's Mujahedin and my publications, there is no chance for me to return to Iran unless the present system is overthrown.

The Iranian Islamic regime. . . suppresses all national minorities and especially Kurdish people. As an active supporter of Komeleh, I might be executed if I return.

Persecution of Bahai's by the government and lack of security in the country.

Political repression, mass executions. . . , and the danger of being imprisoned or killed upon returning.

Dictatorship of mullahs, lack of security, lack of respect for women, lack of freedom of speech and political assembly.

The general state of insecurity, chaos, anarchism, and the dictatorship. The mullahs have made life intolerable for everyone.

The dictatorship of the mullahs. As an educated person, I cannot allow a stupid mullah to tell me I am wrong about everything. I thought that if I returned I would want to speak out about all aspects of Iranian life—which would put me in a dangerous situation.

Because of the on-going political repression in Iran. Having a government in power which is opposed to the basic concepts of freedom and civil liberty has prevented many from going back, even though I believe that I do not belong here either.

[The Khomeini] regime considers women as inferiors. People have no freedom to express their political views. I don't see a chance to employ my education due to the fact that I am an intellectual woman who opposes the government.

Ethiopians and Eritreans
I opposed the military leadership, the way it ran the government, and its mass tortures and imprisonment of the people. This would have happened to me also, especially since I had been out of the country.

(Continues)

Box 3.2

Selected Respondent Explanations for Not Returning to Homeland

(Continued)

Ethiopians and Eritreans

The Derg. . . started harassing nationality and peasant association leaders, who became targets for repression, terrorism, and subjugation. As an external[ly educated] Oromo, I would be under surveillance and would be unable to say what I wanted to my people. I decided I couldn't accept that.

The situation in Eritrea got worse and my involvement in political organizations such as EPLF contributed to my final decision to stay.

My commitment to Eritrea and Mengistu's outlook toward Eritrea and way of approaching it.

Fear of persecution which appeared to be imminent given my capitalistic economic sympathy, democratic political orientation, and strong belief in human rights. Fear that I might speak out if I returned and fall victim to totalitarian injustice.

I decided not to return to Ethiopia. . . because I am against the present regime and its ideology, and because of the general political conditions in my country.

I was worried I might go to jail because of my family's background in Haile Selassie's regime. I didn't want my children to grow up in that environment.

from this table that the overwhelming majority of exiles from Ethiopia and Iran acted primarily on the basis of a political rather than an economic consideration. Indeed, not a single interviewee cited the general state of the homeland economy or income-earning restrictions abroad as the decisive factor shaping the decision to live in exile. About five percent of the sample were most strongly influenced by two pull factors: the presence of family members abroad or overseas educational opportunities.

We further observe from Table 3.7 that there are sharp differences by nationality when it comes to the decisive consideration in the decision to become an exile. Among Eritreans, nationality-movement concerns—principally their movement's failure to achieve its objectives and opposition to the Ethiopian regime's policies on nationality matters—stood out far above all other issues. Only two other items proved decisive among more than 10 percent of the Eritrean interviewees. These are opposition to the regime in power and/or its policies, and general conditions of insecurity in the homeland due to war and other forms of violent conflict.

Box 3.3
Selected Respondent Explanations for Fleeing Homeland

Iranians

The dictatorship of the mullahs had left no room for political activities. Despite this, I was active. But, when I felt that my life was definitely in danger, I left. I was an active supporter of the Organization of Communist Unity. Some of my close friends who were connected with me were arrested. I left with several others to escape persecution and probable execution.

In my classes and in my public speeches, I publicly criticized the present regime of Iran, especially the mullahs. Therefore, I was listed as an active opponent of the regime.

I was politically very active against the regime. As a result, I was imprisoned in 1981. When released, I lost my job. Eventually, when my sister and her husband were arrested, I felt that it would really be dangerous for me to stay in Iran.

The social unrest enticed by the Shah's mistakes and intensified by zealot Shiites had crippled the regime. When I saw that the Shah could not control the country, I decided to leave in order to protect myself and my family.

The mobs were attacking anybody who did not agree with them. As a military officer, I was afraid for my own life and my family's.

By July [1981], I was totally determined to leave in order to save my life. The main reason was that the government was indiscriminately executing the people opposed to Ayatollah Khomeini.

Ethiopians

I was an active member of the EPRP. I felt that before they got me, I should leave the country.

Because my life was in danger. My colleagues were killed or imprisoned and I was the only one left in my resistance [cell]. Also, I had been arrested.

I was imprisoned, physically tortured. So, after I got out of the jail, I was afraid of another imprisonment.

Because of the political insecurity and the imprisonment of my relatives.

Because my father was killed, I was tortured, and my parents' property taken by the government. I had nothing to look forward to there.

They started imprisoning others who refused to attend political education classes. I thought my time is soon going to come. I saw no future for myself in the country because I did not like the government.

(Continues)

Box 3.3
Selected Respondent Explanations for Fleeing Homeland
(Continued)

Ethiopians
I didn't want to live there any more because I hated the government. I saw people suffering all around me—including people who were killed [shot] by the government and left to die in the streets. My older sisters were imprisoned for fifteen days. My family wanted me to be safe.

The general political upheaval of my country and the communist ideology of the military junta are the main causes. . . .

Change was overdue in Ethiopia, but it was abused and the opportunity robbed. The revolution which the people wanted was hampered by the Derg for selfish power greed. So, I saw there was no hope.

Eritreans
I left Eritrea and went to Sudan because of the mass killings.

Because I oppose the Ethiopian colonial regime in Eritrea.

Being an Eritrean sympathetic to the cause of the nationalists, and given the military government's propensity to seek military solutions to situations.

The political oppression of Eritreans inside Ethiopia as well as Eritrea, coupled with the fact that Eritrea was fighting for its independence. This was a movement which I supported wholeheartedly.

The expectation of chaos and personal insecurity; the government's actions made me expect disorder, that the country would fall apart. I lost my sense of belonging. I feared that, as an Eritrean, I could be accused and persecuted easily and my family harmed as well.

While more respondents of all three nationalities reported general conditions of homeland insecurity to be an important contextual factor than mentioned any other consideration (Table 3.2), insecurity heads the list of *decisive* motivating concerns only among Ethiopian exiles (Table 3.7). More than 10 percent of the Ethiopians interviewed also cited ideological commitments, lack of freedoms, political persecution, and nationality-movement concerns[46] as the overriding or most important consideration affecting their decision to leave or not return to Ethiopia. Most of those who selected nationality issues are Oromo.

TABLE 3.7   Overriding or Most Important Factor in Decision to Leave Homeland or Not Return Permanently, by Nationality

Overriding/Most Important Factor in Decision	All Respondents N	All Respondents %Tot	% Iranians (Total N=148)	% Ethiopians (Total N=97)	% Eritreans (Total N=60)
Genl condit of insecurity	45	15.7%	9.2%	27.0%	14.3%
Lack of freedom	40	14.0	17.7	13.5	5.4
Ideol posit, opposit regime in power/its policies	36	12.6	7.8	19.1	14.3
Natlity movemt concern	34	11.9	0.7	11.2	41.1
(Likely) physical danger	32	11.2	17.7	4.5	5.4
(Likely) imprisonment	23	8.0	16.3	0.0	0.0
Abil post-rev reg retain power	20	7.0	8.5	3.4	8.9
Political persecution	16	5.6	2.1	12.4	3.6
Family abroad	10	3.5	5.0	1.1	3.6
Econ,professal deprivation, opports abroad	8	2.8	3.5	2.2	1.8
Educational opports abroad	6	2.1	2.8	2.2	0.0
Other	16	5.6	8.5	3.4	1.8

Source: D.C./L.A.   sample

The Table 3.7 data indicate that Iranian exiles tended to be most affected by lack of freedoms and two additional considerations. When these two related factors are treated together, the results reveal that one-third of the Iranian respondents acted to become an exile primarily because of fear of personal physical danger or imprisonment. This finding is surprising given that a considerably smaller proportion of all Iranian exiles relative to the other two groups identified the threat of physical harm or imprisonment as an important exile decision-making influence (Table 3.2). It suggests that while such fears influenced most of the exiles from Ethiopia and a minority of those from Iran, the threat of physical danger and imprisonment is more likely to prove decisive among Iranians. This is particularly the case among Iranian exiles associated with a leftist political organization. Such respondents are nearly twice as likely as those without leftist sympathies are to list personal/family danger or imprisonment as their most important decision-making consideration (46 versus 26 percent).

122

Primary and Second-Most Important Motives. We next evaluate the relative importance of several particularly interesting exile considerations by including both the primary and second-most important reasons identified by the respondents. The results presented in Table 3.8 show clear differences by nationality that are consistent with the analysis presented above.[47]

TABLE 3.8 Primary and Second-Most Important Reason for Deciding to Become an Exile, by Nationality

Type of Consideration	All Respondents (Top 2) N	%Tot	% Iranians (Total N=148)	% Ethiopians (Total N=97)	% Eritreans (Total N=60)
Ideological reason(s)	186	65.0%	56.0%	67.4%	83.9%
Genl condit insecurity	85	29.7	22.7	44.9	23.2
(Likely)phys dangr,impris	77	26.9	42.6	13.5	8.9
Political persecution	48	16.8	14.2	21.3	16.1
Econ, professional, family reason(s)	50	17.5	27.0	9.0	7.1

Source: D.C./L.A. sample.

Eritreans are most likely to rank ideological considerations— including nationality concerns—among the two most influential factors. Iranians are considerably more likely than the other two groups of interviewees are to place physical danger and/or imprisonment among their top two considerations.[48] Ethiopians are about twice as likely as either Iranians or Eritreans are to list general conditions of insecurity. There are no major variations in terms of the pivotal decisional role of political persecution. However, Iranians are far more likely than the others are to include an economic, professional, or family reason among the two that most influenced their decision to become an exile. In the words of one pre-revolution exile, for instance, "I had my wife and children here. I also was against the Shah's government. And, I had opened a factory [here in the U.S.] which should be run by me."

Gender. Table 3.9 confirms that there are strong parallels among the total sample of male and female household heads in terms of the principal factors which shaped exile decision making. Roughly equal proportions of interviewees of both sexes list ideological commitments, fear of political persecution, and economic, professional, and family reasons among their two uppermost considerations.[49] The major differences are the much greater tendency for Iranian men to be influenced decisively by the threat of

TABLE 3.9   Primary and Second-Most Important Reason for Deciding to Become an Exile, by Gender

Type of Consideration	All Respondents (Top 2) N	%Tot	% Male (Total N=216)	% Female (Total N=89)
Ideological reason(s)	186	65.0%	64.7%	65.9%
Genl condit insecurity	85	29.7	23.0	46.3
(Likely)phys dangr,impris	77	26.9	30.9	17.1
Political persecution	48	16.8	15.7	19.5
Econ, prof, fam reasons	50	17.5	17.2	18.3

Source: D.C./L.A. sample.

physical harm and/or imprisonment and for Ethiopian and Eritrean women to be affected primarily by general conditions of violence and insecurity.[50]

Homeland Economic Status. When all of the exiles interviewed in this study are considered together, one finds no important relationship between homeland-income levels and respondent assessments of the two most decisive factors affecting the decision to become an exile (Table 3.10).[51] Of particular interest, interviewees with high-income backgrounds are not more likely than the low-income exiles are to have acted primarily out of fear of physical harm, imprisonment, or other forms of personal persecution, and those from poor family backgrounds do not select general conditions of insecurity more frequently than their wealthier counterparts do.

When investigated by nationality, however, we find that high- and middle-income Iranians are much more apt to place the general state of insecurity among their two most influential considerations than are their compatriots from poor homeland backgrounds. The converse applies among Ethiopian and Eritrean exiles. Iranian and Eritrean interviewees are more

124

TABLE 3.10 Primary and Second-Most Important Reason for Deciding to Become
an Exile, by Respondent/Family Income Level at Time Left
Homeland

Type of Consideration	All Respondents (Top 2)		Income Level at Time Left		
	N	%Tot	%High (Total N=58)	% Med (Total N=179)	% Low (Total N=54)
Ideological reason(s)	186	65.0%	72.2%	62.6%	65.3%
Genl condit insecurity	85	29.7	27.8	32.0	22.4
(Likely)phys dangr,impris	77	26.9	20.4	31.4	22.4
Political persecution	48	16.8	16.7	15.1	20.4
Econ, prof, fam reason(s)	50	17.5	18.5	18.0	14.3

Source: D.C./L.A. sample.

likely to include personal political persecution among their top two
considerations as homeland-income levels decline, while that pattern is
reversed among Ethiopians. Medium-income Iranians stand out from the
others in terms of their tendency to rank the prospect of being singled out
for personal harm and/or imprisonment among the two most decisive
influences; mid-income Ethiopians and Eritreans, on the other hand, are
substantially less likely to select this item in comparison to those with high-
and low-income backgrounds. Respondents from wealthy family
backgrounds in Iran place greater weight on ideological commitments
relative to their low-income compatriots (74 percent versus 25 percent),
while Ethiopians from poor homeland situations are the most likely to rank
this factor highly. Finally, among those from high-income homeland
contexts, none of the Eritreans and only one Ethiopian (out of 21) rated
economic, professional, or family reasons as the primary or second-most
important consideration in the decision to become an exile. In contrast,
nearly 40 percent of the Iranians from a high-income background admit that
these non-political concerns rank among the two factors that had the
greatest influence on their decision to leave or not return to Iran. In
conclusion, homeland economic status does not exert a consistent impact on
exile-decision making.

Educational Level. From Table 3.11, we observe that educational level exerts little influence on the principal motives for becoming an exile. Respondents with fewer educational attainments at the time of decision are

TABLE 3.11   Primary and Second-Most Important Reason for Deciding to Become an Exile, by Educational Level at Time of Decision

Type of Consideration	All Respondents (Top 2) N	%Tot	% Sec or less (Total N=81)	% Some Post Sec (Total N=66)	% U Degree(s) (Total N=138)
Ideological reason(s)	186	65.0%	65.4%	62.1%	65.9%
Genl condit insecurity	85	29.7	37.0	33.3	23.2
(Likely)phys dangr,impris	77	26.9	13.6	31.8	32.6
Political persecution	48	16.8	22.2	16.7	13.8
Econ, prof, fam reasons	50	17.5	12.3	15.2	21.7

Source: D.C./L.A. sample.

somewhat more likely than their more highly educated counterparts are to act out of fear attributed to the general state of insecurity in the homeland,[52] while those with some exposure to post-secondary education respond more often than do exiles without such attainments to fear of physical danger and political persecution combined.[53] Ethiopians possessing at least one post-secondary degree and Iranians with secondary educational attainments or less are more likely to list economic, professional, and family reasons among their two top concerns than their compatriots are. The most surprising finding, however, concerns the lack of variation by educational level in terms of the priority placed upon ideological commitments. Secondary-school graduates and respondents with less education are as likely to rank ideological concerns among their two principal considerations as are exiles with university education.[54]

Exposure to Revolution. The information set forth in Table 3.12 suggests that exiles who experience revolution are considerably more likely

TABLE 3.12   Primary and Second-Most Important Reason for Deciding to Become an Exile, by Period Exile Left Homeland

Type of Consideration	All Respondents (Top 2)		% Left Prior Regime Overthrow (Total N=161)	% Left After Regime Overthrow (Total N=144)
	N	%Tot		
Ideological reason(s)	186	65.0%	54.6%	76.9%
Genl condit insecurity	85	29.7	25.7	34.3
(Likely)phys dangr,impris	77	26.9	32.2	20.9
Political persecution	48	16.8	19.7	13.4
Econ, prof fam reasons	50	17.5	22.4	11.9

Source: D.C./L.A. sample.

than are migrants who depart prior to the political transformation of the homeland to be influenced primarily by ideological commitments.   This finding applies across all three nationality groups.[55]   Post-revolution migrants also are more likely than the others are to act out of concern over the general state of insecurity prevailing in the homeland following the revolution and are much more apt to include economic or family considerations among their two top reasons for becoming an exile.   The interviewees who did not personally experience the homeland revolution turn out to be more prone than their counterparts are to act out of fear of personal/family danger, imprisonment, and political persecution.

     There are interesting differences in the effect of exposure to revolution by nationality on several of these items.   The finding that refugees who experience revolutionary conditions are more likely than the others are to cite general conditions of insecurity as their principal motivating consideration is attributed to responses from only one of the three groups under study; that is, to Ethiopians who left after the overthrow of the Emperor.   In fact, Iranians who departed prior to the revolution place the general state of insecurity among their top two considerations more frequently than their post-revolution compatriots do (26 percent and 16 percent, respectively).   In addition, the Iranian results differ from those reported by the other two groups when it comes to the inclusion of economic, professional, or family considerations among the uppermost reasons for seeking exile.   While nearly all of the Ethiopians and Eritreans who ranked such non-political considerations among the two most influential had exited from their country of origin prior to its revolutionary political transformation, a higher proportion of the post-revolution migrants from Iran had acted on the basis of economic, professional, or family interests in comparison to those who departed prior to the overthrow of the Shah (35 percent versus 24 percent).[56]

Departure Interval. The Cuban and Vietnamese experiences suggest that most persons who take flight from a post-revolution environment at the time of upheaval or relatively soon afterward leave the homeland strictly out of fear of political persecution. Later departure vintages are likely to include economic migrants and emigrants seeking family reunification, along with the politically disaffected and dispossessed.

The D.C./L.A. study partially confirms this tendency in the case of the Iranian community. Whereas 19 percent of the Iranians who departed between the time of the outbreak of revolutionary conflict and the end of 1982 listed economic, professional, and/or family motives among their top two considerations, exactly one-third of those who left in 1983 and 1984 emphasized such motives. At the same time, however, the percentage of Iranian respondents who ranked fear of physical danger among their two foremost concerns also increased slightly. In striking contrast to the Cuban and Vietnamese experience, none of the interviewed Ethiopians who exited in the latest vintage studied (i.e., 1983 or 1984) placed priority on economic, professional, or family considerations.[57] The overall results from the three study communities indicate that most late post-revolution emigrants are neither economic migrants[58] nor persons primarily interested in family reunification. Both Iran and Ethiopia have continued to be a major source of political emigration long after the conclusion of the revolutionary-upheaval period.

Conclusions

Contrary to popular impression, most refugees are not forced to leave their home country without advance notice and preparation. They typically decide to move or to stay abroad on the basis of carefully weighed deliberations that occasionally extend over a lengthy period of time. Their determinations involve strategies planned amidst tension and crisis which are aimed at ensuring individual or family survival "in a world fraught with uncertainties and controlled by distant forces."[59]

Refugees differ from purely voluntary migrants, however, in that their decision to abandon the homeland is an act of desperation based on political disaffection which they are extremely reluctant to undertake. Egon Kunz has contributed the important insight that "it is the reluctance to uproot oneself, and the absence of positive original motivations to settle elsewhere, which characterises all refugee decisions and distinguishes the refugee from the voluntary migrant."[60] Self-imposed exile is "the last step of a process of political disaffection."[61] In sum, refugees must be understood as "conscious, active human beings"[62] who agonize over ties that bind and forces that expel[63] and act in response to individual experiences and motives, social forces, and national and international events.

In taking the life-transforming step of becoming an exile, refugees from revolution are influenced by multiple and diverse experiences and motives. In this chapter, we probed deeply into the most compelling of these factors with the aid of new data based primarily upon extensive interviews conducted with Iranian, Ethiopian, and Eritrean household heads living in exile in the United States.[64] The new study findings confirm that the overwhelming majority of the family decision makers living in these exile communities responded to mixed motives and pressures,[65] and that they migrated *exclusively* for political reasons. Comparative analysis of Ethiopian, Eritrean, and Iranian refugees reveals that the precise mix of decisive political considerations varies among exiles of differing nationality. While the specific factors responsible for uprooting vary, violence and the fear of life-threatening violence constituted major motives for breaking the homeland bond among most of the exiles interviewed in this project.[66] The exceptions are primarily restricted to the Iranian community; they include some pre-revolution economic migrants and a sizeable minority of the late post-revolution group who acted on the basis of a mix of political and non-political motives. In contrast to the experience with Vietnamese and Cuban quasi refugees,[67] the "pull effect" is not only subordinate to the political situation that compelled individuals to leave Ethiopia, it is entirely inoperative.[68]

Roughly equal proportions of the refugees interviewed for this project listed general conditions of insecurity and fear of individual imprisonment/physical harm as decisive factors in their decision to become an exile. The complex subjective variations identified in this study do not correspond with stronger or weaker objective bases for fearing persecution, however. Moreover, neither gender nor homeland economic status exerted much influence on exile decision making.

National events, regime policies, and/or personal incidents play a decisive role in the decision to live in exile among many refugees from revolution. Exiles respond to a wide variety of political stimuli, however. Among the refugees from Ethiopia and Iran interviewed in the United States, no single intervening factor or cluster of factors proved responsible for the decision to break with one's homeland. The structural conditions generated by revolutionary political change produced a series of events, policies, and incidents which directly and indirectly shaped the individual concerns and ethical positions that motivated exile decision making in the post-revolution period.

Efforts to effectuate a coercive transformation of society, the brutal repression of opposition political factions and suppression of human rights, the presence of random terror and counter-violence, and the heightened persecution of disaffected nationality and religious groups are among the most powerful factors contributing to massive post-revolution refugee migrations. The common bond responsible for generating these developments is the Third World revolution itself. This insight reveals the crucial link between the foreign policy of the United States and post-revolution migration. By supporting "friendly" regimes that suppress pressures for radical social change and preclude peaceful political transition, U.S. foreign-policy actions supply the props that enable unpopular rulers to retain power while revolutionary pressures build until they no longer can be contained. The powerful aftershocks that are unleashed during the successful revolutionary overthrow of a U.S.-supported regime and in its aftermath provide the principal concrete and immediate catalysts for the decision to become an exile.

Finally, ideological commitments turned out to be particularly important for a high proportion of the respondents in the D.C./L.A. study. When one considers that the appeal to higher principles is used to justify revolutionary challenges to existing authority systems,[69] that revolution involves a life-and-death struggle over ideology that yields new winners and new losers, and that the violent suppression of opposition organizations and dissent constitutes a common feature of post-revolution regimes, then the crucial decisional role of ethical standards and differences in political values at the individual level becomes understandable. Nevertheless, the central place of ideological commitment in refugee formation has not been given sufficient recognition by scholars and policy makers.

In addition to identifying the decisive role played by this consideration among the respondents, we discovered that, on a cross-national basis, exposure to revolutionary conditions strengthened the exile's ideological commitment and increased the salience of opposition to the regime in power on ethical grounds as a decisional factor. It is likely that self-awareness and understanding of the fate of other political opponents of the post-revolution regime brings the realization to survivors that their continued presence in the homeland would eventually place them in a position where they would be forced either to act on their commitments, and thereby attract a violent reaction, or to repudiate deeply held values. This insight suggests that the ability to perceive danger, to identify viable alternatives to one's situation, and to react quickly and courageously by exiting before one is completely powerless to avoid physical harm, internment, and other forms of persecution, might be a personality characteristic that distinguishes refugees from those who do not opt for or succeed in exiting.[70]

Egon Kunz reminds us to be attentive to the "recurring elements" in each refugee situation.[71] The analysis undertaken in this chapter unmasked important common experiences in the Cuban, Vietnamese, Ethiopian, and Iranian cases. First and foremost, Third World revolutions that overthrow regimes heavily supported "to the end" by the United States produce refugees who opt for exile primarily for political reasons. Second, those who flee and those who are abroad and later decide not to return possess equally compelling reasons, typically involving reasonable fears of life-threatening violence directed against themselves, for becoming a political exile. The first finding carries important implications for U.S. foreign-policy making that will be considered in Chapter 10, while the latter is relevant to the recurring debate over political asylum—an aspect of immigration policy treated in Chapters 5 and 10.

Notes

1. See, for instance, Richard R. Fagen, Richard A. Brody, and Thomas J. O'Leary, *Cubans in Exile: Disaffection and the Revolution* (Stanford: Stanford University Press, 1968), pp. 79–89.

2. Tabori correctly points out that it does not matter in terms of exile formation if the compulsion experienced consists of being "expelled by physical force" or "making the decision to leave without such an immediate pressure." Paul Tabori, *The Anatomy of Exile: A Semantic and Historical Study* (London: Harrap, 1972), p. 37.

3. Elizabeth G. Ferris, "Overview: Refugees and World Politics," in *Refugees and World Politics*, edited by Elizabeth G. Ferris (New York: Praeger, 1985), p. 15; Gil Loescher, "Introduction: Refugee Issues in International Relations," in *Refugees*

and International Relations, edited by Gil Loescher and Laila Monahan (Oxford: Oxford University Press, 1989), p. 4; Hiram A. Ruiz, *Beyond the Headlines: Refugees in the Horn of Africa* (Washington, D.C.: U.S. Committee for Refugees, 1988), p. 14.

4. Failure to link the structural context of exile formation with individual decision making is especially problematic.

5. See Sidney R. Waldron, "Is there a Future for the Ogaden Refugees?" (paper presented at the Seventh International Conference on Ethiopian Studies, University of Lund, Sweden, 1982); Sidney R. Waldron, "Somali Refugee Background Characteristics: Preliminary Results from the Qoriooley Camps" (unpublished paper in the author's possession, n.d.), pp. 1, 13; Peter J. Schraeder, "Involuntary Migration in Somalia: The Politics of Resettlement," *Journal of Modern African Studies* 24, No. 4 (1986):653; and Leon Gordenker, *Refugees in International Politics* (New York: Columbia University Press, 1987), pp. 63, 188.

6. Robert E. Mazur, "Refugees in Africa: The Role of Sociological Analysis and Praxis," *Current Sociology* 36(2):46–49; also see Roger Zetter, "Refugees and Refugee Studies—A Label and an Agenda," *Journal of Refugee Studies* 1, No. 1 (1988):4.

The Refugee Affairs Coordinator at the U.S. Embassy directed a 1984 'research' project in Sudan, for instance. Mixed among the 1,012 Ethiopian households in Khartoum surveyed in this project are approximately 300 persons who already had been selected for U.S. resettlement and others interviewed at churches, hotels, and clubs. See Jerry L. Weaver, "Sojourners Along the Nile: Ethiopian Refugees in Khartoum," *Journal of Modern African Studies* 23, 1 (1985):148, 150. In 1985, three researchers affiliated with Cultural Survival carried out one of the few studies of refugees in the Sudan that has not relied upon governmental or international-agency support. Unfortunately, their research design was flawed by selective interviewing, failure to ascertain the nationality of respondents, and the deliberate steps taken to exclude Eritrean refugees. See Jason W. Clay and Bonnie K. Holcomb, *Politics and the Ethiopian Famine 1984–1985* (Cambridge: Cultural Survival, Inc., 1985), pp. 18, 25, 38. Moreover, the overtly political reputation of Cultural Survival in promoting nationality interests raises serious questions about possible bias in the interview process. Fortunately, Mekuria Bulcha subsequently published the results of his well-designed and more reliable 1982–1983 study of 413 randomly selected refugee households drawn from eight organized and spontaneous settlement sites in Sudan. See Mekuria Bulcha, *Flight and Integration: Causes of Mass Exodus from Ethiopia and Problems of Integration in the Sudan* (Uppsala: Scandinavian Institute of African Studies, 1988), pp. 91–97. Mekuria's research findings from Sudan, which deal in holistic fashion with refugee formation, flight, and resettlement, provide a useful complement to the results obtained from the D.C. study of refugees from Ethiopia analyzed in this volume.

7. See also Art Hansen, "Self-Settled Rural Refugees in Africa: The Case of Angolans in Zambian Villages," in *Involuntary Migration and Resettlement: The Problems and Responses of Dislocated People*, edited by Art Hansen and Anthony Oliver-Smith (Boulder: Westview Press, 1982), p. 31.

8. Clay and Holcomb (*Famine*, p. 26) point out that inside Ethiopia "the safety of interviewees cannot be guaranteed once the investigator leaves the area. This undoubtedly affects the 'truths' that are to be uncovered." Indeed, the post-revolution penal code subjects persons who directly or indirectly encourage illegal exit from Ethiopia to 5–25 years of "rigorous imprisonment" and, in especially serious cases, to life imprisonment or execution. No responsible researcher would be willing to expose interviewers and interviewees to the risk of such retribution. Also see Alex Inkeles and Raymond A. Bauer, *The Soviet Citizen: Daily Life in a Totalitarian Society* (Cambridge: Harvard University Press, 1959), p. 5; Fagen *et al.*, *Cubans*, pp. 103–109.

While admitting that his conclusions are based on potentially unreliable second-hand reports about family members who remained behind, Mekuria Bulcha (*Flight*, p. 133) speculates that those who did not opt to leave Ethiopia include persons physically unable to exit due to impairments attributed to old age or sickness, and those who can be categorized as "optimists, fatalists and altruists." Fagen *et al.* (*Cubans*, p. 105) hypothesize that "personality characteristics are involved, for some persons are clearly better able to tolerate deprivation, negative experiences, personal insecurity, and change than are others. Furthermore, differing value hierarchies help to explain why revolutionary programs, perceived as intolerable by some, are seen as at least partially necessary and thus not wholly negative by others."

9. Fagen *et al.*, *Cubans*, pp. 9–13, 101.

10. Fagen *et al.*, *Cubans*, pp. 79–93; also see Al Santoli, *New Americans: Immigrants and Refugees in the U.S. Today* (New York: Viking, 1988), pp. 374–375. On the role of personal experiences and hardships in shaping the motives of refugees from the Hungarian uprising of 1956, see Lawrence E. Hinkle, Jr. *et al.*, "Hungarian Refugees: Life Experiences and Features Influencing Participation in the Revolution and Subsequent Flight," *American Journal of Psychiatry*, 116 (July 1959):17.

11. The authors specifically point out that "concern with the long-term *continuation* of political and economic limitations rather than with short-term shortages was the decisive factor for many recent exiles." Alejandro Portes, Juan M. Clark, and Robert L. Bach, "The New Wave: A Statistical Profile of Recent Cuban Exiles to the United States," *Cuban Studies* 7 (1977):1–3, 16–17. Ferris adds that the act of leaving, whatever the reason(s), "meant that henceforth the individual

would be singled out for political persecution." Ferris, "Overview," p. 16; also see Silvia Pedraza-Bailey, "Cuban Exiles: Portrait of a Refugee Migration," *International Migration Review* 19, No. 1 (1985):17.

12. Robert L. Bach, "Cubans," in *Refugees in the United States: A Reference Handbook*, edited by David W. Haines (Westport: Greenwood Press, 1985), pp. 81–85; Aristide R. Zolberg, Astri Suhrke, and Sergio Aguayo, *Escape from Violence: Conflict and the Refugee Crisis in the Developing World* (Oxford: Oxford University Press, 1989), p. 186.

13. Pedraza-Bailey, "Cuban Exiles," 28–30.

14. Gail P. Kelly, *From Vietnam to America: A Chronicle of the Vietnamese Immigration to the United States* (Boulder: Westview Press, 1977), pp. 16–17.

15. Rebecca Allen and Harry H. Hiller, "The Social Organization of Migration: An Analysis of the Uprooting and Flight of Vietnamese Refugees," *International Migration* 23, No. 4 (1985):442.

16. Nguyen Manh Hung, "Vietnamese," in *Refugees in the United States: A Reference Handbook*, ed. by David W. Haines (Westport: Greenwood Press, 1985), pp. 195–199; also see Allen and Hiller, "Refugees," 442–443. According to Robinson, "high expectations about resettlement" constitute the common link among those who have fled from Vietnam in recent years. Court Robinson, "Sins of Omission: The New Vietnamese Refugee Crisis," *World Refugee Survey—1988 in Review* (Washington, D.C.: U.S. Committee for Refugees, 1989), pp. 7–8.

17. Rubén D. Rumbaut and Rubén G. Rumbaut, "The Family in Exile: Cuban Expatriates in the United States," *American Journal of Psychiatry* 133, No. 4 (April 1976):396; Zolberg et al., *Refugee Crisis*, p. 187.

18. The sample is compared with each sending country's population in Chapter 6. A brief discussion of the research design and sampling methodology utilized in the D.C./L.A. study can be found in the Appendix. Girma Negash co-directed the D.C./L.A. project, and Mohammad Amjad worked as principal research assistant in both locations.

These are indeed overwhelmingly exile communities. Only 12 respondents, or 3.8 percent of the total sample, had not decided to live in exile at the time of interview. Unless otherwise noted, the data analysis conducted in the rest of this book is restricted to the 305 self-identified exiles.

19. Poor peasant families also suffer considerable loss when uprooted from their traditional homeland. See Mekuria Bulcha, *Flight*, pp. 140–141.

20. Also see Ferris, "Overview," p. 15; Hinkle et al., "Hungarian," 16–17.

21. See Peter Koehn, Mohammad Amjad, and Girma Negash, "Pre- and Post-Revolution Émigrés and Non Returnees: Ethiopian-Iranian Comparisons" (paper presented at the Joint Meeting of the African and Middle Eastern Studies Associations, New Orleans, November 1985), p. 22. Among Iranian non returnees,

40 percent of those who supported or agreed with a leftist political organization, and 73 percent of the others, had *not* been influenced to become an exile by a particular event or incident.

22. Fagen *et al., Cubans*, p. 76. [italics added]

23. For a list of all incidents and events mentioned by two or more exiles from Ethiopia, see Peter Koehn and Girma Negash, *Resettled Refugees and Asylum Applicants: Implications of the Case of Migrants from Ethiopia for United States Policy* (Arlington: Center for Ethiopian Studies, 1987), p. 56.

24. In contrast, Fagen *et al.* (*Cubans*, pp. 76, 78) found that "the precipitating experiences were personal and proximate" among the vast majority of the post-revolution refugees from Cuba who participated in their survey.

The open-ended responses collected in the D.C./L.A. study are rich in detail. However, the pre-identification of specific key events linked to important social-structural factors would have allowed the formulation of standardized questionnaire items and inquiry with each respondent regarding the influence or lack of influence of particular occurrences.

25. Koehn *et al.*, "Émigrés and Non Returnees," pp. 13–15. See also Hinkle *et al.*, "Hungarian Refugees," 17.

Immigration-related interviews conducted with refugees from Ethiopia selected for resettlement in the United States show a lower level of anti-regime activity. Among the 197 files surveyed by the author at the New York City headquarters of Church World Service, 64 percent contained no mention of anti-regime actions. Only 3 percent of these refugees reported that they had engaged in armed struggle; 9 percent had participated in a strike or public demonstration; 9 percent had spoken out against the regime; 14 percent had violated a rule or regulation; and 3 percent had supported an opposition organization.

26. When pre-revolution émigrés are removed from consideration, Eritreans are still more than twice as likely as Iranians are (56 percent versus 26 percent) to rate the experience of war and/or armed conflict as important in their decision-making process.

27. Among the refugees from Ethiopia interviewed in Sudan by Mekuria Bulcha, 47 percent of those from rural backgrounds and only 29 percent of the respondents who fled from urban settings listed the experience of armed conflict as one of the three top reasons for flight. Mekuria Bulcha, *Flight*, p. 99.

28. Only 10 percent of the émigrés cited personal incidents alone. Fully 43 percent of this group mentioned both personal/family *and* national/regional factors, however. For insight regarding the personal incidents and national political developments that led one high-level defector not to return to Ethiopia in the mid 1980s, see Dawit Wolde Giorgis, *Red Tears: War, Famine and Revolution in Ethiopia* (Trenton: Red Sea Press, 1989), pp. 346–347.

29. For example, see Astri Suhrke, "Global Refugee Movements and Strategies of Response," in *U.S. Immigration and Refugee Policy: Global and Domestic Issues*, edited by Mary M. Kritz (Lexington: D.C. Heath and Company, 1983), p. 159.

30. Moreover, three-quarters of the Ethiopian exiles and nearly half of the other two groups came from homeland situations in which they (or their parents) had possessed more than 10 hectares of rural land, profitted from urban rental property, and/or served on the board of directors of a private corporation or public enterprise. These are revealing indicators of ruling-class status in Third World societies.

In Ethiopia, the Derg's most revolutionary measures involved the nationalization of rural holdings over 10 hectares, all non-owner occupied and privately rented urban housing units, and many industrial establishments. See John M. Cohen and Peter H. Koehn, "Rural and Urban Land Reform in Ethiopia," *African Law Studies* 14 (1977):3–62.

31. Most of the reported links are with transnational capitalist institutions. See Koehn *et al.*, "Émigrés and Non Returnees," p. 11. The percentage reporting ties with these organizations is quite high relative to the entire population in both Iran and Ethiopia.

32. See Koehn *et al.*, "Émigrés and Non Returnees," p. 27.

33. Peter Koehn and Girma Negash, "Iranian Émigrés and Non Returnees: Political Exiles or Economic Migrants?" *Scandinavian Journal of Development Alternatives* 8 (June 1989):88, 103.

34. One must bear in mind, however, that most Iranians opposed to the Shah's rule regarded his "illegitimate political system as a creation of American and British imperialism." Abdolmaboud Ansari, *Iranian Immigrants in the United States: A Case Study of Dual Marginality* (Millwood: Associated Faculty Press, 1988), p. 22.

35. Precise figures are reported in Koehn *et al.*, "Émigrés and Non Returnees," pp. 35–39. The socio-economic policies cited by refugees in Sudan as contributing to their flight from the homeland include imprisonment for inability to pay compulsory contributions, confiscation of property by the state, forced labor, and military conscription. Mekuria Bulcha, *Flight*, pp. 110–111.

36. See Koehn *et al.*, "Émigrés and Non Returnees," pp. 43–45.

The presence of many non returnees in these three exile communities raises the prospect that economic and/or social adaptation in the receiving country might have influenced the decision not to return to Ethiopia or Iran. In assessing the impact of these considerations, it is valuable to compare the adaptation experiences of non returnees at the time they decided to live in exile with the 1984 situation of the 12 non exiles in the sample. In terms of economic adaptation, virtually identical proportions of both types of respondent held full-time employment and were unemployed. Employed non exiles proved more likely to occupy permanent jobs relative to working non returnees (57 and 48 percent, respectively). Moreover, a

136

smaller proportion of the non returnees possessed secure immigrant status (citizenship or permanent residency) at the time they decided not to return than non exiles did at the time of interview (31 to 42 percent). A higher percentage of the non returnees than the non exiles also described their incomes as "low" compared to others in the homeland (21 versus 9 percent) and to others in the United States (65 versus 30 percent). Finally, non returnees proved more likely than their non-exile counterparts did to avoid social interaction with U.S. nationals. The interviews revealed that 17 percent of the non exiles and 36 percent of the non returnees interact with U.S. citizens less than once per week. In sum, these comparative findings strongly suggest that the decision to become or not to become an exile occurs independently of economic and social adaptation in the receiving country.

37. Ferris, "Overview," p. 4.

38. The response from low-income Eritreans accounts for virtually all of the variation on the threat dimension. In addition, there is no difference among Ethiopian exiles of high- and low-income homeland status in terms of reference to political persecution as an important consideration.

39. Indeed, all ten Eritrean interviewees from high-income homeland backgrounds reported that general conditions of insecurity played an important part in their decision. High-income Eritreans also proved considerably more likely than their low-income counterparts to be influenced by the suppression of political activity in Ethiopia (90 percent, versus 68 percent).

40. The Eritrean respondents are exceptional on all three items. Those who left after the overthrow of Emperor Haile Selassie I are far more likely than their counterparts who departed prior to the revolution are to be influenced by general conditions of insecurity (91 versus 69 percent), the suppression of political expression and association (82 versus 56 percent), and ideological commitments (77 versus 38 percent). These results undoubtedly reflect the intensification within Eritrea of armed conflict over nationality issues after the military assumed power in Addis Ababa. In contrast, higher proportions of pre-revolution than post-overthrow Ethiopian migrants reported being influenced by political suppression and ideological commitments. This finding may well be related to the total ban on political activity ruthlessly imposed by the Emperor and to the widespread disgust that Ethiopians held for imperial rule by the end of Haile Selassie's reign.

41. Ethiopian respondents account for all of the observed variation on this factor. While there are no differences by period of departure among Eritrean and Iranian migrants, the Ethiopians who left prior to the Emperor's overthrow proved much more likely to be influenced by economic deprivation in the homeland relative to their post-revolution counterparts (22 percent and 7 percent, respectively). These findings are consistent with Abdolmaboud Ansari's conclusion that pre-revolution migration from Iran to the United States "is not basically a result of economic

hardship." Instead, thousands of Iranian professionals opted for transnational migration "as an outlet for their general alienation from the socio-political system." Ansari, *Iranian Immigrants*, p. 32.

42. Among the Ethiopian interviewees, there are no differences in terms of the role of political persecution. Moreover, the smallest variation (15 percent) on the threat dimension occurs among exiles of Ethiopian nationality; the largest exists among Eritreans (56 percent for those leaving prior versus 93 percent of those who departed after the overthrow of the Emperor).

43. Respondents who did not encounter revolutionary conditions actually are more likely than are those who lived in the homeland following regime overthrow to report that fear of imprisonment/physical danger and political persecution constituted a *decisive* decision-making consideration. See Table 3.12.

44. This treatment follows the identification of leftist groups found in Val Moghadam, "The Left and Revolution in Iran: A Critical Analysis," in *Post-Revolutionary Iran*, edited by Hooshang Amirahmadi and Manoucher Parvin (Boulder: Westview Press, 1988), p. 23.

45. Another illustrative statement comes from an interview with two former Eritrean Liberation Front (ELF) guerrillas conducted by Al Santoli in the Washington, D.C., area: "We made the decision to become refugees because, even though the ELF and the EPLF had successfully counterattacked the Derge and the Soviets, they began to fight each other as well." Santoli, *New Americans*, p. 95.

46. The respondents in the "Ethiopian" group who identified nationality issues as decisive are mainly Oromo.

47. With two exceptions, moreover, the U.S. findings reported in Table 3.8 closely parallel the "top three" reasons identified by refugees from Ethiopia interviewed in Sudan by Mekuria Bulcha. The exceptions are the more frequent reporting of ideological reasons by the U.S. sample and the somewhat greater tendency of the refugees in Sudan to cite economic, professional, and family considerations. Nevertheless, the Sudan sample includes "a relatively large group of refugees who left Ethiopia in defiance of the military, social and economic policies of the government—in particular, conscription, forced labour and involuntary relocation." Mekuria Bulcha, *Flight*, pp. 99–100, 129.

48. Iranians who supported or agreed with leftist political groups are more likely than their counterparts are to list physical danger and/or imprisonment among their two foremost considerations (54 percent to 35 percent). The former also are more apt to emphasize ideological commitment (66 versus 49 percent).

49. There are interesting gender variations by nationality, however. For instance, Ethiopians account for all of the variation in the political-persecution results. While Ethiopian exiles of both sexes respond in similar fashion with respect to ideological commitments, Iranian females and Eritrean males weigh this

138

factor more heavily in comparison with their counterparts (by 13 percent and 24 percent, respectively). Iranian and Eritrean women are somewhat more likely than their male compatriots are to indicate that economic, professional, or family considerations ranked among their uppermost concerns when they opted for exile, while the converse applies in the Ethiopian case.

50. Iranian males and females are equally likely to list general conditions of insecurity among their top two considerations; the same pattern applies to Ethiopian and Eritrean men and women on the physical-danger item.

51. Furthermore, there are no meaningful variations on the five selected items among exiles who had possessed and had not possessed a homeland association with a Western government agency, multinational corporation, or international organization.

52. Ethiopians account for virtually all of the difference on this item.

53. Eritreans with secondary-school education or less account for nearly all of the difference with respect to fear of political persecution.

54. This finding probably is related to the vanguard role played by secondary-school enrollees in the pre-revolution Ethiopian student movement (see Chapter 2). Thus, Iranians differ from the migrants from Ethiopia with regard to the weight of ideological motives among respondents of diverse educational backgrounds. Roughly 60 percent of the Iranians exposed to post-secondary education place ideological commitments among the two most influential considerations, while only 27 percent of their compatriots with a secondary-school education or less responded in this fashion.

55. Moreover, those respondents whose final decision to become an exile has been influenced by a particular incident or event are more likely than their counterparts are to list ideological considerations among their two foremost motives (71 percent and 58 percent, respectively). The former also are less likely to cite general conditions of insecurity (25 percent to 37 percent). Experiencing an influential incident or event bears no relationship to priority rankings for political persecution, physical danger/imprisonment, or economic, family, and professional considerations.

56. This finding challenges the assumption made by Sabagh and Bozorgmehr that Iranians arriving in the United States prior to 1978 are likely to be immigrants rather than exiles. See Georges Sabagh and Mehdi Bozorgmehr, "Are the Characteristics of Exiles Different from Immigrants? The Case of Iranians in Los Angeles," *Sociology and Social Research* 71, No. 2 (January 1987):81.

Analysis by exposure to revolutionary conditions yields offsetting results among Ethiopian and Eritrean exiles in terms of the impact of the two remaining factors. Ethiopians who left prior to the demise of the imperial regime and Eritreans who departed afterward are much more likely than their counterparts are to place political persecution among the two most important reasons for becoming an exile. On the other hand, post-revolution Ethiopian migrants and pre-revolution Eritreans favor fear of physical danger and/or imprisonment as one of the two most important explanations for exile decision making.

57. Moreover, none of the late-departing Ethiopians emphasized physical danger.

58. For the entire D.C./L.A. sample, an identical proportion (11.1 percent) of early and late post-revolution exiles indicated that economic deprivation in the homeland constituted an important decisional consideration.

59. James T. Fawcett, "Migration Psychology: New Behavioral Models," *Population and Environment* 8 (Spring/Summer, 1985–1986):8, 13; Hansen, "Self-Settled," p. 31; Allen and Hiller, "Refugees," 440, 448; Hinkle *et al.*, "Hungarian Refugees," 16–17. This understanding refutes Kunz' early view that "inner force is singularly absent from the movement of refugees. Their progress more often than not resembles the movement of the billiard ball devoid of inner direction. . . ." He acknowledges, nevertheless, the existence of "refugees by choice" who are outside the homeland and refuse to return to their country of origin. Egon F. Kunz, "The Refugee in Flight: Kinetic Models and Forms of Displacement," *International Migration Review* 7, No. 2 (Summer, 1973):131n, 135. Unlike the exiles found in industrialized countries, many of the refugees studied by Mekuria Bulcha in Sudan had been involved in a collective rather than an individual decision to flee and had left without thoroughly assessing the implications of flight or possessing information about conditions in the country of destination. Mekuria Bulcha, *Flight*, pp. 131–132. In any event, neither refugees nor exiles are "passive, faceless, inarticulate. . . member[s] of a mass movement in almost lemming-like, barely comprehensible flight. . . ." Roger G. Thomas, "Exile, Dictatorship and the Creative Writer in Africa: A Selective Annotated Bibliography," *Third World Quarterly* 9, No. 1 (January 1987):272–273.

60. Kunz, "Displacement," 130, 132; Hansen, "Self-Settled," p. 32. This reluctance to leave one's home area is found among pastoralists as well as sedentary peoples. See Mekuria Bulcha, *Flight*, pp. 133, 135.

61. Pedraza-Bailey, "Cuba's Exiles," 8.

62. Robert E. Mazur, "Linking Popular Initiative and Aid Agencies: The Case of Refugees," *Development and Change* 18 (1987):438.

63. Rumbaut and Rumbaut, "Cuban," 396; Gaim Kibreab, *African Refugees: Reflections on the African Refugee Problem* (Trenton: Africa World Press, 1985), p. 5.

64. The unsystematic research on reasons for fleeing that has been conducted to date among refugees from Ethiopia living in Somalia and Sudan is not particularly reliable. Nevertheless, Waldron ("Qoriooley," pp. 5, 7) reports that fear of death in

warfare, particularly from strafing, constituted a major factor among the Oromo and Somali refugees he interviewed in three Somali camps in 1982; also see Ulrich Braukämper, "Ethnic Identity and Social Change Among Oromo Refugees in the Horn of Africa," *Northeast African Studies* 4, No. 3 (1982–83):4. Among those interviewed in Khartoum as part of the study sponsored by the U.S. Embassy's Refugee Affairs Coordinator, most cited the need to escape political persecution and armed conflict as the main reason they left Ethiopia. Weaver, "Sojourners," 150–151. The interviews conducted by members of the Cultural Survival research team with non Eritreans encountered in rural Sudan uncovered a host of explanations for the decision to flee from Ethiopia. These refugees most frequently mentioned fear of imprisonment, reimprisonment, or execution, land confiscation for the government's resettlement scheme, opposition to conscription into military service, lack of freedom to practice their religion, and, among some of the most recently arrived, famine induced by government policies. According to the interviewers, "none of the [Oromo] respondents mentioned warfare as a cause of flight, though individual stories often mentioned forced entry into their houses, burning of their homes and supplies, and public executions of suspected supporters of the OLF." Clay and Holcomb, *Famine*, pp. 47, 142–162.

65. Suhrke, "Global," p. 162.

66. Also see Mekuria Bulcha, *Flight*, p. 225; Hinkle *et al.*, "Hungarian Refugees," 17.

67. Suhrke, "Global," pp. 164–165.

68. These findings are supported by Waldron's 1982 interviews ("Qoriooley," pp. 7–8) with pastoralists and farmers in the Qoriooley camps in Lower Shebelli Province, Somalia. In his survey, "*no* respondents knew of the existence of the camps and their succor when they fled Ethiopia. A recurrent comment was, 'I was fleeing to save my life.'" Also see Gordenker, *Refugees*, p. 188.

A plurality of the farmers and herders from Ethiopia interviewed by Weaver ("Sojourners," 150–151) offered an employment-seeking explanation for their decision to flee to Sudan. Mekuria Bulcha (*Flight*, pp. 99–100, 129) also uncovered a small group of "borderline cases" carried along by the outflow of refugees "who take advantage of the situation created by the mass movement to fulfil [sic] frustrated aspirations for further education and economic betterment." Nevertheless, the weight of the evidence gathered in studies of migrants from Ethiopia does not confirm the assertion by Zolberg *et al.* (*Refugee Crisis*, p. 176) that "an elaborate relief or resettlement apparatus also tends to attract. . . refugee flows. . . ."

69. Zolberg *et al.*, *Refugee Crisis*, p. 9.

70. Mekuria Bulcha, *Flight*, p. 132; Hansen, "Self-Settled," 31; Fagen *et al.*, *Cubans*, p. 106.

71. Kunz, "Displacement," 129.

PART TWO

Post-Revolution Migration Routes

4

Vintages, Steps, and Waves

If we in government or politics are not able to bridle our compassion for the less fortunate people of other lands sufficiently to protect the 'national interest,' then not only will we have failed in our primary official duty, including our duty to the least advantaged in our own nation, but there is a substantial risk that in the long run the American people will be unable or unwilling to respond at all, even when the need is desperate. I refer to this potential unwillingness to respond as 'compassion fatigue.' The signs are all around us that this is already occurring.

—Alan K. Simpson, U.S. Senator and Chairman of the Judiciary
Subcommittee on Immigration and Refugee Policy

Many refugees find the road to safety and security long and arduous. Success in taking flight from one's country of origin does not guarantee a secure destination. Even after reaching a place of refuge, further trauma is encountered[1] and new challenges must be faced. Most refugees languish for years, or even decades, in a neighboring country of first asylum. This situation is graphically described in a passage penned by Gil Loescher:

142

For the majority of these refugees, life in exile is as bad or even worse than the conditions experienced in the countries from which they have fled. Many are confined to camps or ramshackle settlements close to the borders of their home countries where, deprived of opportunities to work or farm their own land, they depend on international charity for survival. Refugees are often separated from members of their families, exposed to the danger of armed attack, subject to many forms of exploitation and degradation, and haunted by the constant fear of expulsion and the forced return to their countries of origin. Vast numbers of children have spent all their lives in [such] refugee camps.[2]

Refugees from Revolution is principally concerned with political migrants who have managed to overcome the barriers to entry maintained by the United States. In general terms, relocation in the industrialized North depends upon individual initiative and the application of receiving-country admission policy. This chapter describes the steps and strategies involved in South-North political migration, and traces the prevailing routes followed by refugees from Third World revolutions. It also investigates the changing composition of post-revolution transnational population flows both in terms of sending-country departure intervals (vintages) and in terms of receiving-country arrival intervals (waves).[3] Chapter 5 provides a detailed analysis of the application and consequences of U.S. refugee-admission policy.

Step Migration

The transnational migration of political exiles encompasses a series of potential steps. The number of moves involved in refugee migration can be many or few. In addition, movement from South to North occurs according to a variety of alternative routes and methods, and each step can be activated by different forces.[4] The distinct paths followed by post-revolution refugees constitute an important dimension of contemporary international migration.

Refugee flows begin with departure from the home country. Flight from the country of one's origin frequently is not easy to arrange, nor is success in this risky and stressful venture assured. The capacity to migrate depends upon judicious decisions and actions that, in turn, require the mobilization of valuable economic and social resources. Rebecca Allen and Harry Hiller suggest that participation in the social organization for flight and in problem solving that overcomes intervening obstacles makes departure feasible.[5] During the flight-preparation process, the household or the extended family often performs vital migration-related functions—reinforcing the decision to depart, providing information about flight opportunities, and linking members to cross-national networks.[6]

In many cases, the transnational movement of refugees is arrested in the country of first asylum. Those who move on often pass through a series of temporary residencies before reaching a place of resettlement. These steps, which might be undertaken illegally, also can involve considerable danger and expense.[7] Although refugees decide to leave or not to return to their country of origin due to expulsive political pressures, their choice of country to live in exile might be influenced by institutional and/or individual attractions.[8] For instance, the process of step migration from South to North is greatly facilitated at the individual level by the presence of social and kinship networks in the receiving country. Once in place, social networks—especially within ethnic enclaves—generate their own "chain migration" incentives.[9] Moreover, the admission practices of receiving countries can encourage entry or present a major barrier to further movement. Finally, third-country resettlement can be the end result of chance encounters and/or the perceived lack of any alternative.

When the locational moves of newcomers take place *within* the country of (re)settlement, the process is referred to as secondary migration. Secondary-migration outcomes are likely to be affected by the dynamics of immediate- and extended-family reunification, the presence or absence of social- and cultural-support systems, access to acceptable employment, and the availability of appropriate housing. Although frequently overlooked, the reasons for not moving also are important in analyzing the extent of secondary migration among refugee populations.[10]

The final potential step in the migration process is repatriation. This chapter treats refugee step migration from the time of departure from the homeland through actual and expected secondary movement within the United States. Repatriation is the subject of Part 4 of the book.

Cuban Migration North

With the exception of some émigrés who entered via Spain and Costa Rica, Cuban refugees have migrated directly to the United States. They have arrived in three distinct waves that closely correspond to a departure vintage.

The First Vintage and Wave

The first vintage of exiles departed following the success of the revolution in 1959,[11] the nationalization of industries in October 1960, and Fidel Castro's moves to create a Marxist-Leninist political order in 1961. This group included discredited political figures in the Batista government and capitalists who had benefitted from the penetration of U.S. capital—the "top layers of prerevolutionary society."[12] The earliest arrivals made their own way north "in an anticipatory refugee movement, spurred by Cuba's nationalization of American industry, agrarian reform laws, and the United States' severance of diplomatic and economic ties with Cuba."[13] Some entered with legal immigrant visas. Others refused to return when their temporary nonimmigrant visas expired and additional migrants "came with no documentation at all."[14] Cuban exiles began to reach Miami, the closest U.S. city, in larger numbers during 1961 and the first nine months of 1962.[15] This second phase of the initial wave of Cuban migration concluded in October 1962 with the cessation of regular flights from Havana to Miami due to the missile crisis and the U.S. blockade. The 1961–1962 group encompassed "middle merchants and middle management, landlords, middle-level professionals, and a considerable number of skilled unionized workers. Members of the economic elite that had earlier been reluctant to leave also departed."[16] In comparison with the Cuban population as a whole, the exiles who reached the United States between 1959 and 1962 "were disproportionately well educated, white, and of upper-echelon occupations and income."[17]

The first wave tended to settle in the Miami metropolitan area, where a majority of the newly arriving exiles were reunited with relatives and close friends.[18] Moreover, "as the refugee community mushroomed and as an atmosphere of 'little Havana' grew in certain sections of Miami, a self-sustaining dynamic of refugee inflow was established."[19]

The Second Vintage and Wave

Over the next few years, a relatively small number of Cubans escaped in boats and rafts and managed to reach the shores of Key West, Florida.[20] The second major wave of refugees from Cuba began to arrive in 1965 with the organization of "freedom flights" from Varadero to Miami in response to the Castro regime's announced willingness to allow the emigration of persons who had families in the U.S.A. and President Lyndon

Johnson's "open door" policy. When the airlift ended in 1973, more than one quarter of a million Cuban exiles had entered the United States.[21]

The social composition of the second vintage differed markedly from the first. Administrative and clerical employees, skilled and semi-skilled workers, and small merchants predominated in the second wave. By 1970, only 12 percent of the arriving Cubans were managers and professionals; more than half came from laborer, service-worker, and agricultural-worker backgrounds.[22]

Although the "freedom flights" had ended, migrants from the second vintage who had first lived in Spain—including a sizeable proportion of the service workers and merchants dispossessed by the Castro regime's extensive nationalization of small businesses—continued to reach the United States from 1973 through 1975 under special parolee status.[23] These exiles were older than the median age of the Cuban population on arrival; they also were overwhelmingly white and Roman Catholic. Roughly 10 percent had visited this country prior to their final departure from the island. Most had several relatives and/or close friends here. The overwhelming majority of this group settled in the greater Miami area and planned to remain there.[24]

The Third Vintage and Wave

After the arrival of exiles who had fled to Spain, the flow of Cuban refugees essentially ceased until the spring of 1980.[25] Following mass demands for political asylum at the Peruvian Embassy, the third vintage began to pour out of Cuba. Assisted by relatives who sent boats from Florida to Mariel Harbor, this wave, which included "social undesirables" forced to leave by government officials, eventually brought another 125,000 Cubans to the United States.[26] The periodic arrival of third-wave exiles continued on a smaller scale throughout the 1980s.[27]

The Mariel exodus involved roughly the same proportion of professionals and craft workers as the second wave did, but fewer service workers and administrators. Robert Bach adds that "the latest wave had an average level of education of approximately eight to nine years, similar to the arrivals in the 1970s and still higher than the average education of the Cuban population."[28] The third wave differed dramatically from its predecessors, however, in that it encompassed a high proportion of semi-skilled and unskilled laborers (roughly 45 percent) and black Cubans (about 40 percent), and because of the heavy representation of young males who had been raised under the revolution.[29]

146

Overall Outcome

Given that nearly all Cuban refugees secured first asylum in the United States, the departure vintages largely coincide with the three arrival waves. This situation heightens the cleavages among the three groups, however. Indeed, one's date of departure from the island provides a common basis for intra-community class and political distinctions based on vintage that bear little relevance to life in the United States. For instance, "they tend to blame each other for having left too soon or stayed too late."[30]

Cuban step migration also is unique in that a single destination point—the Miami metropolitan area—has functioned as a magnet for the overwhelming majority of exiles. Many of the others who initially settled in northern states later opted to relocate in Miami.[31]

Indochinese Step Migration

Although most Indochinese refugees also have resettled in the U.S.A., the transit process has become progressively longer, less direct, and more difficult. Corporations, including ESSO, American Express, and the Chase Manhattan Bank, brought roughly 5,000 Vietnamese employees directly to the United States prior to the fall of Saigon.[32] The first post-revolution vintage left Vietnam under panic conditions associated with the U.S. evacuation. Most members of this group spent time in processing camps in the Pacific and in the continental United States prior to resettlement in local communities with the assistance of voluntary agencies.[33]

Subsequent vintages of refugees from Vietnam, Cambodia, and Laos have encountered long stays in temporary holding camps in Southeast Asia. Poor living conditions typically prevail in these camps—including "little security, limited supplies, and limited opportunity for planning a future in a country of final asylum."[34] The increasing number of Vietnamese who fled by boat starting in 1978 faced additional dangers and insecurity at the hands of regional pirates and inhospitable landing-country governments.[35] Up to half of the boat people have drowned at sea or perished at the hands of attackers "during their journey in search of freedom and compassion." Nguyen Manh Hung adds that "even if they survived the angry waves, mechanical failure, the lack of food and water, multiple robberies, assaults, and rapes, they still had to suffer humiliation, mistreatment, and possibly internment by the countries of first asylum."[36]

Vintages and Waves

There have been five discrete refugee vintages from Vietnam. The next sections discuss each departure vintage within the context of the three U.S. waves of arriving refugees from Indochina.

First and Second Waves. Vietnamese who exited prior to the fall of Saigon and during the evacuation arrived in what can be considered the initial wave of Indochinese migration to the United States. The first vintage consisted primarily of high-ranking South Vietnamese government authorities, military officers and other personnel closely associated with Western advisers, employees of U.S. government agencies and corporations as well as of charitable organizations, and the spouses of U.S. citizens and their relations.[37] The initial group of refugees leaving Laos also primarily consisted of highly educated government officials and military officers.[38] The earliest refugee exodus from Cambodia, which occurred in 1975 before the Pol Pot regime consolidated political power, included ethnic Chinese and peasants from the Thailand border region along with ranking officials in the overthrown Lon Nol government and professionals.[39]

According to Gail Kelly, more than half of the first wave of Vietnamese refugees to reach the United States had been "closely associated with the war either as policymakers or as employees or relatives of the American military and intelligence community in Vietnam."[40] They included a sizeable share of the Vietnamese medical community and roughly half of the nearly 18,000 U.S. government employees. Most of the refugees in this initial group had been born in northern Vietnam; many also had been associated with the French colonial presence. To some extent, therefore, this exodus can be viewed as an extension of the 1954 north-to-south movement of refugees within Vietnam.[41]

The second wave encompasses military personnel without rank, low-level public servants and teachers, farmers and fishers, and small merchants.[42] Although they often arrived together, participants in the second wave left Vietnam in two vintages. Some exited in the midst of the chaotic evacuation; a smaller number fled later in modest boats.[43] The second, and much more massive, exodus of Cambodians commenced with Vietnam's invasion of Kampuchea at the end of 1978.[44]

The preponderance of Vietnamese refugees in the two initial waves were male, Catholic, from urban areas and wealthy families, and young in age. They also tended to be highly educated. Roughly 30 percent of the household heads about whom information is available had attended a university and three-fourths possessed some secondary education.[45]

148

Third Wave. The fourth flow from Vietnam consisted primarily of ethnic Chinese who left the country in 1978 and 1979. Many of the prominent businesspersons who exited in this "unofficial departure" vintage registered with government authorities and purchased space on a boat that would be escorted out of Vietnamese territorial waters.[46] The fifth vintage includes both the Vietnamese escapees who arranged their own perilous exit by land or sea and the small number of former employees and others closely associated with the United States whom the post-revolution government has permitted to leave under the orderly departure program (ODP).[47] Both types of exodus continue to occur.[48] This vintage encompasses minor associates of the pre-revolution regime, teachers, clerks, soldiers, peasants, and fishers.[49] In recent years, the boat traffic to Hong Kong increasingly has been "dominated by northern Vietnamese with no ties to the United States or other resettlement countries."[50]

The fourth and fifth vintages merged into a third wave of post-1978 arrivals from camps in Thailand and elsewhere in Southeast Asia.[51] Among the Vietnamese, in particular, the expanded network of overseas settlers has encouraged continued outmigration and facilitated third-country resettlement in the North—especially of extended family members.[52] At the beginning of the 1990s, a substantial volume of new entrants from Vietnam sustained the third wave of Indochinese refugee movement to the United States.

The educational attainments and employment skills of third-wave Indochinese refugees are considerably below those reported by their predecessors. For the Hmong, for instance, "54 percent of the most recent arrivals have no formal education as compared to 20 percent of the early arrivals."[53] Among the recent arrivals from Indochina of all nationalities, 47 percent have completed an elementary education or less; only 27 percent of their predecessors arrived with educational qualifications at this level. Except for Cambodians, participants in the third wave also tend to come from less urbanized places of residence in comparison to the earlier arrivals.[54] Consequently, the latest wave has "consisted of persons with minimal Western acculturation. . . ."[55]

Secondary Migration

Whereas Cuban exiles congregated in the Miami area, the U.S. government initially went to considerable lengths to disperse Vietnamese refugees throughout the country.[56] The Office of Refugee Resettlement endeavored to place Cambodian refugees in clusters located in twelve diverse urban areas.[57] National voluntary agencies (volags) relied upon their

local branches to sponsor or locate sponsors for new arrivals.[58] In the face
of processing pressures, voluntary agencies split extended families and
accepted some sponsorship situations that resulted in the economic
exploitation of refugee labor.[59] Half of the new arrivals found themselves
in states where Vietnamese refugees numbered less than 3,000 in total at
the end of 1975. However, the largest number still managed to settle in
California and in favored urban centers.[60]

One result of the government's initial distribution policy has been high
rates of self-initiated secondary migration and intra-jurisdictional housing
mobility. This has led to the clustering of Indochinese refugees in a few
preferred cities. Refugees from Indochina moved due to problems with
sponsors, the desire to reunify extended families and/or to link up with or
reestablish viable and supportive communities, climatic preferences,
employment prospects, and considerations involving welfare benefits.[61] A
majority of the secondary migrants headed for California. By 1985, about
one-third of the total resettled Indochinese refugee population lived in
California, and roughly three-fourths resided in only twelve states.[62]
According to Nguyen Hung:

> The nation's capital area. . . has a large number of professionals working
> for international organizations and for federal and local governments.
> Texas and California have. . . entertainers, writers, journalists, English-as-
> a-second-language teachers, and blue-collar workers. Ethnic Chinese tend
> to gather in New York and especially in California, where they are
> engaged in the restaurant business, groceries, retail sales, and commercial
> real estate. Southern California, with its warm climate, its large population
> of Vietnamese refugees, its thriving Vietnamese business community along
> Bolsa Avenue, all the important Vietnamese-language newspapers, and the
> possibility to lead a social life close to the one at home, has been called
> by the Vietnamese 'the refugee's capital.' [63]

In sum, initial U.S. resettlement practices paved the way for the
establishment of viable Vietnamese communities in seventeen major cities
and the development of several ethnic enclaves. On the other hand, the
dispersal strategy precluded population concentration in a single area and
delayed the development of an independent political power base by
Indochinese immigrants.[64]

150

Migration from Ethiopia and Iran

Migration from Iran and Ethiopia to the United States has involved a much smaller proportion of the total refugee population than in the Cuban and Indochinese situations. While the opportunities for Iranians, Ethiopians, and Eritreans to secure official resettlement have been more limited than in the cases explored above, exiles from these three communities have discovered and availed themselves of alternative means of protection and/or immigration. For these reasons, the South-North migration steps followed by Iranians, Ethiopians, and Eritreans are more diverse and often stand in sharp contrast to those that characterize post-revolution movements from Cuba and Indochina.

In the case of the three communities of interest here, the step-migration differences between official refugees and other exiles are sufficiently large to require that the two groups be treated separately. The analysis that follows considers resettled refugees first. Émigrés who did not enter the United States with official-refugee status and non returnees are treated next. The final section presents additional findings about the composition of U.S. arrival waves from Iran and Ethiopia.

Resettled Refugees: Vintages and Waves

It is useful to distinguish three basic vintages of political migration from Iran and Ethiopia: pre-revolution, immediate post-revolution, and late post-revolution. In the Iranian case, the first departure interval ends at the beginning of 1979. The second vintage extends from the termination of monarchical rule in 1979 through the consolidation of Ayatollah Khomeini's leadership and the mass execution and exodus of regime opponents in 1981. The third, or late post-revolution, vintage corresponds with the departure interval 1982 to the present time.

Among migrants from Ethiopia, the pre-revolution vintage draws to a close with the overthrow of Emperor Haile Selassie's regime in 1974. This initial interval includes the first major exodus of 46,000 Eritreans into Sudan in 1967.[65] The immediate post-revolution vintage commences in 1974 and concludes with the virtually complete decimation of armed urban opposition and the consolidation of Mengistu Haile Mariam's rule in 1979. The second exit interval also encompasses the escalation of Ethiopian government attempts to impose a military solution on the Eritrean conflict, a costly but rapidly concluded border war with Somalia, and the "Red Terror" episode in Addis Ababa.[66] During this period, the estimated number of refugees from Ethiopia in Sudan increased by about 300,000; hundreds of thousands of others fled to Somalia and Djibouti.[67] The Sudan component of this vintage consisted of highly educated urban political activists connected with the E.P.R.P., Mei'son, the student movement, and the principal national liberation fronts, along with members of the imperial political order and E.D.U. supporters, the victims of armed conflict between government forces and the nationality movements, economic refugees fleeing poverty and famine, and persons who escaped from a labor camp, involuntary relocation scheme, or threat of military conscription.[68]

The final vintage extends from 1980 until the present time. More than 300,000 Eritreans and Ethiopians have fled to Sudan during this interval, with the largest exodus occurring between 1984 and 1986.[69] In the Ethiopian as well as the Iranian cases, the pre-revolution vintage involved a comparatively small number of exiles and massive outmigration occurred during both the immediate and late post-revolution intervals.

Exiles from Iran and Ethiopia did not gain admission as official refugees as quickly as their Cuban and Vietnamese predecessors did. In fact, the U.S. government did not accept Iranians under the resettlement program until 1983.[70] Nearly 4,000 Iranian refugees entered this country between FY 1983 and FY 1984. New arrivals, processed primarily in Europe, escalated rapidly thereafter. Over the next three years, 13,613 official refugees from Iran arrived in the United States.[71]

The Immigration and Naturalization Service allowed some Ethiopians and Eritreans to enter the country as seventh-preference (refugee) immigrants by the late 1970s.[72] Many others joined the initial wave immediately following enactment of the Refugee Act in 1980. The larger second post-revolution wave of official refugees covers the peak years from 1982 to 1984 through the present. Between 1982 and 1987, 12,551 resettled refugees from Ethiopia arrived in the United States.[73] Annual admissions have declined substantially in recent years, however. This is primarily because INS circuit riders in Sudan usually only approve applicants with U.S. family ties—a criterion that few Africans can meet.[74]

Drawing on data gathered from a sample of official refugee household heads from Iran and Ethiopia,[75] we find that the U.S. resettlement program only encompasses the two post-revolution vintages. At the time of data collection in late 1984, 63 percent of the sample of admitted refugees from Ethiopia and 60 percent of those from Iran had exited the sending country in the latest interval. Virtually all of the others left in the immediate post-revolution vintage.[76] Furthermore, all of the sampled Iranian refugees and nearly 70 percent of the the resettled group from Ethiopia—including 84 percent of the Eritreans—arrived in the United States during the second wave (i.e., after 1981).[77]

The results from the Refugee Data Center bio-data sample of household heads who reached the U.S.A. by 1984 enable us to present some interesting comparisons between the two post-revolution vintages from Iran and Ethiopia and between the first and second waves admitted from Ethiopia. The next sections compare these vintages and waves by nationality, occupation, education, English language ability, and family ties.

Nationality. Among those for whom information about vintage is available, Eritreans constitute a majority of the resettled refugees who fled from Ethiopia in the late post-revolution period. Table 4.1 also indicates that there are few Oromo and "others" in this group. In contrast, the distribution by ethnicity is rather evenly balanced within the immediate post-revolution vintage.

Table 4.1 Ethnicity of Refugee Household Heads from Ethiopia, by Vintage and Wave

| Migration Interval | Ethnicity | | | | |
	Eritrean	Amhara	Tigrean	Oromo	Other
Vintages					
% 1980 or before (N=148)	29.7%	30.4%	23.6%	10.1%	6.1%
% 1981-1984 (N=201)	50.2	28.9	17.4	2.5	1.0
Waves					
% 1981 or before (N=166)	16.9	35.5	16.9	12.7	18.1
% 1982-1984 (N=339)	43.7	25.7	18.6	5.0	7.1

Source: RDC Bio-data sample.

There are striking differences by wave. In this case, we observe (Table 4.1) that refugee household heads identified as Amhara constitute a plurality (36 percent) of the first wave. The rest of this arrival group is roughly evenly split among Eritreans, Tigreans, Oromo, and the combined category of other ethnic groups. Eritreans clearly predominate within the second wave, however. Among those who arrived between 1982 and 1984, 44 percent are Eritrean. During this interval, only 26 percent of the entering refugee household heads are Amhara.[78] The representation of Tigrean refugees remains constant during both waves, but the proportion of Oromo and "others" declines dramatically over time.

Home-Country Occupation. The Table 4.2 data reveal that there are few differences in the principal home-country occupational backgrounds of

Table 4.2 Home-Country Occupational Background of Refugee Household Heads from Iran and Ethiopia, by Vintage

	Vintage			
	Iran		Ethiopia	
Principal Home-Country Occupation	%'82 or prior (N=87)	%'83, '84 (N=130)	%'80 or prior (N=140)	%'81- '84 (N=243)
Professal, top policy maker	11.5%	9.2%	.7%	1.6%
Owner, mgr large business	14.9	7.7	2.1	0.0
Pub servant, teacher, med worker	21.8	25.4	20.7	23.9
Trader, owner small business	5.7	6.2	10.0	6.6
Skilled worker	10.3	13.1	5.7	2.5
Secretarial	0.0	3.8	7.1	9.1
Farmer, worker	5.7	3.1	31.4	17.3
Student only	24.1	21.5	13.6	35.0
Unemployed, homemaker	5.7	10.0	8.6	4.1

Source: RDC Bio-data sample.

immediate and late post-revolution vintage refugees from Iran and Ethiopia who had been resettled in this country by 1984. The most interesting changes are the decline in large businesspersons in the Iranian case and the decrease in exiting farmers and workers (from 31 to 17 percent) within the Ethiopian sample.

In contrast to the published findings for post-revolution refugees from Cuba and Indochina, Table 4.3 shows that there is no substantial decline among household heads from Ethiopia arriving during the second wave in terms of the proportion from high-status occupational backgrounds and no significant increase in the percentage who were farmers and laborers.[79] The only changes are the increase in former students entering as official

154

refugees after 1981 and the decrease in homemakers and the unemployed
from the first to the second wave.

Table 4.3   Home-Country Occupational Background of Refugee Household Heads
from Iran and Ethiopia, by Wave

	Wave		
	Iran	Ethiopia	
Principal Home	%'82-'84	%'81 or prior	%'82-'84
Country Occupation	(N=218)	(N=175)	(N=375)
Professal, top policy maker	10.6%	1.7%	1.7%
Owner, mgr large business	10.6	3.4	.8
Pub servant, teacher, med worker	23.9	23.4	20.8
Trader, owner small business	6.0	7.4	7.2
Skilled worker	11.9	6.3	4.8
Secretarial	2.3	12.0	12.4
Farmer, worker	4.1	18.3	20.3
Student only	22.5	13.1	26.9
Unemployed, homemaker	8.3	14.3	5.3

Source: RDC Bio-data sample.

Educational Attainments. Table 4.4 displays the educational attainments
of the sampled refugees by vintage and wave. We discover, first, that the
late post-revolution vintage from Ethiopia does not conform to the pattern
of declining educational attainments reported for other Third World refugee
migrations.[80]   In comparison with the initial post-revolution group of
political migrants, however, the latest vintage from Iran "tends to be
younger and less highly educated. . . ."[81]

In terms of arrival interval, the Table 4.4 findings indicate that a higher
proportion of second-wave than first-wave refugee household heads from
Ethiopia had at most completed a primary education (26 percent versus 17
percent).[82]   On the other hand, there are more university-educated persons
in the second wave than in the first group (9 percent and 3 percent).

Table 4.4   Educational Attainments of Refugee Household Heads from Iran and
Ethiopia, by Vintage and Wave

Vintages and Waves by Country of Origin	% Primary or less	% Some Post-prim	% Complt Sec or equiv	% Some Post-sec	% Univ 1st or Adv degree
Iranian Vintages					
% 1982 or earlier (N=88)	2.3%	0.0%	47.7%	13.6%	36.4%
% likely 1983, 1984 (N=129)	3.1	0.0	59.7	7.8	29.5
Ethiopian Vintages					
% 1980 or earlier (N=148)	33.8	31.8	19.6	13.5	1.4
% 1981-1984 (N=243)	23.5	21.8	22.2	18.9	13.6
Iranian Waves					
% 1982-1984 (N=218)	2.8	0.0	54.6	10.1	32.6
Ethiopian Waves					
% 1981 or earlier (N=181)	16.6	26.5	33.7	19.9	3.3
% 1982-1984 (N=381)	26.2	24.7	22.3	17.6	9.2

Source: RDC Bio-data sample.

English-Language Ability. The data on the English-language ability of the Ethiopian sample presented by vintage and wave in Table 4.5 are interesting in a couple of respects. First, the pre-1981 vintage contains a higher proportion of non-literate refugees than the late post-revolution vintage does. Nevertheless, the proportion of illiterate refugees arriving in the first wave of resettlement is less than it is for those entering in the second wave. This finding strongly suggests that the increase in non-literate refugees from Ethiopia resettled in the second wave is a result of delayed admission rather than later departure from the home country. Further evidence along the same lines can be found in the tendency for fluent English-language speakers to be less heavily represented in the immediate post-revolution vintage than in the later vintage, but to be admitted in higher proportion during the first wave of resettlement from Ethiopia than in the second.

156

Table 4.5   English-Language Ability of Refugee Household Heads from Iran and Ethiopia, by Vintage and Wave

Vintages and Waves by Country of Origin	Fluent	English Ability (V) Good, Fair	Poor; Literate	Not Literate
Iranian Vintages				
% 1982 or earlier (N=86)	48.8%	7.0%	32.6%	11.6%
% likely 1983, 1984 (N=129)	40.3	.8	38.0	20.9
Ethiopian Vintages				
% 1980 or earlier (N=148)	16.2	31.1	29.1	23.6
% 1981-1984 (N=242)	25.2	32.2	26.0	16.5
Iranian Waves				
% 1982-1984 (N=215)	43.7	3.3	35.8	17.2
Ethiopian Waves				
% 1981 or earlier (N=181)	27.6	34.8	26.0	11.6
% 1982-1984 (N=379)	18.2	37.5	25.6	18.7

Source: RDC Bio-data sample.

Family Ties.   One result that is consistent with expectations based upon the experiences of earlier migrants is the discovery that the principal applicants who left Ethiopia in the late post-revolution interval are more likely to possess a close relative (sibling, spouse, parent, child) already living in the United States than are those who departed in the immediate post-revolution vintage (20 percent versus 10 percent).   However, exactly the same percentage of first- and second-wave refugees admitted from Ethiopia (14 percent) report that they knew of a close relative who resided in the receiving country at the time of application for resettlement.

Resettled Refugees: Strategies and Steps

The D.C./L.A. study included a comprehensive investigation of the step-migration process.   Thus, the responses provided by the 90 refugees in the sample offer valuable insights regarding the steps and strategies which culminated in resettlement in the United States. The discussion that follows rests primarily upon these insights.[83]

The Decision to Leave. Over three-fourths of the resettled Ethiopian refugees in the D.C./L.A. sample (76 percent) made a firm decision to leave the homeland between the time of the Emperor's overthrow and the end of 1979. A slight majority of the Ethiopian respondents left in the initial post-revolution vintage; most of the others exited in the 1980–1984 period (see Table 4.6). In comparison, half of the responding Eritrean refugees reached the decision to flee from Ethiopia in the immediate post-revolution interval. Only 31 percent of the Eritreans actually joined the early vintage (see Table 4.6).[84] For many of the Ethiopian and the Eritrean respondents, then, a

Table 4.6   Vintages and Waves of Resettled Refugee Respondents, by Nationality

Departure and Arrival Intervals	%Iranians (N=10)	%Ethiopians (N=41)	%Eritreans (N=39)
Vintages			
Pre-revol	30.0%		
1979-1981	10.0		
1982-1984	60.0		
Pre-revol		2.4%	5.1%
1974-1979		51.2	30.8
1980-1984		46.3	64.1
Waves			
1983-1984	100.0		
1974-1981		56.1	23.1
1982-1984		43.9	76.9

Source: D.C./L.A. sample.

lengthy time lag existed between the decision to flee the home country and realization of the opportunity to escape.

Table 4.6 also reports on the arrival waves for each group of respondents. As a result of the U.S. government's delay in granting official-refugee recognition to Iranians, all three vintages from that sending country arrived during the second wave. A majority of the sampled Ethiopian refugees entered during the first wave. In contrast, 77 percent of the Eritreans secured third-country resettlement after 1981—a figure that is quite close to the nation-wide proportion (84 percent) for official refugees of Eritrean nationality.

The First Step. Most refugees from Iran and Ethiopia first seek refuge in a neighboring country. Many Iranians move within Iran, across the border, and to a country of temporary asylum with the help of an expensive and risky underground chain of linked agents. According to Mohammad Amjad, "smugglers are the best source of escaping to the outside world for those who can afford spending large sums of money. It costs between three and fifteen thousand dollars to use the services of smugglers."[85] The principal countries of first asylum for Iranian refugees have been Turkey, Afghanistan, Pakistan,[86] and, less frequently, India.

Eritreans generally flee to Sudan. Nearly all of the Eritrean refugees in the D.C./L.A. sample (97 percent) had first sought asylum in Sudan. Ethiopians usually escape to Sudan, Somalia, and Djibouti; occasionally, Ethiopian exiles initially seek refuge in Kenya. A majority (58 percent) of the sampled Ethiopian refugees had first lived in Sudan after fleeing from the home country; another 32 percent had sought asylum elsewhere in the Horn of Africa. In some cases, a non-proximate country, usually in Europe, provides the first refuge for an Iranian, Ethiopian, or Eritrean later accepted under the U.S. resettlement program.[87]

The experiences of Ethiopians and Eritreans in Sudan reveal a great deal about the first and subsequent steps in the refugee-migration process. The trip to Sudan often proves to be harsh and risky. In some cases, families have been forced to sell their property, including their homes, in order to finance the fees charged by guides who lead the journey of a son or daughter through inhospitable terrain across the border with Sudan.[88]

Spontaneous border settlements have existed since the outbreak of fighting in the Eritrean liberation struggle.[89] While the flight of rural refugees tends to be a single-step phenomenon, most urban exiles engage in multiple-step migration. The most highly educated urban migrants usually end up moving on to Khartoum, the nation's capital, in search of employment and third-country resettlement.[90]

First Asylum in Sudan. In 1984, about 80 percent of the refugees from Ethiopia inhabited spontaneous residential circumstances; that is, they were "self-settled and lived scattered among the local population."[91] The remaining 22 percent resided in 23 organized settlements in eastern and central Sudan operated since 1980 by the Sudanese government with international assistance. There are two major categories of organized settlement. In the *land settlements*, refugee families are awarded small plots and expected to subsist through food-crop cultivation, animal husbandry, and occasional wage labor. In the *wage-earning settlements* located in close proximity to large-scale commercial farms or government agricultural schemes, they survive by providing unskilled labor.[92] Exile political organizations provide assistance and educational programs, mobilize refugees and help them preserve their sense of identity, and mediate on their behalf when they must interact with domestic and international agencies.[93]

Upon arrival in Sudan, the refugee from Ethiopia confronts the need to adapt to a different language and culture as well as the challenge of basic survival. "When I entered Kassala," explains an Eritrean who today directs a large state-government program in Nevada, "I had no money, could not speak the language, did not know the culture. I stood in front of a bakery. When people left with bread in their bags, I begged them to give me a piece. Since I could not speak their language, I had to use body language. It was the first time in my life to beg."

Shelter and subsistence top the list of initial problems reported by respondents in six Sudanese settlement sites.[94] Lack of free health care also negatively affects refugees living outside of organized settlements. In two rural spontaneous sites studied by Mekuria Bulcha, 30 percent of the children in the sampled refugee households died within the first year and 20 percent of all family members perished within the space of four years.[95] Laws restricting refugee movement within Sudan and the acquisition of work permits and licences present additional problems. Finally, many are affected by the psychological burdens of separation from close family and isolation from the homeland community that previously provided one's sense of belonging and identity.[96]

Mekuria Bulcha's 1982 interviews in rural Sudan revealed that "above two-thirds of the respondents were unable to achieve economic self-reliance and were therefore on the brink of starvation." Families led by women are the most vulnerable since the rate of unemployment is much higher among female than male household heads.[97] Most household heads rely upon seasonal agricultural employment for five to six months in "good" years. Wages are low and exploitation is widespread.[98] Only 40 percent of all households retained any income after meeting food and shelter expenses alone.[99] Most refugee families are locked in long-term economic dependency and destitution. According to Mekuria, "the incidence of material poverty was as frequent among those who had been in the Sudan between 4 and 8 years as those who had been there just a year or two."[100]

Khartoum's refugees face comparable problems to those experienced by their compatriots living in eastern Sudan. At least 20 percent of these urban refugees were unemployed in 1984, and a higher proportion struggled to subsist through underemployment in low-paying work. In one large-scale survey, "over two-thirds of the sample reported that they received less daily income than is required to provide food, shelter, and basic necessities."[101] Skilled urban refugees, often lacking documents authorizing residence in Khartoum, are subject to exploitation at the hands of Sudanese landlords and employers as well as to arrest and involuntary relocation.[102] Ethiopian and Eritrean refugees are routinely refused credit, barred by law from owning fixed assets, and blamed for Khartoum's economic problems.[103] Marginally integrated into the receiving society and economy, many seek "an external solution to their survival problems." Meanwhile, the Sudanese government provides no assistance to urban refugees and they are virtually ignored by international donor agencies.[104]

The focus on refugee migration to Sudan yields important insights. First, most of the Eritreans and Ethiopians who have sought protection in Sudan have experienced a decline in their standard of living. Nearly everyone left all of their possessions—property and goods—behind. In short, "flight entails instant impoverishment"—even for those who were wealthy in the country of origin.[105] The incidence of unemployment and underemployment is much higher in the new location than prior to flight. When asked to compare their standard of living in Sudan with their pre-flight condition, 74 percent of Mekuria Bulcha's respondents stated that they had become poorer; only 6 percent answered that they were better off.[106]

Downward Occupational Mobility. Using data gathered from the RDC bio-data files, it is possible to document the extent of downward occupational mobility in the place of first asylum that occurred among the principal applicants accepted for refugee resettlement from Ethiopia. Table 4.7 reveals a substantial decline in the proportion of employed persons performing administrative, educational, and skilled work among this group of official refugees. At least 16 percent of the sample had held no remunerated employment in the country of application.[107] Nearly half of the reporting principal applicants had engaged in domestic service or another form of unskilled labor in the country of temporary asylum. If we limit attention to resettled refugees from Sudan, the proportion employed as domestics or in other unskilled capacities increases from 19 percent in Ethiopia prior to departure to 52 percent in the country of first asylum.

The occupational history reported by the sample of refugees assisted by Church World Service (CWS) is even more revealing of the extent of

Table 4.7   Principal Type of Work Performed in Home Country and Country of
Application, by Principal Applicants for Refugee Resettlement from
Ethiopia Sampled in 1984

Type of Work	%Home Country (N=429)	%Country of Application (N=280)
Profssnl, top policy maker	2.1%	.7%
Mgr, owner large bus	2.1	.4
Pub servant, teacher, soc worker	28.2	11.1
Skilled worker	6.8	1.8
Secretarial, clerical	15.6	11.4
Trader, small bus owner	9.3	6.8
Farmer	4.4	2.5
Unskilled laborer	19.1	27.9
Domestic helper	1.9	21.4
Unemployed, homemaker	10.5	16.1
Total	100.0	100.1

Source: RDC Bio-data sample.

downward mobility that occurs following flight to a neighboring country. About 65 percent of the Ethiopian and Eritrean refugees in the CWS sample were not employed in the country of temporary protection; only 10 percent had been unemployed and 30 percent never employed in the homeland. Whereas about half of the CWS-assisted refugees from both communities had functioned in a professional, business, administrative, teaching, or skilled-labor capacity in Ethiopia, only 17 percent of the Eritreans and 13 percent of the Ethiopians occupied such roles in the country of temporary asylum.

Step-migration Motives. Among the resettled refugees interviewed in the D.C./L.A. study, nearly two-thirds reported that they had no intention of migrating to the United States at the time they fled from their country of origin. The absence of a prior inclination to attempt to migrate to the U.S.A. is particularly widespread among Eritreans (72 percent). Conceivably, then, most of the official refugees in these three exile communities might have opted to live in the United States due to expulsive forces in the country of temporary asylum.[108]   When we examine the unstructured explanations they offered for seeking admission under the U.S. resettlement program, however, we discover that over half (58 percent) mention U.S. opportunities and conditions by way of explanation.   Another 21 percent cite the presence of family members or relatives in the receiving country.[109]   Only 11 percent of the 72 responding refugees (15 percent of the Eritreans and 8 percent of the Ethiopians) directly refer exclusively to living conditions in the country of application.   The rest (10 percent) state that they had no other viable alternative.   Box 4.1 contains illustrative statements regarding the reasons why official refugees from the three study communities decided to seek entry to the United States.

The respondents' open-ended indications that perceived conditions in the receiving country provided powerful incentives for step-migration decision making are reinforced by their reactions to a more explicit set of standardized items.   Table 4.8 indicates that the interviewees' general

Table 4.8   Important Considerations in Respondents' Decision to Apply for Refugee Resettlement in the United States, by Nationality

"Important" Considerations	% Total (N=90)	%Iranians (Total N=10)	%Ethiopians (Total N=41)	%Eritreans (Total N=39)
Lack any option	48.9%	40.0%	51.2%	48.7%
Genl impression condits in US	46.1	30.0	45.0	51.3
Presence in US of fam/frnds	30.0	70.0	22.0	28.2
Nature, reputat US educ sys	27.8	10.0	31.7	28.2
Unable provide for self/fam welfare	23.6	10.0	19.5	31.6
Income/empmt opports in US	23.3	50.0	22.0	17.9
Fear of retributn place temp asylum	21.1	20.0	19.5	23.1
Experiences of fam/frnds	20.2	70.0	12.2	15.8

Source: D.C./L.A. sample.

impression of conditions and opportunities in the United States played an important role in migration-decision making among roughly half of the Ethiopian and Eritrean refugees.   The popularity of this explanation is rivaled only by the "lack of any other option" item.   Conditions in the country of temporary asylum at the time of application, although typically

Box 4.1
Selected Respondent Explanations for Seeking U.S. Admission
Under the Refugee Resettlement Program

Iranians

I had heard that I could work in U.S. and earn my living expenses. I thought I could earn enough money to register in a university.

Availability of jobs and my familiarity with the English language.

My oldest brother lived in USA. He had a job and could afford to support me and find a job for me.

As a Kurd, I had a good chance of being granted refugee status. The main reason was because I had a better chance of being secure from retribution and a better chance to make contacts that would serve the cause of the Iranian people in general and the Kurdish issue in particular.

Ethiopians and Eritreans

I appreciated the existence of freedom and education opportunities.

Because I thought that if I have to live in exile, the United States of America would be the best place to exercise my profession and to enjoy the freedom of human rights.

For better life and peace.

I knew a lot about the U.S.; the freedom of speech, etc. I knew a lot of Americans through Kagnew Air Force Base. I could have a decent life in U.S. It would have been difficult to start all over again in France because I didn't know the language. If I could go to school, I knew that it would be an English one in the U.S. and that the U.S. is an English-speaking country.

I had known the country before; I didn't want to take any other chances.

I was informed that the U.S. resettled refugees and helped to rehabilitate them.

The only foreign language I spoke was English; so I decided it would be easier for me to come to a country where I could easily communicate.

Because my brothers and other relatives were already there.

It was the only chance I got.

Because of the living situation in Sudan.

To continue education, and the desire to escape from any physical danger that the Ethiopian government could cause to my life.

harsh and insecure, turn out not to be especially influential in the decision to seek official-refugee status in the United States. In addition to the two items related to the country of application that are listed in Table 4.8, between 82 and 94 percent of the refugee respondents replied in the negative when asked if the following factors played an important part in the decision to apply for admission under the U.S. refugee-resettlement program: camp conditions, discrimination in the country of temporary asylum, inability to use their highest educational training or to practice their profession, and the desire to avoid participating in actions directed against the post-revolution regime in the home country.[110]

The findings do indicate, however, that the type of settlement experienced in the country of first asylum exerted an important influence on third-country resettlement *opportunities* among these official refugees from Ethiopia and Iran. In the D.C./L.A. study, 67 per cent of the Iranians, 76 percent of the Ethiopians, and 87 percent of the Eritreans had never inhabited a designated refugee camp. These figures suggest that placement in a camp situation in the country of first asylum proved to be detrimental, and living in "spontaneous" settlements or in urban areas to be advanta-geous, in terms of the refugee's chance of third-country resettlement.[111]

Among those who could identify a single step-migration consideration that outweighed all others, a slight plurality selected "lack of any option" (29 percent). Two receiving-country attractions (general impression regarding life in the U.S.A. and the presence of family and friends) each are ranked as the overriding consideration in step-migration decision making by 24 percent of the resettled refugees.[112]

Step-migration Strategies. The limited number of admission slots allocated, along with the considerable length of time that typically lapses between exit from the homeland and official resettlement in the United States, provoke several important questions about step migration in the Iranian, Ethiopian, and Eritrean cases. Which countries are resettled members of these three exile communities usually admitted from and what are the prevailing transit routes? How do official refugees succeed in gaining entry to the United States? How important is the presence of family and relatives in the admission process? These questions are addressed in the paragraphs below with principal reference to resettled refugees from Ethiopia.[113]

Securing admission to the United States under the refugee-resettlement program requires participation in a competitive application process. The D.C./L.A. respondents achieved impressive success rates on their initial attempt to obtain official-refugee status. Fully 90 percent of the Eritrean refugees, 89 percent of the Iranians, and 80 percent of the Ethiopians secured admission with their first application.

In many cases, success in gaining entry hinges on utilizing the appropriate admission strategy. This step in the migration process demands some of the same skills that facilitated exit from the home country. Convincing the screening agents—both voluntary agency and U.S. government personnel—that one is an authentic and qualified refugee often presents the principal challenge to the would-be official refugee. The most enterprising individuals cultivate inside contacts and/or utilize the compatriot-community grapevine to discover and refine the stories that secure the highest rate of acceptance. Some resort to covering up participation in anti-regime political organizations whose members the U.S. government has disqualified for admission on the grounds that they have engaged in terroristic acts or in the persecution of others.[114] After an initial rejection, some would-be refugees adopt a complete change of identity and tactics. Forged travel documents are widely available for this purpose.[115]

In the resettlement game, location can be the decisive variable. Success rates in securing admission to the United States frequently fluctuate widely from country to country and from year to year. Prospective and previously unsuccessful applicants quickly learn about places of application where the odds favor admission. When resources permit, some attempt to employ various legal and illegal step-migration strategies aimed at moving closer to favorable application points.

In the case of refugees from Ethiopia, Sudan has provided the location where the greatest number of applicants are awarded third-country resettlement in the United States. Table 4.9 shows that about 60 percent of the principal applicants granted official-refugee status by 1984 entered via Sudan. Since the "R.D.C. Summary" column includes family-reunification cases while the bio-data sample does not, we can infer from the results set forth in this table that individuals petitioning to be reunited with close relations are the most successful when they apply for resettlement from Italy. Most of the unrelated applicants admitted from Europe arrived in the country of application in transit from the Soviet Union, an Eastern European country, or Cuba.[116] Since 1984, the admission of official refugees under the U.S. program increasingly has been restricted to persons who can demonstrate the presence of caring family members who already are legally settled in the receiving country.[117]

A number of particularly enterprising Ethiopian and Eritrean refugees also managed to secure admission from Europe or Canada after first living

Table 4.9   Refugees from Ethiopia Resettled by 1984 in the United States, by Country Admitted From

Country Admitted from	RDC Summary (All Refugees)		RDC Bio-data (Household Heads)		D.C./L.A. Sample	
	N	%	N	%	N	%
Sudan	4,475	56.4%	359	62.2%	49	62.0%
Italy	2,181	27.5	23	4.0	12	15.2
Europe (other than It, Fr)	432	5.4	42	7.3	5	6.3
Djibouti	254	3.2	87	15.1	7	8.9
France	188	2.4	--	-----	4	5.1
Somalia	78	1.0	19	3.3	1	1.3
Other	323	4.1	47	8.1	1	1.3
Total	7,931	100.0%	577	100.0%	79	100.1%

Source: RDC; D.C./L.A. sample.

for a time in the Horn of Africa.[118]   Information available from the Church World Service sample of assisted refugees arriving via Europe allows us to estimate the length of time involved at various stages in this step-migration process.   The majority of resettled refugees assisted by CWS first fled to a neighboring African country.[119]   Those who left Ethiopia in the early and mid 1970s spent more time living in the country of first entry/protection than did those who exited in later years.   For instance, the 12 CWS-assisted refugees who left Ethiopia in 1976 lived, on average, for 3.5 years in the country they first entered.   For those who departed in 1977, 1978, 1979, 1980, and 1981 (N=19, 20, 23, 16, 31), the averages are 2.6, 2.3, 2.1, 1.8, and 1.3, respectively.   The CWS findings also show a relatively steady decrease in the amount of time that lapsed between the date of departure from Ethiopia and the year of application for U.S. resettlement.   Among the principal applicants who left the sending country in 1978, 1979, 1980, and 1981, for instance, the average number of years from time of departure to date of application is 3.2, 2.2, 1.7, and 1.4, respectively.[120]   In virtually all of the sampled CWS-assisted cases, U.S. government gatekeepers approved requests for official-refugee status within a year.[121]   Most successful applicants arrived no longer than 12 months after their request for resettlement had been approved by the INS and nearly everyone reached the United States within eighteen months.[122]

These study results allow us to estimate the total length of time involved in the cross-national step-migration process among successful Ethiopian and Eritrean applicants for refugee status who initially sought protection in a neighboring African country and arrived via Europe. Those who left Ethiopia in the pre- and immediate post-revolution vintages typically spent five years or longer outside of the sending country before they landed on U.S. soil. However, the duration of the transit process shortened considerably for successful applicants who had departed in 1979 or later.[123]

In 1983 and 1984, nearly all of the Iranian refugees resettled in the United States arrived from Europe—especially from Spain.[124] However, 99 percent of the admitted principal applicants for whom data are available (N=109) had first sought protection in a country other than the one they resided in when they finally secured permission to enter the United States. Most of the resettled refugees from Iran initially had fled to Turkey (45 percent) or to Pakistan (35 percent)—countries where the U.S. Immigration and Naturalization Service did not interview candidates for third-country resettlement.[125] Moreover, nearly 25 percent of the successful Iranian applicants had lived in at least three different countries before obtaining admission under the resettlement program.[126] As a result of frequent cross-national movement and the unwillingness of the U.S. government to offer resettlement to Iranians until 1983, the immediate post-revolution vintage experienced a lengthy transition period before arriving as official refugees.

In addition to seeking the most favorable application location, the prospective refugee can attempt to use association with Western institutions as a wedge in gaining access to the resettlement program. In the RDC bio-data sample, for instance, 13 percent of the principal applicants from Ethiopia and over 16 percent of the Iranians possessed at least one personal tie to a Western institution. Over 15 percent of the Iranians had worked for a U.S. or multinational corporation.[127] Three percent of the applicants from Ethiopia had been employed by a U.S. government agency.

A particularly effective strategy for securing third-country resettlement is to work for one of the voluntary agencies that assists refugees in countries of first asylum.[128] John Rogge notes that this situation offers the "advantage of access to information on resettlement or even counseling by well-meaning NGO staff on how best to ensure that. . . [one] be accepted for resettlement."[129] We find, therefore, that an unexpectedly high proportion (8 percent) of the successful applicants from Ethiopia in the

RDC sample (N=387) report that they had been employed by a Western voluntary organization.[130]

We have seen that the U.S. presence of family members and other relatives facilitates acceptance under the resettlement program. Nearly 70 percent of the principal applicants from Ethiopia in the RDC sample gained no benefit from this consideration, however.[131] Only 14 percent of the sampled refugees note that a parent, child, spouse, or sibling resided in the United States at the time of application. A further 17 percent mention a cousin, uncle/aunt, or another distant relation.[132] On the other hand, just over 40 percent of the resettled Ethiopian and Eritrean refugees interviewed in the D.C./L.A. study, and 60 percent of the Iranians, affirm that a member of their extended family had been in the U.S. prior to the date on which they applied for admission under the resettlement program. In this sample, 28 percent of the Eritrean refugees, 12 percent of the Ethiopians, and 40 percent of the interviewed Iranians note that they had a sibling, child, or parent in this country at the time of application. Another 13 percent of the Eritreans, 17 percent of the Ethiopians, and 10 percent of the Iranians refer to a more distant relative. In fact, 20 percent of the Ethiopians and Eritreans report that one of their relatives already had been admitted under the U.S. resettlement program at the time they submitted their own application. Finally, it is interesting with regard to step-migration strategies that approximately one-fourth of the Eritrean and Ethiopian refugees interviewed in Washington, D.C., and two-fifths of the sampled Iranians who had been resettled in the L.A. or D.C. area, confirm that a member of their family had helped them enter this country.

Who Gets In? Comparisons Between Resettled and Non-Resettled Refugees. Only a small proportion of the total number of refugees from Iran and Ethiopia are accepted for resettlement in the North. How do the individual household heads selected by the U.S. INS resemble and/or differ from their compatriots who remain in neighboring countries of temporary asylum? Although the answer to this important question promises to enhance our understanding of the step-migration process, detailed comparative data have not been available in the past. New research findings allow us to address the issue through a focused comparison of resettled and non-resettled refugees from Ethiopia who first received protection in Sudan.

The majority of Eritrean refugees and non Somali-speaking Ethiopians have fled to Sudan. In fact, most of the departing population still dwell within the borders of that neighboring country.[133] In the following comparative analysis, information on refugees who remain in Sudan is drawn from two sources of local field work: Jerry Weaver's 1984 survey of urban refugees from Ethiopia living in the Khartoum area and Mekuria Bulcha's 1982–1983 eastern Sudan sample taken from three organized settlement sites and five spontaneous settlement areas in urban, semi-urban, and rural settings.[134]   For the backgrounds of their third-country counterparts, we refer to findings drawn from the subgroup of 359 resettled-refugee household heads in the 1984 RDC bio-data sample who arrived in the U.S.A. directly from refuge in Sudan.

Table 4.10 presents data on six background characteristics across the three subsets of refugees from Ethiopia.[135]   This table helps us identify the ways in which admitted refugees differ from those who remain in the country of first asylum.   Gender and age are not particularly interesting in this regard, although the household heads admitted by the U.S. government are somewhat more likely to be in their twenties and less likely to be younger.   One striking finding is the tendency for later migrants (i.e., the late post-revolution vintage) to secure resettlement and for the earliest refugees to remain in Sudan.   Table 4.10 also shows that the Amhara and the Christians have succeeded within the Sudan resettlement program in numbers that are disproportionate to their presence in the total pool of refugees living there.   Eritreans and Muslims have been particularly unlikely to obtain third-country resettlement in the United States.

The Table 4.10 data suggest that it is the refugee's educational background, however, that exerts the greatest influence over the prospect of gaining entry to the United States.   For instance, while less than 5 percent of refugees from Ethiopia living in Sudan had attended a university, nearly 20 percent of the resettled household heads had attained this educational level.   At the other end of the educational scale, less than 30 percent of the those in the resettled sample possessed a primary education or less; half of the Khartoum sample and 90 percent of the eastern Sudan group are in this category.

Persons with certain occupational backgrounds also are particularly likely to gain third-country resettlement.   The findings set forth in Table 4.11 indicate that nearly 40 percent of the admitted household heads had worked as a teacher, professional, manager, administrator, secretary, or soldier in Ethiopia; only about 10 percent of those who remained in Sudan reported such occupational backgrounds.   Former subsistence farmers and herders, on the other hand, are the least likely group of migrants to move beyond rural settlements in border regions and are the most underrepresented component of the sending-country labor force in the

170

Table 4.10 Selected Characteristics of Refugees from Ethiopia Still Living in Sudan
and Resettled in the United States by 1984

| | Sudan | | U.S. |
| | Khartoum Study | E. Sudan Study | RDC Bio-data |
Characteristics	(N=1012)	(N=413)	(N=359)
Gender			
Male	90.0%	84.7%	88.9%
Female	10.0[a]	15.3	11.1
Age			
21 or less	21.7	15.3[b]	8.9
22-25	26.8	(44.4[b])	26.3
26-30	24.7		34.4
31 and older	27.3	40.3	30.4
Year Arrived in Sudan			
Prior to 1976	c	10.6	0.0
1976-1979	c	59.6	18.7
1980-1982	c	29.8	63.9
1983-1984	c	----	17.4
Ethnic Identification			
Eritrean	67.1	(59.0[d])	42.2
Tigrean	15.6		22.9
Amhara	14.5	25.0	31.0
Oromo	1.4	16.0	2.8
Other	.4	----	1.1
Religious Identification			
Ethiopian Orthodox			79.8
Other Christian	(82.5)	(80.0)	12.9
Muslim	16.4	20.0	7.3
Educational Attainment			
Completed University	1.3	(2.7)	1.7
Some post-secondary	3.5		16.2
Complt sec or equiv	12.4		24.9
Some post primary	32.1	(7.5)	27.9
Completed primary	21.0	15.0	7.5
Some primary			15.9
No formal	29.2	74.8	5.9

[a]Household heads only.   [b]20 or less; 21-30.
[c]No information available.   [d]Reported only by language spoken.

Source: Weaver, "Sojourners," 149; Mekuria Bulcha, *Flight*, pp. 98, 150, 153-154;
RDC Bio-data sample.

resettled sample. Table 4.11 also suggests that most of the skilled workers in the refugee population managed to gravitate to the capital of the initial receiving country. Although relatively few skilled laborers have been selected for U.S. admission, many have found jobs in the Middle East.[136]

Table 4.11 Homeland Occupational Background of Refugees from Ethiopia Still Living in Sudan and Resettled in the U.S. by 1984

| Homeland Occupation | Sudan | | U.S. |
	Khartoum Study (N=1012)	E.Sudan Study (N=413)	RDC Bio-data (N=345)
Subsistence farmer/herder	7.0%	23.0%	5.5%
Homemaker	18.9	18.9	2.0
Student only	29.2	4.1	22.0
Domestic helper	1.3	6.1	2.3
Unskilled laborer	9.1[a]	11.7	16.8
Trader, artisan	3.6[b]	8.0	5.8
Skilled labor	11.1	.7	2.6
Clerk, secretary	2.0[c]	(d)	9.3
Teacher, clergy	0.0	(d)	11.1
Soldier, police	3.4	(d)	4.1
Public servant	0.0	(d)	10.7
Professional, manager	6.7	(d)	4.0
Other	0.0	8.3	.3
Unemployed	6.8	9.9	4.1
Total	99.1	99.9	100.6

[a]"Service" [b]"Self-employed" [c]"Office" [d]9.2% for all five occupations

Source: Weaver, "Sojourners," 152; Mekuria Bulcha, *Flight*, pp. 155; RDC Bio-data sample.

The suggestive findings reviewed here point to educational and occupational background factors as particularly influential considerations affecting the refugee step-migration process. Although not required to do so by legislation dealing with refugee resettlement, U.S. administrative gatekeepers give preference in the screening process to applicants with backgrounds deemed most conducive to adaptation in the receiving society.[137] It is likely, moreover, that refugees with higher-educational attainments and employment experience in the urban, Westernized sector of the sending country's economy are better prepared than their compatriots are to apply strategies that are effective in securing third-country resettlement in the North.[138]

Resettled Refugees: Secondary Migration

The U.S. government and its authorized resettlement agencies basically followed the dispersed model in the initial location of refugees from Ethiopia.[139] The relocation community placed 21 percent of the 9,486 refugees resettled between August 1980 and the end of September 1984 in the state of California. Over 10 percent initially found themselves in the Washington, D.C., metropolitan area. Texas received 11 percent of the total and New York resettled 7 percent. The placement process scattered the remaining 50 percent among most of the other 47 states in numbers that range from 1 (Utah) to 464 (Illinois).[140] Agencies using the caseworker approach resettled the majority of Ethiopian and Eritrean refugees; church congregations assumed responsibility for most of the others.[141]

Considerable secondary migration occurs among Ethiopian and Eritrean refugees who are separated from their compatriots. Movement within the United States has contributed to the concentration of exiles in a few major urban centers—principally Washington, D.C., Los Angeles, Dallas, and New York City.[142] On 18th Street in the Adams Morgan area of the nation's capital, for instance, one finds an array of Ethiopian and Eritrean restaurants and hears Amharic and Tigrinyan being widely spoken. Data from the D.C. sample provide insights into the factors that have led resettled refugees from Ethiopia to opt for residence in the nation's capital and shed light on their future internal-migration intentions.

The D.C. Case. The majority of official refugees in the D.C. sample originally settled in the nation's capital upon arrival in this country. Three-fourths of the Ethiopians and 85 percent of the Eritreans report that they have never lived anywhere else in the United States. At the time of interview, 35 percent of the Ethiopian refugees had resided in the D.C. area for more than three years, and another 25 percent had lived there for between two and three years. Only 10 percent of the Eritreans had lived in the Washington, D.C., metropolitan area for more than three years.

In contrast to the decisions to become an exile and to seek U.S. resettlement, less than half of the interviewed refugees made their own final decision to settle in the District of Columbia area. Fifty-four percent of the Ethiopians and 62 percent of the Eritreans indicated that a resettlement agency decided on their initial location within the United States. Ten of the 20 Ethiopians and 6 of the 15 Eritreans who *chose* to live in the nation's capital are secondary migrants.

Among the 35 refugee respondents who made or influenced the decision to locate in the D.C. area, 80 percent of the Ethiopians and 87 percent of the Eritreans indicated that the presence of family, relatives, and/or close friends in the area constituted an important consideration in the choice of settlement location. The only other factor rated as important by more than 20 percent of the respondents from either community (33 percent of the Eritreans) is employment and professional prospects. None of the Ethiopian refugees viewed the opportunity to participate in community cultural activities as important, although 17 percent volunteered that the area's status as the nation's capital and its reputation as an international and cultural center had attracted them. When asked to identify the overriding or most important consideration in their decision to select the D.C. area, over two-thirds of both groups indicated the presence of relatives or friends. Employment-related issues served as the overriding consideration in the decision to come or move to Washington, D.C., among 18 percent of the Ethiopians and 13 percent of the Eritrean refugees.

At the time of the survey in 1984, most of the interviewed refugees indicated that they were satisfied or very satisfied with life in the nation's capital. However, 32 percent of the Ethiopian refugees and 26 percent of the Eritreans lacked satisfaction with the city of current residence. When we inquired about their migration intentions, 69 percent of the Eritrean refugees responded that they planned to stay in the local area; 31 percent either intended to move elsewhere or were undecided. The Ethiopian refugees turned out to be less committed to remaining in the D.C. metropolitan area in comparison to the Eritreans. Nearly half (46 percent) revealed that they wanted to move elsewhere or could not make up their mind about whether to stay or move on. These findings suggest that, while a powerful magnet, the nation's capital is not always the terminal point in the step-migration process for resettled refugees from Ethiopia.

In their open-ended explanations for deciding to remain in the area, resettled Ethiopians are most likely to mention educational considerations (37 percent), followed by the presence of family, relatives, and close friends (32 percent) and employment/economic factors (21 percent). Eritrean

refugees favored employment and economic explanations (31 percent); only 19 percent mentioned close relatives or friends and 12 percent referred to matters related to education. Explanations involving educational considerations are the most common type volunteered by refugees who expect to move elsewhere.

Émigrés and Non Returnees: Vintages and Waves

Many exiles from Iran and Ethiopia have arrived in the United States without official status as a resettled refugee. There are two distinct components to this understudied stream of South-North migration: (1) *émigrés*, who, like most official refugees, leave the home country with the intention of living in exile and (2) *non returnees*, who decide to become an exile only after going abroad. The first group are "anticipatory refugees." The latter are sometimes referred to as *sur place* refugees. However, this term implies that only changed conditions at home during the expatriate's stay overseas can provoke the decision not to return.[143] The broader concept of "non returnee" also allows for the situation in which the expatriate himself or herself undergoes changes while abroad that result in the realization that s/he cannot safely return to the home country and, therefore, contribute in a central way to the decision to become an exile.

Three decision/action intervals are of particular interest in the step migration of émigrés and non returnees. They are the date of decision to leave/not to return to the home country, the time of departure from the sending country, and the year of arrival in the receiving land. The findings for the émigrés in the D.C./L.A. sample are presented first in Table 4.12. The results for the Ethiopian and Eritrean respondents indicate that virtually all of the émigrés surveyed decided to leave Ethiopia after the overthrow of the Emperor in 1974. With the exception of a couple of Eritreans, these exiles also departed after the revolution. A plurality of the Eritreans and nearly 70 percent of the Ethiopians belong to the late post-revolution vintage. The Ethiopian émigrés are evenly divided between the first and second post-revolution arrival waves, whereas the Eritreans are scattered among all three waves.

When we turn to the data regarding émigrés from Iran displayed in Table 4.12, we find that a surprisingly high percentage (70 percent) had reached the decision to leave Iran before the overthrow of the Shah. Only 45 percent managed to exit prior to the revolution, however. The others are divided evenly between the immediate and late post-revolution vintages.

Table 4.12 Decision Interval, Departure Interval, and Arrival Interval of Émigré Respondents, by Nationality

Interval	Ethiopians (N=22)	Eritreans (N=9)	Iranians (N=31)
Decision to leave homeland			
Pre-revolution	0.0%	22.2%	70.0%
Post-revolution	100.0	77.8	30.0
Departure from homeland			
Pre-revolution	0.0	22.2	----
1974-1979	31.8	33.3	----
1980-1984	68.2	44.4	----
Pre-revolution	----	----	45.2
1979-1981	----	----	25.8
1982-1984	----	----	29.0
Arrival in U.S.			
1952-1973	0.0	22.2	----
1974-1981	50.0	44.4	----
1982-1984	50.0	33.3	----
1952-1978	----	----	45.2
1979-1982	----	----	29.0
1983-1984	----	----	25.8

Source: D.C./L.A. sample.

Moreover, a plurality of the Iranian émigrés arrived in the pre-revolution wave and most of the others entered the United States in the first post-revolution interval.

Table 4.13 shows that the Iranian non returnees also are the most likely of the three groups to have left the homeland in the pre-revolution period (91 percent) and to have arrived in the United States prior to the overthrow of the Shah (85 percent).   Among non returnees however, the critical threshhold point in terms of both vintage and wave is the decision not to return to the sending country, or *to* become an exile.   Only 16 percent of the Iranian non returnees became exiles prior to the revolution.[144] Fully 96 percent of the Ethiopians and 87 percent of the Eritreans made the decision not to return in the post-revolution interval.

Table 4.13 Departure Interval, Arrival Interval, and Decision Interval of Non-
          Returnee Respondents, by Nationality

Interval	Ethiopians (N=44)	Eritreans (N=16)	Iranians (N=105)
Departure from Homeland			
Pre-revolution	63.6%	87.5%	-
1974-1979	29.5	15.5	-
1980-1984	6.8	0.0	-
Pre-revolution	-	-	90.5%
1979-1981	-	-	5.7
1982-1984	-	-	3.8
Arrival in U.S.			
1952-1973	61.4	68.8	-
1974-1981	34.1	25.0	-
1982-1984	4.5	6.3	-
1952-1978	-	-	84.8
1979-1982	-	-	8.6
1983-1984	-	-	6.7
Decision not to return			
Pre-revolution	4.5	13.3	16.2
Post-revolution	95.5	86.7	83.8

Source: D.C./L.A. sample.

Émigrés and Non Returnees: Strategies and Steps

For the vast majority of émigrés and non returnees in the sample, the
United States is the country of first asylum. This does not necessarily
mean that such migrants move directly to this country from their homeland.

Émigré Steps. About 60 percent of all émigrés interviewed in the
D.C./L.A. study did not live in another country after departing from their
homeland. The remaining 40 percent resided in at least one nation other
than the United States.

Three factors are reported by a majority of the interviewed émigrés to
have played an influential part in their choice of the United States over
other possible countries of destination. These considerations are (1) the
prior U.S. experiences of family members and/or friends; (2) the presence
of family and/or friends in the receiving country; and (3) the general
impression they had concerning conditions in the United States (see Table
4.14). There are differences by nationality in the pattern of responses,

however. For instance, Eritreans are much less likely than the other two groups are to refer to family and friends.

Table 4.14   Important Considerations in Decision to Migrate/Come to the United States, by Nationality

"Important" Considerations	%Total Émigrés (N=48)	%Total Non Rets (N=153)	Iranians		Ethiopians		Eritreans	
			%Émigs (N=27)	%Non Rets (N=101)	%Émigs (N=14)	%Non Rets (N=42)	%Émigs (N=7)	%Non Rets (N=11)
Experience of fam/frds	72.3%	70.7%	96.3%	74.3%	46.2%	63.2%	28.6%	63.6%
Presence in US of fam/frds	64.6	55.6	77.8	64.4	57.1	41.5	28.6	27.3
Genl impress condits in US	59.6	39.9	55.6	35.0	61.5	51.4	71.4	45.5
Nature, reputat US educ sys	48.9	76.0	44.4	76.8	46.2	71.1	71.4	84.6
Income/empmt opports in US	19.1	16.6	25.9	16.8	7.7	13.2	14.3	25.0

Source: D.C./L.A. sample.

Nearly half of the interviewed émigrés report that the nature and reputation of the U.S. higher educational system played an important part in their decision to move here rather than to another country. This consideration is especially likely to have been viewed as important by Eritreans (71 percent). Finally, Table 4.14 shows that U.S. income and employment opportunities served as an important step-migration consideration for only a small minority of the émigrés in the three communities.[145]

The transnational step-migration routes followed by émigrés differ in many cases from those pursued by official refugees. Instead of Pakistan and Turkey, for instance, the vast majority of Iranian émigrés who did not move directly to the United States first lived in Western Europe or Canada after leaving the home country.[146] Nearly half of the Ethiopian émigrés and one-third of the Eritreans who did not migrate directly initially resided outside of the Horn of Africa. The others often followed the same route taken by resettled refugees and entered Sudan before moving on to another country or to the United States.[147]

There are striking differences between the Iranian émigrés intent on living in exile and those from Ethiopia in terms of the length of their sojourn in the country of first residence. Iranians tended to move on quickly from the country of first entry; only 14 percent stayed in the initial transit land for one year or longer. The Ethiopian and Eritrean émigrés, on the other hand, typically lived for two years or longer in the country they first migrated to.[148] Only one of the twelve respondents from Ethiopia in this category had spent less than a year in the place of first residence. Eritreans (14 percent) and Iranians (13 percent) were somewhat more likely than the Ethiopian émigrés (9 percent) were to have resided in at least two other countries in route to the United States.

Non Returnee Steps. Whereas 40 percent of the émigrés had lived elsewhere after departing from Iran or Ethiopia, only 20 percent of the non returnees had not moved directly to the United States. Most of the Iranians had first stayed in England (30 percent) or elsewhere in the North (35 percent); only 25 percent of those who did not come directly had initially lived in Pakistan and Turkey. In addition, all of the Eritrean non returnees who arrived in the United States after at least one stop along the way had initially stayed in Italy; over 60 percent of the "stop-over" Ethiopians first moved to Western Europe or Canada.[149]

Émigré Strategies. At the micro-level, possession of overseas contacts offers a valuable South-North migration resource. In this respect, the Iranian émigrés in the D.C./L.A. sample occupied the most advantageous position. In the first place, nearly 60 percent of this group of respondents had themselves previously lived in or visited the United States before the time they exited from the Iran with no intention of returning. None of the Eritrean émigrés and only 2 Ethiopians (14 percent) had previous personal experience in this country at the time of departure from Ethiopia.

In addition, 93 percent of the Iranian émigrés, versus 64 percent of the Ethiopians and 43 percent of the Eritreans, report that a member of their extended family—usually a sibling—had previously resided in the United States at the time they left the home country. In over three-fourths of the cases where the relatives of Iranians and Ethiopians had been in this country, they still resided here at the time of emigration. A majority of the émigré respondents from all three communities note that this relation, or another family member outside of the receiving country, helped them enter the United States.[150] A minority received personal assistance from a U.S.

citizen—usually someone befriended in the homeland. The Ethiopian interviewees are the most likely to have received help in migrating from a U.S. citizen (36 percent); one-fourth of the Iranians and 14 percent of the Eritreans had obtained such aid.

Non Returnee Strategies. Between 71 percent and 75 percent of each group of non returnees report that they had followed an extended-family member to the United States. In comparison with émigrés, the relation mentioned by non returnees is less likely to be an immediate family member.

In contrast to the patterns that prevailed among émigrés, the Ethiopian and Eritrean non returnees in the sample are more likely to indicate that one or more of their relatives had previously resided in the United States at the time of their departure and the Iranians are less likely to have possessed family members with experience in the receiving country. However, none of the relatives cited by Eritreans remained here on the eve of their departure from the homeland. In 87 percent of the cases where Iranians had been preceeded by a relative, that person still lived in the receiving country when the non returnee exited from Iran;[151] among Ethiopian non returnees, the figure is 59 percent.

Family members helped non returnees enter the United States (mainly for studies) in 69 percent of the Iranian cases, 46 percent of the Ethiopian situations, and 27 percent of the Eritrean cases. On the other hand, a higher proportion of the non returnees from Ethiopia (27 percent) received assistance from a U.S citizen in comparison to the Iranians (7 percent).[152]

Three-fourths of the Iranian non returnees initially arrived under a student visa. The others, including 46 percent of the Ethiopian and Eritrean non returnees, had been admitted under a variety of non-immigrant and immigrant visa situations or, in the case of a handful of Iranians, had entered without inspection.[153] Patricia Fagen points out that subsequent efforts by U.S. consular officers to restrict the issuing of non-immigrant visas to citizens of countries such as Ethiopia and Iran has precluded family visits, business trips, and higher-education opportunities that do not result in overstays, and "encouraged the illegal, expensive and dangerous smuggling operations that bring people into the country who might otherwise come by normal means."[154]

Table 4.15 displays data regarding the immigration and employment status of the non returnees in the sample at the time they made their decision to become an exile. It is important to recognize that about 70 percent of the interviewees of each nationality decided not to return to the homeland at a time when they did not hold secure immigrant status in the

Table 4.15 Immigration and Employment Status of Non Returnees at Time of Decision Not to Return to Homeland, by Nationality

Status	Iranians		Ethiopians		Eritreans	
	N	%	N	%	N	%
Immigration						
Student	49	47.6%	10	25.0%	5	38.5%
Other temporary; none	21	20.4	19	47.5	4	30.8
Perm resident, citizen	33	32.0	11	27.5	4	30.8
Employment						
Part-time, unempld; student	72	68.6	17	41.5	10	71.4
Full-time	33	31.4	24	58.5	4	28.6
Type of Job						
Temporary	29	42.0	22	66.7	5	45.5
Permanent	40	58.0	11	33.3	6	54.5

Source: D.C./L.A. sample.

United States.[155] Nearly half of the Iranian respondents still possessed valid student visas when they made this decision. About half of the Ethiopians who decided not to return only after leaving Ethiopia held another type of non-immigrant visa or were out of legal status at the time they reached that decision. Approximately 30 percent of all non returnees elected to live in exile after they had already become permanent residents or citizens of the United States through various avenues—including marriage to a U.S. citizen and labor certification.

With the exception of the Ethiopian respondents, only a minority of the interviewed non returnees engaged in full-time work at the time they decided not to return home (Table 4.15). Although 59 percent of the Ethiopians worked on a full-time basis at that point, two-thirds of this group only held temporary positions. In sum, most of the non returnees interviewed in this study made the decision to become an exile without first having obtained secure immigration status and a permanent, full-time job.

Non returnees employ a variety of legal and illegal strategies to remain in the United States. Some maintain temporary status, as a student for example, for a lengthy period of time. Others remain without authorization after their visa expires. Many eventually secure permanent residency. In FY 1987, for instance, 7,106 Iranians and 490 Ethiopians who did not arrive as official refugees adjusted to permanent-resident status. A majority in both cases (56–57 percent) had entered the United States with a temporary-visitor visa; most of the others (37 percent of the Iranians and 32 percent of the Ethiopians) had arrived as students.[156] The Immigration Reform and Control Act opened a route to permanent residency for long-term visa abusers. In FY 1987, 4,890 Iranians and 1,070 Ethiopians who had overstayed their non-immigrant visa since 31 December 1981 applied for legalization under the amnesty program.[157]

Émigrés and Non Returnees: Secondary Migration

In general, we can identify three secondary-migration patterns among the interviewed émigrés and non returnees: stationary, single-move, and multiple-move. The stationary pattern fits most Iranians and Ethiopian émigrés. Ethiopian non returnees are divided among all three secondary-migration alternatives and most Eritreans are split between the single-move and multiple-move situations.

Iranian émigrés and non returnees proved more likely than the resettled refugees did to have lived exclusively in the Los Angeles or Washington, D.C., area. It is particularly interesting that 71 percent of the Iranian non returnees, versus 45 percent of the Ethiopians and 17 percent of the Eritreans, had only lived in one U.S. location at the time of interview. In terms of initially settling and staying on in the D.C. area, Ethiopian émigrés (79 percent) stand out from their non-returnee counterparts (45 percent) and from both groups of Eritreans (33 and 17 percent, respectively, for émigrés and non returnees). Less than 20 percent of the Iranian émigrés and non returnees (and less than 15 percent of the Ethiopian émigrés) previously lived outside of New York City, Chicago, or Los Angeles before moving to their present location. In contrast, 45 percent of the Ethiopian non returnees and half of the Eritreans in both categories had moved to the nation's capital from a U.S. city or town other than New York, Chicago, and Los Angeles. Those who engage in secondary migration are likely to have lived in at least two or more other areas before reaching their current location.

Although some émigrés are short-term residents, others have lived in the current area for a considerable length of time. Ethiopians and Iranians are the most likely to have lived for two years or less in their current locale (36 and 31 percent, respectively). Iranian émigrés turn out to be more likely than the other two groups are to have stayed for more than four years (58 percent versus about 30 percent). Since they arrived in the United States earlier, non returnees tend to have resided longer in their current area in comparison to émigrés. Within this group, 58 percent of the Iranian non returnees and half of the Ethiopians and Eritreans had lived in D.C. or L.A. for more than six years.

Reasons D.C. or L.A. Selected. According to the data presented in Table 4.16, a majority of both émigrés and non returnees from all three communities opted to settle in or move to their current metropolitan area in part because of the presence in that setting of family members, relatives, and/or close friends. Two-thirds of the Iranian non returnees also rated

Table 4.16   Reasons Émigrés and Non Returnees Selected Current Metropolitan Area, by Nationality

Important Considerations Dec. to Come/Move this Area	%Total Émigrés (N=56)	%Total Non Rets (N=158)	Iranians %Émigs (N=31)	%Non Rets (N=104)	Ethiopians %Émigs (N=19)	%Non Rets (N=41)	Eritreans %Émigs (N=6)	%Non Rets (N=13)
Presence fam, rels, frnds	73.2%	71.5%	71.0%	74.0%	78.9%	70.7%	66.7%	53.8%
Educational opports	29.1	53.8	36.7	66.3	21.1	28.9	16.7	28.6
Empmt, professal prospects	28.6	27.9	41.9	21.2	10.5	41.7	16.7	42.9
Partic commty cultal actv	32.1	19.5	35.5	10.6	26.3	40.5	33.3	30.8
Cap city, intn/ cultal cntr	18.2	11.5	12.9	5.8	33.3	22.5	0.0	23.1
Offer of employment	10.7	16.1	12.9	11.7	5.3	23.7	16.7	28.6

Source: D.C./L.A. sample.

educational opportunities as an important decisional consideration. None of the other suggested factors, nor the respondent-volunteered "other" item dealing with the international and cultural character of the city of residence, influenced more than 30 percent of all émigrés or non returnees. However, the Table 4.16 results with respect to the role of employment and professional prospects are especially interesting in that non returnees from Ethiopia are much more likely than their émigré counterparts are to have been influenced by that consideration when they decided to migrate to their current U.S. area. Among Iranians, on the other hand, émigrés are more apt than non returnees are to have been affected by prospects for employment and by professional considerations.

When asked to identify the overriding or most important factor in their decision to migrate to the D.C. or L.A. area, a majority (55 percent) of the émigrés who could distinguish a single consideration chose the presence of family, relatives, and/or friends. The non returnees as a whole were more likely to identify educational opportunities as decisive (42 percent, versus 36 percent because of the presence of relations in the area). Among the Ethiopian non-returnee respondents, however, educational opportunites were the least likely consideration to be decisive (11 percent); nearly half of this group indicated that the presence of family, relatives, and/or friends most strongly influenced their decision to migrate to the Washington, D.C., area.

Future Migration Intentions. In terms of future migration intentions, a majority of the interviewees from each community plan to remain in their current metropolitan area. Two groups of respondents stand out from the others on this issue. First, Iranians—especially Iranian émigrés (87 percent)—are considerably more likely than Ethiopians and Eritreans are to express the intention to stay. Second, Ethiopian émigrés are the only group where a majority (59 percent) either expect to move away from the D.C. area or are not sure if they will leave or stay.[158]

We asked the respondents to explain in their own words the reasons for their answer to the question about future internal-migration intentions. The results show that most non returnees, but none of the Ethiopian and Eritrean émigrés, are inclined to stay in the current metropolitan area because of employment or economic considerations. One-third or less of those who have no intention of moving from the two metropolitan areas offered reasons related to educational opportunities and to the presence of family or friends in the area. The presence of ties to other local residents constitutes the most frequently cited consideration among migrants from Ethiopia who intend to remain in the nation's capital, although the percentage who mentioned this factor only ranges between 20 and 33 percent. In comparison, 56 percent of the non returnees and 65 percent of the émigrés from Iran mentioned the presence of family members, relatives, or friends as an important consideration in their decision to continue to reside in the current area.

Among all respondents, Ethiopians constitute the only group with a substantial number of members who intend to move to another U.S. site. Two-thirds of the émigrés in this group and roughly one-third of the non returnees mention both employment/economic considerations and educational objectives as reasons for their decision to leave the Washington, D.C., metropolitan area.[159] Although family unification plays a major role in the initial stage of secondary migration, that motive declines in importance over time.[160]

All Exiles: Composition of U.S. Arrival Waves

The D.C./L.A. sample data allowed us to distinguish among resettled refugees, émigrés, and non returnees in terms of several interesting step-migration issues. These three migrant categories are now merged in order that certain important general attributes of the three principal U.S. arrival waves can be identified and discussed.

Departure Vintages and Arrival Waves. The second wave of U.S. arrivals consists predominantly of migrants who left the homeland in the immediate post-revolution vintage. About 28 percent of this wave departed in the late post-revolution interval in the case of migrants from Ethiopia (12 percent among the Iranian respondents). Another 20 percent of the Eritreans, 8 percent of the Iranians, and 4 percent of the Ethiopians in the initial post-revolution wave had exited the home country in the *pre-revolution* vintage. There are no pre-revolution vintage migrants in the second post-revolution wave (1982–1984) from Ethiopia and over three-fourths of this wave belong to the late post-revolution departure interval. While nearly three-fourths of the Iranian respondents in the second wave (1983–1984) also are from the late post-revolution vintage, the others are most likely to have exited from Iran in the pre-revolution period (21 percent).

Gender, Occupation, and Income. Among the sampled household heads, there are no major differences in the gender of migrants arriving in the three waves. Female household heads from Ethiopia comprise a somewhat higher proportion of the first post-revolution wave than they do for the other two intervals (45 percent versus 33 and 35 percent), while women are present in a slightly higher percentage among the second post-revolution wave from Iran (26 percent, versus 21 percent for the pre-revolution wave and 17 percent for the 1979–1982 period).

Among the Ethiopian and Eritrean respondents, the proportion of professionals and administrators declines in the second post-revolution wave from the previous two influxes, and the number of laborers and farmers increases slightly. There is no last-wave decline in the representation of professionals and administrators in the Iranian case. The major change in migration from Iran is a sharp decrease in businesspersons and finance specialists after the pre-revolution wave.

Table 4.17 sets forth data by wave on the self/family income level of all exiles in the D.C./L.A. sample at the time of departure from Iran or Ethiopia. There is a clear tendency for exiles from self-identified low-income backgrounds in the homeland to constitute a higher proportion of the second post-revolution wave than they do in the first post-revolution arrival interval. The proportion of high-income migrants declines sharply in the last wave among Ethiopians and Eritreans, but not among Iranians.

Table 4.17 Self/Family Income Level of All Exiles at Time Respondent Departed from Homeland, by Wave and Nationality

| | Income Level | | |
Nationality and Wave	High	Medium	Low
Iranians			
% 1952-1978 (N=102)	13.7%	75.5%	10.8%
% 1979-1982 (N=24)	25.0	75.0	0.0
% 1983-1984 (N=19)	21.1	63.2	15.8
Ethiopians			
% 1952-1973 (N=23)	30.4	47.8	21.7
% 1974-1981 (N=45)	31.1	53.3	15.6
% 1982-1984 (N=20)	15.0	55.0	30.0
Eritreans			
% 1952-1973 (N=13)	23.1	61.5	15.4
% 1974-1981 (N=14)	28.6	35.7	35.7
% 1982-1984 (N=31)	9.7	41.9	48.4

Source: D.C./L.A. sample.

Ties to Western Institutions. The data on respondent ties to Western institutions presented in Table 4.18 are quite interesting. In the first place, they reveal a consistent decline in such ties by subsequent arrival wave among members of all three exile communities. While these results confirm that migrants possessing a personal association with a multinational

186

corporation, Western government agency, or international organization are
apt to gain entry to the United States in the first post-revolution wave, they
also suggest that such individuals constitute an even higher proportion of
the pre-revolution arrival group.

Table 4.18 Respondents' Association with a Multinational Corporation, Western
Government Agency, and/or International Organization, by Wave and
Nationality

Nationality and Wave	Report Any Tie	
	Yes	No
Iranians		
% 1952-1978 (N=105)	20.0%	80.0%
% 1979-1982 (N=24)	16.7	83.3
% 1983-1984 (N=19)	10.5	89.5
Ethiopians		
% 1952-1973 (N=27)	22.2	77.8
% 1974-1981 (N=47)	14.9	85.1
% 1982-1984 (N=23)	8.7	91.3
Eritreans		
% 1952-1973 (N=13)	38.5	61.5
% 1974-1981 (N=15)	20.0	80.0
% 1982-1984 (N=32)	12.5	87.5

Source: D.C./L.A. sample.

Political Orientations. Table 4.19 displays the respondents' at-home
orientations toward the pre- and post-revolution regimes by wave and
nationality. The results indicate, first, that the immediate post-revolution
wave of Iranians includes a much higher proportion of supporters of the
Shah's regime in comparison with both the preceeding and the subsequent
waves. However, it is the second post-revolution wave that incorporates the
largest proportion of supporters of the imperial regime in the Ethiopian
case. Moreover, the pre-revolution Ethiopian migrants are much more likely
to have opposed Emperor Haile Selassie's regime in comparison to both
waves of their post-revolution compatriots. The most interesting aspect of
the findings with regard to the Eritrean respondents is the decline in
opponents of the imperial regime during the first post-revolution wave and

the corresponding increase in the proportion of migrants who neither opposed nor supported that political system.

With regard to orientations toward the post-revolution regime, we observe from Table 4.19 that the second post-revolution wave from Iran includes the highest proportion of migrants who initially supported but later opposed the Khomeini regime and of those who had remained neutral while living in the homeland. The second post-revolution wave of Ethiopians is more apt than the first is to have opposed the Derg from the beginning. There are no major differences by wave among the Eritreans.

Table 4.19 Respondents' At-Home Regime Orientations, by Wave and Nationality

	Orientations						
	Pre-revol Regime			Post-revol Regime			
Nationality and Wave	Opposd	Supptd	Neither	Initially Opposd	Later Opposd	Supptd	Neither
Iranians							
% 1952-1978 (N=102)	50.0%	5.9%	44.1%	----	----	----	----
% 1979-1982 (N=24,19)	45.8	33.3	20.8	57.9%	36.8%	5.3%	0.0%
% 1983-1984 (N=19,14)	57.9	5.3	36.8	42.9	42.9	0.0	14.3
Ethiopians							
% 1952-1973 (N=27)	59.3	7.4	33.3	----	----	----	----
% 1974-1981 (N=47,39)	34.0	12.8	53.2	74.4	15.4	2.6	7.7
% 1982-1984 (N=23,23)	30.4	26.1	43.5	100.0	0.0	0.0	0.0
Eritreans							
% 1952-1973 (N=13)	61.5	0.0	38.5	----	----	----	----
% 1974-1981 (N=15,12)	40.0	6.7	53.3	75.0	16.7	0.0	8.3
% 1982-1984 (N=32,31)	68.8	3.1	28.1	87.1	6.5	0.0	6.5

Source: D.C./L.A. sample.

Migrant Motivations. The D.C./L.A. study data also allow us to compare arrival waves by the factors that motivated respondents to emigrate from or not to return to Iran or Ethiopia. We find that the first post-revolution wave of Iranians are more likely than those who preceded and followed them are to have decided to live in exile due in part to the threat of personal or family danger and to fear of political persecution (see Table 4.20). In contrast, these considerations are important among a higher

Table 4.20 Role of Selected Sending-Country Factors in the Decision to Emigrate from or Not Return to the Homeland, by Nationality and Wave

Nationality and Wave	Important Considerations		
	Threat Impris/Danger self/family	Political Persecution	Economic Deprivation
Iranians			
% 1952-1978 (N=105,105,103)	42.9%	46.7%	15.5%
% 1979-1982 (N=24,24,23)	70.8	62.5	17.4
% 1983-1984 (N=19)	52.6	57.9	10.5
Ethiopians			
% 1952-1973 (N=27)	59.3	66.7	22.2
% 1974-1981 (N=47,47,43)	74.5	57.4	9.3
% 1982-1984 (N=23)	82.6	78.3	4.3
Eritreans			
% 1952-1973 (N=13)	61.5	69.2	7.7
% 1974-1981 (N=15,15,12)	73.3	73.3	16.7
% 1982-1984 (N=32,32,30)	96.9	93.8	10.0

Source: D.C./L.A. sample.

proportion of the second post-revolution wave in the case of Ethiopian and Eritrean exiles.

Table 4.20 also reveals that pre-revolution Ethiopian migrants are the most likely of any category, and pre-revolution Eritreans are the least likely, to have been influenced by (prospective) economic deprivation in the sending country. Ideological considerations rank among the top two reasons for becoming an exile among a much higher proportion of the initial than the second post-revolution wave in the case of Iranians and Eritreans; the opposite pattern prevails among the Ethiopians.

These findings caution us against rushing to judgment with regard to the nature of migrant motivations in different arrival waves. Certainly, the evidence does not support the proposition that late arrivals are less likely than initial post-revolution wave migrants are to have become an exile out of fear of personal persecution.

Conclusions

Although people from different countries become a refugee during or after a revolution for similar reasons, the likelihood of securing resettlement in the North and the steps involved in arriving there vary considerably. Most Indochinese political migrants and virtually all Cuban exiles have been admitted by industrialized nations. For the Cubans, and a large number of Vietnamese, the United States of America has served as the country of first asylum. In the usual Cuban situation, "exodus to the United States was. . . coordinated and organized, based on special arrangements between the two governments."[161]

The majority of refugees from other revolutions continue to live in neighboring countries of first asylum in the Third World. Among these groups, methods of entry to the United States are more involved and diverse. The discussions presented in this chapter regarding Cuban and Indochinese refugees on the one hand, and exiles from Iran and Ethiopia on the other, elucidate the different migration patterns and strategies that characterize these five exile communities.

The available information about migrants from Iran and Ethiopia suggests that they differ in important ways from post-revolution migrants to the United States from Cuba and Indochina. To begin with, non returnees and non-resettled refugees constitute a much higher proportion of the total migrant community. Two other particularly important distinctions are (1) the absence of dimunition among Iranians, Ethiopians, and Eritreans in the proportion of political migrants encountered in the late post-revolution departure vintage and in the second post-revolution arrival wave, and (2) the lack of any substantial decline among late-arriving official refugees from Ethiopia in persons with high-status occupational backgrounds, higher-educational attainments, and English-language proficiency.

Many of the arrival-interval differences among post-revolution migrants reviewed in this chapter stem from the inconsistent application of refugee-admission policy by U.S. government gatekeepers. The initial reluctance to offer mass resettlement also produced more heterogeneous post-revolution waves among the Iranian, Ethiopian, and Eritrean communities than encountered among directly and immediately admitted Cubans.[162]

The South-North movement of Iranians, Ethiopians, and Eritreans provides valuable insights regarding the step-migration and secondary-migration processes. Study results confirm that political migrants choose a country of resettlement based on considerations that usually are separate and distinct from the reasons they opt to become an exile. In the case of the refugee-resettlement program, the previous experiences of other family members and the presence of relatives in the receiving country tend to be influential step-migration factors even among groups such as Ethiopians and Eritreans where the formation of immigrant communities is a new phenomenon. In addition, many refugees from revolution take advantage of the opportunity to resettle in the United States because they perceive no other viable option.[163] In 1953, the Shah established English as the exclusive second language in Iran. Emperor Haile Selassie, after returning from exile in England at the end of World War II, ruled that English would be the primary language of instruction at the secondary and university levels and Ethiopia's second national language. These moves, coupled with the extensive presence of U.S. agencies and nationals in both countries and the attendant network-building and cultural familiarity, created the ironic situation where the foreign country responsible for pre-revolutionary exploitation offered the post-revolution exile's best resettlement option. Step-migration motives do not detract in any way from the reasons why political migrants left their home country nor diminish their fear of return, although they are likely to account in large part for the high—and frequently unrealistic—expectations for economic improvement that many exiles bring with them to the United States.

Notes

1. Barry N. Stein, "Refugee Resettlement Programs and Techniques," in U.S., Select Commission on Immigration and Refugee Policy, *U.S. Immigration Policy and the National Interest*, Appendix C to the Staff Report (Washington, D.C.: The Commission, 1981), p. 4.

2. Gil Loescher, "Introduction: Refugee Issues in International Relations," in *Refugees and International Relations*, edited by Gil Loescher and Laila Monahan (Oxford: Oxford University Press, 1989), p. 1. Also see Gervase Coles, "Approaching the Refugee Problem Today," in *Refugees and International Relations*, edited by Gil Loescher and Laila Monahan (Oxford: Oxford University Press, 1989), p. 388; Paul D. Starr and Alden E. Roberts, "Community Structure and Vietnamese Refugee Adaptation: The Significance of Context," *International Migration Review* 16, No. 3 (1982):596. Moreover, "political sponsorship is abandoned in that the refugee rejects the protection of the only government under which he or she has the rights of a citizen. . . ." Art Hansen, "Self-Settled Rural Refugees in Africa: The Case of Angolans in Zambian Villages," in *Involuntary Migration and Resettlement: The Problems and Responses of Dislocated People*, edited by Art Hansen and Anthony Oliver-Smith (Boulder: Westview Press, 1982), p. 120.

3. This terminology is drawn from Egon F. Kunz, "The Refugee in Flight: Kinetic Models and Forms of Displacement," *International Migration Review* 7, No. 2 (Summer 1973):137–139.

4. Kunz, "Displacement," 126.

5. Rebecca Allen and Harry H. Hiller, "The Social Organization of Migration: An Analysis of the Uprooting and Flight of Vietnamese Refugees," *International Migration* 23, No. 4 (1985):446–448; also see Alan B. Simmons, "Recent Studies on Place-Utility and Intention to Migrate: An International Comparison," *Population and Environment* 8, No. 1 & 2 (Spring/Summer 1985/1986):120.

6. Mary M. Kritz, "The Global Picture of Contemporary Immigration Patterns," in *Pacific Bridges: The New Immigration from Asia and the Pacific Islands*, edited by James T. Fawcett and Benjamin V. Cariño (Staten Island: Center for Migration Studies, 1987), p. 46; Marta Tienda, "Socioeconomic and Labor Force Characteristics of U.S. Immigrants: Issues and Approaches," in *U.S. Immigration and Refugee Policy: Global and Domestic Issues*, edited by Mary M. Kritz (Lexington: D.C. Heath and Company, 1983), pp. 220–223.

7. Elizabeth G. Ferris, "Regional Responses to Central American Refugees: Policy Making in Nicaragua, Honduras, and Mexico," in *Refugees and World Politics*, edited by Elizabeth G. Ferris (New York: Praeger, 1985), p. 192.

8. See William S. Bernard, *Chinese Newcomers in the United States: A Sample Study of Recent Immigrants and Refugees* (New York: American Immigration and Citizenship Conference, 1974), p. 11.

9. Alejandro Portes, "One Field, Many Views: Competing Theories of International Migration," in *Pacific Bridges: The New Immigration from Asia and the Pacific Islands*, edited by James T. Fawcett and Benjamin V. Cariño (Staten Island: Center for Migration Studies, 1987), p. 57. As Mary Kritz ("Contemporary Immigration," p. 46) points out, "links between kin and social groups in the sending and receiving communities serve, on the one hand, as channels for communicating information about opportunities and, on the other, as the means for facilitating the transfer and settlement of migrants." See also Wayne A. Cornelius, "Mexican Migration to the United States," *Proceedings of the Academy of Political Science* 34, No. 1 (1981):69–70, 76; Demetrios G. Papademetriou and Nicholas DiMarzio, "An Exploration into the Social and Labor Market Incorporation of Undocumented Aliens: The Case of the New York Metropolitan Area" (report to the Center for Migration Studies and the Tinker Foundation, November 1985), p. 15; John M. Goering, "The 'Explosiveness' of Chain Migration: Research and Policy Issues," *International Migration Review* 23, No. 4 (1989): 804, 809.

10. David Haines, Dorothy Rutherford, and Patrick Thomas, "The Case for Exploratory Fieldwork: Understanding the Adjustment of Vietnamese Refugees in the Washington Area," *Anthropological Quarterly* 54, No. 2 (1981):99; Daniel T. Lichter and Gordon F. De Jong, "The United States," in *International Handbook on Internal Migration*, edited by Charles B. Nam, William J. Serow, and David F. Sly (Westport: Greenwood Press, 1990), pp. 403, 405.

192

11. During the first year, "only those who had substantial wealth or who had been members of the inner circle of the Batista government" exited. Robert L. Bach, "Cubans," in *Refugees in the United States: A Reference Handbook*, edited by David W. Haines (Westport: Greenwood Press, 1985), p. 82.

12. Bach, "Cubans," p. 82; Silvia Pedraza-Bailey, "Cuba's Exiles: Portrait of a Refugee Migration," *International Migration Review* 19, No. 1 (1985):9–10; Gil Loescher and John A. Scanlan, *Calculated Kindness: Refugees and America's Half-Open Door, 1945 to Present* (New York: Free Press, 1986), p. 62. Many in this initial group brought substantial capital assets with them. Kenneth L. Wilson and Alejandro Portes, "Immigrant Enclaves: An Analysis of the Labor Market Experiences of Cubans in Miami," *American Journal of Sociology* 86, No. 2 (September 1980):302.

13. Pedraza-Bailey, "Cuba's Exiles," 10.

14. Loescher and Scanlan, *Kindness*, p. 61.

15. Richard R. Fagen, Richard A. Brody, and Thomas J. O'Leary, *Cubans in Exile: Disaffection and the Revolution* (Stanford: Stanford University Press, 1968), p. 113.

16. Pedraza-Bailey, "Cuba's Exiles," 11; Bach, "Cubans," p. 83. See also Richard R. Fagen and Richard A. Brody, "Cubans in Exile: A Demographic Analysis," *Social Problems* 11 (Spring 1964):395–398.

17. David M. Reimers, *Still the Golden Door: The Third World Comes to America* (New York: Columbia University Press, 1985), p. 164; also Rubén D. Rumbaut and Rubén G. Rumbaut, "The Family in Exile: Cuban Expatriates in the United States," *American Journal of Psychiatry* 133, No. 4 (April 1976):396.

18. Fagen *et al.*, *Cubans in Exile*, p. 102. Among those who settled in West New York, the presence of relatives and friends also constituted the principal attraction. Eleanor M. Rogg, *The Assimilation of Cuban Exiles: The Role of Community and Class* (New York: Aberdeen Press, 1974), pp. 29, 132.

19. Fagen *et al.*, *Cubans in Exile*, p. 102; Aristide R. Zolberg, Astri Suhrke, and Sergio Aguayo, *Escape from Violence: Conflict and the Refugee Crisis in the Developing World* (Oxford: Oxford University Press, 1989), p. 188. See also Al Santoli, *New Americans: Immigrants and Refugees in the U.S. Today* (New York: Viking, 1988), pp. 378–379.

20. On this period, see Pedraza-Bailey, "Cuba's Exiles," 14–16.

21. Pedraza-Bailey, "Cuba's Exiles," 16.

22. Pedraza-Bailey, "Cuba's Exiles," 16, 18. The second wave also included "most of Cuba's active academic and scholarly community. . . ." José Llanes, *Cuban Americans: Masters of Survival* (Cambridge: Abt Books, 1982), p. 99.

23. Pedraza-Bailey, "Cuba's Exiles," 18–20; Bach, "Cubans," p. 84.

24. Alejandro Portes, Juan M. Clark, and Robert L. Bach, "The New Wave: A Statistical Profile of Recent Cuban Exiles to the United States," *Cuban Studies* 7 (1977):9, 11–12, 17–18, 25.

25. Bach, "Cubans," p. 84.

26. Pedraza-Bailey, "Cuba's Exiles," 21–22; Bach, "Cubans," pp. 84–86.

27. See, for instance, *New York Times*, 26 July 1990, p. A6.

28. Bach, "Cubans," p. 85.

29. Pedraza-Bailey, "Cuba's Exiles," 23–27.

30. Pedraza-Bailey, "Cuba's Exiles," 11, 18; Llanes, *Cuban Americans*, p. 197. This situation is anticipated by Kunz in "Displacement," 138–139.

31. Wilson and Portes, "Miami," 303.

32. Gail P. Kelly, *From Vietnam to America: A Chronicle of the Vietnamese Immigration to the United States* (Boulder: Westview Press, 1977), p. 56.

33. David Haines, "Initial Adjustment," in *Refugees in the United States: A Reference Handbook*, edited by David W. Haines (Westport: Greenwood Press, 1985), p. 22; Kelly, *Vietnamese Immigration*, pp. 57, 61.

34. Haines, "Adjustment," pp. 22–23.

35. Haines, "Adjustment," p. 23.

36. Nguyen Manh Hung, "Vietnamese," in *Refugees in the United States: A Reference Handbook*, edited by David W. Haines (Westport: Greenwood Press, 1985), pp. 201–202.

37. Kelly, *Vietnamese Immigration*, pp. 1–2, 53; Robert L. Bach, "Third Country Resettlement," in *Refugees and International Relations*, ed. by Gil Loescher and Laila Monahan (Oxford: Oxford University Press, 1989), p. 315; Hung, "Vietnamese," p. 200; Loescher and Scanlan, *Kindness*, pp. 111–112.

38. John van Esterik, "Lao," in *Refugees in the United States: A Reference Handbook*, ed. by David W. Haines (Westport: Greenwood, 1985), pp. 154–155.

39. May Ebihara, "Khmer," in *Refugees in the United States: A Reference Handbook*, edited by David W. Haines (Westport: Greenwood Press, 1985), p. 133.

40. They included individuals who had played an important role in Operation Phoenix. Kelly, *Vietnamese Immigration*, pp. 1–2, 16. Members of the first wave from Cambodia also tended to be connected to the war effort and/or to U.S. institutions or citizens. Ebihara, "Khmer," pp. 134–135.

41. Kelly, *Vietnamese Immigration*, pp. 14–15, 47, 51–53.

42. Kelly, *Vietnamese Immigration*, pp. 2, 36; Ebihara, "Khmer," pp. 133–134.

43. Kelly, *Vietnamese Immigration*, p. 36; Astri Suhrke and Frank Klink, "Contrasting Patterns of Asian Refugee Movements: The Vietnamese and Afghan Syndromes," in *Pacific Bridges: The New Immigration from Asia and the Pacific Islands*, edited by James T. Fawcett and Benjamin V. Cariño (Staten Island: Center for Migration Studies, 1987), p. 88.

194

44. Ebihara, "Khmer," pp. 133–134.

45. Calculated from Table 3 in Kelly, *Vietnamese Immigration*, p. 48; also see pp. 41–47, 54.

46. Hung, "Vietnamese," p. 200. Many of the workers, peasants, and fishers who fled at this time went to the People's Republic of China. Zolberg *et al.*, *Refugee Crisis*, p. 164.

47. Norman L. Zucker and Naomi F. Zucker, *The Guarded Gate: The Reality of American Refugee Policy* (San Diego: Harcourt Brace Jovanovich, 1987), p. 79; Hung, "Vietnamese," pp. 200–201. For an informative personal account that describes in detail the planning and execution of a dangerous sea escape from Vietnam, see Bui Van Cao, "Planning Escape, 1978," in *Refugee: The Vietnamese Experience*, edited by Lesleyanne Hawthorne (Melbourne: Oxford University Press, 1982), pp. 238–241.

48. Robinson, "Crisis," p. 9; *New York Times*, 14 September 1988, p. A16; 1 August 1989, p. A4; 17 April 1990, p. A4; William Shawcross, "A Tourist in the Refugee World," in *Forced Out: The Agony of the Refugee in Our Time*, compiled by Carole Kismaric (Washington, D.C.: Human Rights Watch and the J. M. Kaplan Fund, 1989), p. 30.

49. Suhrke and Klink, "Vietnamese and Afghan," p. 89; Reimers, *Golden Door*, p. 181.

50. Court Robinson, "Sins of Omission: The New Vietnamese Refugee Crisis," in *World Refugee Survey—1988 in Review* (Washington, D.C.: U.S. Committee for Refugees, 1989), p. 8.

51. Paul J. Strand and Woodrow Jones, Jr., *Indochinese Refugees in America: Problems of Adaptation and Assimilation* (Durham: Duke University Press, 1985), p. 79. The post-1978 wave of Cambodian refugees includes a number of female household heads and unaccompanied children. Ebihara, "Khmer," pp. 135–136.

52. Suhrke and Klink, "Vietnamese and Afghans," p. 90; Zolberg *et al.*, *Refugee Crisis*, p. 165; Haines *et al.*, "Vietnamese Refugees," 98; W. R. Smyser, *Refugees: Extended Exile* (New York: Praeger, 1987), p. 115. Also see Joseph Cerquone, *Refugees from Laos: In Harm's Way* (Washington, D.C.: U.S. Committee for Refugees, 1986), p. 13.

53. Strand and Jones, *Indochinese Refugees*, pp. 79, 85.

54. Strand and Jones, *Indochinese Refugees*, pp. 79–80, 108.

55. Suhrke and Klink, "Vietnamese and Afghan," p. 91; Zolberg *et al.*, *Refugee Crisis*, p. 165.

56. Haines, "Adjustment," p. 24. In 1975, the distribution by state of the Indochinese refugee population "was almost identical to the geographic concentration of the general U.S. population." Susan F. Forbes, "Residency Patterns and Secondary Migration of Refugees," *Migration News* (March 1984):2.

57. Ebihara, "Khmer," p. 135.

58. The U.S. Catholic Conference resettled nearly half of all Indochinese refugees assisted by volags as of 1976. In place of a sponsor, employers directly resettled between 8,000 and 10,000 new arrivals possessing over $4,000 per family member. Kelly, *Vietnamese Immigration*, pp. 146–152.

59. Strand and Jones, *Indochinese Refugees*, p. 41; Kelly, *Vietnamese Immigration*, pp. 146, 202.

60. Connections with U.S. government agencies and defense contractors in Vietnam, as well as with pre-revolution migrants, brought many Vietnamese to the Washington, D.C., metropolitan area. Kelly, *Vietnamese Immigration*, pp. 153–157.

61. Strand and Jones, *Indochinese Refugees*, pp. 41–46, 81–82; Hung, "Vietnamese," p. 202; Kelly, *Vietnamese Immigration*, pp. 157, 200–202; Susan S. Forbes, *Adaptation and Integration of Recent Refugees to the United States* (Washington, D.C.: Refugee Policy Group, 1985), p. 25; Forbes, "Secondary Migration," 6–7; Timothy Dunnigan and Douglas O. Olney, "Hmong," in *Refugees in the United States: A Reference Handbook*, edited by David W. Haines (Westport: Greenwood Press, 1985), p. 118; Bach, "Resettlement," p. 325.

62. Forbes, *Adaptation*, p. 25; Forbes, "Secondary Migration," 5, 7; Hung, "Vietnamese," p. 202. The largest concentration of Khmer is in the Long Beach area. Other sizeable communities can be found in the states of Washington, Oregon, Texas, and in the nation's capital. Ebihara, "Khmer," p. 135. On the secondary migration of Hmong refugees to the central valley region in California and to Minneapolis, see Nicholas Tapp, "The Reformation of Culture: Hmong Refugees from Laos," *Journal of Refugee Studies* 1, No. 1 (1988):33.

63. Hung, "Vietnamese," pp. 202–203. Also see Santoli, *Strangers*, p. 303.

64. Kelly, *Vietnamese Immigrants*, pp. 157, 203; Forbes, "Secondary Migration," 12–13.

65. Tessa Williams, "Sudan: Twenty Years on," *Refugees* 72 (February 1990):31; also see Ahmed Karadawi, "The Problem of Urban Refugees in Sudan," in *Refugees: A Third World Dilemma*, edited by John R. Rogge (Totowa: Rowman & Littlefield, 1987), pp. 117–118.

66. By 1977, the EPLF had gained control of virtually the entire countryside and many towns in Eritrea. On this period, see Mekuria Bulcha, *Flight and Integration: Causes of Mass Exodus from Ethiopia and Problems of Integration in the Sudan* (Uppsala: Scandinavian Institute of African Studies, 1988), pp. 107–110; Karadawi, "Urban Refugees," p. 118. During the second interval, "many of the substantial Eritrean population of professionals, civil servants, and students in Ethiopian cities fled abroad or into the guerrilla zones." Crawford Young, "Comparative Claims to Political Sovereignty: Biafra, Katanga, Eritrea," in *State*

Versus Ethnic Claims: African Policy Dilemmas, edited by Donald Rothchild and Victor A. Olorunsola (Boulder: Westview Press, 1983), p. 216.

67. Mekuria Bulcha, *Flight*, p. 28. Hiram Ruiz maintains that "reprisals by victorious Ethiopian troops against the Somali and Oromo population of the Ogaden and southern provinces sparked the mass outflow of refugees." Hiram Ruiz, *Beyond the Headlines: Refugees in the Horn of Africa* (Washington, D.C.: U.S. Committee for Refugees, 1988), pp. 22, 32.

68. In Mekuria Bulcha's sample, which consists predominantly of second-vintage refugees, radical political activists account for less than 10 percent of the total. The number of beneficiaries of the imperial order and persons who joined the refugee stream for economic reasons is "small." The dislocated victims, mainly peasants and herders, constitute over half of the sample. Finally, there is a relatively large group of refugees who sought to escape the negative personal consequences of the Derg's military and economic policies. Mekuria Bulcha, *Flight*, pp. 98, 127–129. To this list, Ahmed Karadawi ("Urban Refugees," p. 121) adds deserters from the Ethiopian army, former liberation-front fighters who grew disillusioned by internal factionalism and/or the protracted nature of the struggle, and *sur place* refugees.

69. This group includes an increased number of famine-related migrants as well as many Ethiopian Jews who subsequently resettled in Israel. Mekuria Bulcha, *Flight*, pp. 27–28, 128; Peter Koehn and Girma Negash, *Resettled Refugees and Asylum Applicants: Implications of the Case of Migrants from Ethiopia for United States Policy* (Arlington: Center for Ethiopian Studies, 1987), p. 9; *New York Times*, 14 July 1990, p. 3. Many Tigrean famine victims returned to the homeland in 1985 and 1986. Ruiz, *Refugees*, pp. 32, 36.

70. Allen K. Jones, *Iranian Refugees: The Many Faces of Persecution* (Washington, D.C.: U.S. Committee for Refugees, 1984), p. 17. The refugees interviewed by McSpadden spent an average of nearly four years outside of Ethiopia before reaching the United States. Lucia A. McSpadden, "Ethiopian Refugee Resettlement in the Western United States: Social Context and Psychological Well-Being" (Ph.D. dissertation, University of Utah, 1988), p. 130.

71. United States, INS, *Statistical Yearbook of the Immigration and Naturalization Service, 1987* (Washington, D.C.: U.S. GPO, 1988), p. 50; Patricia W. Fagen, *Resource Paper on Political Asylum and Refugee Status in the United States* (Washington, D.C.: Refugee Policy Group, 1985), p. 8.

The large number of officially admitted refugees and Iranians granted asylum in the United States refutes Sabagh and Bozorgmehr's blanket assertion that "the status of Iranian exiles has a sociological rather than a legal or political basis." Georges Sabagh and Mehdi Bozorgmehr, "Are the Characteristics of Exiles Different from

Immigrants? The Case of Iranians in Los Angeles," *Sociology and Social Research* 71, No. 2 (January 1987):77.

72. The Immigration and Nationality Act of 1965 allowed the "conditional" entry of 6 percent of the total annual immigration quota (i.e., about 17,000 principal applicants and 25,000 persons) under a seventh-preference category established for those who had fled communist-dominated political systems, or a Middle Eastern country. John A. Scanlan, "First Final Research Report Submitted to the Select Commission on Immigration and Refugee Policy," in *U.S. Immigration Policy and the National Interest*, Appendix C to the Staff Report (Washington, D.C.: The Commission, 1980), pp. 105–106.

73. U.S., INS, *1987 Yearbook*, p. 50.

74. Beverly G. Hawk, "Africans and the 1965 U.S. Immigration Law" (Ph. D. dissertation, University of Wisconsin-Madison, 1988), pp. 112-114, 161, 287; Carole Kismaric, compiler, *Forced Out: The Agony of the Refugee in Our Time* (Washington, D.C.: Human Rights Watch and the J. M. Kaplan Fund, 1989), p. 127.

75. On the nature of the RDC bio-data sample, see Chapter 6.

76. The sample is classified by vintage on the assumption that the year of homeland departure (about which information is not reported) corresponds with the date of arrival in the country from which the household head applied for admission to the United States (information which usually is recorded). This is a safe assumption in the Ethiopian case since almost 90 percent of the sample arrived directly from an African country. However, the proportion of immediate post-revolution vintage Iranians is certainly higher than reported using this method of classification given that many refugees from Iran experienced a period of exile in a neighboring land before moving on to the European nation where they applied for resettlement in the United States.

77. The actual date of arrival usually is not recorded in the bio-data files. In its place, we relied upon the year in which an applicant received approval to enter the United States since this corresponds in most cases with the year of arrival.

78. These data do not support Beverly Hawk's assertion ("Africans," p. 126) that most resettled refugees from Ethiopia are Amhara.

79. The available FY 1987 data continue to support this conclusion. See U.S., INS, *1987 Yearbook*, p. 40.

80. See Reimers, *Golden Door*, p. 182.

81. Annabelle Sreberny-Mohammadi and Ali Mohammadi, "Post-revolutionary Iranian Exiles: A Study in Impotence," *Third World Quarterly* 9, No. 1 (January 1987):128.

82. There are noteworthy variations by ethnicity, however. The educational levels attained by admitted Eritreans decline considerably from the first to the second wave. To a lesser extent, this pattern also prevails among the Amhara in

198

the sample. Among the Oromo and "other" groups, however, educational attainments actually increase from the first to the second wave.

83. In light of the small number of refugee respondents, particularly in the Iranian case, the results of this study must be viewed as suggestive. When available, the D.C./L.A. sample findings are supplemented by data from the other sources consulted in this study.

84. Several of the resettled Iranian refugees in the sample had departed just prior to the termination of monarchical rule; most of the others left in the late post-revolution vintage (Table 4.6).

85. Mohammad Amjad, "Post-revolutionary Migration of Iranians Abroad" (paper presented at the 7th Third World Studies Conference, Omaha, October 1984), pp. 20–22.

86. Jones, *Iranian Refugees*, pp. 10, 13; Amjad, "Iranians Abroad," pp. 24–26; Kismaric, *Forced Out*, pp. 144, 147. Patricia Fagen (*Political Asylum*, p. 8) reports that Iranians have experienced particularly difficult and frequently dangerous conditions in Pakistan. Also see Loescher, "Issues," p. 16; Zolberg *et al., Refugee Crisis*, p. 154.

87. Among the D.C./L.A. sample, for instance, 3 percent of the responding Eritrean refugees, 11 percent of the Ethiopians, and 43 percent of the Iranians had initially lived in an non-proximate country after exiting from the sending country.

88. See Mekuria Bulcha, *Flight*, pp. 106, 132–141; Lucia A. McSpadden, "Ethiopian Refugee Resettlement in the Western United States: Social Context and Psychological Well-Being," *International Migration Review* 21, No. 3 (1987):804. On the experiences of Somali refugees, who tended to flee in small groups, see Sidney R. Waldron, "Somali Refugee Background Characteristics: Preliminary Results from the Qoriooley Camps" (mimeo, 1983), p. 7.

89. Leon Gordenker, *Refugees in International Politics* (New York: Columbia University Press, 1987), p. 147.

90. Mekuria Bulcha, *Flight*, pp. 136–138. Of course, some rural migrants also make their way to the larger towns in Sudan. See Karadawi, "Urban Refugees," pp. 116, 119–120.

In discussing the results of one local study, Jerry Weaver refers specifically to the goal of resettlement in the United States. Jerry L. Weaver, "Sojourners Along the Nile: Ethiopian Refugees in Khartoum," *Journal of Modern African Studies* 23, No. 1 (1985):150–151. An earlier research project (cited in Mekuria Bulcha, *Flight*, p. 138) also found considerable interest in migration to Europe and the Middle East. Also see Karadawi, "Urban Refugees," pp. 121–122.

91. Mekuria Bulcha, *Flight*, p. 30.

92. Mekuria Bulcha, *Flight*, p. 30; John R. Rogge, "When is Self-Sufficiency Achieved? The Case of Rural Settlements in Sudan," in *Refugees: A Third World*

Dilemma, edited by John R. Rogge (Totowa: Rowman & Littlefield, 1987), pp. 90–92; Ruiz, *Refugees,* p. 32; Karadawi, "Urban Refugees," p. 118.

93. Karadawi, "Urban Refugees," pp. 121–122; Ruiz, *Refugees,* p. 35. On the other hand, many Eritreans encounter continued agitation from political activists who pressure them to serve as a rear-support group for the guerrilla forces. Mekuria Bulcha, *Flight,* pp. 82–83.

94. Mekuria Bulcha, *Flight,* p. 140.

95. Over half of the interviewees who complained of poor personal health had contracted their affliction after arrival in Sudan. Mekuria Bulcha, *Flight,* pp. 141, 171.

96. Mekuria Bulcha, *Flight,* pp. 142–143, 198–199.

97. Mekuria Bulcha, *Flight,* pp. 162–164. On the barriers to employment of women outside of service and domestic jobs in Khartoum, see Weaver, "Sojourners," 152–153.

98. Moreover, the exploitation of refugee labor has negative consequences for the income-earning prospects of the local poor. Mekuria Bulcha, *Flight,* pp. 172–173, 192.

99. Yet, they "still were not free from malnutrition." Mekuria Bulcha, *Flight,* pp. 155, 170.

100. Mekuria Bulcha, *Flight,* pp. 163, 200.

101. Weaver, "Sojourners," 152–153.

102. Weaver, "Sojourners," 153–155; Gordenker, *Refugees,* p. 148; Santoli, *New Americans,* p. 95; Kismaric, *Forced Out,* p. 127. The EPLF provides some relief and a certain degree of protection for Eritrean refugees.

103. Weaver, "Sojourners," 154–155. Specifically, they are blamed for the shortage of housing and rising rents, pressures on public services, and insufficient supplies of consumer goods. Karadawi, "Urban Refugees," pp. 124, 116; Santoli, *New Americans,* p. 96. One local study revealed the misdirected nature of these charges. See Ruiz, *Refugees,* pp. 34–35.

104. Weaver, "Sojourners," 147–148; Karadawi, "Urban Refugees," p. 126.

105. Mekuria Bulcha, *Flight,* p. 200.

106. In addition, 67 percent had owned productive assets in Ethiopia, whereas only 12 percent possessed such property in Sudan. Mekuria Bulcha, *Flight,* p. 171.

107. The actual unemployment rate undoubtedly is much higher than 16 percent since most of the applicants for whom no information on employment is recorded are likely to have been unemployed in the country of application.

108. Egon Kunz ("Displacement," 133) predicts this outcome.

109. Ethiopians are more likely than Eritreans are to refer to U.S. attractions (67 percent versus 50 percent) and less likely to mention family considerations (14 to 23 percent).

110. These findings refute Kunz's contention ("Displacement," 132–133) that, in cases of further migration, push forces in the country of temporary refuge will be "always more decisive than the pull of the country where the refugee eventually goes." Also see Barbara E. Harrell-Bond, "Repatriation: Under What Conditions is it the Most Desirable Solution for Refugees? An Agenda for Research," *African Studies Review* 32, No. 1 (1989):54.

111. However, the refugees from Ethiopia who arrived in Dallas in 1984 and 1985 mainly came from first-asylum camps. Few in this group spoke much English at the time of arrival. Donald J. Cichon and Tesfaye Shiferaw, "Dallas Ethiopians," in *The Economic and Social Adjustment of Non-Southeast Asian Refugees*, Volume II (Falls Church: Research Management Corporation, 1986), p. 16.

112. In addition, 14 percent of the official refugees from Ethiopia rated the U.S. educational system as the single most important factor in their decision to seek admission under the resettlement program.

113. The main reason for the absence of comparable data on Iranian refugees is the fact that few Iranians had been accepted for U.S. resettlement at the time of project fieldwork in 1984 and 1985.

114. For an exceptional situation, see Santoli, *New Americans*, p. 97. This provision has been invoked most frequently to exclude suspected participants in the Khmer Rouge who are currently living in camps in Thailand. Arthur C. Helton, "Asylum and Refugee Protection in the Bush Years," in *World Refugee Survey—1988 in Review* (Washington, D.C.: U.S. Committee for Refugees, 1989), p. 27; Fagen, *Political Asylum*, p. 8.

115. *New York Times*, 26 May 1987, p. 6; Karadawi, "Urban Refugees," p. 127.

116. Nearly 80 percent of non-reunified applicants in the RDC bio-data sample followed this path. For some time after 1982, the INS only processed refugees from Ethiopia in Western Europe when they arrived there directly from an Eastern European country. Zucker and Zucker, *Guarded Gate*, p. 85. Toward the end of the 1980s, African refugee admissions from Sudan declined and those from Europe increased. Hawk, "Africans," p. 125.

117. See Donald J. Cichon, Elzbieta M. Gozdziak, and Jane G. Grover, *The Economic and Social Adjustment of Non-Southeast Asian Refugees*, Vol. I (Falls Church: Research Management Corporation, 1986), p. 29.

118. In the D.C. sample, 19 percent of the resettled Ethiopians and 13 percent of the Eritreans used this step-migration strategy.

119. In the CWS sample, 23 percent of the Ethiopians and 67 percent of the Eritreans first fled to Sudan. Another 30 percent of the CWS-assisted Ethiopians and 8 percent of the Eritreans initially received protection in Djibouti, Somalia, or Kenya.

120. In Lucia McSpadden's western-U.S. sample of single male refugees from Ethiopia, the mean number of years spent outside of Ethiopia prior to arrival in the United States was 3.7. McSpadden, "Resettlement," 804.

121. The approval process consumed slightly more time for a few of the Ethiopian and Eritrean refugees in the D.C. sample who applied in 1981 and 1982.

122. The D.C./L.A. study data confirm this finding for the 90 resettled refugees in the sample. In addition, less than three years elapsed from the time of application to the time of U.S. entry in the step-migration experience reported by all but two of these official refugees. The two exceptions both belong to the Eritrean community.

123. As of 1985, about three-fourths of the CWS-assisted refugees who had left Ethiopia in 1982 reached the United States within two years.

124. Spain accounted for slightly more than one-third of the Iranian official-refugee total according to the RDC bio-data sample.

125. Fagen, *Political Asylum*, p. 7; Jones, *Iranian Refugees*, pp. 12, 14.

126. The exploratory D.C./L.A. data provide further confirmation that Iranians are especially likely to make several moves before being accepted for resettlement in the United States. Over seventy percent of the responding official refugees from Iran had lived in more than one other country after leaving the homeland and prior to arrival in the U.S.A. In contrast, 76 percent of the Ethiopians and 86 percent of the Eritreans had been resettled directly from the country of first asylum.

127. Fifteen percent is the minimum figure. No employment history is available for 185 principal applicants from Iran in the RDC bio-data files.

128. For a personal example, see Santoli, *New Americans*, pp. 96–97. Also see Hawk, "Africans," p. 122.

129. Rogge, "Sudan," p. 97.

130. Almost all resettled refugees also are assisted in one way or another by a voluntary agency; non-governmental resettlement agencies helped 85 percent of the Ethiopian official refugees in the D.C. sample and 95 percent of the Eritreans. The U.S. Catholic Conference assisted about 45 percent of both groups. Church World Service aided 18 percent of the Ethiopians and 10 percent of the Eritreans. For background on these two volags, see Norman L. Zucker, "The Voluntary Agencies and Refugee Resettlement in the United States" in U.S., Select Commission on Immigration and Refugee Policy, *U.S. Immigration Policy and the National Interest*, Appendix C to the Staff Report (Washington, D.C.: The Commission, 1981), pp. 524–525, 543–544.

131. No data on U.S. family relations are recorded on the bio-data forms for Iranians.

132. There are no major variations between Ethiopian and Eritrean applicants in terms of the U.S. presence of close and distant relatives.

133. In 1990, Sudan accommodated roughly 660,000 refugees from Ethiopia—mainly Eritreans and Tigreans. Some of these refugees have lived in Sudan for over 20 years. Williams, "Twenty Years," 31.

134. See Weaver, "Sojourners," 147–150; Mekuria Bulcha, *Flight*, pp. 92–97. Most refugees from Ethiopia live in eastern Sudan. An estimated 200,000 inhabit Sudan's largest cities of Khartoum, Gedaref, Kassala, and Port Sudan. Williams, "Twenty Years," 31. Mekuria Bulcha's research included the town of Gedaref.

135. The RDC sample consists of principal applicants for refugee status—almost all of whom are heads of household or independent. About 35 percent of the Khartoum group are the spouses of male household heads who were away at work at the time that Weaver's survey took place. Weaver, "Sojourners," 150. Mekuria Bulcha's team also interviewed some wives in place of absent male household heads. He found it necessary to make such substitutions in nearly 20 percent of the sampled households in two of the three organized settlements. Mekuria Bulcha, *Flight*, p. 95.

136. Also see Mekuria Bulcha, *Flight*, p. 138.

137. It also is conceivable that the narrow definition of "refugee" that guides U.S. admission practice amounts to a formidable class barrier to further migration. However, Chapter 5 shows that overseas gatekeepers generally have not applied a particularly narrow definition in the refugee-resettlement process.

138. Also see Weaver, "Sojourners," 155.

139. Iranian refugees also have dispersed throughout the country upon arrival, with a plurality selecting the Los Angeles-Long Beach area. U.S., INS, *1987 Yearbook*, p. 37.

140. "Demographic Data for Ethiopian Refugees: Arrivals 08/1/80–9/30/84 by State" (report prepared for the author by the Refugee Data Center, New York City, 1984).

141. Mc Spadden, "Resettlement," 797.

142. Comparing the state of residence of refugees from Ethiopia granted permanent-resident status in FY 1987 with the 1980–1984 placement figures cited above suggests that the exile population from Ethiopia has declined in California and increased in D.C.-Maryland-Virginia as the result of secondary migration. Iranian refugees, on the other hand, have tended to move to California. U.S., INS, *1987 Yearbook*, pp. 54–55. On the net in-migration of refugees from Ethiopia to the Los Angeles metropolitan area, see Cynthia J. Gimbert and Tesfay Shiferaw, "Los Angeles Ethiopians," in *The Economic and Social Adjustment of Non-Southeast Asian Refugees*, Volume II (Falls Church: Research Management Corporation, 1986), p. 10.

143. Egon Kunz ("Displacement," 142–143) uses the related concept of "displacement by absence" to refer to "individuals who left their country of origin

peacefully, under normal circumstances, but who refused to return there after the turn of events."

144. The findings discussed in this paragraph reveal the hazards inherent in a methodology that imputes migration motives according to time of arrival in the receiving country. For an example of the type of misleading assumptions that can result from an approach based upon census data, see Sabagh and Bozorgmehr, "Iranians," 77.

145. Iranians are the most likely to have opted to migrate to the United States due in part to considerations related to employment and income.

146. About 70 percent of these Iranians also secured their entry visa from Canada or a Western European country. U.S. diplomatic missions in Turkey reject 75 percent of the visa applications submitted by Iranians each year. On the informal strategies used by Iranians in Turkey in the quest for admission to the United States, see *New York Times*, 26 May 1987, pp. 1, 6.

147. Two-thirds of the Eritrean émigrés who did not arrive in the United States directly from Ethiopia and 56 percent of the Ethiopians secured their entry visa from a neighboring country in the Horn of Africa. The rest entered via Western Europe.

148. Over three-fourths of the Ethiopian émigrés who stopped in route (78 percent) and two-thirds of the Eritreans had resided for at least two years in the country of initial habitation.

149. Only one Ethiopian non-returnee respondent had initially lived in the Horn of Africa (Kenya).

150. In this case, Iranians were slightly less likely to receive help from a family member than the others were (53 percent versus 57 percent).

151. These findings, which consider extended-family ties, challenge Abdolmaboud Ansari's earlier conclusion that the movement of Iranians to the United States "does not involve chain migration." Abdolmaboud Ansari, *Iranian Immigrants in the United States: A Case Study of Dual Marginality* (Millwood: Associated Faculty Press, 1988), pp. 32, 66.

152. Once again, most of those providing assistance are people whom the non returnee knew personally in Ethiopia—Peace Corps volunteers, for instance.

153. The GAO study of 1984 Iranian asylum applicants discovered that 43 percent had entered on student visas, 44 percent as visitors, and the rest either without inspection or on an undeterminable basis. U.S., General Accounting Office, *Asylum: Uniform Application of Standards Uncertain—Few Denied Applicants Deported* (Washington, D.C.: GAO, 1987), p. 17; also see Sabagh and Bozorgmehr, "Iranians," 78. Some Iranians fly to Mexico City on a tourist visa and, then, attempt to cross the border without documentation. See Santoli, *New Americans*, p. 264. On the widespread availability of fake documents for purchase by

undocumented immigrants, see *New York Times*, 4 August 1990, p. A8; 26 November 1990, p. A11.

154. Fagen, *Political Asylum*, pp. 14–15. On the border-crossing dangers experienced by undocumented Salvadorean migrants, see Margarita B. Melville, "Salvadoreans and Guatemalans," in *Refugees in the United States: A Reference Handbook*, edited by David W. Haines (Westport: Greenwood Press, 1985), p. 174.

155. Nearly all of the Eritrean political-asylum applicants in the sample applied between 1976 and 1978. In contrast, virtually all of the others submitted asylum applications in the 1980s.

156. U.S., INS, *1987 Yearbook*, p. 20.

157. U.S., INS, *1987 Yearbook*, p. 44.

158. If we consider the entire sample of exiles from Ethiopia, the group of migrants who are dissatisfied with living conditions in the nation's capital are the most likely to be inclined to move elsewhere (50 percent) or to be undecided about their future migration intentions within the receiving country (another 50 percent). Less than half of those who are neither satisfied nor dissatisfied in their current locale express the firm intention to remain in the Washington, D.C., metropolitan area. About 70 percent of the satisfied migrants from Ethiopia intend to remain.

159. Furthermore, considering all of the exiles who report that the presence of family or friends served as the decisive reason for migrating to the current place of residence, we find that, with the exception of Ethiopian respondents, this group is not particularly likely to mention local ties of an inter-personal nature as an important consideration in the decision to *remain* in the D.C. or L.A. area.

160. The results regarding the motives that prevail after initial secondary migration are consistent with findings on the reasons for inter-jurisdictional movement among the U.S. population as a whole. Lichter and De Jong, "United States," p. 403.

161. Silvia Pedraza-Bailey, *Political and Economic Migrants in America: Cubans and Mexicans* (Austin: University of Texas Press, 1985), p. 16.

162. This is consistent with the expectation for vintage mergers set forth in Kunz, "Displacement," 139.

163. Also see the findings of UNHCR consultant Gilbert Jaeger cited in Dennis Gallagher, Susan F. Martin, and Patricia W. Fagen, "Temporary Safe Haven: The Need for North American-European Responses," in *Refugees and International Relations*, edited by Gil Loescher and Laila Monahan (Oxford: Oxford University Press, 1989), pp. 341–342.

5

Applications of U.S. Admission Policy

Procedures to determine who is and who is not a refugee are now being used to accept as few as possible and not to determine who needs protection and who does not.
—Jean-Pierre Hocké, former U.N. High Commissioner for Refugees

Only a small fraction of the world's refugees and displaced persons resettle in North America, Western Europe, or Japan. In the face of formidable government barriers to immigration in these regions, most persons who flee from revolution find that transnational movement terminates in the Third World country that they first enter. Chapter 4 dealt with the strategies employed by the few who manage, through legal or unauthorized step migration, to reach the United States and described the composition of various arrival waves. The focus here is on the screening process that allows some exiles to secure official permission to settle in the North and denies it to others.

On what grounds are refugees who gain entry to industrialized nations admitted? When admission is selective, which post-revolution political migrants are accepted for third-country resettlement and awarded asylum? What does process analysis reveal in terms of admission outcomes and the prevailing acceptance policy? What difference does officially recognized refugee status make? This chapter addresses these important policy-application questions with primary reference to the United States.

The Policy Context

Authorized in-migration to the United States occurs within three broad categories: (1) immigrant visas issued under a preference system subject to a 270,000 annual ceiling and a maximum per country of 20,000; (2) immediate relatives of U.S. citizens; and (3) refugee admissions.[1] The U.S. government grants refuge from persecution to a limited number of exiles either by arranging entry as an official—or resettled—refugee, or by awarding political asylum to petitioners who apply at the port of entry or from within the country. Thus, the United States both engages in the process of third-country resettlement and serves as a country of first asylum.

The Parole Power

Prior to passage of the Refugee Act in 1980, Congress imposed a ceiling of 17,400 on admissions in the seventh preference (refugee) category.[2] However, the executive branch frequently admitted much higher numbers of refugees under the attorney general's "parole power." Between 1956 and 1980, roughly eight times as many parolees as seventh-preference entrants arrived in the U.S.A. In total, "parole accounted for over a million entrants. . ." during this period.[3] Cubans, Indochinese, Hungarians, Jewish émigrés from the Soviet Union, and some Chinese have constituted the principal beneficiaries of the executive's parole authority.[4] Although members of Congress complained about the executive branch's use of the parole power, they eventually enacted assistance programs for the new arrivals and passed legislation enabling them to become permanent residents.[5]

Third-Country Resettlement

Under the terms of the 1980 Refugee Act, the President sets an annual ceiling on refugee admissions after consultation with Congress.[6] The number of persons accepted for resettlement usually falls short of the ceiling figure and there is no carry-over of numbers from one year to the next. Between 1980 and 1982, the INS approved the resettlement of 424,000 refugees. After this initial influx, annual refugee admissions averaged 63,000 through FY 1987.[7] In FYs 1990 and 1991, the United States resettled approximately 125,000 officially processed refugees from selected countries.[8]

Political Asylum

The wealthy receiving nations dominate the international system of third-country resettlement in much the same fashion as they control commodity prices on the world market and the distribution of global capital. Asylum seekers already located in the West operate outside the global resettlement system and press their claims directly with the national bureaucracy. However, prospective asylum seekers from the Third World[9] have found it increasingly difficult to gain entry to Western European countries—a situation which most governments firmly intend to reinforce on the occasion of European integration in 1993.[10]

Refugee Recognition and Admission: The Foreign-Policy Factor

The 1980 Refugee Act changed the U.S. government's officially recognized definition of a refugee by removing the reference in earlier legislation to flight from "any Communist or Communist-dominated country or area" and replacing it with the internationally accepted standard of "persecution or a well-founded fear of persecution on account of race, religion, nationality, membership in a particular social group, or political opinion. . . ."[11] In spite of this legal change, humanitarian impulses remained subordinate to ideological and foreign-policy calculations both in the refugee-admission program[12] and in the treatment of political-asylum applications within the United States.

The U.S. Resettlement Program

Under the resettlement program, government decisions on qualifying countries and regional numerical ceilings are largely shaped by the U.S. Refugee Coordinator's recommendations and are greatly influenced by political considerations.[13] Given the locus of the Coordinator's office within the State Department, it is not surprising to discover that most of the refugees resettled since 1980 continue to come from communist countries.[14] Admissions are used to embarrass and discredit nations defined as "adversaries" by the foreign policy-making establishment.[15] Norman and Naomi Zucker correctly point out that "a well-founded fear of persecution from the left is no more pernicious than it is from the right."[16] Nevertheless, individuals with equally convincing or more compelling cases for resettlement who are fleeing from non-communist countries and from repressive regimes that the State Department considers friendly to the United States have not secured equitable access to the refugee-admission program. Prominent among those excluded from the resettlement program established by the 1980 Refugee Act, as well as among those denied parole status, are persons who have fled persecution in Chile during General

Pinochet's rule, South Africa, South Korea, El Salvador, Haiti, and the Philippines under Ferdinand Marcos.[17]

In addition, the Reagan and Bush administrations have consistently set disproportionately low admission ceilings for refugees from two regions of the world: Africa and Latin America. In FY 1984, for instance, "Latin America and Africa, regions with enormous refugee populations, together received only 5 per cent of the total."[18] According to the State Department's own statistics for 1987, African refugees comprised 27 per cent of the world total and only 3 per cent of the 66,000 persons authorized to resettle in the United States.[19] Africa and Latin America jointly still accounted for 5 percent of total refugee admissions in FY 1988 and for 6 percent of authorized FY 1991 admissions.[20]

Over the past decade, the allocation-numbers game has favored refugees from Indochina, the Soviet Union, and Eastern Europe. These areas supplied 84 percent of all refugees admitted in FY 1988.[21] As a consequence of U.S. policy-application actions, therefore, *bona fide* refugees from other regions of the world are precluded from consideration under the resettlement program. In addition, emigrants from the Soviet Union, Eastern Europe, and Vietnam who do not satisfy refugee criteria continue to be admitted under the attorney general's parole authority.[22] Deciding on the privileged few to admit as refugees remains an intensely political matter in the United States.

Political-Asylum Seekers and Other Exiles in the United States

For refugees from Third World areas with small or non-existent allocations under the resettlement program who seek third-country protection or resettlement in the North, the dangerous, expensive, and uncertain option of unauthorized entry remains a compelling alternative. Upon entry, or at a later date, these exiles might attempt to obtain political asylum on an individual basis.[23] Concomitantly, the United States has become the country of first asylum for an increasing number of political migrants from the Western Hemisphere. In 1984, persons who entered on student or visitor visas presented 51 percent of the total number of asylum applications filed in the United States; individuals who entered or attempted to enter without inspection submitted most of the others.[24]

The drafters of the 1980 Refugee Act did not anticipate the growth in the number of in-country demands for refugee status experienced throughout the 1980s. Even though the budget allotted to the Immigration and Naturalization Service more than doubled to over one billion dollars under the Reagan administration, the executive branch assigned minimal resources and low priority to processing political-asylum claims. A massive backlog resulted from the failure of State Department and INS officers to cope with the volume of asylum requests.[25]

"Non-resettled" refugees include exiles who declare an intention to seek political asylum at the time of entry, externally displaced persons who cross the U.S. border without permission in search of a safe haven, and visitors who fear to return to their home country because of revolutionary or other drastic and personally threatening political changes. In the absence of legally conferred refugee status, thousands of exiles typically function under one of several temporary and tenuous situations. Non-resettled refugees most commonly hold student visas, enjoy "tolerance" status (e.g., grants of extended voluntary departure), are political-asylum applicants, or are undocumented migrants—including those who secretly "entered without INS inspection" (EWI), visa abusers who overstayed their permitted temporary-admission period, and genuine refugees unfairly refused asylum who are never deported by the INS.[26] The focus of the following discussion is on migrants who formally apply for political asylum.[27]

While governments retain discretionary authority to grant or deny political asylum, signatory countries must respect the *non-refoulement* provisions incorporated into article 33 of the 1951 Convention Relating to the Status of Refugees.[28] Domestic practices also are scrutinized for conformity with the treatment one advocates for first-asylum applicants elsewhere in the world. When the United States rejects deserving asylum seekers, it undermines the world-wide refugee-protection system—"one of the most humanitarian systems the international community has yet constructed."[29] In light of the obligation to shelter political-asylum seekers, the legislative and executive branches possess less control over the number of asylum awards than they do over resettlement ceilings. Moreover, the U.S. judiciary has become increasingly involved in extending legal protections to asylum seekers and in reviewing their treatment by the INS.[30]

To date, ideological and foreign-policy considerations have prevailed in the U.S. government's treatment of asylum applications. Lawrence Fuchs, former executive director of the Select Commission on Immigration and Refugee Policy, reports that foreign policy shapes the "invariably conclusive" advisory opinions on asylum applications provided by the State Department's Bureau of Human Rights and Humanitarian Affairs.[31] When consulted, the country desk officer at State usually is "unwilling to admit that persecution occurs" because "the desk officer's primary mission is to maintain the best possible relationship with the country in question."[32]

TABLE 5.1 Proportion of Political Asylum Cases Filed with INS District Directors Granted and Denied in FY 1984, by Applicant's Country of Origin[a]

Country	Cases Granted No.	%	Cases Denied No.	%	Total No. Granted and Denied	Number Pending
"Adversary"						
Iran	5,016	60.9	3,216	39.1	8,232	
Soviet Union	45	51.1	43	48.9	88	
Albania	186	40.9	269	59.1	455	
Romania	158	39.1	246	61.9	404	
Czechoslovakia	36	36.3	72	66.7	108	
Poland	721	32.7	1,482	67.3	2,203	
Hungary	62	27.9	160	72.1	222	
Libya	11	26.2	31	73.8	42	
Ethiopia	305	23.1	1,014	76.9	1,319	
Afghanistan	8,277	20.4	32,344	79.6	40,621	(138,598)
Vietnam	19	19.4	79	80.6	98	
Syria	21	13.5	135	86.5	156	
Nicaragua	1,018	12.3	7,274	87.7	8,292	(1,644)
Cuba	16	3.3	472	96.9	488	(121,937)
"Friendly"						
Bangladesh	0	0.0	283	100.0	283	
India	0	0.0	164	100.0	164	
Chile	0	0.0	46	100.0	46	
Egypt	1	.2	467	99.8	468	
Guatemala	3	.4	758	99.6	761	
Jordan	1	1.3	75	98.7	76	
Israel	1	2.4	41	97.6	42	
El Salvador	328	2.5	13,045	97.5	13,373	(1,335)
Honduras	4	2.6	135	97.1	139	
Lebanon	16	3.0	518	97.0	534	
Pakistan	7	3.0	224	97.0	231	
Liberia	5	4.0	119	96.0	124	
Haiti	23	6.1	352	93.9	375	(7,265)
Peopls Rep of China	15	7.2	192	92.8	207	
Yugoslavia	12	8.8	124	91.2	136	
Philippines	36	25.0	108	75.0	144	

[a] Only clearly "adversary" and "friendly" countries with 40 or more cases granted and denied are included in this table. Each case may include one or more individuals.

Source: United States, Department of Justice, Immigration and Naturalization Service, "Asylum Cases Filed with District Directors Pursuant to Section 208 INA (Consolidated FY 1984, October 1983--September 1984)."

Using INS figures for FY 1984 asylum cases granted and denied as an example, it is clear that applicants from "adversary" countries nearly always fared considerably better in percentage and numerical terms in comparison to those from "friendly" countries (see Table 5.1).[33] Among the 30 nations with significant numbers of cases, only 2 (Iran and the Soviet Union) recorded approval rates that exceeded 50 percent.[34] Between 19 percent and 41 percent of the petitioners from nine other adversary countries succeeded in securing political asylum. These are individuals or families from Albania, Rumania, Czechoslovakia, Poland, Hungary, Libya, Ethiopia, Afghanistan, and Vietnam. In contrast, the INS denied 91 percent or more of the applications submitted by persons from 15 nations where governments, often in exchange for extensive military assistance, maintained relatively positive relations with the United States. In addition to El Salvador (98 percent) and Haiti (94 percent), this group includes Chile (100 percent), Guatemala (99.6 percent), Honduras (97 percent), Pakistan (97 percent), and Liberia (96 percent)—along with two communist countries viewed as independent of Soviet influence (China and Yugoslavia).[35] Table 5.1 also shows that the INS awarded asylum to over 1,000 Nicaraguans. Only applicants fleeing Afghanistan and Iran received more grants in FY 1984. On 16 April 1986, moreover, Perry Rivkind, INS District Director in Florida, refused to order the deportation of any more Nicaraguans on the grounds that they might be persecuted by the Sandinista government and because their asylum claims are "difficult to prove."[36] Salvadoreans, Guatemalans, and Haitians remained subject to deportation in Florida.[37]

Table 5.2 presents more recent figures—including data made available for the first time by the Executive Office of Immigration Review on the decisions reached by certain immigration judges.[38] The Table 5.2 results are interesting for several reasons. First, they confirm that, when compared to the immigration judges, district directors generally approve a higher proportion of asylum requests. The overall FY 1988 approval rate for the directors is 39.1 percent, while it is 22.6 percent for the judges.[39] However, there are some striking exceptions to the overall pattern, including the far greater willingness of immigration judges to grant asylum to applicants from Afghanistan (73 percent versus 40 percent among the district directors). Asylum seekers from Mexico, Guatemala, El Salvador, and Liberia also fared better in FY 1988 under the judges than they did under the directors, although the approval rate remains low in all three cases.

TABLE 5.2 Proportion of Political Asylum Cases Approved by INS District Directors and Immigration Judges in FY 1988, by Applicant's Country of Origin[a]

| Country | District Directors | | Immigration Judges[b] | |
	Total # of Cases Awarded & Denied	% Awarded	Total # of Cases Awarded & Denied	% Awarded
"Adversary"				
U.S.S.R.	51	84.3%	N.A.	----
Romania	416	82.9	27	59.3%
Ethiopia	572	77.0	73	65.7
Iran	1018	75.0	368	60.9
Libya	85	72.9	27	63.0
Syria	38	65.7	13	38.5
Poland	806	53.7	200	20.5
Nicaragua	5241	53.1	1358	37.4
Panama	53	49.1	N.A.	----
Afghanistan	91	39.5	110	72.7
Cuba	94	31.9	647	13.9
Hungary	83	28.9	17	41.2
"Friendly"				
Mexico	60	0.0	21	14.3
El Salvador	3932	2.7	2786	12.0
Guatemala	471	5.0	408	14.5
Honduras	135	7.4	101	6.9
Yugoslavia	65	9.2	141	9.9
Philippines	40	10.0	38	13.2
Liberia	20	15.0	21	33.3
India	20	15.0	77	6.5
Haiti	19	31.5	115	3.5
Lebanon	153	36.6	80	30.0
Sri Lanka	77	44.2	58	29.3
Pakistan	57	57.9	N.A.	----
Peopls Rep of China	86	69.8	N.A.	----

[a] Only clearly "adversary" and "friendly" countries with 40 or more cases granted and denied are included in this table. Each case may include one or more individuals.
[b] Data are available only for offices with computer capability.

Source: U.S., Department of Justice, Immigration and Naturalization Service, "Asylum Cases Filed with District Directors (Fiscal Year 1988)"; *Refugee Reports*, 19 May 1989.

A comparison of the findings displayed in Table 5.2 with the Table 5.1 results suggests that some important changes occurred between 1984 and 1988 in political-asylum processing before INS district directors. In the first place, the directors acted upon a smaller total number of cases in FY 1988. As a consequence, the number of asylum awards are far fewer than the FY 1984 figures. To take an extreme example, over 8,000 applicants from Afghanistan received political asylum in FY 1984; only 36 were so fortunate in FY 1988. On the other hand, the approval *rates* are higher virtually across-the-board.[40] The earlier conclusion regarding the favored treatment of applicants from "adversary" sending countries continues to be supported by the more recent data. However, the disinclination of district directors to grant asylum to claimants from "friendly" nations was no longer as uniform in 1988 as it had been in the past. Specifically, the directors approved over 30 percent of the cases acted upon that had been submitted by petitioners from the People's Republic of China, Pakistan, Lebanon, and Haiti; in FY 1984, asylum seekers from these four sending countries had been successful no more than 7 percent of the time. On the other hand, Salvadoreans experienced the most rejections and nearly the lowest approval rate in spite of the continuation of widespread hostilities in that "friendly" sending country.[41]

Resettled Refugees and Political Asylum Applicants: Process Distinctions

Legal recognition of the refugee condition is determined by prevailing public policy. Under the 1980 Refugee Act, U.S. law defines a "refugee" in a manner that conforms with the United Nations' definition and, as John Scanlan informs us, "the U.N. definition makes no distinction between 'asylees' and 'ordinary' refugees, and provides no analytical basis for so distinguishing. . . ."[42] Nevertheless, until forced to adopt changes at the end of the 1980s by legal challenges and political pressures, the INS employed substantially different standards in admitting refugees from overseas than it did when ruling on asylum petitions submitted by persons already in the United States.

Evidence and Documentation

In the first place, most political-asylum seekers must provide evidence of individualized persecution that is not required of overseas applicants for refugee status.[43]   For instance, decision makers frequently dismiss uncorroborated personal testimony as inherently self-serving.[44]   Some INS examiners even have insisted that asylum applicants produce written proof (e.g., official documents) and/or eye witnesses in order to substantiate their claims.[45]   Although State Department officers have rendered decisive "advisory" judgments regarding the validity of political-asylum cases, they generally rely on interview summaries and blanket assumptions rather than examine the claimant in person or refer the case for verification or further investigation to the U.S. embassy in the applicant's country of origin.[46]   The hidden political agenda intrudes at the documentation stage of the review process.   Thus, Norman and Naomi Zucker suggest that "if the asylum applicant comes from a country in which the United States does not officially acknowledge political repression, or asserts that human rights are improving, that individual will be required to present an almost unattainable level of documentation."[47]

In the case of the refugee-resettlement program, officers conducting overseas interviews at times apply standardized group profiles; they do not expect concrete documentation of personal persecution or insist upon corroborative evidence because to do so would be "unrealistic and unfair."[48] Thus, the case for official-refugee admission typically rests on the applicant's own statements about group membership, experiences, and motives.[49] If the petitioner's statements are credible and consistent with the gatekeeper's knowledge of conditions in the sending country, they usually are accepted as sufficient proof.[50]   The Commission on Immigration and Refugee Policy found that "a person who belongs to a group qualified for refugee status is accorded a strong presumption of eligibility. . . , and is primarily examined to ensure only that he/she is not excludable from the United States."[51]   In short, "a refugee begins with a presumption of merit; an applicant for asylum begins with a presumption of deceit."[52]   Until recently, this blanket presumption of eligibility included "'any refugee from the Soviet Union who wishes to resettle in this country.'"[53]

Refugee Resettlement: The "Priority" System.   In contrast to the procedures followed in evaluating asylum claims, "the review of refugee credentials seems to be generous indeed if an applicant fits into one of the [six] priority categories."[54]   The categories encompass refugees whose lives are in immediate danger (mainly political prisoners)—priority #1, family-reunification cases (#3 & #5), former U.S. government employees (#2), persons with ties to U.S. corporations, educational organizations, foundations, voluntary agencies, and other institutions (#4), and those whose admission is otherwise in the U.S. "national interest" (#6).[55] Norman and Naomi Zucker explain that:

> Priorities are not preferences. Processing for an entire national group takes place within all the approved priorities. Thus, someone in priority two does not usually get preference over someone in priority three. . . and so on. If an applicant satisfies any priority being processed, he [sic] gains a place in the pool of eligible applicants. On the other hand, no matter how well-founded a refugee's fear of persecution may be, if he does not fit into a priority for his country, he is ineligible for consideration.[56]

In practice, the family-reunification priorities provide the basis for most admissions under the U.S. refugee-resettlement program.[57] Over time, the result for Cuban and Indochinese refugee admissions has been to transform the resettlement process into an extension of the regular immigration-preference system. Throughout the second wave of orderly (i.e., pre-screened) Cuban migration, for instance, "the proportion of refugees who had relatives already living in the United States was consistently above 90 percent."[58] In Thailand, moreover, the process of screening for third-country resettlement has been plagued by "a misplaced emphasis on immigration, rather than refugee, criteria."[59]

Embassy and consular officers only present petitioners in authorized priority categories to INS personnel. The latter then assess each applicant's eligibility for refugee status and determine the order in which qualified refugees will be processed for travel to the United States in accordance with the priority scheme. Thus, the priority system principally operates as a mechanism for including or excluding persons with certain backgrounds on a *regional* basis. The specific priorities awarded to a particular region of the world again are largely determined by the State Department's foreign-policy positions.[60] Thus, refugees from the Soviet Union and Eastern Europe, along with those from East Asia who arrived in a country of first asylum prior to April 1982, have been processed in all six categories. In contrast, only persons in priorities one and two—political prisoners and former U.S. government employees—have been eligible from Latin America.[61] Refugees from Ethiopia can acquire eligibility through the first five priorities. Although Iranians have been limited to categories one through four, the State Department has "expanded priority four [other ties to the United States] to include persons who could show they suffered persecution because of their religion, making Baha'is, Jews and Christians from Iran. . . eligible."[62] In FY 1984, the INS approved 65 percent of the

Iranian applicants for resettlement interviewed overseas. In practice, Iranians who can establish membership as Baha'i have been "virtually assured INS approval." Other Iranians "who do not have members of their immediate families in the United States and lack other close ties are ineligible for resettlement. . . ."[63]

Process Inconsistencies and Biases in Refugee Admissions. Inconsistent adjudication characterizes the refugee-admission decisions made by inadequately trained and understaffed INS circuit riders.[64] According to Zucker and Zucker, similar applications in the same office are decided differently by government gatekeepers according to the time of receipt. Specifically, "early in the year, there is a tendency to apply the criteria for refugee status stringently; later in the year, if the numbers allotted to the office have not been used, the standards of proof may be relaxed, allowing migrants to qualify as refugees."[65]

The Refugee Data Center bio-data sample suggests that certain selection biases also are at work in the refugee-resettlement process. For instance, males constituted 88 percent of the principal applicants from Iran and Ethiopia granted admission by overseas gatekeepers. Among those who entered under the Ethiopian ceiling, 35 percent identified themselves as Eritreans, 29 percent as Amhara, 18 percent as Tigrean, 8 percent as Oromo, and 11 percent belonged to other or mixed ethnic groups. Relative to the proportion they constitute of the total pool of refugees from Ethiopia, these figures suggest that Tigreans are the most overrepresented among those selected for third-country settlement in the United States and that Somali speakers are the most underrepresented.

High-level Defectors. Another set of rules applies to high-level defectors. This group need not prove that they feared persecution prior to requesting asylum; it is the act of seeking refuge in the United States which is presumed to ensure punishment if they return to the home country. In addition, requests from high-level defectors "are approved within a matter of days, and they are never detained or required to defend their claims in an immigration court."[66] This type of special treatment is routinely granted to renown athletes and artists who seek asylum for economic and/or professional reasons. After defecting in 1975, for instance, the Czechoslovakian tennis star Martina Navratilova bluntly stated that "'politics had nothing to do with my decision. It was strictly a tennis matter.'"[67]

Assessment. In sum, the U.S. refugee-admission process is replete with crucial process disparities. Governments typically neither admit nor broadcast their individual persecution intentions. People who flee grave threats, physical abuse, and political harassment usually are in no position to gather sworn statements from eyewitnesses or supporting documentary evidence of personal persecution.[68]   Indeed, Patricia Fagen reminds us that "people who are genuinely afraid very often dispose, as quickly as possible, of anything in writing that might identify them as dissenters or opponents, and they are especially reluctant to take such material with them if they decide to flee."[69]   Relatives and others in the homeland who could provide evidence frequently fear reprisals if they cooperate.   Faced with the prospect of jeopardizing the lives of family members, friends, and colleagues still in the homeland, applicants are inclined to withhold certain details that are vital to substantiating their case during political-asylum proceedings.[70] Under the standards of evidence required of asylum claimants, therefore, it is extremely difficult for the rank-and-file political activist to establish that s/he has been the special target of state persecution.[71]

Interviews

Important differences also appear in the interview process.   Whereas the overseas applicant for resettlement usually is asked to describe the ways in which s/he has been or would be mistreated in the home country, the inquiry to the asylum seeker might well be "Why did you come to the United States?"[72]   In addition to the obvious presumptive biases attached to each line of questioning, the query about movement to the U.S.A. is likely to elicit a response that refers to step-migration motives.   We discovered in Chapter 4 that the reasons official refugees, émigrés, and non returnees move to this country usually are unrelated to the political factors that lead members of all three groups to depart from or not return to their country of origin.   Thus, the deliberate confusion of step-migration motives with reasons for becoming an exile amounts to an unfair attempt to weaken or undermine the asylum seeker's case.

In spite of the legal complexities and the difficulty involved in winning an asylum case, only a small proportion of all applicants are represented by legal counsel.[73]   The availability of legal counsel is particularly problematic for persons detained at border crossings.[74]   This situation seriously undermines due-process protection for many non-resettled refugees who apply for political asylum in the United States.[75]

The interview process provides a useful occasion to assess the veracity and conviction of an applicant's persecution claim.   Consistency between the petitioner's personal account and conditions in the sending country should be weighed as an important piece of corroborative evidence.[76]   It is appropriate that contradictions in testimony that have a central bearing on the claim to fear of persecution carry considerable weight. Too often, however, inconsistencies that are peripheral to the issue of well-founded fear of persecution serve as the basis for denying political asylum.[77]

The Application of Differential Screening Standards

Finally, U.S. gatekeepers evaluate asylum appeals according to more stringent standards than those employed when considering overseas requests for resettlement.[78] Until recently, for instance, the INS required that political asylees show "clear probability of persecution" in their country of origin. Under this standard, persecution must be a near certainty.[79] In an internal report, one district director acknowledged that "'if we used that [clear probability standard] all the time, no one would be given asylum.'"[80] In practice, recourse to such a strict standard allows variables unrelated to fear of persecution to constitute the decisive basis for decision making and provides a rationale that masks arbitrary and biased treatment. The outcome has been the inconsistent application of standards by poorly prepared INS district directors and immigration judges among petitioners from different countries and even among applicants of the same nationality and family.[81] The only consistent variable in the treatment of asylum claims has been U.S. foreign-policy orientations; the quality of documentation argument has provided a convenient smokescreen for inherent biases.

The U.S. Supreme Court's landmark decision on 9 March 1987 in *INS v. Cardoza-Fonseca* clearly applied the terms of the 1980 Refugee Act to the political asylum decision-making process. Specifically, the Court ruled that "well-founded fear" of persecution and not the "clear probability" standard must be applied in determining an applicant's eligibility for political asylum in the United States. Justice John Paul Stevens, who authored the majority opinion in the 6-3 ruling, referred to past treatment as well as "good reason" to fear future persecution as the tests to apply in assessing the objective grounds for well-founded fear of persecution.[82]

The U.S. Board of Immigration Appeals (BIA) reacted to the *Cardoza-Fonseca* decision by adopting a narrow interpretation of the term persecution that "renders it more difficult to establish an asylum claim, especially when the applicant is from a country engulfed in civil war."[83] The principal effect of the BIA's new rulings is to deny political asylum to persons who demonstrate a reasonable fear of harm based on a political position of *neutrality* in the context of conflict between government and guerrilla forces. In one case involving a Salvadorean farmer who refused to take sides, the Board found that the fear and possibility of physical harm involved did not stem from a political opinion that he held or that his possible persecutors assumed he held. This ruling does not conform with two federal circuit courts of appeal that have recognized ideological neutrality as a political opinion, however.[84]

Alternative Explanations for Differential Outcomes

In FY 1985, INS district directors granted 24 per cent of the 18,757 first-asylum claims that they acted upon.[85] In percentages, the overall approval rates among overseas candidates for official-refugee status for FYs 1984, 1985, 1986, and 1987 are: 83, 76, 84, and 82, respectively.[86]

In attempting to justify current practice, some of those involved defend the use of stricter standards in political-asylum cases as necessary in order to ferret out frivolous claims by persons who have arrived in the United States without having been preselected for resettlement by the government or its representatives.[87] U.S. government authorities are prone to charge that imposters are driven to submit fradulent asylum claims solely in order to secure work authorization while their applications are under review.[88] Others contend that evenhandedness in the treatment of asylum applications would reward individuals who have "jumped queue" at the expense of those awaiting admission as an official refugee.[89]

In 1986, the Deputy Assistant Secretary of the State Department's Bureau of Human Rights and Humanitarian Affairs, Laura Dietrich, advanced both of these arguments. First, she contended that "a great number of people who apply for asylum in the United States each year are not refugees—that is, not people who are seeking to escape persecution. Rather, they are economic migrants, people who are hoping to make a better life in America than they can in their country of origin."[90] Dietrich further alleged that:

"hundreds of thousands, if not millions, of people have tried to leapfrog over our immigration procedures and over their fellow countrymen who are attempting to conform to such procedures. The great majority of these people have crossed our borders illegally; many of these people, and some who entered legally, have tried to remain in the United States by claiming asylum."[91]

Such charges are noteworthy in that they are never substantiated by reference to reliable empirical data regarding political-asylum seekers and claims.[92] When issued by officials in positions of authority, moreover, they sow "confusion in the public mind" between the special situation of refugees and that of the millions of others who enter this country legally or illegally.[93]   In fact, a relatively small number of persons participate in the political-asylum process.   Whereas the INS apprehended 1.3 million undocumented aliens in FY 1985, it received only 16,622 asylum petitions during that year.[94]   Although there is no fixed limit or ceiling on the number of people who can be granted asylum annually, all awards are at the discretion of the U.S. attorney general.   INS district directors only approved 18,701 cases between June 1983 and September 1986.   In FY 1989, 9,229 persons received political asylum in the United States.[95]

There is a plausible alternative explanation for the dramatic differences consistently encountered in approval rates that merits testing. That is, U.S. gatekeepers, when acting on claims by political-asylum petitioners who possesses an equal or even more compelling basis for admission under the Refugee Act of 1980 in comparison with overseas applicants for official-refugee status, might insist on evidential requirements and definitional standards which are extremely difficult or even impossible to satisfy.   The discriminatory application by administrative officials of more stringent rules in deciding political-asylum cases is likely to stem from "floodgate fears."[96] Whatever the motivation, the practice directly contradicts the country's legislative enactments and humanitarian objectives.[97]

The next section reviews data dealing with exiles from Ethiopia gathered independently of government sources. The findings enable us to ascertain whether or not justifiable grounds exist for the differential treatment of applications for political asylum and resettled-refugee status.

The Ethiopian Case

Fleeing a Marxist regime offers an exile no guarantee of being awarded political asylum in the United States.[98]   In FY 1981, 83 per cent of the Ethiopian[99] applicants for official-refugee status and 40 per cent of the asylum claimants received a favorable result.[100]   In FY 1984, INS officials rejected 77 percent of the Ethiopian asylum applications they acted upon and denied 40 percent of the petitions for refugee admission which they reviewed.[101]   The 60 percent resettlement-approval figure is below average and quite modest compared to Afghanis (85 percent), Vietnamese (93 percent), Soviet émigrés (97 percent), and others.[102]   Even though the INS approved only 23 percent of their claims, moreover, asylum seekers from the Marxist state of Ethiopia ranked quite high (ninth) in overall rate of success among petitioners from countries with 40 or more cases acted upon in FY 1984 (Table 5.1).

The Ethiopian case is particularly instructive in seeking explanations for the wide discrepancies observed in resettled-refugee and asylee approval patterns because several possible justifications for the recurrent differential treatment can be ruled out from the start. In the first place, the majority of exiles from Ethiopia who claim political asylum, along with many others who could have applied but elected not to for various reasons, came to the United States as students and were living here when events occurred in the homeland that gave rise to fears of personal persecution.[103] For them, the United States is the place of first asylum.

The Ethiopian situation also provides a useful basis for resettled-refugee/asylee comparisons because the U.S. government did not possess friendly relations with Mengistu Haile Mariam's communist regime. Thus, mutual interests and/or ideological affinity at the official level do not underlie the denial of asylum claims submitted by Ethiopians. Furthermore, most resettled refugees from Ethiopia have not possessed family or other ties to the United States.[104] The absence of a major "family reunification" bias leaves lack of well-founded fear of persecution itself as the only reasoned ground for the differential treatment of asylum cases.

If discrimination is not at work, the household heads admitted from Ethiopia as official refugees will be more likely than asylum seekers and other exiles living here are to be motivated by persecution and/or well-founded fear of political persecution in the homeland. According to the UNHCR's *Handbook on Criteria for Determining Refugee Status*, which the U.S. INS has implicitly adopted as an authoritative source through distribution to all officers assigned to hear asylum cases, "well founded" is an objective term, while "fear" is subjective.[105] In ascertaining whether an objective basis exists for well-founded fear of persecution, an assessment should be made of conditions in the sending country and of the applicant's background, character, and past experience. In addition, section 43 of the *Handbook* provides that what "happened to his [sic] friends and relatives and other members of the same racial or social group may well show that his fear that sooner or later he also will become a victim of persecution is well founded."[106] In short, it is not necessary for one to experience persecution in order to possess a legitimate "well-founded" fear of it. This understanding is central to the asylum claims presented by most *sur place* refugees and to the survival prospects of anticipatory refugees. On the subjective side, Egon Kunz writes that "the validity of fear for one's safety which is the creator of all refugees can after all never be tested; it is the individual's interpretation of events and self-perceived danger or revulsion. . . which motivates the refugee and justifies his [sic] stand."[107] Furthermore, as Roger Winter points out, evaluators do not possess "the moral right to underestimate refugee pain."[108]

While there must be a real basis for well-founded fear of persecution, the UNHCR *Handbook* stresses that the claimant's subjective state of mind constitutes the primary variable and provides the most conclusive evidence.[109] Therefore, when the case is not clear from the documents available and the facts on record, but the applicant's account is judged to be credible, s/he should "be given the benefit of the doubt."[110] The comparative analysis that follows focuses on the subjective state of mind of migrants from Ethiopia; that is, on the factor(s) that triggered the decision to leave or not to return to the home country.

Political Persecution and Perceived Threats

The presence of fear of personal persecution constitutes the most crucial consideration that qualifies an individual for admission to the United States under the Refugee Act of 1980. In the D.C. sample, exactly 81 per cent of both the responding resettled refugees and the asylum petitioners indicated that (likely) political persecution played an important part in the decision to leave or not return to Ethiopia. In short, applicants for political asylum and officially admitted refugees are equally apt to have been motivated in part by fear of political persecution in Ethiopia.

Home Country Political Involvement. The degree of one's involvement in an opposition capacity and a person's association with an anti-regime organization are other particularly relevant factors in terms of likely political persecution. Table 5.3 presents the distribution of organizational supporters and sympathizers among the D.C. sample at the time of departure from the homeland or time of decision not to return to Ethiopia. Overall, there are no discernable differences between resettled refugees and asylum petitioners in terms of active support for an opposition political organization or nationality movement. Asylum seekers are more likely than official refugees are to have supported the political organization (EPRP) that provided the main opposition to the Derg in the 1970s. Most of those who had supported the Eritrean People's Liberation Front (EPLF), and all of the Eritrean Liberation Front (ELF) and Tigray People's Liberation Front (TPLF) activists in the sample, are resettled refugees. Taken together, however, about half of the official refugees neither supported nor agreed with the objectives of a nationality movement at the time they left Ethiopia

TABLE 5.3 Active Support for Political Organization/Nationality Movement at Time
Left Ethiopia/Decided Not to Return

Organization, By Type	Official Refugee N	Official Refugee %	Asylum Applicant N	Asylum Applicant %
Type of Migrant				

Organization, By Type	N	%	N	%
Opposition Political Organization				
EPRP	10	12.5%	8	24.2%
EDU	0	----	0	----
Me'ison	1	1.3	0	----
Other	3	3.8	1	3.0
None	66	82.5	24	72.7
Nationality Movement				
EPLF	13	16.3	4	12.1
ELF	9	11.3	0	----
OLF	6	7.5	6	18.2
TPLF	2	2.5	0	----
Other	1	1.3	0	----
None	49	61.3	23	69.7

Source: D.C./L.A. sample.

and three-fourths had not been involved with or sympathetic to an opposition political organization. Among the activists, a slightly higher proportion of respondents in the asylum category (11 percent) had exercised a leadership role in an opposition political organization or nationality movement relative to the resettled group (8 percent).

Table 5.4 reports data collected by the author from the written application forms found in (1) a sample of 193 files for resettled refugees from Ethiopia who received assistance in Europe from Church World Service personnel[111] and (2) a sample of 59 files involving political-asylum cases submitted primarily in the New York City and Washington, D.C. metropolitan areas.[112] The results show that a high proportion of the sampled asylum applicants (83 percent) had personally engaged in some act of opposition to the post-revolution regime prior to departure from the sending country. Many of these individuals had manifested their opposition in a serious manner—that is, through armed struggle or by joining a public

TABLE 5.4 Personal Actions in Opposition to Post-revolution Regime Reported by Resettled Refugees and Applicants for Political Asylum That Would Likely Result in Political Persecution in Ethiopia

Action Cited in Petition	%Resettled Refugees (N=193)[a]	%Asylum Applicants (N=59)[b]
Participated in armed struggle	3.1%	16.9%
Participated in demonstration/strike	8.3	20.3
Spoke out, violated regime rule(s)	21.8	23.7
Supptd opposition polit organiz at home	2.1	18.6
Supptd opposition polit organiz abroad	.5	3.4
None reported	64.2	16.9
TOTAL	100.0	99.8

Source: [a]Church World Service sample. [b]Author's asylum-case sample.

protest demonstration or strike. In contrast, 64 percent of the resettled-refugee files did not mention a single opposition act. Less than 12 percent of the official refugees had engaged in armed combat or participated in a public-protest action. While only 11 percent of the resettled sample cited a specific political organization that they had supported in Ethiopia, 19 percent of the asylum seekers had supported the EPRP, 21 percent had been aligned with a national-liberation front, and 23 percent specifically mentioned another opposition group.

Ties to the United States. Previous ties to the United States constitute another factor that might invite individual persecution following a revolution. Recognition of this relationship undoubtedly lies behind the fact that four of the six priorities that guide the INS in deciding which refugees to admit to this country from overseas refer to family reunification, past employment by U.S. government agencies, business firms, and voluntary agencies, or education and training under U.S. auspices.[113] In defending this emphasis, officials contend that "'the United States owes first allegiance to those who are in danger of persecution because of their ties to this country'" and "'adaptation to life in this country is facilitated by the admission of people who either have family [here] or are already familiar with the country.'"[114] Let us, then, examine the strength of the case for priority admission presented by those admitted as resettled refugees from Ethiopia relative to asylum applicants in terms of these considerations.

First, employment by Western government agencies is not an important factor among either migrant category. However, a considerably higher proportion of the applicants for asylum than the resettled refugees (25 percent versus 4 percent) possessed ties to a U.S. or multinational firm.

Personal and family visits to the United States indicate ties to and familiarity with this country's citizens and institutions. Table 5.5 presents

TABLE 5.5 Previous U.S. Visit by Relative(s) Before Respondent Last Left Homeland

| | Type of Migrant | | | |
| | Official Refugee | | Asylum Applicant | |
Relation of U.S. Visitor	N	%	N	%
Parent(s) & sibling(s)	1	1.3%	3	9.1%
Parent(s)	1	1.3	2	6.1
Sibling(s)	10	12.5	7	21.2
Other relative(s) only	18	22.5	11	3.3
None	50	62.5	10	30.3

Source: D.C./L.A. sample.

comparative data on U.S. visits by relatives prior to the respondent's final departure from Ethiopia.[115] Only 37 percent of the official refugees, versus 70 percent of the others, indicate that one or more of their relatives had come to the United States. Furthermore, more than twice the proportion of asylum petitioners relative to resettled refugees report that a member of their *nuclear family* had been in this country prior to their departure from the homeland.

Family reunification also has not been a factor of overwhelming importance in overseas admissions from Ethiopia. Only 28 of the resettled refugees in the D.C. sample (35 percent of the total) report that a member of their extended family lived in this country at the time they applied for admission as a refugee. Sixteen of these interviewees indicate that a relative had already been admitted as an official refugee when they submitted their own application. Applicants for political asylum were more likely than resettled refugees were to possess personal and family ties to the United States—including children who are U.S. citizens.

In contrast to the recently resettled refugee who encounters difficulties adapting to life in this country, most of the migrants from Ethiopia who did not enter with refugee status have lived here for over a decade, speak fluent English, and have been educated at U.S. universities. In conclusion, the officially admitted refugees in the D.C. sample do not possess a stronger

TABLE 5.6   Threat to Self and/or Family Member Important in Decision to Leave/Not Return to Ethiopia

| | | Type of Migrant | | |
| | Official Refugee | | Asylum Applicant | |
Type/Basis of Threat	N	%	N	%
(1) Decision to Emigrate				
Imprisonment	4	5.4	0	----
Physical Danger	3	4.1	1	9.1
Both	60	81.1	9	81.8
Neither	7	9.5	1	9.1
(2) Decision Not to Return				
Imprisonment	NA	----	2	9.5
Physical Danger	NA	----	0	----
Both	NA	----	12	57.1
Neither	NA	----	7	33.3
(3) Primary Basis of Threat if Did Not Leave				
Treatmt self	10	15.6	3	33.3
Treatmt family member	12	18.8	1	11.1
Background of self	4	6.3	3	33.3
Treatmt others sim self	7	10.9	0	----
Genl insecurity, repress	31	48.4	2	22.2
(4) Primary Basis of Threat if Returned				
Treatmt family member	NA	----	2	14.3
Background of self	NA	----	8	57.1
Treatmt others sim self	NA	----	3	21.4
Genl insecurity, repress	NA	----	1	7.1

NA = Not applicable

Source: D.C./L.A. sample.

case for priority admission or special consideration relative to asylum
petitioners in terms of family reunification, corporate ties, identification with
the United States, or potential for social and economic adaptation.

Perceived Threat and Prior Mistreatment. In the comparative analysis
of official refugees and asylum seekers, it also is useful to explore the
extent to which each type of migrant felt compelled to flee or not return to
Ethiopia due to perceived threats or danger to themselves or to a member
of their immediate family.   From Table 5.6, we observe that asylum
applicants who left Ethiopia with no intention of returning are just as likely
as resettled refugees are to base their decision partly on fear of
imprisonment and/or physical danger.   The data reported in the last two
sections of Table 5.6, moreover, reveal that asylum seekers are considerably
more likely than recognized refugees are to attribute their fear of
imprisonment and/or physical danger primarily to factors related directly to
themselves or to a member of their family.   Official refugees, in contrast,
refer most often to general conditions of insecurity and repression as the
principal source of the threat they faced if they did not flee from
Ethiopia.[116]

Furthermore, the official-refugee/asylum-seeker comparisons presented in
Table 5.7 reveal that a much higher proportion of the New York City and

TABLE 5.7 Type of Personal Mistreatment at Hands of Post-Revolution Regime
Reported, by Resettled Refugees and Applicants for Political Asylum
from Ethiopia

Type of Mistreatment	%Resettled Refugees (N=193)[a]	%Asylum Applicants (N=59)[b]
Tortured	14.5%	37.3%
Imprisoned	16.1	16.9
Detained	14.0	----
Other	9.3	32.2
None reported	46.1	13.6
TOTAL	100.0	100.0

Source: [a] Church World Service sample.   [b] Author's asylum-case sample.

228

D.C.-area asylum applicants, as compared with the sampled CWS-assisted refugees, report personal experiences of torture at the hands of the post-revolution authorities. Whereas 46 percent of the CWS group had been imprisoned or detained, about 54 percent of the asylum seekers had been political prisoners in Post-Revolution Ethiopia. More than three-fourths (79 percent) of the asylum claimants, versus only one-quarter of the resettled refugees, indicate that they had been mistreated due to (suspected) membership in a particular opposition organization; two-thirds of the political-asylum group and only 20 percent of the CWS-assisted sample had experienced persecution in Ethiopia as a result of the political opinions they held. Finally, nearly half of the official refugees (46 percent), but only 14 percent of the asylum petitioners, fail to report a single incident of personal mistreatment.

The results presented in Table 5.8 are particularly informative because family ties are especially strong in Ethiopia. Consequently, one typically can expect to receive the same type of (mis)treatment from the regime in

TABLE 5.8 Mistreatment of Family Member and/or Relative at Hands of Post-Revolution Regime Reported, by Resettled Refugees and Applicants for Political Asylum from Ethiopia

Mistreated Relation and Type of Mistreatment	%Resettled Refugees (N=193)[a]	%Asylum Applicants (N=57-59)[b]
Parent		
Any mistreatment	32.6%	51.7%
Killed/imprisoned	26.9	32.8
Sibling		
Any mistreatment	25.4	59.6
Killed/imprisoned	21.8	50.9
Other Relative		
Any mistreatment	18.1	50.0
Killed/imprisoned	15.5	N.A.
Any Family Relation Mistreated	46.1	86.4

N.A. = Not available.

Source: [a]Church World Service sample. [b]Author's asylum-case sample.

power as government authorities have doled out to one's close relatives. The findings indicate that the asylum applicants from Ethiopia are much more likely than the resettled refugees are to possess a family member who had been mistreated by the post-revolution regime. Over half of the asylum seekers report that a brother or sister had been killed or imprisoned, while only 22 percent of the CWS-assisted group share this family experience. In total, 86 percent of the applications submitted by the former and less than half (46 percent) of the official-refugee files mention at least one family relation who had been mistreated at the hands of the post-revolution government. While about 15 percent of the resettled refugees note that a relative had been harmed due to membership in an opposition group, nearly 80 percent of the asylum petitioners cite this situation. Finally, 69 percent of the asylum seekers report that one or more relatives had suffered because of political opinion; only 5 percent of the CWS group mentioned a relative who had experienced mistreatment at the hands of the post-revolution regime due to his or her political views.[117]

Overriding Consideration. Interviewee responses to the series of questions concerning motivations for departing or not returning to Ethiopia reveal that more than one consideration played an important part in the decisional calculations of many migrants. When respondents in the D.C. sample identify the factor of overriding or greatest importance in their decision, officially admitted refugees are much more likely than asylum petitioners are to refer to (1) issues related to the struggle for independence in Eritrea and (2) general conditions of insecurity in Ethiopia; asylum seekers make a disproportionate number of references to (1) fear of personal physical danger at the hands of the Mengistu regime and (2) the imprisonment, torture, or disappearance of a family member or close friend.[118]

Principal Fear If Returned to Ethiopia. In comparing the impact of persecution and personal danger on asylum claimants and resettled refugees, the Church World Service sample and the New York/D.C. cases offer useful insights related to the principal fear that applicants expressed when asked what they expect would happen to them should they be forced to return to Ethiopia. Table 5.9 reveals that the asylum applicants are much more likely than the others are to mention the fear of being killed and the prospect of being imprisoned by the post-revolution regime. Moreover, 13 percent of the admitted refugees in the CWS sample failed to report any fear over the prospect of returning to the sending country.

230

TABLE 5.9 Principal Fear If Returned to Homeland Reported, by Resettled
Refugees and Applicants for Political Asylum from Ethiopia

Principal Fear	%Resettled Refugees (N=193)[a]	%Asylum Applicants (N=58)[b]
Killed, arrested and killed	18.7%	32.8%
Imprisoned, maybe killed	39.9	46.6
Imprisoned only	20.2	20.7
Denial free polit expression	4.1	0.0
Other	4.1	0.0
None reported	13.0	0.0
TOTAL	100.0	100.1

Source: [a]Church World Service sample. [b]Author's asylum case sample.

Overall Results

The results of this comparative analysis demonstrate conclusively that
asylum claimants from Ethiopia are in no sense less motivated than
officially admitted refugees are by fear of individual political persecution
and personal physical danger. In fact, resettled refugees from Ethiopia,
particularly Eritreans, are considerably more likely than applicants for
political asylum are to act primarily out of concern over nationality issues
and due to insecure conditions brought about by war or political
repression.[119] There is no support among the study findings for the charge
levied by government officials and others[120] that most asylum seekers are
economic migrants attempting to bypass immigration laws.

In sum, this study found no evidence that resettled refugees have a
stronger claim to well-founded fear of personal persecution and, therefore,
should be treated differently than asylum applicants. In the case of
migrants from Ethiopia, persons requesting political asylum in the United
States are as likely to have acted out of fear of imprisonment as are those
admitted as official refugees, and they are even more likely to perceive the
threat(s) they face primarily in personal terms rather than in terms of the
general state of insecurity and armed conflict prevailing in the homeland.
On the basis of respondent motivations, then, we find that the asylum

claimants from Ethiopia fit the prevailing legal definition of a refugee even more closely than the individuals granted resettlement by the U.S. government.

The Refugee/Asylee Contradiction

In the post-World War II period, the United States has been generous in terms of admitting certain externally displaced populations. However, at the same time that the U.S. government protests the wholesale rejection of refuge seekers by other countries and proposes to grant entry to as many as 30,000 special immigrants annually who are not refugees but whose admission would be in its "foreign-policy interest,"[121] its gatekeepers consistently deny legitimate claims for political asylum on arbitrary grounds. Certainly, the asylum-review process has not functioned to uphold the refugee definition embodied in U.S. and international law. Persons with legitimate fears of political persecution are regularly denied asylum status. The arbitrary and secretive nature of the review process leaves ample room for foreign-policy considerations, discrimination, and deterrence goals to flourish as the principal bases for treating first-asylum claims.

The political asylum application process is a particularly revealing public-policy arena. Here, actions that would be consistent with standards of international law formally adopted by the U.S. government, as well as with publicly embraced humanitarian concerns, come into conflict with bilateral foreign-policy calculations and with the domestic-policy objective of restricting and discouraging South-North migration. The record is mixed, but the prevailing tendency is heavily oriented toward deterring future population movements rather than making reasoned distinctions among first-asylum applicants. Even refugees from Marxist revolutions, who are often treated generously when they apply for resettlement in the United States, find it difficult to break through the barriers that surround the political-asylum process.

1990 Reforms

In July 1990, the Bush administration instituted several important administrative reforms in the decade-old asylum-review process. The procedural changes, which are intended to ensure that political-asylum rulings are "fair and sensitive," address some of the shortcomings in past practice identified in this chapter. First, the new rules created the position of asylum officer within the Office of Refugees, Asylum, and Parole in INS.[122] A corps of 70–90 INS asylum officers has been trained to specialize in hearing and deciding upon political-asylum petitions. These officers deal exclusively with asylum cases and are encouraged to issue rulings that are not dependent upon the State Department's advisory recommendations.[123] In addition, a documentation center containing information about human-rights conditions in sending countries has been established.[124]

The 1990 rules also introduced revisions in evidential requirements and in screening standards. With regard to evidence, an applicant henceforth is allowed to qualify for political asylum on the basis of his/her own testimony, without needing to produce corroboration, if the personal account is "credible in light of general conditions" in the country of origin. In terms of decisional standards, the 1990 INS "Asylum and Withholding of Deportation Procedures" specifically acknowledge two distinct methods of establishing oneself as a refugee: (1) actual past persecution and (2) well-founded fear of (future) persecution. With regard to the first avenue, the regulations state that "if the applicant establishes past persecution, the burden is then on the government to show (by a preponderance of evidence) that conditions have changed so substantially that the applicant would not have a well-founded fear if he [sic] were to return."[125] Asylum seekers on the basis of well-founded fear no longer need to prove that they would be singled out for individual persecution if there is a "pattern or practice of persecuting the group of persons similarly situated" in the home country and they establish that they are included in or identified with the persecuted group. Moreover, "the Asylum Officer or Immigration Judge must also take into account whether the applicant's country persecutes those persons who leave without permission or seek asylum elsewhere."[126]

Other far-reaching reforms emerged six months later under the terms of a legal settlement reached between the government and the plaintiffs in a class-action suit filed in San Francisco's Federal District Court. The suit claimed, with reference to exiles from Guatemala and El Salvador, that the INS had decided political-asylum cases on the basis of foreign-policy considerations in contravention of the 1980 Refugee Act. Under the terms of the settlement to the *American Baptist Churches vs. Thornburgh* case, the INS agreed to cease the practice of deferring to State Department advisory opinions, to reconsider all cases decided since 1980 under the new rules adopted in July 1990, and to stop deporting and detaining undocumented migrants from El Salvador and Guatemala.[127] Most important, the government stipulated that foreign-policy considerations, flight from a U.S.-supported country, its opinion of the ideological position held by the applicant, and domestic influx-control pressures would no longer affect eligibility determinations in political-asylum cases.[128]

Amnesty and Political Migrants

The amnesty provisions of the *Immigration Reform and Control Act of 1986* applied to political exiles as well as to economic migrants who could prove continuous unlawful resident status in the United States since 31 December 1981.[129] During the brief window of opportunity that commenced in May 1987, over three million undocumented migrants received legal permission to remain in this country under section 201 of the 1986 act.[130] Although principally advanced to benefit illegal workers, an unknown number of genuine refugees who had elected not to apply for political asylum, as well as many of those who had not been deported after INS officials had rejected their asylum claim for foreign-policy reasons, also qualified for legalization.

The immediate benefit of amnesty is possession of the prized document that authorizes one to work legally. Aside from becoming a necessity in the new era of strictly enforced employer sanctions ushered in by the same 1986 law,[131] employment permission reduces the likelihood that workers will put up with excessive exploitation by unscrupulous employers. In addition, all qualified and timely applicants became eligible for permanent residency eighteen months after receiving temporary-resident status—provided that they had not engaged in an act that constitutes grounds for exclusion under the 1986 statute.[132]

Section 902 of the *Foreign Relations Authorization Act* for fiscal years 1988 and 1989 advanced the amnesty qualifying dates for nationals granted entended voluntary departure status at any time during the five-year period ending 1 November 1987. This legislation allowed continuously resident nationals from Ethiopia, Afghanistan, Poland, and Uganda, regardless of whether or not they personally had received EVD from the INS, to obtain legalization if (1) they entered with non-immigrant visas and either applied for political asylum before 21 July 1984 or could prove that their authorized stay expired prior to 21 January 1985, or (2) entered with a status that is not clearly non-immigrant—such as parole, EWI, etc.—and could prove arrival before 21 July 1984.[133]

Exiles who are not nationals of EVD countries and who arrived in the United States on 1 January 1982 or later, as well as those who arrived earlier but held a valid visa subsequent to the cut-off date, are not eligible for amnesty. In February of 1990, however, the Bush administration agreed to allow the spouse and unmarried children of residents legalized under section 201 of the *Immigration Reform and Control Act of 1986* who had been "continuously resident since before 7 November 1986" to remain in the country under voluntary-departure status.[134] Persons covered under this policy can secure employment authorization. Until such time as the individuals granted voluntary departure acquire permanent residency via some other avenue, this change amounts to a partial and transitional remedy for the commonly encountered splitting of family members into documented and undocumented groups.[135] New immigration legislation enacted late in 1990 reserved 55,000 visas over the next three years for the spouses and children of persons granted amnesty.[136]

Nevertheless, many political migrants living in the United States remain ineligible for amnesty for one reason or another; others constantly arrive in a clandestine manner.[137] These exiles, for whom there is little hope that new amnesty legislation will be enacted in the near future, must continue to function without legal status or take their chances with the political-asylum process.

Implications for Third-World Exiles Who Reach the United States

Admission-status distinctions are of far more than academic importance and theoretical interest for the individuals affected. As Robin Cohen notes, "nowadays, one's legal or national status. . . operate as indelible stigmata, determining a set of life chances. . ." in the receiving North.[138] The value of official-refugee admission and award of political asylum is immediately apparent when one considers the rights and benefits that recipients possess in comparison to exiles who reside in the United States under less secure immigration status.

The Undocumented

Among all types of residents, the undocumented and the non immigrant possess the fewest rights and are eligible for the least benefits in the United States.[139] The Carter administration's 1979 effort to identify and deport Iranian students who were out of status and its directive to INS officials encouraging discretionary measures against Iranians—including revocation of authorization for temporary stay or employment—provide a case in point.[140]

Aside from the threat of deportation, lack of lawful employment amounts to the most important disadvantage faced by undocumented migrants. As a result of strict enforcement of the employer sanctions contained in the 1986 legislation, job opportunities and working conditions have deteriorated even further for persons who do not possess employment authorization.[141] Moreover, neither the undocumented nor unsuccessful applicants for political asylum are eligible to receive any of the benefits provided by programs designed specifically to assist refugees.[142] Without legal status, refugees are denied automatic access to private voluntary sponsors who serve as effective links in this society to job and housing markets, public-assistance programs, and language and occupational-training opportunities.[143] In a study with broader implications, Sylvia Pedraza-Bailey has documented how recognition as an official refugee generated a process of cumulative advantage for Cubans and how its denial has resulted in cumulative disadvantage for migrants from Mexico.[144]

Extended Voluntary Departure

The Departments of Justice and State occasionally decide to grant extended voluntary departure status to resident nationals from countries where State deems conditions to be so violent and unstable that their lives would be endangered if they had to return upon expiration of their temporary non-immigrant visa.[145] EVD applicants tend to be university graduates whose safe return home has been jeopardized by altered internal conditions.[146]

In initiating an EVD ruling, the State Department places greatest weight on foreign-policy objectives.[147] The INS issues extended voluntary departure for short intervals in anticipation that the unstable and unsafe circumstances it addresses are likely to improve over time. EVD is the in-country equivalent of parole in that the executive branch determines who should receive it.[148] By 1990, gatekeepers had granted blanket voluntary-departure status to nationals from Ethiopia who arrived in the U.S.A. on or before 30 June 1980, to Poles who departed after the imposition of martial law, and to nationals of Uganda and Afghanistan.[149]

The main advantages of coming forward to claim recognized EVD status when one's temporary visa is no longer valid are that holders (1) are assured that they will not be deported as long as the blanket provision remains in effect, (2) receive work permits, and (3) avoid what has been a highly visible and risky process of claiming political asylum and proving individual persecution.[150]   Nevertheless, individuals granted EVD remain indefinitely in illegal status unless they later qualify for permanent residency through another immigration avenue—such as marriage to a U.S. citizen/permanent resident, or amnesty.   Moreover, EVD can be revoked at any time, with short notice and without a hearing, by the executive branch.[151]

Award or denial of legal permanent residency in the United States is of crucial importance in the lives and future of refugees from revolution.[152] Without permanent residency, EVD holders are left in an indefinite state of limbo.   While many dare not return to their homeland out of fear of personal harm, they concomitantly possess neither the constitutionally guaranteed rights of permanent residents and citizens nor assurance of securing them.[153]   The status and aid afforded to explicitly recognized refugees, the opportunity to reunify a divided family through the regular admission preferences that govern U.S. immigration law, and access to international travel documents[154] are three particularly valuable benefits withheld from persons in EVD status.

Individuals who are granted EVD status and "visa abusers" who entered the United States legally can establish social-security eligibility.   Both groups also can qualify to receive benefits under a few federally funded programs, such as AFDC, which are open to persons indefinitely residing in the United States "under color of law" as long as the INS is not proceeding against their continued stay in this country.[155]   All children of undocumented residents possess the right to a public-school education under the Supreme Court's ruling in *Plyler vs. Doe* and those born in the U.S.A. are eligible to benefit from social-service programs.[156]

Political Asylees

Until 1990, some INS districts granted political-asylum claimants permission to work during the application-review process; a growing number of petitioners did not receive such authorization.[157]   Since asylum proceedings (including appeals) often drag on for years, it is difficult to envision how the INS expected a claimant denied work authorization to support himself or herself other than through illegal employment.   In short, denial of work authorization amounts to a thinly disguised means of deterring applications for political asylum that should be considered on their merits.[158]   In 1990, however, the INS issued regulations that mandated renewable one-year grants of employment authorization to "applicants who are not in detention and who file asylum applications which the Asylum Officer determines not to be. . . manifestly unfounded or abusive.'"[159]

Successful political-asylum seekers are treated quite generously in comparison with their compatriots who hold EVD, are undocumented, or retain non-immigrant visas while not intending to return to the homeland.[160] The former are immediately granted work permits, are eligible for special cash and medical assistance that lasts 12 (formerly 18) months, may participate in language training and educational programs, and are entitled to general public assistance.[161] Upon becoming permanent residents, they can secure international travel papers and acquire most of the constitutionally protected rights possessed by U.S. citizens.[162]

While successful asylum petitioners immensely improve their legal standing, they remain temporarily disadvantaged relative to official refugees. In the first place, they are likely to experience delays that can extend beyond the mandatory one year waiting period in securing permanent residency due to the annual limit of 5,000 (now 10,000) adjustments of status that Congress has imposed on asylees.[163] Unlike resettled refugees, moreover, political asylees are not assisted by voluntary agencies in social integration and in locating suitable employment.[164]

Resettled Refugees

Resettled refugees are in the most privileged situation. In addition to possessing all of the rights and benefits that accrue to the successful asylum claimant, the refugee admitted from overseas attends specially designed training courses operated by voluntary agencies even before arriving in the U.S.A. and the family's transportation costs are borne by the U.S. government. Official refugees are received, placed, and counseled by experienced resettlement agencies that operate with support from government grants.[165] Sponsors provide for their immediate relocation needs.[166] They are eligible for the same cash- and medical-assistance programs that are available to U.S. citizens as well as for special federally subsidized social services operated by state and local governments.[167] The 1980 Refugee Act provides that resettled refugees can be assisted on a preferential basis when such assistance is likely to encourage self-sufficiency or reduce the long-term costs of public support.[168] The result has been creation of "a distinctive class of immigrants that has access to a much larger array of state aid programmes than any other group to come before it."[169]

Notes

1. People with close relatives in the United States also benefit the most from the preference system that drives the first category. See, for instance, Michael J. Piore, *Birds of Passage: Migrant Labor and Industrial Societies* (Cambridge: Cambridge University Press, 1979), p. 178; U.S., Immigration and Naturalization Service, *Statistical Yearbook of the Immigration and Naturalization Service, 1987* (Washington, D.C.: U.S. Government Printing Office, 1988), p. xvii. The lack of numerous recent "anchor" relatives has primarily constitued a barrier to immigration from Africa. See Demetrios G. Papademetriou, "Contending Approaches to Reforming the U.S. Legal Immigration System" (paper prepared for the NYU/Rockefeller Foundation Conference on Migration, Ethnicity, and the City, November 1990), pp. 23–24.

The two latter categories are exempt from the 270,000 ceiling. See Charles B. Keely, "Current Status of U.S. Immigration and Refugee Policy," in *U.S. Immigration and Refugee Policy: Global and Domestic Issues*, edited by Mary M. Kritz (Lexington: D.C. Heath, 1983), pp. 340–349; Demetrios G. Papademetriou and Mark J. Miller, "U.S. Immigration Policy: International Context, Theoretical Parameters, and Research Priorities," in *The Unavoidable Issue: U.S. Immigration Policy in the 1980s*, edited by Demetrios G. Papademetriou and Mark J. Miller (Philadelphia: Institute for the Study of Human Issues, 1983), p. 12.

2. David M. Reimers, *Still the Golden Door: The Third World Comes to America* (New York: Columbia University Press, 1985), p. 161.

3. John Scanlan, "First Final Research Report Submitted to the Select Commission on Immigration and Refugee Policy," in *U.S. Immigration Policy and the National Interest*, Appendix C to the Staff Report of the Select Commission on Immigration and Refugee Policy (Washington, D.C.: Commission, 1980), pp. 105–107, 113; also see Reimers, *Golden Door*, pp. 161–162.

4. For years, the U.S. government "let virtually any Cuban enter the United States without legal formalities." Gil Loescher and John A. Scanlan, *Calculated Kindness: Refugees and America's Half-Open Door, 1945 to the Present* (New York: Free Press, 1986), pp. 61, 75. Also see Scanlan, "Research Report," p. 107; Reimers, *Golden Door*, pp. 158–161, 176, 178–180; Gail P. Kelly, *From Vietnam to America: A Chronicle of the Vietnamese Immigration to the United States* (Boulder: Westview Press, 1977), pp. 21, 36. Between 1968 and 1980, only 7,150 persons who did not flee from Cuba, the U.S.S.R., Indochina, or Eastern Europe, were accommodated under the attorney general's parole power. They came from Lebanon, Uganda, and other Latin American nations. Arthur C. Helton, "Political Asylum under the 1980 Refugee Act: An Unfulfilled Promise," *University of Michigan Journal of Law Reform* 17, No. 2 (Winter 1984):246, 248.

5. Reimers, *Golden Door*, pp. 162–163, 172, 176–180; Loescher and Scanlan, *Kindness*, p. 68.

6. Reimers, *Golden Door*, pp. 192–193; Elizabeth Hull, *Without Justice for All: The Constitutional Rights of Aliens* (Westport: Greenwood Press, 1985), p. 120. In practice, the mandated prior consultation has been dominated by the U.S. Coordinator for Refugee Affairs and the State Department. The State Department's annual report on "Proposed Refugee Admissions and Allocations" for the next fiscal year serves as the principal basis for discussion with congressional committees. See Norman L. Zucker and Naomi F. Zucker, *The Guarded Gate: The Reality of American Refugee Policy* (San Diego: Harcourt Brace Jovanovich, 1987), pp. 72–74.

7. U.S., INS, *1987 Yearbook*, p. 50; George Shultz, "Proposed Refugee Admissions for FY 1987," *Current Policy* 866 (1986):1–5; *New York Times*, 27 March 1989, p. 6. On the efforts of H. Eugene Douglas, U.S. Coordinator of Refugee Affairs from March 1982 through October 1985, to "manage down" refugee admissions and the resistance he encountered, see Zucker and Zucker, *Guarded Gate*, pp. 127–128.

Cubans in the third (Mariel) wave secured entry under special legislation. The Carter administration created the ad hoc category of "entrant—status pending" for this group, partly in order to avoid national government responsibility for reimbursing resettlement costs. Robert L. Bach, "Cubans," in *Refugees in the United States: A Reference Handbook*, edited by David W. Haines (Westport: Greenwood Press, 1985), pp. 87–88; Robert L. Bach, "Third Country Resettlement," in *Refugees and International Relations*, edited by Gil Loescher and Laila Monahan (Oxford: Oxford University Press, 1989), pp. 319, 323.

8. See Lawrence S. Eagleburger, "Proposed FY 1991 Refugee Admissions Levels," *Current Policy* 1307 (October 1990):3; *New York Times*, 16 October 1990, p. A5.

9. Gervase Coles maintains that "in Western practice after 1950 an interpretation was widely given to persecution in relation to Eastern Europeans that was so broad as to amount to a liberal immigration policy. . . ." Gervase Coles, "Approaching the Refugee Problem Today," in *Refugees and International Relations*, edited by Gil Loescher and Laila Monahan (Oxford: Oxford University Press, 1989), p. 385.

10. The principal method of enforcement has involved insistence on admission criteria at the borders that are impossible for many asylum seekers to fulfill—for instance, possession of valid travel documents and all needed visas. In 1988, West Germany turned away an estimated 124,000 foreigners. Some Western European immigration officials require airline employees to deny boarding passes to suspected immigrants and/or refuse to allow potential asylum claimants to step off arriving flights. Such actions, which fail to discriminate between genuine political migrants

and imposters, threaten the very principal of political asylum. Similarly, the U.S. government has automatically placed many Central American asylum seekers who arrive without proper documents under lengthy detention and has been found to intimidate and coerce Salvadoreans into abandoning their asylum claims. It is pertinent in this regard that U.S. gatekeepers admitted only 6 individuals fleeing Haiti by boat out of 21,461 intercepted. See *New York Times*, 27 March 1989, p. 6; 16 March 1990, p. A10; 12 August 1990, p. 16; *World Refugee Survey—1988 in Review* (Washington, D.C.: U.S. Committee for Refugees, 1989), p. 87; Gil Loescher, "Introduction: Refugee Issues in International Relations," in *Refugees and International Relations*, edited by Gil Loescher and Laila Monahan (Oxford: Oxford University Press, 1989), p. 16; Roger P. Winter, "The Year in Review," in *World Refugee Survey—1988 in Review* (Washington, D.C.: U.S. Committee for Refugees, 1989), p. 4; W. R. Smyser, *Refugees: Extended Exile* (New York: Praeger, 1987), pp. 96–97; Johan Cels, "Responses of European States to *de facto* Refugees," in *Refugees and International Relations*, edited by Gil Loescher and Laila Monahan (Oxford: Oxford University Press, 1989), p. 191; *Refugees*, August 1989, p. 24; Bill Frelick, "No Place to Go: Controlling Who Gets In," in *Forced Out: The Agony of the Refugee in Our Time*, compiled by Carole Kismaric (Washington, D.C.: Human Rights Watch and J. M. Kaplan Fund, 1989), pp. 163, 165, 168; Annick Billard, "Second European Assizes on the Right of Asylum," *Refugees* 41 (May 1987):11; Aristide R. Zolberg, Astri Suhrke, and Sergio Aguayo, *Escape from Violence: Conflict and the Refugee Crisis in the Developing World* (Oxford: Oxford University Press, 1989), p. 280. On the June 1990 Schengen agreement, which harmonizes the entry procedures for Third World nationals—including refugees and political-asylum applicants—and will be enforced by Germany, France, Belgium, Luxembourg, and the Netherlands at the most restrictive level, see Sarah Helm, "Europe Sans Frontires?" *Refugees* 78 (September 1990):15–17.

In addition, Western governments increasingly have resorted to deporting acknowledged refugees who are alleged to have qualified for first asylum elsewhere. See Dennis Gallagher, Susan F. Martin, and Patricia W. Fagen, "Temporary Safe Haven: The Need for North American-European Responses," in *Refugees and International Relations*, edited by Gil Loescher and Laila Monahan (Oxford: Oxford University Press, 1989), pp. 341, 348.

11. Michael Posner, "Refugees and Asylum: An Assessment of U.S. Policy and Practice," in U.S., Select Commission on Immigration and Refugee Policy, *U.S. Immigration Policy and the National Interest*, Appendix C to the Staff Report (Washington, D.C.: The Commission, 1981), pp. 19–20. On the history of this legislation, see Reimers, *Golden Door*, pp. 190–191.

12. Dennis Gallagher, Susan S. Forbes, and Patricia W. Fagen, *Of Special Humanitarian Concern: U.S. Refugee Admissions Since Passage of the Refugee Act*

(Washington, D.C.: Refugee Policy Group, 1985), p. 11. See also Hull, *Without Justice*, pp. 119–120.

13. Scanlan, "Research Report," pp. 123–124.

14. Gallagher *et al.*, *Refugee Admissions*, p. 6. See also Michael S. Teitelbaum, "Immigration, Refugees, and Foreign Policy," *International Organization* 38 (Summer 1984):430; Lawrence H. Fuchs, "The Search for a Sound Immigration Policy: A Personal View," in *Clamor at the Gates: The New American Immigration*, edited by Nathan Glazer (San Francisco: Institute for Contemporary Studies, 1985), p. 35; Patricia W. Fagen, *Resource Paper on Political Asylum and Refugee Status in the United States* (Washington, D.C.: Refugee Policy Group, May 1985), p. 24. Elizabeth Hull reports that, in FY 1984, "less than 14 per cent of the proposed allocations were reserved for noncommunist areas." Hull, *Without Justice*, p. 122. In FY 1988, "the only noncommunist country worldwide to produce more than a token number of refugee admissions to the United States was Iran, also viewed as a foreign-policy adversary by the U.S. government." Arthur C. Helton, "Asylum and Refugee Protection in the Bush Years," in *World Refugee Survey—1988 in Review* (Washington, D.C.: U.S. Committee for Refugees, 1989), p. 26. Historically, the State Department's Bureau of East Asian and Pacific Affairs has been an effective internal advocate for increased Indochinese admissions. Loescher and Scanlan, *Kindness*, p. 138.

15. Teitelbaum, "Policy," 439; Zucker and Zucker, *Guarded Gate*, p. 74; Astri Suhrke and Frank Klink, "Contrasting Patterns of Asian Refugee Movements: The Vietnamese and Afghan Syndromes," in *Pacific Bridges: The New Immigration from Asia and the Pacific Islands*, edited by James T. Fawcett and Benjamin V. Cariño (Staten Island: Center for Migration Studies, 1987), pp. 91, 97.

16. Zucker and Zucker, *Guarded Gate*, p. 94.

17. Reimers, *Golden Door*, pp. 185–189, 194; Loescher and Scanlan, *Kindness*, p. 69; Gallagher *et al.*, *Refugee Admissions*, pp. 38–43; Hull, *Without Justice*, pp. 140, 142; Zucker and Zucker, *Guarded Gate*, p. 268; Hanson, "Asylum Practice," 124. See also Mark J. Miller and Demetrios Papademetriou, "Immigration and U.S. Foreign Policy," in *The Unavoidable Issue: U.S. Immigration Policy in the 1980's*, edited by Mark J. Miller and Demetrios Papademetriou (Philadelphia: Institute for the Study of Human Issues, 1983), p. 177; Scanlan, "Research Report," pp. 112–113, 123; Zolberg *et al.*, *Refugee Crisis*, p. 175.

18. Hull, *Without Justice*, p. 122. In some recent years, moreover, the ceiling on African resettlement has not been approached. Thus, only 1,315 official refugees from Africa entered the United States in FY 1986 even though the congressional allocation authorized 3,000 persons. *Refugee Reports*, 20 February 1987, pp. 3, 16; also see Jonathan Moore, "Perspectives on U.S. Refugee Programs," *Current Policy* 981 (June 1980):4. This situation arises, in part, as a result of administrative

decisions that affect processing outcomes. Since 1982, for instance, only exiles from Ethiopia who come directly from Eastern Europe or the Soviet Union have been interviewed at Western European posts. For the vast majority of African refugees, including applicants from southern Africa, resettlement processing has been possible only in Khartoum, Sudan. Fagen, *Political Asylum*, p. 4. Although the distribution of INS processing facilities largely predetermines the nationality of persons resettled in the United States, the criteria used in determining where such centers will be located have not been publicly articulated. The failure of U.S. embassies and consular posts that lack both permanently attached INS staff and circuit riders to process substantial numbers of refugees for resettlement on their own also requires explanation.

Within the African ceiling, there has been "an ongoing presumption in favor of Ethiopians." Zucker and Zucker, *Guarded Gate*, pp. 91–92, 150. For instance, refugees from Ethiopia comprised 98 percent of the FY 1986 admissions from the continent. *Refugee Reports*, 20 February 1987, pp. 3, 16. The Latin American resettlement program has been essentially limited to Cubans. Fagen, *Political Asylum*, pp. 4, 9.

19. George Shultz, "Proposed Refugee Admissions for FY 1988," *Current Policy* 1004 (1987):1–3. In FY 1987, moreover, the State Department transferred 3,000 admission slots from the Latin American total and 1,500 from the African ceiling to Eastern Europe, the Soviet Union, and the Near East/South Asia. Moore, "Perspectives," 4. In FY 1991, President George Bush authorized U.S. government assistance for 50,000 refugees from the Soviet Union. In the previous fiscal year, religious organizations had provided the financial support for 10,000 Soviet refugees and Cuban-American groups had paid for the resettlement of 3,000 applicants from Cuba. Eagleburger, "FY 1991," 4; *New York Times*, 16 October 1990, p. A5.

Africans constituted an even smaller proportion (2.2 percent) of the FY 1986 total, and 2 percent of the combined FY 1980–1985 figure. U.S., Immigration and Naturalization Service, *Statistical Yearbook of the Immigration and Naturalization Service, 1987* (Washington, D.C.: U.S. Government Printing Office, 1988), p. 50. One reason for these low admission numbers, as well as for the lengthy delays encountered in processing applications, has been the assignment of only one INS circuit rider from the Rome Office to handle all applications submitted in Africa—until the 1988 appointment of an INS officer in Nairobi. Beverly G. Hawk, "Africans and the 1965 U.S. Immigration Law" (Ph.D. dissertation, University of Wisconsin-Madison, 1988), pp. 127–128, 132, 279; George Shultz, "Proposed Refugee Admissions for FY 1989," *Current Policy* 1103 (September 1988):5.

The bias against refugee admissions from Africa is not surprising given that between 1820 and 1979, according to Lynn Norment, Africans accounted for less than 150,000 of the 49 million persons allowed to enter the United States as immigrants. Lynn Norment, "Are Black Refugees Getting a Dirty Deal?" *Ebony* 38 (October 1983):136.

20. *New York Times,* 27 March 1989, p. 6; 16 October 1990, p. A5.

21. *New York Times,* 27 March 1989, p. 6; 22 November 1989, p. A7; also see Zucker and Zucker, *Guarded Gate,* p. 86; May Ebihara, "Khmer," in *Refugees in the United States: A Reference Handbook,* edited by David W. Haines (Westport: Greenwood Press, 1985), p. 135. They accounted for 89 percent of the Bush administration's FY 1989 refugee-admission proposal. Jonathan Moore, "Update on Immigration and Refugee Issues," *Current Policy* 1163 (April 1989):2–3. In November 1989, representatives of the Bush administration announced that the U.S. government would sharply curtail the admission of Poles and Hungarians as refugees in light of changes in these countries that had reduced the fear of political persecution. *New York Times,* 22 November 1989, pp. A1, 7.

22. Robert L. Funseth, "Orderly Departure of Refugees from Vietnam," *Current Policy* 1199 (June 1989):4; Robert L. Funseth, "U.S.-Vietnam Relations and Emigration," *Current Policy* 1238 (November 1989):5. In 1989, the Bush administration proposed legislation that would accord parolees "the full rights of other permanent residents of the United States—including the right to qualify for citizenship." Moore, "Update," 2.

23. Reimers, *Golden Door,* p. 194; Zucker and Zucker, *Guarded Gate,* pp. 85, 149, 151–152, 269; Fagen, *Political Asylum,* p. 10.

24. U.S., General Accounting Office, *Asylum: Uniform Application of Standards Uncertain—Few Denied Applicants Deported* (Washington, D.C.: GAO, 1987), p. 17.

25. See, for instance, Reimers, *Golden Door,* p. 197; Doris Meissner, "Statement Before the Subcommittee on Immigration, Refugees, and International Law of the Committee on the Judiciary, U.S. House of Representatives" (mimeo, 9 March 1989), p. 7; Helton, "Bush Years," p. 26; Zucker and Zucker, *Guarded Gate,* pp. 173–174; *New York Times,* 14 December 1988, p. 15.

26. Also see Coles, "Refugee Problem," p. 386; Reimers, *Golden Door,* p. 199. The INS had not begun deportation proceedings against roughly 80 percent of the denied asylum applicants in the 1984 GAO study. U.S., GAO, *Asylum,* p. 3. Also see Christopher T. Hanson, "Behind the Paper Curtain: Asylum Policy Versus Asylum Practice," *New York University Review of Law and Social Change* 7 (Winter 1978):121.

27. For an analysis of the reasons why *non returnees* from Iran and Ethiopia in the D.C./L.A. sample fear political persecution in the home country, see Peter Koehn, Mohammad Amjad, and Girma Negash, "Pre- and Post-Revolution Émigrés and Non Returnees: Ethiopian-Iranian Comparisons" (paper presented at the joint meeting of the African and Middle Eastern Studies Associations, New Orleans, November 1985), p. 27. In comparison with their émigré counterparts who left the

sending country with no intention of returning, the non returnees proved even more likely to report that fear of political persecution due to their ideological position and/or opposition to the regime in power on ethical grounds constituted an important consideration in the decision to become an exile.

28. The United States acceded to the Convention when it signed the 1967 United Nations Protocol Relating to the Status of Refugees (19 U.S.T. 6257). Also see James Silk, *Despite a Generous Spirit: Denying Asylum in the United States* (Washington, D.C.: U.S. Committee for Refugees, 1986), pp. 3, 11.

29. Winter, "Year in Review," p. 3.

30. Zucker and Zucker, *Guarded Gate*, p. 137.

31. Fuchs, "Immigration Policy," p. 36. Department of Justice decisions conformed with the State Department's advisory opinion in 96 percent of the cases acted on in 1984. Iranian applications recorded one of the lowest conformity rates (87 percent). U.S., GAO, *Asylum*, p. 22. See also Paul Cowan, "America Denied: The Plight of People Seeking Political Asylum," *Village Voice*, 13 November 1984, pp. 15–18; Gilburt Loescher and John Scanlan, "Human Rights, U.S. Foreign Policy, and Haitian Refugees," *Journal of Inter-American Studies and World Affairs* 26 (August 1984):314–315, 335, 349; John Scanlan, "Issue Summaries Submitted to the Select Commission on Immigration and Refugee Policy," in *U.S. Immigration Policy and the National Interest*, Appendix C to the Staff Report of the Select Commission on Immigration and Refugee Policy (Washington, D.C.: Commission, 1980), p. 51; John Scanlan, "Who is a Refugee? Procedures and Burden of Proof Under the Refugee Act of 1980," in *In Defense of the Alien*, Vol. V, edited by Lydio F. Tomasi (Staten Island: Center for Migration Studies, 1983), pp. 28–30; Austin T. Fragomen, "New Asylum Regulations," *International Migration Review* 13 (Summer 1979):351; Patricia W. Fagen, *Applying for Political Asylum in New York: Law, Policy, and Administrative Practice* (New York: New York University's Center for Latin American and Caribbean Studies, 1984), pp. 2, 13, 16, 56; Zucker and Zucker, *Guarded Gate*, pp. 157–158.

32. Hanson, "Asylum Practice," 134. Also see Posner, "Asylum," pp. 28–29; Loescher and Scanlan, *Kindness*, p. 82.

33. An asylum applicant's country of origin proved to be more decisive in 1984 than the experience of torture, political imprisonment, or threats to his/her life. U.S., GAO, *Asylum*, p. 22.

34. Also see Allen K. Jones, *Iranian Refugees: The Many Faces of Persecution* (Washington, D.C.: U.S. Committee for Refugees, 1984), pp. 16, 18. During the Shah's reign, INS officials denied most asylum applications filed by Iranian petitioners. It is doubtful, however, that the level of suffering in Iran is any greater today than under the Shah, or that there is any more to fear from the Islamic Republic regime than from SAVAK. The different foreign-policy situation, then,

presents the most powerful explanation for the dramatic change in the treatment of Iranian asylum petitions by U.S. gatekeepers. See Peter Korn, "Hiding in the Open," *Student Lawyer* 14, No. 5 (January 1986):26; Hanson, "Asylum Practice," 117–118, 121.

On the overriding motives for Jewish emigration from the Soviet Union since 1973, see Laurie P. Salitan, "Domestic Pressures and the Politics of Exit: Trends in Soviet Emigration Policy," *Political Science Quarterly* 104, No. 4 (1989/90):675–686.

35. The cumulative statistics for June 1983 through September 1986 (reported in *Refugee Reports* 7 (December 1986):14) confirm the findings presented in Table 5.1. In every instance, the proportion of granted cases either remained the same or increased over the three-year period among petitioners from adversary nations. Indeed, the figure for Cuban asylum applicants rises to 10.3 per cent—and this excludes nearly 35,000 persons granted permanent residency via the Cuban Adjustment Act of 1966. In the "friendly" column, the longer time frame only changes the approval percentages for Liberia (8.4 percent), Pakistan (6.5 percent), Philippines (20.9 percent), and Haiti (1.6 percent).

36. According to former INS Commissioner Doris Meissner ("Statement," pp. 4–5), officials in the Miami office interviewed asylum applicants, but did not schedule denied cases for deportation hearings. The Reagan administration raised no objections to Rivkind's action. Indeed, Attorney General Edwin Meese ruled in July 1987 that Nicaraguans seeking work permits should receive them on an expedited basis, directed INS offices to reinterview sympathetically all asylum claimants from that country, and authorized stays of deportation for asylum applicants. President Reagan later publicly declared that the U.S. government would accept responsibility for Nicaraguan "contras" living in Honduran camps. *New York Times*, 14 December 1988, p. 15. The Department of Justice even considered adopting new regulations that would grant persons who flee "totalitarian" (i.e., communist) countries a presumption of having met the well-founded fear of persecution standard required for obtaining political asylum. See Silk, *Denying Asylum*, p. 8; *New York Times*, 17 March 1986, p. A1; 22 April 1986, p. A10; and 8 May 1986, p. A27; Loescher and Scanlan, "Haitian Refugees," 346–347; Zucker and Zucker, *Guarded Gate*, p. 93.

A flood of first-asylum applications from newly arriving Nicaraguans not connected to the contras led immigration officials to reassess the no-deportation policy in late 1988 and to give the petitions cursory review in order to deny work permits to "frivolous" claimants. *New York Times*, 14 December 1988, pp. 1, 15.

37. Congressman Peter Rodino, among others, criticized the inconsistent and ideologically biased nature of Rivkind's actions. See Zucker and Zucker, *Guarded Gate*, pp. 93–94.

38. In addition to those who file after being apprehended, persons denied asylum by an INS district director possess the right to raise their request again in deportation hearings before an immigration judge. The decisions of immigration judges, but not those of district directors, can be appealed to the Board of Immigration Appeals and the Board's actions can be taken to the U.S. district court or to the court of appeals. Only one percent of the judges' decisions have been appealed to the Board. See the helpful chart depicting both paths in the U.S. asylum-seeking process found in Silk, *Denying Asylum*, p. 5; also see U.S., GAO, *Asylum*, pp. 10–11; Fagen, *Political Asylum*, p. 11; Zucker and Zucker, *Guarded Gate*, pp. 156–157. District directors have handled over three-fourths of all asylum applications in the past. U.S., GAO, *Asylum*, p. 2.

39. *Refugee Reports*, 19 May 1989. The GAO uncovered the following approval rates in 1984: district directors (27 percent), cases originating before EOIR judges (6 percent), and cases initially denied by a district director and renewed before an immigration judge (11 percent). U.S., GAO, *Asylum*, p. 19.

40. Only petitioners from the Philippines, an exceptional case in FY 1984, recorded a lower success rate in FY 1988.

41. The sanctuary movement constituted a citizen response to the policy openly pursued by successive U.S. administrations of denying Salvadoreans political asylum and official recognition as refugees eligible for resettlement. See Korn, "Hiding," 27–31; Todd Howland and Richard Garcia, "The Refugee Crisis and the Law: The 'City Sanctuary' Response," in *Refugee Law and Policy: International and U.S. Responses*, edited by Ved P. Nanda (Westport: Greenwood Press, 1989), pp. 185–194.

42. John Scanlan, "Issue Summaries," p. 47. Also see Fuchs *et al.*, 1981, p. 7; Helton, "Unfulfilled Promise," 251; Hull, *Without Justice*, p. 121.

43. Fagen, *Applying*, pp. 50–52; Fagen, *Political Asylum*, pp. 9, 20; Scanlan, "Issue Summaries," p. 46; Zucker and Zucker, *Guarded Gate*, p. 153.

44. *Refugees*, August 1989, p. 24.

45. Fuchs, "Policy," p. 35; U.S., Select Commission on Immigration and Refugee Policy, *U.S. Immigration Policy and the National Interest*, Final Report and Recommendations of the Select Commission (Washington, D.C.: The Commission, 1981), p. 170; Margarita B. Melville, "Salvadoreans and Guatemalans," in *Refugees in the United States: A Reference Handbook*, edited by David W. Haines (Westport: Greenwood Press, 1985), p. 176.

46. Fuchs, "Policy," p. 36; Loescher and Scanlan, "Human Rights," 334–335; Scanlan, "Burden of Proof," pp. 28, 34; "Issue Summaries," pp. 52–53; Gil Loescher and John Scanlan, "Human Rights, Power Politics, and the International Refugee Regime: The Case of U.S. Treatment of Caribbean Basin Refugees" (paper presented at the annual meeting of the International Studies Association, Washington, D.C.,

March 1985), p. 12; Silk, *Denying Asylum*, p. 30.   In evaluating asylum claims, untrained BHRHA officials rely "solely on information provided by government sources, and tend to ignore diverging assessments of human rights violations compiled by independent human rights organizations or country experts."   Fagen, *Political Asylum*, p. 19.   They also typically communicate their decision in a form letter that does not provide specific reasons for the conclusion reached.   Only 16 percent of the State Department's 1984 advisory opinions sampled by the General Accounting Office included an explanation for the conclusion rendered.   U.S., GAO, *Asylum*, p. 3.

47. Zucker and Zucker, *Guarded Gate*, p. 154.

48. Gallagher *et al., Refugee Admissions*, pp. 55, 58; Scanlan, "Issue Summaries," p. 43.   The group-profile method of review principally benefitted Indochinese resettlement seekers.   See Court Robinson, "Sins of Omission: The New Vietnamese Refugee Crisis," in *World Refugee Survey—1988 in Review* (Washington, D.C.: U.S. Committee for Refugees, 1989), p. 8.

49. See Patricia W. Fagen, "U.S. Refugee Admissions: Processing in Europe," *Migration News* 4 (March 1985):61.

50. Zucker and Zucker, *Guarded Gate*, p. 153.

51. U.S., Select Commission, *Immigration Policy*, p. 169.   Also see Hull, *Without Justice*, p. 121.   On the other hand, "refugee applicants are not given any reason for denial of admission, and they have no effective way to appeal or review denials."   Helton, "Bush Years," p. 27.

52. Zucker and Zucker, *Guarded Gate*, p. 147.

53. Cited in Reimers, *Golden Door*, p. 194.   Also see Loescher and Scanlan ("Caribbean Basin Refugees," p. 8) on Cuban admissions.

54. Gallagher *et al., Refugee Admissions*, pp. 8–9.   Zucker and Zucker (*Guarded Gate*, pp. 155, 269) cite evidence that INS overseas examiners—especially those seeking to fill the Eastern Europe allocation—even have treated insufficient educational and employment opportunities and lack of food as acceptable evidence of persecution.

55. For a detailed description of each category, see Fagen, *Political Asylum*, p. 25.

56. Zucker and Zucker, *Guarded Gate*, pp. 76–77.   Also see Fagen, *Political Asylum*, p. 16.

57. Zucker and Zucker, *Guarded Gate*, pp. 77, 90.   By the start of the decade of the 1980s, over three-fourths of the resettled refugees from Southeast Asia, Cuba, the U.S.S.R., and Eastern Europe possessed family members already living in the United States.   Cited in Barry N. Stein, "Refugee Resettlement Programs and Techniques," in U.S., Select Commission on Immigration and Refugee Policy, *U.S.*

Immigration Policy and the National Interest, Appendix C to the Staff Report (Washington, D.C.: The Commission, 1981), p. 407.

58. According to Robert Bach ("Cubans," pp. 82–83), "relatives of people already living in the United States were given preference according to the following ranking: spouses, parents, and then siblings."

59. Robinson, "Crisis," p. 11. Zolberg *et al. (Refugee Crisis*, p. 167) make the same argument with regard to the Orderly Departure Program.

60. Zucker and Zucker, *Guarded Gate*, p. 77.

61. Fagen, *Political Asylum*, p. 5; Zucker and Zucker, *Guarded Gate*, pp. 77–78. For background on the open-ended processing system used to admit Vietnamese refugees, see Suhrke and Klink, "Vietnamese and Afghan," pp. 90, 96. In recent years, the system has been limited to those in priorities 1–5 who can establish a well-founded fear of persecution. However, the U.S. government remains willing to resettle from first-asylum countries up to half of the newcomers from Vietnam who are determined to be refugees. It also is committed to expanding and accelerating orderly departures (thus far, predominantly family-reunification cases) from Vietnam. Robinson, "Crisis," pp. 7, 9; Lawrence S. Eagleburger, "Indochina Refugee Situation: Toward a Comprehensive Plan of Action," *Current Policy* 1184 (June 1989):1–2; James Baker, "ASEAN: Challenges and Opportunities," *Current Policy* 1190 (July 1990):3. This decision could bring to the United States well over 100,000 family members of U.S. citizens, former reeducation-camp detainees, previous U.S. government or organization employees, and former civilian or military personnel closely associated with the U.S. presence in South Vietnam (along with their families). The orderly departure effort allows processing under three subprograms: regular, Amerasian, and reeducation-center detainee. Funseth, "Orderly Departure," 2–4; Funseth, "Emigration," 5; *New York Times*, 1 August 1989, p. A4.

62. Zucker and Zucker, *Guarded Gate*, p. 78.

63. Fagen, *Political Asylum*, pp. 3, 7, 24. Non-Muslims, including Baha'i (11 percent), comprised 35 percent of the RDC bio-data sample of principal applicants resettled from Iran by late 1984.

64. Helton, "Bush Years," p. 27.

65. Zucker and Zucker, *Guarded Gate*, p. 85; also see Miller and Papademetriou, "Immigration," p. 177.

66. Zucker and Zucker, *Guarded Gate*, p. 148. There have been a number of high-level Ethiopian defections. In the first thirteen years following the revolution, according to one insider's account, "21 ministers, 18 deputy ministers, and 26 ambassadors defected." Dawit Wolde Giorgis, *Red Tears: War, Famine and Revolution in Ethiopia* (Trenton: Red Sea Press, 1989), p. 357.

67. *Boston Globe*, 8 September 1975, p. 2, cited in Hanson, "Asylum Practice," 125. On the immediate award of asylum to the Romanian gymnast Nadia Comaneci in 1989, see *New York Times*, 2 December 1989.

68. See Richard Deutsch, "The Ethiopian Controversy," *Africa Report* 27 (May/June 1982):50; Leon Gordenker, *Refugees in International Politics* (New York: Columbia University Press, 1987), p. 31. The difficulty of providing documentary evidence is compounded for asylum seekers who file an application years after leaving the sending country.

Recently, the Board of Immigration Appeals has further required that petitioners produce evidence that their persecutors possessed no legitimate prosecutorial basis for their actions. Deborah Anker and Kate T. McGrath, "The New Battleground of Asylum Eligibility," in *World Refugee Survey—1988 in Review* (Washington, D.C.: U.S. Committee for Refugees, 1989), p. 31.

69. Fagen, *Applying*, p. 50.

70. See Carolyn Waller, "Statement to the House Committee on Foreign Affairs, Subcommittee on Africa and Human Rights" (March 1982), p. 3. Under INS procedures issued in 1990, applications can be disclosed without the written consent of the individual claimant to "U.S. government officials or contractors with the need to know" as well as to "any other official when the Attorney General deems it appropriate." *Federal Register* 55, No. 145 (27 July 1990):30676.

71. Fagen, *Applying*, p. 51.

72. Zucker and Zucker, *Guarded Gate*, p. 154.

73. *New York Times*, 16 March 1990, p. A10. The voluntary agencies that interview candidates for resettlement overseas, on the other hand, often act as the applicant's advocate as well. Stein, "Resettlement," pp. 395, 406; Fagen, "Processing," 48–49.

74. Furthermore, "immigration lawyers' fees tend to be high in relation to refugees' resources" and many asylum (and amnesty) petitioners have paid "large sums for services of questionable value." Fortunately, dedicated attorneys at some large law firms represent indigent asylum seekers on a *pro bono* basis and voluntary agencies and law-school students provide legal and other forms of assistance. Fagen, *Political Asylum*, pp. 13, 20; Patricia W. Fagen, "California Dreaming," *Refugees* 82 (January/February 1991):21.

75. The particularly egregious violations of due process which occurred in the 1978–1979 INS treatment of asylum petitions from 5,000 Haitians are reviewed in Hull, *Without Justice*, pp. 128–130.

76. Also see Theodore Cox, "'Well-founded Fear of Being Persecuted': The Sources and Application of a Criterion of Refugee Status," *Brooklyn Journal of International Law* 10 (Summer 1984):375–376.

77. *Refugees*, August 1989, p. 24.

78. Zucker and Zucker, *Guarded Gate*, p. 155.

79. Theodore Cox, who makes this point, also reports that "the State Department, in giving advisory opinions to immigration judges, recommends granting asylum only to persons who face a 'high likelihood of persecution.'" Cox, "Well-founded Fear," 372.

80. Cited in Helton, "Unfulfilled Promise," 253.

81. Silk, *Denying Asylum*, pp. 8, 31–32; U.S., GAO, *Asylum*, p. 14; Helton, "Unfulfilled Promise," 252–253, 260; Zucker and Zucker, *Guarded Gate*, p. 162; U.S. Select Commission, *Immigration Policy*, pp. 173–174. In some Eastern European cases, State Department desk officers have admitted accepting "career limitations" as a basis for recommending asylum. Hanson, "Asylum Practice," 125. Iranians claiming fear of persecution on the basis of religious affiliation secured a much higher approval rate (87 percent) in 1984 in comparison with their compatriots who cited fears based upon political opinion, membership in an opposition group, or another consideration. The GAO's study of 1984 decisions also revealed that while 58 percent of all applicants who entered under a student visa and 30 percent of those arriving with a visitor visa received asylum, only 2 percent of the petitioners who entered or attempted to enter without inspection were successful. U.S., GAO, *Asylum*, pp. 17, 21. On the lack of special training for examination officers and immigration judges (many of whom are former INS attorneys), see Zucker and Zucker, *Guarded Gate*, p. 157; Fagen, *Political Asylum*, pp. 18–19.

82. See *New York Times*, 10 March 1987, pp. 1, 11; 107 S. Ct. 1217 (1987). The *Cardoza-Fonseca* ruling does not alter the inherent class bias in the prevailing definition of political persecution. Thus, "the emphasis on loss of existing rights implied in the term persecution tends to favor disposed elites, while persons who normally possess few, if any, rights would not as readily qualify." Astri Suhrke, "Global Refugee Movements and Strategies of Response," in *U.S. Immigration and Refugee Policy: Global and Domestic Issues*, edited by Mary M. Kritz (Lexington: D.C. Heath and Company, 1983), p. 159.

83. Anker and McGrath, "Asylum Eligibility," p. 29.

84. This issue is of particular importance due to the prevailing military strategy employed on contesting sides of contemporary liberation struggles in the Third World. Both government and guerrilla forces utilize "tactics that attempt to remove support for the opposing group by directly attacking those civilians they suspect of supporting, or even sympathizing with, their opponents and often by forcibly relocating such persons out of contested areas." Lance Clark, "Internal Refugees—The Hidden Half," in *World Refugee Survey—1988 in Review* (Washington, D.C.: U.S. Committee for Refugees, 1989), p. 20. Although thousands of former soldiers and guerrillas have been admitted in the past, the BIA also recently ruled that combatants are not refugees since "'virtually all participants on

either side of an armed struggle could be characterized as persecutors'" who are ineligible for asylum. Anker and McGrath, "Asylum Eligibility," pp. 29–30.

85. *Refugees* 25 (January 1986):7. The approval figure for FY 1989 is 23 percent. *New York Times*, 19 July 1990, p. A10. While the U.S. percentage has remained relatively constant, asylum-approval rates have declined precipitously in Western Europe. With the exception of France (at 32 percent), most Western European governments granted asylum in less than 15 percent of the cases they reviewed by 1988. *New York Times*, 27 March 1989, p. 6; Frelick, "Who Gets In," p. 165.

86. U.S., INS, *1987 Yearbook*, p. 49. At processing posts, voluntary-agency personnel working under contract with the State Department screen persons interested in third-country resettlement, prepare their initial dossier, and assist them in preparation for the INS interview. Fagen, *Political Asylum*, pp. 17–18; Hawk, "Africans," pp. 120–121. The number of potential applicants for resettlement who are rejected by voluntary-agency staff during the screening phase does not appear to be great. See, for example, Fagen, "Processing," 55, 57, 59. However, no reliable figures dealing with this dimension of the admission process are available in the published literature.

87. See Fagen, *Political Asylum*, p. 21; Hanson, "Asylum Practice," 136. On the damage caused by frivolous claims, see Zucker and Zucker, *Guarded Gate*, p. 153.

88. See Meisner, "Statement," pp. 3–4, 12; Alan C. Nelson, "Prepared Statement," in U.S., Congress, Senate, Committee on the Judiciary, Subcommittee on Immigration and Refugee Policy, *S. 377. Hearings*, 99th Congress, 1st session, 1985, pp. 50–51.

89. Fagen, *Political Asylum*, p. 10. Zucker and Zucker (*Guarded Gate*, p. 152) maintain that line jumpers usually are "motivated by desperation."

90. Laura J. Dietrich, "U.S. Asylum Policy," in *World Refugee Survey—1985 in Review* (Washington, D.C.: U.S. Committee for Refugees, 1986), p. 9.

91. Dietrich, "Asylum Policy," p. 9. Also see the quite similar allegations set forth by Canada's Minister of Employment and Immigration in Benoît Bouchard, "The Refugee Challenge: Time for a World Response," in *Human Rights and the Protection of Refugees under International Law*, edited by Alan E. Nash (Halifax: Institute for Research on Public Policy, 1988), pp. 21–22.

92. Cels ("Responses," p. 205) makes a similar point regarding Western European government allegations that they are being flooded with manifestly unfounded applications. A comprehensive analysis conducted for the U.N.H.C.R. found that the proportion of genuinely abusive asylum requests is small. That agency also has expressed concern over exaggerated allegations of fraudulent claims

by industrialized-country governments. Cited in Gallagher *et al.*, "Safe Haven," p. 341.

93. Silk, *Denying Asylum*, pp. 10–11.

94. Silk, *Denying Asylum*, p. 11; U.S., Immigration and Naturalization Service, *1985 Statistical Yearbook of the Immigration and Naturalization Service* (Washington, D.C.: U.S.G.P.O., 1986), p. 72. Also see Arthur C. Helton, "The Refugee Act's Unfulfilled Asylum Promise," in *World Refugee Survey—1985 in Review* (Washington, D.C.: U.S. Committee for Refugees, 1986), p. 7. Applicants, 85 percent of whom came from Latin American nations, filed a record 101,679 claims in FY 1989. *New York Times*, 19 July 1990, p. A10.

95. Silk, *Denying Asylum*, pp. 6, 9; *New York Times*, 19 July 1990, p. A10. Clearly, not all of the asylum cases denied by U.S. immigration authorities are without merit. Nearly one-third of the refugees recently admitted to Canada are individuals who have been refused asylum in the United States. Patricia W. Fagen, "Resettlement: A Modest Option," *Refugees* (March 1989):29.

96. Zucker and Zucker, *Guarded Gate*, pp. 146, 156, 162–163.

97. Also see Scanlan, "Research Report," p. 133; Silk, *Asylum*, pp. 39, 2, 7.

98. See Reimers, *Golden Door*, p. 196.

99. In its reports, the U.S. government classifies Eritreans and Oromo as "Ethiopian." In this chapter, "migrant from Ethiopia" is used to designate the sending country rather than nationality identification.

100. Cited in Waller, "Statement," pp. 3, 5. Arthur Helton ("Unfulfilled Promise," 260) quotes an internal INS report which states that examiners accepted 99 percent of the Ethiopians processed for admission as refugees from overseas at the beginning of FY 1982.

101. Fagen, *Political Asylum*, p. 24. During the first six months of the 1983 fiscal year, INS officers authorized the admission of 55 percent of the persons presented by the International Catholic Migration Commission in Sudan. *ICMC Newsletter* 8, No. 2 (1984):7. In FY 1986, INS circuit riders approved 60 per cent of the refugee applicants for resettlement whom they interviewed in Africa. One circuit rider interviewed 1,300 Ethiopian petitioners in a 13-day period. *Refugee Reports*, 20 February 1987, p. 4. The FY 1987 figures show a 68 percent approval rate among refugee-status applicants from Ethiopia. The success rate for Iranians was 84 percent in that year and 66 percent in FY 1984. U.S., INS, *1987 Yearbook*, p. 49; U.S., Immigration and Naturalization Service, *1984 Statistical Yearbook of the Immigration and Naturalization Service* (Washington, D.C.: INS, 1985), p. 71. Approval and refusal statistics for FY 1984 among Iranians and Ethiopians interviewed in Rome, Vienna, and Frankfurt are presented in Fagen, "Processing," 54–59.

102. Fagen, *Political Asylum*, p. 24.

103. In the D.C. sample, 55 percent of the asylum claimants had left Ethiopia prior to the revolution; roughly half had arrived in the United States in 1974 or earlier.

104. In the Church World Service sample of Ethiopian and Eritrean refugees resettled from Europe, 19 percent of the applicants mention a brother or sister who lived in the United States and 17 percent of the files contain reference to a relative outside of the refugee's nuclear family. The figures for the RDC bio-data sample are 14 percent (member of nuclear family) and 17 percent (another family relation). In terms of special ties, 5 percent of the CWS-assisted refugees from Ethiopia had benefitted personally from a U.S. government-sponsored program; 3 percent had worked for a U.S. government agency (also 3 percent of the RDC sample); 13 percent had worked for a U.S. or multinational business firm (2 percent, RDC); and 4 percent had been employed by an external voluntary agency or foundation (8 percent, RDC).

105. United Nations, Office of High Commissioner for Refugees, *Handbook on Procedures and Criteria for Determining Refugee Status* (Geneva: U.N.H.C.R., 1979), sections 37 and 38, pp. 11–12; Scanlan, "Burden of Proof," pp. 25–26. The Board of Immigration Appeals also has accepted the *Handbook* as persuasive authority on the determination of asylum claims.

106. U.N.H.C.R., *Handbook*, pp. 12–13; Scanlan, "Burden of Proof," p. 26.

107. Egon F. Kunz, "The Refugee in Flight: Kinetic Models and Forms of Displacement," *International Migration Review* 7, No. 2 (Summer 1973):136.

108. Winter, "Year in Review," p. 3.

109. U.N.H.C.R., *Handbook*, pp. 11–12; Fagen, *Applying*, pp. 51–52.

110. Scanlan, "Burden of Proof," p. 27; also see Silk, *Denying Asylum*, p. 32. Although the *Handbook* clearly is more flexible than U.S. practice, application of its principles would not allow undeserving petitioners to gain asylum. See Scanlan, "Refugee Act," p. 31.

111. For details regarding this sample, see Chapter 6. The sampled files typically contained a summary statement prepared by the CWS staff member who interviewed and assisted the applicant. This source is used rather than the RDC bio-data sample because the latter does not usually include information on the principal applicant's qualifications for refugee status.

112. In addition to the N.Y.C. and D.C. districts, several of the sampled petitions were filed in Arlington, Baltimore, Newark, and a few other districts. This data set is not based upon systematic sampling; it simply consists of all available files. It is important to note that the application material submitted by nearly all of the asylum claimants had been prepared with the assistance of legal counsel. Of course, Church World Service counsellors had aided all of the applicants for resettlement. Another difference concerns the outcome of the process. The CWS

sample deals with principal applicants who had been accepted as refugees and resettled in the United States by 1985. The on-going asylum sample includes cases filed as late as 1989. Although the fears confronted by this group are more compelling than those uncovered for the successful refugee applicants, INS district directors had denied *60 percent* of this set of asylum requests. Many of the other cases are pending.

113. See Gallagher *et al., Refugee Admissions,* p. 45.

114. Cited in Gallagher *et al., Refugee Admissions,* p. 47.

115. Only three of the resettled refugees had traveled to the United States prior to fleeing from Ethiopia.

116. Among the successful refugees in the CWS sample, only 15 percent of the Eritreans and 7 percent of the Ethiopians reported that they had been the victims of war and/or other forms of armed conflict in Ethiopia. However, 68 percent of all the files contained representations of personal danger due to conditions of insecurity in the homeland.

117. However, 12 percent of the CWS sample reported that they had a relative who had been persecuted because of his/her position in Haile Selassie's regime.

118. For more detailed analysis, see Peter Koehn and Girma Negash, *Resettled Refugees and Asylum Applicants: Implications of the Case of Migrants from Ethiopia for United States Policy* (Arlington: Center for Ethiopian Studies, 1987), pp. 68–69.

119. A plurality of the official refugees cited nationality movement concerns as the overriding or most important consideration in their decision to emigrate. Ninety per cent of this group simultaneously feared personal political persecution. More resettled refugees mentioned Eritrean liberation or persecution issues than any other factor when describing the reason they fled from Ethiopia. Among the resettled Eritrean household heads interviewed in the D.C. study, EPLF supporters constituted the largest group of those who had been politically involved in the homeland.

The resettlement of such applicants stands in sharp contrast to the U.S. State Department's recommendations with respect to certain Eritrean asylum seekers. In the fall of 1986, the Bureau of Human Rights and Humanitarian Affairs suddenly began issuing detailed "advisory" opinions that recommended against granting political asylum to EPLF members. The Bureau based its decisions, in part, on the argument that the United States "supports the existing borders of Ethiopia, and does not encourage the movement for Eritrean secession." Advisory opinion by Edward H. Wilkinson, Director, Office of Asylum Affairs, BHRHA, U.S. Department of State, in an Arlington District case, November 1986, p. 2.

120. See Silk, *Denying Asylum,* p. 10.

121. *New York Times,* 6 April 1989, p. 1.

122. *Federal Register* 55, No. 145 (27 July 1990):30676.

123. *Federal Register* 55, No. 145 (27 July 1990):30676–30677. Michael Posner ("Asylum," p. 22) had recommended this reform measure in 1980.

124. *Federal Register* 55, No. 145 (27 July 1990):30676; *New York Times*, 19 July 1990, p. A10.

125. *Federal Register* 55, No. 145 (27 July 1990):30678.

126. *Federal Register* 55, No. 145 (27 July 1990):30678; *New York Times*, 19 July, 1990, p. A10.

127. Under this agreement, the U.S. government agreed to conduct new hearings for about 150,000 claimants from Guatemala and El Salvador as well as for an estimated 350,000 undocumented migrants who never applied for asylum because the process had been stacked against them. *New York Times*, 20 December 1990, p. A10. The *Immigration Act of 1990*, signed by President Bush on 29 November, explicitly grants Salvadoreans in this country since 19 September 1990 temporary protected status for 18 months and eligibility to receive work authorization in 12-month increments. Demetrios G. Papademetriou, "The Immigration Act of 1990" (Washington, D.C.: U.S. Department of Labor, Bureau of International Labor Affairs, December 1990), p. 12.

128. In addition, the settlement stipulates that the churches and civil-rights groups that initiated the suit will designate representatives to participate in training programs on international human-rights issues specifically designed for the new asylum officers and for immigration judges. *New York Times*, 20 December 1990, p. A10.

129. U.S., INS, *1987 Yearbook*, p. xv. On the long history of this legislation and the positions taken by various interested groups, see Demetrios Papademetriou, "Attempting Immigration Reform: An American Quandary," *Migration* 1, No. 1 (1987):142–155.

130. *New York Times*, 5 March 1990, p. A12. In a 1991 majority opinion, Supreme Court Justice Stevens ruled that the government cannot deny amnesty to illegal migrants without due process of law. *New York Times*, 21 February 1991, pp. A1, 10.

131. See Meissner, "Statement," p. 3.

132. With the exception of the handicapped, and the under-aged or pregnant seeker of Medicaid coverage, amnesty recipients are barred from most national government public-assistance programs for five years following legalization. U.S., INS, *1987 Yearbook*, p. xv.

133. In the case of nationals from EVD countries, residence since 21 July 1984 need not be continously unlawful. For details, see *Federal Register* 53, No. 54 (21 March 1988):9274–9280.

134. An estimated 1.5 million undocumented migrants could benefit from this decision. *New York Times*, 5 March 1990, p. A12.

256

135. See Reimers, *Golden Door*, pp. 217, 224.

136. *New York Times*, 29 October 1990, p. A13.

137. See, for instance, *New York Times*, 2 January 1990, p. A9 and 27 February 1990, p. A5.

138. Robin Cohen, "Citizens, Denizens and Helots: The Politics of International Migration Flows in the Post-War World" (paper presented at the International Symposium on Cultural Changes in the Period of Transformation in the Capitalist World System, Hitotsubashi University, Tokyo, September 1988), pp. 14–16. Also see Bach, "Resettlement," p. 322.

139. See Hull (*Without Justice*, pp. 85–88, 93), who also points out (p. 147) that "temporary visitors—so-called 'nonimmigrants'—and even undocumented aliens are entitled to due process and most of the Constitution's substantive rights."

140. These acts of retribution ultimately failed to produce the intended results mainly due to the inability of the INS to identify Iranians studying in the United States at that time. Hull, *Without Justice*, pp. 66–68.

141. See, for instance, *New York Times*, 2 January 1990, p. A9; 3 January 1991, p. A11.

142. Fagen, *Political Asylum*, p. 12; David S. North, "Impact of Legal, Illegal, and Refugee Migrations on U.S. Social Service Programs," in *U.S. Immigration and Refugee Policy: Global and Domestic Issues*, edited by Mary M. Kritz (Lexington: D.C. Heath, 1983), p. 280.

143. Bach, "Resettlement," pp. 323–324.

144. Sylvia Pedraza-Bailey, *Political and Economic Migrants in America: Cubans and Mexicans* (Austin: University of Texas Press, 1985), pp. 13, 40.

145. Fagen, *Applying*, pp. 43–45; Dale S. de Haan, "Statement on Salvadoran Refugees, Extended Voluntary Departure, and S. 377," in U.S., Congress, Senate, Committee on the Judiciary, Subcommittee on Immigration and Refugee Policy, *S. 377 Hearings*, 99th Congress, 1st sess., 1985, pp. 76–104.

146. Ronald Copeland and Patricia W. Fagen, *Political Asylum: A Background Paper on Procedures and Problems* (Washington, D.C.: Refugee Policy Group, 1982), pp. 28–30.

147. Zucker and Zucker, *Guarded Gate*, pp. 217–219.

148. Reimers, *Golden Door*, p. 198.

149. Nationals from Ethiopia who arrived at a later date, along with Lebanese, could receive EVD on a case-by-case basis. Koehn and Girma Negash, *Resettled Refugees*, pp. 21–22; also see Gallagher *et al.*, "Safe Haven," pp. 346–347; Zucker and Zucker, *Guarded Gate*, pp. 218–219. Since 1960, EVD also has been issued for varying periods to nationals of Cuba, Dominican Republic, Czechoslovakia, Chile, Cambodia, Vietnam, Laos, Hungary, Romania, Iran, and Nicaragua.

Interpreter Releases 64, No. 36 (21 September 1987):1093; Hanson, "Asylum Practice," 119.

150. See Scanlan, "Issue Summaries," pp. 72–73. The INS's reputation for arbitrary and unfair adjudication of asylum petitions, and the desire to return to the home country, discourage many genuine refugees from applying for political asylum. See Gallagher *et al.*, "Safe Haven," pp. 333–334.

151. See Hanson, "Asylum Practice," 119; Loescher and Scanlan, *Kindness*, p. 196. In 1981, the State Department did announce that blanket EVD had been withdrawn for nationals of Ethiopia. However, widespread protests from civil-rights groups and others brought about the reinstatement of EVD less than one year later. See Koehn and Girma Negash, *Resettled Refugees*, p. 22.

152. Also see Hanson, "Asylum Practice," 119, 138; Zucker and Zucker, *Guarded Gate*, p. 175.

153. The same conclusions generally apply with respect to persons granted temporary safe haven in most Western European countries. It is noteworthy in this connection that "Eastern Europeans almost always have been able to remain in Western European countries of first asylum. . . ." See Gallagher *et al.*, "Safe Haven," pp. 334, 342, 348; Smyser, *Refugees*, p. 103. After they have resided in a European country for a long time, however, these "B-status" refugees "will often be granted residence permits of unlimited duration since, for humanitarian reasons, they cannot be returned." Cels, "Responses," pp. 192–193.

154. Gallagher *et al.*, "Safe Haven," p. 147.

155. Carolyn Waller, "Aliens and Public Benefits: New Developments and Policy Considerations," *Migration Today* 10, No. 2 (1981):23–25; Fagen, *Political Asylum*, p. 12; also see *New York Times*, 15 July 1986, p. 13.

156. Demetrios G. Papademetriou and Nicholas DiMarzio, "An Exploration into the Social and Labor Market Incorporation of Undocumented Aliens: The Case of the New York Metropolitan Area" (report to the Center for Migration Studies and the Tinker Foundation, New York, 1985), p. 72; Hull, *Without Justice*, pp. 89–93.

157. Fagen, *Political Asylum*, p. 11.

158. This tactic, along with reduction of welfare benefits and long-term lodging in cramped quarters, has been adopted by Western European countries bent upon discouraging asylum petitions. Cels, "Responses," p. 191; Guy S. Goodwin-Gill, "Refugees: The Functions and Limits of the Existing Protection System," in *Human Rights and the Protection of Refugees under International Law*, edited by Alan E. Nash (Halifax: Institute for Research on Public Policy, 1988), p. 152; *New York Times*, 27 March 1989, p. 6; Billard, "Asylum," 11–12; also see Silk, *Denying Asylum*, p. 26. In 1990, the United States Court of Appeals for the Ninth Circuit found an INS regulation that called for the detention of persons working without

authorization while awaiting deportation hearings "'harsh and inhumane'" and ruled it illegal. *New York Times*, 12 September 1990, p. A14.

159. *Federal Register* 55, No. 145 (27 July 1990):30676–30677.

160. In at least one crucial respect, those who maintained legal non-immigrant status after 1981 are the most disadvantaged group because they were ineligible for amnesty under the 1986 Immigration Reform and Control Act. See *New York Times*, 8 November 1986, pp. 1, 7.

161. Fagen, *Political Asylum*, pp. 6–7; Copeland and Fagen, *Asylum*, p. 25; North, "Social Service," pp. 272–273; U.S., Select Commission, *Immigration Policy*, p. 179. The Reagan administration reduced the period of eligibility for refugee cash and medical assistance from 18 to 12 months in 1988. *World Refugee Survey—1988 in Review*, p. 86.

162. Permanent residents are subject to all the obligations of citizenship, but are not entitled to all of the rights. They are not allowed to vote or hold elected office, are barred from sensitive government jobs, and are not guaranteed reentry when they venture outside the United States. Furthermore, "they live with the knowledge that they can be deported on any of 700 grounds" and that Congress could order the blanket deportation of permanent residents and drastically restrict their employment options. Most fundamentally, permanent residents are vulnerable because they are politically powerless. Hull, *Without Justice*, pp. 29–36, 52.

163. 8 USC 1159; Scanlan, "Issue Summaries," p. 84; Scanlan, "Research Report," p. 112. Iranians secured over 60 percent of the 5,000 adjustments to permanent residency issued in FY 1987. U.S., INS, *1987 Yearbook*, p. xxix.

164. Fagen, *Political Asylum*, p. 12.

165. Fagen, *Political Asylum*, p. 6.

166. Paul J. Strand and Woodrow Jones, Jr., *Indochinese Refugees in America: Problems of Adaptation and Assimilation* (Durham: Duke University Press, 1985), p. 40.

167. Fagen, *Political Asylum*, pp. 6–7; U.S., Select Commission, *Immigration Policy*, p. 179.

168. See Susan S. Forbes, *Adaptation and Integration of Recent Refugees to the United States* (Washington, D.C.: Refugee Policy Group, 1985), p. 2.

169. This assessment is particularly applicable in California, where broadly interpreted regulations allow a high-level of participation in the AFDC-Unemployed Parent program. Robert L. Bach, "State Intervention in Southeast Asian Refugee Resettlement in the United States," *Journal of Refugee Studies* 1, No. 1 (1988):40, 45, 52.

Third-World Exiles in Industrial Societies: The U.S. Reception

6

Profiles: Post-Revolution Exile Communities in the United States

A basic measure of a civilized society is the way it treats strangers.

—Arthur C. Helton

Persons fleeing revolutionary political change constitute an important, but often misunderstood dimension of recent South-North population movements. Part 3 explores key dimensions of the U.S. reception of Cuban, Vietnamese, Iranian, Ethiopian, and Eritrean exiles.

What are the backgrounds of the refugees from revolution who are received by the United States? Based upon available demographic data, Chapter 6 profiles the five migrant communities that are of special concern in this book and identifies the key differences that exist between the entire population of persons who break with their homeland and the few who reach the United States. In light of the paucity of previously published information about the "new" exiles from Iran and Ethiopia,[1] they are the central focus of attention here. Following an overview of refugees from Cuba and Indochina based on research findings reported in secondary sources, available data regarding the demographic characteristics of the

Iranian, Ethiopian, and Eritrean migrant communities are used to construct the detailed profiles presented for the first time in the next section.

The Cuban and Indochinese Exile Communities

Profile: Cuban Refugees in the United States

Prior to the post-revolution influx, more than 100,000 Cubans lived in the United States—including persons born here as well as some exiles from the U.S.-supported Batista regime.[2] By 1990, over one million people of Cuban ancestry resided in this country. They comprise about 5 percent of the raidly expanding and increasingly politically influential Hispanic-American population.[3] Most exiles from Cuba settled in Dade County, Florida. Other large Cuban-American settlements exist in West New York and in Union City, New Jersey.[4]

The Cuban exile population in the United States includes many former professionals, government officials, and relatively wealthy members of the urban society.[5] The capital city of Havana, which encompassed 21 percent of the total population, constituted the pre-departure place of residence for 62 percent of the exiles. Only 2 percent of the refugees sampled in 1963 had fled from homes in the Cuban countryside even though over 40 percent of the nation's population lived in rural areas. In comparison with the occupational distribution of the home-country population, professionals and semiprofessionals were overrepresented and farmers and fishers grossly underrepresented within the refugee community at the end of 1962. At that time, more than 35 percent of the sampled exiles in Miami had at least completed the equivalent of a secondary-school education; only 4 percent of the adult population in Cuba had attained this level of education. Whereas over half of the national population possessed less than a fourth-grade education in 1953, only four percent of the refugees were in this situation.[6]

Later waves of entrants changed the composition of the Cuban population in the United States. The more recent arrivals include carpenters and others with working-class backgrounds, along with lawyers, doctors, and teachers.[7] Subsistence farmers and fishers remain a small fraction of the total pool of migrants, but intermediate- and low-level clerical and service workers make up an increasing proportion of the Cuban-American community. Without question, the more recent arrivals are less wealthy than are those who left in the early post-revolution period.[8] The later waves also incorporated a much larger share of black Cubans.[9] Although the vast majority of migrants continued to leave from residency in Havana and other large cities, nearly half had been born in a town or rural area. Educational attainment levels declined and most refugees knew little or no English upon arrival.[10] Nevertheless, 83 percent of the Cuban-American population had completed secondary school by 1988, and 24 percent reported four or more years of university education.[11]

José Llanes suggests that approximately 10 percent of the Cuban exile families earned over $45,000 per year in the early 1980s and that about 40 percent lived below the poverty line.[12] The economic success of Cuban exiles in Miami is widely reported. Less is known about the poor.[13] According to Llanes, "the Cuban working poor constitute a large majority of the seasonal workers in tourism and services in Miami." Thousands of others are agricultural workers in Florida and Louisiana and are "employed 'off the books'" in New York and New Jersey sweatshops.[14] Reflecting on 25 years of refugee influx, Robert Bach concludes that "many of the dimensions of social organization that stand out in the predominant Miami and New Jersey Cuban communities, including the social and economic inequalities, recall the social order of Havana in the 1950s."[15]

Profile: Indochinese Refugees in the United States

The presence of large numbers of Indochinese migrants in the United States is a recent development. Prior to the collapse of the U.S.-supported Republic of Vietnam in 1975, for instance, less than 20,000 Vietnamese—including students—resided in this country.[16] The four leading settlements for Vietnamese refugees are Los Angeles, Santa Ana, Houston, and Washington, D.C.[17] The largest U.S. concentrations of Khmer are in southern California, Washington, Oregon, Texas, and the nation's capital.[18]

At the time of arrival, Indochinese refugees have been quite young in comparison with migrants from Cuba and the U.S. population.[19] Since many families managed to migrate together, or were able to reunite later, household size tends to be large.[20] Whereas Catholics comprised 10 percent of the population of South Vietnam, 40 percent of the early Vietnamese refugee arrivals adhered to that faith. This group also came from urban, ruling-class family backgrounds.[21] About one-third of the migrants who had been in the sending-country labor force possessed professional or technical occupational backgrounds; only 5 percent of the early group of Vietnamese household heads possessed fishing or agricultural skills.[22]

Data from a survey of Indochinese refugee household heads conducted in Illinois indicate that only 7 percent lacked any formal education. A large proportion had at least completed a secondary education, although only 8 percent had graduated from a college or university.[23] While Vietnamese household heads resemble the total U.S. population in terms of their educational background, they clearly come from the ranks of the educated elite in the homeland. According to Gail Kelly, the comparable school-age participation rates for the population of South Vietnam were 3 to 16 percent (secondary) and 1 to 2.5 percent (university).[24] Exiles from Vietnam tend to be more highly educated than Laotians and Cambodians.[25] Nevertheless, the initial group of refugees from Laos included many of the country's most highly educated and trained people.[26] Many recent Khmer arrivals are former peasants and workers with no formal schooling. Their English-language skills tend to be poor.[27]

Chinese refugees from Indochina tend to be older than others from that region and to come from urban settings. Most possess backgrounds as skilled or unskilled laborers, or as urban service providers. According to one study, more than half of the adult Chinese refugees from Vietnam had at most attained a primary-school education; only 4 percent had studied at the university level. Over 90 percent of the households reported that none of their members knew English fairly well at the time of entry.[28]

The Iranian Exile Community

Consideration of the Iranian exile community is divided into two parts. First, we will examine available data on the national migrant population. Then, we will focus on the local communities in the Los Angeles and Washington, D.C., metropolitan areas.

National Population Characteristics

Approximately 110,000 U.S. residents reported that they possessed Iranian ancestry in the 1980 census. This figure excludes many Iranians of Armenian, Turkish, and Kurdish ethnicity.[29] On the other hand, not all of these self-identified Iranians are first-generation migrants.

The U.S. government granted permanent residency to 29,820 Iranian immigrants between 1958 and 1975.[30] Most of these early arrivals are highly educated professionals—particularly physicians and engineers.[31] During the period 1976–1984, U.S. gatekeepers admitted about 75,000 new immigrants from Iran.[32] A dramatic increase in the number of political-asylum awards from October 1981 through September 1984 benefitted an additional 16,000 Iranians.[33] During 1983 and 1984, the U.S. government resettled 3,829 official refugees from Iran.[34] Perhaps 29,000 Iranian migrants lived here with undetermined or undocumented immigration status.[35] Finally, we might speculate that half of the approximately 17,500 Iranians holding student visas in 1984 had no intention of returning to their home country.[36] Adding each of the estimates presented above yields a total projected national population size for the Iranian migrant community of approximately 171,000. This 1984 estimate does not include children born in the United States.

Iranian migrants tend to concentrate in a few states—especially California, New York, and Texas—and in certain metropolitan areas. The Los Angeles and Washington, D.C., areas are two of the most popular residential locations for exiles from Iran.[37]

Resettled Refugees. The U.S. government began to resettle a small number of Iranian refugees in 1983. In 1984, the author coded available information from the Refugee Data Center (RDC) bio-data files for a 14 percent random sample with a systematic start of principal applicants for resettlement from Iran who had been admitted as official refugees from Spain, France, Italy, and the Near East via other European countries. The data collected provide a reliable profile of the initial group of about 1,500 resettled household heads from Iran.[38]

In the first place, 189 of the 219 principal applicants (86 percent) are men. In addition, this group of refugees is predominantly middle-age or older. Persons under 26 years of age only make up 25 percent of the sample; 50 percent are over 30. The breakdown by religious affiliation is 65 percent Muslim, 11 percent Baha'i, 9 percent Protestant, 8 percent Jewish, and 8 percent other. Fourteen of the official refugees (6 percent) are Armenian. Only 3 percent had not completed secondary school; 55 percent had finished secondary or equivalent education, one-third possessed a university degree (including 12 percent with an advanced degree), and 10 percent had received some post-secondary education without completing a degree. Nearly half of the principal applicants (44 percent) report being fluent in English. However, 17 percent are not literate in the English language and another 36 percent are literate but speak English poorly.

Roughly 70 percent of the sampled refugees had been active in the homeland labor force; 23 percent had only been students and the rest had not been employed. Among those in this early group of resettled refugees who had worked in Iran, a wide range of occupations are represented. Skilled workers comprise the largest category (17 percent). Other major occupational groups are school teachers and professors (14 percent), public servants (14 percent), members of the armed forces and police (13 percent), owners/top managers of a large business (11 percent), traders/tailors/small-business owners (8 percent), professionals (7 percent), and unskilled laborers (5 percent). There is only one farmer in the employed sample, and no members of the clergy. The sample of admitted refugees included 3 SAVAK officers, a colonel in the Imperial Guard, and 33 former employees of a U.S. or multinational corporation.

The L.A. and D.C. Metropolitan Areas

This section presents a profile of the household heads from Iran interviewed in the D.C./L.A. study. Roughly half of these migrants lived in the nation's capital or in the surrounding area. A majority (68 percent) of the respondents had arrived in the United States between 1974 and 1981. Exactly three-quarters of the interviewed migrants had left Iran permanently prior to the revolution; the majority departed from the homeland in the interval just prior to the deposition of the Shah.

In 1984, males comprised approximately 80 percent of the sampled Iranian household heads. Two-thirds of the household heads in the D.C./L.A. exile communities were between 25 and 39 years of age in 1984; another 23 per cent had passed their 40th birthday. Although 78 percent of the respondents never had been married prior to their final departure from Iran, only 35 percent remained unmarried at the time of interview. An additional 14 percent reported that they were divorced or separated. Two-thirds of the married respondents had an Iranian spouse and 22 percent were wed to a U.S. citizen; 9 interviewees had married a non citizen who was not Iranian. A slight majority of the respondents lived in households of three or more persons at the time of interview.

Six of the interviewed household heads from Iran identified themselves as Kurdish and eight as Turkish; all of the others reported Iranian nationality identification. Table 6.1 sets forth the religious identification of respondents. At the time of final departure from Iran, the majority of interviewees (73 percent) adhered to Shiite Islam. However, less than half of the non returnees maintained this religious affiliation at the time they decided to live in exile. The Table 6.1 findings reveal that a sizeable proportion of the Iranian community had abandoned Islam without embracing another religious faith after leaving the homeland.[39] While a minute fraction of the population of Iran are granted access to higher education,[40] nearly half of these migrants (46 percent) had attended or graduated from a university prior to departing from the home country—

TABLE 6.1   Religious Identification of Iranian Respondents at Time Departed Iran
and at Time Non Returnees Decided to Live in Exile

Religious Identification	Time Left Iran N	%	Time NRs Decd Live in Exile N	%
Muslim (Shiite)	111	72.5%	51	48.6%
Baha'i	7	4.6	5	4.8
Muslim (Sunni)	5	3.3	3	2.9
Jewish	3	2.0	3	2.9
Zorastrian	2	1.3	2	1.9
None	25	16.3	39	37.1
Agnostic	--	--	2	1.9
Total	153	100.0%	105	100.1%

Source: D.C./L.A. sample.

including 10 percent who possessed an advanced degree at that point in their lives.

Class Backgrounds. We also are interested in the class backgrounds and origins of Iranian migrants who currently are settled in the United States. Most (55 percent) of their fathers worked primarily in the private sector; 61 per cent of this group had owned a small business. The fathers of 25 interviewees either owned or worked for large business firms—mainly manufacturing, construction, and commercial companies. Among the fathers of Iranian exiles who principally worked in the public sector, six percent had occupied a high-level political position. Only 12 percent of the respondents reported that their mother had ever accepted a salaried job outside of the home.

The data presented in Table 6.2 offer a clearer picture of the social origins of Iranian migrants. Nearly two-thirds of the interviewees report that their father either had held a supervisory or administrative position in government, or had been the owner/manager of a private enterprise. While one in every four Iranian migrants came from a professional family, there are only two children of small farmers among the respondents. A substantial proportion of the interviewees (10 percent) note that their father had worked in a clerical or secretarial capacity at the time of the revolution. The sons and daughters of skilled and unskilled laborers are under-

TABLE 6.2 Type of Work Performed by Father of Respondents from Iran at Time of the Revolution[a]

Father's Type of Work	No.	%
Policy, law making	1	0.7%
Professional, technical, teaching	34	24.8
Mgt., supervision, administration	52	38.0
Large-scale farming	4	2.9
Financial, commercial	12	8.8
Clerical, secretarial	13	9.5
Skilled labor	5	3.6
Unskilled labor	4	2.9
Small-scale farming	2	1.5
Retired	10	7.3
TOTAL	137	100.0%

[a]Information concerning fathers who had passed away by the time of the revolution is not included in this table.

Source: D.C./L.A. sample.

represented given Iran's relatively industrialized economy. Considered as a group, these migrants do not possess family backgrounds associated with severe economic subjugation and exploitation in Iran.

In terms of their own employment history, slightly more than half of the respondents never worked in Iran. Among those who had been employed, 54 percent had occupied private-sector jobs. Most of the privately employed migrants (59 percent) had been affiliated with large businesses. Three out of every ten private-sector respondents had *owned* a large or small business. The sample also includes 5 former members of the armed forces and 4 top-level policy makers. Table 6.3 shows that about half of the exiles who had worked in Iran engaged in administrative work, financial/commercial activities, or teaching. Only 11 percent had been laborers, and a single interviewee had belonged to a labor union. None of the migrants from Iran interviewed in L.A. and D.C. came from the ranks of small-scale agricultural producers in the homeland.

Class origins can be explored further utilizing information collected regarding homeland income. Nearly three-fourths of the respondents

TABLE 6.3 Principal Type of Work Performed in Homeland by Respondents from Iran

Type of Work	No.	%
Policy, law making	1	1.4%
Diplomacy	3	4.2
Professional (law, med., engineer)	5	6.9
Technical, scientific	6	8.3
Teaching, academic	10	13.9
Management, supervision, admin.	18	25.0
Financial, commercial	11	15.3
Art, entertainment, sports	3	4.2
Clerical, secretarial	7	9.7
Skilled labor	5	6.9
Unskilled labor	3	4.2
TOTAL	72	100.0%

Source: D.C./L.A. sample.

assessed their (their family's in the case of students) income level as "medium" relative to others living in Iran at the time they left. Less than 10 percent identified their income level as "low." Exactly one-tenth of the respondents had profited from urban house rents themselves, and 38 percent indicate that their parents had possessed city rental property. In addition, the parents of 10 percent of these migrants served on the board of directors of a private corporation.

In terms of association with Western employers, 30 percent of the émigrés and 17 percent of the non returnees had worked for a multinational corporation in Iran. Two others (3 percent) admitted that they had worked for a Western government agency before leaving the home country. In addition, 10 percent of the sample report that their father had worked for a firm with U.S. and/or transnational corporate ties.

Only 9 percent of the Iranian respondents who received some post-secondary education before departing from their country of origin had attended an educational institution run by foreigners. However, 21 percent of the interviewees had already visited the United States before their final departure. Most had come for study or training programs, although six respondents had made business trips and nine others had come only as a tourist or visitor. The findings on travel by relatives show that the parent(s) of 36 percent of the interviewees had visited the United States prior to the exile's departure from Iran, while an additional 33 percent could think of one or more other relatives who had come to this country. Most of the Iranian migrants, then, belong to families that were familiar with and, in one way or another linked to, the United States.

Social Background Summary. The findings presented thus far are suggestive of several important ways in which migrant household heads from Iran who reach the United States differ from their compatriots who continue to live in the homeland. In comparison with the sending-country population, the U.S. exiles are younger, more highly educated, more often the children of small business owners, managers, or professionals and to have been business owners/managers or teachers themselves, and more likely to possess upper- and middle-class backgrounds.[41] Household heads with subordinate class backgrounds—particularly peasant farmers and unskilled laborers—are grossly underrepresented. Finally, the interviewed members of the Iranian migrant community are clearly distinguished from their home-country counterparts by their much greater tendency to possess pre-departure family contacts with the United States and to have been employed by a multinational corporation while living in Iran.

Political Orientations. Exactly half of the Iranian migrants had opposed the pre-revolutionary regime, although only 28 percent of them did so actively. A small minority (10 percent) indicate that they had supported the Shah. Among those who held pro-regime orientations, about 40 percent had been active in their support for the monarchy.

About 17 percent of the interviewed migrants report that they actively supported an opposition political organization during the Shah's reign; another 19 percent had agreed with an opposition group. Most of this politically involved minority supported or identified with the People's Mujahedin and the People's Fedayii-e, or agreed with the National Front. About 20 percent of the sampled exiles had participated in the student movement at home prior to the overthrow of the Shah.

Although nearly 40 percent of the respondents who lived in Iran after the overthrow of the monarch initially supported the revolution, roughly 90 percent ended up opposing the new political order. Moreover, 59 percent of the latter group engaged in anti-regime activity. For the sample as a whole, 88 percent opposed Khomeini's regime in 1984, 3 percent expressed support, and 9 percent took no position.

In comparison with the pre-revolution period, a considerably higher proportion of those living in Iran after the revolution indicated support for an opposition political organization. Fully 44 percent of the interviewed migrants (N=36) report that they participated in an opposing group—mainly the People's Mujahedin and the People's Fedayii-e, Minority faction—in the post-revolution period. Roughly the same proportion of the non returnees either actively promoted (32 percent) or agreed with (13 percent) an anti-regime organization.

TABLE 6.4 Political Organizations Supported and Agreed with in Past and in 1984 by Iranian Respondents

	Time Period			
	Time Exile Decision		1984	
Political Organization	N	%	N	%
People's Fedaii-e (Minority)	42	38.2%	5	13.5%
People's Mujahedin	22	20.0	12	32.4
Both Mujahedin and Fedaii-e (Minority)	5	4.5	-	-
National Front	9	8.2	-	-
Iran Novin, Rastaklez	5	4.5	-	-
Organization of Communist Unity	4	3.6	3	8.1
Peykar	4	3.6	-	-
Tudeh Party	3	2.7	1	2.7
Muslim Brotherhood, IRP (Imam Khomeini)	3	2.7	3	8.1
Democratic Party of Kurdistan	2	1.8	1	2.7
Komeleh	2	1.8	3	8.1
Tenpest (Toofan)	2	1.8	-	-
Front for Liberation of Iran (Amini)	1	0.9	4	10.8
Communist Party of Workers & Peasants	1	0.9	1	2.7
Natl Resist Movemt of Iran (Bakhtiar)	-	-	1	2.7
Bakhtiar's and Amini's Groups	-	-	1	2.7
Shah's Party (Mardon)	1	0.9	-	-
People's Fedaii-e (Majority)	1	0.9	1	2.7
Peykar and Fedaii-e (Minority)	1	0.9	-	-
Mujahedin and National Front	-	-	1	2.7
Not specified	2	1.8	-	-
TOTAL	110	99.7%	37	99.9%

Source: D.C./L.A. sample.

Table 6.4 lists the specific political organizations that Iranian respondents supported or identified with at the time they decided to become an exile and in 1984. All of the groups that played important roles during the revolution and in the post-revolution period are represented here.[42] Over 80 per cent of the respondents who identified with or participated in a political organization at the time they decided to live in exile mention a leftist group.[43] The results reveal a decided decline in respondent support for opposition political organizations after leaving Iran or deciding to remain in the United States. The People's Fedayii-e (Minority) suffered the most dramatic loss of supporters (from 42 to 5). Although the number of respondents who identified with the People's Mujahedin also had declined by 1984, this organization attracted the greatest level of support among those who named a political organization at the time of the interview (32 percent). Only two groups recorded a numerical increase: (1) supporters of Amini's Front for the Liberation of Iran and (2) Komeleh.

U.S. Position. Any profile of the Iranian exile community would be incomplete without identifying the U.S. social and economic position of members living in the two study areas. This section treats the respondents' educational attainments, immigration and employment status, type of work, and income level at the time of interview in the mid 1980s.

TABLE 6.5   Immigration Status of Iranian Respondents

Immigration Category	N	%
A. Naturalized citizen/permanent resident	73[a]	46.8%
B. Official refugee	10[b]	6.4
C. Political asylee	15	9.6
D. Asylum applicant	3[c]	1.9
E. Undocumented	26	16.7
F. Valid non immigrant	29	18.6
TOTAL	156	100.0%

[a] Includes 2 respondents who had become permanent residents by 1984.
[b] Includes 12 respondents who had become permanent residents by 1984.
[c] Includes 2 respondents who entered without valid documents or INS inspection and 5 respondents whose asylum claim had been denied.

Source: D.C./L.A. sample.

Most of the household heads from Iran are highly educated. Only 3 respondents (2 percent) had not completed secondary school. Three-fourths of the interviewees possessed at least one university degree, and 45 percent had received an advanced degree.

The data set forth in Table 6.5 indicate that nearly half of the D.C./L.A. sample had secured U.S. permanent residency without arriving as a resettled refugee or claiming political asylum (i.e., by marriage or other family relationship to a U.S. citizen or permanent resident, through labor certification, as a "qualified investor" prior to 1978, etc.).[44] This figure includes 11 naturalized citizens (7 percent of the interviewed community members).[45] Only 6 percent were resettled refugees; another 10 percent had received political asylum. The Table 6.5 results also suggest that a sizeable proportion of the migrant household heads from Iran possess undetermined or undocumented immigration status (19 percent of the sample) and non-immigrant visas (19 percent).[46]

TABLE 6.6 Iranian Respondents' Current (1984) Work in U.S.

Type of Employment	N	%
Business owner	17	14.3%
Food, drink, hotel worker	13	10.9
Mgr., supervisor, administrator	11	9.2
Engineer	10	8.4
Driver	9	7.6
Research or teaching assistant	8	6.7
Skilled worker, mechanic	7	5.9
Accountant, financial administrator	6	5.0
Lawyer, physician	6	5.0
Salesperson	6	5.0
Store Clerk, cashier	5	4.2
Nurse, social worker	3	2.5
Unskilled service worker	3	2.5
Technical worker	3	2.5
Artist, clergy, other professional	3	2.5
Teacher, academic	3	2.5
University professor	2	1.7
Secretarial worker	1	0.8
Laborer, guard	1	0.8
Financial analyst, econ researcher	1	0.8
Retired	1	0.8
TOTAL	119	99.6%

Source: D.C./L.A. sample.

In terms of participation in the U.S. work force, roughly two-thirds of the interviewed migrants worked full-time and another 16 per cent held a part-time job.[47] The others either exclusively pursued studies (8 percent) or were unemployed at the time of interview (10 percent). Table 6.6 reports the latest type of work performed by employed respondents in the D.C. and L.A. metropolitan areas. Iranian exiles engaged in a wide variety of different economic activities. The largest group (14 percent) owned business enterprises. Another 11 percent of those who provided information about their current employment worked for food, beverage, or lodging establishments. Professional engineers (8 percent) and administrators (9 percent) also are well represented in the sample.

From Table 6.7, we observe that 15 percent of the 121 interviewed migrants from Iran who answered the self/family income query received in excess of $50,000 in 1984. Roughly one-third of the interviewees in this

TABLE 6.7 Reporting Iranian Respondents' Self/Family Total Income from All Sources in 1984

Total Income (U.S. $)	N	%
None - 9,000	14	11.6%
$10,000 - 19,000	29	24.0
$20,000 - 28,000	32	26.4
$30,000 - 38,000	17	14.0
$40,000 - 48,000	11	9.1
$50,000 - 120,000	18	14.9
TOTAL	121	100.0%

Source: D.C./L.A. sample.

category are established pre-revolution non returnees, while another third consists of post-revolution émigrés—many of whom undoubtedly brought considerable wealth out of Iran. Only 36 percent of the respondents report total annual family-income levels below $20,000. Three-fourths of the household heads earning less than $20,000 had recently decided not to return to Iran.

The Community of Exiles from Ethiopia

The overthrow of Haile Selassie's regime in September 1974 marks a critical threshold in the history of migration from the Horn of Africa to the United States. Prior to the revolution, only a handful of Ethiopians, Eritreans, and Oromo had settled in the United States. Most Ethiopians were unfamiliar with the very concept of a "refugee" and repelled by the idea of moving abroad permanently.[48] Virtually all students and temporary visitors returned to Ethiopia in the pre-revolution period.[49] As a result, a community of immigrants had not been established in the United States when the Derg terminated monarchial rule in 1974.[50]

A dramatic reversal of this pattern commenced within a short time after the revolution. Instead of returning, thousands of students remained in this country upon completing their studies. In the early 1980s, roughly 80 percent of the students, 60 percent of the businesspersons, and 20 percent of the tourists from Ethiopia who entered the United States did not exit upon the expiration of their temporary non-immigrant visas.[51] In addition, defections consistently occurred among the diplomatic corps, official delegates on government business, and touring artists and performers.[52] Only a small proportion of the non returnees who elected to live in self-imposed exile have later changed their mind and moved back to Ethiopia.

National Characteristics of the Current Exile Community

Beginning in the late 1970s, official refugees from Ethiopia began to enter the United States under the seventh-preference immigration category. After 1980, the Refugee Act provided the principal resettlement avenue for Ethiopians, Eritreans, and Oromo. Refugees from Ethiopia regularly make up over 90 percent of all arrivals under the annual African ceiling. The total number of exiles from Ethiopia resettled in this country under the Refugee Act of 1980 reached 4,993 in 1982[53] and rose to 10,674 by 1 October 1984.[54] By the end of 1989, the United States had provided a place of resettlement for about 20,000 official refugees from Ethiopia.[55]

Accurate statistics do not exist for the non refugees from Ethiopia who are currently living in the United States. Ethiopians and Eritreans are not enumerated in the national census and the INS has not maintained reliable population records. Various sources crudely estimated the number of persons from Ethiopia who qualified for extended voluntary departure in 1982 at between 10,000 and 40,000, although only 3,000 individuals actually registered for EVD status with the INS.[56] Roughly 5,000

274

individuals whose country of origin is Ethiopia applied for political asylum between FY 1981 and FY 1984.[57] Some of these asylum seekers also qualified for EVD status at the time of application. Perhaps 2,000 Ethiopians and Eritreans still held valid student visas in 1985;[58] most of them had no intention of returning. An unknown number of others—including former EVD holders and some of those reported as students—have become permanent residents through amnesty, marriage, or other legal means independent of the political-asylum and refugee-resettlement processes.[59] Finally, there is a small community of undocumented migrants—mainly visa abusers who entered after 1 January 1982.

In sum, the available statistics suggest that a conservative estimate would place the total population of migrants from Ethiopia living in the United States in 1989 at 40,000.[60] The entire community, including children born here, is considerably larger.

Focus: Official Refugees. Two sets of data concerning resettled refugees from Ethiopia made available by the Refugee Data Center in New York City allow for more detailed sociological analysis. In the first place, the Center provided certain summary demographic information (RDC "Summary") regarding all refugees who arrived between 1 August 1980 and 25 October 1984. In addition, the author coded available information related only to household heads and independent applicants from a 10 percent sample of the refugee bio-data forms received by 1984 at the Refugee Data Center (RDC "Bio-data" sample). These forms are numbered sequentially and arranged by date of entry in the United States and by country (or area) of application for admission as an official refugee. The procedure for this study involved a systematic sample with a random start from the 12 file boxes of applicants from Sudan, 2 of Djibouti applicants, and one each for refugees from Somalia, Kenya, Egypt, and via Europe.

TABLE 6.8 Age in 1984 of Official Refugees from Ethiopia

Age in 1984	Sampled Household Heads	
	N	%
From 15 to 22	84	14.6%
From 23 to 26	212	36.7
From 27 to 30	141	24.4
From 31 to 34	67	11.6
Thirty-five and over	73	12.7

Source: RDC Bio-data sample.

Two-thirds of the official refugees from Ethiopia who arrived in this country between January 1980 and September 1984 are males. The majority are quite young. Over half of the resettled household heads were 26 years of age or younger at the time of admission; only 13 percent had reached 35 years of age (see Table 6.8). In addition, the majority (69 percent) had no relatives in the United States at the time of their arrival.

Over half of all the refugees from Ethiopia admitted by 1984 belonged to one-person households. Two-thirds adhered to Ethiopian Orthodox Christianity, 22 percent identified themselves as Muslim at the time of application, and 11 percent were Roman Catholic or Protestant. In terms of ethnicity, more than 35 percent of the resettled refugees are Eritrean; approximately 29 percent are Amhara, 18 percent Tigrean, 8 percent Oromo, 6 percent Harari, 4 percent Somali, and 2 percent Gurage and other.

Table 6.9 shows that less than 10 percent of the refugees resettled by 1984 possessed a university degree. However, over 40 percent had completed secondary school or an equivalent post-primary education. Around 20 percent of the official refugees from Ethiopia had not completed

TABLE 6.9 Highest Education Attained by Official Refugees from Ethiopia at Time of Application for Resettlement in the United States

Highest Education Attained	Household Heads (RDC Bio-data)		All Refugees (RDC Summary)	
	N	%	N	%
Advanced university degree	4	0.7%	36	0.8%
University first degree	37	6.5	314	6.7
Some post-secondary	106	18.7	1917	40.9
Completed secondary or equiv	147	25.9	1917	40.9
Some post-primary	143	25.2	1456	31.0
Completed primary	37	6.5	1456	31.0
Some primary, literacy	71	12.5	972	20.7
No formal	22	3.9	972	20.7
TOTAL	567	99.9%	4695[a]	100.1%

[a]No information available for an additional 5,294 refugees

a primary-school education. Eritreans are the most likely, and Amhara the least likely, to arrive with a primary-school education or less (35 percent and 16 percent, respectively). The resettled Oromo refugees proved most likely to possess some post-secondary education at the time of entry (32 percent, versus, for example, 17 percent of the Eritreans).

The overwhelming proportion of the refugees from Ethiopia resettled in the United States by the mid 1980s possessed urban backgrounds. For data on place of birth, we turn to the sampled Church World Service files. The findings reveal that 35 percent of the arriving refugees from Ethiopia assisted by CWS were born in Asmara; another 31 percent report Addis Ababa as their place of birth. In addition to these two primate cities, 14 percent of the resettled refugees were born in another major urban center—Dessie, Dire Dawa, Jimma, Mekele, Nazareth, or Harar. Other towns and rural areas served as the birthplace for only 20 percent of the sample.[61]

Only 31 percent of the principal applicants for official-refugee status from Ethiopia had never worked at home. The main type of work performed by those who had been employed is displayed in Table 6.10. Unskilled laborers and professionals are particularly well represented among

TABLE 6.10 Principal Type of Work Performed in Homeland by Principal Applicants for Refugee Resettlement from Ethiopia Sampled in 1984

Type of Work	Household Heads	
	N	%
Policy, law making	1	0.3%
Management, administration	36	9.4
Teaching, academic	47	12.3
Skilled, technical, professional	75	19.6
Financial, commercial	30	7.8
Clerical, secretarial	67	17.5
Unskilled labor	108	28.2
Farming	19	5.0
TOTAL	383	100.1%

Source: RDC Bio-data sample.

the resettled refugees. Relative to the distribution of the labor force in the sending country, small-scale farmers are grossly underrepresented in the U.S. admission total.[62]

The CWS files yield interesting supplemental information regarding the duration of the work last performed in Ethiopia by refugees admitted from Europe. The sampled files reveal that a majority of the refugees in each major employment category had been firmly established in their chosen line of work at the time they decided to leave Ethiopia.

The D.C. Metropolitan Area

The nation's capital is both the location of the largest concentration of exiles from Ethiopia and the site of the field research which informs the findings reported in this book. Using the three area telephone directories, membership counts provided by six community associations, two Howard University conference registration sheets, local lists of refugees maintained by 12 public- and private-assistance agencies (including the national Refugee Data Center), and two of the principal sources of legal assistance for asylum applicants in the area, we identified, after the elimination of duplicate names, a total of 2,754 household heads whose country of origin is Ethiopia. This figure slightly underestimates the actual total since it does not include heads of household who live in the D.C. area but are not found on any roster and do not have listed telephone numbers. In any event, the 1984 rough estimate most widely cited by community leaders for the total number of Ethiopians, Eritreans, and Oromo resident in the Washington, D.C., metropolitan region (i.e., 10,000) is not out of line with the figure that the sampling frame yields under the assumption of an average household size of three.[64]

Sample Characteristics

Results from the D.C. sample enable us to report on the basic demographic characteristics of the community of exiles from Ethiopia. The D.C. sample is overwhelmingly populated by post-revolution migrants. Only 7 percent of the non returnees who decided to remain in this country, and only 4 percent of the refugees and other émigrés who left Ethiopia with no intention of returning, took that action prior to the Derg's overthrow of Emperor Haile Selassie. Approximately 65 percent of the interviewed Ethiopian migrants and 75 percent of the Eritreans had lived in the sending country following the revolution. In fact, one-third of the Ethiopian respondents and one-half of the Eritrean interviewees did not leave Ethiopia until the 1980s. Most of the Ethiopians (48 percent) arrived in the United States between 1974 and 1981, while a majority of the Eritreans (53 percent) entered during the 1982-1984 interval.

About three-fourths of the respondents were below 35 years of age at the time of the survey. There are approximately twice as many interviewees who are below 25 years of age than there are in the 40-and-above age bracket. The gender split among these household heads is 64 percent male and 36 percent female.

Nearly 60 percent of the household heads had never been married in 1984; another 12 percent were widowed, divorced, or separated from their spouse. Three-quarters of the married Ethiopians and 85 percent of the Eritreans were wed to a person from their homeland; all the others had married U.S. citizens. Roughly half of the interviewed Ethiopian and Eritrean community members lived in households of one or two persons. In sharp contrast to the prevailing pattern in the home country, the refugee household both in Sudan and in the West is "small, incomplete and disorganized."[65]

TABLE 6.11 Homeland Educational Backgrounds of Interviewed Exiles from Ethiopia Living in the Washington, D.C., Area and the 1970 Ethiopian School-Aged Population as a Whole

Educational Background	Total Population in 1970		D.C. Respondents	
	N	%tot	N	%tot
University education	3,870	[a]	54	33.5%
Sec or specialized school	98,420	0.8%	79	49.1
Primary school (Gr 1-6)	513,981	4.8	22	13.7
No formal	10,551,429	94.5	6	3.7
TOTAL	11,167,700	99.9	161	100.0

[a] = less than 0.1%

Source: Ethiopia, Central Statistical Office, Ethiopia: Statistical Abstract 1970 (Addis Ababa: C.S.O., n.d.), pp. 27, 198; D.C. sample.status.

The sample includes 62 self-identified Eritreans (39 percent of the total and 49 percent of the official refugees), 60 Amhara (37 percent of the total, but only 28 percent of all refugees), 16 Tigrean respondents (10 percent), and 14 Oromo (9 percent).[66] In terms of religious affiliation at the time of departure from the homeland, 72 percent of the Ethiopians and 69 percent of the Eritreans reported Coptic Christianity. Another 7–8 percent were Muslims. Nearly 20 percent of the Eritreans identified themselves as Roman Catholics, while the Ethiopian group included roughly equal proportions of Catholics (7 percent) and Pentecostalists (5 percent).[67]

The D.C. research results indicate that the exile community has been drawn predominantly from the tiny intellectual elite of the sending country (see Table 6.11). While less than 1 percent of the total school-age population in Ethiopia attended secondary schools and the university around the time of the revolution, 90 percent of the interviewed Ethiopian household heads and 69 percent of the Eritreans had received at least some secondary education before they left the home country.[68]

Class Backgrounds. In an effort to identify the class backgrounds and origins of the exiles from Ethiopia residing in the D.C. area, we inquired regarding the respondent's (and his/her parents') home-country economic activities and status. First, over half (55 percent) of the fathers of migrants from Ethiopia worked primarily in the private sector—principally as farmers.[69] The fathers of 19 interviewees either owned or worked for large private business firms; these are mainly commercial, service, and manufacturing enterprises. Among those with fathers who principally worked in the public sector, an exceptionally high proportion (30 percent) report that he had occupied a high-level political position. The data presented in Table 6.12 reveal a decided split in the social origins of these migrants. For instance, roughly equal proportions mentioned that their father (1) had held a supervisory or administrative position in government or (2) had engaged in small-scale agriculture. Although many respondents are the sons or daughters of peasants, the children of fathers who belong to the dominant class outnumber the others.

Slightly more than half of the respondents never had worked in the homeland. Among those who had been employed at home, 65 percent worked for public agencies. The sample includes 2 former members of the armed forces and 3 top-level policy makers. In addition, 35 percent of the

280

TABLE 6.12 Type of Work Performed by Father of Respondents from Ethiopia at Time of the Revolution[a]

Father's Type of Work	N	%
Policy, law making	9	6.3%
Professional, technical, teaching	14	9.8
Mgt., supervision, administration	36	25.0
Financial, commercial	17	11.8
Large-scale farming	5	3.5
Clerical, secretarial	4	2.8
Skilled labor	6	4.2
Unskilled labor	9	6.3
Small-scale farming	35	24.3
Retired	9	6.3
TOTAL	144	100.3%

[a]Information regarding fathers who had passed away by the time of the revolution is not reported in this table.

Source: D.C./L.A. sample.

privately employed exiles had been affiliated with large businesses. Table 6.13 is even more revealing of the class backgrounds of respondents who had worked in their country of origin. Teaching, administration, and financial/commercial activities constitute the three main types of work engaged in by the interviewees.

These migrants, then, are overwhelmingly from the dominant class. Less than 20 percent came from laboring-class or clerical backgrounds. By comparing the findings in Table 6.13 with those presented in Table 6.12, moreover, we immediately notice that the one striking cross-generational change that occurred in class backgrounds is the move out of small-scale agriculture and into academic, professional, and technical employment.

Class origins can be further defined from information collected regarding homeland income, and access and ties to important sources of private domestic capital. When asked to provide a self-assessment of their (their family's in the case of students) income level relative to others living in Ethiopia at the time they left home, about half of the respondents

TABLE 6.13 Principal Type of Work Performed in Homeland by Respondents from
Ethiopia

Type of Work	N	%
Policy, law making	3	4.2%
Diplomacy	2	2.8
Professional (law, med., engineer)	3	4.2
Technical, scientific	7	9.9
Management, supervision, admin.	12	16.9
Teaching, academic	16	22.5
Political organizing	1	1.4
Art, entertainment, sports	2	2.8
Nursing	1	1.4
Financial, commercial	10	14.1
Large-scale farming	1	1.4
Clerical, secretarial	7	9.9
Skilled labor	2	2.8
Unskilled labor	4	5.6
Small-scale farming	0	0.0
TOTAL	71	99.9%

Source: D.C./L.A. sample.

percent) selected "medium." However, a substantial minority (27 percent) identified their income level as "low." On the other hand, slightly more than half of the interviewees report that their parents owned more than 10 hectares of rural land at the time of the revolution and over 50 percent also admit that their parents received rent income from urban housing. Seven percent of the exiles from Ethiopia had profited from urban house rents themselves, and ten percent had personally owned more than 10 hectares of rural land. Control over land constituted an important indicator of dominant-class status in pre-revolutionary Ethiopia.[70]

Table 6.14 reveals sharp differences in class backgrounds between *resettled refugees* from Ethiopia and the rest of the migrant community in the D.C. sample. First, a much higher proportion of the official refugees report a low level of income in the homeland. Moreover, exiles who did not enter under the resettlement program are more likely to be children of

282

TABLE 6.14 Indicators of Homeland Economic Status Among Resettled Refugees and Other Exiles from Ethiopia

Status Indicators	Resettled Refugees N	%	All Others N	%
Self/Family Income Level Time Left Homeland				
High	11	14.5%	25	33.8%
Medium	33	43.4	40	54.1
Low	32	42.1	9	12.2
Respondent Owned More Than Ten Hectares Rural Land				
Yes	3	3.8	13	16.3
No	75	96.2	67	83.8
Parent(s) Owned More Than Ten Hectares Rural Land				
Yes	32	40.0	50	64.1
No	48	60.0	28	35.9
Respondent had Rent Income from Urban Housing				
Yes	5	6.3	6	7.4
No	75	93.8	75	92.6
Parent(s) had Rent Income from Urban Housing				
Yes	36	45.6	47	60.3
No	43	54.4	31	39.7

Source: D.C./L.A. sample.

the landlord class. Nevertheless, at least half of the resettled refugees come from families which either possessed more than 10 hectares of rural land or controlled urban rental units.

The prospect that association with Western institutions plays a role in Third World exile formation and migration to the United States has attracted considerable attention. It is particularly interesting to point out in this regard that 19 percent of the reporting migrants who had worked at home indicate a personal affiliation with a multinational corporation. In light of the limited extent of transnational corporate penetration, less than one percent of the labor force in Ethiopia had such connections. Three other respondents (4 percent of those employed at home) admit that they had worked for a Western government agency before exiting. In addition, 8 percent report that their father had worked for a firm with U.S. and/or transnational corporate ties. In sum, persons associated with Western institutions operating in Ethiopia, particularly multinational firms, are overrepresented within the community of exiles living in the nation's capital relative to their numerical position in the pre-revolution work force in the homeland.

Furthermore, the D.C. survey uncovered extensive links to Western social institutions. For instance, 15 percent of the exiles who received some post-secondary education before departing from Ethiopia had studied at an educational institution run by foreigners (including religious groups). The figures for those taught at expatriate-controlled institutions rise to 23 percent at the secondary-school level and to 30 per cent when primary education is considered.

International travel patterns provide an indication of initial network building in the West. Before final departure from their country of origin, 7 percent of the respondents from Ethiopia had previously studied in the United States. The findings on travel by relatives show that a much larger group of migrants had possessed family contacts and ties with the West. Slightly more than half of the respondents mentioned that at least one relative (often a parent or sibling) had visited the United States prior to departure from their home country.

Social Background Summary. The national and D.C. community data reviewed here suggest that exiles from Ethiopia who succeed in entering the United States differ from their homeland counterparts in terms of several important background variables. In comparison with the home-country population, the U.S. migrants are younger, more likely never to have married, far more highly educated, more often from families with high-level political contacts, more likely to have been teachers, administrators, or employees of large business firms in Ethiopia, and more likely to possess propertied-class backgrounds. While most households in Ethiopia survive by engaging in small-scale agricultural activities, none of the sampled migrants living in D.C. had been a peasant farmer prior to departure from the sending country. Finally, the interviewees are clearly distinguished from the population of Ethiopia as a whole by their much greater tendency to belong to families that possessed pre-departure ties to the United States, to have been affiliated with a multinational business firm operating in Ethiopia, and to have been exposed to Western educational influences in the homeland.

Political Orientations. Political orientations and homeland activities constitute potentially decisive factors in exile formation with important consequences for overseas migrant communities. Nearly half of the D.C. sample had opposed Haile Selassie's regime. Most of the others had not taken a position. Only eleven percent indicated that they had supported the Emperor. Among those with pro-regime orientations, about 40 percent had *actively* supported the monarchy in the homeland. Two-thirds of the exiles who opposed the pre-revolutionary regime had been *actively* involved in an anti-regime capacity.

The proportion of respondents who neither supported nor opposed the regime in power declined drastically in the post-revolution period. Over 90 percent of the respondents who lived in Ethiopia after the overthrow of the monarch opposed the new political order, and 59 percent did so actively. Non returnees also overwhelmingly opposed the Derg at the time they decided to live in exile (92 percent), although many (25 percent) had initially supported the revolution.[71]

At the time of their interview, none of the respondents supported Mengistu Haile Mariam's rule. Only 10 interviewees (6 percent) held a neutral position. The vast majority (94 percent) of Ethiopian and Eritrean exiles opposed the post-revolution regime.

We can discern a great deal about the specific and shifting ideological orientations that prevail within the exile community by identifying the opposition political organizations that members support and become involved in. About one-fourth (23 percent) of the interviewees report that they actively supported an anti-regime political organization prior to the Emperor's overthrow; another 20 percent "agreed with" a particular opposition group. Virtually all of the pre-revolution political engagement on the part of migrants from Ethiopia involved nationality fronts, mainly the Eritrean People's Liberation Front (EPLF) and the Eritrean Liberation Front (ELF). Since the Emperor did not allow political organizations to function, the record of participation in the student movement helps to fill out the picture of pre-revolution political activity. The interview data reveal that 15 percent of the respondents had frequently participated in demonstrations and other forms of student political action, while another 21 percent occasionally had become involved in such activities.

A somewhat higher proportion of those living in Ethiopia after the overthrow of the monarchy supported a specific political organization that opposed the post-revolution regime. Roughly 40 percent either participated in or agreed with an opposition political structure (principally the Ethiopian People's Revolutionary Party, or EPRP) following the revolution. In addition, 28 percent of the respondents personally assisted and another 18 percent agreed with a national liberation movement (mainly the EPLF and the ELF) in the post-revolution period. Non returnees exhibit patterns of organizational support and agreement that are similar to these "at home" responses. Nearly 40 per cent indicated that they had actively supported an opposition political structure operating within Ethiopia at the time they decided not to return home (principally the EPRP, EPLF, and Oromo Liberation Front). Furthermore, 44 percent of the non returnees indicated that they personally supported an anti-regime political organization operating *outside* of their homeland at the time they elected to become an exile. Among those who had been active in an exile political organization, fully 46 percent of the non returnees from Ethiopia had served in a leadership capacity by the time they reached the decision not to go home.

The past and present distribution of respondents from Ethiopia by self-designated association with political organizations is presented in Table 6.15. In the table, supporters and sympathizers of groups promoting nationality movements are distinguished from those who joined and agreed with organizations based strictly on anti-regime objectives.[72] Given the strict ban on association for political purposes enforced during Haile Selassie's reign, virtually all of the organizations appearing on the top half of this table are of post-revolution origin. The Derg's decimation of organized opposition within Ethiopia is responsible for the decline in support following the time of departure or decision not to return. The falloff in supporters is most dramatic for the EPRP, which had ceased operating within Ethiopia by 1984. By comparison, national liberation movements have succeeded in retaining most of their supporters within the exile community. This is particularly the case for the EPLF and the TPLF. The ability of these two movements to retain overseas followers is partly a result of their success in the field. The contributions made by supporters living in exile, in turn, have helped to sustain the liberation efforts.

In summary, the D.C. exile community from Ethiopia is sharply divided according to political background and orientations. First, the sizeable group of immigrants who neither actively supported nor even agreed with an opposition political organization when they lived in their home country co-exists with committed and experienced activists. These findings suggest that the community of exiles from Ethiopia is split into those with apolitical and those with intensely political backgrounds at home and in the United States. There also is a particularly strong relationship between ethnic identification and homeland ties to a national-liberation struggle. Two-thirds of the Eritrean respondents who exited prior to the revolution and 71 percent of those who left subsequently either had actively supported or agreed with the EPLF, or the ELF, while living in Ethiopia. Similarly, two-thirds of the

TABLE 6.15 Political and National Liberation Organizations Supported and Agreed with in Past and in 1984 by Ethiopian and Eritrean Respondents

Political Organizations and National Liberation Fronts	Time Period			
	Time Exile Decision		1984	
	N	%	N	%
Ethiopian People's Revolutionary Party (EPRP)	42	71.2%	5	33.3%
Ethiopian Democratic Union (EDU)	4	6.8	4	26.7
Mecha Tulema	4	6.8	--	----
Echa'at	2	3.4	--	----
Meison	2	3.4	--	----
EPDM	--	----	1	6.7
Both EPDM + EPDA	--	----	1	6.7
Not Specified	5	8.5	4	26.7
TOTAL	59	100.1%	15	100.1%
Eritrean People's Liberation Front (EPLF)	37	48.7%	36	56.3%
Eritrean Liberation Front (ELF)	19	25.0	8	12.5
Oromo Liberation Front (OLF)	13	17.1	7	10.9
Tigrean People's Liberation Front (TPLF)	4	5.3	3	4.7
Western Somali Liberation Front (WSLF)	--	----	1	1.6
EPLF & ELF	2	2.6	2	3.1
EPLF & OLF	--	----	2	3.1
EPLF & TPLF	--	----	1	1.6
EPLF, OLF, SLF	--	----	1	1.6
All but ELF	--	----	1	1.6
All	--	----	2	3.1
Not specified	1	1.3	--	----
TOTAL	76	100.0%	64	100.1%

Source: D.C./L.A. sample.

Oromo who departed after the revolution had associated with the OLF. In contrast, 38 percent of the Tigrean interviewees reported pre-revolution ties with a national-liberation organization (EPLF or TPLF) and only 13 percent of the Tigreans who emigrated in the post-revolution period had supported or identified with the TPLF. None of the Amhara had even agreed with a national-liberation movement while living in the homeland.

In 1990, the militants were divided into two principal groups—those who supported a nationality movement and those who only worked to overthrow the Mengistu regime. Some factional disputes, such as the bitterness between former supporters of the ELF and the EPLF, had moderated over time and were being "expressed through avoidance rather than through confrontation."[73] As the fighting grew closer to Addis Ababa, the exile community's cleavage on the nationalities issue took a public turn in 1990. Although the national-liberation forces threatened to overthrow the despised post-revolution regime, local leaders of the Ethiopian community organized a large demonstration in the nation's capital in support of unity and maintenance of the Ethiopian state.

U.S. Position. To complete this profile of the exile community from Ethiopia, we need to explore certain socio-economic aspects of the respondents' position in the mid 1980s. This investigation includes educational levels, immigration status, employment status, type of job, and income.

With regard to educational attainments, the data found in Table 6.16

TABLE 6.16 Ethiopian and Eritrean Respondents' Highest Educational Attainment in 1984

Educational Level	Ethiopians		Eritreans	
	N	%	N	%
No formal education	1	1.0%	3	5.0%
Some primary school	1	1.0	7	11.7
Completed primary school	3	3.0	3	5.0
Some post primary school	2	2.0	3	5.0
Complt secondary school or equiv	14	14.1	11	18.3
Some post secondary	28	28.3	18	30.0
University first degree	23	23.2	4	6.7
Masters, law degree	25	25.3	9	15.0
Ph.D., M.D., advanced medical	2	2.0	2	3.3
TOTAL	99	99.9%	60	100.0%

Source: D.C./L.A. sample.

288

suggests that the community of migrants from Ethiopia can be divided into three groups. The first category consists of the minority (15 percent)—mainly recently settled Eritrean refugees—who have not completed secondary school. A roughly equal percentage of respondents (16 percent) have graduated from a secondary-level institution, but have not studied at the post-secondary level. Finally, 79 percent of the Ethiopian exiles and 55 percent of the Eritreans have attended a college or university.

Table 6.17 shows that the D.C. sample is split evenly between those (80) admitted to the United States as official refugees and those (81) who

TABLE 6.17 Immigration Status of Respondents from Ethiopia

Immigration Category	Respondents N	%
A. Citizen/permanent resident	24[a]	14.9%
B. Official refugee	80[b]	49.7
C. Political asylee	14	8.7
D. Asylum applicant	12	7.5
E. Denied asylum	7[c]	4.3
F. EVD	9	5.6
G. Undocumented	3	1.9
H. Valid non immigrant	12	7.5
TOTAL	161	100.1%

[a] Includes 53 respondents who entered as official refugees and had become permanent residents by the time of the interview.
[b] Includes 11 respondents who reported that they had become permanent residents by the time of the interview.
[c] Includes 2 respondents who held EVD status at the time they decided to become an exile, but reported that they had become permanent residents by the time of the interview.

Source: D.C. sample.

entered via other avenues.[74] The non-resettled group includes 24 respondents (category A) who secured permanent residency under normal immigration procedures without first being granted refugee or asylee status. Only two interviewees in the sample had obtained U.S. citizenship. This is in line with national trends.[75]   Even though they possess non-immigrant (student) visas, most of the individuals in category H have no intention of returning to Ethiopia.

Categories C-E involve past and present applicants for political asylum. Roughly 40 percent of the claimants had succeeded in securing asylum. Category G is restricted to respondents who arrived after 30 June 1980 and were out of status in 1984.   There are no illegal entrants (persons who entered the United States without inspection) among the interviewees. While there is no reliable way of estimating the distribution of visa abusers and EWI among migrant populations resident in the United States, sources close to the Ethiopian and Eritrean communities in Washington, D.C., held the consensus view that undocumented immigrants are not commonly encountered among their members.[76]

The community of migrants from Eritrea, with its higher proportion of resettled refugees,[77] proved more likely to possess legal immigrant status in comparison with the Ethiopian exiles (86 percent and 68 percent, respectively).   Twenty-six percent of the Ethiopian respondents were in an undetermined or undocumented immigration position versus only seven percent of the Eritreans.   Finally, 7–8 percent of the interviewed members of both communities were non immigrants.

Turning to indicators of participation in the U.S. work force, we first observe from Table 6.18 that a higher proportion of Ethiopian than Eritrean

TABLE 6.18 Employment Status of Ethiopian and Eritrean Respondents in 1984

| | Ethiopians | | Eritreans | |
	N	%	N	%
Unemployed	9	9.1%	14	23.0%
Student only	9	9.1	7	11.5
Part Time	15	15.2	6	9.8
Full Time	66	66.7	34	55.7
TOTAL	99	100.1%	61	100.0%

Source: D.C./L.A. sample.

respondents are engaged in full-time and part-time employment.   The list of employers includes hotels, banks, electronics firms, labor unions, volags and interest groups, schools and universities, and the local, state, and national government. Roughly 10 percent of both groups are full-time students. The unemployment rate is much higher among Eritreans (23 percent) than it is among Ethiopian migrants (9 percent).

Table 6.19 focuses on the latest type of work performed by employed respondents. Migrants from Ethiopia living in the nation's capital have located a wide range of jobs—from dishwasher to World Bank economist. A plurality (13 percent) of those who provided information concerning their current employment are working for food, beverage, or lodging establishments. Another seven per cent are (mainly taxi cab) drivers.

TABLE 6.19   Ethiopian and Eritrean Respondents' Current (1984) Work in U.S.

Type of Employment	N	%
Food, drink, hotel worker	12	12.9%
Nurse, social worker	11	11.8
Driver	7	7.5
Unskilled service worker	7	7.5
Manager, supervisor, administrator	6	6.5
Store clerk, cashier	6	6.5
Technical worker	6	6.5
Business owner	5	5.4
Artist, clergy, other professional	5	5.4
Secretarial worker	5	5.4
Skilled worker, mechanic	4	4.3
Teacher, academic	4	4.3
Accountant, financial administrator	3	3.2
Laborer, guard	3	3.2
Financial analyst, econ researcher	3	3.2
Research or teaching assistant	2	2.2
University professor	2	2.2
Engineer	1	1.1
Lawyer, physician	1	1.1
TOTAL	91	100.2%

Source: D.C./L.A. sample.

Exiles from Ethiopia are less likely than Iranians are to be business owners and engineers, but are more apt to fill social-service jobs and to be employed as nurses. Among the group of employed migrant household heads from Ethiopia, 30 percent work in low-wage, service-sector jobs.

Table 6.20 lists reporting respondents by their specific annual-income

TABLE 6.20 Reporting Ethiopian and Eritrean Respondents' Self/Family Total Income from All Sources in 1984

Total Income (U.S. $)	Ethiopian		Eritrean	
	N	%	N	%
None - $ 9,500	18	28.1%	17	42.5%
$10,000 - 18,000	24	37.5	9	22.5
$20,000 - 28,000	10	15.6	3	7.5
$30,000 - 38,000	7	10.9	7	17.5
$40,000 - 50,000	4	6.3	4	10.0
$95,000	1	1.6	0	0.0
TOTAL	64	100.0	40	100.0

Source: D.C./L.A. sample.

levels. Under 11 percent of the interviewed household heads in both communities received annual incomes that exceed $40,000. Roughly two-thirds of the reporting Ethiopian and Eritrean interviewees earned $18,000 or less in 1984. The gap between relatively wealthy and impoverished household heads in most pronounced within the Eritrean community. Nearly all of the respondents earning less than $10,000, and two-thirds of those in the two lowest income categories, are official refugees.

Conclusions

In general, U.S. communities of refugees from revolution are disproportionately populated by members of the pre-revolution elite. Exile household heads from Cuba, Indochina, Iran, and Ethiopia tend to be highly educated relative to both the sending and receiving populations. Many were

292

prominent, successful, and highly trained individuals in their homeland, and most were self-sufficient.[78]

Exiles who have settled in emergent global cities, such as Los Angeles, Washington, D.C., Miami, and New York, generally have been incorporated either into the ethnic-enclave economy or into the expanding and polarized post-industrial producer-service sector. The latter group is split into the few who occupy professional and managerial positions in the central-control network and the many who provide the requisite underclass of workers that services the office and personal needs of the managerial elite in poorly paid and unprotected jobs with limited or nonexistent advancement opportunities.[79]

Notes

1. In particular, recent migrant communities from Africa have been virtually ignored by scholars. Vincent N. Parrillo, *Strangers to These Shores: Race and Ethnic Relations in the United States*, 3rd ed. (New York: Macmillan, 1990), p. 383.

2. David M. Reimers, *Still the Golden Door: The Third World Comes to America* (New York: Columbia University Press, 1985), p. 157.

3. Rafael Valdivieso and Cary Davis, *U.S. Hispanics: Challenging Issues for the 1990s* (Washington, D.C.: Population Reference Bureau, 1988), pp. 1, 3–4, 14.

4. Reimers, *Golden Door*, p. 165.

5. Richard R. Fagen, Richard A. Brody, and Thomas J. O'Leary, *Cubans in Exile: Disaffection and the Revolution* (Stanford: Stanford University Press, 1968), pp. 21–22; Reimers, *Golden Door*, pp. 164–165.

6. Fagen *et al., Cubans*, pp. 18–19, 22–23.

7. José Llanes, *Cuban Americans: Masters of Survival* (Cambridge: Abt Books, 1982), pp. 98–99.

8. Alejandro Portes, Juan M. Clark, and Robert L. Bach, "The New Wave: A Statistical Profile of Recent Cuban Exiles to the United States," *Cuban Studies* 7 (1977):14–16.

9. Robert L. Bach, "Cubans," in *Refugees in the United States: A Reference Handbook*, edited by David W. Haines (Westport: Greenwood Press, 1985), p. 86.

10. Portes *et al.*, "Profile," 11–13.

11. Valdivieso and Davis, *U.S. Hispanics*, p. 7.

12. Llanes, *Cuban Americans*, p. 196.

13. See Sylvia Pedraza-Bailey, "Cuba's Exiles: Portrait of a Refugee Migration," *International Migration Review* 19, No. 1 (1985):18.

14. Llanes, *Cuban Americans*, p. 196.

15. Bach, "Cubans," p. 86.

16. David Haines, Dorothy Rutherford, and Patrick Thomas, "The Case for Exploratory Fieldwork: Understanding the Adjustment of Vietnamese Refugees in the Washington Area," *Anthropological Quarterly* 54, No. 2 (1981):95.

17. Haines *et al.*, "Vietnamese Refugees," 95. According to Douglas Pike, "'there are a lot of generals and officers in Washington, a lot of field grade, upper grade, officers either in Texas or in the Los Angeles area, and in the lower Bay area of San Francisco you tend to have enlisted men and sergeants.'" Cited in *New York Times*, 25 August 1989, p. A7.

18. May Ebihara, "Khmer," in *Refugees in the United States: A Reference Handbook*, edited by David W. Haines (Westport: Greenwood Press, 1985), p. 135.

19. The median age was less than 20 for refugees who had arrived from Southeast Asia by 1975. David W. Haines, "Initial Adjustment," in *Refugees in the United States: A Reference Handbook*, edited by David W. Haines (Westport: Greenwood Press, 1985), p. 18. Also see Paul J. Strand and Woodrow Jones, Jr., *Indochinese Refugees in America* (Durham: Duke University Press, 1985), p. 76.

20. In one sample of Indochinese refugees, the mean nuclear-family size was about 4.5 persons and the total household consisted of 6 people. Strand and Jones, *Indochinese Refugees*, p. 76. Also see Paul D. Starr and Alden E. Roberts, "Community Structure and Vietnamese Refugee Adaptation: The Significance of Context," *International Migration Review* 16, No. 3 (1982):604.

21. Gail P. Kelly, *From Vietnam to America: A Chronicle of the Vietnamese Immigration to the United States* (Boulder: Westview Press, 1977), pp. 47, 50–51; Nguyen Manh Hung, "Vietnamese," in *Refugees in the United States: A Reference Handbook*, edited by David W. Haines (Westport: Greenwood Press, 1985), p. 202. Also see Starr and Roberts, "Community Structure," 604.

22. Kelly, *Vietnamese Immigration*, pp. 52–53. In comparison, approximately 15 percent of the U.S. labor force report professional or technical occupations. Haines, "Adjustment," pp. 18–19.

23. Haines, "Adjustment," p. 19. Starr and Roberts ("Community Structure," 603) derived similar results from their interviews with Vietnamese heads of household in northern California and the Gulf Coast.

24. Kelly, *Vietnamese Immigration*, pp. 49–50.

25. Haines, "Adjustment," p. 19; Strand and Jones, *Indochinese Refugees*, pp. 78, 108.

26. John L. Van Esterik, "Lao," in *Refugees in the United States: A Reference Handbook*, edited by David W. Haines (Westport: Greenwood Press, 1985), p. 155.

27. Ebihara, "Khmer," p. 137; Strand and Jones, *Indochinese Refugees*, p. 80.

28. John K. Whitmore, "Chinese from Southeast Asia," in *Refugees in the United States: A Reference Handbook*, edited by David W. Haines (Westport: Greenwood Press, 1985), pp. 68–69; also see Hung, "Vietnamese," p. 202.

29. Jamshid Momeni, "Size and Distribution of Iranian Ethnic Group in the United States: 1980," *Iran Nameh* 2 (Winter 1984):17, 20.

30. Calculated from Hossein Askari, John T. Cummings, and Mehmet Izbudak, "Iran's Migration of Skilléd Labor to the United States," *Iranian Studies* 10, Nos. 1–2 (Winter-Spring 1977):6.

31. Askari *et al.*, "Skilled Labor," 22; Abdoulmaboud Ansari, *Iranian Immigrants in the United States: A Case Study of Dual Marginality* (Millwood: Associated Faculty Press, 1988), pp. 30, 32, 44, 66; Reimers, *Golden Door*, p. 118.

32. Calculated from Table 1.3 in United States, Immigration and Naturalization Service, *1984 Statistical Yearbook of the Immigration and Naturalization Service* (Washington, D.C.: U.S. GPO, [1985]), pp. 6, 23, 74; also see Table 9.1 in Parrillo, *Strangers*, p. 306; Reimers, *Golden Door*, p. 118. Many Iranians continue to enter under occupational preferences. About one-third of the previously employed Iranian immigrants admitted in 1984 were professionals. The occupational backgrounds of the others were managers and administrators (27 percent), service workers (20 percent), skilled and unskilled laborers (13 percent), and salespersons (8 percent). Only 0.2 percent of the total came from farming, fishing, or forestry backgrounds. U.S., INS, *1984 Yearbook*, pp. 16, 65.

Members of minority groups who migrate to the United States from Iran often enter with immigrant visas for purposes of family reunification. See Ansari, *Iranian Immigrants*, p. 66. The Baha'i National Center in the United States places the size of the Iranian Baha'i community alone at 7,000. Cited in Allen K. Jones, *Iranian Refugees: The Many Faces of Persecution* (Washington, D.C.: U.S. Committee for Refugees, 1984), p. 6.

33. See Jones, *Iranian Refugees*, p. 16.

34. The number of annually resettled Iranian refugees exceeded 3,000 in FY 1985 and 1986 and, then, jumped to 7,075 in FY 1987. United States, Immigration and Naturalization Service, *Statistical Yearbook of the Immigration and Naturalization Service, 1987* (Washington, D.C.: U.S. GPO, 1988), p. 50.

35. This figure is reached by applying the percentage holding undetermined and undocumented status in the D.C./L.A. sample (19 percent) to the estimated community of immigrants from Iran as of 1984 (153,000—assuming 1 percent mortality). Another indication of undetermined and undocumented status comes from the number of rejected and pending asylum claims. See Jones, *Iranian Refugees*, p. 16. On non-immigrant admissions for FY 1984, see U.S., INS, *1984 Yearbook*, pp. 117–118. In FY 1987, about 5,200 Iranians (300 of whom had

entered the United States illegally prior to 1982) applied for amnesty. U.S., INS, *1987 Yearbook*, p. 44.

36. The 17,500 figure is derived by assuming that half of the 35,000 Iranians studying the United States in 1984 would not be permanent residents, asylum applicants, etc. The twin "fifty percent assumptions" that underlie this particular estimate are simply guesses. On Iranian student enrollment, see Ansari, *Iranian Immigrants*, p. 120.

37. Momeni, "Distribution," 18–19; Parrillo, *Strangers*, p. 333; Annabelle Sreberny-Mohammadi and Ali Mohammadi, "Post-revolutionary Iranian Exiles: A Study in Impotence," *Third World Quarterly* 9, No. 1 (January 1987):127. Indeed, L.A. and D.C. ranked first and second, respectively, as "areas of intended residence" among immigrants from Iran admitted in FY 1984 and in FY 1987. Roughly thirty percent of the arriving immigrants indicated that they planned to settle in these two metropolitan areas. U.S., INS, *1984 Yearbook*, p. 63; *1987 Yearbook*, p. 37.

38. Over half (58 percent) of the sample had secured admission in 1984; the remaining 42 percent arrived in 1983.

39. Over 91 percent of the respondents reported that they no longer attended organized religious services at the time of the interview. Also see Abdoulmaboud Ansari, "A Community in Process: The First Generation of the Iranian Professional Middle-class Immigrants in the United States," *International Review of Modern Sociology* 7 (January-June 1977):95. Although they have received considerable public attention, only a small percentage of all Iranian exiles in the United States are Baha'i or Jewish. See Parrillo, *Strangers*, p. 332.

40. For 1973 figures, see Askari *et al.*, "Skilled Labor," 29.

41. On the last point, also see Ansari, *Iranian Immigrants*, p. 117.

42. See Chapter 2 for a discussion of the historical role of these organizations. Also see Nozar Alaolmolki, "The New Iranian Left," *Middle East Journal* 41, No. 2 (Spring 1987):220–232; Val Moghadam, "The Left and Revolution in Iran: A Critical Analysis," in *Post-Revolutionary Iran*, edited by Hooshang Amirahmadi and Manoucher Parvin (Boulder: Westview Press, 1988), pp. 23, 31–32.

43. Assignment of Table 6.4 organizations into leftist and non-leftist categories follows Moghadam, "The Left," p. 23.

44. As one would expect given their earlier U.S. arrival, the Iranian permanent residents proved more likely than the Ethiopians and Eritreans did to have secured that immigration status prior to 1982 (73 percent, 46 percent, and 56 percent, respectively). Prior to the overthrow of the Shah, about 50,000 Iranian students were enrolled at U.S. educational institutions. Parrillo, *Strangers*, p. 332. Marriage to a U.S. citizen is the most common avenue to permanent residency among non-returning Iranian students. Askari *et al.*, "Skilled Labor," 15–16.

45. Between 1958 and 1975, 14 percent of the Iranian migrants receiving U.S. permanent residency opted to become citizens. Calculated from Askari *et al.*, "Skilled Labor," 6, 9.

46. Although the undocumented are likely to be underenumerated in the sample, legal and illegal migrants with similar demographic backgrounds frequently are found in the same North American household. Demetrios G. Papademetriou and Mark J. Miller, "U.S. Immigration Policy: International Context, Theoretical Parameters, and Research Priorities," in *The Unavoidable Issue: U.S. Immigration Policy in the 1980s*, edited by Mark J. Miller and Demetrios G. Papademetriou (Philadelphia: Institute for the Study of Human Issues, 1983), p. 23.

47. Many employed Iranians also are students.

48. Tsehaye Teferra, cited in Nicholas Van Praag, "From Ethiopia to the USA: A Difficult Transition," *Refugees* 25 (January 1986):15; Akalou Wolde-Michael, "The Advent, Dilemma, and Prospects of Ethiopians in America" (paper presented at the 15th Annual Conference of the National Association for Ethnic Studies, San Diego, February 1987), pp. 9–10.

49. See Richard Lapchick, Benjamin Hooks, and Franklin Williams, "Racial Implications of U.S. Immigration Policy," *Issue* 12, No. 1/2 (1982):14; Akalou Wolde-Michael, "Ethiopians," p. 6.

50. Al Santoli, *New Americans: Immigrants and Refugees in the U.S. Today* (New York: Viking, 1988), p. 87.

51. Cited in Carolyn Waller, "The Simpson-Mazzoli Bill and Its Impact on Ethiopian Refugees" (paper presented at the Conference on Ethiopian Refugees in the United States, Washington, D.C., September 1983).

52. By 1986, an estimated 22 ambassadors, 40 senior diplomats, and 14 cabinet ministers had defected in the West. One of the most celebrated cases involved Dawit Wolde Giorgis, the former military governor of Eritrea and Commissioner of Relief and Rehabilitation during the 1984-1985 famine. *Wall Street Journal*, 12 November 1986; *New York Times*, 23 December 1988, pp. B1–2.

53. Figures provided by the U.S. Department of State, Bureau of Refugee Affairs, November 1982.

54. Summary data provided by the Refugee Data Center.

55. See, for instance, U.S., INS, *1987 Yearbook*, p. 50.

56. Richard Deutsch, "The Ethiopian Controversy," *Africa Report* 27 (May/June 1982):49; Ethiopian Committee on Immigration, "Human Rights Violations in Ethiopia: The Case for Permanent Adjustment of Immigration Status for Ethiopians in the United States," *Issue* 12 (Spring/Summer 1982):20; *Washington Post*, 22 May 1982.

57. Deutsch, "Controversy," 50.

58. Marianthi Zikopoulos, editor, *Open Doors: 1984/85: Report on International Educational Exchange* (New York: Institute of International Education, 1985), p. 116.

59. The number of non-resettled refugees from Ethiopia adjusted to permanent-resident status by the INS increased from 273 in FY 1984 to 490 in FY 1987. U.S., INS, *1984 Yearbook*, p. 39 and *1987 Yearbook*, p. 20.

60. This estimate places migrants who are not resettled refugees at numerical parity with the official refugees. Estimating the resettled-refugee and non-refugee groups at equal size is consistent with the sampling frame constructed in 1984 for the survey-research project in the Washington, D.C., metropolitan area. In that case, official refugees constituted 48 percent of all identified household heads. See Appendix; Van Praag, "Transition," 15.

Between 1984 and 1991, more official refugees than other migrants from Ethiopia entered the United States. In FY 1984, for instance, the U.S. government admitted 363 non-immigrant students, 621 persons on temporary business visas, and 2,784 visitors from Ethiopia. Applying the liberally estimated non-return percentages for the early 1980s to these figures yields 1,220 new additions to the migrant community. Only 443 Ethiopians entered as immigrants under non-refugee provisions of U.S. immigration law. In comparison, 2,347 refugees from Ethiopia arrived in this country in FY 1984. U.S., INS, *1984 Yearbook*, pp. 16, 24, 74, 119.

Approximately 10,000 exiles from Ethiopia lived in Canada in 1990. John Sorenson, "Politics of Social Identity: 'Ethiopians' in Canada," *Journal of Ethnic Studies* (forthcoming).

61. For similar findings on the urban backgrounds of refugees from Ethiopia sampled in the Los Angeles area, see Cynthia J. Gimbert and Tesfaye Shiferaw, "Los Angeles Ethiopians," in *The Economic and Social Adjustment of Non-Southeast Asian Refugees*, Vol. II (Falls Church: Research Management Corporation, 1986), p. 7. The characteristics of the sample of 59 resettled male household heads from Ethiopia interviewed by McSpadden in California, Nevada, and Washington are quite similar to the RDC results in terms of urban/rural origin, ethnic identification, religion, educational attainments, and at-home occupation. See Lucia A. McSpadden, "Ethiopian Refugee Resettlement in the Western United States: Social Context and Psychological Well-Being" (Ph.D. dissertation, University of Utah, 1988), pp. 123–125.

62. However, see Lesley R. Drake, "Ethiopians in California: Aspirations and Reality," *Refugees* 44 (August 1987):17.

63. In the CWS sample, 28 per cent of the 121 respondents for whom information is available worked in one of these three high-status capacities; 26 per cent were the owners/employees of large firms and 26 per cent of small businesses.

Five per cent had been occupied with other kinds of work and 16 per cent reported unemployment as their job status at the time of exit.

64. The actual mean household size among those interviewed in the D.C. study is 2.72.

65. Mekuria Bulcha, *Flight and Integration: Causes of Mass Exodus from Ethiopia and Problems of Integration in the Sudan* (Uppsala: Scandinavian Institute of African Studies, 1988), p. 153.

66. For detailed breakdowns by first language and immigration status, see Peter Koehn and Girma Negash, *Resettled Refugees and Asylum Applicants: Implications of the Case of Migrants from Ethiopia for United States Policy* (Arlington: Center for Ethiopian Studies, 1987), pp. 41, 71.

67. Whereas only 2 percent of the sampled Ethiopians report possessing no religious faith at the time they left Ethiopia, 21 percent of the non returnees had gravitated to this position by the time they decided to become an exile.

68. Also see McSpadden, "Resettlement," pp. 127–128. Between 1968 and 1970, 3,154 students graduated from Haile Selassie I University. Ethiopia, CSO, *Statistical Abstract 1970*, p. 197. If the Ethiopian educational system produced an average of 1,000 university graduates during the years 1960–1984 (a highly inflated assumption), 0.2 percent of these graduates are included in the D.C. sample.

69. Only 8 percent of the interviewees from Ethiopia report that their mother had ever held a salaried job outside the home.

70. Prior to 1974, a small landlord class accumulated capital by exploiting tenant and contract farmers in rural areas and/or by renting houses and commercial units in urban areas. In terms of rural-land ownership, possession of more than ten hectares signified a relatively large holding. These variables also allow us to identify respondents who suffered adverse economic consequences from the land-reform measures enacted by the Provisional Military Administrative Committee in 1975. The new regime nationalized rural land and set a 10-hectare ceiling on possessory rights. The Derg also nationalized any "extra" urban houses that had been utilized for rental purposes. See John M. Cohen and Peter H. Koehn, "Rural and Urban Land Reform in Ethiopia," *African Law Studies* 14 (1977):3–62.

71. For details, see Koehn and Girma Negash, *Refugees*, pp. 13–17.

72. On the role of specific opposition organizations in Ethiopia, see Chapter 2. Me'ison and Echa'at are two leftist factions that the Derg treated favorably for a short period following the revolution. The Ethiopian Democratic Union (EDU) provided the only organized conservative opposition to the revolution. None of these groups offered a viable alternative within Ethiopia by 1990. The sample of migrants also includes four persons who held leadership positions in urban *kebele* associations and one peasant association leader under the post-revolution regime.

73. Sorenson, "Canada."

74. Although the latter categories include individuals who clearly meet the definition of a refugee adopted in the Refugee Act of 1980 (as well as those who certainly do not), for purposes of comparison the entire group of respondents who have not arrived in the United States under the resettlement program are occasionally referred to as "non refugees" (a shorthand term for "not admitted as an official refugee" or "not granted the legal status and benefits of a resettled refugee").

75. Only 925 persons out of the total community of migrants from Ethiopia had elected to become a naturalized citizen of the United States by 1984. U.S., INS, *1984 Yearbook*, p. 145.

76. In FY 1987, only 55 migrants from Ethiopia *nation-wide* applied for amnesty on the basis of a pre-1982 entry without inspection. U.S., INS, *1987 Yearbook*, p. 44.

77. Sixty-three percent of the interviewed Eritreans, versus forty-one percent of the Ethiopians, arrived as official refugees.

78. Also see Barry N. Stein, "Refugee Resettlement Programs and Techniques," in United States, Select Commission on Immigration and Refugee Policy, *U.S. Immigration Policy and the National Interest*, Appendix C to the Staff Report (Washington, D.C.: The Commission, 1981), p. 387. He argues that expellees might not possess these characteristics.

79. See Saskia Sassen-Koob, "The New Labor Demand in Global Cities," in *Cities in Transformation: Class, Capital, and the State* (Beverly Hills: Sage Publications, 1984), pp. 140–151, 154–164; Tables 6.6 and 6.19 above; *New York Times*, 23 June 1989.

7

Economic Adjustment and Social Adaptation

The face that looks back sees displacement, separation, uprooting, loss, nostalgia, and, in a certain sense, even death, because some things die inside us when we are forced to abandon our homeland without the possibility of returning at will. The face that looks forward sees new horizons, unknown environments, strangers with unfamiliar customs and languages, real and imaginary perils, a vigorous challenge to survive, adapt, and grow, and even the opportunity of constructing a new identity in sudden anonymity.
—Rubén D. Rumbaut and Rubén G. Rumbaut

Conceptual Approaches

Economic adjustment and social adaptation constitute the principal challenges that confront newcomers to a host society. *Economic adjustment* involves the ability of migrants to find employment, the attainment of self-sufficiency, and the transfer of home-country occupational skills to the new employment context. In the face of barriers to occupational transfer, "the jobs that refugees initially obtain usually involve severe downward mobility and low incomes."[1]

Adjustment to mainstream economic institutions can occur independently of social integration.[2] Assimilation and cultural pluralism, the two prevailing perspectives on *social adaptation*, envision dramatically different outcomes. In the assimilationist model, the adaptation process encompasses adoption of receiving-society values and behavioral norms, amalgamation through intermarriage with host-country nationals, structural—including political—participation in core-society institutions, and development of a common national identity.[3] In theory, the possible end results in the United

States are either "Anglo-conformity," or the blending of in-coming and receiving cultures into a new "melting pot."[4] In practice, however, assimilation has required adherence to the dominant culture and neglect of one's "foreign" identity, and the concept of a malleable and changing core culture has remained a myth.[5]

With the discrediting of the melting-pot thesis, largely due to lack of structural assimilation, scholars devoted greater attention to the cultural-pluralist alternative to mainstream conformity.[6] The cultural-pluralist approach recognizes that migrants can retain and maintain much of their own distinctive culture and that one outcome of such an adaptive response is the existence of "multiple melting pots."[7] Moreover, "this perspective on immigrant adaptation emphasizes ethnic consciousness and the resilience of ethnic culture as instruments of political resistance by exploited minorities."[8] For political migrants, who initially confront adaptation demands within a context of "deprivation and anxiety,"[9] the availability of an ethnic community can limit the extent of resocialization and new learning that is needed in the short run.

Milton M. Gordon contends that structural pluralism is essential for maintaining cultural uniqueness. He asserts that "it is not possible for cultural pluralism to exist without the existence of separate subsocieties. . . which provide the framework for communal existence—their own network of cliques, institutions, organizations, and informal friendship patterns."[10] Exclusive interaction in community-based institutions is aptly referred to as the *ethnic-enclave*, or ethnic-solidarity, adaptive response. In certain U.S. urban areas, residential districts resemble "distant provinces" of the sending country. Residents remain preoccupied with "the political happenings, economic events, sports, gossip—even the latest dance music and hit tunes—of the country left behind."[11] For some migrants, ethnic enclaves have proven particularly advantageous in terms of economic competition with mainstream firms. They create jobs with upward-mobility avenues and offer an available alternative basis for organizing vertically integrated enterprises that rely upon community-supplied and constantly replenished resources and serve "their own ethnic market and/or the general population."[12] Ethnic enclaves have enabled certain "first-generation groups to be economically successful despite their evident lack of acculturation. These groups tend to preserve their cultural identity and internal solidarity."[13]

The existence of separate subsocieties does not preclude migrants from participating concurrently in mainstream structures. In fact, the ethnic community can facilitate adjustment by mediating between the new arrival and dominant-society institutions.[14] This possibility reveals the third major form of immigrant adaptation: biculturalism. Biculturalism is clearly the most demanding type of adaptation. Bilingualism, along with frequent contact with homeland nationals as well as with members of the receiving society, are prerequisites for this adaptive response. The need to satisfy two distinct, and at times conflicting, sets of social and economic expectations requires substantial energy, considerable creativity, and the ability to tolerate a high level of cognitive dissonance. The adoption of bi-structural participation strategies offers another means of preserving and enriching cultural uniqueness.[15] Unlike the assimilationist and cultural-pluralist models, the bi-cultural alternative does not assume that migrants will adopt U.S. citizenship and become integrated into the formal political system. The rise of bi-cultural situations indicates movement in the direction of a multi-cultural, trans-national society.

Cubans and Indochinese

Most of the published field research and evaluation work on refugee adaptation in the United States deals with the experiences of Indochinese and Cuban migrants.[16] After reviewing the most important results, this chapter presents new information about exiles from Iran and Ethiopia.

Cuban Exiles

Kin relations and the organized ethnic community have contributed in key ways to the economic adjustment and social adaptation of refugees from Cuba and Indochina.[17] Even among the first wave, the majority of Cuban refugees had close friends and relatives in the United States at the time they arrived and "problems of language, employment, and social adjustment were mitigated by the size and social supportiveness of the Cuban community. . . ."[18] The U.S. government also provided an exceptionally high level of adjustment-assistance services.[19]

Many Cuban refugees have utilized the ethnic-enclave strategy of economic adjustment and advancement.[20] The rate of participation in the economy by male and female exiles quickly outstripped the figure for U.S. nationals.[21] Secondary migrants returning to Florida from the northern states added their savings to capital brought from Cuba to consolidate the economic enclave. As a result, "Cuban-owned enterprises in the Miami area increased from 919 in 1967 to about 8,000 in 1976."[22] In 1979, "Cuban-Americans had a median family income of $17,538, compared with

$14,569 for other Spanish-origin groups and $19,965 for non-Spanish-origin groups."[23]   By 1987, the median Cuban family-income level of $27,300 approached the non-Hispanic figure.[24]

The Cuban enclave in Miami "consists of a highly differentiated, vertically integrated set of economic activities. . . ."[25]   About one-third of the businesses in Miami are owned and/or operated by Cuban-Americans. Enclave firms initially focused on construction, finance, textiles, leather, furniture, cigars, restaurants, supermarkets, clinics, private schools, funeral parlors, and law firms.[26]   In Little Havana, the Southwest Eighth Street area of Miami, more than 20,000 Cuban-owned businesses generated about $2.5 billion worth of sales in 1986.   Increasingly, upward-mobile Cubans have directed their entrepreneurial, technical, and managerial skills toward the Latin market within the adopted country and abroad.   Miami currently serves as the U.S. headquarters for domestic and multinational business ventures in Latin America—including a multi-billion dollar annual export-import trade, tourism, and international banking.[27]   Today, it has become "difficult for the Anglos to adapt" to life in Miami.[28]

For many Cuban exiles who arrived in the 1960s and 1970s, adaptation required coping with "future shock" combined with culture shock.   Young people showed greater flexibility in facing these challenges in comparison with the elderly.[29]   As the prospect of returning to the homeland faded, Cubans began to interface with mainstream culture and institutions.[30] Bilingualism became the norm.[31]   By the 1980s, "Cuban-Americans overwhelmingly had already become U.S. citizens or. . . had decided to adjust their status.   As citizens, they registered to vote and exercised that option at levels much higher than the average U.S. population."[32]

James Pisarowicz and Vicki Tosher report that studies conducted among Cuban refugees in Miami indicate that a "bicultural orientation is the most adaptive form of acculturation" and that maladjustment is more prevalent among migrants "who are monocultural, either in their original Hispanic culture or in their adopted American culture."[33]   Biculturalism introduces new problems, however.   In the words of Pedro Reboredo, Mayor of West Miami: "My family has assimilated well, but I have mixed emotions.   As we get closer to our fellow American brothers, I don't want to lose our ties to Cuba."[34]

Indochinese Exiles

The lack of an established ethnic base at the time the first wave of refugees arrived made adjustment in the United States more difficult for

304

groups from Southeast Asia, including the Vietnamese, in comparison to the Cuban experience.[35] By 1977, however, the rate of participation in the labor force among Indochinese refugees resembled the general U.S. population.[36] Over time, "sharing networks" based upon extended-family ties and/or ethnic enclaves assumed increasing economic importance among the Indochinese exile communities.[37] Economic undertakings include, for Vietnamese refugees, business and banking enclaves in the Los Angeles area, merchant restoration of the Argyle Street business strip in Chicago and the Clarendon section of Arlington into prosperous "Little Saigons," and cooperative fishing ventures along the Gulf Coast.[38]

Students of refugee adjustment agree that professionals suffer considerable initial downward mobility in the receiving society.[39] According to one study, only ten percent of the refugees who were professionals in Southeast Asia located professional employment in the United States. Instead, most worked as operatives or in service-industry jobs that require few skills—such as cleaners, or food-preparation and distribution workers.[40] In addition to outright job discrimination, Third World refugees are barred from entry into many professional fields by licensing requirements, inflexibility regarding the recognition of overseas credentials, and employer ignorance concerning the appropriateness of past employment in the home country.[41] Based upon the experience of Indochinese and Cuban exiles, Barry Stein concludes that even though refugees may eventually surpass their former standard of living (due in part to multiple wage-earner strategies), their occupational status, which tends to advance rapidly during the first four years of resettlement, will never return to the homeland level.[42] For Southeast Asian refugees, this has meant a substantial shift away from white-collar work. As a result of the combination of unfulfilled individual expectations and rigid occupational-entry barriers, job satisfaction often is elusive for the political migrant who does not participate in an ethnic enclave.[43]

Downward occupational mobility and problems locating employment in the host economy result in a tenuous income situation. Indochinese wage earners with numerous non-working dependents find economic self-sufficiency particularly difficult to achieve. In most early-arrival cases, nevertheless, household income among refugees from Indochina exceeded the national poverty line by the third year of residence and continued to rise subsequently.[44]

In terms of incorporation into mainstream economic institutions, lack of English-language competence has presented the most serious barrier for Southeast Asian refugees.[45] Paul Strand and Woodrow Jones cite the results of a San Diego study showing that family separation and English skills rank as the two most serious problems in the estimation of Indochinese refugees themselves. Others have identified housing for large families, educational assistance, and vocational skills as priority needs.[46] Southeast Asian refugees record relatively high rates of dependence on public-assistance programs.[47] However, many households remain economically active at the same time. Robert Bach concludes that "public aid helps to establish a reasonable standard of living for many who work."[48]

Vietnamese refugees who possess "greater educational attainment, higher social status, greater English proficiency, and less traditional Vietnamese outlook, people generally thought of as better equipped for adjustment, tend to earn higher income, but also have more serious mental problems."[49] For Vietnam's former political, managerial, and technical elite, adapting to U.S. culture essentially involves "adjusting to a change in class position."[50] The exile community remains divided politically, moreover. In particular, proponents of normalized relations between the United States and the post-revolution regime in Vietnam have been threatened or attacked.[51]

The Vietnamese refugee community in the United States has created numerous mutual-assistance associations to promote economic and social adjustment.[52] The level of social interaction with mainstream nationals usually is not extensive. Newcomers spend most off-work hours with family members or other compatriots.[53] The children of first-generation migrants are serious students who readily embrace visible aspects of the dominant culture.[54]

Between 1980 and 1984, 19 per cent of the eligible Southeast Asian refugees opted for naturalization.[55] The number of Cambodians, Vietnamese, and Laotians who decided to become U.S. citizens increased dramatically beginning in 1986.[56] Moreover, younger people have formed local organizations that "work in support of certain legislation or political candidates, especially in areas in which there are heavy concentrations of Vietnamese."[57]

Ethiopians, Eritreans, and Iranians

Two broad questions related to the U.S. experiences of migrants from Ethiopia and Iran are addressed from a comparative perspective in this section. First, we are interested in discovering *which of the three types of adaptive responses to life in the receiving society discussed above prevails among the three study communities.* Second, *what are the key variables affecting economic adjustment and social adaptation?* The D.C./L.A. survey results presented in this section are informative with respect to both questions. However, in light of the role of the Washington, D.C., and Los Angeles areas as centers for migrants from Ethiopia and Iran, and the exceptionally large size of the community of exiles living there, it is not possible to generalize from these findings beyond the two research sites.[58]

Operationalization

One can identify three discrete aspects of migrant incorporation. To begin with, there are the familiar issues of economic and social adjustment. An additional, albeit often implicit, consideration involves the depth of commitment to the host society relative to one's homeland.[59] The presence or absence of commitment bears directly on the permanency of adaptation to the new environment. In the following discussion of exile adjustment, each dimension of the adaptation experience reported by individual household heads is operationalized utilizing a rich mix of behavioral and attitudinal indicators.

Economic-Adjustment Indicators. Economic adjustment is conceptualized in three related parts. The first involves the migrant's *employment and occupational status.* Secure employment status is revealed by full-time work and by hiring on a permanent rather than a temporary basis.[60] Occupational position is measured by employment or non employment in a high-status activity (professional, businessperson, manager) and by the extent to which one's knowledge and skills are utilized in the current job. The ability to satisfy basic family needs without external assistance provides a strong indication of economic adjustment.[61] *Economic self-sufficiency* is measured in terms of (1) reliance upon self/spouse earnings and/or savings as the primary source of family income and (2) attainment of an annual family income from all sources of $20,000 or greater. Finally, *perceived economic status* involves assessment of one's annual family income relative to others in the homeland and in the receiving society.

Social-Adaptation Indicators. In exploring the applicability of alternative models of immigrant social and cultural adaptation in the United States, several indicators merit special attention. The initial concern is with the extent of interface with mainstream structures and culture among the interviewed migrants. This is measured, first, by reference to English-language ability and in terms of two crucial types of participation in large-scale U.S. institutions: educational and employment.[62] The degree of integration or assimilation into mainstream society is investigated objectively by reference to (1) the extent of residential integration and (2) the frequency of social interaction with U.S. nationals.[63] The subjective dimension of mainstream interaction is reflected in primary identification with host nationals.

The analysis of involvement within the migrant community follows. This effort explores participation in community-organized associations,[64] support for exile political organizations, residency and employment in ethnic enclaves, and the frequency of social interaction with other Iranians, Ethiopians, or Eritreans. The subjective dimension is measured by primary identification with members of the migrant community. The social-interaction and self-identification results enable us to distinguish social enclavist, integrator, and bi-cultural respondents.

Permanent-Attachment Indicators. Michael Piore shows how attitudes toward the permanency of attachment can exert an important effect on adaptation outcomes.[65] The final series of items explored here are utilized in an effort to estimate the likely permanence of adaptation to life in the receiving society—a temporal condition that occurs independently of assimilation, cultural pluralism, or biculturalism. With in-person visitation out of the question for most political exiles, relevant indices of permanent attachment include homeland ties and contacts (the presence of a parent living in Ethiopia or Iran, the act of sending money to someone in the home country within the past year)[66] and identification indicators (degree of satisfaction with life in the United States, the presence or absence of aspirations to return home permanently).

Economic Adjustment

African refugees face particularly strong structural barriers to incorporation in the mainstream economy of the United States. Two formidable obstacles are the lack of pre-existing kin/ethnic support networks and encounters with racial discrimination.[67] Throughout the 1980s, Iranians also encountered a particularly hostile reception in the United States in the wake of the hostage crisis.[68] However, the multi-cultural and international composition of the population of the nation's capital and the Los Angeles area mitigated the adaptive significance of racial and nationality discrimination in the two primary study sites.[69] In addition, most exiles from Ethiopia and Iran benefit from a relatively high level of English-language proficiency.[70]

308

The economic-adjustment data are set forth in Table 7.1. On the whole, the interviewees demonstrated an impressive ability to adjust to economic conditions in an industrialized society.

TABLE 7.1 Economic Adjustment Indicators, by Respondent Nationality

Economic Adjustment Indicators	All Respondents		%Iranians (Total N=148)	%Ethiopians (Total N=97)	%Eritreans (Total N=60)
	N	%tot			
Employment and Occupation					
Employed full time	197	65.0%	66.7%	67.0%	57.6%
Permanent job	175	73.5	69.4	70.5	92.3
Curr emplyd busnsperson, professal,adminor	113	53.3	59.7	48.2	40.5
Use highest educ/skills curr job	124	51.9	55.4	53.2	38.5
Self-sufficiency					
Self/spouse earns/savs prim source inc	247	85.1	91.1	83.3	72.2
Ann fam inc all sources $20,000 or more	110	50.7	65.2	34.9	33.3
Perceived status					
Curr inc high/med compared others homeld	211	75.1	80.3	74.4	64.4
Curr inc high/med compared others in US	135	46.1	65.2	31.6	22.8

Source: D.C./L.A. sample.

Employment. At the time of their interview in the mid-1980s, most migrant household heads were employed full-time in jobs they regarded as permanent. Furthermore, more than half of all employed respondents occupied professional, administrative, or business positions and confirm that they use their highest education and skills in the current job. Of course, most did not start there, but had advanced from entry-level positions in the service sector at the bottom of the job ladder.[71]

Self-sufficiency. Most interviewed members of the three exile communities quickly attained economic self-sufficiency.[72] Fully 85 percent of the sample report that family earnings and savings constitute their primary source of income (Table 7.1). Moreover, half of all the respondents received total annual family incomes in excess of $20,000.[73]

Perceived Status. Economic adjustment involves subjective as well as objective considerations. Three-fourths of the interviewees assess their total U.S. family-income level as high or medium compared with others living in the homeland and almost half (46 percent) regard their current earnings as high or medium relative to others in the United States.

Community Differences. There are interesting variations in the economic-adjustment experiences reported by members of the three exile communities. The Eritrean respondents stand out from the others in terms of employment and occupation (Table 7.1). They are the least likely to be employed on a full-time basis. However, the Eritreans who are employed proved to be the most likely to view their current position as a permanent one (92 percent versus 70 percent for the others). The interviewed Eritrean migrants also are the least likely to have located U.S. employment as a professional, administrator, or businessperson, and are considerably more likely than the two other groups are to be working in a job that does not utilize their skills and education. One contributing factor in this connection is that over half of the Eritrean respondents (53 percent) had arrived in the United States within the previous three years, whereas 85 percent of the Iranians and 77 percent of the Ethiopians had lived in this country for at least four years. Finally, Eritreans are the group that is most likely to be employed by a large mainstream organization and least likely to be self-employed or to work for a small business.

Overall, half of the interviewed exiles from Ethiopia report that they "never" use their highest education in their present job. Another 25 percent only occasionally employ their education and skills. The dissatisfaction which this engenders, particularly among professionals, undermines the adaptive effect of securing employment in the mainstream economy.[74]

Lucia McSpadden's study of 59 single male refugees from Ethiopia living in northern California, Seattle, and Reno indicates that most of the individuals resettled by agencies and caseworkers held "entry-level jobs with no supportive schooling or training for future change," whereas those assisted by church-congregation volunteers were more likely to be employed in professional or "acceptable status" jobs.[75] Congregational volunteers played a more active role than the agency personnel did in connecting refugees with employment opportunities, explaining how the system works, and opening doors that would otherwise remain closed to new migrants. The emphasis they placed upon pursuing U.S. higher education proved to be particularly effective in securing professional employment that is compatible with refugee aspirations.[76] The successful church-sponsored refugee would "go to school all day, and juggle one or more jobs part-time."[77] In contrast, the caseworker-assisted newcomer typically did not receive useful advice about how to improve his situation or effective assistance in opening appropriate employment and educational doors. The outcome tends to be incorporation into the lower class "without structural access to other resources to enable upward class mobility."[78]

In terms of income levels and the role of earnings/savings, the Iranian migrants show higher rates of self-sufficiency when compared with the interviewed Ethiopians and Eritreans. The Table 7.1 results reveal that over 90 percent of the Iranians relied on family earnings and savings as their primary income source. Only 83 percent of the Ethiopians and 72 percent of the Eritreans report this degree of economic self-sufficiency.[79] At the time, the national rate for cash-assistance dependency among resettled refugees from Ethiopia was 26 percent; among all official refugees, it was 55 percent.[80]

The income-distribution findings are even more striking. Among those who provided specific information regarding annual family income from all sources, roughly two-thirds of the Iranians and only one-third of the other two groups received more than $20,000. These family-income results must be viewed in the context of the extremely high overall living costs that prevail in the two metropolitan areas.[81] Among the resettled refugees from Ethiopia, the key economic-survival strategy has been shared living arrangements and even vehicles.[82]

The income results are related to the different perceptions interviewed migrants hold regarding their relative economic status in the United States. While nearly two-thirds of the Iranians view their current income as high or medium compared to most other U.S. families, only 32 percent of the Ethiopians and 23 percent of the Eritreans share this assessment.[83] From the perspective of most household heads belonging to the Ethiopian and Eritrean communities, then, the income-parity dimension of economic adaptation clearly had not yet been achieved.

Ethnic Enclaves. A defining characteristic of an ethnic enclave is that "a significant proportion of the immigrant labor force works in enterprises owned by other immigrants."[84] The ethnic-enclave economic strategy is only moderately developed within these three exile communities. In the D.C./L.A. sample, 29 percent of the employed Eritreans worked for a small business or on their own. At most, 40 percent of the Ethiopians and 44 percent of the Iranians worked in community-owned and operated enterprises.[85]

Nevertheless, by 1988 a wide variety of small firms owned and managed by exiles from Ethiopia existed in the Washington, D.C., metropolitan area. They included restaurants; law, accounting, and tax-preparation offices; gift shops; delivery, taxi, limousine, and towing services; a computer-software company; private physicians; laundries and cleaning services; automobile dealers and repair shops; financial and investment consultants; bands and night clubs; import-export companies; publishers; a travel agency; child- and home-care providers; a beauty salon; bakeries, food markets, convenience stores, and caterers; copying and duplicating firms; liquor stores; a home decorator; parking-lot companies; gift shops; photography studios; and service stations.[86]

In sum, a clear majority of the interviewed household heads from Iran and Ethiopia are employed in the mainstream economy. Self-employment is popular among all three exile groups and there has been limited development of an ethnic-enclave economy.

Downward Occupational Mobility. From largely impressionistic and anecdotal information, it is widely accepted that professionals who have migrated from Ethiopia to the United States have experienced the same downward occupational mobility that other refugees have encountered.[87] The D.C. interview results reveal that 53 per cent of the household heads employed both in Ethiopia and in the United States are former professionals and administrative managers who continued to hold the same type of position. A sizeable minority (29 percent) of the former professionals and managers occupied service jobs in the D.C. area. Nearly half of the others had started out in the service sector.

Without question, it is difficult for professionals from Ethiopia to locate jobs in their field in this country.[88] Moreover, 40 percent of the homeland professionals from Ethiopia interviewed in the D.C. area earned less than $15,000 in annual family income. However, the findings of this study indicate that an exceptionally high percentage of the experienced migrants from Ethiopia living in the nation's capital have been able to overcome existing barriers to entry into professional occupations. One contributing reason for this outcome is that "employers are usually very happy with the hard work and good attitudes of their Ethiopian workers." Consequently, job opportunities open up for newcomers in occupations and workplaces where others from Ethiopia are employed.[89]

Social Adaptation

Table 7.2 provides a breakdown of the D.C./L.A. study findings with regard to seven separate dimensions of social adaptation. The next sections briefly review these results.

Interface with Mainstream Society. We observe, first, that there is considerable interface with mainstream institutions and culture. Eighty-four percent of the interviewees who possessed some post-secondary education had attended a university or college in the United States.[90] Exactly 60 percent of the employed members of the sample work in a large, mainstream organizational setting. Over half of the interviewed migrants live in a residential area where fewer than five separate households of people from the homeland can be found within a short walking distance. Finally, two-thirds of the interviewees report that they spend at least an hour more than once per week in social interaction with U.S. nationals.[91]

English-language competency greatly facilitates interface with the mainstream society at both secondary and primary levels. Fluency in English is associated with social adaptation as well as with economic success outside of the ethnic enclave. The vast majority of migrants from these three communities do not face major barriers to structural interaction in mainstream institutions or to establishing smooth inter-personal relations with members of the host society due to English-language deficiencies.[92] In the D.C./L.A. sample, over 80 percent of the interviewees rated their English-language ability as excellent or good.

Identification with the Mainstream Society. Although the Table 7.2 results indicate that a majority of the interviewed migrants interact with U.S. nationals frequently at the primary-friendship level as well as in secondary institutions, these experiences have not resulted in individual identification with the dominant receiving society in most cases. Only a minority of the respondents (10 percent) report that they are closer to U.S. nationals than they are to their fellow migrants. On the basis of their primary identification, this small group constitutes the committed "integrators" among the sampled community members.[93]

Involvement with the Migrant Community. A minority of the total sample of migrant household heads are actively engaged in organized community activities or employed in ethnic businesses. Table 7.2 reveals that 38 percent of the interviewees participate in a community self-help association, cultural group, or place of worship.[94] Less than one-fourth of the sampled migrants support an exile political organization.

313

TABLE 7.2 Social Adaptation Indicators, by Respondent Nationality

Social Adaptation Indicators	All Respondents N	%tot	%Iranians (Total N=148)	%Ethiopians (Total N=97)	%Eritreans (Total N=60)
Interface with mainstream society					
Exc/good Eng lang	245	80.9%	78.9%	90.7%	69.5%
Attended US post-sec	203	83.5	86.8	78.9	80.6
Curr emplyd lg US/intn org	117	60.0	55.7	61.1	71.4
Few people from homeld live area of res	161	54.8	74.6	38.9	31.6
Soc interact at least 1x week US natls	201	66.8	54.1	84.5	69.0
Identification with mainstream society					
Feel closer US natls	29	9.5	6.8	15.5	6.7
Involvement with homeland community in US					
Partic community org(s)	116	38.0	29.1	44.3	50.0
Support exile polit org	65	22.4	21.4	16.0	35.7
Curr self-emplyd or sm bus	78	40.0	44.3	38.9	28.6
Live among homeld natls	133	45.2	25.4	61.1	68.4
Soc interact at least 1x week homeld natls	273	90.1	91.2	90.7	86.4
Identification with homeland community in US					
Feel closer compatriots	256	83.9	89.2	74.2	86.7
Type of migrant based on social interaction and identification					
Enclavist	97	31.8	44.6	13.4	30.0
Integrator	29	9.5	6.8	15.5	6.7
Biculturalist	179	58.7	48.6	71.1	63.3
Homeland ties					
Parent still living homeld	241	79.8	83.7	76.8	75.0
Remitted within past yr	71	23.7	14.4	28.1	39.7
Identification with homeland					
Dissatisfied living in US	188	63.1	55.5	66.7	76.3
Hope return homeld perman	178	59.1	74.1	47.9	40.0

Source: D.C./L.A. sample.

In late 1984, exactly forty percent of the employed respondents worked on their own (e.g., as self-employed professionals) or for a small business—including restaurants, import firms, and other ventures owned and managed by their compatriots. Furthermore, less than half of the interviewed exiles resided in an area with a concentration of people from the homeland. On the other hand, ninety percent of the sampled community members spent an hour or more socially at least twice each week with others from the homeland who are not part of their household. Most of these respondents engaged in such social interaction daily.

Identification with the Migrant Community. All three exile groups are fragmented politically and the migrants from Ethiopia are divided ethnically and linguistically as well.[95] While involvement in organized community undertakings is limited, the survey findings show that the vast majority of the household heads continue to identify principally with their fellow migrants.[96] Over 80 per cent of the respondents report that they feel closer to other community members from their homeland rather than to U.S. nationals. In light of the vital connection between language and culture, however, it is important to note that only 54 per cent of the interviewees with offspring evaluate their children's ability in a homeland language as excellent or good. This suggests that sustaining the homeland culture and the prevailing identification pattern is likely to become increasingly problematic in the future—particularly if the volume of new migrants diminishes.[97]

Type of Migrant. Creating a typology based upon social interaction and identification offers a convenient way of summarizing the social-adaptation findings presented up to this point. In the typology utilized here, an *integrator* frequently interacts on a social basis with U.S. nationals and identifies primarily with members of the dominant society. The *social enclavist* rarely meets U.S. nationals and feels closer to fellow migrants than to members of the mainstream society. Finally, the *biculturalist* personally interacts with U.S. friends on a frequent basis, but either still identifies primarily with the community of exiles from the home country or cannot decide which group s/he feels closer to. In the D.C./L.A. study, a majority of the respondents (59 percent) turned out to be biculturalists. Slightly less than one-third can be classified as social enclavists, and only one-tenth are integrators (see Table 7.2).

Homeland Ties. There are two family considerations that bear heavily on the decision to resettle permanently in this country among many exiles and refugees. One is separation from parents living in the sending country.[98]

This source of considerable unhappiness can be removed by bringing one's parents to live here, but such a move is not achieved easily and the elderly person's acceptance of U.S. life is far from guaranteed. The presence of one or more parents in the homeland generates resistance to adaptation in order to keep alive the dream of reunion in the sending country. The second factor is the practice of remitting money to persons in the country of origin. In this study, eighty percent of the interviewed community members report that at least one of their parents still lived in the sending country at the time of the interview. However, less than one-quarter of the interviewees had sent money to someone residing in the homeland within the past year (Table 7.2).

Children, on the other hand, can be an important consideration promoting long-term attachment to the place of exile.[99] In this case, the child(ren)'s lack of ability in the parent(s)' first language is the key factor. Parents realize that their children's adaptation in the homeland will be greatly complicated if they are not competent in one or more indigenous languages. Among the respondents with offspring, 46 per cent of the household heads report that their child(ren)'s command of the mother and/or father's first language ranges from fair to none.[100]

Identification with the Homeland. Cultural identification with the homeland remains strong among many members of the three exile communities. Exiles from Ethiopia, in particular, are reported to experience psychological distress over separation from homeland needs; concern about the welfare of relatives left behind; loss of autonomy, power, and daily social reinforcement; and the impersonal and culturally insensitive treatment they encounter in the United States.[101] Over 60 percent of the respondents in the D.C./L.A. study express dissatisfaction with life in the receiving country. In addition, nearly three-fifths of the interviewed migrants retain hope of returning permanently to Iran, Ethiopia, or Eritrea. These findings suggest that strong homeland orientations persist among many refugees from revolution living in the West.

At the behavioral level, naturalization statistics provide further evidence of lack of long-term commitment to the host society. In the sample, 13 persons (4 percent of the total, and 21 percent of those who were eligible after five years of permanent residency) had become a U.S. citizen by 1984. Eligible permanent residents from Ethiopia have been particularly reluctant to adopt citizenship.[102] Between the 1975 and 1987 fiscal years, only 2,371 migrants from Ethiopia elected to become citizens of the United States. In comparison, 25,871 Iranians became naturalized citizens over the same thirteen-year period.[103] The number of Ethiopians and Eritreans adopting

U.S. citizenship showed a dramatic increase beginning in 1985, however. In the eight years prior to that point in time, an average of 103 immigrants became naturalized citizens. The numbers for FYs 1985, 1986, and 1987 are 258, 474, and 714, respectively.[104]

Summary of General Findings. In summary, there is extensive interface with mainstream culture and institutions among the interviewed household heads living in the nation's capital and in the Los Angeles metropolitan region. Only a small proportion of the respondents show evidence of integration into mainstream society, however. While interaction in community-based organizations is restricted to a minority of the sample and there is limited use of ethnic-enclave economic strategies, identification with the homeland culture and with one's compatriots is widespread.

The findings also suggest that biculturalism is a popular adaptive response among migrants in the three studied communities. A major proportion of the interviewed exiles from Ethiopia and Iran participate in mainstream institutions and willingly interact with U.S. nationals, but most continue to identify with the community of migrants from the homeland.[105] On the whole, these migrants from Iran and Ethiopia can be characterized as "soft" adaptors. Although they generally have been successful in the United States, many continue to nurture the dream of repatriation.

Community Differences. The D.C./L.A. findings also suggest that there are some important differences among the three study communities in terms of social adaptation. The interviewed members of the Ethiopian community are the most likely to report excellent or good facility in the English language and to interact socially with U.S. nationals. The Iranian migrants are considerably more prone to live in neighborhoods where few or none of their compatriots reside.[106] Nevertheless, they report less frequent primary interactions with members of the dominant society than do interviewees from the two other communities. The Ethiopian respondents also are more than twice as likely as the Eritreans and Iranians are to identify most closely with U.S. nationals (see Table 7.2).

In terms of involvement with the community of migrants from the homeland, Iranian respondents are the least likely of the three groups to participate in self-help or cultural associations and to live among their compatriots.[107] They are the most inclined to work for themselves or for a family/Iranian small business, however. Table 7.2 shows that, unlike their Iranian counterparts, a solid majority of the migrants from Ethiopia chose to live in close proximity to their fellow nationals.[108] Eritreans are the most actively involved group—both in community organizations and in exile political action.[109] We observed in Chapter 4 that most exiles from

Ethiopia prefer to live in the nation's capital because of the presence of family members and/or the existence of employment and professional opportunities. An emphasis on personal and family needs might account, in part, for the finding that less than half of the Ethiopian respondents participate regularly in community organizations.[110] Of course, virtually everyone in the area attends community-based weddings and funerals on a periodic basis. Likewise, Iranians are loath to miss the annual Persian New Year (*Now-ruz*) celebration.[111]

There are striking differences among the three groups in classification by predominant type. Nearly half (45 percent) of the Iranian interviewees are social enclavists, while less than 30 percent of the others can be placed in this category (Table 7.2). Yet, Iranians rarely live in close proximity to one another. For many Iranian exiles, their current situation might be best described as "a state of dual detachment from both home and host societies . . . ."[112] Ethiopian migrants are the most likely to be integrators and biculturalists.[113]

Finally, several interesting variations in terms of homeland ties and identification merit consideration. The Eritrean migrants, for instance, are more likely than members of the other groups are to have sent money to someone in the homeland within the past year, to support an exile political organization, and to be dissatisfied with life in the United States. Although the interviewed Iranians are the least likely to have maintained homeland ties through remittances and to be dissatisfied living in the receiving nation, they are much more likely than the others are to nurture the hope of returning to live permanently in the home country (see Table 7.2).[114]

Key Variables Affecting Economic Adjustment and Social Adaptation

In this section, the goal is to identify the factors that exert the strongest influence on economic and social adaptation among migrants from Iran and Ethiopia. It is useful in this regard to distinguish between two basic sets of variables with the potential to affect adaptation outcomes in the country of resettlement. These are (1) pre-migration experiences and characteristics and (2) post-migration situations and individual characteristics in the receiving society.[115] Of particular interest here is the relationship to economic adjustment and social adaptation of six *pre*-migration factors:

- employment experience;
- principal type of work;
- family-income level;

- homeland ties to Western institutions;
- departure period;
- role of political persecution in the decision to become an exile;

as well as eight *post*-migration variables:

- length of time spent in the United States;
- gender;
- age in 1984;
- educational attainments;
- family-income level;
- refugee status;
- immigration position;
- marital status.

    Economic Adjustment: Pre-Migration Factors. Among the D.C./L.A. respondents, some pre-migration factors are consistently related to economic-adjustment outcomes and others are not. The most influential pre-migration variable is period of departure from the homeland. Migrants who left Iran and Ethiopia prior to the overthrow of the monarchy proved considerably more likely than did those who experienced post-revolution conditions in the sending country to be working on a full-time basis (76 versus 52 percent), to be employed in a high-status job (65 to 33 percent), to utilize their highest education and skills in their current work (59 versus 40 percent), to rely primarily upon family earnings as a source of support (98 to 70 percent), to possess annual family incomes of $20,000 or more (63 versus 35 percent), and to describe their income position as high/medium relative to most others living in the United States (61 percent and 29 percent, respectively).[116]

    Family-income level in the sending country is another pre-migration variable that generally is related to all three dimensions of economic adaptation. Most of the variations are less pronounced than the differences observed by period of departure, however. Specifically, respondents who report that they belonged to low-income families in the homeland are considerably less likely than their medium- and high-income counterparts are to be employed in high-status jobs where they use their education and training, to receive annual family incomes of at least $20,000, and to assess their economic position as medium or high compared with most others living in the receiving country.[117] Among the migrants from Ethiopia, those who came from low-income family backgrounds are three times as likely as the others are to be unemployed and to be supported by a volag or welfare agency. Relative to their counterparts from high-income family backgrounds, moreover, these low-income migrants are twice as likely to be earning less than $7,500 per annum and to hold jobs in the service sector.

A third pre-migration factor of interest is the respondent's employment status in the homeland. On every indicator, except for skills utilization, migrants who had been employed in Ethiopia or Iran possess a slight edge in terms of economic adaptation when compared with their previously unemployed compatriots. Two findings related to Ethiopian and Eritrean migrants deserve special mention. In comparison to respondents who had worked in Ethiopia, twice the proportion of household heads who had never been employed there relied primarily upon agency financial support in 1984. Secondly, the previously employed respondents proved to be far more likely than those who had not occupied paid positions in Ethiopia to view their current standard of living as "high" relative to persons residing in the homeland (54 and 26 percent, respectively).

There are several interesting differences among the total sample according to the interviewee's previous type of employment. Migrants who had worked as laborers or farmers in Ethiopia or Iran are the least likely to hold full-time positions, to earn at least $20,000 per annum, to be supported principally by family income, and to evaluate their current economic position as high or medium. None of the former laborers and farmers had secured high-status employment in the D.C. or L.A. area. In contrast, 69 percent of those employed in financial or commercial jobs in the sending country, and 64 percent of the former professionals and administrators, occupied high-status positions in the United States.[118]

Table 7.3 suggests that pre-migration ties to Western institutions also are conducive to economic success in the United States. A slightly higher proportion of the respondents who possessed a personal or parental link in the sending country to a multinational corporation, Western government agency, and/or international organization held an advantageous position on every indicator of economic adjustment in comparison with the interviewed migrants who reported no such ties.

The final pre-migration variable considered here is the role of political persecution in the respondents' decision to live in exile. Those who state that (fear of) political persecution did *not* play an important part in their decision to become an exile are consistently more likely than their counterparts are to occupy an advantageous economic position in the D.C. or L.A. area. Indeed, they are *substantially* more apt to be employed as a

TABLE 7.3 Economic Adjustment Indicators, by Homeland Tie to Western Government Agency, Multinational Corporation, and/or International Organization

Economic Adjustment Indicators	All Respondents		% Self, Parent Tie (Total N=54)	% No Tie (Total N=251)
	N	%Tot		
Employment and occupation				
Employed full time	197	65.0%	77.8%	62.2%
Permanent job	175	73.5	82.2	71.5
Curr emplyd busnsperson, professal, adminor	113	53.3	64.0	50.0
Use highst educ/skls cur job	124	51.9	64.4	49.0
Self-sufficiency				
Self/spouse earns/savings prim source income	247	85.2	90.7	83.9
Ann fam inc all sources $20,000 or more	110	50.7	58.3	48.5
Perceived status				
Curr inc high/med compared to others homeland	211	75.1	94.1	70.9
Curr inc high/med compared to others in US	135	46.1	62.3	42.5

Source: D.C./L.A. sample.

professional, businessperson, or administrator (70 percent, versus 44 percent of the interviewed migrants who indicate that political persecution did constitute an important decisional consideration), to obtain incomes equal to or in excess of $20,000 per year (69 versus 40 percent), and to perceive their economic position as high or medium relative to most others living in the host country (63 to 36 percent).

Economic Adjustment: Post-Migration Factors. Table 7.4 indicates that migrants from Iran and Ethiopia who reached the United States between 1952 and 1973 typically are at least twice as likely as those who arrived after 1982 are to be in an advantageous position in the receiving country in terms of employment and occupation, economic self-sufficiency, and per-

TABLE 7.4 Economic Adjustment Indicators, by Period Arrived in United States

Economic Adjustment Indicators	All Respondents		% Early 1952-73 (Total N=64)	% Middle 1974-81 (Total N=163)	% Late 1982-84 (Total N=78)
	N	%tot			
Employment and occupation					
Employed full time	197	65.0%	90.6%	65.4%	42.9%
Permanent job	175	73.5	84.1	73.1	58.5
Curr emplyd busnsperson professal, adminor	113	53.3	78.2	53.3	16.2
Use highst ed/skls cur job	124	51.9	70.3	50.7	26.8
Self-sufficiency					
Self/spouse earns/savings prim source income	247	85.2	100.0	92.9	55.6
Ann fam inc all sources $20,000 or more	110	50.7	78.0	48.3	29.4
Perceived status—evaluation of current income level					
High/med re. others homeld	211	75.1	96.7	75.2	56.9
High/med re. others in US	135	46.1	74.2	46.2	21.9

Source: D.C./L.A. sample.

ceived status.[119] On each of the economic-adjustment indicators listed in Table 7.4, moreover, respondents who entered between 1974 and 1981 are found in the middle of the other two groups in terms of their current position. The differences in type of employment and in income are particularly pronounced. For instance, nearly 80 percent of those who had lived in this country for 11 years or longer reported annual family earnings of $20,000 or more. In contrast, less than 30 percent of the migrants who had arrived within the past three years had reached this income level. Almost half of the recent arrivals are not financially self-sufficient. This category includes a substantial number of newly resettled refugees. Overall, the post-migration variable of time of arrival in the United States turns out to be more influential than period of departure is in terms of the selected economic-adjustment indicators.

In general, community members who reach the United States by means other than official resettlement under the government's refugee program are more likely to possess secure employment and to enjoy economic self-sufficiency as well as higher perceived status in the receiving country. For instance, refugees were much more likely than non-resettled migrants were to be unemployed in 1984. Nearly three-fourths of the non-resettled group (73 percent) engaged in full-time employment; less than half of their refugee counterparts (46 percent) had located full-time jobs. Over 60 percent of the employed non-resettled respondents had secured work as a professional, businessperson, or administrative manager by 1984, whereas only 19 percent of the officially admitted refugees occupied such positions. A similar gap in percentages separated the two groups in terms of annual family income when $20,000 is used as the cutoff point. In addition, 81 percent of the reporting refugee households from the Ethiopian and Eritrean communities earned $14,000 or less per year, whereas only 29 percent of the others did not exceed the $14,000 income level. Most remarkably, non-resettled Ethiopian and Eritrean migrants accomplished these feats even though over half of them (53 percent) report that their current immigration or visa status adversely has affected their ability to find and retain jobs they are trained for; only 3 official refugees (4 percent) encountered problems as a result of this barrier. In terms of perceived economic status, considerably higher proportions of the non-resettled migrants than the official refugees view their current income level as high/medium relative to most others living in their home country and in the United States (83 and 59 percent, versus 56 and 15 percent). Finally, a higher proportion of the resettled refugees than the non-resettled group (37 versus 6 percent) are financially dependent upon loans or agency support, and do not primarily support their households through family earnings.

Educational level is another post-migration variable that is clearly related to economic adjustment among the three study communities.[120] From Table 7.5, we observe that there is a remarkably consistent relationship between higher-educational attainments and every indicator of economic adjustment with the exception of job permanency. Those holding university degrees are particularly likely to be employed in high-status positions.[121] In contrast, nearly half (48 percent) of the Ethiopian and Eritrean respondents in the less-than-secondary-complete group were unemployed at the time of the interview. Almost two-thirds of the reporting household heads who possess an advanced degree received at least $20,000 in annual income, while less than 30 percent of their counterparts who had never attended a university earned this much.[122]

With the exception of the income-related variables, the patterns observed in Table 7.5 apply across the three exile communities. With

TABLE 7.5 Economic Adjustment Indicators, by Highest Educational Attainment

Economic Adjustment Indicators	All Respondents		%Adv U Degree (Total N=102)	%U Degree (Total N=72)	%Some Post Sec (Total N=69)	%Sec Or Less (Total N=59)
	N	%tot				
Employment and occupation						
Employed full time	197	65.0%	74.5%	76.4%	56.5%	45.8%
Permanent job	175	73.5	68.1	76.2	77.1	78.8
Curr emplyd busnsperson, professal, adminor	113	53.3	73.0	63.2	22.0	12.5
Use highst ed/skl cur job	124	51.9	69.1	57.8	31.3	21.2
Self-sufficiency						
Self/spouse earns/savings prim source income	247	85.2	97.1	95.7	77.8	58.2
Ann fam inc all sources $20,000 or more	110	50.7	64.0	54.0	39.1	29.4
Perceived status						
Curr inc high/med compared others homeland	211	75.1	84.2	84.6	71.9	53.6
Curr inc high/med compared others in US	135	46.1	61.6	59.4	31.8	20.7

Source: D.C./L.A. sample.

regard to annual family income from all sources, the interviewed Iranians possessing secondary education or less actually are considerably more likely than their compatriots are to earn at least $20,000 (80 percent versus slightly more than 60 percent).[123] In sharp contrast with the results for Iranian migrants, only 11 percent of the Ethiopians and 7 percent of the Eritreans without a university education reported incomes equal to or in excess of $20,000.[124]

None of the other post-migration factors selected for study are strongly and consistently associated with the indicators of economic adjustment. However, younger respondents are less likely to possess secure employment status and to occupy high-status positions. For instance, only 11 percent of those under 25 years of age were employed as a businessperson, professional, or administrator. Nearly four-fifths (77 percent) of the migrants who had reached their 35th birthday report that they worked in one of these high-status jobs. The youngest group of respondents are the least likely to be economically independent and held the most unfavorable perceptions of their current economic standing relative to other people living in the homeland and the United States. In the case of migrant economic adjustment, however, age typically serves as a proxy for other variables—particularly length of residence in the United States and educational level.[125]

Married and single household heads do not differ greatly in terms of employment and occupational status. It is likely, therefore, that the tendency for married respondents to report higher family incomes (62 percent at $20,000 or more, versus 42 percent for single migrants) and to be more apt to view their economic standing as high/medium relative to others living here (61 to 36 percent) is primarily a function of the availability of two or more wage earners.

There is surprisingly little difference within the sample between migrants who are on a firm track toward permanent residency and those who are not.[126] The respondents who possess secure immigrant status are only slightly more likely than other exiles are to be employed in a high-status profession and to earn at least $20,000 per year.[127]

Finally, a higher proportion of the female than the male household heads use their highest education or training in the current job. Males are more likely than females are to hold full-time jobs, to be employed in pretigious professions, and to report annual incomes of $20,000 or greater. The overall results mask important differences by nationality, however, on two of these items. First, Ethiopian males and females are equally likely to be employed on a full-time basis (two-thirds of both groups). Iranian and Eritrean male interviewees, in contrast, are considerably more likely than their female counterparts are to hold full-time jobs (74 and 63 percent, versus 41 and 47 percent). In the second place, male Iranian household heads are much more likely than their female compatriots are to report annual family incomes equal to or in excess of $20,000 (69 to 42 percent). The difference by gender is not nearly as pronounced among Eritrean respondents (37 versus 25 percent) and disappears completely in the Ethiopian case (34 percent of the males and 35 percent of the females possess incomes in this category).

Social Adaptation: Pre-Migration Factors. Among the interviewed migrants from Iran and Ethiopia residing in the D.C. and L.A. areas, pre-migration variables are not consistently related to social-adaptation outcomes across the categories identified for analysis. With respect to the presence or absence of homeland ties to a Western agency or corporation, there are no important adaptation variations.

The respondents' principal type of homeland work and family economic standing at the time of departure are related to some, but not all, of the indicators of interface and identification with mainstream U.S. society. Thus, persons with sending-country backgrounds as farmers or laborers are the least likely group of interviewees to assess their English language competency as excellent or good (71 percent, versus 90 percent for former professionals and administrators), to interact socially on a weekly basis with U.S. nationals (43 percent, versus 78 percent for respondents employed in financial or commercial positions), and to feel closer to host-country nationals than to their fellow migrants (0 percent, versus 13 percent for the professionals/administrators). The interviewed migrants who evaluated their self/family income position as "low" at the time of exit from the home country are less likely than their high- and medium-income counterparts are to possess competency in English language (68, 85, and 84 percent, respectively); they also are the least likely to report closer ties with U.S. nationals than with their compatriots (4 percent, versus 16 and 8 percent).

In terms of involvement and identification with the community of migrants from the home country, respondents from low-income backgrounds are more prone to support exile political organizations and to feel closer to the expatriate community than are persons from high- and medium-income situations in Iran and Ethiopia.[128] The group of interviewed migrants possessing subordinate-class backgrounds in the sending country are the most likely to support exile political organizations operating in the United States (50 percent, versus only 6 percent for those with financial/commercial backgrounds and around 20 percent for the others). However, homeland professionals and administrators participate most frequently in migrant-community organizations (48 percent, versus roughly 30 percent for each of the other three groups).[129] Respondents who cite political persecution in the homeland as an important factor in the decision to become an exile are considerably more likely than their counterparts are to participate in community-organization activities, to support an exile political organization,[130] and to live among other migrants from the homeland (48, 32, and 54 percent, versus 22, 8, and 32 percent for those who rated homeland persecution as personally unimportant).[131]

On the basis of patterns of social interaction and identification, the former farmers and laborers in the D.C./L.A. sample prove most likely to be enclavists in their new society (57 percent to about 30 percent for the others) and least likely to be biculturalists (43 percent to 53 percent and higher) or integrators.[132] The homeland farmers/laborers also are somewhat more prone to reside among fellow nationals in the host society, although they are not particularly likely be employed in ethnic enclaves.[133]

Turning to homeland ties and identification, we discover that the migrants who left Iran or Ethiopia prior to the overthrow of the monarchy are considerably more apt than their counterparts who exited after the revolution are to have remitted within the past year (31 to 16 percent) and to maintain hope of returning to live in the homeland (74 to 43 percent).[134] They are less likely than the others are to be dissatisfied with life in the United States, however (58 to 69 percent).[135] The homeland-identification results also are mixed in terms of type of work in the country of origin. Former farmers and laborers, for instance, are the most likely to have a parent still living in Iran or Ethiopia and to be dissatisfied with U.S. life, but are the least likely group of respondents to have sent money home within the past year and to sustain hope of returning to live in the sending country. One's economic standing in the home country exerts no impact on current homeland ties, with the exception of the tendency for respondents from middle-income backgrounds to continue to hope for eventual repatriation (67 percent, versus 51 percent for high-income and 42 percent for low-income migrants).

Social Adaptation: Post-Migration Factors. Post-migration factors tend to be more closely related than pre-migration variables are to social-adaptation outcomes among the interviewed migrants from Iran and Ethiopia, although the connections are neither as consistent nor as strong as we observed in the case of economic adjustment. The most interesting post-arrival variables are length of residence in the receiving country, educational attainments, and refugee status. Current economic standing and secure immigration status each are associated with only one of the three broad social-adaptation categories. There are no important differences at all among males and females or among married and unmarried respondents.[136] Age, which is likely to be a proxy for other variables, is strongly but inconsistently related to several indicators.[137]

The findings presented in Table 7.6 reveal that the social-adaptation position of the most recent migrants from Iran and Ethiopia is strikingly different from that reported by their counterparts who have resided for a longer time in this country. In comparison with respondents who had lived here for between 4 and 33 years, those who arrived in 1982 or later are considerably less likely to be competent in English,[138] to have attended a U.S. institution of higher education, and to live in residential areas where

TABLE 7.6   Social Adaptation Indicators, by Period Arrived in United States

Social Adaptation Indicators	All Respondents N	%tot	% Early 1952-73 (Total N=64)	% Middle 1974-81 (Total N=163)	% Late 1982-84 (Total N=78)
Interface with mainstream society					
Exc/good Eng lang ability	245	80.9%	96.9%	85.8%	57.1%
Attended US post-sec inst	203	83.5	95.3	88.0	45.9
Curr emplyd US/intn org	117	60.0	72.2	57.3	48.4
Few people from homeld live area of res	161	54.8	56.5	60.1	41.9
Soc interact at least 1x week US natls	201	66.8	80.6	63.6	62.3
Identification with mainstream society					
Feel closer to US natls	29	9.5	14.1	7.4	10.3
Involvement with expatriate community in U.S.					
Partic commun org(s)	116	38.0	57.8	32.5	33.3
Support exile polit org	65	22.4	26.2	16.7	31.5
Curr self-emplyd or sml bus	78	40.0	27.8	42.7	51.6
Live among homeld natls	133	45.2	43.5	39.9	58.1
Soc interact at least 1x week homeld natls	273	90.1	81.3	93.2	90.9
Identification with expatriate community in U.S.					
Feel closer to compatriots	256	83.9	70.3	88.3	85.9
Type of migrant based on social interaction and identification					
Enclavist	97	31.8	15.6	36.2	35.9
Integrator	29	9.5	14.1	7.4	10.3
Bicultural	179	58.7	70.3	56.4	53.8
Homeland ties					
Parent still living homeld	241	79.8	62.5	82.5	88.5
Remitted within past yr	71	23.7	45.2	21.7	10.4
Identification with homeland					
Dissatisfied life in US	188	3.1	61.7	60.2	70.1
Hope return homeld perman	178	59.1	68.3	66.9	35.9

Source: D.C./L.A. sample.

there are few compatriots.[139] Moreover, the interviewees who have resided in the U.S.A. for at least 12 years are much more apt than those who have spent fewer years living here are to work for a large employer in the mainstream economy,[140] to interact often on a social basis with U.S. nationals,[141] and to identify with members of the dominant society.[142]

In terms of migrant-community adaptation, Table 7.6 shows that recent arrivals interact frequently with other migrants from the homeland and are the most likely to live in ethnic neighborhoods and to work for ethnically based businesses.[143] The group of respondents with the longest U.S. residency reports the highest rate of participation in community-organization activities;[144] they are the least likely to be employed by ethnic businesses[145] and to interact frequently and identify with other expatriates.[146]

In general, respondents who had lived in the United States for longer than eleven years proved more likely to be bi-cultural adaptors and integrators in comparison with the interviewed migrants who had arrived in 1974 or later (70 and 14 percent, versus 56 and 8 percent). The overall study findings suggest that the level of participation in ethnic enclaves will decline and the bi-culturalist adaptation strategy increasingly will be employed over time. However, there are interesting variations by nationality in the relationship between duration of U.S. residency and type of migrant. Iranians who reached the receiving country after 1981 were particularly likely to be social enclavists (78 percent, versus 12 percent of the earliest arrivals). The most recent group of Ethiopian migrants, on the other hand, showed a greater tendency to be integrators than did their compatriots who had arrived prior to 1974 or between 1974 and 1981 (26, 7, and 15 percent, respectively). Finally, Eritreans with short-term residency were more apt, in comparison with those who reached the U.S.A. prior to 1982, to be bi-cultural adaptors (69 percent versus 57 percent).

The Table 7.6 data regarding long-term adaptation prospects indicate that the recently arriving exiles are weakly tied to the homeland in terms of remitting behavior and with regard to the two identification items. Migrants who entered the United States prior to 1974 are the most apt to have sent money to someone in the homeland within the past year[147] and to hope to return to live in the country of origin.[148]

Educational attainments are related to many of the selected indicators of social adaptation. The Table 7.7 data show that respondents with some exposure to university education possess superior English-language skills,[149] are more likely to work for large mainstream economic institutions,[150] and are more apt to live among U.S. nationals than are migrants who have not

TABLE 7.7   Social Adaptation Indicators, by Highest Educational Attainment

Social Adaptation Indicators	All Respondents N	%tot	%Adv U Degree (Total N=102)	%U Degree (Total N=72)	%Some Post Sec (Total N=69)	%Sec Or Less (Total N=59)
Interface with mainstream society						
Exc/good Engl lang abil	245	80.9%	93.1%	86.1%	88.4%	45.8%
Attended US post-sec inst	203	83.5	88.2	81.9	78.3	-
Curr emplyd US/intn org	117	60.0	62.8	58.5	63.9	45.0
Few people from homeland live in area of res	161	54.8	62.2	64.8	51.5	33.9
Soc interact at least 1x week US natls	201	66.8	66.0	65.3	71.0	66.1
Identification with mainstream society						
Feel closer to US natls	29	9.5	9.8	8.3	11.6	8.5
Involvement with expatriate community in U.S.						
Partic comm org(s)	116	38.0	53.4	33.3	23.2	33.9
Support exile polit organz	65	22.4	24.5	15.9	18.5	31.6
Curr self-emplyd or sml bus	78	40.0	37.2	41.5	36.1	55.0
Live among homeland natls	133	45.2	37.8	35.2	48.5	66.1
Soc interact at least 1x week homeland natls	273	90.1	88.2	90.3	92.8	89.8
Identification with expatriate community in U.S.						
Feel closer to compatriots	256	83.9	80.4	88.9	82.6	88.1
Type of migrant based on social interaction and identification						
Enclavist	97	31.8	32.4	33.3	29.0	32.2
Integrator	29	9.5	9.8	8.3	11.6	8.5
Bicultural	179	58.7	57.8	58.3	59.4	59.3
Homeland ties						
Parent still living homeld	241	79.8	74.3	86.1	79.4	81.0
Remitted within past year	71	23.7	34.0	18.3	21.7	13.6
Identification with homeland						
Dissatisfied life in US	188	63.1	53.1	65.3	70.6	68.4
Hope return homelnd perm	178	59.1	70.3	69.4	55.2	32.8

Source: D.C./L.A. sample.

attended an institution of higher education. Nevertheless, there are no major variations by educational-attainment level in terms of the extent of social interaction with members of the dominant society or in personal identification.[151]

We also observe from Table 7.7 that the interviewees from Iran and Ethiopia who have completed no more than a secondary-school education are more likely than their counterparts are to support an exile political organization, to work by themselves or for a small (ethnic) business, and to live in an ethnic neighborhood. Individuals holding an advanced university degree are the most apt to participate in community mutual-assistance associations, however.[152] The differences by educational level in social interaction with others from the sending country and in identification with the expatriate community are negligible.[153] In addition, the distribution of the respondents by type of migrant is virtually identical across all four educational categories. Controlling for nationality reveals three distinct patterns, however. Eritreans who have earned an advanced degree are much more likely than their compatriots are to be social enclavists and much less likely to be biculturalists and integrators. Among the interviewed Iranian migrants, however, increasing levels of formal educational attainment are associated with declining proportions identified as enclavists—ranging from 73 percent (completed secondary education or less) to 35 percent (possession of an advanced university degree). Conversely, Iranians with an advanced degree are the most likely, and those without any university education are the least likely, to be biculturalists and integrators. There are no variations by educational level among the Ethiopian respondents.

The findings are mixed with regard to the association of educational attainment with homeland ties and identification. Among the interviewed migrants in the D.C./L.A. sample, persons possessing an advanced degree are the most likely to have remitted within the past year[154] and to have sustained the hope of returning to live in the country of origin (see Table 7.7).[155] They are the least likely to be dissatisfied with life in the United States, however.[156] The group with the lowest level of formal education shows the smallest incidence of recent remitting and possesses the least hope regarding repatriation prospects.

Although *resettled refugees* are expected to have a head start on social adaptation as a result of the special attention and resources they receive,[157] we observe from Table 7.8 that respondents *without official-refugee status* from these three communities are more likely to be competent in English, to have interacted in U.S. institutions of higher education, and to live in neighborhoods settled predominantly by host-society nationals. Resettled

TABLE 7.8   Social Adaptation Indicators, by Official Immigration Status as Resettled Refugee

Social Adaptation Indicators	All Respondents N	%tot	% Refugees (Total N=90)	% Non Refugees (Total N=215)
Interface with mainstream society				
Exc/good English lang abil	245	80.9%	65.2%	87.4%
Attended US post-sec instit	203	83.5	51.2	90.1
Curr emplyed US/intn org	117	60.0	64.9	58.9
Few people from homeland live in area of res	161	54.8	38.4	61.5
Soc interact at least 1x week US natls	201	66.8	73.0	64.2
Identification with mainstream society				
Feel closer to US natls	29	9.5	8.9	9.8
Involvement with expatriate community in U.S.				
Participate in community org(s)	116	38.0	35.6	39.1
Support exile polit org	65	22.4	29.8	19.4
Curr self-emplyd or sml bus	78	40.0	35.1	41.1
Live among homeland natls	133	45.2	61.6	38.5
Soc interact at least 1x week homeland natls	273	90.1	92.1	89.3
Identification with expatriate community in U.S.				
Feel closer to compatriots	256	83.9	84.4	83.7
Type of migrant based on social interaction and identification				
Enclavist	97	31.8	25.6	34.4
Integrator	29	9.5	8.9	9.8
Biculturalist	179	58.7	65.6	55.8
Homeland ties				
Parent still living homeld	241	79.8	84.1	78.0
Remitted within past year	71	23.7	15.7	27.0
Identification with homeland				
Dissatisfied living in US	188	63.1	70.1	60.2
Hope return homeld permanently	178	59.1	33.0	70.0

Source: D.C./L.A. sample.

refugees are slightly more apt than the others are to work for a large employer in the mainstream economy and to engage in frequent social interaction with receiving-country citizens—including congregational sponsors. The only differences between the two groups in terms of adaptation to the community of migrants are the greater tendency for the former to support an exile political organization and to live in ethnic neighborhoods. Overall, official refugees are somewhat less likely than other types of migrants are to be social enclavists and slightly more likely to be biculturalists.

In terms of long-term adaptation prospects, Table 7.8 shows mixed results by official immigration status as a resettled refugee. Official refugees are slightly more prone to be dissatisfied with U.S. life in comparison with other migrants. However, those who did not enter this country as a resettled refugee are substantially more apt than the others are to maintain the hope of repatriation.[158]

The remaining variables are less strongly and consistently associated with variations on several social-adaptation indicators. With regard to mainstream adaptation, for instance, respondents possessing secure immigration status are more likely than their counterparts are to engage in weekly social interaction with members of the dominant society (73 versus 53 percent) and to identify with U.S. nationals (11 to 7 percent). In addition, the interviewed migrants without permanent-residency prospects are somewhat more apt than the others are to work for themselves or for a small (ethnic) business (47 to 37 percent), to feel closer to migrants from their homeland than to U.S. nationals (91 to 81 percent), to be social enclavists (47 versus 25 percent), and to maintain the hope of returning to the sending country (67 to 56 percent).

A respondent's family-income level relative to most others living in the United States is one measure of economic adaptation in the receiving society. In this study, no consistent relationship exists between "high" and "medium" U.S. economic standing and indicators of adaptation to mainstream society or behavior associated with social enclavists. However, interviewees with "low" family incomes are less likely than their wealthier counterparts are to have sent money home recently (17 versus 32 percent), to be dissatisfied with life in the United States (60 to 67 percent), and to retain hope of returning to live in the country of origin (52 to 69 percent).

Finally, the youngest respondents are the least likely to be competent in English (54 percent, versus 86 percent for those 25 years of age and older), and the most likely to live among other migrants from the homeland (64 to 42 percent), to interact socially with their compatriots at least weekly (98 percent, versus 93 percent for those between 25 and 34 years of age and 83 percent for those 35 and older), and to feel closer to people from the homeland (89 percent to 82 percent for those above 24 years of age). Those aged 17 to 24 also are less likely than their elders are to have remitted within the past year (7 to 26 percent) and to continue to hold repatriation hopes (43 to 63 percent).

Conclusions

The experience of exile involves "an extraordinarily stressful process of dislocation and relocation, loss and rediscovery, and uprootedness and new growth."[159] The mental-health problems that all groups of resettled refugees from revolution have encountered in the North increasingly are related to difficulties "of transition to a new society rather than the aftereffects of exodus."[160] Downward occupational mobility ranks among the most common initial problems refugees have experienced in the United States. Exiles who are able to transfer their occupational skills generally adapt socially in more rapid fashion in comparison to their compatriots.[161] Nevertheless, Third World refugees have demonstrated a remarkable capacity for economic adjustment and social adaptation in the North. Lack of achievement, particularly in terms of occupational transfer, is primarily a consequence of structural constraints and failure to accommodate cultural strangers on the part of the receiving society rather than an indication of individual failure or a negative reflection on the abilities and determination of refugees themselves.[162]

The D.C./L.A. study results confirm that nationality is related in interesting ways to economic-adjustment and social-adaptation outcomes among the interviewed refugees. However, they also show that both processes are strongly influenced by factors that transcend national identification.[163]

Post-Migration Factors

In the study of exiles from Iran and Ethiopia, post-migration variables showed stronger and more consistent association with incorporation in the receiving industrial society—particularly economic adjustment—than did pre-migration influences.[164] Among the variables tested, length of U.S. residency and current educational level proved to be the most powerful. The importance of higher education as a factor in adaptation to life in

Western industrialized countries is understandable given that "as the economic and social environment becomes more complex, education augments the capacity to decode, interpret, and make decisions based on new technical and economic information."[165]

Bicultural Adaptation

The study of randomly selected migrant household heads living in the Washington, D.C., and Los Angeles metropolitan areas provides evidence of bi-cultural adaptation on the part of many community members. Most Iranian, Ethiopian, and Eritrean exiles and refugees are competing effectively in the mainstream economy and are involved with large-scale institutions. Many live among U.S. nationals and are comfortable interacting frequently with them on a social basis. In short, they have friends in the dominant society. Concomitantly, most members of the three communities interact socially with fellow migrants and feel closer to their compatriots than to U.S. nationals. We also discovered that most respondents are dissatisfied with life in the receiving country and a plurality retain the hope of returning to the homeland. Many would like to keep alternative adaptation options open for themselves and their children.

The spread of biculturalism among migrants from Ethiopia and Iran is particularly interesting. Although the requisite population concentration, sources of finance, and supply of labor[166] certainly exist in the D.C. and L.A. areas, the incidence among the three studied communities of economic success achieved by operating within an ethnic enclave is surprisingly limited. Neither rigid structural separation from mainstream society, integration into a dominant melting pot, nor political assimilation are widespread among these refugees from Third World revolutions. Clearly, the prevailing adaptive response of exiles from Iran and Ethiopia differs dramatically from patterns uncovered in earlier studies of Japanese, Chinese, Indochinese, Korean, and Cuban migrants.[167]

Economic Adjustment

Most of the D.C./L.A. respondents have opted to participate in rather than to compete with mainstream economic institutions. The accomplishments of Ethiopian and Eritrean exiles are especially impressive given the absence of an established generation of prior immigrants and a supportive kin community, the extreme poverty that prevails in the country they fled from,[168] and the tenuous legal status that many had to surmount.

The findings of the D.C./L.A. study, which indicate that many Iranian, Ethiopian, and Eritrean political migrants have achieved considerable economic success and rapid occupational advancement, raise a fundamental challenge to Barry Chiswick's generalizations that denigrate the economic-adjustment potential of Third World refugees based upon aggregate statistics.[169] In particular, there is no empirical support here for the argument that economic migrants admitted on a kinship basis will "have a more successful economic adjustment than refugees with the same demographic characteristics. . . ."[170] Refugees are unique in that "all their inner resources have been fully tested, their dormant qualities and potentials have been evoked, and their purposes and goals have been challenged."[171] Consequently, the refugee survivor is likely to be resourceful in mastering the new environment of the Western society, to respond to employment-related challenges with exceptional motivation and levels of accomplishment, and to become self-reliant in relatively short order.[172] In the long run, then, there are a number of strong similarities in the impact that refugees and other immigrants exert on the host economy and society.[173]

Recent Developments

By 1990, a decided shift had occurred within the Ethiopian and, to a lesser extent, the Eritrean community away from intense preoccupation with political objectives. In place of ideological fervor, many exiles are consumed by plans for capital accumulation and by the desire to acquire material possessions.[174] Former political activists dwell on economic-advancement strategies and dedicated Marxists have become business owners. In the Washington, D.C., area, the most visible manifestation of this tendency is the news that it has become fashionable to purchase one's own house—a previously unthinkable act that symbolizes joining the capitalist land-owning class and abandoning the commitment to returning home.[175] There even are some indications that resistance among migrants from Ethiopia to adopting U.S. citizenship is weakening on a nation-wide basis.[176] In the nation's capital, exiles "talk openly about taking citizenship"—principally because of the strategic advantages offered, but also because they have finally accepted that they will continue to live in this country.[177]

Many Iranian migrants also are turning increasingly toward personal pursuits—education, employment, capital accumulation—and away from opposition political activity. The others either approach the exile condition as an opportunity for learning, reflection and analysis, and revamping

336

political organizations, or become involved in a gradual process of repatriation.[178]

The findings reviewed in this chapter regarding the economic-adjustment and social-adaptation experiences of Iranian, Ethiopian, and Eritrean migrants to the United States suggest the presence and viability among refugees from revolution of diverse modes of incorporation in the Western receiving society. At the same time that they demonstrate strong adaptive capacity and a growing interest in property acquisition and capitalist investment, many of the interviewed refugees are not happy with life in the United States, identify primarily with other expatriates from the country of origin, seek to preserve their culture and language, resist acquiring U.S. citizenship, evidence little interest in participating in the host country's political system, maintain ties to the sending country, and are reluctant to rule out returning to their homeland.[179] In recent years, dedicated community members have organized popular non-political study groups that are devoted to renewing cultural traditions, reviving linguistic facility, discussing literary works, and publishing in the vernacular. Many exiles are growing increasingly comfortable with an adaptation strategy that seeks to maximize options through biculturalism.

In the United States, the importance of cultural diversity is receiving renewed attention. Increasingly, ethnic assertiveness is publicly expressed.[180] Refugees from Third World revolutions have made a major contribution to the growing diversity of the host population. The multicultural resettlement strategies collectively practiced by political exiles and other immigrants offer newcomers acceptable, promising, and increasingly appropriate adaptation options at the same time time that they continue to influence the receiving population's social vision.

Notes

1. Gertrud Neuwirth, "Socioeconomic Adjustment of Southeast Asian Refugees in Canada," in *Refugees: A Third World Dilemma*, edited by John R. Rogge (Totowa: Rowman & Littlefield, 1987), p. 325.

2. See Vincent N. Parrillo, *Strangers to these Shores: Race and Ethnic Relations in the United States*, 3rd ed. (New York: Macmillan Publishing Company, 1990), pp. 317, 338–339.

3. Milton M. Gordon, *Assimilation in American Life: The Role of Race, Religion, and National Origins* (New York: Oxford University Press, 1964), pp. 71, 81; Alejandro Portes, "One Field, Many Views: Competing Theories of International

Migration," in *Pacific Bridges: The New Immigration from Asia and the Pacific Islands*, edited by James T. Fawcett and Benjamin V. Cariño (Staten Island: Center for Migration Studies, 1987), p. 63; Paul J. Strand and Woodrow Jones Jr., *Indochinese Refugees in America: Problems of Adaptation and Assimilation* (Durham: Duke University, 1985), p. 130.

4. Gordon, *Assimilation*, p. 85; Parrillo, *Strangers*, p. 54.

5. Gordon, *Assimilation*, pp. 72–73, 89, 90, 105, 125–129; Leon F. Bouvier and Anthony J. Agresta, "The Future Asian Population of the United States," in *Pacific Bridges: The New Immigration from Asia and the Pacific Islands*, ed. by James T. Fawcett and Benjamin V. Cariño (Staten Island: Center for Migration Studies, 1987), p. 299; Parrillo, *Strangers*, pp. 55, 57; Strand and Jones, *Indochinese*, p. 128.

The cultural-assimilation model "implicitly devalues the immigrant's cultural heritage and traditions by basically measuring the degree to which they have adopted the dominant cultural practices and thus abandoned their customary ones." Neuwirth, "Adjustment," p. 326. For the assimilationist, a refugee's failure to adapt results in "dual marginality"—estrangement from the receiving and the sending society. See Abdolmaboud Ansari, *Iranian Immigrants in the United States: A Case Study of Dual Marginality* (Millwood: Associated Faculty Press, 1988), pp. x, 4, 14, 34, 46.

6. Gordon, *Assimilation*, pp. 85, 110–114, 125, 127, 158; Bouvier and Agresta, "Population," p. 299; Eleanor M. Rogg, *The Assimilation of Cuban Exiles: The Role of Community and Class* (New York: Aberdeen Press, 1974), p. 3; Kenneth L. Wilson and Alejandro Portes, "Immigrant Enclaves: An Analysis of the Labor Market Experiences of Cubans in Miami," *American Journal of Sociology* 86, No. 2 (September 1980):296.

7. Gordon, *Assimilation*, pp. 130–131; Parrillo, *Strangers*, p. 57.

8. Portes, "International Migration," p. 64; also see Alejandro Portes, Robert N. Parker, and José A. Bobas, "Assimilation or Consciousness: Perceptions of U.S. Society Among Recent Latin American Immigrants to the United States," *Social Forces* 59, No. 1 (September 1980):220.

9. Art Hansen, "Self-Settled Rural Refugees in Africa: The Case of Angolans in Zambian Villages," in *Involuntary Migration and Resettlement: The Problems and Responses of Dislocated People*, edited by Art Hansen and Anthony Oliver-Smith (Boulder: Westview Press, 1982), pp. 32–33.

10. Gordon, *Assimilation*, p. 158.

11. Elsa M. Chaney, "Migrant Workers and National Boundaries: The Basis for Rights and Protections," in *Boundaries: National Autonomy and Its Limits*, edited by Peter G. Brown and Henry Shue (Totowa: Rowman and Littlefield, 1981), p. 57.

12. Alejandro Portes, "Modes of Structural Incorporation and Present Theories of Labor Immigration," in *Global Trends in Migration: Theory and Research on*

International Population Movements, ed. by Mary M. Kritz, Charles B. Keely, and Silvano M. Tomasi (New York: Center for Migration Studies, 1981), pp. 290–292; Wilson and Portes, "Miami," 301–302, 314–315; David W. Haines, "Toward Integration into American Society," in *Refugees in the United States: A Reference Handbook*, ed. by David W. Haines (Westport: Greenwood Press, 1985), pp. 47–48. According to Portes ("International Migration," pp. 62–65), ethnic enclaves "show how immigrants may respond to the threat of exploitation in the open capitalist market with a capitalism of their own." Also see Strand and Jones, *Indochinese Refugees*, p. 131; Susan S. Forbes, *Adaptation and Integration of Recent Refugees to the United States* (Washington, D.C.: Refugee Policy Group, 1985), p. 21.

About five percent of the exclusively Korean firms located in the Los Angeles area have prospered by trading imports from the home country. Illsoo Kim, "Korea and East Asia: Premigration Factors and U.S. Immigration Policy," in *Pacific Bridges: The New Immigration from Asia and the Pacific Islands*, edited by James T. Fawcett and Benjamin V. Cariño (Staten Island: Center for Migration Studies, 1987), p. 339. On Korean-owned shops and businesses in New York City, see Al Santoli, *New Americans: Immigrants and Refugees in the U.S. Today* (New York: Viking, 1988), pp. 164, 177. Ethnic enclaves also provide "a protective environment for undocumented workers who originate from the same place as legal, established migrants." Marta Tienda, "Socioeconomic and Labor Force Characteristics of U.S. Immigrants: Issues and Approaches," in *U.S. Immigration and Refugee Policy: Global and Domestic Issues*, edited by Mary M. Kritz (Lexington: D.C. Heath and Company, 1983), p. 223.

13. Bouvier and Agresta, "Asian Population," p. 299. They achieve these ends, in part, through reliance on "rituals that emphasize continuity with the past." Elizabeth Colson, "Introduction: Migrants and Their Hosts," in *People in Upheaval*, edited by Scott M. Morgan and Elizabeth Colson (New York: Center for Migration Studies, 1987), p. 3.

14. Haines, "Integration," p. 47; Forbes, *Adaptation*, p. 20; Gordon, *Assimilation*, p. 242.

15. Also see Asmarom Legesse, "Eritrea and Ethiopia: The Prospects for a New Political Framework" (paper presented at the U.S. Institute of Peace seminar, Washington, D.C., August 1989), p. 4; *New York Times*, 11 September 1990, p. A21.

16. See Forbes, *Adaptation*, p. 3; Donald J. Cichon, Elzbieta M. Gozdiak, and Jane G. Grover, *The Economic and Social Adjustment of Non-Southeast Asian Refugees*, Volume I (Falls Church: Research Management Corporation, 1986), p. 1.

17. See, for instance, Rubén D. Rumbaut and Rubén G. Rumbaut, "The Family in Exile: Cuban Expatriates in the United States," *American Journal of Psychiatry* 133, No. 4 (April 1976):398; Alejandro Portes, Juan M. Clark, and Robert L. Bach,

"The New Wave: A Statistical Profile of Recent Cuban Exiles to the United States," *Cuban Studies* 7, No. 1 (1977):18, 24; Rogg, *Cuban Exiles*, pp. 29, 132–133, 136.

18. Richard R. Fagen, Richard A. Brody, and Thomas J. O'Leary, *Cubans in Exile: Disaffection and the Revolution* (Stanford: Stanford University, 1968), p. 102.

19. Silvia Pedraza-Bailey, *Political and Economic Migrants in America: Cubans and Mexicans* (Austin: University of Texas, 1985), pp. 11, 13, 17, 40–41, 46–49, 78, 96, 126–127; José Llanes, *Cuban Americans: Masters of Survival* (Cambridge: Abt Books, 1982), p. 99; David W. Haines, "Initial Adjustment," in *Refugees in the United States*, ed. by David W. Haines (Westport: Greenwood Press, 1985), p. 30.

20. Wilson and Portes, "Miami," 307, 309–310, 313; Llanes, *Cuban Americans*, p. 198; Robert L. Bach, "Cubans," in *Refugees in the United States*, ed. by David W. Haines (Westport: Greenwood, 1985), p. 89; Rogg, *Cuban Exiles*, pp. 132–133; Rafael Valdivieso and Cary Davis, *U.S. Hispanics: Challenging Issues for the 1990s* (Washington, D.C.: Population Reference Bureau, 1988), p. 7.

21. Haines, "Adjustment," p. 27.

22. Wilson and Portes, "Miami," 303.

23. Bach, "Cubans," p. 88.

24. Valdivieso and Davis, *U.S. Hispanics*, p. 7.

25. Bach, "Cubans," pp. 88–89.

26. Wilson and Portes, "Miami," 303–304.

27. Santoli, *New Americans*, pp. 368–370; Llanes, *Cuban*, pp. 99, 198.

28. Santoli, *New Americans*, p. 370.

29. Rumbaut and Rumbaut, "Cuban," 396–397; Sylvia Pedraza-Bailey, "Cuba's Exiles: Portrait of a Refugee Migration," *International Migration Review* 19, No. 1 (1985):18.

30. Pedraza-Bailey, "Cuba's Exiles," 17; Rogg, *Cuban Exiles*, p. 138.

31. Valdivieso and Davis, *U.S. Hispanics*, p. 9.

32. Bach, "Cubans," p. 91.

33. James A. Pisarowicz and Vicki Tosher, "Vietnamese Refugee Resettlement: Denver, Colorado, 1975–1977," in *Involuntary Migration and Resettlement: The Problems and Responses of Dislocated People*, ed. by Art Hansen and Anthony Oliver-Smith (Boulder: Westview, 1982), p. 79; Llanes, *Cuban Americans*, p. 198.

34. Santoli, *New Americans*, pp. 370–371. On inter-generational tensions related to cultural adaptation, see Rogg, *Cuban Exiles*, pp. 133–134. U.S.-born Cuban-Americans have engaged in a high incidence of out-group marriage. Bach, "Cubans," p. 90.

35. Haines, "Adjustment," p. 24; Gail P. Kelly, *From Vietnam to America: A Chronicle of the Vietnamese Immigration to the United States* (Boulder: Westview, 1977), p. 54; May Ebihara, "Khmer," in *Refugees in the United States: A Reference Handbook*, ed. by David W. Haines (Westport: Greenwood, 1985), pp. 137–138.

36. Haines, "Adjustment," p. 27. By 1982, Indochinese refugees who had lived here for five years or longer participated in the labor force at an even higher rate than the rest of the U.S. population. Nguyen Manh Hung, "Vietnamese," in *Refugees in the United States*; ed. by David W. Haines (Westport: Greenwood Press, 1985), p. 203; also see Strand and Jones, *Indochinese Refugees*, pp. 115–117.

37. Haines, "Integration," p. 47; Robert L. Bach, "State Intervention in Southeast Asian Refugee Resettlement in the United States," *Journal of Refugee Studies* 1, No. 1 (1988):46–47, 50; Hung, "Vietnamese," pp. 203, 205; Van Esterik, "Lao," in *Refugees in the United States: A Reference Handbook*, ed. by David W. Haines (Westport: Greenwood, 1985), p. 156.

38. Haines, "Integration," p. 48; Santoli, *New Americans*, pp. 104–107; *New York Times*, 26 October 1989, p. A10; Ronald Takaki, *Strangers from a Different Shore: A History of Asian Americans* (Boston: Little, Brown and Company, 1989), p. 459. In addition to business transactions, "the Vietnamese-owned stores in Clarendon. . . house a great many non-economic and tangentially economic activities such as information exchanges, employment advisement, training, and simple social interactions within the Vietnamese community." David Haines, Dorothy Rutherford, and Patrick Thomas, "The Case for Exploratory Fieldwork: Understanding the Adjustment of Vietnamese Refugees in the Washington Area," *Anthropological Quarterly* 54, No. 2 (1981):96–98.

39. See, for example, Portes *et al.*, "Profile," 22–23; Eleanor Rogg, "The Influence of a Strong Refugee Community on the Economic Adjustment of Its Members," *International Migration Review* 5, No. 4 (1971):477–478; Rogg, *Cuban Exiles*, pp. 69, 91, 105–108, 129; Strand and Jones, *Indochinese Refugees*, pp. 83–84; Barry N. Stein, "Occupational Adjustment of Refugees: The Vietnamese in the United States," *International Migration Review* 13, No. 1 (1979):28, 41–42; Haines, "Integration," pp. 40, 42; John K. Whitmore, "Chinese from Southeast Asia," in *Refugees in the United States: A Reference Handbook*, ed. by David W. Haines (Westport: Greenwood Press, 1985), p. 70.

40. Cited in Forbes, *Adaptation*, p. 7; also see Kelly, *Vietnamese*, pp. 175–178; Haines, "Integration," p. 39; Hung, "Vietnamese," p. 203.

41. Haines, "Integration," p. 43; Neuwirth, "Adjustment," p. 325; Ebihara, "Khmer," p. 137; Pedraza-Bailey, *Migrants*, p. 46; Rogg, *Cuban Exiles*, pp. 17–18. Several studies conducted following enactment of the employer-sanction provisions in the 1986 Immigration Reform and Control Act have uncovered widespread, nation-wide job discrimination against individuals with a "foreign appearance or accent." See *New York Times*, 30 March 1990, pp. A1; 22 March 1990, p. A17; 12 January 1990, pp. A1, 10.

42. Stein, "Vietnamese," 41–42; also see Haines, "Integration," p. 38; Bach, "State Intervention," 40–41, 48; Kelly, *Vietnamese Immigration*, pp. 178–179;

Neuwirth, "Adjustment," p. 326. However, Bach ("Cubans," p. 89) contends that most early arrivals from Cuba recovered their temporarily lost occupational status.

43. Haines, "Integration," pp. 39, 43–44.

44. Haines, "Integration," pp. 41–42. Among all Southeast Asian refugees, wage levels are lowest for the Khmer and Lao. Van Esterik, "Lao," pp. 155–156.

45. Haines, "Adjustment," pp. 28–30; Forbes, *Adaptation*, p. 10; Kelly, *Vietnamese Immigration*, p. 56.

46. Strand and Jones, *Indochinese Refugees*, pp. 115, 132, 82; Haines, "Integration," p. 45; Haines *et al.*, "Vietnamese Refugees," 98; Parrillo, *Strangers*, p. 303; Haines, "Adjustment," pp. 25, 29–30; also see Hung, "Vietnamese," p. 206.

47. David S. North, "Impact of Legal, Illegal, and Refugee Migrations on U.S. Social Service Programs," in *U.S. Immigration and Refugee Policy*, ed. by Mary M. Kritz (Lexington: D.C. Heath and Company, 1983), p. 273; Robert L. Bach, "Third Country Resettlement," in *Refugees and International Relations*, ed. by Gil Loescher and Laila Monahan (Oxford: Oxford University Press, 1989), p. 326; Bach, "State Intervention," 40, 43; Santoli, *New Americans*, p. 121; Parrillo, *Strangers*, p. 303; Hung, "Vietnamese," p. 203. Among Vietnamese refugee households, a high proportion of women also joined the work force—"many at jobs better paying than men's and ones that had more potential for advancement." Kelly, *Vietnamese*, pp. 180–183, 175–176.

48. Moreover, "a slower pace, combined with greater use of job training, creates an opportunity for much greater achievement in a truly self-sufficient future." Bach, "State Intervention," 44–55.

49. Hung, "Vietnamese," pp. 203–204.

50. Kelly, *Vietnamese Immigration*, p. 199.

51. *New York Times*, 25 August 1989, pp. A1, 7; also see Hung, "Vietnamese," p. 204; *New York Times*, 25 September 1990, p. A14. On the extortion of arriving Hmong refugees by General Van Pao's resistance organization in California, see *New York Times*, 7 November 1990, p. A9. Southeast Asian refugees also have been subjected to racial hostility from some U.S. citizens. See Parrillo, *Strangers*, p. 535; Takaki, *Asian Americans*, pp. 454–455; Gil Loescher and John A. Scanlan, *Calculated Kindness: Refugees and America's Half-Open Door, 1945 to the Present* (New York: Free Press, 1986), pp. 116–117.

52. Kelly, *Vietnamese*, pp. 203–204; Santoli, *New Americans*, p. 121.

53. Strand and Jones (*Indochinese*, pp. 134–135) found that the "Hmong perceived themselves as facing much greater problems in acculturation" than did the Vietnamese, Cambodians, and Lao in their sample.

54. Hung, "Vietnamese," p. 205; Santoli, *New Americans*, p. 121; Gordon, *Assimilation*, p. 245.

55. Cited in Linda W. Gordon, "Southeast Asian Refugee Migration in the United States," in *Pacific Bridges: The New Immigration from Asia and the Pacific Islands*, edited by James T. Fawcett and Benjamin V. Cariño (Staten Island: Center for Migration Studies, 1987), p. 168.

56. The increases between FY 1985 and FY 1986 are from 860 to 1,847 (Cambodians), from 1,616 to 3,426 (Laotians), and from 18,060 to 30,840 (Vietnamese). U.S., Immigration and Naturalization Service, *Statistical Yearbook of the Immigration and Naturalization Service, 1987* (Washington, D.C.: U.S. Government Printing Office, 1988), p. 90.

57. Hung, "Vietnamese," p. 205.

58. Moreover, relatively positive employment prospects, particularly in the personal- and professional-service sector, prevailed through 1984 in both study areas. See, for instance, Saskia Sassen-Koob, "The New Labor Demand in Global Cities," in *Cities in Transformation: Class, Capital, and the State*, edited by Michael P. Smith (Beverly Hills: Sage Publications, 1984), pp. 140–150; Patricia R. Pessar, "The Socio-Economic Incorporation of Greater Washington, D.C.'s Latino Population: The Case of Immigrant Entrepreneurs" (report prepared for the U.S. Department of Labor, Bureau of International Labor Affairs, Washington, D.C., November 1990), p. 64; *New York Times*, 23 June 1989. In comparison to regions experiencing severe economic decline, therefore, conditions in D.C. and L.A. might have expanded the range of possible attainments for migrants and increased receptivity to newcomers. See Kennell A. Jackson, "The Old Minorities and the New Immigrants: Understanding a New Cultural Idiom in U.S. History," in *U.S. Immigration and Refugee Policy*, ed. by Mary M. Kritz (Lexington: D.C. Heath, 1983), p. 329. The public sector, which usually requires U.S. citizenship, is the principal employer in the D.C. area, however. At the end of the 1980s, moreover, the construction industry and the private-service sector experienced workforce reductions. Larry Yunck, "Capital Concerns," *Refugees* 82 (January/February 1991):27–28.

59. This important relationship is "largely ignored" by students of adaptation. Mary C. Sengstock, "Social Change in the Country of Origin as a Factor in Immigrant Conceptions of Nationality," *Ethnicity* 4, No. 1 (March 1977):54, 56. Although not treated here, the additional consideration of value convergence among the newcomers and their mainstream hosts presents a fruitful, but complex area for future inquiry among Third World exile communities in the North.

60. Part-time and short-term employment also generally precludes refugees from receiving important benefits—including health insurance and pensions. See Forbes, *Adaptation*, p. 7.

61. Also see Mekuria Bulcha, *Flight and Integration: Causes of Mass Exodus from Ethiopia and Problems of Integration in the Sudan* (Uppsala: Scandinavian Institute of African Studies, 1988), pp. 88, 149.

62. On the last, see Stein, "Vietnamese," 27.

63. Susan Forbes (*Adaptation*, p. 20) maintains that "the capacity to socialize with native-born U.S. residents, and the interest in doing so, are important marks of cultural and social assimilation." Also see Neuwirth, "Adjustment," p. 326; Bach, "Resettlement," p. 316.

64. Such organizations include community-based religious institutions (e.g., the Ethiopian Orthodox Church) as well as mutual-assistance associations (MAAs)—multi-functional self-help groups that offer social, cultural, and educational activities, cushion separation from family and country, and/or provide training, employment, financial assistance, and other services to members and to the wider exile community. See Forbes, *Adaptation*, p. 20; Mekuria Bulcha, *Flight*, pp. 174–175. Some self-help associations are affiliated with a particular exile political organization. See, for instance, Mekuria Bulcha, *Flight*, pp. 185–186.

65. Michael J. Piore, *Birds of Passage: Migrant Labor and Industrial Societies* (Cambridge: Cambridge University Press, 1979), pp. 64–65. Also see Strand and Jones, *Indochinese Refugees*, pp. 130–131.

66. Also see Demetrios G. Papademetriou and Nicholas DiMarzio, "An Exploration into the Social and Labor Market Incorporation of Undocumented Aliens: The Case of the New York Metropolitan Area" (report to the Center for Migration Studies and the Tinker Foundation, November 1985), p. 152. In addition, support for an exile political organization indicates the persistence of a homeland orientation to the extent that it reflects commitment to bringing about political changes that will enable one to return to the country of origin.

67. Lucia A. McSpadden, "Ethiopian Refugee Resettlement in the Western United States: Social Context and Psychological Well-Being," *International Migration Review* 21, No. 3 (1987):796, 800, 816; Maigenet Shifferraw and Getachew Metaferia, "Trained Manpower Exodus from Ethiopia to the United States and Adjustment Issues in the United States" (paper presented at the 31st Annual Meeting of the African Studies Association, Chicago, October 1988), p. 20; Cichon *et al., Adjustment*, pp. 42–43; John Sorenson, "Opposition, Exile and Identity: The Eritrean Case," *Journal of Refugee Studies* (forthcoming). On the involvement of skinheads and the White Aryan Resistance in the 1988 Portland beating death of Mulugetta Seraw, see *New York Times*, 24 October 1989, p. A8; also see Bach, "Resettlement," p. 327.

68. See, for instance, Parrillo, *Strangers*, p. 333.

69. Foreign-born residents comprise roughly 13 percent of the population in the Washington, D.C., metropolitan area. *Washington Post*, 13 December 1987, p. A20.

By 1990, the white population no longer constituted a majority in the Los Angeles area. Margaret S. Boone, "The Social Structure of a Low-density Cultural Group: Cubans in Washington, D.C.," *Anthropological Quarterly* 54, No. 2 (1981):107; Paul D. Starr and Alden E. Roberts, "Community Structure and Vietnamese Refugee Adaptation: The Significance of Context," *International Migration Review* 16, No. 3 (1982):607–609; *New York Times*, 16 June 1990, p. 7; *Chronicle of Higher Education*, 12 September 1990, p. A1.

On the other hand, a 1990 GAO study reported that 29 percent of the employers in Los Angeles had formally adopted discriminatory hiring practices—one of the highest rates uncovered. *New York Times*, 30 March 1990, p. C18. Also see Cynthia J. Gimbert and Tesfaye Shiferaw, "Los Angeles Ethiopians," in *The Economic and Social Adjustment of Non-Southeast Asian Refugees*, Volume II (Falls Church: R.M.C., 1986), p. 18.

The relatively small size of the community of migrants from Ethiopia also could be a factor reducing the extent of discrimination among host-society nationals. Akalou Wolde-Michael, "Ethiopians in the United States: Adjustment Issues" (paper presented at the 31st Annual Meeting of the African Studies Association, Chicago, October 1988), p. 15. Jane Grover and Tesfaye Shiferaw report that refugees from Ethiopia "tend not to attribute problems with Americans to racism, but rather to the fact that they are foreigners" and suggest that "this indicates that insofar as racial discrimination is directed at Ethiopians, its demoralizing effects have not yet reached the Ethiopian community in a conscious way." Jane G. Grover and Tesfaye Shiferaw, "Virginia/DC Ethiopians," in *The Economic and Social Adjustment of Non-Southeast Asian Refugees*, Volume II (Falls Church: R.M.C., 1986), p. 31; also see Gimbert and Tesfaye Shiferaw, "Los Angeles Ethiopians," p. 18.

70. McSpadden, "Resettlement," 804-813; Cichon, *Adjustment*, p. 37.

71. Also see McSpadden, "Resettlement," 805; Santoli, *New Americans*, pp. 87, 99; Cichon *et al., Adjustment*, pp. 3, 31–33.

72. Resettled refugees from Ethiopia "are active labor force participants and in most cases are motivated to seek work as soon as possible after arrival." Grover and Tesfaye Shiferaw, "Ethiopians," p. 7.

73. There is a strong association between high-income level and mastery of the English language among the migrants interviewed in this study. On the economic value of speaking only English in the home, see James V. Koch, "The Incomes of Recent Migrants: A Look at Ethnic Differences," *Social Science Quarterly* 68 (June 1987):303–304.

74. See Grover and Tesfaye Shiferaw, "Ethiopians," pp. 1, 9, 19–20. Among many refugees from Ethiopia, the problem of downward occupational mobility is compounded by high expectations for employment in the United States. See McSpadden, "Resettlement," 800, 803, 814.

75. McSpadden, "Resettlement," 811–813. Also see Cichon *et al., Adjustment,* p. 3. Church-congregation volunteers have aided "considerably less than half of the refugees resettled in the United States." On the congregational model of resettlement, see Lucia A. McSpadden, "Ethiopian Refugee Resettlement in the Western United States: Social Context and Psychological Well-Being" (Ph.D. dissertation, University of Utah, 1988), pp. 8–12, 126, 132–133, 139, 178–179. In the Washington, D.C., metropolitan area, only two or three volags utilized the church-congregation method of resettlement. The D.C. Refugee Services Center, operated by the U.S. Catholic Conference with matching funds from the Office of Refugee Resettlement, assisted the largest number of refugees from Ethiopia. See Grover and Tesfaye Shiferaw, "Ethiopians," pp. 21, 23.

76. McSpadden, "Resettlement," pp. 136–137, 181, 191, 267. Among Iranians, Baha'i and Jewish refugees who join established U.S. religious communities have the advantage of access to similar types of assistance. Allen K. Jones, *Iranian Refugees: The Many Faces of Persecution* (Washington, D.C.: U.S. Committee for Refugees, 1984), p. 18.

77. McSpadden, "Resettlement," 814; also see Cichon *et al., Adjustment,* p. 37; Grover and Tesfaye Shiferaw, "Ethiopians," pp. 8, 26.

78. McSpadden, "Resettlement," pp. 230, 136, 138, 154, 225, 235. In the D.C. area, refugees assisted by a caseworker from Ethiopia reported more favorably on the services they received in comparison to those aided by volags without compatriot employees. Grover and Tesfaye Shiferaw, "Ethiopians," p. 25.

79. The sample of respondents from Ethiopia included 21 official refugees still being supported by a resettlement or welfare agency; the others in the dependent category relied upon loans and/or relatives.

Other studies also indicate that refugees from Ethiopia generally become financially independent in short order and record a low welfare-dependency rate. Moreover, community members assist one another in times of emergency need. See Cichon *et al., Adjustment,* p. 33; Grover and Tesfaye Shiferaw, "Ethiopians," pp. 7, 11, 13, 16, 19.

80. Grover and Tesfaye Shiferaw, "Ethiopians," p. 11.

81. In the mid 1980s, applicants needed to earn at least $20,000 per year "to meet the terms of a lease to rent an apartment" in northern Virginia. For details on area living costs, see Jane G. Grover and Mohammad Bashir, "Virginia/DC Afghans," in *The Economic and Social Adjustment of Non-Southeast Asian Refugees,* Vol. II (Falls Church: R.M.C., 1986), pp. 20-21, 32; Grover and Tesfaye Shiferaw, "Ethiopians," p. 18; Cichon *et al., Adjustment,* p. 34; Yunck, "Capital," 27.

82. Cichon *et al., Adjustment,* pp. 4, 34.

83. Only two Ethiopian exiles (no Eritreans) selected "high" on this item. In contrast, 12 Iranians (9 percent) rated their current income level as high compared

to most others living in the United States. The Iranians also are the most likely to evaluate their income level as high/medium relative to most others living in the homeland. However, more than half of the others share this perception (see Table 7.1). This finding undoubtedly reflects Ethiopia's position as one of the world's poorest countries.

84. Portes, "Labor Immigration," p. 291.

85. The D.C./L.A. study did not specifically ask respondents about the nationality of their employer.

86. Tsehaye Teferra, compiler, *1988 Ethiopian Business Directory* (Arlington: Ethiopian Community Development Council, 1988), pp. 4–44.

87. See Cichon *et al., Adjustment*, p. 91; Grover and Tesfaye Shiferaw, "Ethiopians," p. 19; Santoli, *New Americans*, p. 100. In a highly publicized case of downward bureaucratic mobility, the former head of Ethiopia's Relief and Rehabilitation Commission, Dawit Wolde Giorgis, located a job as project analyst in New Jersey's Department of Human Services. *New York Times*, 23 December 1988, pp. B1, 2.

88. See Grover and Tesfaye Shiferaw, "Ethiopians," pp. 9, 31; Gimbert and Tesfaye Shiferaw, "Los Angeles Ethiopians," p. 21.

89. Grover and Tesfaye Shiferaw, "Ethiopians," p. 10.

90. Moreover, the school-age children of the interviewed exiles have experienced no trouble advancing in the U.S. school system.

91. By 1985, however, little interaction and few ties had developed among exiles from Ethiopia and the African-American community in the Washington, D.C., metropolitan area. Grover and Tesfaye Shiferaw, "Ethiopians," p. 30. As one would expect, McSpadden ("Resettlement," 816–817) found a higher degree of personal interaction and friendship with U.S. citizens among refugees from Ethiopia who initially had been sponsored by church congregations in comparison with the agency-assisted interviewees.

In contrast to the U.S. findings, only 19 percent of Mekuria Bulcha's total sample of refugees from Ethiopia living in Sudan (10 percent of the female respondents) reported that they maintained informal personal relations with Sudanese nationals. Mekuria Bulcha, *Flight*, pp. 176–177.

92. Also see Georges Sabagh and Mehdi Bozorgmehr, "Are the Characteristics of Exiles Different from Immigrants? The Case of Iranians in Los Angeles," *Sociology and Social Research* 71, No. 2 (1987):80; McSpadden, "Resettlement," p. 126. Cichon *et al.* (*Adjustment*, pp. 41, 79) agree that competency in English (particularly the spoken language) generally is not a problem among migrants from Ethiopia. The emphasis on spoken English which characterized most language-training programs in the D.C. area did not address the principal needs of refugees from Ethiopia. Grover and Tesfaye Shiferaw, "Ethiopians," p. 27.

93. In terms of intermarriage, a strong indicator of assimilation, 21 percent of the married respondents (9 percent of the total sample) had entered a marital relationship with a U.S. national. Nearly 80 percent had married a person from their homeland; the rest had chosen a partner of another nationality. While 46 percent of the Iranian permanent residents had secured immigrant status via marriage, only 17 percent of the Eritreans and 10 percent of the Ethiopians had become permanent residents by marrying a citizen or a U.S. permanent resident. Also see Ansari, *Iranian Immigrants*, p. 42. In FY 1987, 549 Iranians and 21 migrants from Ethiopia secured naturalization papers via marriage to a U.S. citizen. U.S., INS, *1987 Yearbook*, p. 88.

94. The two principal mutual-assistance associations serving the Ethiopian community in the nation's capital are the Ethiopian Community Development Council (ECDC) in Arlington and the Ethiopian Community Center in the district. By 1988, eight community-focused churches served exiles from Ethiopia living in the D.C. area. See Tsehaye Teferra, *Directory*, pp. 4–5; Grover and Tesfaye Shiferaw, "Ethiopians," pp. 16, 22–23. On Ethiopian and Eritrean mutual-assistance associations in the L.A. area, see Gimbert and Tesfaye Shiferaw, "Los Angeles Ethiopians," pp. 27–28.

95. Also see John Sorenson, "Politics of Social Identity: 'Ethiopians' in Canada," *Journal of Ethnic Studies* (forthcoming).

96. Some exiles from Ethiopia strive to maintain aspects of the homeland culture through religious activities, by distributing periodicals in their own language, by attending weddings and funerals, by teaching children, and through familiar food, music, and sports. See Maigenet Shifferaw and Getachew Metaferia, "Exodus," pp. 25–26; Cichon et al., *Adjustment*, p. 41.

97. Also see Annabelle Sreberny-Mohammadi and Ali Mohammadi, "Post-revolutionary Iranian Exiles: A Study in Impotence," *Third World Quarterly* 9, No. 1 (January 1987):129; Maigenet Shifferaw and Getachew Metaferia, "Exodus," pp. 26–27, 29, 31; Sorenson, "Eritrean Case;" Gordon, *Assimilation*, pp. 107, 159, 244.

98. Akalou Wolde-Michael ("Ethiopians," p. 10) characterizes the bond that ties families as "deeply ingrained in the Ethiopian psyche."

99. Also see Piore, *Migrant Labor*, pp. 66, 118.

100. Also see Ansari, *Iranian Immigrants*, pp. 108–109.

101. See McSpadden, "Resettlement," pp. 17–18, 259. She adds ("Resettlement," 818) that "with a higher level of employment and/or access to higher education, comes a higher level of psychological well-being." Also see Cichon et al., *Adjustment*, pp. 35, 42. The important role played by congregational volunteers in reducing refugee stress by locating valued employment is described in McSpadden, "Resettlement," pp. 154, 166–169, 182, 267.

348

The death of a distant parent, when one cannot even attend the funeral in Ethiopia, is a particularly troubling experience. See, for instance, Santoli, *New Americans*, p. 101. Psychological adjustment is most difficult for refugees who are deprived of the means of existence, not involved in decision making about their own future, and lack political power in their new environment. Mekuria Bulcha, *Flight*, pp. 88–89, 216–218.

102. Akalou Wolde-Michael, "Adjustment," p. 11.

103. Calculated from U.S., Immigration and Naturalization Service, *1984 Statistical Yearbook of the Immigration and Naturalization Service* (Washington, D.C., 1985), pp. 144–145; U.S., INS, *1987 Yearbook*, p. 90.

104. The number of Iranians who opt for naturalization also has increased constantly—from 601 in FY 1975, to 1,868 in FY 1983, to 4,277 in FY 1987. While those adopting U.S. citizenship within the most recent three-year interval constitute 61 percent of the thirteen-year total in the Ethiopian case, they only amount to 47 percent of the total among Iranians. Calculated from U.S., INS, *1984 Yearbook*, pp. 144–145 and *1987 Yearbook*, p. 90.

105. Further insight into patterns of social adaptation among migrants from Ethiopia is obtained by investigating relationships between responses on key indicators of interaction and identification. In the first place, 69 percent of the respondents who interact socially on a daily basis with U.S. nationals also come together every day with people from their homeland. Nearly half (47 percent) of the interviewees who do not engage in daily social interaction with host-society nationals also do not interact every day with their compatriots. In addition, respondents who get together socially with citizens at least once per week are less likely than the others are to identify primarily with migrants from Ethiopia (79 versus 97 percent). The daily socializers also are slightly more likely to have given up the hope of returning permanently to their homeland. Finally, there is no relationship between participation in D.C.-area community organizations and respondent identifications. Virtually identical percentages of those who do and do not take part in community-association activities feel closer to people from the homeland (86 percent and 85 percent, respectively).

106. Also see Abdoulmaboud Ansari, "A Community in Process: The First Generation of the Iranian Professional Middle-class Immigrants in the United States," *International Review of Modern Sociology* 7 (January-June 1977):93; Ansari, *Iranian Immigrants*, pp. 65, 86, 89. Similar findings are reported for Armenians living in the D.C. area. See Ingrid P. O'Grady, "Shared Meaning and Choice as Components of Armenian Immigrant Adaptation," *Anthropological Quarterly* 5, No. 2 (1981):77.

A narrower study, based only upon members of community associations, found 16 percent of the migrants from Ethiopia living in non-clustered situations in the

Houston-Galveston area. Akalou Wolde-Michael, "The Advent, Dilemma, and Prospects of Ethiopians in America" (paper presented at the 15th Annual Conference of the National Association for Ethnic Studies, San Diego, February 1987), pp. 12, 17.

107. Also see Ansari, "Iranian Professional," 95, 97–98; Ansari, *Iranian Immigrants*, pp. 67–69.

108. In the D.C. area, resettled refugees from Ethiopia tend to live in clusters rather than in a single neighborhood. Santoli, *New Americans*, p. 87. Agency-resettled families usually are placed initially in large, refugee-exclusive apartment complexes in low-income areas. See Grover and Tesfaye Shiferaw, "Ethiopians," p. 19; McSpadden, "Resettlement," pp. 126, 131. In Dallas, most Eritrean and Ethiopian refugees "live in apartments in two neighborhoods not far from the center of the city." Donald J. Cichon, "Dallas Ethiopians," in *The Economic and Social Adjustment of Non-Southeast Asian Refugees*, Vol. II (Falls Church: Research Management Corporation, 1986), pp. 7–8. Most refugees from Ethiopia in the L.A. area "live in apartments in mixed neighborhoods which are often heavily Hispanic." The community is dispersed geographically in different sections of Los Angeles. Gimbert and Tesfaye Shiferaw, "Los Angeles Ethiopians," pp. 8–9.

109. John Sorenson ("Eritrean Case") reports that ten distinct Eritrean community voluntary associations are functioning in the Toronto metropolitan area.

110. This finding lends support to Akalou Wolde-Michael's observation ("Ethiopians," pp. 12–13) regarding the absence of "cohesive community spirit or. . . strong self-help community based organizations even when such organizations appear advantageous." He further maintains that "the great handicap in building such associations is the unwillingness of individuals to commit themselves to long term obligations."

111. See Ansari, *Iranian Immigrants*, p. 67.

112. Ansari, "Iranian Professional," 99.

113. It is relevant to note McSpadden's finding ("Resettlement," 815, 818) in this regard that the congregation-volunteer method of refugee resettlement facilitates a higher level of psychological adaptation when compared with the agency-caseworker approach.

114. Also see Farah Gilanshah, "Iranians in the Twin Cities," *Journal of the Institute of Muslim Minority Affairs* (January 1986):120. In research conducted prior to the revolution, Abdoulmaboud Ansari ("Iranian Professional," 95, 99) found that 70 percent of the interviewed Iranian migrants had paid two recent visits to their families in Iran.

Cichon *et al.* (*Adjustment*, pp. 92–93) suggest that unfulfilled aspirations with regard to employment and living standards, along with loneliness and lack of

350

hospitable treatment by host-country nationals, contribute to feelings of disappointment and dissatisfaction among migrants from Ethiopia.

115. Pisarowicz and Tosher, "Vietnamese," p. 79.

116. In comparison with those who departed in the post-revolution interval, Eritreans who left Ethiopia prior to the revolution are especially likely to hold full-time jobs (94 to 44 percent), to be employed as a businessperson, professional, or administrator (73 versus 18 percent), to report family incomes of $20,000 or more per year (64 to 16 percent), to use their highest education and skills in their current job (60 versus 25 percent), and to describe their economic standing as high/medium relative to others in the homeland and in the United States (88 and 56 percent, versus 56 and 10 percent). The results for Ethiopian respondents are similar on all three income indicators. However, Iranians who departed prior to the Shah's overthrow are only slightly more likely than their counterparts who experienced the revolution are to earn at least $20,000 (67 to 61 percent); they are somewhat *less* likely to regard their economic attainments as high/medium relative to others living in Iran and in the host country (79 and 65 percent, versus 85 and 69 percent).

117. The interviewees from low-income homeland backgrounds also are less likely to be engaged as full-time employees, to be supported primarily by family earnings, and to view their current income level as high or medium relative to most others living in the home country.

118. However, only 69 percent of the former professionals/administrators consider their current position to be a permanent one. In contrast, 94 percent of the respondents employed as businesspersons in the home country view their reported U.S. employment as permanent.

119. The same general pattern of results applies among respondents from all three exile communities. Although the percentages frequently are especially impressive for those who *secured permanent residency prior to 1974*, they are not reported here because of the small number of respondents (10) who fall into this category.

120. In this section, we use current (1984) educational level rather than homeland attainments in order to account for the accomplishments of the many non returnees in the sample. Higher education in the refugee's country of origin also plays an important role in facilitating employment in the North. See Forbes, *Adaptation*, pp. 9–11.

121. The interviewed household heads from Ethiopia who possess a university degree are far more likely than the others are to be constrained by their current immigration or visa status in finding and keeping the type of work they have trained for. See Peter Koehn, "Exiles from Ethiopia: Economic and Social Adaptation in the Nation's Capital" (paper presented at the 31st annual meeting of the African Studies Association held in Chicago, October 1988), p. 28.

122. Indeed, over half of the reporting Ethiopians and Eritreans who have not attempted post-secondary education live on family incomes of less than $7,500 per year.

123. This is a most unusual finding. Using national census data for 18 identifiable national groups, James V. Koch ("Incomes," 301) concludes that "the percentage of immigrants who are college educated is a significant predictor of immigrants' income."

124. These differences by nationality also are reflected in the perceived-status findings. Iranians with no exposure to university education comprise the group that is most likely to perceive their current income as high or medium in comparison with others living in the sending country and in the United States (89 and 73 percent, respectively). Eritreans in this educational category are the least likely to take this view of their current income level (41 and 7 percent, respectively).

125. Koch, "Incomes," 305.

126. The relationship between lack of secure immigrant status and economic-adjustment difficulties is discussed in Gordon, "Refugee Migration," p. 168; Robin Cohen, "Citizens, Denizens and Helots: The Politics of International Migration Flows in the Post-War World" (paper prepared for the International Symposium on Cultural Changes in the Capitalist World System, Hitotsubashi University, Tokyo, September 1988), pp. 15–16; and Saskia Sassen-Koob, "Towards a Conceptualization of Immigrant Labor," *Social Problems* 29 (October 1981):72.

127. Also see Papademetriou and DiMarzio, "Undocumented Aliens," p. xvi.

128. Persons with low-income social backgrounds in the homeland also are slightly more apt to participate in community-organization activities, but are slightly less likely to engage in weekly social interaction with other expatriates.

129. They also are the least likely to feel closer to fellow migrants than to U.S. nationals.

130. In contrast with the Iranian and Eritrean respondents, there are no differences on this item among the Ethiopians who report that political persecution constituted and did not constitute an important decisional consideration.

131. Eritrean migrants are exceptional on this score; their responses do not differ according to the role of political persecution in the decision to live in exile.

132. None of the homeland farmers/laborers (or clerical/secretarial employees) could be classified as integrators, whereas over 10 percent of the other two groups fit into this category.

133. Former employees in the financial or commercial sector are the group that is most likely to be self-employed or to work for a small (potentially ethnic-based) firm (56 percent, versus between 30 and 37 percent for the other three groups). They are the least likely to live among other nationals from the sending country, however (29 percent, versus between 44 and 50 percent for the others).

134. The difference in response to the remittance question is especially pronounced among Eritreans and Ethiopians. Moreover, nearly equal percentages of Iranians who left before and after the overthrow of the Shah continued to hope they would return permanently to Iran.

135. There is no difference in the overall response pattern for this item among Ethiopian interviewees.

136. Large household size proved to be related to social interaction among Vietnamese refugees living in the Denver metropolitan area in the late 1970s. See Pisarowicz and Tosher, "Vietnamese," p. 79. However, this variable is not associated with increased social interaction and community-association membership among the interviewed exiles from Ethiopia. Indeed, the sampled heads of large (4–7 person) nuclear and extended-family households are less likely than singles and two-person households are to interact more than once per week with other migrants from the home country and with U.S. nationals; a slightly smaller proportion of these respondents also participate in community organizations relative to singles.

137. Specifically, the youngest group of respondents (i.e., those between 17 and 24 years of age in 1984) are much less likely to be competent in English (54 percent, versus above 85 percent for the others), are more likely to live in ethnic neighborhoods (64 percent to 42 percent for the others) and to interact at least once per week with other expatriates (98 percent, versus 83 percent for those 35 and older and 93 percent for the 25–34 year-old category), and are the least likely to continue to remit and to hope for permanent return to the sending country (7 percent, versus 26 percent for those older in the first instance, and 43 versus 63 percent in the second). At the same time, the oldest group of interviewees are the least likely to have interacted with host-country nationals in U.S. institutions of higher education (76 percent, versus 96 percent of those in the youngest category who attended a post-secondary school), the most likely to participate in community-based organizations (53 percent, versus less than 35 percent for the others), the least likely to interact on a frequent social basis with other migrants from the home country, the least likely to have a parent still living in the country of origin (64 percent, versus 86 percent for their younger counterparts), and the least apt to be dissatisfied living in the United States (58 percent, versus 66 percent for the others). There are no differences by age on the other social-adaptation indicators selected for analysis.

138. This tendency is most striking among Iranians. Little variation exists on this item among Ethiopians who entered at different intervals.

139. No differences exist among the early-, middle-, and late-arriving Ethiopian interviewees in terms of area of residence.

140. This pattern is most pronounced among Iranians; there are no differences by arrival interval among Ethiopian respondents.

141. Iranians account for this finding. No differences exist among Ethiopian exiles by period of entry and Eritreans are somewhat *less* likely to interact socially with U.S. nationals at least once per week as the duration of their stay in this country increases.

142. *Late*-arriving Ethiopians are much more likely than the earliest entrants are to feel closer to U.S. nationals than to other migrants from Ethiopia (26 versus 8 percent).

143. The group of late-arriving migrants from Iran are much more likely than their compatriots are to be self-employed or to work for a small business. In contrast, Ethiopians who have lived for three years or less in this country are not as likely as the other two groups are to hold these kinds of jobs.

144. This pattern is most pronounced for Ethiopian-community respondents.

145. This tendency is most pronounced among the interviewed Eritreans.

146. Long-term residents from Iran are much less likely than others in the migrant community are to interact frequently on a social basis with fellow Iranians. There are no differences by length of residence among the Ethiopian respondents. Moreover, the Ethiopian interviewees are unusual in that the group which reached the United States between 1982 and 1984 is much less likely than the others are to identify primarily with the expatriate community.

147. This finding is most pronounced among Eritrean respondents and weakest for Iranians.

148. More discriminating data analysis shows that long-term Ethiopian and Eritrean residents are much more likely to cling to the hope of return, whereas the strongest sentiment to this effect among the Iranian interviewees is present among those with 4 to 11 years of U.S. residence.

149. As one would expect, the results found in Table 7.7 concerning English language competency prevail among all three nationality groups.

150. The Ethiopian respondents differ from the others in that those with secondary education or less are the most likely to work for a large U.S. or international employer and interviewees possessing an advanced degree are the least apt to be employed by such organizations.

151. Among Iranians, however, the extent of frequent social interaction with U.S. nationals diminishes consistently at declining levels of educational achievement. In contrast, Eritreans holding an advanced university degree are the least likely group within that exile community to interact socially at least once per week with members of the receiving society.

In terms of personal identification, none of the Eritreans who completed a university degree and none of the Iranians with the equivalent of a secondary-school education or less report that they feel closer to U.S. nationals than to other migrants from the homeland. Among the Ethiopian respondents, the least educated group

354

contains the highest proportion of household heads who identify primarily with host-society nationals. These mixed results do not consistently support Kunz' prediction that "the highly educated, in the long run, may remain more impervious to assimilationist pressures than less educated compatriots." Egon F. Kunz, "Exile and Resettlement: Refugee Theory," *International Migration Review* 15, No. 1 (Spring 1981):51.

152. The widest variation in participation rates occurs among Ethiopian interviewees—from 88 percent for those with an advanced degree to 14 percent for migrants with secondary education or less. Among Iranians, respondents with no university education are as likely as those who possess an advanced degree are to take part in community-association activities.

153. It is important to note, however, that all of the Iranians and 96 percent of the Eritreans with no university educational experience feel closer to other migrants from the home country than to U.S. nationals.

154. This pattern is especially pronounced among the Eritrean respondents; all of the interviewees with an advanced degree, but only 15 percent of those who had not been educated beyond the secondary level, had sent money to someone in the homeland during the year prior to the interview date. Sharp declines in remitting also are associated with decreased educational attainments among the Ethiopian household heads. However, there are no differences on this item among Iranians in each of the four categories of formal educational accomplishment.

155. Iranians also prove exceptional on this item in that respondents with no university exposure are not less likely to hope for repatriation and those possessing an advanced degree are the least likely to cling to the hope of returning to live in the country of origin.

156. More discriminating analysis reveals that this statement applies to Iranians and Eritreans, but not to the interviewed Ethiopians.

157. See Forbes, *Adaptation*, p. 21.

158. Exactly half of the official refugees have given up the hope of returning to live in the homeland; the rest of those not accounted for in Table 7.8 are unsure.

159. Rumbaut and Rumbaut, "Cuban," 397. Also see Barbara E. Harrell-Bond, "Repatriation: Under What Conditions is it the Most Desirable Solution for Refugees? An Agenda for Research," *African Studies Review* 32, No. 1 (1989):62–63. Since 1985, The Center for Victims of Torture in Minneapolis has addressed the special problems encountered by refugees who have been psychologically and physically tortured in the homeland. See *Refugees* 82 (January/February 1991):16–17.

160. Haines, "Integration," p. 49. This is confirmed by mental-health professionals and other service providers who work with exiles from Ethiopia. Grover and Tesfaye Shiferaw, "Ethiopians," p. 13. For some Iranians, as one exile

who has worked with refugees explains, "being in the U.S. feels like living in the enemy's zone. After combatting U.S. imperialism, one cannot evade the stress involved in living in the country we struggled against."

161. Neuwirth, "Adjustment," p. 325.

162. Neuwirth, "Adjustment," p. 326; also see Grover and Tesfaye Shiferaw, "Ethiopians," pp. 14–15.

163. Among political migrants from Indochina, the most important factors have been length of time in the United States, education and occupation in the sending country, proficiency in English language, and household composition. Whitmore, "Chinese," p. 72.

164. Future research should aim to advance upon the limited slice-in-time perspective available from these findings by investigating the complex issue of how pre- and post-migration factors "interact over time and space to lead to successful or unsuccessful cultural and psychosocial integration into the new social environment." Pisarowicz and Tosher, "Vietnamese," p. 81.

165. Vernon W. Ruttan, "Integrated Rural Development Programs: A Skeptical Perspective," *International Development Review* 17, No. 4 (1974/75):13. The technological gap between Third World and Western societies forms an important dimension of the adaptation challenge for many migrants. Neuwirth, "Adjustment," p. 325. For instance, this gap has complicated the adjustment process for most Hmong migrants. Parrillo, *Strangers*, p. 304.

166. See Bouvier and Agresta, "Asian Population," p. 299; Pessar, "Incorporation," p. 1.

167. See Ivan Light, "Immigrant Entrepreneurs in America: Koreans in Los Angeles," in *Clamor at the Gates: The New American Immigration*, edited by Nathan Glazer (San Francisco: Institute for Contemporary Studies, 1985), pp. 172–176; Strand and Jones, *Indochinese Refugees*, pp. 131, 138; Portes, "Labor Immigration," p. 291; Portes et al., "Profile," 18; Santoli, *New Americans*, pp. 164–178; Bach, "Resettlement," p. 328; Whitmore, "Chinese," pp. 71–73.

However, the economic-adjustment and social-adaptation responses of Cuban refugees residing in the Washington, D.C., area, where the migrant community is small, more closely resemble those discovered in the D.C./L.A. study of exiles from Iran and Ethiopia than they do the experience of other Cubans living in the Miami area. Two differences are (1) the tendency for Cubans in the D.C. area to split into separate residential groups based upon racial background and (2) the inter-generational preservation of a fundamental Latino/Anglo distinction in the formation of close friendships and marriage relationships. Boone, "Cubans," 103–108; also see Pessar, "Incorporation," pp. 11, 59. Llanes (*Cuban Americans*, p. 202) also reports substantial intermarriage among white Cubans and other Latin American migrants in the New York City area.

168. See Stein, "Vietnamese," 37.

169. Barry R. Chiswick, "The Economic Progress of Immigrants: Some Apparently Universal Patterns," in American Enterprise Institute, *Contemporary Economic Problems 1979* (Washington, D.C.: A.E.I., 1979), pp. 365–366, 398.

170. Chiswick, "Economic Progress," p. 399.   Chiswick's argument is particularly problematic when applied to resettled refugees who are assisted by church-congregation volunteers and to non returnees.

171. Rumbaut and Rumbaut, "Cuban," 397.

172. Rumbaut and Rumbaut, "Cuban," 397; Boone, "Cubans," 106–107; Starr and Roberts, "Community Structure," 599, 605; Weinstock cited in Rogg, *Cuban Exiles*, p. 18.

173. Based upon his extensive research among undocumented migrants in the New York City metropolitan area, Demetrios Papademetriou has reached the same conclusion. Personal communication, 8 October 1986. For detailed study findings, see Papademetriou and DiMarzio, "Undocumented Aliens."

174. See Akalou Wolde-Michael, "Adjustment," p. 10.

175. Interview conducted by the author with Tsehaye Teferra, Director, Ethiopian Community Development Council, 23 October 1989; also see Maigenet Shifferraw and Getachew Metaferia, "Exodus," p. 21; Akalou Wolde-Michael, "Adjustment," p. 9. In the D.C. area, according to Tsehaye, "there has been a frenzy of house buying as Ethiopians try to break into real estate."

176. Although it has increased, the rate of naturalization (and political participation) among migrants from Ethiopia remains far below the national average. Naturalized citizens constituted "over half of *all* foreign-born residents counted in the 1980 census." Leon F. Bouvier and Robert W. Gardner, "Immigration to the U.S.: The Unfinished Story," *Population Bulletin* 41, No. 4 (November 1986):34. [emphasis added] Also see Bach, "Resettlement," p. 322.

177. Tsehaye Teferra, interview, 23 October 1989. On the limited *social* benefits realized in practice through the adoption of U.S. citizenship, see Anthony P. Maingot, "Ideology, Politics, and Citizenship in the American Debate on Immigration Policy: Beyond Consensus," in *U.S. Immigration and Refugee Policy*, ed. by Mary M. Kritz (Lexington: D.C. Heath and Company, 1983), p. 371.

178. Annabelle Sreberny-Mohammadi, "Iranian Opposition in Exile: A Study in Political Communication" (paper presented at the joint meeting of the African Studies Association and the Middle Eastern Studies Association, November 1985).

179. Also see Akalou Wolde-Michael, "Ethiopians," p. 11; Grover and Tesfaye Shiferaw, "Ethiopians," p. 15; Ansari, *Iranian*, pp. 118–119; Getachew Metaferia and Maigenet Shifferraw, "Democracy in Ethiopia: The Quest" (paper presented at the Midwest Political Science Association Annual Meeting, Chicago, 1988), p. 15.

180. See *New York Times*, 11 September 1990, p. A21.

PART FOUR

Repatriation

8

The Decision to Return

Selam America!
heaven at a distance
hell within a grasp
kingdom of hope
land of verbal equality
but, in practice of empty promise
place of exploitation
withering away my culture, my pride, my spirits

—Mulugeta Worku

Returning to live in the homeland constitutes a potential final step in the migration process.[1] The act of repatriation effectively terminates the condition of exile. For nearly everyone involved in assisting refugees, as well as for most migrants, secure voluntary repatriation is unquestionably the "preferred solution" to the tragic condition of external dislocation.[2]

Nevertheless, the return of refugees to their homeland is an uncommon event in international politics. Most cases of mass repatriation have involved peoples dislocated as a result of anti-colonial struggles that eventually succeed in evicting foreign subjugators.[3] Refugees from revolution do return voluntarily to their country of origin, but in trickles rather than droves.[4]

This chapter returns to the individual level of analysis in search of insights into three crucial questions regarding Third World exile communities in the industrialized West:

How likely are refugees from revolution to return to live in their homeland?
Why do some members of these migrant communities go back to their country of origin?
What is required to convince the others to return home?

While external sources can provide vital information and means of support, each exile must undertake an individual act of voluntary repatriation. The D.C./L.A. study explored the specific considerations that are important to Iranian, Ethiopian, and Eritrean exiles when they contemplate repatriation. Chapter 8 analyzes the information provided by respondents, while Chapter 9 assesses prospects for repatriation by relating the study findings to the national and transnational preconditions and protections needed to stimulate return migration.

Orientations Toward Returning to Live in the Homeland

The range of repatriation options available to migrants can be placed on a continuum bounded at one end by the act of returning to live in the sending country and at the other by determination never to go back. Only orientation points within these two extremes are relevant, however, when one is interested in repatriation *prospects*. The key points are (1) made firm decision to return; (2) gave serious consideration to returning within the past year; (3) hope to go back at some future time; (4) doubtful, but have not entirely given up hope of returning; and (5) have lost hope of being able to live in the homeland again. Although far from a perfectly reliable measure, one can suggest hypotheses concerning the likelihood that an exile will return to the country of origin from the position of his/her expressed orientation on this continuum. For instance, we would expect migrants at the lower end of the scale (i.e., 1–2) to be more likely to opt for repatriation relative to those at the upper end (4–5).[5]

In the D.C./L.A. study, only ten respondents (3 percent of the total sample) had decided to return to live in their country of origin. Another 30 community members (10 percent) had seriously considered moving back to the homeland within the past year. This means that nearly 90 percent of the interviewed household heads were not entertaining the idea of returning to Iran or Ethiopia at the time of the survey.

Nevertheless, many of the respondents refused to give up the dream of repatriation completely. Over half of the migrants (59 percent, including the group that seriously considered going home) clung tenaciously to the hope, however remote, that they would one day be able to reside in their home country again. Another 14 percent were not certain that they wanted to return and not sure that they could stay away.[6] Finally, 80 interviewees (27 percent) indicated that they no longer hoped to return to their homeland.[7]

Loss of hope must not be confused with rejection of repatriation among the members of these exile communities. Even when they had lost hope that any viable prospect for return would arise, nearly everyone interviewed still could identify developments that would lead them to rejoin their compatriots in the sending country. By admitting loss of hope, an Iranian exile explained, one actually means "let's say that I am staying here for the rest of my life for the time being." She added that this position is less psychologically threatening and distressing than preoccupation with returning home—especially when one has children who do not know the homeland.

Nationality

Respondents from the Iranian community proved to be far more positively inclined toward repatriation relative to the Ethiopian and Eritrean interviewees.[8] For instance, 16 percent of the Iranians (excluding those who were committed to returning) had seriously considered moving back to Iran within the past year. In comparison, only 6 percent of the Ethiopians and 2 percent of the Eritreans had devoted serious thought to repatriation. Moreover, while nearly three-fourths of the interviewed household heads from Iran continued to hold out hope that they would live at home again,[9] only 48 percent of the Ethiopian respondents and 40 percent of the Eritreans took this position. Nearly half (48 percent) of the interviewed Eritreans no longer hoped to return to their homeland; slightly more than 20 percent of the other two groups felt this way.[10]

A critical factor affecting repatriation decision making among exiles who are parents is the ability of children to (re)adjust to the home society. If the children are not fluent in a home-country tongue, it is much less likely that the family will return. The D.C./L.A. study results again suggest that Iranian migrants are more likely to return to the country of origin than the other two groups are based upon this consideration. Slightly more than two-thirds of the Iranian parents rated their child(ren)'s language ability in Farsi as excellent or good. In comparison, more than sixty percent of the reporting Ethiopians and Eritreans graded their child(ren)'s ability in the first language of their parent(s) as fair, poor, or nonexistent.[11]

Length of Exile Interval

The D.C./L.A. survey data do not support the idea that exiles become less inclined to return to the country of origin over time. In fact, respondents who left Ethiopia prior to the revolutionary overthrow of the old regime are much more apt than their counterparts who exited after the revolution are to possess hope that they will reside in the home country again and to have given serious consideration to the idea of returning (see Table 8.1).[12] Furthermore, the Table 8.2 data indicate that the earliest

TABLE 8.1 Orientations Toward Repatriation, by Period of Departure from Homeland

Orientations	All Respondents		Prior Revol Overthrow		After Revol Overthrow	
	N	%Tot	N	%Tot	N	%Tot
Made firm dec to repatriate	10	3.2%	7	4.2%	3	2.0%
Seriously considered within past year	31	10.3	25	15.6	6	4.3
Hope at some future time?						
Yes	178	59.1	118	73.8	60	42.6
Don't know, not sure	43	14.3	15	9.4	28	19.9
No	80	26.6	27	16.9	53	37.6

Source: D.C./L.A. sample.

arrivals in the United States (prior to 1974) are the most likely to have decided to go back and to have considered taking that action within the past year. They also are the least likely to have given up all hope of living in the homeland at some future time.[13] Late arrivals, particularly resettled refugees, exhibit the opposite tendencies. Roughly one-third of all official

TABLE 8.2 Repatriation Orientations, by Period of Arrival in United States

| | All Respondents | | Arrival Period | | | | | |
| | | | Early 1952-1973 | | Middle 1974-1981 | | Late 1982-1984 | |
Orientations	N	%Tot	N	%Tot	N	%Tot	N	%Tot
Made firm decision to return homeland	10	3.2%	4	5.9%	5	3.0%	1	1.3%
Seriously considered within past year	31	10.3	10	15.9	18	11.3	3	3.8
Hope at some future time?								
Yes	178	59.1	43	68.3	107	66.9	28	35.9
Don't know; not sure	43	14.3	10	15.9	20	12.5	13	16.7
No	80	26.6	10	15.9	33	20.6	37	47.4

Source: D.C./L.A. sample.

refugees, and the same proportion of the group of migrants who entered after 1981 (see Table 8.2), hoped to return to the home country.[14]

Social Background Characteristics and Adaptation Experiences

Educational attainments provide the most striking and surprising association with repatriation hopes. From Table 8.3, we observe that 70 percent of the respondents who had completed a university degree, but only one-third of those with a secondary education or less, have sustained the expectation of rejoining their compatriots in the sending country.[15] All of the interviewees who had decided to return, moreover, had at least attended a post-secondary institution and the majority had completed a university degree.

It is interesting to observe that migrants categorized as "integrators" are far less likely than their "enclavist" and "bicultural" counterparts are to sustain hope for returning to live in the home country (31 percent, versus 69 percent and 59 percent). While integrators tend not have lost hope entirely, they are much more likely than the others are to be unsure about repatriation prospects. However, they also are the most likely of the three groups to have made a firm decision to return to live in the sending country and to have given serious thought to relocating there within the past year.

362

TABLE 8.3   Orientations Toward Repatriation, by Highest Educational Attainment

	All Respondents		Adv U Degree		U Degree		Some Post Sec		Sec or Less	
Orientations	N	%Tot	N	%Tot	N	%Tot	N	%Tot	N	%Tot
Made firm decision to return homeland	10	3.2%	5	4.7%	2	2.7%	3	4.2%	0	0.0%
Seriously considered within past year	31	10.4	13	12.9	10	13.9	6	9.0	2	3.4
Hope at some future time?										
Yes	177	59.4	71	70.3	50	69.4	37	55.2	19	32.8
Don't know, not sure	43	14.4	9	8.9	10	13.9	16	23.9	8	13.8
No	78	26.2	21	20.8	12	16.7	14	20.9	31	53.4

Source: D.C./L.A. sample.

The findings presented in Table 8.4 should be considered in connection with the hypothesis that economic success in the receiving society reduces the motivation to return home. Iranian migrants offer a striking contrast with members of the two other exile communities in this regard. On every indicator of economic adjustment in the United States, the less successful Iranian respondents are more likely than their compatriots are to nurture the hope of returning to Iran and to have considered repatriation seriously within the prior year. In sharp contrast, economically successful Ethiopian and Eritrean exiles are *more* likely than their counterparts are to be positively inclined toward returning to the homeland. The differences are particularly striking on the variables related to income.

Finally, the respondents who express dissatisfaction with life in the United States are *less* likely to retain the hope of repatriation and to have contemplated returning within the past year in comparison with their counterparts who report that they are not dissatisfied. This finding applies consistently across all three exile communities.[16]

The Decision to Return

Six Iranians, two Ethiopians, and two Eritreans interviewed in the D.C./L.A. study had made a firm decision to return to their home country.[17] These ten respondents make up a small comparison group that

TABLE 8.4 Respondent Repatriation Orientations, by Selected Indicators of Economic Adjustment in the United States

Economic Adjustment Indicators	% Seriously Considered Return			% Hope to Return		
	Iranians (N=18-24)	Eths (N=3-6)	Erits (N=1)	Iranians (N=87-108)	Eths (N=3545)	Erits (N=19-24)
Annual Inc. More $20,000						
Yes	13.5%	9.1%	0.0%	74.3%	68.2%	61.5%
No	22.5	7.3	3.8	80.0	48.8	46.2
Inc High/Med Re. Others US						
Yes	14.3	10.0	0.0	72.5	60.0	69.2
No	20.4	4.8	2.3	79.6	43.5	34.1
Inc High/Med Re. Others Homeld						
Yes	14.3	9.4	2.6	74.3	60.9	50.0
No	19.2	0.0	0.0	84.6	13.0	23.8
Prime Source Income						
Self/spouse	15.9	8.3	2.6	74.2	58.3	43.6
Other	23.1	0.0	0.0	76.9	13.3	33.3
Curr Empld Busperson, Professnl, Adminor						
Yes	15.7	7.4	6.7	72.9	70.4	73.3
No	20.8	3.6	0.0	75.0	57.1	45.5
Nature present job						
Perm	14.5	7.5	2.8	77.1	56.6	44.4
Temp	16.2	9.1	0.0	78.4	59.1	100.0
Use highest educ, skills cur job						
Yes	13.6	9.8	0.0	74.2	51.2	46.7
No	16.7	5.7	4.2	81.5	65.7	50.0

Source: D.C./L.A. sample.

offers valuable preliminary indications about repatriation decision making. The question of paramount interest is: *Why do some members of the migrant community decide to return to the homeland?*

Table 8.5 provides some tentative insights that are useful in addressing this question. First, individuals who have decided to go home nearly universally indicate that homeland political features are *not* important in the

364

TABLE 8.5 Important Factors in the Decision to Return, by Nationality

Factor	All Respondents N	%Tot	Iranian % Total	Ethiopian % Total	Eritrean % Total
Able help people homeld	9	90.0%	83.3%	100.0%	100.0%
Presence relatives, frds homeld	7	78.8	100.0	50.0	50.0
Cultural, relig activities homeld	7	78.8	80.0	50.0	100.0
Able use educ, practice profess homeld	6	60.0	66.7	50.0	50.0
Unable pract profess US	4	44.4	60.0	50.0	0.0
Problems adjusting to US life	4	44.4	80.0	0.0	0.0
Experience of discrim US	4	44.4	60.0	50.0	0.0
No discrim in homeld	3	33.3	60.0	0.0	0.0
Soc/econ pols implemted homeld	3	33.3	60.0	0.0	0.0
Econ deprivation US	2	22.2	40.0	0.0	0.0
No econ depriv homeld	2	22.2	40.0	0.0	0.0
Ability post-revol regime to retain power	2	22.2	40.0	0.0	0.0
Unable partic in US polit sys	2	22.2	20.0	50.0	0.0

Source: D.C./L.A. sample.

decision to return to live in one's country of origin.[18] Four sending country socio-cultural items stand out from the others in terms of their consistent presence as influential factors among committed returnees from all three migrant communities. This small group, at least, is motivated to return by the desire to help their compatriots at home, by the attractions of relatives and cultural/religious events and activities,[19] and by the perceived ability to utilize their education and professional skills in the homeland.

At least half of the Iranian and Ethiopian respondents have been influenced by a particular set of experiences in the receiving country. These are the inability to practice their profession in the United States, encounters with discrimination, and problems of adjustment to life in this country. Neither of the Eritrean interviewees report that these host-society experiences affected their repatriation deliberations, however. The remaining items presented receive support from a minority or none of the respondents in the committed-returnee category.[20]

When asked to identify the most important factors affecting the decision to return to live in the homeland, all of the Ethiopians, two-thirds of the Iranians, and half of the Eritreans rank the opportunity to be of service to one's compatriots among their two foremost decisional considerations. No other item receives more than one "vote," with the exception of the presence of relatives and friends in the sending country (3), the ability of the post-revolution leadership to retain power (2), and the opportunity to use one's education and expertise at home (3).

BOX 8.1
Reasons Selected Respondents Decided to Return to the Homeland
Iranians
•I visited Iran. . . [and] found that I could be helpful there. All my family lives there. I belong to that culture. Above all, at present, a regime is in power which is not corrupted and is giving full independence to Iran. I have dignity there and I can live as a human being and be respected. Life has a meaning. I am tired of living here as a foreigner and doing cheap work.
•I belong to Iran, and I feel responsible to my family and my people. My family lives there and I can identify myself with everything and everybody.
•Because my family is back home. I don't think that because the government has changed this means that the social patterns among people have changed to the degree that makes it impossible for a committed and yet idealistic person like me to live in Iran.

Ethiopians and Eritreans
•I have to go to my country and try to contribute as much as possible. I want to go home and work.
•I feel that I can make a more worthwhile contribution in Ethiopia than anywhere else and that my services are more needed there than anywhere else. I do also love my country.
•Because my goal is to serve the people after I take proper education and training in the U.S.
•To rejoin my family, even if I can't get a satisfactory job.

In sum, responses from the comparison group suggest that committed returnees from these three communities are motivated primarily by social and cultural attractions present in the home country. The desire to assist people in one's homeland is a particularly compelling factor among this group. This also is evident from the self-initiated explanations presented in Box 8.1. Political motives generally are not evaluated as important by returning respondents and push factors operating in the industrialized receiving country are not prominent among the two foremost considerations in the decision to go home.

Important Repatriation Considerations

We now return to the analysis of exiles who have not made the decision to return to live in their home country. *Under what circumstances are they likely to go back?* The D.C./L.A. study followed the same approach used with regard to exile decision making in exploring repatriation considerations. After assessing the importance of various factors in terms of personal decision making, respondents identified their overriding or most important, and second most important, considerations. An open-ended explanation supplemented responses to the standardized questions.

Exiles encounter little difficulty distinguishing among factors which are and are not relevant in terms of personal repatriation decision making. All of the most frequently cited considerations involve changes in homeland conditions. For some respondents, implementation of the identified changes would lead them to return. In all cases, they would provoke serious contemplation and discussion of voluntary repatriation. Most of the respondents, incidentally, were pessimistic regarding the likelihood that the developments which they view as important would be forthcoming.

The top part of Table 8.6 presents respondent assessments concerning the importance of 22 possible repatriation considerations. One factor, *political change resulting in a new homeland regime*, stands out from the others in terms of the proportion of household heads who identify it as a consideration that would play an important part in their decision about returning permanently to the country of origin. Over 80 percent of all respondents, and more than half of the interviewees of each nationality, indicate that their deliberations over repatriation would be greatly influenced by political changes that result in a new regime in Ethiopia and Iran which they do not oppose.[21] Although no other item received such broad-based support, two factors proved important for an exceptionally high proportion of the respondents from a single community. Roughly two-thirds of the interviewed Ethiopians rate the opportunity to help one's people in a meaningful way in the homeland as important[22] and the same proportion of the Eritreans report that realization of the goals of their nationality movement would influence the repatriation decision.[23] The results displayed in Table 8.6 also reveal that only one additional factor, freedom of political expression and association, is evaluated as important by more than 40 percent of the respondents. We shall see, however, that the interviewed community members do not consider political freedoms in the homeland to be especially influential in comparison with other factors when repatriation decision making is involved.

There is limited support in these results for the thesis that elimination of specific exile-inducing conditions, including political persecution, would provide refugees with a strong incentive to return home.[24] Iranians are considerably more likely than the other two groups are to place importance on changes in the homeland regime's socio-economic policies, improved economic conditions in the country of origin, economic deprivation in the United States, and the return of relatives; they are less inclined to emphasize freedom of movement and the end of armed conflict. Table 8.6 further indicates that Eritreans are less apt than the other two groups are to emphasize the opportunity to practice one's profession in the homeland[25] and academic/artistic freedom. In comparison with the others, a higher proportion of the Ethiopian migrants view the removal of restrictions on international business operations as an important repatriation factor. Finally, 80 percent or more of the interviewees from each community indicate that 9 items on the list which had not been influential exile-decision factors among most of the interviewed migrants (including all those related to economic conditions) also would not play an important part in the decision about returning to live in the homeland.

Most Important Repatriation Considerations

Although the information set forth in the upper part of Table 8.6 is helpful in enabling us to distinguish important factors from those which are not influential in repatriation decision making, it provides no indication of the relative weight attached to considerations rated as important. Respondent choices when asked to identify the one consideration of overriding or greatest importance confirm that regime change is the most crucial repatriation factor. Nearly two-thirds (64 percent) of the interviewed household heads identify political change resulting in a new regime which they do not oppose as the one development that would most decisively affect their decision about returning to live in the home country.[26] The only other item that a substantial group of respondents (16 percent) rank first in influence is realization of the goals of a nationality movement.[27] The finding that more than half of the Eritreans (54 percent) view this

368

factor as the most decisive in their deliberations confirms that the outcome
of their nationality struggle is uniquely vital to this group of exiles.

TABLE 8.6 Repatriation Considerations, by Nationality

Considerations	All Respondents N	%Tot	Iranian % Total	Ethiopian % Total	Eritrean % Total
Important considerations affecting repatriation decision making					
Polit chg resultng new regime	244	81.1%	90.4%	83.3%	54.2%
Able to help one's people	156	52.5	49.3	67.7	36.2
Freedom political express, assn	121	41.0	41.5	45.7	32.2
Gen condit security improve	101	33.3	36.7	32.3	26.7
End of discrimination in homeld	89	29.7	28.6	31.2	30.0
No political persecution	83	27.7	30.1	28.1	20.7
Freedom of movement (natl/intn)	79	26.5	16.4	36.2	36.2
Goals nationality movmnt realized	78	25.9	7.5	29.2	66.1
Able use educ, pract profession	58	19.3	24.0	18.9	8.5
Presence acad/artistic freedom	56	18.7	22.4	19.1	8.6
Change regime's socio-econ pol	53	17.6	24.0	11.5	11.9
End of armed conflict	49	16.5	9.0	22.6	25.4
Change regim policy natlity iss	42	13.9	6.2	16.8	28.4
Improved econ condit homeld	34	11.3	14.3	9.4	6.9
No econ depriv in homeld	33	11.0	15.1	8.4	5.1
Milit conscript homeld unlikely	30	10.0	12.3	6.4	10.0
Relatives return to homeland	29	9.8	17.2	3.2	1.7
Economic deprivation abroad	29	9.7	14.5	7.4	1.7
No income-earn restrict homeld	24	8.0	9.5	8.5	3.4
Relations with US govt change	23	7.7	5.5	10.6	8.6
Freedom to practice religion	20	6.7	8.9	5.3	3.4
No restrict intn bus activity	15	5.0	2.7	10.5	1.7
Ranks among two foremost considerations in decision to return					
Polit chg resulting new regime	199	71.1	86.0	68.2	39.3
Help people; use educ; pract prof	57	20.4	14.0	33.0	16.1
Goals nationlty movmnt realized	51	18.2	1.5	19.3	57.1
End armd conflict; imprv security	43	15.4	9.6	21.6	19.6
No political persecution	28	10.0	14.7	6.8	3.6

Source: D.C./L.A. sample.

Five factors principally shaped repatriation decision making among 10 percent or more of the exiles interviewed in the D.C./L.A. study. The next sections of this chapter are concerned with exploring variations in response on these items among migrants with different background characteristics.

Nationality

The findings found in the lower part of Table 8.6 reveal that nearly all Iranian exiles include homeland regime change among their two foremost repatriation considerations. The open-ended responses received from the interviewees reinforce this conclusion. From Box 8.2, we observe that while the type of regime required for repatriation varies (socialist, Islamic, and monarchist alternatives all receive mention), the vast majority of statements make reference to a "democratic" political system. Respect for fundamental human rights and for the status of women are other oft-cited themes.

Ethiopian exiles are nearly as likely as the Iranians are to view regime change as a decisive repatriation factor. "If only the present regime is overthrown for the better" are the words used by one Ethiopian interviewee when asked to describe the conditions under which he would return to the sending country. Another exile referred to the need to eliminate "fear of one's own government." According to this respondent, "there can be no guarantees when the protector is the abuser." Box 8.3 highlights other characteristic open-ended explanations of the principal repatriation considerations cited by exiles from Ethiopia. Regime change, with several different twists, is the prevailing response. In addition to the need for a new political system that they do not oppose, Ethiopian respondents are particularly likely to cite opportunities to help people, use their education, and practice their profession in the homeland.

Returning to the two foremost considerations identified by the D.C./L.A. migrants, we observe from the second section of Table 8.6 that Ethiopians are much more likely than the other two groups are to include helping one's people and using one's training as a top repatriation motive. Whereas roughly half of the responding Iranians view this item as important, only 14 percent place it among their two top considerations. While Ethiopian and Eritrean interviewees select security issues about twice as often as Iranians do, the latter are the most likely to report that an end to political persecution in the homeland ranks among the two most powerful factors affecting the decision to return to the country of origin. Iranians who supported or agreed with a leftist political group are especially likely to

BOX 8.2

Explanations by Selected Iranian Respondents of Conditions Under Which They Would Return to Live in the Homeland

•Change of government to one that does not persecute the Baha'i.

•If present regime is replaced by a moderate regime and Kurdish people gain self-determination and achieve their objectives.

•The mullahs are overthrown and monarchy is restored in Iran.

•When Reza Shah II comes into power.

•If there is a national democratic regime which respects political and social freedom, I would return.

•If a progressive, nationalistic, social-democratic regime which would create a united, independent Iran and respect political freedom for everyone comes into power.

•If there is a democratic regime which does not violate human rights.

•If a democratic regime came to power which guarantees democracy, social welfare, and, most importantly, equality for all men and women.

•When there is no more persecution in the society and freedom of speech, assembly, and political activity is not restricted.

•If a democratic regime comes into power. I prefer the Islamic Democratic Republic suggested by the Mujahedin organization.

•If a socialist regime comes to power which guarantees the distribution of income among the people and also respects freedom of speech, assembly, and political participation for everybody.

•If a democratic regime composed of progressive Iranian organizations comes to power. The government must be secular and non-sectarian.

•If I'm not in danger of imprisonment or physical harm; freedom of speech.

•When it is safe and secure to go back. Also, when women are respected as equals to men.

•When I feel that my life is not in danger.

•The present system changes and there is an atmosphere where an educated woman can live as a human being.

•Economic security, absence of oppression as a woman and as a Baha'i, and lack of political repression.

•Whenever I feel I can be useful for my country.

•If I could work in my field.

•If the country becomes independent. I have thought seriously about returning because of the experience of discrimination here and because I cannot practice my profession here.

•If I could find a very good job with a very good salary.

BOX 8.3
**Explanations by Selected Ethiopian Respondents of Conditions
Under Which They Would Return to Live in the Homeland**

•If a government that I do not oppose takes over.
•Under a new regime which I fully support.
•If the political situation in Ethiopia changes to my liking.
•Atmosphere of fear and political restrictions have to be relaxed. Physical and mental repression must be ended.
•When the political, economic, and social situations improve to my satisfaction and there is an end to armed conflict.
•Change of government, the guarantee of personal freedom, and the establishment of a democratic (non-communist) state.
•After the military government is changed and substituted with a democratic government which offers human rights and freedom to the people of Ethiopia.
•If there is a democracy. If people can say what they want to say and feel secure. If people can come and go as they please. If there is security where no one can take you away arbitrarily. If justice prevails. No ethnic oppression.
•If there is a return to civilian rule. If leaders of the country are not socialist. If there is freedom of speech, writing, etc.
•Under a liberal democratic national government—which is a dream.
•When the present regime is done away with and pre-revolutionary regime is re-established.
•Only if it changes to a Haile Selassie-like regime.
•The primary factor is that there has to be a change in government. The new government will have to show the potential to resolve some of the serious political issues which exist.
•Full national freedom for Tigray.
•If political situation is democratically settled, particularly in regard to the nationalities question. If there is a democratic government with civil rights and protections, and no persecution on the basis of ethnic background. Oromo liberation may be an essential condition for this.
•Only if Oromia became independent.
•When I am called upon to fight to destroy Ethiopian colonialism or to rebuild our nation of Oromia.
•If absolute personal security—political and economic—exists, and if I am able and allowed to contribute something to the people.
•If I could work in my field, get a job there and a place to live. If it would be safe for me to go back.

372

include political persecution (22 percent, versus 10 percent of their non-leftist compatriots).

The lower Table 8.6 results also indicate that the Eritrean community is split among those who would seriously consider returning to Ethiopia in the event of regime change in Addis Ababa and those who view repatriation in terms of a liberated Eritrea. Thus, 61 percent of the interviewed Eritreans do not consider regime change in Ethiopia to be a decisive development in terms of repatriation planning, while 43 percent of their compatriots do not rank the realization of nationality goals among their two foremost considerations. This division is reflected in the unstructured answers that Eritrean exiles provided when asked to identify the conditions under which they would return permanently to the homeland (refer to Box 8.4).

BOX 8.4

Explanations by Selected Eritrean Respondents of Conditions Under Which They Would Return to Live in the Homeland

• When Eritrea gains its independence.

• If the Eritrean struggle is resolved and aspirations of the Eritrean people are realized through winning the war or diplomacy.

• If there is unity within the Eritrean liberation movement and the Eritrean people have a free choice to decide the type of government they wish to have.

• If Eritrea achieves independence, or there is a negotiated settlement (like confederation) agreed to by the EPLF and the Ethiopian government.

• Change. . . to a democratic government along with the guarantee of full independence [for Eritrea].

• If the regime in power is overthrown and peaceful conditions arise.

• If there is peace.

• If a democratic government is established which acknowledges human rights and security.

• When a pro-people government is established.

Period of Arrival in the United States

Among the three migration waves identified in Table 8.7, the middle group, who arrived during the height of the Ethiopian and Iranian revolutions, is much more inclined than the others are to place regime change among their two foremost considerations in repatriation decision making.[28] The late arrivals, who reached the United States at a time of continued fierce fighting in Eritrea, are the most likely to view the

TABLE 8.7 Two Foremost Considerations in Exile's Decision to Return, by Period of Arrival in the United States

Ranks Among 2 Top Considerations	All Respondents		Early 1952-1973		Middle 1974-1981		Late 1982-1984	
	N	%Tot	N	%Tot	N	%Tot	N	%Tot
New regime	199	71.1%	28	50.0%	127	84.7%	44	59.5%
Help people, use ed/profess	57	20.4	17	30.4	24	16.0	16	21.6
Realize natlity movemt goals	51	18.2	11	19.6	15	10.0	25	33.8
End conflict; security	43	15.4	9	16.1	21	14.0	13	17.6
No polit persec	28	10.0	5	8.9	17	11.3	6	8.1

Source: D.C./L.A. sample.

attainment of nationality goals as decisive.[29] The pre-revolution arrivals are more apt than respondents from the two other migrant waves are to emphasize helping people, using their education, or practicing their profession in the country of origin.[30] There are no meaningful differences by period of arrival in terms of the two remaining considerations.[31]

Retention of Hope

When we limit attention to community members who have not lost hope of going back to the homeland permanently, fully 70 percent of the respondents indicate that political change resulting in a regime which they do not oppose constitutes the foremost consideration affecting the decision to return. In contrast, 45 percent of the interviewed household heads who have given up the hope of repatriation rank political-system change as the overriding or most important decisional factor.[32]

Furthermore, those exiles who still expect to live in the homeland, or do not rule out the possibility, prove to be *less* likely to view the realization of nationality movement goals as a decisive consideration in comparison with respondents who have lost hope. The only other major difference is the tendency for Ethiopian and Eritrean interviewees who have not lost the hope of return to be more likely than their compatriots are to consider homeland service to be a key factor in repatriation decision making. The converse pattern applies among Iranians.

Unrelated Characteristics

Most other respondent characteristics are not related to attitudes about the foremost repatriation considerations. With regard to regime change, for instance, there are no consistent associations with educational levels or age brackets. Other variables are only weakly related to inclusion of this item among the two foremost repatriation considerations; they include family-income level at the time of departure from the homeland,[33] principal type of work performed in the country of origin,[34] current family income,[35] and type of migrant.[36] Finally, there are virtually no variations in attitudes concerning the role of regime change between males and females,[37] between those holding secure permanent residency and individuals with no prospect of securing such status, between respondents with and without a homeland tie to a foreign organization, and among those who, in part, initially decided/did not decide to become an exile out of fear of political persecution or due to the threat of physical danger.[38]

Conclusions

Most refugees who desire to go home will take the step of returning to the sending country when their perception of the homeland situation is congruent with certain self-imposed preconditions. Among political exiles, the relevant preconditions usually involve changes that must occur in the homeland. The results of the D.C./L.A. study of migrant household heads from the Iranian, Ethiopian, and Eritrean exile communities suggest that there is one particular change that would appeal to a majority of those who are willing to consider repatriation. That development is replacement of the existing regime with a new political system acceptable to the individual exile. Other policy and institutional changes may be necessary, but they are expected to emerge out of fundamental regime transformation.[39] The fact that few exiles from these migrant communities had returned by the end of 1990, even following the death of Ayatollah Khomeini,[40] is consistent with the lack of regime change in Iran and Ethiopia.

Only one other change might be decisive among a substantial proportion of the exiles who are willing to entertain the prospect of living in the homeland again. This precondition involves the opportunity to provide homeland service by helping one's people, using one's educational attainments, and/or practicing one's profession.

While it is conceivable that refugees might be "propelled" to return home by negative forces associated with the place of exile, the D.C./L.A. findings indicate that key push forces are not operative among most of the U.S.-based exiles who participated in the study. For instance, 90 percent of the respondents did not view economic deprivation in the United States as an important consideration affecting repatriation calculations. It is particularly revealing in this regard that 80 percent of the Iranians, 93 percent of the Ethiopians, and 100 percent of the Eritreans who did not possess secure immigrant status reported that denial of the opportunity to remain legally in this country would *not* have an important effect on their decision about returning to live in the homeland. The discovery that economic deprivation is of little consequence when one contemplates going back to the country of one's origin is not surprising since economic motives did not prompt most of these migrants to emigrate or refuse to return to the home country in the first place.[41] In addition, none of the comparison group of respondents who had made a firm decision to go back indicated that political persecution abroad had influenced that choice. The absence of political persecution and the chance to reside in a relatively peaceful and secure environment generally are treasured as two of the few positive outcomes of the transnational-migration experience.[42] On the other hand, former political activists, particularly in the Iranian exile community, often find it difficult to live in the "imperialist camp" and to interact with proponents of U.S. foreign policy.

Although many respondents place considerable weight on the desire to help their compatriots and/or to practice their profession at home, the main difference between the small group who decided to repatriate and the others is that those in the non-repatriating category also hold strong political convictions that override the impulse to return to Iran or Ethiopia. Their convictions and related fears are connected to the reasons that led most community members to elect to become exiles in the first place. Based upon these findings, then, one would predict that exiles who rank helping people in the homeland as a decisive consideration affecting the decision to return will be the most likely group to return home once the political barriers which lead them to rule out repatriation are removed or drastically reduced.

Finally, the findings presented in this chapter indicate that exiles often remain ambivalent about their current status. The hope and urge to return home remains strong—especially among the earliest arrivals. Many are torn between the desire to be of help to their compatriots and to be near to their family on the one hand and the fear of personal danger and committed opposition to the post-revolution regime on the other. While material comforts and cherished freedoms may be available in Western countries, it is often difficult for refugees from revolution to find satisfaction and sound mental health in the new land.[43] In the context of a desperately poor home country, such as Ethiopia, the contrast between personal life style abroad and the condition of those at home is especially acute. This situation compounds the agony of exile.

Notes

1. Of course, re-emigration may occur. However, this would be conceptualized as the start of a new migration process.

2. Jacques Cuénod, "Refugees: Development or Relief?" in *Refugees and International Relations*, edited by Gil Loescher and Laila Monahan (Oxford: Oxford University Press, 1989), p. 242; Leon Gordenker, *Refugees in International Politics* (New York: Columbia University Press, 1987), p. 126.

3. The most recent example is the return of thousands of Namibians from exile to participate in the United Nations-supervised transition to independence. See Ngila R. L. Mwase, "The Repatriation, Rehabilitation and Resettlement of Namibian Refugees at Independence," *Community Development Journal* 25, No. 2 (April 1990):113–120. In other types of repatriation situations, a number of Ugandans returned to their homeland after the fall of Idi Amin and thousands of refugees crossed back into Ethiopia from Somalia in 1988. See Gordenker, *Refugees*, p. 127; Robert Gersony, "Why Somalis Flee: Conflict in Northern Somalia," *Cultural Survival* 13, No. 4 (1989):45, 55.

4. Little is known about the few who return and it is often not possible to follow up on their homeland reception and subsequent experiences.

5. Strict adherence to procedures that guarantee respondent anonymity and the protection of sources constituted essential and irrevocable conditions for the successful execution of research among the exile communities chosen in the D.C./L.A. project. Unfortunately, these requirements preclude the longitudinal type of analysis needed to test this hypothesis.

6. Abdolmaboud Ansari reports that some Iranian pre-revolution migrants to the United States found it difficult to reach a definitive decision on repatriation because they received contradictory advice from different sources. Specifically, the migrant "has a reference group which consists of his friends who returned home and found themselves disappointed. . . . He has also another reference group which includes those friends who feel they should have returned home and found themselves

disappointed." Abdolmaboud Ansari, *Iranian Immigrants in the United States; A Case Study of Dual Marginality* (Millwood: Associated Faculty Press, 1988), p. 47.

7. Eleanor Rogg's study of Cuban exiles reports results that closely parallel these findings. See Eleanor M. Rogg, *The Assimilation of Cuban Exiles: The Role of Community and Class* (New York: Aberdeen Press, 1974), p. 93.

8. In his study of Iranian professionals who migrated to the United States prior to the revolution, Ansari (*Iranian Immigrants*, p. 96) also found that the "predominant orientation of the majority of the immigrants toward the home society is the expectation of eventual return."

9. Iranians who had been associated with a leftist political organization are more apt to retain the hope of homeland return than their non-leftist compatriots are (84 percent versus 68 percent).

10. This finding lends some support to Egon Kunz's thesis that minority-group members who experience discrimination in the sending country "seldom entertain the hope, and only rarely the wish, to return to live among their former compatriots." Egon F. Kunz, "Exile and Resettlement: Refugee Theory," *International Migration Review* 15, No. 1 (Spring 1981):43. Moreover, the émigrés in the D.C./L.A. sample who rated discrimination in their country of origin as an important factor affecting the decision to leave are more likely to lack any hope of repatriation in comparison with the émigrés who did not perceive homeland discrimination to be influential (45 versus 28 percent). Among non returnees, however, the responses do not differ according to the perceived importance of discrimination.

11. The percentage of respondents reporting "none" ranges from 25 (Eritreans) to 12 and 9 (Iranians and Ethiopians, respectively).

12. Nearly identical proportions of Iranian respondents who departed prior to and following the Shah's overthrow answered "yes" when asked if they hoped to resettle in Iran at some future time.

Some early migrants undoubtedly cling to an outdated and idealized view of life in the home country. On this point, also see Ansari, *Iranian Immigrants*, p. 98.

13. Iranians again constitute an exception on this score. Among this group, respondents who arrived between 1974 and 1981 proved least likely to have lost hope of returning to Iran.

14. According to Tsehaye Teferra (interview conducted by the author in Arlington, 23 October 1989), recently arriving exiles who suffered for a long time under the Mengistu regime, are "even more bitter about the whole experience" than are those who left Ethiopia soon after the revolution.

15. Higher levels of education are consistently associated with more widespread hope for return among Ethiopians and Eritreans, but not among Iranians. See Peter Koehn, "Exiles from Ethiopia: Economic and Social Adaptation in the Nation's Capital" (paper presented at the 31st Annual Meeting of the African Studies

Association, Chicago, October 1988), p. 43. These findings suggest the possibility that Ethiopian and Eritrean migrants might become more favorably disposed toward returning to the homeland once they have succeeded in preparing themselves academically in ways "which will enhance their position there as well as be of use to their country. . . ." Jane G. Grover and Tesfaye Shiferaw, "Virginia/DC Ethiopians," in *The Economic and Social Adjustment of Non-Southeast Asian Refugees*, Vol. II (Falls Church: Research Management Corporation, 1986), p. 2.

16. On the "hope to return" dimension, the breakdown, with percentages for not-dissatisfied interviewees listed first, is as follows: Eritreans (64 versus 31); Iranians (88 versus 64); and Ethiopians (61 versus 41).

17. Ten of the twelve interviewees who maintained that they were not exiles had made this determination.

18. The principal exception is the finding that three Iranians view the socio-economic policies implemented by the post-revolution regime as important in their decision to go back.

19. Also see Alex Inkeles and Raymond A. Bauer, *The Soviet Citizen: Daily Life in a Totalitarian Society* (Cambridge: Harvard University Press, 1959), p. 33.

20. Only one Iranian selected "no political persecution in the homeland," "no association with an opposition political organization," "freedom of political expression, association in Iran," "government policies on nationality issues," and "the general state of the Iranian economy." One Ethiopian mentioned "if not allowed to work legally in the United States." None of the committed returnees identified the following as important considerations: unlikely military conscription in the homeland, the general state of personal security in the sending country, and freedom of movement (national and international).

21. Regime change also proved to be the decisive factor uncovered among most of the refugees from Ethiopia in Sudan questioned by Cultural Survival interviewers. See Jason W. Clay and Bonnie K. Holcomb, *Politics and the Ethiopian Famine 1984–1985* (Cambridge: Cultural Survival, 1985), pp. 150, 162.

22. Also see Maigenet Shifferraw and Getachew Metaferia, "Trained Manpower Exodus from Ethiopia to the United States and Adjustment Issues in the United States" (paper presented at the 31st Annual Meeting of the African Studies Association, Chicago, 1988), p. 32.

23. A considerably smaller percentage of the interviewed Eritreans (28 percent) rate changes in Addis Ababa's policy on nationality issues as an important repatriation consideration in comparison with the results on the "realization of nationality objectives" item.

24. Gordenker, *Refugees*, pp. 127, 130.

25. On the strong professional orientation possessed by some Iranian immigrants, see Ansari, *Iranian Immigrants*, pp. 34–35, 104. This author also notes

(p. 33) that professional considerations are not divorced from the political situation at home since the public sector constitutes the principal source of potential employment.

26. Iranians were especially likely to select this factor (76 percent). Regime change ranked as most important among only 32 percent of the interviewed Eritreans.

27. Iranians show virtually no interest in this item. Among the Ethiopian interviewees, 15 percent rank the realization of nationality goals as their first concern in terms of repatriation. Most of these respondents are Oromo.

A few Iranians felt that the absence of political persecution would be most crucial, while several exiles from Ethiopia selected an end to armed conflict or improved security conditions in the homeland.

28. Iranians who arrived between 1982 and 1984 are as likely as their middle-wave compatriots are to respond in this fashion.

29. There are no major variations by time of arrival among the Ethiopian interviewees on this item.

30. In the case of the interviewed Ethiopians, a higher proportion of the 1982–1984 entrants than either of the other waves rank this item among their two top considerations. In contrast, the late-arriving group is the least likely to report homeland service as a key factor among Eritreans.

31. Among Iranians, late arrivals are the most likely to view the absence of political persecution as decisive, whereas Ethiopians who entered after 1981 are the least likely migrant wave from that country to emphasize this consideration.

32. This difference only occurs among Iranians and Eritreans, however.

33. Iranian and Ethiopian interviewees from low-income families are less likely than those from medium- and high-income backgrounds are to view regime change as a crucial factor; Eritrean respondents present the opposite pattern.

34. Those with backgrounds in financial and commercial work are the most likely to rank regime change among their top two repatriation considerations.

35. Heads of high- and medium-income families are somewhat more likely than their low-income counterparts are to include political change that produces an acceptable regime.

36. Integrators are more likely than enclavists and biculturalists are to assess homeland regime change as decisive. Eritrean enclavists, incidently, are especially prone to place realization of nationality objectives, but not regime change, among their two top repatriation considerations.

37. With the exception of Ethiopian women—who are far more likely than their male compatriots are to place regime change among the two foremost repatriation considerations.

38. Those who left due in part to a perceived threat to their or a member of their family's safety, or due in part to fear of personal political persecution, are no more likely than the others are to include regime change as one of the two foremost factors affecting the decision to return permanently to the home country. The economic deprivation motive also makes no meaningful difference in this regard.

39. See Gordenker, *Refugees*, p. 130.

40. John H. Kelly, "The U.S. Approach to Iran: Outlook for the Future," *Current Policy* 1231 (1989):1; U.S., Department of State, *Country Reports on Human Rights Practices for 1989* (Washington, D.C.: U.S. GPO, 1990), p. 113. Moreover, the ultra-religious factions in Iran "oppose the idea of asking the hundreds of thousands of professionals and intellectuals who left Iran after the revolution to return." Bahram Alavi, "Rafsanjani Faces Crucial Struggle," *Washington Report on Middle East Affairs* 8, No. 2 (June 1989):15.

41. Only 8 percent of all respondents who indicate that they had not been influenced to become an exile by material deprivation in the homeland report that economic hardship abroad might contribute to the decision to return home permanently, whereas 21 percent of those influenced by economic hardship in Iran or Ethiopia rate deprivation in the receiving country as an important repatriation consideration. The difference in response between those who had not and had been affected by economic deprivation in the sending country is more pronounced when analysis is limited to the Ethiopian interviewees (3 versus 36 percent).

42. On this point, also see Freda Hawkins, *Critical Years in Immigration: Canada and Australia Compared* (Kingston and Montreal: McGill-Queen's University Press, 1989), p. 279.

43. Also see Nguyen Manh Hung, "Vietnamese," in *Refugees in the United States: A Reference Handbook*, edited by David W. Haines (Westport: Greenwood Press, 1985), p. 204; Ronald Takaki, *Strangers from a Different Shore: A History of Asian Americans* (Boston: Little, Brown and Company, 1989), p. 455.

9

State and Transnational Barriers to
Refugee Repatriation

*The voluntary character of repatriation is. . . the necessary correlative to the
subjective fear that gave rise to flight.*

—*Guy S. Goodwin-Gill*

Voluntary repatriation, the most highly regarded solution to the problem
of external population displacement by receiving countries and the
international community, potentially involves refugees who find themselves
in first-asylum situations as well as those who have been resettled in the
North. In both instances, the termination of exile depends upon changes in
the forces and conditions that generated flight.[1] This chapter examines the
"inherent, stubborn structural barriers"[2] to homeland return confronted by
refugees living in neighboring as well as distant countries of asylum along
with the pre-conditions needed to induce return migration.

Repatriation Pre-Conditions

The analysis of individual exile considerations presented in Chapter 8
suggests that three types of obstacles preclude widespread return migration:
(1) perpetuation in power of the regime responsible for creating conditions
that prompted the decision to become an exile in the first place; (2)
continuous or intermittent armed conflict and/or lack of resolution of the
underlying bases for nationality or inter-nation struggle; and (3) the absence
of acceptable readaptation opportunities. The first two barriers can operate
independently of each other, but both require the availability of attractive
repatriation conditions in order to provide sufficient motivation for return.

Regime Change

Continuation of the post-revolution regime constitutes the most serious obstacle to refugee repatriation. As Leon Gordenker points out, "governments which oppress certain groups or individuals so heavily that they choose to leave the country will not readily take up initiatives leading to the return of emigrants."[3] From the perspective of the refugee, change in political authorities without fundamental alterations in the nature of the regime usually will not suffice to induce return migration. After the death of Ayatollah Khomeini, for instance, political repression continued and arrests and executions escalated. Few Iranian exiles returned.[4] Thus, the reacceptance of regime opponents is facilitated by, and often is contingent upon, the establishment of a new political system.

We observed in Chapter 8 that nearly all of the Iranian exiles in the D.C./L.A. study, two-thirds of the Ethiopians, and 40 percent of the Eritreans view transformation of the home-country regime as a decisive factor which is likely to alter their outlook on returning. Whether this group of refugees actually would return to Iran and Ethiopia in the event of regime change is by no means assured, however. While most agree on the need to witness the demise of the present regime, there is no consensus on the exact type of replacement that would inspire repatriation.[5] Moreover, economic adjustment and social adaptation in the United States might override the strong desire to return to the country of origin. In the words of one Cuban exile, "through the 1970s, even though Cubans in Miami wanted to go back to our homeland in our hearts, we cared more about the material things that we earned here."[6] Some community members seriously question whether many of their exiled compatriots, who have adopted acquisitive values and an individualistic life style shaped by years of residence in a capitalistic high-technology society, *ought* to return to the home country.

Homeland regime change has a greater chance of resulting in the mass repatriation of refugees who remain in neighboring countries of first asylum—usually the vast majority of the externally displaced population—than it does among those who have secured third-country resettlement. This prospect is partly due to the relative lack of integration into the host society which characterizes camp settlements. It also is related to the capacity of refugees living together in close proximity to the sending country to maintain their cultural identity. Removal of the underlying factors responsible for refugee formation remains the prior condition for mass reverse migration from neighboring countries. Thus, repeated declarations of amnesty by Mengistu Haile Mariam convinced few Ethiopians to return home.[7]

Regime transformation, and the institutionalization of a legitimate replacement political system, are matters primarily determined by the outcome of *internal* struggle and negotiation. External forces that attempt to terminate a post-revolution regime through destabilization measures rarely succeed in achieving their objectives. Moreover, exile organizations in the North usually are too far removed in time and space from local action to exert much impact on regime change. There is a tendency for self-exiled activists "to become frozen in opposition, increasingly out of touch with the mood 'back home' and increasingly integrated into the life of the host country."[8] In addition, opposition groups rarely overcome their fragmentation in exile.[9] Thus, while exit as a political strategy has the potential to contribute to the success of efforts to overthrow the post-revolution regime, it is more probable that overseas support mobilization and migrant remittances will perpetuate an inconclusive struggle. By living abroad and dealing with foreign authorities who are unpopular at home, the leaders of exile organizations risk alienating their support base within the domestic population.

Conflict Resolution

Perpetual political violence in the cities and armed struggle in the countryside constitute the second major obstacle to voluntary return which is embedded in the social structure of certain post-revolution societies. Exiles have no desire to return to a situation where their life and the lives of their immediate family would be in danger. The political activist devoted to the goals of a liberation movement is exceptional in this regard. Some of these individuals are *sur place* refugees in the North who decide to return to the homeland in order to join an opposition fighting force. It is more common, however, to encounter "refugee-warrior communities" on the borders of the sending country where exiles committed to armed struggle possess opportunities to mobilize material resources, tap a conducive and readily available recruitment pool, sustain the movement's ideological fervor, train eager young fighters, and engage the home-country military.[10]

The struggle of guerrilla forces against the post-revolution regime frequently is fueled by nationality or religious objectives. In such situations, mass repatriation awaits resolution of the underlying sources of conflict as well as settlement of the immediate dispute. For the majority of the Eritrean respondents in the D.C. sample, for instance, realization of the goals of the Eritrean liberation movement constituted the overriding or most important consideration affecting repatriation decision making. Among the refugees interviewed in Sudan by Mekuria Bulcha, moreover, "those who identified with the liberation movements, particularly the ELF, EPLF and the OLF, often gave the independence of their territories as a precondition to repatriation."[11]   The limited volume of repatriation from Djibouti and Somalia in the years immediately following the termination of hostilities at the end of the 1978 war between Ethiopia and Somalia suggests that failure to resolve the underlying sources of territorial conflict between nations, when coupled with refugee distrust of ruling political authorities, also constitutes a formidable barrier to voluntary return.[12]

Cessation of armed hostilities and vastly diminished prospects for renewed conflict are the structural prerequisites for repatriation among exiles concerned about inter-group violence and/or motivated by nationality or religious objectives.[13]   It is likely that regime change, or at least a new set of political authorities, will be a necessary first step in order to clear the way for conflict resolution.   Only a popular and legitimate regime will be able to negotiate and enforce a long-term settlement.

The recent historical record offers little room for optimism regarding the resolution of deep and long-standing social conflicts.   Neither intra-national, regional, nor superpower-sponsored efforts have been effective in removing the underlying bases for nationality and religious strife. Nevertheless, one can discern, in general terms, the most promising path to the long-term resolution of such conflicts.   First and foremost, an agreement that will secure the interests of the local populations—particularly their impoverished component—must be fashioned and implemented.   Mass empowerment and a significant realm of local self-determination are essential.[14]   All sides must be convinced that the benefits of peace and disarmament outweigh the possible gains of armed struggle.   For these conditions to be introduced, it is necessary that external military involvement be terminated and the sale of instruments of violence be effectively curtailed.   Certainly, the most effective diplomatic skills of international negotiators—preferably including widely respected exiles—will be at a premium both during and subsequent to conflict-resolution efforts.

Homeland-Readaptation Opportunities

The fact that most contemporary refugees have lived in exile for a decade or longer suggests that substantial individual readjustment to the home country will be necessary in order for repatriation to succeed.   In a reference to economic migrants in the industrialized world that also applies to many political exiles, Michael Piore maintains that "returnees are tied to their home area by nostalgia rather than by realistic experience. They often have problems of cultural assimilation which are as extreme as those of other foreigners. . . ."[15] This situation requires that serious attention be devoted within the sending country to issues of refugee readaptation.

The study of individual repatriation motives presented in Chapter 8 indicates that the provision of professional opportunities to participate in a meaningful way in rebuilding the homeland would be a powerful incentive among certain refugees—including many of those who have settled in the North.[16] About one-third of the Ethiopian exiles in the D.C. sample, for instance, ranked the ability to help their compatriots in Ethiopia, and concomitantly to use their education and practice their profession, as one of the two foremost considerations that would affect the repatriation decision. This also turned out to be a decisive factor for several respondents among the small group who already had decided to return. Three additional homeland-readaptation measures are likely to be instrumental in promoting repatriation: (1) likely responsiveness to the educational and social needs of children who may never have lived in their parents' country of birth;[17] (2) involvement of refugees themselves in the planning of and preparation for reincorporation; and (3) establishment of culturally sensitive and economically viable rehabilitation projects.

In particular, the opportunity to participate in promising local development projects sponsored by dynamic government agencies and/or by non-governmental organizations, or to invest in small-business operations, would be attractive to exiles who reside in the North.[18] For many exiles living in neighboring countries of first asylum, the investment of financial resources in sustainable rural-development projects and in the reconstruction of areas destroyed or disrupted by fighting offers the most appealing rehabilitation strategy.[19]

In light of changes that occur during the lengthy period of exile, repatriation as a durable solution "involves more than a return to a place and a people; it is a process of creating a new home and new conditions which fulfil [sic] promises and expectations of a secure and prosperous future."[20] At minimum, adequate living conditions, appropriate employment and educational opportunities, and attention to basic human needs are essential ingredients in an effective economic-readjustment approach. Impoverished Third World countries—such as Ethiopia, which ranks among the world's poorest—are in no position to undertake the required readjustment projects without substantial foreign assistance. Furthermore, "people who have stayed on through the fall of one regime and the emergence of another may be antagonistic towards the expenditure of scarce resources on those who fled."[21] Provided that it is responsive to indigenous needs, external support for rehabilitation ventures can help overcome such attitudes.[22] In order to promote peaceful reintegration, moreover, subordinate-class members of the sending society who did not exit must possess access to equivalent development opportunities. One way to avoid giving preferential treatment to returnees and provoking resistance among those who remained behind is by allocating "development aid to a returnee-affected *area*" on a long-term basis.[23] Donor aid and internal investment must be accompanied by drastic reductions in the level of domestic military spending. As an incentive, external creditors could match progress in cutting military expenditures with significant debt-relief measures.

There are potential drawbacks to national reabsorption of Third World refugees who have resided for a lengthy period of time in the North. Exiles are likely to have lost touch with the aspirations of those who remained behind, to have acquired Western values and imported tastes that are expensive for the home country to sustain,[24] and to encounter difficulty adjusting to a life style devoid of multiple technological conveniences. On the positive side of the ledger, many exiles living in the North have collected educational attainments and professional skills that are desperately needed in the sending country.[25] Moreover, the level of commitment to the homeland, as distinct from the post-revolution regime, remains strong. From the D.C./L.A. sample results, we discovered that the exile's hope of returning to the country of origin is likely to increase rather than diminish with prolonged residence in the receiving country.[26] Finally, the resourcefulness of the successful refugee, along with his/her proven ability to survive and often prosper in the extremely different cultural context of the West, augurs well for the prospect of readaptation in the homeland.

Conclusions

For the individual refugee, repatriation is a move with high stakes attached. The obstacles that must be overcome, both domestic and international, are deeply imbedded and often reinforced rather than removed by the prevailing norms that shape the conduct of international relations, regional interaction, and local politics. Consequently, "success in repatriation has been and probably will remain patchy."[27]

Nevertheless, secure voluntary repatriation—even by exiles who have resettled in the United States—remains a viable future option if the preconditions and post-change protections discussed in this chapter and in Chapter 11 are brought into place. The historical record indicates that regime change and resolution of the underlying sources of nationality, religious, and class conflicts present the most formidible obstacles to return migration in post-revolution circumstances. At the end of the 1980s, a few political developments occurred—including the thaw in relations among the superpowers—that are consistent with the goal of reversing refugee flows. A peaceful change of government in Nicaragua attracted some repatriation. The governments of Somalia and Ethiopia resumed diplomatic relations and demilitarized their border.[28] In 1991, the EPLF won control over all of Eritrea and TPLF/EPRDF forces replaced Mengistu Haile Mariam's regime in Addis Ababa.[29]

Notes

1. Guy S. Goodwin-Gill, "Refugees: The Functions and Limits of the Existing Protection System," in *Human Rights and the Protection of Refugees under International Law*, edited by Alan E. Nash (Halifax: Institute for Research on Public Policy, 1988), p. 163; Norman L. Zucker and Naomi F. Zucker, *The Guarded Gate: The Reality of American Refugee Policy* (San Diego: Harcourt Brace Jovanovich, Publishers, 1987), p. 49.

2. Leon Gordenker, *Refugees in International Politics* (New York: Columbia University Press, 1987), p. 128.

3. Gordenker, *Refugees*, p. 128. Also see Gervase Coles, "Approaching the Refugee Problem Today," in *Refugees and International Relations*, edited by Gil Loescher and Laila Monahan (Oxford: Oxford University Press, 1989), p. 404.

4. See Roger P. Winter, "The Year in Review," in *World Refugee Survey—1988 In Review* (Washington, D.C.: U.S. Committee for Refugees, 1989), p. 4.

5. In the short run, moreover, change in the post-revolution regime is likely to provoke additional conflict and a small new vintage of refugee outmigration. Jacques Cuénod, "Refugees: Development or Relief?" in *Refugees and International Relations*, edited by Gil Loescher and Laila Monahan (Oxford: Oxford University Press, 1989), p. 242.

6. Al Santoli, *New Americans: Immigrants and Refugees in the U.S. Today* (New York: Viking, 1988), pp. 379, 382; also see Michael J. Piore, *Birds of Passage: Migrant Labor and Industrial Societies* (Cambridge: Cambridge University Press, 1979), pp. 118–119.

7. Mekuria Bulcha, *Flight and Integration: Causes of Mass Exodus from Ethiopia and Problems of Integration in the Sudan* (Uppsala: Scandinavian Institute of African Studies, 1988), pp. 21, 128.

388

8. Annabelle Sreberny-Mohammadi and Ali Mohammadi, "Post-revolutionary Iranian Exiles: A Study in Impotence," *Third World Quarterly* 9, No. 1 (January 1987):129, 126.

9. Annabelle Sreberny-Mohammadi, "Iranian Opposition in Exile: A Study in Political Communication" (paper presented at the Joint Meeting of the African Studies Association and the Middle Eastern Studies Association, New Orleans, 24 November 1985).

10. External powers are prone to support refugee-warrior activities in an effort to overthrow the post-revolution regime or weaken its patrons. U.S. military assistance for Afghan *mujahedin* guerrillas in Pakistan and for *contra* forces in Costa Rica and Honduras provide two prominent examples of this strategy. See Aristide R. Zolberg, Astri Suhrke, and Sergio Aguayo, *Escape from Violence: Conflict and the Refugee Crisis in the Developing World* (Oxford: Oxford University Press, 1989), pp. 152–154, 169, 218, 275–277.

11. Mekuria Bulcha, *Flight*, p. 128.

12. See Gordenker, *Refugees*, pp. 128–129; Peter J. Schraeder, "Involuntary Migration in Somalia: The Politics of Resettlement," *Journal of Modern African Studies* 24, No. 4 (1986):649, 659–660; Hiram Ruiz, *Beyond the Headlines: Refugees in the Horn of Africa* (Washington, D.C.: U.S. Committee for Refugees, 1988), pp. 28–29. Likewise, the agreement which produced an end to the fighting between Iran and Iraq did not result in substantial return migration to Iran. In both situations, however, the volume of new refugees declined in the wake of the suspension of hostilities.

13. Also see Mekuria Bulcha, *Flight*, p. 129.

14. For one proposal regarding Eritrea, see Asmarom Legesse, "Eritrea and Ethiopia: The Prospects for a New Political Framework" (paper presented at the United States Institute of Peace seminar, 11 August 1989), pp. 9–10.

15. Michael Piore, *Migrant Labor*, p. 119. Also see Barbara E. Harrell-Bond, "Repatriation: Under What Conditions is it the Most Desirable Solution for Refugees? An Agenda for Research," *African Studies Review* 32, No. 1 (1989):42. Robert Bach adds that international agencies also "construct idyllic images of 'home', based on conditions that only existed prior to the crises that spawned the outflow." Robert L. Bach, "Third Country Resettlement," in *Refugees and International Relations*, edited by Gil Loescher and Laila Monahan (Oxford: Oxford University Press, 1989), pp. 313–314.

16. This includes refugees who hope to return to an area under the control of a liberation front. It is important to bear in mind that, from the refugee's perspective, "voluntary repatriation means going 'home', and not going to a regime or to a political entity. . . ." Jeffery Crisp, editor, *Refugees: The Dynamics of Displacement* (London: Zed Books, 1986), p. 62.

17. See Piore, *Migrant Labor*, p. 118.

18. On the former, see Peter H. Koehn, *Public Policy and Administration in Africa: Lessons from Nigeria* (Boulder: Westview Press, 1990), pp. 290–295. On past experience with returning economic migrants, see Piore, *Migrant Labor*, pp. 117, 189.

19. See Cuénod, "Development," p. 243; Crisp, *Refugees*, p. 59. On the rehabilitation approach that UNHCR provided for returning Ethiopian refugees from Djibouti, see Guy Goodwin-Gill, "Voluntary Repatriation: Legal and Policy Issues," in *Refugees and International Relations*, edited by Gil Loescher and Laila Monahan (Oxford: Oxford University Press, 1989), pp. 267–270.

20. Bach, "Resettlement," p. 314. Sidney Waldron points out, with particular reference to refugees from Ethiopia living in Somalia, that children brought up in a dependent "refugee-camp culture" will find reverting to pastoral or agricultural activity especially difficult. Sidney R. Waldron, "Somali Refugee Background Characteristics: Preliminary Results from the Qoriooley Camps" (mimeo, 1983), p. 6. Also see Jeffrey Crisp, "Somalia: Solutions in Sight," *Refugees* (December 1989):7.

21. Dennis Gallagher, Susan F. Martin, and Patricia W. Fagen, "Temporary Safe Haven: The Need for North American-European Responses," in *Refugees and International Relations*, edited by Gil Loescher and Laila Monahan (Oxford: Oxford University Press, 1989), p. 352.

22. UNHCR currently provides rehabilitation aid, but normally places a one-year limit on direct assistance to returnees. Cuénod, "Development," p. 243; Crisp, *Refugees*, p. 59; Harrell-Bond, "Repatriation," 56, 58.

23. Cuénod, "Development," p. 243 [emphasis added]; Crisp, *Refugees*, pp. 59–61.

24. See Piore, *Migrant Labor*, pp. 116–117.

25. For this reason, President Hojatolislam Ali Rafsanjani appealed to Iranian exiles with specialized skills to join in the reconstruction of Iran following the end of the war with Iraq. See *New York Times*, 6 February 1989, p. 5. On the downside, some talented exiles have opted to work at unskilled jobs in industrialized societies for purposes of immediate monetary gain and consumer gratification.

26. Nevertheless, the longer the period one lives in exile, the more difficult the transition to the country of origin—both socially and politically—is likely to become. Sreberny-Mohammadi, "Exile."

27. Gordenker, *Refugees*, p. 131. Also see Barry N. Stein, "ICARA II: Burden Sharing and Durable Solutions," in *Refugees: A Third World Dilemma*, edited by John R. Rogge (Totowa: Rowman & Littlefield, 1987), p. 56.

28. Some refugee-initiated repatriation ensued. Crisp, "Solutions," 8.

29. See *New York Times*, 30 May 1991, p. A10. On the other hand, post-war fighting in Iraq forced hundreds of thousands of Kurds and Shiites to flee to Iran

390

and Turkey. Although multi-party international negotiations involving Cambodia and Afghanistan held out the slight prospect that the regimes in power might be transformed via the electoral process, the conditions for safe return were not yet in place. Jewel S. Lafontant, "Refugees and Conflict Victims: Meeting their Critical Needs," *Current Policy* 1252 (February 1990):4; *New York Times*, 10 September 1990, p. A1.

PART FIVE

Conclusions

10

Policy Implications for the United States

Our ultimate goal is to allow people to remain in their homelands and to live there in dignity and without fear.
—Jewel S. Lafontant, U.S. Coordinator for Refugee Affairs

Compassion Fatigue is a truly terrifying sickness. Those it afflicts do not waste away physically—it is their humanity that is harmed. The fatalities are among those with whom the infected deal, or fail to deal: refugees or the starving.
—William Shawcross

Principal Conclusions

The interactive application of social-structural and individual analysis provides important insights regarding South-North migration from areas of the world that experience revolutionary political change. Personal explanations for decision making at each step of the migration process help us to assess the strength of underlying contextual forces identified through historical investigation. By approaching the issue of refugee formation at the global, national, and individual levels of analysis, we gain a more complete picture of the factors involved in post-revolution political migration.

This section provides a concluding assessment of refugee formation, U.S. admission policy, reception issues, and repatriation considerations. The rest of Chapter 10 explores the major policy implications for the United States suggested by a deeper understanding of these dimensions of the South-North migration process.

Origins of Refugees from Revolution

The overwhelming majority of refugees from revolution flee from, or do not return to, their country of origin and remain in exile due to political considerations. In the absence of the threat of serious personal physical danger and/or bitter and hardened political opposition, most exiles would prefer living and working conditions in their own homeland over those they have experienced in the United States.

The Iranians, Ethiopians, and Eritreans interviewed in the D.C./L.A. study generally became exiles in response to a variety of political motives. Fear of political persecution, physical danger and/or the threat of imprisonment, and opposition to the regime in power are especially likely to be encountered together. Respondents who acted primarily on the basis of nationality-movement concerns often feared persecution by the regime in power as well. While the specific factors associated with uprooting vary, violence and the fear of life-threatening violence are frequently responsible for the decision to sever ties with one's homeland among post-revolution refugees. These exiles also share a common bond in that they are victims of underlying U.S. foreign-policy interventions in the Third World. Finally, the Ethiopian and Eritrean community findings reveal that economic motives are not always mixed with considerations of personal or family safety among refugees who depart in *late* post-revolution vintages.

Foreign Policy

As Michael Teitelbaum points out, the effect of superpower foreign policy on international migration is "far more important than generally perceived. . . ."[1] In fact, U.S. foreign-policy actions rank among the most powerful "root causes" of Third World refugee flows. Although external military and political interventions frequently stimulate displacement and mass migration, foreign-policy makers "rarely evaluate such effects seriously when considering intervention." Specifically, the intervening-country government fails to incorporate the future need to accommodate externally displaced persons as a "serious cost" of policy implementation.[2] The consequences of population dislocation have been experienced most acutely as a result of the consistent refusal by U.S. administrations in the post-World War II period to appreciate the growing importance of revolutionary change and nationalist sentiments in Third World societies wracked by decades of repressive rule.[3]

On rare occasions, such as in the case of Vietnamese migration, the connection between external involvement and refugee creation is direct and highly visible. However, the superpowers usually intervene indirectly.[4] The prevailing low-risk strategy relies on proxy wars and the arming of rival factions. While the nature of superpower involvement is less visible in this type of situation, the consequences are likely to be as serious in terms of refugee formation.[5] In Iran, Ethiopia, Central America, and elsewhere in the Third World, extensive U.S. military aid has provided repressive regimes with the tools of political persecution and with the means of forcibly resisting popular movements and ignoring pressures to resolve underlying local problems. By delaying the withdrawal or overthrow of leaders who lack domestic support and legitimacy, such props only increase the level of violence required to bring about political change and result in sharper cleavages and intensified conflict in post-revolution societies.[6] Individual-level research reveals that events and incidents unleashed during the revolutionary overthrow of a U.S.-supported regime and in its immediate aftermath play an important part in the decision to break with the homeland among many post-revolution exiles.

Furthermore, superpower foreign-policy actions in the post-revolution period tend to exacerbate rather than to diminish emigration pressures. First, the United States typically endeavors to overturn or to isolate, both diplomatically and economically, Marxist regimes.[7] Such actions typically cut off and reduce the influence of leaders and citizen activists in post-revolution societies who are concerned with protecting human rights. At the same time, the superpower-rivalry, or globalist, perspective has resulted in competitive arming by the United States and the Soviet Union of pro-and anti-regime forces.[8] The consequences are prolonged instability, the exacerbation of nationality and other conflicts, diversion of scarce resources into militaristic activity, stricter repression, expansion of the conflict zone, and increased numbers of victims of violence. These outcomes are directly related to an immediate surge in post-revolution refugees and are indirectly responsible for the economic devastation which later sustains outmigration. Following a revolution, moreover, emigration is tacitly encouraged by U.S. foreign-policy makers who score each refugee who elects to "vote with

394

his/her feet" as a propaganda victory at the same time that they decry the burden which results.[9]

Finally, pre- and post-revolution foreign-policy interventions create new domestic immigration and political pressures. Political-economic involvement abroad on the part of the receiving country resulted in massive South-North population movements from Indochina and Cuba. In these instances, the U.S. government proved unable or unwilling to halt inmigration because of "inability to control the flow at its source (Cuban); concern for the effect of refugees on friendly first-asylum countries (Southeast Asian); sensibility to the reaction that stopping the flow would produce among previously settled refugees (Cuban); and humanitarian concerns (both groups)."[10] Growing involvement by post-revolution refugee communities in host-country politics also can complicate receiving-country efforts to address the root causes of exile formation given the tendency of certain migrants to remain particularly hostile toward the regime that brought about their exile.[11] In particular, Cuban-Americans have vocally and effectively opposed changes in U.S. foreign policy that involve movement in the direction of establishing normal relations with the Castro regime.[12] Furthermore, the Carter and Reagan administration's public statements throughout the hostage crisis and the Iran-Contra controversy indirectly exacerbated refugee flows by fanning anti-Iranian feelings among the populace and, thereby, making it more difficult to establish productive diplomatic relations with the sending country's post-revolution regime.[13]

Admission Policy

In terms of admission to the United States, persons fleeing from revolution have enjoyed an edge over other Third World refugees. Since 1980, the U.S. government has resettled more post-revolution exiles than it has refugees from countries not experiencing revolution. The allocation for Vietnam alone has vastly exceeded the admission numbers awarded to official refugees from other countries since passage of the Refugee Act in 1980. Within Africa, refugees from Ethiopia have received most of the small number of available slots. U.S. immigration authorities have granted favored treatment to Nicaraguans, but not to Salvadoreans. Even though this country's refugee policy is based upon the assumption that the United States will serve as a land of resettlement, but not as a country of initial reception and protection,[14] the executive branch has used the parole power to admit on a first-asylum basis nearly one million exiles fleeing the Cuban revolution and its aftermath.

Step Migration. The discussion of step migration presented in Chapter 4 reviewed the different strategies employed by political migrants who gain entry to the United States. Cuban exiles are the only group to be admitted on a first-asylum basis in large numbers. In the case of Cuban refugees, departure vintages most clearly correspond with arrival waves, and there has been limited secondary migration within the receiving country. Indochinese refugees have benefitted the most from the resettlement program in terms of admission numbers and assistance upon arrival. The U.S. government's early emphasis on the dispersed settlement of Indochinese refugees has been reversed by high rates of secondary migration to a limited number of preferred cities. Finally, exiles from Iran and Ethiopia have employed a diverse and innovative set of strategies to overcome admission barriers. Many have passed through the demanding political-asylum process; others have taken advantage of the 1986 amnesty legislation. The migration routes followed by refugees from Iran and Ethiopia who reach the United States usually have involved more steps, greater complications, and longer intervals in comparison with the Cuban situation. As a result, the post-revolution arrival waves from Iran and Ethiopia encompass more than one vintage and are quite heterogeneous in social and political composition.

The third-country acceptance of exiles immediately following a revolution exerts a powerful impact on future South-North migration patterns. Networks are established in the receiving country which encourage and facilitate further refugee resettlement. Over time, family ties also expand the immigration pathways available to compatriots who are not refugees. When the base number of initially admitted refugees is large to begin with—as in the case of Cubans and Vietnamese—subsequent migration pressures escalate. For African petitioners, however, family ties "are limited by the severe cultural amputation of the slave period" and only small numbers have been admitted as refugees. The increasing dedication of allocations under the refugee-resettlement program for family reunification results in *de facto* discrimination against applicants from Africa and other places without a tradition of extensive recent immigration.[15]

Refugee-Asylee Comparisons. The resettled refugees from Ethiopia interviewed in the Washington, D.C., area are most likely to have left the homeland in order to distance themselves from general conditions of war, violence, or repression, and out of concern for nationality issues. One-fourth of the official refugees, but only 3 percent of the asylum applicants, report that armed conflict and the general state of insecurity constituted the most crucial consideration in their decision to become an exile. The resettled refugees also are somewhat more likely than asylum petitioners are to have experienced danger and insecure conditions at home. However, *fear of personal persecution* remains the key to qualifying for admission as a refugee or asylee under the Refugee Act. On this score, the asylum seekers are in no sense less motivated than resettled refugees are by fear of individual political persecution and personal physical danger. It is misleading and irresponsible, therefore, to confuse post-revolution asylum seekers with economic migrants.[16]

We also observed that pre-screened emigrants from Ethiopia who apply for refugee status from overseas are nearly three times more likely to be successful than their compatriots are who seek political asylum within the United States. Nevertheless, the author's comparative study of motivations for becoming an exile found that asylum petitioners are every bit as deserving of refugee status under the 1980 Act as are those resettled from abroad. Asylum applicants, on the whole, also possess an even stronger objective basis for claiming well-founded fear of political persecution in terms of certain personal background attributes—including ties to the United States, pre-revolution position of self or member of one's immediate family, association with an opposition political organization such as the EPRP, and connection with a Western government agency or multinational corporation in Ethiopia.

These in-depth case-study findings suggest that institutionalized biases account in large part for the much lower INS approval rate across-the-board for asylum applications in comparison with the acceptance rate for heads of households who apply for refugee status overseas.[17] Clearly, governmental obsession with stemming the tide of illegal entrants has been displaced upon genuine political-asylum seekers.[18] Asylum-review practices prior to the 1990 reforms violated both the Refugee Act of 1980 and this country's humanitarian objective of responding to the plight of victims of political persecution.

Reception Issues

At the institutional level, refugees from revolution have received a mixed reception in the United States. Nearly all Indochinese have benefitted from the special cash-assistance and public-welfare programs that the U.S. government makes available to official refugees. Nguyen Hung credits public and voluntary agencies with "a remarkable job in resettling a massive influx of Vietnamese refugees into the United States in the aftermath of an unpopular war." This accomplishment "has been aided partly by the traditional American compassion for refugees, partly by

Vietnamese culture, which emphasizes the need to live in 'harmony with the environment,' and partly by the refugees' capability (gained throughout their turbulent history) to accommodate to changing circumstances."[19]

Nevertheless, a large number of exiles from Third World countries experiencing revolution have neither entered the United States as a refugee nor been granted political asylum. This group of unrecognized refugees is ineligible for most special-benefit programs. Their adaptation prospects are further conditioned by immigration status. Exiles with temporary or tenuous status, as well as those who possess no legal documentation as immigrants, typically encounter the most serious barriers to economic adjustment.

There also are generic structural constraints, such as racial discrimination and xenophobia, which restrict the adjustment potential of all members of certain exile communities. Ethiopians, Eritreans, and Indochinese have been especially likely to experience racial discrimination and hostility; many Iranians have encountered extreme xenophobia.[20] Moreover, U.S. resettlement-agency staff often are culturally unprepared to assist the members of new exile communities.[21] There is a pressing need, therefore, to involve members of migrant communities in the staffing of refugee-assistance programs and in resettlement-policy making.[22]

Research at the exile-community level reveals that many of the refugees from revolution who succeed in reaching the United States possess an extraordinary capacity for economic adjustment. On the whole, the Cuban exile community has employed an enclavist strategy to develop a unique economic niche and to compete effectively in the U.S. economy. Many Vietnamese refugees also have prospered in this manner. The enterprising, committed, and survivalist qualities associated with escape from a revolutionary society and successful migration to an industrialized nation undoubtedly contribute to economic adaptation in the receiving country. In less than a decade, exiles from Iran and Ethiopia compiled an impressive record in terms of occupational advancement and economic self-sufficiency. The role of academic accomplishments and employment assistance in the achievements of these recent migrants merits greater recognition.[23]

Social and psychological adjustment have proven more elusive. Among refugees from revolution, one encounters two prevailing patterns of social adjustment: (1) enclavists and (2) biculturalists. Exiles from Ethiopia, in particular, are able to participate in mainstream institutions and to interact with U.S. citizens without shedding primary identification with their compatriots. Such biculturalism constitutes an interesting migrant response to the challenge of adapting to Western society. The ability of a minority community to sustain such behavior beyond the first generation is problematic, however.

It is important to emphasize that economic- and social-adjustment studies reveal that refugees from revolution do encounter problems in the United States. Many occupy vulnerable and/or exploited economic positions and remain personally insecure. The incidence of psychological illness is considerably higher than one finds in the home country. Disaffection with Western culture and one's current life-style abounds. For the exile, the required sacrifices are many and the pain of separation from the country of one's birth runs deep. In sum, "contemporary refugees resettled in North America and Western Europe learn that the streets are not paved in gold, and that life there can be hard, alienating, and troublesome."[24]

An important consolation is the new-found political tranquility and physical security. Robert Bach astutely points out that "if durable solutions are evaluated according to the extent to which they protect human lives, then there is little doubt that resettlement in a third country, usually in the advanced industrial world, is more valuable than any other option."[25] For most post-revolution exiles living in the United States, continued third-country residence is the currently preferred alternative. However, it will never provide an adequate substitute for life in the homeland.

Refugees from Third World revolutions have contributed considerable ethnic, racial, and cultural diversity to the receiving U.S. population. At the same time that exiles are swelling the ranks of permanently resident non citizens and being subjected to unsupported charges that they are responsible for domestic problems, they continue to make lasting and increasingly vital economic and social contributions to their host communities at small cost in terms of overall national, state, and local government budgets.[26] In the United States, moves in the direction of a multi-cultural future generated by arriving refugees are posing critical new challenges and opportunities for the polity.[27]

Repatriation Considerations

Repatriation constitutes a potential final step in the refugee-migration process. Only a small fraction of the world's post-revolution refugees have returned to live in their homeland, however. The majority have resided in another country or countries for more than a decade.

One might assume that each year spent abroad, particularly in the wealthy industrialized world, would reduce the exile's interest in repatriation. Interviews with Iranian, Ethiopian, and Eritrean household heads do not support this assumption. In fact, those who have lived in the United States longer are *more likely* than their recently arrived compatriots are to retain some hope of living permanently in the home country again, to have decided to go back, and to have given serious consideration to returning during the year prior to their interview.

The D.C./L.A. study also revealed the weakness of host-country push forces and the strength of homeland developments as factors affecting repatriation decision making. Many refugees from revolution who have reached the United States strongly desire to be reunited with their family, to be of help to people in their homeland, and to practice their profession at home. However, these goals are outweighed by fear of personal danger and opposition to the post-revolution regime. Political change which produces a new and acceptable regime is the development singled out by most respondents as indispensable for repatriation. Although there are deeply held differences of opinion within the community of exiles from Iran and Ethiopia regarding the required nature of the new regime, most of the D.C./L.A. sample articulated some notion of democratic process, respect for human rights, and individual security. In addition, a large segment of the Eritrean community, and many Oromo, insist upon independence for their homeland as a prerequisite for return.

Policy Recommendations

The debate over refugee policy in the United States occurs within the overarching context of conflicting objectives and a pluralistic policy-making system that frequently issues inconsistent and even contradictory messages.[28] At issue are ethical and humanitarian concerns (including this country's historical tradition of providing a haven for the persecuted), fundamental and contentious national interests, current and future international agreements and relations, and individual human rights.[29] This political discourse, which involves representatives of non-governmental organizations as well as public-policy makers, must be informed by a penetrating and inclusive understanding of the multiple underlying transnational and national forces responsible for refugee migration.

The finding that U.S. involvement in the case countries constituted a common ingredient affecting the post-revolution migration process carries serious public-policy implications.[30] Specifically, the principal conclusions reviewed above suggest the need for comprehensive and mutually reinforcing changes in U.S. foreign, immigration, and refugee policy. The recommendations set forth in the following sections are guided by conviction that national and international policy makers have been and will be affected by revolution and its attendant human consequences. They are fortified by the prospect that "the reassessments and reflections brought about by upheaval in turn produce actions heavily influenced by an overwhelming sense of moral conviction and responsibility for the values of freedom, justice, and respect for all. . . ."[31]

Global Level: Changes in U.S. Foreign Policy

The connection between foreign involvement and international migration has both immediate and long-term implications for U.S. policy making. Governments are inclined to emphasize short-term objectives such as strategic influence, winning wars and negotiating the cessation of hostilities, and resource/profit extraction; they tend to ignore both long-term social impacts and the human consequences of international politics. Repeated experience has demonstrated that it is not an accident that the leading Third World sources of immigration to the United States—including unauthorized labor migrants, regular immigrants, and resettled refugees—are countries that host (or had hosted before a revolution) a high presence of U.S. personnel, capital investment, and military or security assistance. Therefore, those who make and influence immigration policy in this country must be prepared to accept responsibility for the social costs in the form of transnational human dislocations that accompany failed foreign-policy interventions, massive military and security aid, inappropriate foreign-assistance programs, and large-scale corporate investments abroad.[32]

Short-term Responsibilities. On ethical grounds, "to the extent that the United States has contributed to causes for the flow of refugees, whether directly or by proxy, there is a special responsibility to grant safe refuge."[33] This important principle is neither entirely novel nor inherently unacceptable to the body politic in Western countries. A broadly based sense of obligation to help those affected by U.S. military actions already undergirds the unusually high number of admission slots which this country has consistently awarded to refugees from Vietnam.[34] The ethical challenge is to accept responsibility for interventions that are less direct.

It is interesting that, in justifying the priorities that guide admissions under the Refugee Act, government officials explicitly maintain that "the United States owes its first allegiance to those who are in danger of persecution because of their ties to this country."[35] In practice, this position has been given the most narrow interpretation possible. Acting in an ethically responsible manner requires that the principle of giving preference to persons of "special humanitarian concern" to the United States consistently be held to encompass *those who are in danger because of the overseas actions of this country's government agencies or corporations.*[36] Certainly, the extent of U.S. government intervention in assisting repressive pre-revolution regimes and in attempting to destabilize post-revolution ones implies that refugees from revolution merit special consideration under prevailing policy guidelines. This expanded interpretation should guide asylum determinations and other dimensions of U.S. immigration law as well as resettlement decisions and the provision of refugee assistance.[37] Linking admission decisions to the government's foreign-policy actions would rightly focus domestic pressures arising from the costs associated with refugee assistance on the factors that stimulate population dislocation in the first place.

All political migrations have serious economic repercussions. The transnational approach to the study of contemporary world politics reveals that once processes have been set in motion that generate mass population movements, state efforts to stem migration flows will be largely ineffectual.[38] This situation occurs, in part, because "rapid changes in technology and transportation continually challenge those countries which want absolute sovereign control over who can and who cannot enter a state. . . ."[39] The U.S. government's futile attempts to arrest illegal immigration provide a case in point.[40]

Furthermore, the costs associated with enforcement exercises directed at undocumented migrants are prohibitive—in terms of scarce resources, human rights, international relations, and transformation of the target country into a garrison society.[41] For instance, Barry and Carmel Chiswick suggest that tougher penalties offer the only potentially effective way of reducing illegal immigration. They specifically advocate detention of those apprehended for the duration of the harvest season.[42] The Chiswicks' approach fails to address the principal pressures that underlie South-North population movement, including entrenched economic disparities and inequities, and rests on the questionable assumption that lengthy detention will stem the flow across the southern border of the United States.[43] At 1990 rates of apprehension, moreover, the Chiswicks' recommendation would require the investment of substantial public funding in new prison facilities capable of holding about one million citizens of other countries.[44] In a related finding, the General Accounting Office reported in 1990 that the employer-sanction "deterrent" built into the 1986 Immigration Reform and Control Act has resulted in widespread discrimination by employers against people with a "foreign" appearance or accent.[45] The overall conclusion from this analysis is that continuing to treat the symptoms and avoiding the causes of population outmigration in the Third World only ensures that the immigration-policy decisions facing the United States will become increasingly difficult, costly, and problematic.[46]

Initiatives of Long-term Consequence. For all parties affected, refugee flows are "never a good thing."[47] Behind each refugee lies the resort to violence, personal tragedy, social and environmental costs, and political failure.

The most promising and urgently needed responses to involuntary international migration require fundamental modifications in U.S. foreign policy as well as in global economic relations.[48] Foreign-policy options, particularly those involving political and military interventions abroad, must be evaluated and debated both in terms of their potential to provoke mass international population flows, and out of concern for the obligation to receive those who will be displaced.[49] Within the government, this discussion and debate should involve functional as well as geographic bureaus of the Department of State, the Defense Department, the National Security Council, other agencies that deal with international trade, investment, or assistance, relevant congressional committees and subcommittees, the Immigration and Naturalization Service, and representatives of state and local government units that participate in resettling refugees.[50] Requiring agency preparation of "refugee-impact statements" would provide one means of ensuring that this concern is considered by the foreign-policy establishment. Impact statements should be prepared and addressed whenever military intervention or assistance and the application of economic sanctions is contemplated as well as when programs of development assistance, international finance, and relief aid are reviewed. A contemplated policy or action in any of these realms "must be measured against the yardstick that it does not directly contribute to the creation of future refugees. . . ."[51]

The primary objective of U.S. policy should be to avoid external involvement in or support for actions and programs that contribute to political and economic dislocation in the first place.[52] First and foremost, therefore, foreign-policy makers must guard against the types of direct and proxy political and military interventions that help to create refugee situations.[53] From this perspective, prohibiting military and security assistance to repressive regimes and overcoming the obsession with crushing leftist opposition would constitute farsighted foreign-policy actions.

Nevertheless, a non-interventionist foreign policy that emphasizes local
conflict resolution is unlikely by itself to avert future refugee flows.

The U.S. government also must adopt and support innovative policies
and diplomatic strategies that effectively restrain mass expulsions, block the
introduction of weapons by external sources, discourage political persecution
and encourage respect for fundamental human rights, and promote labor-
intensive rural and urban economic undertakings that attack the underlying
factors responsible for gross disparities in the distribution of resources
without disrupting traditional work patterns.[54]   In some cases, the capacity
to exert influence in matters affecting population dislocation and emigration
requires that diplomatic relations be maintained or reestablished with
revolutionary—even communist—Third World regimes.[55]   At other times,
the U.S. government can fill the need for a creative, energetic, and honest
peace broker at the intra-nation or regional level.[56]   In the Horn of Africa,
for instance, the United States could press multilateral lending institutions to
freeze all monetary transfers until sustainable peace agreements are reached
and enforced.[57]   Whenever possible, foreign-policy leaders should pursue
opportunities to cooperate with Soviet diplomats in promoting mutual
restraint, reducing regional tensions, preventing armed intervention by
regional powers, and engaging in crisis prevention and management.[58]   The
success of such superpower diplomatic initiatives in the South also requires
leadership by example at home because the response to a country's
international refugee-policy overtures is shaped, in part, by the nature and
internal application of immigration regulations and the domestic treatment
afforded to new migrants.[59]

There are other underlying sources of refugee formation that the U.S.
government has a particularly promising opportunity to address.   A
productive response requires, first of all, explicit rejection of the globalist
view on foreign policy in favor of a perspective that assigns primacy to
indigenous aspirations and culture, focuses on South-North relations,
recognizes the relative autonomy of local conflicts, and appreciates the
creative possibilities as well as the human consequences of revolutionary
change.[60]   To avoid contributing to future refugee outflows, U.S. foreign-
policy actors also must support local efforts to resolve Third World conflicts
in a non-violent fashion, embrace ideological diversity, and refrain from
opposing political participation by leftist groups.[61]

A genuine reduction in the arms race and in hostility between the
superpowers, restraints on weapons sales to the Third World, and an end to
proxy wars, anti-terrorist counter strikes, and military and security assistance
for repressive regimes are actions consistent with a foreign-policy

perspective that would substantially mitigate the conditions that promote population dislocation and outmigration.[62] These objectives entail a mix of practical realism and international morality, of "power and principle."[63] U.S. foreign-policy makers will find it necessary to treat such drastic changes in current practice more seriously than they have in the past as the domestic and international-relations costs associated with failing to deal with the determinant factors responsible for the new migration continue to mount in an increasingly interdependent world where even a superpower cannot control its own borders.[64]

Developments in Afghanistan, Angola, and Eastern Europe indicate that the Soviet Union is guided primarily by pragmatic political considerations and that the domestic concencus undergirding such calculations has shifted in fundamental ways under Mikhail Gorbachev.[65] In the Horn of Africa, Afghanistan, Indochina, and southern Africa, the new Soviet position presents a window of opportunity for massive reductions in levels of armament, for negotiating durable settlements to devastating regional military conflicts, and for arranging the termination of oppressive and fruitless superpower intervention. Continued efforts to destabilize revolutionary regimes via extensive external intervention and economic pressure, coupled with lack of interest in appropriate and sustainable development strategies, only fuel further hostilities and perpetuate population displacement and South-North migration.[66]

Although the United States "could accommodate many more refugees than it now admits without significantly jeopardizing the public's standard of living,"[67] the country cannot successfully resettle an unlimited number of political migrants. In any event, most people quite naturally and understandably want to continue to participate in the cultural environment they are brought up, or socialized, in. In the words of the U.S. Coordinator for Refugee Affairs, Jewel Lafontant, "people prefer to live in the society and culture that they are accustomed to, and they only uproot themselves when persecution or strife forces them to leave their own country."[68] Moreover, transnational movement, which can be dangerous and entail personal as well as financial costs for the Third World refugee, frequently results in a "nerve-wracking life in a foreign community that is often coldly indifferent, if not openly hostile," and is filled with "difficulties, deprivations, and humiliations."[69] It takes an intolerable set of experiences and expectations to make an individual decide to live in exile. The key to a politically responsive and ethically responsible refugee policy that poses minimal threat to other important values, then, is the promotion of actions that reduce or eliminate the well-founded fears of Third World populations.

Through the anguish of exile, many refugees are sustained by the hope of returning to live in the homeland.[70]   If the voluntary repatriation of refugees living in the North is to become a reality, the findings of the D.C./L.A. study point to the importance of strategies that facilitate regime change and opportunities for exiles to be of service to the people of their home country.   In terms of this objective, institutionalized hostility directed against post-revolution regimes and external intervention are counter-productive.   Such actions typically provoke arms build-up, requests for Soviet props, and generate a measure of domestic support for repressive governments that adopt anti-imperialist measures.   A foreign policy designed to promote refugee repatriation would scrupuously refrain from overt and covert intervention in domestic political affairs, avoid the temptation to arm opposition groups, assert the primacy of respecting fundamental human rights, and work effectively within multi-lateral contexts to overcome structural barriers to the secure reintegration of displaced citizens.

National Level: Initiatives in U.S. Immigration and Refugee Policy

Transnational refugee flows of reduced scale are likely to continue even in the face of determined efforts to avert situations that produce them.[71]   Moreover, as long as the fundamental changes in U.S. foreign policy outlined above are not forthcoming, this country carries a particularly heavy responsibility for assisting the surviving victims of political conflict in the Third World.   Enlightened and humane refugee and immigration policies offer the principal available vehicle for dealing with this responsibility and for addressing vital human needs.   Given that no legitimate basis exists for the drastically different outcomes that first-asylum and overseas-refugee applicants have experienced at the hands of U.S. government gatekeepers, changes must be implemented in immigration policy and practice that will result in more equitable and ethically responsible treatment of genuine political refugees.

Political Asylum. Research among refugees from revolution reveals a pressing need for domestic reforms in U.S. political-asylum policy and practice.   In the first place, precisely the same standards and evidential requirements used in making refugee-admission decisions must be followed in asylum determinations.   As John Scanlan points out, "nothing in the Refugee Act of 1980, or in the 1967 [U.N.] Protocol [ratified by the U.S. in 1968], or in Article 32 or 33 of the 1951 UN Convention Relating to the Status of Refugees" justifies imposing what amounts a "heavier burden of proof on asylum applicants than on those allocated refugee slots."[72]   Since the grounds on which petitioners are to be granted or denied asylum are identical to those applicable among persons requesting admission as a refugee,[73] the same standards and procedures should be followed in both cases. This means that the sending government's foreign-policy positions, the interests of Western financial institutions, and U.S. strategic objectives and calculations must be given no place in individual asylum determinations.[74] When the executive branch fails to adhere to this country's international commitments and to demonstrate moral leadership by strictly abiding by non-discriminatory regulations, then the judicial branch must ensure that the appropriate standards are applied.

In terms of procedure, the principles set forth in the UNHCR's *Handbook on Procedures and Criteria for Determining Refugee Status* must govern the treatment of asylum claims. Thus, examiners must recognize "the difficulty of producing documentary or tangible evidence." In light of the circumstances that political exiles find themselves in when they are applying for asylum, evidential requirements should not be "too strictly applied."[75] Certainly, examiners should neither insist upon nor expect the presentation of eyewitnesses, wanted lists, and sworn statements from relatives and friends still living in the homeland. Furthermore, they should give the applicant "the benefit of the doubt" when his/her statements are not susceptible of proof—as long as the account appears credible and there are no good reasons to the contrary. The hearing officer must carefully test and assess the claimant's credibility without imposing "an impossible burden of persuasion" by requiring that the applicant "rebut the frequently held (and frequently stated) assumption that all his [sic] assertions, because self-serving, are inherently incredible."[76]

Members and supporters who have not held leadership positions in trade unions, peasant associations, student movements, opposition political and nationality organizations, and other persecuted groups—especially those residing abroad at a time of radical change in the homeland regime—are particularly disadvantaged under current procedures. They typically find that their only recourse in asylum proceedings is to demonstrate that people like themselves have been imprisoned, tortured, killed, and otherwise harassed by agents of the government and/or that the regime in power has mistreated others who return or are sent home after applying for political asylum abroad, associating with an opposition exile organization, or accusing homeland authorities of violating human rights.[77] Allowing non-elite applicants to establish well-founded fear of persecution by reference to the experiences of relatives, friends, and others with backgrounds similar to their own, coupled with placing great weight on the presence of the subjective state of fear itself, are changes that would bring U.S. government practice in political-asylum cases in line with the UNHCR's *Handbook* as well as its own treatment of official-refugee applications.

Other initiatives in asylum practice and policy also merit adoption. For instance, it is a mistake to assume that opposition to the regime in power on ideological or ethical grounds exists independently from fear of political persecution and threat of imprisonment and/or physical danger as an important motive for becoming an exile. This understanding is explicitly acknowledged in sections 82 and 83 of the UNHCR's *Handbook on Procedures and Criteria for Determining Refugee Status*:

> Due to the strength of his [sic] convictions, . . . it may be reasonable to assume that his opinions will sooner or later find expression and that the applicant will, as a result, come into conflict with the authorities. Where this can reasonably be assumed, the applicant can be considered to have fear of persecution for reasons of political opinion.

These opinions need not have been known by the government before the petitioner left the homeland. In such situations, which apply to most non returnees, "the test of well-founded fear would be based on an assessment of the consequences that an applicant having certain political dispositions would have to face if he returned." Therefore, when expressed as a reason for fearing persecution by applicants for refugee or asylum status, political opposition on ideological and ethical grounds should be treated seriously and not dismissed as "mere dislike." Opponents of the regime in power are likely to be especially prone to commit the kind of acts at home or abroad that provoke political persecution. Self-awareness of this tendency constitutes a reasoned and legitimate basis for well-founded fear of personal political persecution.[78]

Furthermore, serious consideration must be devoted to providing an explicit means by which individuals who fear physical danger due to generalized violence, oppression, and the denial of basic human rights either qualify for admission as a political asylee or are granted secure refuge when relief from personal suffering only is possible outside of the homeland. The research findings presented in this book show that, in practice, many decisions involving overseas applicants for refugee status recognize such fears. In addition, the EVD program and the government's unwillingness to deport many unsuccessful asylum seekers provide indirect recognition of the validity of the claims presented by potential victims of violence.[79] The goal of greater equity in admissions also is served by enabling lower-class petitioners, who possess few existing rights that can be taken away and usually are not singled out for persecution, to gain asylum or safe haven when they demonstrate a credible fear of becoming a personal victim of politically inspired violence and/or deliberately indiscriminate acts of terrorism committed by agents of the state, quasi-official vigilante groups, external agents, or guerrilla forces.[80] On the other hand, granting political asylum to accomplished artists, athletes, and others who principally desire to practice their professional calling in a market-oriented society discredits the entire process.

To support implementation of the recommended changes in political-asylum practices, several related measures need to be adopted. First, asylum claimants must be allowed to support themselves through legal employment as long as their application is under consideration or adjudication.[81] The opportunity to sustain oneself throughout legal proceedings is essential in order that legitimate refugees will be able and willing to come forward and request official asylum. In addition, Congress should rescind its arbitrary limit on the number of persons granted political asylum who are allowed to adjust their status to legal permanent resident each year.[82] In practice, award of asylum is a permanent act, and neither the asylee nor U.S. society benefits from delay in the adjustment-of-status process. Finally, Congress should seriously consider transfering initial political-asylum determinations to specialized adjudicators who belong to an Asylum Admissions Board that operates independently of the Immigration and Naturalization Service and of the State Department.[83] Decisions reached by members of the Asylum Admissions Board should be explained and documented in full and subject to appeal before an Asylum Appeals Board set up outside of the Justice Department.[84] Sufficient resources should be committed to ensure that political-asylum adjudications are conducted in an expeditious manner, that legal counsel is available to indigent applicants, and that due process is respected.[85]

The proposed initiatives require official recognition that U.S. refugee policy encompasses political migrants who initially seek asylum in this country[86] and that "the responsibility to provide first asylum is at least as important as the responsibility to resettle refugees from other first asylum countries."[87] Asylum seekers must not be confused with economic migrants or the victims of natural disaster,[88] and standards must be applied without regard to foreign-policy considerations. Well-trained and broadly informed gatekeepers should continue to make case-by-case determinations regarding who qualifies as a *bona fide* refugee.[89] All applications must be treated strictly on the basis of the merits of the case. The outcome will be consistent and efficient policy application, greater equity in the processing of first-asylum and overseas applications, and the demonstration of increased support for internationally recognized human rights.

These reforms undoubtedly would result in a short-term increase in applications from and in awards to persons who are legitimate political migrants. However, it is the failure to refrain from foreign-policy intrusions that generate and exacerbate sending-country conditions conducive to refugee formation, and not the just and equitable treatment of pleas for political asylum, that is responsible for producing asylum applicants. In the search for appropriate policies, U.S. decision makers must bear in mind that "the modern refugee problem is not one of eligibility criteria or of immigration controls; the problem is, basically, that of the adverse conditions within the country of origin which are forcing people to flee."[90] In short, changes are needed on both the immigration and foreign-policy fronts. If broadening the definition of a refugee to include those who are not protected by the state from violence in their country of origin invites asylum applications in numbers that are too large to be acceptable in Northern receiving societies, then this situation should produce heightened efforts to remove the underlying sources of exile formation rather than provoke restrictive and increasingly less effective short-term measures aimed at deterring political migration.

Admission Under the Refugee-Resettlement Program. Revolutionary conditions compel non participants to flee their homeland for multiple reasons. During and following a successful revolution, one's vulnerability to random acts of violence increases. Pre-existing systems of individual and/or family protection and security break down.

In addition to regime, ideology, and class conflicts, other types of struggles often are simultaneously at work in revolutionary situations. Some Third World peoples concomitantly are subject to hostility on the basis of religion (Cambodia, Iran, Ethiopia) or ethnicity (Eritreans, Kurds, Hmong). Others are trapped in the cross-fire of nationality movements, pro- and counter-insurgency struggles, border conflicts, ecological devastation, and the often deliberate violent destruction of their means of sustenance.[91] In Mozambique, millions of citizens have found it necessary to flee acts of violence directed against them by a terrorist guerrilla force that pursues no coherent social and political policies of its own.[92]

In addition to targeted persecution, therefore, "flight-inducing violence may. . . arise as an incidental consequence of external or internal conflict, or some combination of both, and affect groups that are not even parties to that conflict."[93] Such conflicts are exacerbated when post-revolution rulers attempt to eliminate all opposition or potential opposition to revolutionary objectives and to the new regime. Transnational population flows also increase when regional nationality struggles and border conflicts become linked to larger superpower rivalries.[94]

Astri Suhrke points out that "the definitional question is crucial because persons identified as refugees typically have special protection and benefits that are not accorded those identified as migrants. This preferential status is recognized in international law on the grounds that the refugee is a person in need who cannot turn to his [sic] government for protection."[95] Refining the official definition of a refugee to encompass displaced persons fleeing intolerable conditions out of *fear of uncontrolled violence* brought about by war, acts of terrror directed at civilian populations, and political repression would bring U.S. refugee and asylum law in line with the OAU Charter, UNHCR actions already supported by the international community, and the experiences of Third World refugees from revolution who have arrived in the United States.[96] Nevertheless, most countries have maintained a narrow interpretation that is based upon persecution principally "to preclude overwhelming numbers" from qualifying for this preferential status.[97]

The political-military strategies of indiscriminant acts of violence, guerrilla warfare, counter insurgency, and state and state-sponsored terrorism that are commonly employed in the Third World produce victims of armed conflict whose only hope of finding safety and protection lies in the drastic act of abandoning the homeland. Moreover, general conditions of extreme repression, the absence of law and order, and widespread violations of basic human rights can easily and abruptly turn into a situation of personal persecution and abuse. This understanding shapes exile decision making in many instances. Finally, there is no basis in terms of the degree of human need for continuing to adhere to a policy that denies official recognition as "refugee" to persons who have been externally dislocated as the result of political repression and life-threatening violence directed against those who struggle to protect human rights.[98] In desperation, many of today's political migrants have sought to distance themselves from revolution, ethnic or religious strife, and/or state repression "where there is a good likelihood that they could be the victims of random or organized violence."[99]

Furthermore, it is important that decisions regarding refugee numbers, profiles, and qualifying countries be insulated from foreign-policy pressures.[100] For this reason, the Office of the U.S. Coordinator for Refugee Affairs should be removed from the Department of State and elevated to a prominent place within the Executive Office of the President.[101] Concomitantly, the public debate over refugee policy needs to be informed by accurate descriptions that convey the personal histories of individual exiles and clearly explain the differences between undocumented economic migrants, immigrants, and refugees.[102]   The effort to develop understanding and empathy is particularly important because:

> Bound culturally, socially, psychologically, and spiritually to our culture, we cannot reconcile our lives with the injustice and poverty that characterize a world so radically different from our own.   We cannot identify with the modern refugee, and we are reluctant to imagine his [sic] fate as ours.[103]

Empathy must be accompanied by political will and leadership.   The President's Executive Office is uniquely situated to mobilize these resources.

Refugee-admission decisions are part of the larger fabric of population issues that increasingly will occupy the attention of public-policy makers in the United States.[104]   The U.S. Congress needs to deal with the issue of refugee numbers within the context of a politically determined overall volume of immigration.[105]   This will involve difficult policy choices between the competing objectives of refugee resettlement, economic welfare, occupational adjustment, and extended-family reunification.[106]   In this regard, the current *de facto* emphasis upon family reunion, even among applicants for official-refugee status,[107] deserves critical scrutiny.   If Congress would grant refugees who are eligible for admission on a family-reunification basis priority under the regular immigration ceiling, then other qualified overseas applicants without family in the United States can be accepted for refugee resettlement.   This reform would have the effect of reestablishing the resettlement program as a means of assisting persons in need of refuge who do not fit the normal criteria for admission as an immigrant and simultaneously would remove the incentive to apply for refugee status when one is principally interested in family reunification.[108]

Congress also needs to assert its authority to establish a more equitable standard for allocating regional and country refugee-admission numbers than the foreign-policy driven ceilings supplied by the executive branch.   The idea of setting the U.S. resettlement figure for each sending country at a level proportional to the world-wide refugee total merits serious consideration in this connection.[109]   To reinforce the goal of responsibility in foreign policy, admissions could be linked directly to the record of U.S. involvement or non intervention in the sending country.   The next step is to adopt clear and justifiable guidelines "for choosing among the many who qualify."[110]   A proposal set forth by Norman and Naomi Zucker would give

412

priority in resettlement to individual refugees with the most acute needs—regardless of their country of origin.[111] The combination of a need-based priority scheme within a proportional numbers-allocation system merits discussion as an alternative to the existing family-reunification emphasis and to a resettlement program where admission ceilings are determined by foreign-policy objectives.

Notes

1. Michael S. Teitelbaum, "International Relations and Asian Migrations," in *Pacific Bridges: The New Immigration from Asia and the Pacific Islands*, edited by James T. Fawcett and Benjamin V. Cariño (Staten Island: Center for Migration Studies, 1987), p. 73.

2. Michael S. Teitelbaum, "Immigration, Refugees, and Foreign Policy," *International Organization* 38 (Summer 1984):433. See also Mark Miller and Demetrios Papademetriou, "Immigration and U.S. Foreign Policy," in *The Unavoidable Issue: U.S. Immigration Policy in the 1980s*, ed. by Mark Miller and Demetrios Papademetriou (Philadelphia: Institute for the Study of Human Issues, 1983), pp. 155–157, 176–177.

3. Peter J. Schraeder, "Concepts, Relevance, Themes, and Overview," in *Intervention in the 1980s: U.S. Foreign Policy in the Third World*, edited by Peter J. Schraeder (Boulder: Lynne Rienner Publishers, 1989), p. 11; Harry Piotrowski, "The Structure of the International System," in *Intervention in the 1980s: U.S. Foreign Policy in the Third World*, edited by Peter J. Schraeder (Boulder: Lynne Rienner Publishers, 1989), pp. 177–178; Peter J. Schraeder, "U.S. Intervention in Perspective," in *Intervention in the 1980s: U.S. Foreign Policy in the Third World*, edited by Peter J. Schraeder (Boulder: Lynne Rienner Publishers, 1989), p. 289.

4. George Shepherd, "The Tributary State and 'Peoples' Rights' in Africa: The Banjul Charter and Self-Reliance," *Africa Today* 32, Nos. 1 & 2 (1985):42. In the post-Vietnam era, U.S. administrations also have favored and increasingly employed the strategy of sudden and short attack or incursion by U.S. armed forces. This includes "terrorism counteraction" and anti-drug operations. These militarist responses show scant regard for national sovereignty, are deeply resented abroad, and entail obvious risks of escalation. See Michael T. Klare, "The Development of Low-Intensity Conflict Doctrine," in *Intervention in the 1980s: U.S. Foreign Policy in the Third World*, edited by Peter J. Schraeder (Boulder: Lynne Rienner Publishers, 1989), pp. 39–43.

5. John Scanlan and Gilburt Loescher, "Mass Asylum and Human Rights in American Foreign Policy," *Political Science Quarterly* 97 (Spring 1982):52.

6. See, for instance, Eric Hooglund, "Iran," in *Intervention in the 1980s: U.S. Foreign Policy in the Third World*, edited by Peter J. Schraeder (Boulder: Lynne Rienner Publishers, 1989), pp. 218–219.

7. See Dennis McNamara, "The Origins and Effects of 'Humane Deterrence' Policies in South-east Asia," in *Refugees and International Relations*, edited by Gil Loescher and Laila Monahan (Oxford: Oxford University Press, 1989), p. 133.

8. On the situation in Afghanistan, see Astri Suhrke and Frank Klink, "Contrasting Patterns of Asian Refugee Movements: The Vietnamese and Afghan Syndromes," in *Pacific Bridges: The New Immigration from Asia and the Pacific Islands*, edited by James T. Fawcett and Benjamin V. Cariño (Staten Island: Center for Migration Studies, 1987), pp. 96–97; Aristide R. Zolberg, Astri Suhrke, and Sergio Aguayo, *Escape from Violence: Conflict and the Refugee Crisis in the Developing World* (New York: Oxford University Press, 1989), p. 267.

9. For instance, Ronald Reagan's initial nomination-acceptance speech before the Republican National Convention referred to the U.S.A. as "'a refuge for all those in the world who yearn to be free. . . ,'"—specifically including "'the boat people of. . . Haiti.'" Cited in Lawrence H. Fuchs, "Immigration, Pluralism, and Public Policy: The Challenge of the *Pluribus* to the *Union*," in *U.S. Immigration and Refugee Policy: Global and Domestic Issues*, edited by Mary M. Kritz (Lexington: D.C. Heath, 1983), p. 289; also see Gil Loescher, "Introduction: Refugee Issues in International Relations," in *Refugees and International Relations*, edited by Gil Loescher and Laila Monahan (Oxford: Oxford University Press, 1989), p. 12; Silvia Pedraza-Bailey, *Political and Economic Migrants in America: Cubans and Mexicans* (Austin: University of Texas Press, 1985), p. 154. Even though "there was no basis to suppose that larger numbers of people would flee leftist governments," the Reagan administration later found it useful to fan domestic fears of massive inmigration in the event of successful revolutions in Latin America at the same time that U.S. vessels turned back virtually all Haitians interdicted at sea. Gil Loescher and John A. Scanlan, *Calculated Kindness: Refugees and America's Half-open Door, 1945 to the Present* (New York: Free Press, 1986), p. 192; Bill Frelick, "No Place to Go: Controlling Who Gets In," in *Forced Out: The Agony of the Refugee in Our Time*, compiled by Carole Kismaric (Washington, D.C.: Human Rights Watch and J. M. Kaplan Fund, 1989), p. 165. In another expression of the "propaganda victory" sentiment, the Assistant Secretary for Near Eastern and South Asian Affairs in the U.S. Department of State heralded the "long lines of Iranian visa applicants at our embassies and consulates" as proof that "America remains a beacon of hope to many Iranians." John H. Kelly, "The U.S. Approach to Iran: Outlook for the Future," *Current Policy* 1231 (1989):3.

10. Kevin F. McCarthy and David F. Ronfeldt, "Immigration as an Intrusive Global Flow: A New Perspective," in *U.S. Immigration and Refugee Policy:*

Global and Domestic Issues, edited by Mary M. Kritz (Lexington: D.C. Heath, 1983), pp. 391–392; also see Loescher, "Issues," p. 12; Zolberg *et al., Refugee Crisis,* p. 190.

11. Robert L. Bach, "Third Country Resettlement," in *Refugees and International Relations,* edited by Gil Loescher and Laila Monahan (Oxford: Oxford University Press, 1989), p. 329; Teitelbaum, "Foreign Policy," 442.

12. Robert L. Bach, "Cubans," in *Refugees in the United States: A Reference Handbook,* edited by David W. Haines (Westport: Greenwood Press, 1985), p. 91. Vietnemese refugees are sharply divided over the issue of U.S. political and economic relations with the post-revolution regime. See *New York Times,* 25 August 1989, pp. A1, 7.

13. See Vincent N. Parrillo, *Strangers to these Shores: Race and Ethnic Relations in the United States,* 3rd edition (New York: Macmillan Publishing Company, 1990), p. 333.

14. Charles B. Keely, "Current Status of U.S. Immigration and Refugee Policy," in *U.S. Immigration and Refugee Policy: Global and Domestic Issues,* edited by Mary M. Kritz (Lexington: D.C. Heath, 1983), p. 350.

15. Beverly G. Hawk, "Africans and the 1965 U.S. Immigration Law" (Ph.D. dissertation, University of Wisconsin-Madison, 1988), pp. 27–28, 112, 163, 287. Also see Teitelbaum, "Foreign Policy," 447.

16. Also see James Silk, *Despite a Generous Spirit: Denying Asylum in the United States* (Washington, D.C.: U.S. Committee for Refugees, 1986), pp. 10–11.

17. Also see Patricia W. Fagen, *Resource Paper on Political Asylum and Refugee Status in the United States* (Washington, D.C.: Refugee Policy Group, May 1985), p. 20.

18. Bach, "Resettlement," p. 322. According to Zucker and Zucker, "in the end, the single question most likely to influence an asylum decision is, Will a grant of asylum to this individual encourage others like him [sic] to enter the United States?" Norman L. Zucker and Naomi F. Zucker, *The Guarded Gate: The Reality of American Refugee Policy* (San Diego: Harcourt Brace Jovanovich, Publishers, 1987), p. 146. In 1986, the U.N. High Commissioner warned that refugees and asylum seekers must not be victimized by measures taken to control illegal economic migration. See Dennis Gallagher, Susan F. Martin, and Patricia W. Fagen, "Temporary Safe Haven: The Need for North American-European Responses," in *Refugees and International Relations,* edited by Gil Loescher and Laila Monahan (Oxford: Oxford University Press, 1989), p. 340.

19. Nguyen Manh Hung, "Vietnamese," in *Refugees in the United States: A Reference Handbook,* edited by David W. Haines (Westport: Greenwood Press, 1985), p. 206.

20. The expression of anti-Iranian sentiments by members of the U.S. public peaked during the hostage crisis from November 1979 through January 1981. Abdolmaboud Ansari, *Iranian Immigrants in the United States: A Case Study of Dual Marginality* (Millwood: Associated Faculty Press, 1988), p. 120.

In France and elsewhere in Europe, extreme right-wing political parties have used hostility toward new immigrants as a major campaign theme. Jonas Widgren, "Europe and International Migration in the Future: The Necessity for Merging Migration, Refugee, and Development Policies," in *Refugees and International Relations*, edited by Gil Loescher and Laila Monahan (Oxford: Oxford University Press, 1989), pp. 52–53; Johan Cels, "Responses of European States to *de facto* Refugees," in *Refugees and International Relations*, edited by Gil Loescher and Laila Monahan (Oxford: Oxford University Press, 1989), p. 191; *New York Times*, 27 March 1989, p. 6.

21. Bach, "Resettlement," p. 318; Donald J. Cichon, Elzbieta M. Gozdziak, and Jane G. Grover, *The Economic and Social Adjustment of Non-Southeast Asian Refugees*, Vol. I (Falls Church: Research Management Corporation, 1986), pp. 4, 39.

For culturally sensitive suggestions with regard to assisting refugees from Ethiopia, see Lucia A. McSpadden, "Ethiopian Refugee Resettlement in the Western United States: Social Context and Psychological Well-Being" (Ph.D. dissertation, University of Utah, 1988), pp. 211, 252–253, 257, 306ff.

22. The recent designation of the Ethiopian Community Development Council in Arlington as a volag authorized to sponsor refugees for resettlement constitutes an important step in this direction.

23. Cichon *et al.*, *Adjustment*, p. 4. This includes "taking the need for status upward mobility seriously. . . ." Lucia A. McSpadden, "Ethiopian Refugee Resettlement in the Western United States: Social Context and Psychological Well-Being," *International Migration Review* 21, No. 3 (1987):817–818. On the mobilization of employment and educational resources in support of refugee adjustment, see McSpadden, "Resettlement," pp. 211, 241–244, 256, 260, 263, 277.

24. Bach, "Resettlement," p. 314.

25. Bach, "Resettlement," p. 313.

26. Zucker and Zucker, *Guarded Gate*, p. 137; Bach, "Resettlement," pp. 317, 326; David M. Reimers, *Still the Golden Door: The Third World Comes to America* (New York: Columbia University Press, 1985), pp. 226, 249–250; Jewel S. Lafontant, "Refugees and Conflict Victims: Meeting their Critical Needs," *Current Policy* 1252 (February 1990):1. This conclusion encompasses *de facto* refugees who possess undocumented immigration status. See Demetrios G. Papademetriou and Nicholas DiMarzio, "An Exploration into the Social and Labor Market Incorporation of Undocumented Aliens: The Case of the New York Metropolitan Area" (report to the Center for Migration Studies and the Tinker Foundation, November 1985), pp.

416

149, 178. On recent Canadian and Australian experience with immigrant labor, see Freda Hawkins, *Critical Years in Immigration: Canada and Australia Compared* (Kingston and Montreal: McGill-Queen's University Press, 1989), pp. 268, 273.

27. Anthony P. Maingot, "Ideology, Politics, and Citizenship in the American Debate on Immigration Policy: Beyond Consensus," in *U.S. Immigration and Refugee Policy: Global and Domestic Issues*, edited by Mary M. Kritz (Lexington: D.C. Heath, 1983), p. 375.

28. Richard H. Feen, "Domestic and Foreign Policy Dilemmas in Contemporary U.S. Refugee Policy," in *Refugees and World Politics*, edited by Elizabeth G. Ferris (New York: Praeger, 1985), p. 115.

29. See Paul G. Lauren, *Power and Prejudice: The Politics and Diplomacy of Racial Discrimination* (Boulder: Westview Press, 1988), p. 278.

30. This point also is made with regard to South-North emigration for economic reasons by Saskia Sassen-Koob, "Direct Foreign Investment: A Migration Push-Factor?" *Environment and Planning C: Government and Planning* 2, No. 4 (1984):413.

31. Lauren, *Power and Prejudice*, p. 286.

32. Teitelbaum, "Foreign Policy," 433; Michael S. Teitelbaum, *Latin Migration North: The Problem for U.S. Foreign Policy* (New York: Council on Foreign Relations, 1985), pp. 50–51.

33. Charles S. Milligan, "Ethical Aspects of Refugee Issues and U.S. Policy," in *Refugee Law and Policy: International and U.S. Responses*, edited by Ved P. Nanda (Westport: Greenwood Press, 1989), p. 172. See also Zucker and Zucker, *Guarded Gate*, p. 267; Patricia W. Fagen, *Applying for Political Asylum in New York: Law, Policy, and Administrative Practice* (New York: Center for Latin American and Caribbean Studies, New York University, April 1984), pp. 57–58; Christopher T. Hanson, "Behind the Paper Curtain: Asylum Policy Versus Asylum Practice," *New York University Review of Law and Social Change* 7 (Winter 1978):109–110.

34. Gail P. Kelly, *From Vietnam to America: A Chronicle of the Vietnamese Immigration to the United States* (Boulder: Westview Press, 1977) pp. 15–19, 35–37, 53–56; Dennis Gallagher, Susan Forbes, and Patricia W. Fagen, *Of Special Humanitarian Concern: U.S. Refugee Admissions Since Passage of the Refugee Act* (Washington, D.C.: Refugee Policy Group, 1985), pp. 15–25, 38–39; Suhrke and Klink, "Vietnamese and Afghan," pp. 91–92; Michael Walzer, "The Distribution of Membership," in *Boundaries: National Autonomy and Its Limits*, edited by Peter G. Brown and Henry Shue (Totowa: Rowman and Littlefield, 1981), p. 20.

35. Gallagher *et al.*, *Refugee Admissions*, pp. 44–47. Also see Elizabeth Hull, *Without Justice for All: The Constitutional Rights of Aliens* (Westport: Greenwood Press, 1985), p. 119.

36. This clause is specifically intended to encompass victims of brutal regimes supported by the United States as well as victims of corporate exploitation.

37. Moreover, "the point of departure for illegal alien policy making should be a recognition that the U.S. bears a heavy share of responsibility for the present situation." Wayne A. Cornelius, "Mexican Immigration: Causes and Consequences for Mexico," in *Sourcebook on the New Immigration: Implications for the United States and the International Community*, edited by Roy S. Bryce-Laporte (New Brunswick: Transaction Books, 1980), p. 72.

38. Miller and Papademetriou, "Immigration," pp. 157–158, 161; Wayne A. Cornelius, "Mexican Migration to the United States," *Proceedings of the Academy of Political Science* 34, No. 1 (1981):67, 71.

39. Howard Adelman, "Refuge or Asylum: A Philosophical Perspective," *Journal of Refugee Studies* 1, No. 1 (1988):10.

40. Scanlan and Loescher, "Mass Asylum," 42; Bach, "Resettlement," p. 321; Cornelius, "Mexican Migration," 75; Al Santoli, *New Americans: Immigrants and Refugees in the U.S. Today* (New York: Viking, 1988), p. 256; Parrillo, *Strangers*, p. 535. See also *New York Times*, 26 June 1986, pp. 1, 10; 24 June 1988, pp. 1, 4; and 26 November 1990.

41. Miller and Papademetriou, "Immigration," pp. 161, 181; Hull, *Without Justice*, pp. 113–114; Cornelius, "Mexican Migration," 75.

As an example of a single dimension of this problem, efforts to assist in the economic reconstruction of El Salvador would be seriously undermined by the large-scale deportation of Savadoreans given that an estimated one-third of the families in that Central American nation currently rely for half or more of their annual income upon remittances from relatives living illegally as well as legally in the United States. Doris Meissner, "Statement before the Subcommittee on Immigration, Refugees and International Law of the Committee on the Judiciary, U.S. House of Representatives" (mimeo, 9 March 1989), p. 13.

42. Barry and Carmel Chiswick, "Illegal Immigrants Should be Punished to Stem Tide," *Missoulian*, 13 October 1985, p. 6.

43. Cornelius, "Mexican Migration," 70–71, 76–77; Papademetriou and DiMarzio, "Undocumented Aliens," pp. 185–186; *New York Times*, 3 July 1986, p. 27.

44. See *New York Times*, 26 November 1990, p. A11.

45. *New York Times*, 30 March 1990, p. 1. Studies conducted by agencies of the California and New York state governments reached similar conclusions. See *New York Times*, 26 February 1990, p. A17.

46. See, for instance, Miller and Papademetriou, "Immigration," p. 181; Rafael Valdivieso and Cary Davis, *U.S. Hispanics: Challenging Issues for the 1990s* (Washington, D.C.: Population Reference Bureau, 1988), pp. 14–15.

47. Gervase Coles, "Approaching the Refugee Problem Today," in *Refugees and International Relations*, edited by Gil Loescher and Laila Monahan (Oxford: Oxford University Press, 1989), pp. 388–389.

48. See Scanlan and Loescher, "Mass Asylum," pp. 47, 56. On strategies to reduce economic migration, see Susan George, *Ill Fares the Land: Essays on Food, Hunger, and Power* (Washington, D.C.: Institute for Policy Studies, 1984), pp. 11–14; Alejandro Portes, "Illegal Immigration and the International System: Lessons from Recent Legal Mexican Immigrants to the United States," *Social Problems* 26 (April 1979):435; Sidney Weintraub, "Treating the Causes: Illegal Immigration and U.S. Foreign Economic Policy," in *The Unavoidable Issue: U.S. Immigration Policy in the 1980s*, edited by Demetrios G. Papademetriou and Mark J. Miller (Philadelphia: Institute for the Study of Human Issues, 1983), pp. 190–209.

49. Teitelbaum, "Foreign Policy," 450; Roger P. Winter, "The Year in Review," in *World Refugee Survey—1988 in Review* (Washington, D.C.: U.S. Committee for Refugees, 1989), p. 4.

50. Also see Teitelbaum, *Latin Migration*, p. 70.

51. Zolberg *et al., Refugee Crisis*, pp. 278, 282.

52. Miller and Papademetriou, "Immigration," p. 181.

53. See Scanlan and Loescher, "Mass Asylum," 52; Miller and Papademetriou, "Immigration," pp. 155–157, 176–177, 181; Charles F. Doran, "The Globalist-Regionalist Debate," in *Intervention in the 1980s: U.S. Foreign Policy in the Third World*, edited by Peter J. Schraeder (Boulder: Lynne Rienner Publishers, 1989), pp. 55–56; Aristide R. Zolberg, Astri Suhrke, and Sergio Aguayo, "International Factors in the Formation of Refugee Movements," *International Migration Review* 22, No. 2 (Summer 1986):167–168; Zolberg *et al., Refugee Crisis*, p. 265. While the possibility of benign results cannot be completely denied, past experience indicates that there is a much higher probability that external military intervention will lead to or exacerbate population dislocation.

54. Schraeder, "U.S. Intervention," p. 293; Teitelbaum, "Foreign Policy," 433–434, 450; Zolberg *et al., Refugee Crisis*, pp. 264–265. Appropriate development strategies encompass the democratization of international and national institutions as well as mass empowerment and participation in decision making. Development-assistance projects should be consistent with goals of self-reliance, diversification, decentralization, equitable resource distribution, accountability, and ecological sustainability. Donors need to pursue debt relief and forgiveness aggressively and without imposing structural-adjustment conditionalities. South-South economic and political cooperation and interaction should be encouraged and facilitated, and the presence of Western agencies and personnel minimized. See Fantu Cheru, *The Silent Revolution in Africa: Debt, Development and Democracy* (London and New Jersey: Zed Books, 1989), pp. 142–145, 151–154, 160–163; Peter

H. Koehn, *Public Policy and Administration in Africa: Lessons from Nigeria* (Boulder: Westview Press, 1990), pp. 134–136, 290–295; Josh DeWind and David H. Kinley III, *Aiding Migration: The Impact of International Development Assistance on Haiti* (Boulder: Westview Press, 1988), p. 154.

55. Scanlan and Loescher, "Mass Asylum," 47–48; Doran, "Debate," p. 54.

56. Internal conflicts in Sudan, Ethiopia, Somalia, Mozambique, and Cambodia offer particularly compelling opportunities for the exercise of this role. See Hiram A. Ruiz and Bill Frelick, "Africa's Uprooted People: Shaping a Humanitarian Response," *Issue* 18, No. 1 (Winter 1989):33–35; *New York Times*, 24 October 1990; 30 January 1991, p. A2.

57. This idea is drawn from John Prendergast's suggestion for resolving hostilities between the Sudan government and the Sudanese People's Liberation Army. He adds that "at the same time, a reconstruction fund should be created and held in escrow, not to be released until peace is achieved. The conditions for assistance from this fund should. . . stress food security at the household level, environmental protection and restoration, decentralization, broad participation in government and greatly reduced military budgets." John Prendergast, "A Famine in the Making in Sudan," *Wall Street Journal*, 2 January 1990.

58. In 1990, cooperative efforts occurred with respect to the Eritrean conflict, food-distribution needs in the Horn, and in negotiations concerning a peaceful settlement of the fighting in Angola. See *New York Times*, 4 June 1990, p. A11; 13 December 1990, p. A11.

The role of peace broker might well require that the superpowers apply pressures and sanctions against favored regional states—including South Africa, Israel, Iraq, and Vietnam—that are bent on destabilizing their neighbors.

59. Miller and Papademetriou, "Immigration," pp. 165, 170–171; Teitelbaum, "Foreign Policy," 436, 439, 443–449.

60. Doran, "Debate," pp. 45, 48–49, 53, 57; Schraeder, "U.S. Intervention," pp. 286–287; Zolberg *et al., Refugee Crisis*, p. 263; Hooshang Amirahmadi, "Middle-Class Revolutions in the Third World," in *Post-Revolutionary Iran*, ed. by Hooshang Amirahmadi and Manoucher Parvin (Boulder: Westview Press, 1988), p. 239.

61. Schraeder, "U.S. Intervention," pp. 288–289.

62. See, for instance, Holly Burkhalter, "Human Rights in Sudan," in U.S., Congress, House, Select Committee on Hunger and Subcommittee on Africa, *Politics of Hunger in the Sudan, Joint Hearings*, 101st Congress, 1st session, 1989, pp. 85–86; Peter J. Schraeder, "Paramilitary Intervention," in *Intervention in the 1980s: U.S. Foreign Policy in the Third World*, edited by Peter J. Schraeder (Boulder: Lynne Rienner Publishers, 1989), pp. 122–123.

The realization of these objectives requires vigilance against the inclination of the U.S. military-industrial establishment to "manufacture urgent reasons for its expansion on the North-South axis of conflict when the East-West axis appears less threatening." Klare, "Low-Intensity Conflict," p. 41.

63. See Lauren, *Power and Prejudice*, pp. 289–290.

64. McCarthy and Ronfeldt, "Global Flow," pp. 389, 391; Miller and Papademetriou, "Immigration," p. 165; Alejandro Portes, "Migration and Underdevelopment," *Politics & Society* 8, No. 1 (1978):41; Reimers, *Golden Door*, pp. 203–204; *New York Times*, 6 March 1989, pp. 1, 8; 21 April 1990, p. 7.

65. The changes include official sceptism concerning "the use of force as a political instrument in the Third World." See S. Neil Macfarlane, "Superpower Rivalry in the 1990s," *Third World Quarterly* 12, No. 1 (January 1990):12–15, 20.

66. Also see Zolberg *et al., Refugee Crisis*, p. 261.

67. Hull, *Without Justice*, p. 145; Miller and Papademetriou, "Immigration," 181.

68. Jeff Crisp, "Interview: Jewel S. Lafontant," *Refugees* (October 1989):40. Also see the conclusion to Chapter 3 above.

Even most economic migrants "prefer not to emigrate, particularly if they have to do it illegally." United States, Agency for International Development, "The Relationship of U.S. Aid, Trade, and Investment to Migration Pressures in Major Countries of Origin," in U.S., Select Commission on Immigration and Refugee Policy, *U.S. Immigration Policy and the National Interest*, Appendix B to the Staff Report (Washington, D.C.: Commission, [1981]), p. 13.

69. Coles, "Refugee Problem," p. 387.

70. Coles, "Refugee Problem," p. 388.

71. Zolberg *et al., Refugee Crisis*, pp. 269, 263.

72. John A. Scanlan, "First Final Research Report Submitted to the Select Commission on Immigration and Refugee Policy," in *U.S. Immigration Policy and the National Interest*, Appendix C to the Staff Report of the Select Commission on Immigration and Refugee Policy (Washington, D.C.: The Commission, 1980), pp. 133–136.

73. United States, Select Commission on Immigration and Refugee Policy, *U.S. Immigration Policy and the National Interest; Final Report and Recommendations of the Select Commission* (Washington, D.C.: The Commission, March 1981), p. 171.

74. Also see Hanson, "Asylum," 141; Scanlan, "Report," pp. 133–144. The rules issued by the Bush administration in July 1990 showed progress in this direction. In the December 1990 settlement reached in a federal district court case concerning asylum applicants from El Salvador and Guatemala, moreover, the government stipulated that foreign-policy and influx-control considerations, as well as U.S. political support for the sending-country, would no longer be acceptable factors in determining eligibility for political asylum. See *New York Times*, 19 July 1990, p. A10; 20 December 1990, p. A10.

75. See John A. Scanlan, "Who is a Refugee? Procedures and Burden of Proof Under the Refugee Act of 1980," in *In Defense of the Alien*, Vol. V, edited by Lydio F. Tomasi (Staten Island: Center for Migration Studies, 1983), p. 26.

76. Scanlan, "Proof," pp. 27–28, 33, 36. Also see Theodore N. Cox, "Well-founded Fear of Being Persecuted: The Sources and Application of a Criterion of Refugee Status," *Brooklyn Journal of International Law* 10 (Summer 1984):375–377. In the late 1980s, "asylum interviews remain generally brief with officers spending most of the time being sure forms are correctly completed rather than skilfully [sic] probing the line separating political from economic migration." Meissner, "Statement," p. 7.

77. Also see Fagen, *Applying*, p. 51; Silk, *Denying Asylum*, p. 43.

78. In addition, John Scanlan argues that if a petitioner for political asylum "has a 'well-founded fear of persecution' *based upon the political act of filing an asylum application* abroad, that fact should support the applicant's claim that he [sic] meets the relevant refugee definition." John A. Scanlan, "Issue Summaries Submitted to the Select Commission on Immigration and Refugee Policy," in *U.S. Immigration Policy and the National Interest*, Appendix C to the Staff Report of the Select Commission on Immigration and Refugee Policy (Washington, D.C.: The Commission, 1980), p. 75. [emphasis in original]

79. Zolberg *et al.*, *Refugee Crisis*, p. 270.

80. Also see Zolberg *et al.*, *Refugee Crisis*, pp. 30, 33. Providing "temporary" safe haven status alone is a far less satisfactory alternative to recognizing political migrants as refugees. Persons granted EVD or other forms of indefinite refuge in the North occupy a decidedly inferior economic and political position. For political and humanitarian reasons, host governments typically find themselves unable to return these exiles to the sending country. Consequently, their second-class status tends to be perpetuated indefinitely. Also see Cels, "Responses," p. 193; Teitelbaum, *Latin Migration*, p. 64. For an argument in favor of EVD, see Zucker and Zucker, *Guarded Gate*, pp. 220–222; also see Gallagher *et al.*, "Safe Haven," pp. 342, 351. New U.S. immigration legislation enacted in 1990 with a 1992 effective date grants temporary safe haven to Salvadoreans. *Washington Post*, 28 October 1990, p. A1.

81. See Silk, *Denying Asylum*, p. 27. The majority of asylum seekers "eventually stay in the country where they have submitted their application. People who have been locked up, humiliated and deprived of employment for two years or more" are likely to encounter difficulty becoming "self-sufficient members of their new society." Jeffery Crisp, editor, *Refugees: The Dynamics of Displacement* (London: Zed Press, 1986), p. 41.

82. Also see Ronald Copeland and Patricia W. Fagen, *Political Asylum: A Background Paper on Procedures and Problems* (Washington, D.C.: Refugee Policy

422

Group, December 1982), p. 20. With effect in FY 1991, the *Immigration Act of 1990* raised the limit from 5,000 to 10,000. Demetrios G. Papademetriou, "The Immigration Act of 1990" (Washington, D.C.: U.S. Department of Labor, Bureau of International Labor Affairs, December 1990), p. 12.

83. Neither the U.S. Department of State nor the INS "speaks for the humanitarian concerns of the refugee. . . ." Zucker and Zucker, *Guarded Gate*, p. 159. The State Department's strictly advisory and case-justified input could comprise one component in a multiple-source information network that should encompass human-rights groups and agencies, affidavits prepared by other refugees, scholars who are area experts, and additional sources that are disclosed to petitioners and do not assess conditions related to political migration in terms of foreign-policy considerations. See Scanlan, "Summaries," pp. 7–16, 84–85; Silk, *Denying Asylum*, p. 42; Lawrence H. Fuchs, "The Search for a Sound Immigration Policy: A Personal View," in *Clamor at the Gates: The New American Immigration*, edited by Nathan Glazer (San Francisco: Institute for Contemporary Studies, 1985), p. 36; Peter Koehn, "Persistent Problems and Political Issues in U.S. Immigration Law and Policy," in *Refugee Law and Policy: International and U.S. Responses*, edited by Ved P. Nanda (Westport: Greenwood Press, 1989), p. 77. Hull (*Without Justice*, p. 144) recommends that the State Department no longer submit advisory opinions at all "since in so doing it unduly politicizes the process." Instead, she proposes that asylum-review officers rely upon UNHCR recommendations. Also see Michael H. Posner, "Refugees and Asylum: An Assessment of U.S. Policy and Practice," in *U.S. Immigration Policy and the National Interest*, Appendix C to the Staff Report of the Select Commission on Immigration and Refugee Policy (Washington, D.C.: The Commission, 1980), p. 29; Arthur C. Helton, "Political Asylum under the 1980 Refugee Act: An Unfulfilled Promise," *University of Michigan Journal of Law Reform* 17, No. 2 (Winter 1984):263.

By 1989, even a former Commissioner of the INS "reluctantly" concluded that "the asylum mandate will not be properly carried out unless it is removed from the hands of both INS and the Department of State." She recommended that this function be carried out by a specialized corps of asylum officers, backed by a research staff, who would be located in the Justice Department's Executive Office for Immigration Review. Meissner, "Statement," pp. 8–9. Over the objections of the INS itself, the Bush administration decided to establish a specially trained corps of asylum officers in July 1990. See *New York Times*, 19 July 1990, p. A10; Arthur C. Helton, "Asylum and Refugee Protection in the Bush Years," in *World Refugee Survey—1988 in Review* (Washington, D.C.: U.S. Committee for Refugees, 1989), p. 26.

84. The Asylum Appeals Board would replace the dual system of immigration judges and the Board of Immigration Appeals. Former INS administrators and trial

attorneys should be ineligible to serve on the new body. See Fuchs, "Policy," p. 36; Scanlan, "Summaries," pp. 20–23; Fagen, *Applying*, p. 16. Further recommendations along these lines are presented in Helton, "Bush Years," p. 28.

85. Helton, "Bush Years," p. 28. Doris Meissner ("Statement," p. 13), among others, argues for the swift return of persons judged unqualified for political asylum as an "effective immigration control and deterrence" measure.

86. See Kelly, *Vietnamese*, p. 350.

87. Silk, *Denying Asylum*, p. 34.

88. Elizabeth Ferris points out that "by lumping the economically deprived with the politically persecuted, there is a risk that governments will close the door to all." Elizabeth G. Ferris, "Overview: Refugees and World Politics," in *Refugees and World Politics*, edited by Elizabeth G. Ferris (New York: Praeger, 1985), p. 5. In the same vein, Andrew Shacknove argues that an "overly inclusive conception" will "financially exhaust relief programs and impune the credibility of the refugee's privileged position among host populations, whose support is crucial for the viability of international assistance programs." However, Shacknove then proceeds to advocate a refugee definition that encompasses all persons "whose home state has failed to secure their basic needs" and who have "no remaining recourse other than to seek international restitution of these needs. . . ." Andrew E. Shacknove, "Who is a Refugee?" *Ethics* 95 (January 1985):276–284. See also Crisp, *Refugees*, p. 42. From the perspective of Zolberg et al. (*Refugee Crisis*, pp. 33, 261), "most victims of malnutrition and slow starvation. . . should not be considered as refugees because most of them can be assisted *in situ* in their own countries." However, "people cast abroad by famine are refugees" if they are unable "to meet subsistence needs because of unsafe conditions, or the refusal of the state to accept international assistance."

89. The findings discussed in Chapter 3 of this book suggest that social-background indicators and U.S. ties are not consistently related to exile motivations.

90. Coles, "Refugee Problem," p. 387; also see Frelick, "No Place," p. 165.

91. Zolberg et al. ("Refugee Movements," 164) note that "states facing separatist guerillas [sic] typically exercise violence against the source group as a whole, any member of which is considered an actual or potential supporter of insurgency." Also see Ferris, "Overview," p. 4.

92. Ruiz and Frelick, "Uprooted," 33; James H. Mittelman, *Out from Underdevelopment: Prospects for the Third World* (New York: St. Martin's Press, 1988), pp. 148–149.

93. Zolberg, Suhrke, and Aguayo, "Refugee Movements," 153.

94. Zolberg, Suhrke, and Aguayo, "Refugee Movements," 163, 165–166.

95. Astri Suhrke, "Global Refugee Movements and Strategies of Response," in *U.S. Immigration and Refugee Policy: Global and Domestic Issues*, edited by Mary

M. Kritz (Lexington: D.C. Heath and Company, 1983), p. 157. Also see Shacknove, "Refugee?" 276.

96. See Suhrke, "Refugee Movements," p. 160; Gallagher *et al., Refugee Admissions*, p. 54; Shacknove, "Refugee?" 276; Hull, *Without Justice*, p. 119; Zolberg *et al., Refugee Crisis*, pp. 29–30; Lance Clark, "Internal Refugees—The Hidden Half," in *World Refugee Survey—1988 in Review* (Washington, D.C.: U.S. Committee for Refugees, 1989), p. 20.

97. Zolberg *et al., Refugee Crisis*, p. 25. Zucker and Zucker (*Guarded Gate*, p. 146) maintain that "the floodgates fear outweighs even foreign policy considerations and pressure from support groups."

98. See Leon Gordenker, *Refugees in International Politics* (New York: Columbia University Press, 1987), pp. 63–64; Suhrke, "Refugee Movements," pp. 159–160; Zolberg *et al., Refugee Crisis*, pp. 31, 33.

99. Gallagher *et al.*, "Safe Haven," p. 350; Elizabeth G. Ferris, "Regional Responses to Central American Refugees: Policy Making in Nicaragua, Honduras, and Mexico," in *Refugees and World Politics*, edited by Elizabeth G. Ferris (New York: Praeger, 1985), p. 193.

100. Also see Hull, *Without Justice*, p. 122. Michael Teitelbaum (*Latin Migration*, p. 63) argues the contrary position on this issue.

101. This recommendation also is made in U.S., Select Commission on Immigration and Refugee Policy, *Final Report*, pp. 198–200.

102. See Zucker and Zucker, *Guarded Gate*, p. xvii.

103. Carole Kismaric, compiler, *Forced Out: The Agony of the Refugee in Our Time* (Washington, D.C.: Human Rights Watch and the J. M. Kaplan Fund, 1989), p. 183.

104. See, for instance, Leon Bouvier, "U.S. Immigration: Effects on Population Growth and Structure," in *U.S. Immigration and Refugee Policy: Global and Domestic Issues*, edited by Mary M. Kritz (Lexington: D.C. Heath, 1983), p. 208; Keely, "Policy," p. 340.

105. For restrictionist views on this issue, see Constance Holden, "Debate Warming Up on Legal Migration Policy," *Science* 241 (15 July 1988):288–289. On the other side, some economic demographers contend that future prosperity in the North will depend upon the continued reception, integration, and education of migrant laborers and that the comparative strength of the United States in attracting needed workers is the tradition of an immigrant society in a "non-homeland state." By 1990, the latter view clearly prevailed among top-level Bush administration advisors. See Julian L. Simon, "More Immigration Can Cut the Deficit," *New York Times*, 10 May 1990, p. A27; *New York Times*, 29 October 1990, p. A13; Leon F. Bouvier and Robert W. Gardner, "Immigration to the U.S.: The Unfinished Story," *Population Bulletin* 41, No. 4 (November 1986):32; Walker Connor, "Who are the

Mexican-Americans? A Note on Comparability," in *Mexican-Americans in Comparative Perspective*, edited by Walker Connor (Washington, D.C.: The Urban Institute Press, 1985), p. 9; Demetrios G. Papademetriou, "Contending Approaches to Reforming the U.S. Legal Immigration System" (paper prepared for the NYU/Rockefeller Foundation Conference on Migration, Ethnicity, and the City, November 1990), pp. 1–8, 27–43. On the disutility of applying cost-benefit analysis in the national debate over immigration policy, see McCarthy and Ronfeldt, "Global Flow," p. 394.

In October 1990, the U.S. Congress enacted new immigration legislation that President Bush signed into law on 29 November. The 1990 legislation expands the total number of immigrant visas issued from 500,000 to 714,000 (excluding refugees) in 1992 and to 675,000 beginning in 1995. Papademetriou, "Immigration Act," p. 1.

106. The 1990 legislation increases allowable legal permanent immigration for skilled migrants and for those admitted on the basis of family relationship. For details, consult Papademetriou, "Immigration Act," pp. 1–12; Papademetriou, "Reforming," pp. 9–26. The policy debate over this measure essentially ignored findings that the majority of refugees from Third World revolutions are neither illiterate nor unskilled, and that they show a remarkable ability to adjust in short order to the economic conditions encountered in the United States. See note 108.

107. See Teitelbaum, *Latin Migration*, p. 63; Robert L. Bach, "State Intervention in Southeast Asian Refugee Resettlement in the United States," *Journal of Refugee Studies* 1, No. 1 (1988):41; Holden, "Debate," p. 287. An argument in favor of strict adherence to an expanded Orderly Departure Program from Vietnam is set forth by Court Robinson, "Sins of Omission: The New Vietnamese Refugee Crisis," in *World Refugee Survey—1988 in Review* (Washington, D.C.: U.S. Committee for Refugees, 1989), pp. 9–10.

108. See Hawk, "Africans," pp. 114–115. For instance, Bach ("Cubans," p. 82) notes, with reference to Cuban migration, that "as each wave separated larger numbers of family members, sorting desires to reunite with family from political disaffection became increasingly difficult."

Moreover, the findings presented in Chapter 7 demonstrate that, if past experience is a guide to future outcomes, bi-culturally oriented refugees without family ties in the host country will not experience considerably greater difficulty adjusting economically or adapting to U.S. society than those who arrive on a family-reunification basis. The key to successful adaptation has been placement with U.S. congregations and families rather than exclusive reliance upon agency resettlement staff. See McSpadden, "Resettlement," 817–818. However, the extended-family household plays a vital role in economic adjustment among some refugees—especially those who pursue an ethnic-enclave adaptation strategy. Bach,

426

"State Intervention," 53. Another criticism of the approach advocated here, which resembles unimplemented recommendations set forth for the Indochinese resettlement program by the Ray Panel, is that "designating a genuine refugee as an immigrant ignores the special needs of the refugee, among them the need for resettlement assistance." Zucker and Zucker, *Guarded Gate*, pp. 90–91.

109. This recommendation would result in a dramatically expanded ceiling for refugees from Africa, Central America, and Afghanistan. In FY 1987, for instance, African refugees constituted about 27 percent of the world's total and 3 percent of the U.S. resettlement allocation. George Shultz, "Proposed Refugee Admissions for FY 1988," *Current Policy* 1004 (September 1987):1, 3; also see U.S., Immigration and Naturalization Service, *Statistical Yearbook of the Immigration and Naturalization Service, 1987* (Washington, D.C.: U.S. GPO, 1988), p. 50. Implementation of this recommendation would require the training and deployment of additional refugee-admission officers. See Helton, "Bush Years," p. 26. As Beverly Hawk ("Africans," pp. 129, 279) points out, "the location of refugee processing facilities is a political choice."

110. Zucker and Zucker, *Guarded Gate*, p. 268.

111. Their method of distinguishing need would award highest priority to refugees who already have experienced persecution and face clear threats of further abuse if they should return home. Cases where persecution had not yet occurred, but would be quite probable, would fall in the middle of the scale. The "lowest numbers would go to refugees who are fleeing generalized violence. . . . Applicants whose claims of refugee status were found to be totally unsupported would be given no number whatsoever. . . ." These authors further recommend the establishment of an independent refugee authority to adjudicate resettlement requests. Zucker and Zucker, *Guarded Gate*, pp. 267, 270–273. An alternative proposal based upon discovering "degrees of desperation" is proposed by Hull (*Without Justice*, pp. 144–145). Zolberg, Suhrke, and Aguayo (*Refugee Crisis*, pp. 31, 270) suggest that "the more immediate and intense the life-threatening violence is, the more clearly a person is a refugee rather than a migrant." Their position (pp. 269–271) is clearly distinguished from the priority scheme advanced by the Zuckers in that "the activists, the target, and the victim have an equally valid claim to protection. . . . [by] the international community." It would be a mistake, however, to create a third-country resettlement procedure that rewards and, thereby, encourages exposure to personal danger and violence. One must not be required to experience and survive persecution in order to be recognized as a refugee.

11

Looking Toward the Future:
Refugees and International Relations

I am convinced that we will have a future with much more movement of people.
—Thorvald Stoltenberg, U.N. High Commissioner for Refugees

Neither government policies nor international conventions have kept pace with the new international migrations.

—Myron Weiner

Growing numbers of refugees, economic migrants, and desperate people with mixed motives will move across national borders during the 1990s. As Western Europe braces for an influx from the east,[1] migrants from the South continue to head North. The resource and ethical dilemmas posed by mass international migration will place increasingly difficult policy choices on the global agenda into the 21st century.[2]

The contemporary challenges of transnational refugee flows are not confined to matters of U.S. policy. This chapter considers prospects for additional international population movements and critically examines prevailing responses to cross-border displacement. With a view toward preparing for the future, we then will explore the implications of refugee formation for the South, the North, and for the conduct of international relations.

Post-Revolution Refugee Migration:
Determinant Factors and Future Prospects

Refugees from revolution account for a major share of the world's externally displaced population. The experience of contemporary Vietnamese, Cuban, Iranian, and Ethiopian migration suggests that the Third

World revolution sets in motion a protracted process of mass refugee creation. The future of global political migration, therefore, rests in large measure upon the frequency of revolutionary transformation.

What are the prospects for revolution in additional Third World countries? In their book on the refugee crisis, Aristide Zolberg, Astri Suhrke, and Sergio Aguayo maintain that, outside of the Middle East, "the situations most likely to explode into full-fledged revolutions have already done so. . . ." Instead of revolution, they argue, "the developing countries are likely to experience more limited types of social order conflicts that will produce some refugees."[3] A contrasting assessment is presented here.

Through the method of focused comparison, we discovered that the volatile mix of extreme economic inequity and class conflict, repression by an authoritarian regime, dependency, and external intervention constitute an invitation for revolution.[4] These prerequisites for political transformation are present in many Third World contexts. Often, the crucial missing ingredient is politically astute leadership that is capable of mobilizing a successful mass-based challenge to a U.S.-supported regime. Although the absence of such leadership makes it difficult to predict revolutionary outcomes, "revolution-prone" countries can be identified on the basis of the presence of the other shaping conditions.

There are many places in the Third World where conditions are ripe for revolution. Zolberg, Suhrke, and Aguayo identify some of these countries themselves. They include the kingdoms and principalities of the Middle East, the remaining traditional monarchies in Nepal and Morocco, the Southeast Asian states of Thailand, Indonesia, and the Philippines, authoritarian political systems based on control over land in Pakistan, El Salvador, and Guatemala, and the minority-ruled state of South Africa.[5] One can add to this list, especially in light of the extensive and extended U.S. presence, South Korea, Zaire, Kenya, and even Mexico.[6] In addition, Hong Kong presents the unique prospect of a negotiated revolution with substantial advance notice. Coupled with the British government's refusal to grant full citizenship and residency rights in the United Kingdom to nearly all of the 3.25 million "dependent territory" passport holders,[7] the political, social, and economic transformation of the former colony that will accompany integration into the mainland in 1997 and beyond is likely to provoke a substantial segment of Hong Kong's current population of 5.7 million people to opt for exile.

Under what conditions are refugees from future Third World revolutions apt to resettle in the United States? First, South-North migration is greatly facilitated by the presence of social networks, especially family ties, in the receiving country.[8]   On the basis of the immediate availability of interlocking networks shaped by prior economic migration, potential political migrants from the Philippines, South Korea, Hong Kong, El Salvador, and Mexico would be the most likely to gain entry to the United States. To the extent that personal wealth enables a refugee to "purchase" admission to the North, exiles from the Middle East, South Africa, and Hong Kong would be in an advantageous position relative to other refugees from Third World revolutions.   Finally, some people will secure access to industrialized countries by virtue of regional resistance to providing asylum, official sympathy for flight from a communist post-revolution regime or from invading armed forces, and/or growing public recognition of external responsibility for refugee formation.

Alternative Responses

The so-called *durable solutions* to refugee flows are permanent acceptance and integration in the country of first asylum, third-country resettlement, and voluntary repatriation.[9] Although secure repatriation is the preferred alternative, it usually is the most difficult to arrange.[10]

The Quest for Durable First-asylum Solutions

Most future refugees from revolution are likely to seek refuge in poor neighboring Third World countries.[11] By 1990, the primary activity of the U.N. High Commission for Refugees had shifted from assisting with third-country resettlement to feeding and accommodating vast numbers of refugees—including the victims of war and civil strife—in places of first asylum.[12] UNHCR currently allocates more than half of its roughly $400 million annual budget on care and maintenance activities and UNWRA continues to expend in excess of $200 million on basic assistance to Palestinian refugees.[13] Providing adequate relief assistance that meets basic needs is essential "so that any decisions the refugees reach about whether or not to repatriate will be based on their assessment of conditions in their home country, rather than on a lack of resources in their country of refuge."[14]

Involuntary Return. Early in 1990, U.N. High Commissioner Thorvald Stoltenberg accepted the need to repatriate illegal "economic" migrants in order to ensure receiving-country willingness to grant asylum to recognized refugees.[15] The principal danger inherent in this involuntary-repatriation approach is that political migrants mistakenly or deliberately will be returned to situations of personal persecution because of the difficulties involved in distinguishing among diverse and interconnected motives for flight and/or due to local political or financial considerations.[16] Implementation of this policy also increases the likelihood that people who fear persecution will subject themselves to considerable risk in their homeland "rather than opt to go to a country where they will be subject to harsh treatment."[17]

Permanent Local Integration. Holding dislocated populations indefinitely in externally dependent camps constitutes the least desirable method of assisting refugees.[18] When the prospects for repatriation are remote, immediate-assistance programs must be replaced by permanent settlement and national integration.[19] This effort is necessary for the long-term well-being of the refugee and the receiving society even though "investment in one solution, for example, local integration, may make another solution, such as repatriation, appear less attractive by comparison."[20]

UNHCR has endeavored to replace emergency-relief operations with projects that directly incorporate refugees into the host country's economy and development process "on an equal footing with the surrounding population. . . ."[21] This approach requires cooperation with international and bilateral donor agencies as well as with NGOs.[22] UNHCR seeks to play the catalyst and coordinating roles in such ventures and to avoid performing the functions of a development agency. The results have been limited as the idea of linking refugee aid to sustainable-development projects "has not yet been generally accepted by the donor community."[23]

Additional constraints, including host-country resistance, limit the application of an integrated approach to refugee assistance in first-asylum countries.[24] First, sustainable-development efforts are greatly complicated by the massive numbers of externally displaced persons who overload settlement sites and damage fragile natural resources in the receiving areas. Moreover, U.S. and voluntary-agency assistance has been inadequate—particularly in several African contexts.[25] On the other hand, the success of highly motivated exiles commonly provokes resentment within the surrounding population[26] and the tensions that stem from donor assistance that excludes poor host communities exacerbate the hostility and insecurity experienced by refugees.[27] As a result of these and other concerns, some governments oppose the use of urgently needed and limited development funds on refugee-oriented projects.[28] In certain situations, refugee warriors and others regarded by the government of the receiving society as a threat to national security actually have been contained and guarded.[29]

Impacted-area Assistance. In order to defuse the resentment factor, host nationals must also benefit from development-assistance programs introduced specifically to address the needs of the local poor and to replace vital resources depleted by the population influx.[30] As Mekuria Bulcha points out, "local integration efforts cannot be effective unless they are carried out simultaneously with the economic and infrastructural development of the regions in question."[31]

Participation in Development Projects. When linking refugee aid with self-reliant development, the strategy for involving the local migrant community requires careful attention. In the past, refugees have been excluded from participation in project planning, staffing, and in the making of important administrative decisions. They frequently have been subjected to the imposition of "solutions" by patronizing agency staff.[32] The consequences are increased powerlessness, diminished self-confidence, and greater dependency. From the start, therefore, refugees and the local poor must be centrally involved in project initiation and selection, budgeting and revenue raising, supervision, implementation decision making, evaluation, and monitoring.[33]

The Nature and Extent of Third-country Resettlement

According to the UNHCR, resettlement in third countries, while a "'necessary solution in certain circumstances, is the least desirable and most costly solution'" for externally dislocated populations.[34] The international organization also admits, however, that it is not possible to provide durable solutions within the region of origin for many Third World refugees.[35] Local integration rarely occurs "because the countries of asylum do not have the resources, particularly arable land, necessary to make it politically feasible to absorb the increased population."[36] In light of the difficulties that have been encountered arranging durable first-asylum situations, "every major region but Africa has had a period of significant budgeting for the resettlement of refugees to third countries, often in other continents."[37]

An important advantage of third-country resettlement in the North is that the full costs of economic adjustment and social adaptation are borne by wealthy receiving countries.[38] Furthermore, it typically results in secure immigrant status.[39] Even though Northern countries are geographically and culturally remote, they usually provide an opportunity for Third World refugees to rebuild their lives—as Chapter 7 revealed in the case of most

432

post-revolution exiles who have managed to enter the United States. Moreover, "resettlement removes refugees from the scene of their greatest hardships and frequently provides the only alternative to their languishing in border camps."[40]   The opportunity to start over in a location that is free from fear of retribution and forced repatriation is a highly valued outcome of the third-country resettlement process for refugees from political environments that show little prospect of regime change.   On the whole, then, third-country resettlement has worked well and often constitutes the best available response to the plight of refugees.[41]

Western industrialized countries have moved vigorously, however, to limit the availability of this attractive and effective option to a select few. For instance, the U.S. Coordinator for Refugee Affairs bluntly maintained in 1987 that "resettlement can be a solution for only about 1% of the world's refugees."[42]   Member governments in the European Community have acted unilaterally and collectively to curb non-European asylum applicants and have aggressively sought "means to regionalize the protection of Third World asylum-seekers (i.e. to expand refugee protection in regions *outside* of Western Europe) so that few will arrive."[43]   Beyond limiting admission, "on a bilateral basis, and to a limited extent within the Council of Europe, understandings have been concluded concerning the return of refugees to countries of first asylum, often in return for assistance in helping to deal with the refugees."[44]   Other potential resettlement countries, including Japan and the Soviet Union, have accepted virtually no Third World refugees within their borders. The UNHCR's position in favor of regional settlement over placement in the North lends legitimacy to the exclusionary emphasis adopted by relatively wealthy nations.[45]

Comparative Assessment

The search for durable first-asylum solutions in poor countries has been unproductive—although the North continues to advocate this response as an alternative to resettlement within their own lands.   Meanwhile, as the burden they must shoulder continues to mount, Asian and African countries have demonstrated less willingness to accept refugees from their region.[46] In many cases, this reluctance is quite understandable. The United States would need to admit 15 million refugees in a year, for instance, to equal the per capita population burden placed upon Malawi by the exodus of political migrants from Mozambique in 1988.[47]

The magnitude of the contemporary refugee crisis ensures that out-of-homeland approaches to resettlement will continue to be insufficient.[48]

Durable solutions, including voluntary repatriation, can only be arranged when the conditions that produce refugee flows in the first place are altered to such an extent that the external need shrinks to a manageable and acceptable level in the South as well as the North. When it comes to eliminating or allievating the conditions that result in human dislocation, however, the international community as well as the U.S. government has a "poor record"[49] and humanitarian NGOs lack understanding of and the ability to focus attention on critical preventative measures.[50]

Implications for the South

The South-North movement of refugees exerts considerable impact on sending countries. The flight of talented, highly trained, and committed individuals constitutes an obvious loss to post-revolution societies.[51] On the other hand, political migration promises some relief from employment pressures and demands for educational and other public services.[52] It also offers the prospect of obtaining hard-currency remittances from expatriates.[53] Although remittances have improved the economic standing of families possessing members who have emigrated, they generally have not had a major positive impact on indigenous development. Remittances principally are invested in the purchase of land, housing, and consumer goods. Such investments distort the real-estate market and increase pressures to import luxury foreign products.[54]

In spite of the drawbacks in terms of distortion of the local economy, some post-revolution governments have been favorably disposed toward political emigration because it is perceived as a means of removing regime opponents from the local scene, it provides a short-term opportunity to confiscate the assets of departing dissidents, and/or it promotes the exodus of a religious, ethnic, or racial minority.[55] Silvia Pedraza-Bailey concludes, for instance, that the refugee exodus from Cuba "performed an important political function: it lessened the capacity of those politically disaffected from the revolution to undermine it."[56] In the long-run, moreover, "trained people flee, but new generations—initially with less training, but with a much different and higher level of consciousness—step into the breach."[57]

Finally, the burdens of first asylum are heavy for poor Third World countries that receive large numbers of political migrants from neighboring lands and possess most of the world's refugee-camp populations.[58] In addition to overwhelming the administrative capacity of the host government to serve mass needs over the short and/or long term, refugees tax limited local resources and, at times, cause irreparable damage to the surrounding environment.[59]   Moreover, the selective admission process employed by Northern nations often removes the few skilled refugees who are prepared to assume vital community-development roles in first-asylum countries.[60]

Implications for the North

The outlook for the future involves increased South-North migration pressures for political as well as economic reasons.   Repression and revolution in the Third World are inexorably linked to cross-national refugee flows.   Regional conflicts, civil wars, and other internal political conflicts threaten to overwhelm first-asylum countries with externally displaced neighbors.[61]

Many of the next generation of refugees, particularly those from urban backgrounds, will find their way North.[62]   Entry will occur regardless of whether or not changes are made in the definition of a refugee to encompass victims of violence.   Economic opportunities, social contacts, the availability of living space, the toleration of political dissent, and individual freedoms and security will continue to attract political migrants to the North.[63]

Some of the politically dislocated will arrive legally as resettled refugees or via established family networks.[64]   Others will join the influx of undocumented entrants who continue to penetrate Northern borders in spite of elaborate and expensive attempts to keep them out.[65]   The overall effects, when combined with concurrent economic migration, will be to enhance the multi-cultural composition of industrialized countries and to advance the timetable for political-power sharing with rapidly increasing numbers of new citizens and non citizens possessing Third World roots.[66]   As a result of the 1986 amnesty legislation, for instance, roughly three million previously undocumented migrants will become eligible for U.S. citizenship in the 1990s.[67]   In the future, then, refugee-related issues will command an even larger place on the domestic and foreign public-policy agenda in the North.[68]

Political Migration: Challenges for International Relations

In the new era of receding Superpower tensions, South-North relations have emerged as the paramount nexus of global politics.   Refugee flows and the movement of economic migrants have become recurrent elements in international relations with impacts of the same magnitude as trade and capital transfers.[69]   International migration generates and reinforces interlocking population networks and individual actions that frequently defy state control. Demographic and cultural counter-penetration of the North by Southern populations constitutes a particularly dynamic and unsettling dimension of this interlocking system.[70]

The phenomenon of millions of Third World refugees is neither a coincidence nor an aberration.   In Africa, Asia, and the Middle East, massive camp populations have been a familiar feature of the refugee landscape for more than two decades. Without fundamental changes in South-North relations, the migration of refugees from Third World revolutions, joined by the victims of warfare and repressive state policies, will be sustained and even increase. The argument developed in the next sections of this chapter holds that the prevailing international approaches to refugee situations have not been effective in alleviating political-migration pressures.   The international community needs to adopt a new refugee program that focuses on avoiding flight from one's homeland in the first place, on promoting conditions that will encourage voluntary return, and, when the prior alternatives are not feasible, on facilitating the acquisition of a new country.[71]

Regionalization and Repatriation Without Sending-country Political Change: Outmoded Northern Designs

The prevailing Northern response to political migration in the South is flawed on several grounds. To begin with, the conditions responsible for generating refugee exodus are likely to remain operative for long periods of time in post-revolution societies.   Under such circumstances, it is unconscionable for Northern governments or the UNHCR to push repatriation.[72]

Moreover, proponents advocate the favored regionalization policy based on the unsupported assumption that refugees adjust more readily to life in a neighboring country than in an industrialized Western society. Virtually all internationally displaced persons encounter serious adaptation difficulties. As Barbara Harrell-Bond reports, "there is no evidence to indicate that, say, an Eritrean from the cool highlands, who speaks Tigrinia. . . , practices Christianity, and eats different food, will have an easier time adjusting to the climate, culture and economy of the Sudan than to the conditions of an industrialized country."[73]   Furthermore, Astri Suhrke warns that "if it appears that the rich countries are giving aid in order to avoid accepting Third World refugees in their own states, conflict may be shifted to another level, North-South relations."[74]   The West is vulnerable to unauthorized "refugee-initiated solutions"[75] in this event as the result of porous borders, uncertainty over what constitutes a "nation" at a time of considerable flux in political identification and growing economic interdependence, and due to the lack of an undergirding justification for national sovereignty in liberal-democratic systems that extol the virtue of autonomous individuals.   On what ethical grounds is one who is inside a particular political boundary entitled to much more than one who is not?[76]

Toward a Workable South-North Approach

The resources commanded by the North, as well as the contributions made by certain industrialized states to refugee-producing conditions in the Third World, underlie the obligation that wealthy nations bear to assume a major share of the global asylum burden.[77] This responsibility needs to be pursued simultaneously in tested and novel ways.

Most political-asylum seekers prefer to reside in their region of origin. Donors must ensure that minimum standards for the material welfare of refugees are fulfilled and that UNHCR and other relief agencies are granted sufficient resources to meet this objective. Given that the vast majority of refugees will remain in the South, expanded support for sustainable-development efforts that promote the well-being of refugee and host populations in Third World contexts constitutes another vital element in an integrated, shared approach.[78]

Industrialized nations also must accept a more equitable share of the world's refugees through receptivity both to third-country resettlement and to their own first-asylum situations.[79] James Silk accurately notes that "any failure of developed countries to provide asylum offers a strong justification for others to curtail their hospitality toward refugees."[80] In short, the world's wealthy nations, including Japan, cannot "buy themselves out of" a refugee-settlement role through financial assistance to impoverished first-asylum countries.[81]

Furthermore, major bilateral foreign-policy changes are essential because, as Jonathan Moore admits, "the same nation-states which are providing significant humanitarian assistance to refugees may, at the same time, be pursuing policies that have the effect of generating refugees."[82] In particular, the lack of effective concern for human rights in U.S. foreign-policy actions continues to exacerbate the conditions that push Third World citizens to head North.

The international political community needs to respond in a creative, coordinated, and prevention-oriented fashion to challenges affecting refugee policy that have been avoided in the past. In other words, "the resilience of the uprooted must be matched by ingenuity on the part of policy makers. . . ."[83] In which novel policy directions should the global refugee regime look for promising approaches to managing cross-national political migration?

Third-country Resettlement Policy. With regard to third-country resettlement, agreement should be reached on an expanded, UNHCR-operated quota system of admissions to industrialized countries. Zolberg, Suhrke, and Aguayo suggest that "for the asylee, a quota system means less uncertainty regarding the future; for the country of final settlement, it means greater control in the admission process; and for the first asylum country, it means that asylum can be extended with some assurance that the refugee burden will eventually be shared."[84] At present, the United States assumes responsibility for roughly half of all refugees resettled each year. However, it ranks behind Australia, Canada, Sweden, and Denmark in its refugee-to-host population ratio.[85] The new reception scheme should be based on equitable sharing of the resettlement burden according to the size of each receiving country's population and should involve all industrialized countries—including Japan and the Soviet Union.

Broad agreement on an expanded UNHCR-administered quota would result in a decline in the number of political migrants who are turned away at regional destination points. The prevailing alternative of attempting to deter asylum seekers merely diverts refugee flows without resulting in a long-term reduction in total numbers.[86]

Tackling Root Causes. To date, "the international refugee regime has been largely ineffective in dealing with the root causes of refugee problems."[87] It is time, therefore, that international cooperation "be directed primarily towards the prevention of refugee movements and towards return."[88] The factors contributing to exile formation are both external and internal to refugee-generating countries. The external forces that the international community must address include the arms race and defects in the global economic system.[89] Until the involvement of external powers is recognized as an important source of political migration and precluded through concerted diplomatic action, "little headway will be made towards a resolution of refugee problems."[90] Similarly, effective dispute-settling techniques must be used to avert situations of international violence that provoke refugee flows.

International agencies traditionally have refrained from dealing directly with the factors that produce refugees in countries of origin. Deference to national sovereignty has kept U.N. institutions from acting to prevent human-rights abuses and from sanctioning those in positions of authority who are responsible for them. They only have reacted after flight occurs.[91] From a humanitarian perspective that affirms the rights of victims and potential victims of persecution and other forms of violence as well as the concerns held by states of refuge and the international community as a whole, a more proactive approach is both feasible and essential if the roots of the refugee crisis are to be addressed.

A more assertive approach requires willingness to focus on internal conditions in potential sending countries. One step in this direction would be amendment of the U.N. Refugee Convention to incorporate human-rights obligations in the country of origin and the individual right of return to one's homeland. In fact, commitment to protection of human rights should serve as the underlying basis for all aspects of international refugee policy.[92]

Enforcing a Prevention-Oriented Approach. The most challenging aspect of preventing refugee situations is enforcement. Prospective tools of enforcement include careful investigation into local conditions, in-country educational efforts based upon national values and self-interest, the glare of international publicity, the withholding of foreign assistance, and "a system of international order which disciplines governments failing to meet their obligations to humanity."[93] On the latter score, Ved Nanda calls for application of an international instrument that specifies the liability of officials "who permit and encourage mass expulsions."[94] Daniel Derby shows that other available measures can have a deterrent effect. They include holding states that engage in persecution and officials who participate in forced displacement responsible for international crimes, "assisting refugees in obtaining compensation from their home states for property losses resulting from their flight," and requiring that asylum countries be compensated by the governments of sending countries "for expenses incurred in accommodating refugees."[95]

UNHCR should play the leading role in refugee prevention. This means that displacement in sending countries must no longer be considered as falling outside the scope of its mandate.[96] The guiding principle should be "the avoidance or the remedy of conditions which, if left unchecked, would cause people to leave their country and to seek refuge elsewhere."[97]

Facilitating Secure Repatriation. In addition to the regime-change preconditions elaborated upon in Chapter 9, the durable and safe return of exile populations requires certain key protections in the period following transformation of the political system. In the first place, there must be independent verification that the requisite regime changes actually have occurred.[98] It is particularly important that this step involve advance fact-finding visits to the country of origin by refugee representatives.[99] Concomitantly, it is necessary that the agencies involved in facilitating the return-migration process "evaluate and confirm the voluntary character of the decision to repatriate."[100] Finally, refugees—particularly refugee women, who often constitute the bulk of the returning population—must be deeply involved in establishing and reviewing repatriation plans.[101]

Next, the fundamental human rights of the returning population must be guaranteed. International negotiations with authorities in the country of origin can play a vital role in securing formal human-rights guarantees following regime change.[102] In light of the intensity of their political commitments, firm assurances of free political expression and association are likely to be instrumental in the successful repatriation of former exiles. The new regime's willingness to allow public scrutiny and independent monitoring and auditing of its human-rights record in all areas of resettlement would go a long way toward overcoming any lingering hesitation to return to the homeland. Returnees must be individually identified, accepted, and available for follow-up contacts. Finally, UNHCR must be granted unhindered, long-term access to returnees in order to ensure that they are not mistreated,[103] that their rights to political participation are protected, and that rehabilitation efforts and objectives are not subverted—in short, "to monitor fulfillment of such guarantees as may have encouraged them to repatriate."[104]

Internal Political Conditions. Although the international community has an important role to play in focusing attention on the underlying factors that promote refugee formation and in overseeing secure repatriation, "what governments do of their own accord or with their eye on other governments will have the greatest effect in encouraging or obviating forced migration."[105] Moreover, "if states want their people to return, *they* must create conditions which are conducive."[106]

The principal internal conditions necessary for avoiding political outmigration and encouraging repatriation are establishment of a regime that is committed to tolerating dissent and diversity, institutionalization of constraints on the use of coercion, and the termination of class subjugation and exploitation. A political system built on principles of equality, popular participation, and the public accountability of officials holding positions of authority would be conducive to the realization of these conditions. Ironically, the difficult process of introducing and perfecting such a system is likely to be conflictual.[107] For this reason, a revolution "should not be judged merely by the tragic but historically necessary fact that it produces refugees."[108] If they are not destabilized by external interests, overthrown by reactionary forces, or coopted by self-serving autocrats, dogmatic factions, and bureaucratic elites, Third World revolutions "create enormous possibilities"[109] for the type of social and political transformation that, over the long run, will reduce outmigration pressures.

Notes

1. See *New York Times*, 14 December 1990, p. A6.

2. According to the U.S. Coordinator for Refugee Affairs, the Horn of Africa certainly will be "at the top of the list" of refugee-crisis situations during the decade of the 1990s. Jewel S. Lafontant, "Refugees and Conflict Victims: Meeting their Critical Needs," *Current Policy* 1252 (February 1990):2.

3. Aristide R. Zolberg, Astri Suhrke, and Sergio Aguayo, *Escape from Violence: Conflict and the Refugee Crisis in the Developing World* (New York: Oxford University Press, 1989), pp. 178, 251–255.

4. In an earlier publication, Zolberg, Suhrke, and Aguayo adopted a position that differs markedly from the argument set forth in their book. In the initial article, they concluded that "extreme structural inequality prevails in most of Latin America and parts of Asia, so that revolutionary challenges are likely to continue arising in those regions in the foreseeable future." Aristide R. Zolberg, Astri Suhrke, and Sergio Aguayo, "International Factors in the Formation of Refugee Movements," *International Migration Review* 22, No. 2 (Summer 1986):158, 167.

5. Zolberg *et al.*, *Refugee Crisis*, pp. 178, 206, 208, 213, 236, 253, 255. On El Salvador, also see Peter J. Schraeder, "U.S. Intervention in Perspective," in *Intervention in the 1980s: U.S. Foreign Policy and the Third World*, edited by Peter J. Schraeder (Boulder: Lynne Rienner Publishers, 1989), p. 289. On the prospect of mass white refugee flows from South Africa, see Kevin F. McCarthy and David F. Ronfeldt, "Immigration as an Intrusive Global Flow: A New Perspective," in *U.S. Immigration and Refugee Policy: Global and Domestic Issues*, edited by Mary M. Kritz (Lexington: D.C. Heath and Company, 1983), p. 397.

6. See Doug Bandow, "Economic and Military Aid," in *Intervention in the 1980s: U.S. Foreign Policy and the Third World*, edited by Peter J. Schraeder (Boulder: Lynne Rienner Publishers, 1989), pp. 78–79; James T. Fawcett and Benjamin V. Cariño, "International Migration and Pacific Basin Development," in *Pacific Bridges: The New Immigration from Asia and the Pacific Islands*, edited by

James T. Fawcett and Benjamin V. Cariño (Staten Island: Center for Migration Studies, 1987), p. 11.

7. See *New York Times*, 21 December 1989, p. A3; 2 March 1990, p. A3.

8. The *initial* establishment of migrant communities in industrialized societies frequently is the result of prevailing patterns of global economic migration.

9. Astri Suhrke, "Global Refugee Movements and Strategies of Response," in *U.S. Immigration and Refugee Policy: Global and Domestic Issues*, ed. by Mary M. Kritz (Lexington: D.C. Heath and Company, 1983), p. 167; Jeffery Crisp (ed.), *Refugees: The Dynamics of Displacement* (London: Zed Books, 1986), p. 57.

10. See Chapter 9; Sheila A. McLean, "International Institutional Mechanisms for Refugees," in *U.S. Immigration and Refugee Policy: Global and Domestic Issues*, edited by Mary M. Kritz (Lexington: D.C. Heath and Company, 1983), p. 180.

11. Also see McLean, "Refugees," p. 181.

12. While some argue that, by virtue of its status as part of the United Nations organization, UNHCR is obligated to honor and to promote respect for the Universal Declaration of Human Rights and to offer protection without discrimination "between the claim of one who has a well-founded fear of persecution and one who flees civil conflict or a general breakdown of law and order. . . , others contend that persons displaced by civil wars are the responsibility of the International Committee of the Red Cross—even though opposing parties do not always permit ICRC staff to operate in areas of armed conflict. Guy S. Goodwin-Gill, "Refugees: The Functions and Limits of the Existing Protection System," in *Human Rights and the Protection of Refugees under International Law*, edited by Alan E. Nash (Halifax: Institute for Research on Public Policy, 1988), pp. 155, 159; Roger P. Winter, "Ending Exile: Promoting Successful Reintegration of African Refugees and Displaced People" (U.S. Committee for Refugees Issue Brief, November 1990), p. 10; *New York Times*, 29 May 1989, p. A3; Martin Power, "Assistance for Refugees and Displaced Persons—Opportunities and Constraints," *Courrier* 121 (May/June 1990):91.

13. Jacques Cuénod, "Refugees: Development or Relief?" in *Refugees and International Relations*, edited by Gil Loescher and Laila Monahan (Oxford: Oxford University Press, 1989), p. 219. In spite of this focus, serious deficiencies have been encountered in the level of UNHCR assistance to some refugee populations—particularly in Africa. See John Seaman, "Assistance: The System Breaks Down," *Refugees* 8 (December 1990):12–13.

14. Hiram A. Ruiz and Bill Frelick, "Africa's Uprooted People: Shaping a Humanitarian Response," *Issue* 18, No. 1 (Winter 1989):34.

15. *New York Times*, 12 August 1990, p. 16.

16. A January 1990 report prepared by an Amnesty International delegation following a visit to Hong Kong faulted the screening process utilized by the

442

government to distinguish refugees from "economic migrants" on the grounds that it could not correctly identify persons who deserved refugee status. According to the *New York Times* (16 January 1990, p. A3), "the report cited the example of a young Vietnamese Protestant who was refused refugee status despite the fact that he was facing a five-year prison sentence in Vietnam because of his political views. The man had studied in Czechoslovakia, where he had been briefly jailed because of his involvement in the human rights movement and then deported back to Vietnam. On arrival, he was arrested, mistreated and tried for 'crimes against the state.' He escaped to Hong Kong before his prison sentence could be imposed. . . ."

17. Cuénod, "Development," p. 223.

18. John R. Rogge, "Introduction," in *Refugees: A Third World Dilemma*, ed. by John R. Rogge (Totowa: Rowman & Littlefield, 1987), p. 45; Cuénod, "Development," p. 240.

19. See, for instance, Jonathan Moore, "Refugees Worldwide and U.S. Foreign Policy: Reciprocal Impacts," *Current Policy* 1036 (November 1987):2; Joseph Cerquone, *Refugees from Laos: In Harm's Way* (Washington, D.C.: U.S. Committee for Refugees, 1986), p. 17. In light of the competitive implications of permanent integration for poor host communities, local authorities often prefer to refer to this process as a "lengthy prelude to return." Leon Gordenker, *Refugees in International Politics* (New York: Columbia University Press, 1987), p. 135.

20. Astri Suhrke, "Global Refugee Movements and Strategies of Response," in *U.S. Immigration and Refugee Policy: Global and Domestic Issues*, edited by Mary M. Kritz (Lexington: D.C. Heath and Company, 1983), p. 167.

21. UNHCR informal report of 1986, cited in Cuénod, "Development," pp. 229–231; *New York Times*, 29 May 1989, p. A3.

22. Ved P. Nanda, "The Challenge: Averting Flows of Refugees and Providing Effective Protection and Durable Solutions," in *Refugee Law and Policy: International and U.S. Responses*, edited by Ved P. Nanda (New York: Greenwood Press, 1989), pp. 204–205. By 1985, NGOs provided the basic health services utilized by one-third of the refugees in Pakistan. Helga Baitenmann, "NGOs and the Afghan War: The Politicisation of Humanitarian Aid," *Third World Quarterly* 12, No. 1 (January 1990):65.

23. Cuénod, "Development," pp. 231, 234, 245. Also see Gordenker, *Refugees*, p. 136; Barbara E. Harrell-Bond, "Repatriation: Under What Conditions is it the Most Desirable Solution for Refugees? An Agenda for Research," *African Studies Review* 32, No. 1 (1989):51. On the lack of self-sufficiency and integration among refugees from Ethiopia living in Sudan, especially those inhabiting organized settlements, see Mekuria Bulcha, *Flight and Integration: Causes of Mass Exodus from Ethiopia and Problems of Integration in the Sudan* (Uppsala: Scandinavian Institute of African Studies, 1988), pp. 170, 178–179.

24. Barry N. Stein, "ICARA II: Burden Sharing and Durable Solutions," in *Refugees: A Third World Dilemma*, edited by John R. Rogge (Totowa: Rowman & Littlefield, 1987), p. 57; Sadruddin Aga Khan and Hassan bin Talal, "Foreward," in *Refugees: The Dynamics of Displacement*, edited by Jeffery Crisp (London: Zed Books, 1986), p. xv.

25. Gordenker, *Refugees*, pp. 132, 147–148. However, see Shelly Pitterman, "Determinants of International Refugee Policy: A Comparative Study of UNHCR Material Assistance to Refugees in Africa, 1963–1981," in *Refugees: A Third World Dilemma*, edited by John R. Rogge (Totowa: Rowman & Littlefield, 1987), pp. 25, 27, 35. According to Crisp (*Refugees*, p. 65), an estimated 60 per cent "of the refugees in Africa remain outside the international aid umbrella."

26. Eritrean refugees in eastern Sudan offer an example of this point. See Gordenker, *Refugees*, p. 134.

27. Harrell-Bond, "Repatriation," 51; Mekuria Bulcha, *Flight*, p. 193; Crisp, *Refugees*, p. 16.

28. Cuénod, "Development," p. 229.

29. On Honduras, see *New York Times*, 29 May 1989, p. A3. On the other hand, critics accused the Siad Barré regime, before its overthrow, of pressing refugees into military service against the opposition Somali National Movement in the northern part of Somalia. *New York Times*, 28 January 1989.

30. Cuénod, "Development," pp. 241, 244; Mekuria Bulcha, *Flight*, p. 192.

31. Mekuria Bulcha, *Flight*, p. 24.

32. Mekuria Bulcha, *Flight*, p. 187; Robert E. Mazur, "Refugees in Africa: The Role of Sociological Analysis and Praxis," *Current Sociology* 36, No. 2 (1988):54, 59; John R. Rogge, "When is Self-Sufficiency Achieved? The Case of Rural Settlements in Sudan," in *Refugees: A Third World Dilemma*, edited by John R. Rogge (Totowa: Rowman & Littlefield, 1987), p. 97.

33. Also see Mazur, "Refugees in Africa," 59; Robert E. Mazur, "Linking Popular Initiative and Aid Agencies: The Case of Refugees," *Development and Change* 18 (1987):451–452. For additional recommendations, see Maxine E. Olson, "Refugees as a Special Case of Population Redistribution," in *Population Redistribution: Patterns, Policies, and Prospects* (New York: U.N. Fund for Population Activities, 1979), p. 147. Sidney Waldron adds the important point that "without some culturally informed, socially sensitive research on the facts of life of the refugees, the direction of planning and administration will continue to be from the top down." Sidney R. Waldron, "Working in the Dark: Why Anthropologists are Essential in Refugee Relief" (paper presented at the American Anthropological Association Annual Meeting, December 1986), p. 9.

34. UNHCR informal report of 1986, cited in Cuénod, "Development," p. 233. The U.S. government also views resettlement in the North, in the words of former

444

U.S. Coordinator for Refugee Affairs, Jonathan Moore, as "the last option to be considered." Jonathan Moore, "Refugees and Foreign Policy: Immediate Needs and Durable Solutions," *Current Policy* 945 (April 1987):3.

35. Cited in Dennis Gallagher, Susan F. Martin, and Patricia W. Fagen, "Temporary Safe Haven: The Need for North American-European Responses," in *Refugees and International Relations*, edited by Gil Loescher and Laila Monahan (Oxford: Oxford University Press, 1989), p. 340.

36. Hiram Ruiz, *Beyond the Headlines: Refugees in the Horn of Africa* (Washington, D.C.: U.S. Committee for Refugees, 1988), p. 4; also see Jeff Crisp, "Somalia: Solutions in Sight," *Refugees* (December 1989):7. Poverty-stricken Third World countries rarely offer citizenship to political migrants from neighboring areas. Michel Moussalli, "Refugees in the World Today: Main Characteristics and Outlook for the Future," *Courrier* 121 (May/June 1990):70.

37. Shelly Pitterman, "International Responses to Refugee Situations: The United Nations High Commissioner for Refugees," in *Refugees and World Politics*, edited by Elizabeth G. Ferris (New York: Praeger, 1985), pp. 51–52.

38. Cuénod, "Development," p. 246.

39. Gordenker, *Refugees*, pp. 138–140; also revisit Chapter 5 of this book.

40. Robert L. Bach, "Third Country Resettlement," in *Refugees and International Relations*, edited by Gil Loescher and Laila Monahan (Oxford: Oxford University Press, 1989), p. 313. On the fears that beset refugees from Ethiopia who have sought first asylum in Sudan, including anticipation of forced repatriation, see Mekuria Bulcha, *Flight*, pp. 208–211.

41. William R. Smyser, *Refugees: Extended Exile* (New York: Praeger, 1987), p. 115.

42. Moore, "Durable Solutions," 3.

43. Gallagher *et al.*, "Safe Haven," p. 343; Goodwin-Gill, "Protection System," p. 152. On U.S. government adherence to this policy, see Norman L. Zucker and Naomi F. Zucker, *The Guarded Gate: The Reality of American Refugee Policy* (San Diego: Harcourt Brace Jovanovich, 1987), p. 49; Richard H. Feen, "Domestic and Foreign Policy Dilemmas in Contemporary U.S. Refugee Policy," in *Refugees and World Politics*, edited by Elizabeth G. Ferris (New York: Praeger, 1985), p. 117. The European preference for "regionalization" explains the pressures placed on the Bush administration in 1991 unilaterally to create a refugee zone within northern Iraq for displaced Kurds.

44. Johan Cels, "Responses of European States to *de facto* Refugees," in *Refugees and International Relations*, edited by Gil Loescher and Laila Monahan (Oxford: Oxford University Press, 1989), p. 212.

45. Cels, "Responses," p. 212.

46. Beverly G. Hawk, "Africans and the 1965 U.S. Immigration Law" (Ph.D. dissertation, University of Wisconsin-Madison, 1988), p. 277; Moore, "Durable Solutions," 3.

47. Ruiz and Frelick, "Uprooted People," 34.

48. Also see McLean, "Refugees," p. 181.

49. Moore, "U.S. Foreign Policy," 2; Moore, "Durable Solutions," 3.

50. See, for instance, Michael J. Schultheis, "Refugees in Africa: The Dynamics of a Global Justice Issue" (paper presented at the 30th Annual Meeting of the African Studies Association, 1987), p. 20. Likewise, Sheila McLean ("Refugees," p. 183) argues persuasively that it is not possible to address the condition of Third World refugees effectively "without a comprehensive and long-term appreciation of the social, economic, and political facts that made them refugees, control their relationships with their host governments and neighboring populations, and. . . generate their self-image, which affects so strongly the prospects for constructive resolution of their situations."

51. On Cuba's loss of skilled citizens, see Richard R. Fagen and Richard A. Brody, "Cubans in Exile: A Demographic Analysis," *Social Problems*, 11 (Spring 1964):400; Robert L. Bach, "Cubans,'" in *Refugees in the United States: A Reference Handbook*, edited by David W. Haines (Westport: Greenwood Press, 1985), p. 83. Dawit Wolde Giorgis writes that there are reportedly "more Ethiopian physicians in the United States than in Ethiopia, and more still in Europe." Dawit Wolde Giorgis, *Red Tears: War, Famine and Revolution in Ethiopia* (Trenton: Red Sea Press, 1989), p. 357. Also see Edward Girardet, *Afghanistan: The Soviet War* (New York: St. Martin's Press, 1985), p. 208; Crisp, *Refugees*, p. 16.

52. See Elsa M. Chaney, "Migrant Workers and National Boundaries: The Basis for Rights and Protections," in *Boundaries: National Autonomy and Its Limits*, ed. by Peter G. Brown and Henry Shue (Totowa: Rowman and Littlefield, 1981), p. 57.

53. See, for instance, Michael S. Teitelbaum, "Immigration, Refugees, and Foreign Policy," *International Organization* 38, No. 3 (Summer 1984):447.

54. See Demetrios G. Papademetriou, "International Migration in a Changing World," *International Social Science Journal* 36, No. 3 (1984):418, 423; Mark J. Miller and Demetrios G. Papademetriou, "Immigration and U.S. Foreign Policy," in *The Unavoidable Issue: U.S. Immigration Policy in the 1980s*, edited by Demetrios G. Papademetriou and Mark J. Miller (Philadelphia: Institute for the Study of Human Issues, 1983), pp. 174–175.

55. Teitelbaum, "Foreign Policy," 447–448; Zolberg *et al., Refugee Crisis*, p. 167. In the pre-Gorbachev period, authorities in the Soviet Union shared this perspective. See Laurie P. Salitan, "Domestic Pressures and the Politics of Exit: Trends in Soviet Emigration Policy," *Political Science Quarterly* 104, No. 4 (1989/90):677.

446

56. Silvia Pedraza-Bailey, "Cuba's Exiles: Portrait of a Refugee Migration," *International Migration Review* 19, No. 1 (1985):7.

57. Richard R. Fagen, Carmen D. Deere, and José L. Coraggio, "Introduction,'" in *Transition and Development: Problems of Third World Socialism* (New York: Monthly Review Press, 1986), p. 16.

58. Zolberg *et al., Refugee Crisis,* p. 231; Crisp, *Refugees,* p. 16; *World Refugee Survey—1988 in Review* (Washington, D.C.: U.S. Committee for Refugees, 1989), p. 35.

59. See W. R. Smyser, "Refugees: A Never-Ending Story," *Foreign Affairs* 64, No. 1 (Fall 1985):160; Alan J. Simmance, "The Impact of Large-Scale Refugee Movements and the Role of UNHCR," in *Refugees: A Third World Dilemma,* edited by John R. Rogge (Totowa: Rowman & Littlefield, 1987), pp. 12–13; Girardet, *Afghanistan,* p. 207; Crisp, *Refugees,* p. 16; Crisp, "Solutions," 7.

60. See Hawk, "Africans," pp. 122–123; Rogge, "Sudan," p. 97; "Conference and Symposia Reports," *Journal of Refugee Studies* 1, No. 1 (1988):83; Howard Adelman, "Refuge or Asylum: A Philosophical Perspective," *Journal of Refugee Studies* 1, No. 1 (1988):8.

61. Papademetriou, "International Migration," 417.

62. See Mekuria Bulcha, *Flight,* p. 138.

63. On the space issue, see Freda Hawkins, *Critical Years in Immigration: Canada and Australia Compared* (Kingston and Montreal: McGill-Queen's University Press, 1989), pp. 268–269. On the effect of personal and historical connections with the United States on future migration from Cuba, see Bach, "Cubans," pp. 91–92. Also see Miller and Papademetriou, "Immigration," p. 163.

64. On the latter, see Mary M. Kritz, "The Global Picture of Contemporary Immigration Patterns," in *Pacific Bridges: The New Immigration from Asia and the Pacific Islands,* edited by James T. Fawcett and Benjamin V. Cariño (Staten Island: Center for Migration Studies, 1987), p. 46.

65. See, for instance, *New York Times,* 23 June 1989, p. A10.

66. Also see Leon F. Bouvier and Anthony J. Agresta, "The Future Asian Population of the United States," in *Pacific Bridges: The New Immigration from Asia and the Pacific Islands,* ed. by James T. Fawcett and Benjamin V. Cariño (Staten Island: C.M.S., 1987), p. 300; *New York Times,* 10 January 1990, p. A4.

67. *New York Times,* 30 September 1989, p. 8.

68. Also see Gil Loescher, "Refugee Issues in International Relations," in *Refugees and International Relations,* edited by Gil Loescher and Laila Monahan (Oxford: Oxford University Press, 1989), p. 8.

69. Also see Bach, "Resettlement," p. 329.

70. Ali A. Mazrui, "The New Interdependence: From Hierarchy to Symmetry," in *The U.S. and World Development: Agenda for Action 1975,* ed. by James W.

Howe (New York: Praeger, 1975), p. 126. For instance, the Los Angeles area "now has the largest concentration of people of Mexican origin, about three million, anywhere outside Mexico City." *New York Times*, 8 December 1989, p. A1.

71. Gervase Coles, "Approaching the Refugee Problem Today," in *Refugees and International Relations*, edited by Gil Loescher and Laila Monahan (Oxford: Oxford University, 1989), p. 395; Zolberg *et al., Refugee Crisis*, p. 268.

72. Harrell-Bond, "Repatriation," 62.

73. In fact, there are "few, if any, language courses or cultural programs for refugees in developing countries. For refugees resettling in industrialized countries, it is assumed that such services must be made available." Harrell-Bond, "Repatriation," 54–55.

74. Suhrke adds that "aid would appear particularly racist and mercenary if the rich countries simultaneously accepted European [or white South African] refugees in large numbers." Suhrke, "Movements," p. 167. Also see Harrell-Bond, "Repatriation," 62, 66n.

75. Adelman, "Refuge," 10.

76. I am indebted to Albert Borgmann for this insight.

77. On this point, also see Zolberg *et al., Refugee Crisis*, p. 279.

78. Zolberg *et al., Refugee Crisis*, p. 282. For examples of promising projects in Sudan, see *Refugees* 80 (November 1990):27, 36. Also see Seaman, "Assistance," 12.

79. The former UNHCR High Commissioner, Jean-Paul Hocké, forcefully argued this position. See Gallagher *et al.*, "Safe Haven," p. 340. Also see James Silk, *Despite a Generous Spirit: Denying Asylum in the United States* (Washington, D.C.: U.S. Committee for Refugees, 1986), p. 34.

80. Silk, *Denying Asylum*, pp. 7, 2.

81. Zolberg *et al., Refugee Crisis*, p. 279.

82. Moore, "Durable Solutions," p. 3.

83. Khan and Talal, "Forward," p. xv.

84. Zolberg *et al., Refugee Crisis*, p. 281.

85. See *World Refugee Survey—1988 in Review*, p. 36; Jewel S. Lafontant, "Refugees and Conflict Victims: Meeting their Critical Needs," *Current Policy* 1252 (February 1990):1.

86. Crisp, *Refugees*, p. 41.

87. Loescher, "Issues," p. 18.

88. Coles, "Refugee Problem," p. 392.

89. Harrell-Bond, "Repatriation," 63.

90. Loescher, "Issues," p. 19; Zolberg *et al.*, "Refugee Movements," 167. On the 1983 Contadora Initiative for Central America, see Zolberg *et al., Refugee Crisis*, p. 266.

91. Loescher, "Issues," pp. 18, 19.

92. Coles, "Refugee," pp. 389–390, 395; Nanda, "Averting Flows," p. 204.

93. Stephen B. Young, "Who is a Refugee? A Theory of Persecution," in *In Defense of the Alien*, Vol. V, edited by Lydio F. Tomasi (Staten Island: Center for Migration Studies, 1983), p. 52.

94. Nanda, "Averting Flows," p. 204.

95. Daniel H. Derby, "Deterring Refugee-Generating Conduct," in *Refugee Law and Policy: International and U.S. Responses*, edited by Ved P. Nanda (New York: Greenwood Press, 1989), pp. 44–45, 47–52. Derby points out (p. 51) that "increased deterrence through criminal law can be achieved only if more states enact statutory proscriptions against such conduct and also make them enforceable against conduct beyond their territory. The most logical extension of such proscriptions would be their application to conduct abroad that causes a local influx of refugees."

96. Coles, "Refugee," p. 394. Also see Nanda, "Averting Flows," p. 205.

97. This conception of prevention specifically excludes measures designed to *restrict* transfrontier movement. Coles, "Refugee Problem," pp. 395, 404.

98. Goodwin-Gill, "Protection System," pp. 163–164; Ruiz, *Refugees*, p. 40.

99. Guy Goodwin-Gill, "Voluntary Repatriation: Legal and Policy Issues," in *Refugees and International Relations*, edited by Gil Loescher and Laila Monahan (Oxford: Oxford University Press, 1989), p. 264.

100. This recommendation stems from UNHCR's controversial experience with repatriation from Djibouti to Ethiopia. See Goodwin-Gill, "Voluntary Repatriation," pp. 278–279, 284; Harrell-Bond, "Repatriation," 56.

101. Catherine O'Neill, "Women: Shaping Their Own Destiny," *Refugees* 81 (December 1990):17.

102. Gordenker, *Refugees*, p. 127.

103. In this regard, there is a need to develop "practical and effective methods of monitoring the security of those returning." Goodwin-Gill, "Voluntary Repatriation," p. 285.

104. Goodwin-Gill, "Protection," pp. 163–164; Bach, "Resettlement," p. 314.

105. Gordenker, *Refugees*, p. 178.

106. Harrell-Bond, "Repatriation," 61.

107. Richard R. Fagen, "The Politics of Transition," in *Transition and Development: Problems of Third World Socialism*, ed. by Richard R. Fagen, Carmen D. Deere, and José L. Coraggio (New York: Monthly Review, 1986), pp. 261, 158.

108. Zolberg *et al.*, *Refugee Crisis*, p. 262.

109. Hooshang Amirahmadi, "Middle-Class Revolutions in the Third World," in *Post-Revolutionary Iran*, edited by Hooshang Amirahmadi and Manoucher Parvin (Boulder: Westview Press, 1988), pp. 239–240.

Appendix:
The D.C./L.A. Study—Research Design and Sampling Results

This appendix is devoted to presenting a brief description of the D.C./L.A. study which provided much of the primary-source data base referred to in *Refugees from Revolution*. The author, along with Girma Negash, co-directed the research project under a grant from the Rockefeller Foundation. The discussion set forth here is limited to the survey component of a multi-dimensional project that also involved interviews with resettlement-agency personnel, government officials, legal-service providers, and exile-community leaders, along with systematic data collection utilizing resettled-refugee and asylum-applicant files and information gathered from agency reports and records. The Iranian study is treated separately given the somewhat different approach followed for that community.

Ethiopian and Eritrean Exile Communities

The findings reported for the Ethiopian and Eritrean communities are based upon survey research carried out in the Washington, D.C., metropolitan area during the last half of 1984. In total, the project staff conducted 161 extensive oral interviews, typically two to three hours in duration, with resettled refugees and other migrant household heads.[1]

Survey Sampling Procedures

Budgetary constraints necessitated that geographical limits be placed on the survey-research aspect of the project. Awareness that there are more migrants from Ethiopia living in the nation's capital than in any other U.S. metropolitan area greatly influenced the decision to concentrate on the Washington, D.C., area. Promises of support for the research project from local community leaders constituted another important consideration.

The absence of an adequate sampling frame constituted the principal barrier that had to be overcome in order to select interview respondents through random-sampling procedures. There is, quite simply, no single list of individuals or families who belong to these highly mobile exile communities. The first task, therefore,

450

entailed compiling a reasonably comprehensive sampling frame of household heads living in the Washington, D.C., metropolitan area whose country of origin is Ethiopia. The focus on household heads stemmed from the project's theoretical interest in factors affecting the decision to become an exile.

The co-directors began by identifying and numbering every name of Ethiopian origin encountered on each page of the three 1984 telephone directories for the D.C. metropolitan area. The fact that the interchangeable given and family names of non Muslims from Ethiopia are easily and unmistakably distinguished from all other nationalities facilitated this effort. The project directors were aware of the weaknesses inherent in utilizing telephone directories as one's sampling frame.[2] In addition to class and religious biases, we expected that the telephone books would underrepresent migrants who work without legal permission and request unlisted numbers. As we anticipated, it also turned out that many official refugees did not have a current telephone listing under their own name in the local directories. This situation reflects their relatively poor economic standing, lack of residential stability, and, in the case of recent arrivals in the process of resettlement, placement either in units containing multiple households or among relatives and U.S. sponsors.

These drawbacks convinced us that it would be unwise to rely exclusively on the local telephone directories.[3] We set out, therefore, to compile a more complete list of household heads by supplementing the set of individuals identified from the telephone books with names from other available sources. However, we first ruled out all government sources, whether U.S. or Ethiopian, on the grounds that reference to official lists would cast suspicion on the project and cause many of the subjects selected for study to refuse to cooperate. In any event, we anticipated little methodological gain from referring to census-track or alien-registration data in constructing the sampling frame for a relatively small, highly mobile, and rapidly expanding Third World migrant community that includes a sizeable number of political exiles possessing insecure immigration status. Conversations with Jeffrey Passel of the U.S. Census Bureau (5 July 1983) and Robert Warren of the National Academy of Science's Committee on National Statistics (13 July 1983) had confirmed that both of the above sources lacked utility for our purposes given their generalized and outdated nature, and in light of unrectifiable underreporting flaws.

Instead of relying upon government sources, we turned to community organizations and leaders for assistance in constructing the sampling frame. As the first step in this process, we attempted to identify all functioning associations of persons from Ethiopia in the Washington, D.C., metropolitan area. Between them, the project directors possessed extensive contacts in the Ethiopian and Eritrean communities which facilitated accomplishment of this task. After explaining the project's nature, objectives, and funding sources to the leader(s) of each community group, we requested his/her assistance in building the sampling frame by providing us with a complete and up-to-date membership list along with each individual's telephone number. We received a variety of reactions to this request, ranging from enthusiastic cooperation to *de facto* noncompliance. While no community organization gave an outright refusal, we experienced several unfulfilled promises of cooperation and a couple of obvious "put offs."

One organization we turned to for assistance, the local Ethiopian Orthodox Church, reported that it did not maintain a membership roll. Most of the other community associations expressed serious reservations about providing us with a list of their members. The desirability of eliminating duplicate names from the final sampling frame constituted the sole reason for asking organizations for complete membership information. Ultimately, we decided to sacrifice the ability to do this whenever an association objected to giving over their full roster of names. In such cases, we generally followed a strategy that respected the confidentiality of the organization's membership to the maximum extent and supplied us only with what we absolutely needed to know. Specifically, we asked the association to number consecutively the names of all household heads living in the metropolitan area and report the total to us. We then entered the total numbers assigned onto our master list. Later, once we had randomly selected the sample by number from that group's list, the organization provided the project directors, or one of the interviewers directly, with the name and telephone number of the members whom we had chosen. Using this approach, we ended up with a partially "blind" sampling frame for four community associations (a total of about 300 names).

Final Sampling Frame

In the end, we compiled a master list consisting of 2,603 household heads. The specific breakdown of usable lists, after the elimination of duplicate names, is: three area telephone directories (572 names), six community lists (600 names),[4] three non-community sources (181), and nine resettled refugee-exclusive lists (1,250). Thus, the sampling frame is roughly balanced in terms of names secured from non refugee-specific sources (which include some refugees) and those obtained from refugee-exclusive lists. With considerable effort, we managed to increase its size by nearly four fold over the results secured by consulting the telephone directories alone. We are particularly gratified by and appreciative of the cooperation received from exile-community associations.

By employing a conservative estimate of the likely degree of duplication with other rosters, we estimate that the final sampling frame omitted approximately 151 household heads from Ethiopia whose names appear on seven lists that we had to exclude for various reasons. There is no way to estimate with certainty the number of additional Ethiopian, Eritrean, and Oromo heads of households living in the area

452

in 1984 who were not associated with any of our sources, but it is likely to be relatively small. While the project cannot claim to have succeeded in identifying the total population of migrant heads of household from Ethiopia living in the Washington, D.C., metropolitan area, the final master list utilized in this study is sufficiently comprehensive and unbiased to serve as a scientifically valid sampling frame.

Iranian Exile Community

In order to conserve scarce project resources, the co-directors initially decided to limit their survey to the large Iranian exile community living in the Washington, D.C., metropolitan area. An Iranian research assistant conducted the name-identification exercise for the 1984 District of Columbia telephone book, while the Foundation for Iranian Studies provided the names its staff had culled from the Maryland and Virginia suburb directories.

At the same time, research assistants undertook the process of identifying functioning local associations composed of and/or catering to migrants from Iran. The project directors' request for cooperation received a mixed reaction from Iranian community-association leaders. On the positive side, we secured three organizational lists. The Director of the Foundation for Iranian Studies shared the list of subscribers to the organization's publications. The Iran-American Friendship Foundation, headed by a former minister in the Shah's government, provided its mailing list. Finally, the Confederation of Iranian Students contributed a combined membership, contact, and telephone-book enumeration. From these sources, we incorporated into the sampling frame those local household heads who could be contacted at home or at work by telephone.

In addition to the official submissions, local arrangements allowed access to three lists which remained closed to all project staff except for a trusted interviewer. The Iranian Women's Committee made available a "blind" roll of over 60 names. Two individuals provided an unofficial list of Iranians close to the local People's Fedaii-e (Minority). Finally, a community leader in Virginia submitted names of local household heads of diverse political persuasion and persons associated with non-cooperating organizations.

The project study did not succeed in securing either an official or an unofficial list from several identified community groups. These are the Muslim Iranian Students' Society (MISS), Student Supporters of Revolutionary Socialism, the Iranian Students' Association, the Muslim Students' Association, the Committee for Defense of Democratic Rights in Iran, the Iranian Cultural Society, and the Kurdistan Committee. The local MISS members whom we contacted insisted that we first obtain approval from the organization's leadership in Paris. This condition could not be satisfied given the logistical, financial, and time constraints that the project directors operated under. Although the Iranian Cultural Society never fulfilled its promise to provide us with a membership list, we expect that a high degree of overlap exists between its roster and others we did access. The remaining associations showed little interest in cooperating with the project. They found ways of not responding to repeated requests for help without explicitly refusing to cooperate.[5]

We received no assistance from extra-community organizations in building the Iranian sampling frame. A prominent and busy immigration lawyer who had handled many asylum-application cases never followed through on the blind-list arrangement worked out at an initial meeting. Extensive efforts to elicit the cooperation of the Baha'i community ultimately did not yield a list of Iranian Baha'i living in the metropolitan area.[6] Finally, lack of cooperation on the part of local international-student advisors restricted efforts to incorporate students into the sampling frame.

A relatively small number of official refugees from Iran had arrived in the area during the initial eighteen-month period of eligibility for resettlement. Four refugee-exclusive sources (the D.C. government's Office of Refugee Resettlement, the Virginia Department of Public Health, UNHCR, and HIAS) reported being in contact with a total of 34 resettled Iranians.

Eliminating duplicate names produced a final master list for the D.C. area that consisted of 1,673 heads of household from Iran. With an average family size of three, the sampling frame would cover a total migrant population that slightly exceeds 5,000 persons. This figure does not fall far below estimates projected from 1980 census results regarding the *foreign-born* population of Iranians living in the Washington, D.C., area.[7]

The project's District of Columbia enumeration encompasses exile groups with monarchist and liberal-democratic political leanings (FIS and IAFF) as well as other opposition organizations, and female Iranian household heads. Nevertheless, the final master list for the D.C. area proved deficient in several respects. In particular, it underrepresented leftist exile organizations and certain nationality and minority religious groups (particularly Kurdish people and those adhering to the Baha'i faith). Conceivably, the D.C. sampling frame also did not adequately represent students, asylum applicants, and politically independent professionals. Therefore, we decided to incorporate several accessible and important lists of Iranians residing in the Los Angeles metropolitan area.

We discovered via the District of Columbia sampling experience that virtually all formal associations of Iranian exiles have a political bent.[8] The leadership of political associations tend to be even more suspicious of outsiders than are the heads of other types of migrant-community groups. They guard the names of their members particularly carefully, and often attempt to conceal the total number of active supporters. Under such circumstances, researchers must possess personal contacts with influential members of each organization in order to secure cooperation with one's study. Mohammad Amjad, principal research assistant for the Iranian study, managed to obtain informal lists in Los Angeles from persons who had been affiliated with three different exile associations of radical persuasion. In addition, we incorporated four lists of local contacts and clients provided by independent businesspersons and professionals as well as a supplemental listing of area university students who had not been enumerated elsewhere. These lists also encompass members of religious and national minorities. Finally, we included ten official refugees from Iran identified by a member of the Anti-War Committee. The master list of household heads in the L.A. metropolitan area consists of approximately 1,300 names—bringing the total Iranian sampling frame to almost 3,000 persons.[9]

In comparison with the master list for the Ethiopian and Eritrean communities, the final Iranian sampling frame relies more heavily on informal sources. This is unavoidable given the tendency for Iranian exiles to organize themselves along political lines and the greater sensitivity attached to membership records under such circumstances. Although some of their adherents are encompassed by the general lists, the project directors did not manage to secure access to specific membership rosters (official or unofficial) for three important groups of exiles. These are the Muslim Iranian Students' Society (supporters of the People's Mujahedin), Kurds, and Baha'i. However, one of the informal lists from Los Angeles covered supporters of Peykar, a Marxist splinter group of the Mujahedin. The project also did not succeed in including individuals affiliated with the Muslim Students' Association (supporters of the Ayatollah Khomeini's regime). Nevertheless, the master list did incorporate non exiles, including some who supported the post-revolution regime.

The final Iranian sampling frame employed in this study expands considerably upon the telephone directories. As in the Ethiopian case, no more reliable and inclusive list exists. Although there are no firm aggregate statistics regarding the migrant population from Iran that can be used to assess the comprehensiveness of the D.C./L.A. master list, it clearly covers the spectrum of exile political opinion reflected in organizational form, from the far right to the far left, as well as unaffiliated businesspersons and professionals. Moreover, the considerable effort invested in constructing a sampling frame allowed us to avoid reliance upon the inferior system of soliciting volunteers as respondents.[10]

Sampling Results

Given the diverse nature of the sources comprising these master lists, as well as the logistical problems and time delays encountered in acquiring several of the promised rosters, the project directors found it necessary to select the sample on a list-by-list basis. We based the number of names chosen from each list on the size of the particular roster relative to the entire sampling frame. Then, utilizing the table of random numbers, the directors selected prospective respondents.

The two sampling frames differ in one important respect. Only three lists are relatively homogeneous in the Ethiopian case, and these nationality and evangelical church rosters are quite small. In contrast, a majority of the lists comprising the Iranian sampling frame are homogeneous in terms of political organization, an important stratification variable. Thus, although we followed the same procedure in both cases, the different nature of the lists employed in constructing the two sampling frames resulted in random sampling among the Ethiopian community and a methodology that is more accurately described as stratified random sampling for migrants from Iran.

Among the individuals from Ethiopia randomly selected from the sampling frame and contacted for an interview, we obtained an 86.6 per cent overall positive response rate.[11] At least 70 per cent of those contacted from every list agreed to participate in the interview. The final sample of respondents consists of 161 migrant household heads from Ethiopia, or 6.2 per cent of the sampling frame. The distribution of the total sample in terms of key demographic characteristics (age, sex, marital status, time of arrival, and ethnic or nationality identification) is consistent with what is generally known about the Ethiopian and Eritrean exile communities.[12]

For the Iranian migrant community, the overall response rate is 76 per cent, and at least 60 per cent of the contacted household heads from every list consented to be interviewed. The final sample consists of 156 Iranians, or 5.3 per cent of the sampling frame.[13] The occupational backgrounds of the interviewed household heads are quite similar to those reported by all U.S. immigrants from Iran in FY 1984.[14]

Notes

1. On the value of oral interviews for securing sensitive and confidential information, see Alex Inkeles and Raymond A. Bauer, *The Soviet Citizen: Daily Life in a Totalitarian Society* (Cambridge: Harvard University Press, 1959), p. 54.

2. Earl Babbie, *The Practice of Social Research*, 4th edition (Belmont: Wadsworth Publishing Company, 1986), p. 156.

3. In contrast, Strand and Jones opted for the telephone directory as the population list in their study of Indochinese refugees in the San Diego area. For a justification of their decision, see Paul J. Strand and Woodrow Jones, Jr., *Indochinese Refugees in America: Problems of Adaptation and Assimilation* (Durham: Duke University Press, 1985), pp. 73–74.

4. These lists include the D.C.-area members of the National Oromo Association and of the Research and Information Center on Eritrea.

5. To the best of our knowledge, no group ever openly or privately attacked the research project. For a contrasting experience, see Inkeles and Bauer, *Soviet Citizen*, pp. 11–12.

6. Also see Farah Gilanshah, "Iranians in the Twin Cities," *Journal of the Institute of Muslim Minority Affairs* 7 (January 1986):120.

7. See the figures for all persons of Iranian heritage presented in Jamshid Momeni, "Size and Distribution of Iranian Ethnic Group in the United States: 1980," *Iran Nameh* 2 (Winter 1984):18–20.

8. In Abdolmaboud Ansari's words, "the entire structural relationship of Iranians in America tends to be infused with politics." Abdolmaboud Ansari, *Iranian Immigrants in the United States: A Case Study of Dual Marginality* (Millwood: Associated Faculty Press, 1988), p. 77.

9. There is no obvious reason to expect that exiles on the eight L.A. lists we utilized differ from individuals who would be found on parallel D.C.-area rosters in any important respects related to refugee formation. In any event, we had to choose between incorporating available L.A.-area lists of important groups of exiles from Iran or excluding such names entirely from the sampling frame due to lack of access in the Washington, D.C., area. We opted for inclusion largely on the grounds that this strategy would enable us to take advantage of the larger population size and attendant heterogeneity that exists in the L.A. area, allow us to gain representation from the principal subgroups known to exist within the exile community, and because we had no theoretical interest in testing the effect of present geographical location within the United States on the decision to become an exile.

The Iranian community in Los Angeles is the largest in the country. Counting individuals born in the United States, persons of Iranian heritage constitute the second largest ethnic minority, after Mexican-Americans, in the L.A. area. Georges Sabagh and Mehdi Bozorgmehr, "Are the Characteristics of Exiles Different from Immigrants? The Case of Iranians in Los Angeles," *Sociology and Social Research* 71, No. 2 (January 1987):77–78.

10. On the latter, see Inkeles and Bauer, *Soviet Citizen*, p. 15.

11. This result is identical to the 87 percent completion rate reported by Strand and Jones for Vietnamese refugees. Their completion rates for Lao, Hmong, and Cambodian refugees all are right around 98 percent. Strand and Jones, *Indochinese Refugees*, p. 75.

12. See Peter Koehn and Girma Negash, *Resettled Refugees and Asylum Applicants: Implications of the Case of Migrants from Ethiopia for United States Policy* (Arlington: Center for Ethiopian Studies, 1987), pp. 29–39.

13. In comparison, the widely cited self-administered study of Cubans in Miami carried out by Fagen *et al.* is based on a final sample of 209 exclusively male household heads, or about .4 per cent of their single-source sampling frame. Richard R. Fagen, Richard A. Brody, and Thomas J. O'Leary, *Cubans in Exile: Disaffection and the Revolution* (Stanford: Stanford University Press, 1968), pp. 11–13. Only 42 percent of the 250 Iranians identified by Ansari through friends and personal contacts proved willing to be interviewed when he contacted them. Ansari, *Iranian Immigrants*, pp. 122, 126.

The total number of respondents in the D.C./L.A. study proved to be sufficient for most of the inter- and intra-group comparisons we were interested in.

14. See U.S., Immigration and Naturalization Service, *Statistical Yearbook of the Immigration and Naturalization Service, 1984* (Washington, D.C.: INS, 1985), p. 65.

Further Reading

Students of international relations and U.S. public policy are confronted by an explosion of publications that examine South-North population movements and related issues. This section offers a brief overview of the most important recent books.

Several works treat the new immigration to the United States. For general, but not probing, historical background that would not cover important recent developments, one might consult David M. Reimers, *Still the Golden Door: The Third World Comes to America* (New York: Columbia University Press, 1985) and Nathan Glazer, editor, *Clamor at the Gates: The New American Immigration* (San Francisco: Institute for Contemporary Studies, 1985). A lively account, based on interviews with a member of most new migrant communities, is Al Santoli, *New Americans: Immigrants and Refugees in the U.S. Today* (New York: Viking, 1988).

The groundbreaking work in the overview category is Mary M. Kritz, editor, *U.S. Immigration and Refugee Policy: Global and Domestic Issues* (Lexington: D.C. Heath, 1983). This anthology tackles most of the theoretical and policy issues that continue to engage scholars concerned with international migration. The editor emphasizes the importance of identifying determinant factors in population movement and the need to undertake carefully crafted social-science research. No systematic treatment of the connection between external intervention or revolutionary change and refugee formation is presented, however. Another outstanding anthology, edited by Peter J. Schraeder, *Intervention in the 1980s: U.S. Foreign Policy in the Third World* (Boulder: Lynne Rienner Publishers, 1989), serves as a valuable companion piece to the Kritz book. The Schraeder volume is essential reading for those who seek to understand the underlying political forces responsible for large-scale population dislocation in the Third World.

Refugees provide the specific focus for seven relatively recent titles. An excellent treatment of settlement issues facing Third World receiving countries, with extensive references to the role of international organizations, is Gil Loescher and Laila Monahan, editors, *Refugees and International Relations* (Oxford: Oxford University Press, 1989). Another thoughtful and detailed study that explores refugee formation from the perspective of international relations is Leon Gordenker, *Refugees in International Politics* (New York: Columbia University Press, 1987). A more generalized account by a high official in the refugee-assistance establishment is W. R. Smyser, *Refugees: Extended Exile* (New York: Praeger, 1987).

For a useful review of U.S. refugee-policy making and outcomes, students of the subject should read Norman Zucker and Naomi F. Zucker, *The Guarded Gate: The Reality of American Refugee Policy* (San Diego: Harcourt Brace Jovanovich, 1987). A thorough historical documentation of refugee policy in the United States is Gil Loescher and John Scanlan, *Calculated Kindness: Refugees and America's Half-Open Door, 1945 to Present* (New York: Free Press, 1986). A more critical volume, which analyzes deficiencies in current U.S. law and policy and sets forth alternatives, is Ved P. Nanda, editor, *Refugee Law and Policy: International and U.S. Responses* (Westport: Greenwood Press, 1989).

No one interested in the relationship of international relations, national politics, and refugee formation should ignore the seventh volume in this category, which represents the culmination of several years of collaborative work by three well-informed authors with complementary perspectives. The reference is to Aristide R. Zolberg, Astri Suhrke, and Sergio Aguayo, *Escape from Violence: Conflict and the Refugee Crisis in the Developing World* (Oxford: Oxford University Press, 1989). Their book attempts a comprehensive, theoretically grounded structural explanation for refugee migrations. Its principal shortcoming lies in the failure to incorporate micro-level, individual analysis. The authors treat all major regions of the world other than the Middle East and develop novel typologies based upon the characteristics of previous refugee flows.

Political-asylum seekers have received less attention in the published literature relative to their resettled-refugee counterparts. One of the few available works that examines admission biases in the execution of asylum policy and provides recommendations for reform is James Silk, *Despite a Generous Spirit: Denying Asylum in the United States* (Washington, D.C.: U.S. Committee for Refugees, 1986). Readers interested in the rights of political-asylum petitioners, official refugees, and other immigrants should not fail to consult a more comprehensive and insightful volume: Elizabeth Hull, *Without Justice for All: The Constitutional Rights of Aliens* (Westport: Greenwood Press, 1985).

Only a few of the book-length studies that deal with post-revolution migrants treat both sending and receiving conditions. One such work is Gail P. Kelly, *From Vietnam to America: A Chronicle of the Vietnamese Immigration to the United States* (Boulder: Westview Press, 1977). Also highly recommended is the volume edited by James T. Fawcett and Benjamin V. Cariño which carries the title *Pacific Bridges: The New*

460

Immigration from Asia and the Pacific Islands (Staten Island: Center for Migration Studies, 1987). The classic early study of Third World exiles in the United States is Richard R. Fagen, Richard A. Brody, and Thomas J. O'Leary, *Cubans in Exile: Disaffection and the Revolution* (Stanford: Stanford University Press, 1968). A valuable comparative work is Silvia Pedraza-Bailey, *Political and Economic Migrants in America: Cubans and Mexicans* (Austin: University of Texas Press, 1985). An excellent attempt to link social-structural and historical analysis with individual explanations for flight obtained through systematic interviews among refugees living in first-asylum situations in Africa is Mekuria Bulcha, *Flight and Integration: Causes of Mass Exodus from Ethiopia and Problems of Integration in the Sudan* (Uppsala: Scandinavian Institute of African Studies, 1988). This highly recommended volume also includes useful information regarding trans-border migration processes and refugee responses to different settlement conditions in Sudan.

Index

462

Immigration Act of 1990, 255n, 421n,
425n
Immigration and Nationality Act of
196n5, 197n
Immigration Control and Reform Act of
1986, 27n, 181, 233–235, 258n,
340n, 395, 401, 434
India, 158
Indonesia, 32n, 428
INS v. Cardoza-Fonseca, 218, 250n
Intergovernmental Committee for
Migration, 35n
International Committee of the Red
Cross (ICRC), 441n
International relations, 2–3, 18, 19–20n,
23n, 38–39, 427
Iraq, 7–9, 12, 28n, 32n, 70, 72–73,
388–389n, 419n, 444n
Israel, 33n, 75, 81, 196n, 419n
Italy, 165, 178

Japan, 21n, 26n, 64, 205, 432, 436–437
Johnson, Lyndon B., 145
June 1981 massacre, 106–107, 150

Kennedy, John F., 60
Kenya, 158, 200n, 242n, 428
Khamenei, Ali, 71
Khomeini, Ruhollah, 65, 67–71, 73,
90n, 108–110, 150, 374, 382
Kuwait, 9, 28n

Lamm, Richard, 23n
Lebanon, 7, 213, 238n
Liberia, 30n, 211, 245n
Libya, 211
Low-intensity conflict, 8

Malawi, 12, 432
Malaysia, 32n
Mauritania, 30n
Mengistu Haile Mariam, 77–81, 98n,
106, 150, 221, 383
Mexico, 25n, 203n, 211, 235, 428–429
Migration
East-West, 20n, 427
South-North, 2–6, 14, 38, 142–143,
150, 174, 178, 189, 231, 259,
391, 394–395, 401, 404, 416n,
427–428, 433–435
South-South, 2, 20n

Morocco, 428
Mosaddeq, Mohammad, 64
Mozambique, 8–12, 28n, 31n, 55n, 409,
419n, 432
Myanmar, 29n

Namibia, 376n
Nepal, 428
Networks, 48, 57n, 143, 148, 191n,
203n, 395, 428–429, 434–435
Nicaragua, 9–12, 31n, 53n, 55n, 63,
211, 245n, 387, 394
Nixon, Richard, 90n
Nol, Lon, 62, 147

Office of Refugee Resettlement (ORR),
17, 148, 345n
Orderly Departure Program (ODP), 13,
33n, 102, 248n, 425n
Organization of African Unity (OAU),
7, 410

Pahlavi, Mohammad Reza, 64–67, 71,
73, 87n, 90n, 92n, 190, 244n
Pahlavi, Reza, 69
Pakistan, 9, 12, 31n, 158, 167, 178,
198n, 211, 213, 245n, 388n, 428,
442n
Palestinians, 8–9, 429
Panama, 53n
Philippines, 24n, 32n, 208, 245–246n,
428–429
Plyler vs. Doe, 236
Poland, 233, 235, 243n
Pol Pot regime, 62, 147
Privatization, 41

Rafsanjani, Hojatolislam, 71, 389n
Rajavi, Masud, 68, 72
Reagan, Ronald, 23n, 73, 81, 208–209,
258, 394, 413
Reagan Doctrine, 31n, 55n, 63
Red Terror, 77, 94–95n, 106–107, 150
Refugee Act of 1980, 16–17, 24n, 34n,
151, 206–208, 213, 218, 220, 222,
232, 237, 273, 299n, 394, 396,
400, 405

Sanctuary movement, 246n
SAVAK, 64, 67, 70, 244n, 264
Schengen Agreement, 240n